MOVIES
—AND—
MONEY

Lessons from the
Motion Picture Marketplace
for the 21st Century

David Sikich

Movies and Money
Lessons from the Motion Picture Marketplace
for the 21st Century

© 2012 David Sikich
All Rights Reserved. Published 2012.
Printed in the United States of America
21 20 19 18 17 16 15 14   3 4 5

ISBN: 978-0-9836035-3-5

Published by First Flight Books
A division of Bruce Bendinger Creative Communications, Inc.
2144 N. Hudson • Chicago, IL 60614
773-871-1179 • www.adbuzz.com

Cover Design: Patrick Aylward & Bruce Bendinger

This book is dedicated to all those who have ever worked in the
trenches of a film distribution company or movie theatre circuit.

Acknowledgments

My sincere gratitude goes out to the 16 industry professionals who took the time out of their busy schedules to be interviewed about their jobs, the state of the industry, and lessons learned over the many years they've worked in the motion picture marketplace. The book would not have been the same without the involvement and insight of Richard Abramowitz, Kenny Bahr, Jeff Blake, Vinnie Bruzzese, Ira Deutchman, Steve Friedlander, Chris Johnson, Dean Kerasotes, Tony Kerasotes, Ziggy Kozlowski, Mitch Lowe, Burt Rast, Paul Silk, Doug Stone, Chuck Viane and Clark Woods. An added thank you goes out to Doug Stone who provided many of the grosses and numbers used in the book.

My years of teaching at Columbia College Chicago have played an important role in making this book possible. All my students, past and present, have inspired me to always be at the top of my game and have kept me young in spirit over the years. I have to thank the late Fred Fine who believed in me and gave me my first opportunity to teach in the AEMM department he created in 1978, and for the chairs of the department that have followed, Carol Yamamoto, Dennis Rich and Philippe Ravanas for their continued support and guidance.

I would like to give a special thank you to the two individuals who impacted my career in the film industry more than anyone else, Paul Silk and John Iltis. Paul was an early mentor of mine and hired me for my first two jobs in film distribution at Avco Embassy and Filmways (later to become Orion Pictures) and has remained a good friend and confidant through the years. John Iltis exemplified the highest standards of the movie industry each day of the 30 years he ran his company, John Iltis Associates. Being able to work next to him for 13 years and to call him partner was a privilege and an honor that I'm eternally grateful for. Thank you my friend for everything you've done for me and for always having my back, regardless of the situation or outcome of one of my decisions.

My gratitude goes out to Tom Hudson and Harvey Moshman from the morning television show, *First Business*. My weekly visits discussing the movie industry evolved into the "Movies and Money" segments, which formed the basic framework of this book. I had a lot of fun with Tom on the air; he always was prepared and brought a wit and style to our conversations that elevated whatever topic we were discussing and made it better.

I'm very grateful to my publisher, *First Flight Books* in Chicago, for their work and assistance in making this book a reality. My gratitude goes out to Bruce Bendinger, Patrick Aylward, Lorelei Bendinger and proofreader Stefanie Crawford.

Above all, I want to thank my wife Joy, who for 39 years has stood by my side with her love and support.

Contents

INTRODUCTION

In September, 1973, I was 23 years old, recently married, unemployed and badly in need of a job. It had been over a year since I graduated from Columbia College's Film Program in Chicago. I instinctively knew I didn't have the talent, ambition and makeup to pursue a career in filmmaking, but I loved movies and kept my eyes and ears open for a different way to break into the business. I found it when I opened the Chicago Sun-Times on that September morning and saw a want ad which read Wanted: ASST. MGR. FOR LOOP MOVIE THEATRE. I answered the ad and got the job at the Woods Theatre in downtown Chicago working the night shift between 6:00pm and 2:00am. It was the height of the Blaxploitation era and the Woods was a prime landing spot for many of these movies. On that September day walking up to the theatre for the first time, the 50 foot high neon marquee cut through the night sky blaring out the ad copy which is ingrained deep in my mind "HE'S GOT THE MAN ON THE PAN AND HE'S GOING TO FRY HIM GOOD." The name of the movie playing was "Black Jack." The job paid $135 a week and I was happy to get it. You have to start somewhere.

Thus started a 35 year career working in and around the theatrical motion picture industry. The Woods proved to be a good way to learn the business from the ground level up, from inside a movie theatre, dealing with the public, learning about niche marketing and audiences, managing employees, feeling the excitement of opening night, being there at the start of a movie's commercial lifespan. What will it do? Who will show up? Will it be a hit or a bomb? Working in a movie theatre was the place to be to experience that success or failure first hand, up close and personal. The moment of truth arrives quickly. The audience is either there or it isn't. Regardless of predictions, critics, stars, marketing, campaigns expectations, you learn a movie has to just open to prove itself. It can be thrilling, it can be heartbreaking. What I learned early on was the marketplace was fickle, unforgiving at times, challenging. I was hooked. I wanted to learn more, to do more, to understand how the movie business worked. This was an industry I wanted to stake my claim in.

My period as a theatre manager only lasted a couple of years at the Woods and later at the more upscale Carnegie Theatre about a mile north of the Chicago downtown district. Even though I absolutely loved my time at the Carnegie (the first 16 weeks played the exclusive run of Mel Brooks "Young Frankenstein"), I had my eye on getting a day job in either distribution or exhibition and in 1976 I was offered a sales position at Avco Embassy Pictures Chicago office and gladly jumped at it. Just as I had previously experienced the last gasp of the giant downtown theatres in the 1970s, at Avco it was a different sort of trip down memory lane. My first job was selling the company's movies to small town and 2nd run theatres throughout the Wisconsin territory. That entailed filling the car up with press kits and posters and hitting the road, meeting independent theatre owners in their dens and kitchens and trying to sell them current attractions, double features of older films or drive-in programs, whatever I could move. Speaking to the old timers, this was the weekly routine for film salesmen, leave on Tuesday morning and come back to the office on Friday to fill the orders, but eventually, the trips became fewer and fewer with more business being conducted over the phone. Also during my Avco Embassy years, I heard that Columbia College Chicago was looking for someone from the local film industry to teach a part time course on the movie business and when the person who was going to teach it left town to take another job, I stepped in and agreed to teach it. Even though I didn't have much experience at the time, I looked at it as another opportunity to expand my horizons and to research the other aspects of the business. This proved to be one of the best decisions I ever made.

After five years at Embassy in various sales positions, I took a job at Filmways Pictures, formerly American International Pictures, and in 1982 Orion Pictures came in and bought the struggling company. The 1980s was a great decade of growth for the film industry with the rise of home video fueling revenues and there was no better company to work for than Orion. I became the Chicago Branch Manager and in an eight year span, the company won four Best

Picture Awards with "Amadeus," "Platoon," Dances With Wolves,' and "Silence of the Lambs." It was a wonderful ride that came to a screeching halt in December 1991 when Orion filed for bankruptcy protection which led to the closing of the distribution offices in May, 1992. This surprised a lot of people who only looked at the surface of successful Oscar winning films but had little or no knowledge of the problems brewing behind the scenes for a stand -alone independent company with no corporate safety net to lean on. It wasn't the greatest time to be out of a job at a time when some studios were beginning to close their Chicago branch sales offices and consolidating them into the Western divisions. After 16 years working in distribution, I was wondering what my next move would be.

Being able to fall back on teaching helped but I was looking for another full time job and wanted it to be in a different direction. It took awhile to find a solution. I pitched an offbeat idea to my friend John Iltis who ran a full service publicity, promotion and advertising agency in Chicago which did work for various film studios and independent distributors. My pitch involved setting up a subsidiary producers rep company which would represent filmmakers looking for distribution. The early '90s were a tremendous growth period for the independent film business and more and more filmmakers were making films without having a distributor in place. We would be the middle men in helping filmmakers market and sell their films to distributors. John agreed to try it for six months and Iltis Sikich Associates was born in June, 1993. This was exactly what I was looking for, something more entrepreneurial, more challenging , less corporate and doing some things I had never done before. Some would say timing in life is everything and in this instance that was true. Three Chicago filmmakers were at the tail end of finishing five years of work on a basketball documentary called "Hoop Dreams" when they walked into our office soon after we opened for business. They showed us a three and a half hour video cut of the movie and we were hooked immediately. It was nothing like we ever saw before in our lives and we knew we had to get involved in this unique project. It took several months before we became official reps on the film and it became an exhilarating introduction into the film festival acquisition world. There will be more on "Hoop Dreams" in the book. So the timing was perfect to jump start our new firm and it was an exciting time to get involved in the independent film business. The six month trial period turned into thirteen years and a distribution company, ISA Releasing, would be added in 1995. As President of Marketing and Distribution of ISA, the stakes got much bigger and the decisions became much more risky and expensive. Doing battle in the motion picture marketplace as a micro distributor was the most difficult, challenging portion of my career. Never easy, always nerve wracking. The companies would continue to June, 2006 when the parent company John Iltis Associates closed its doors after 30 years in business. I would continue to book films for an independent theatre for another year to officially close out a 35 year career in the film business. I'm proud of the fact that my entire career has been spent working in Chicago, a city I love and where I was born and raised, in an industry that is largely based in Los Angeles and New York.

Working, teaching, trying to make sense of how the movie industry operates, has been a lifetime of work for me. I've been fortunate to have not one career but dual careers which ran side by side over a 30 year period. I am now starting my 35th year teaching film distribution and marketing courses at Columbia College. For many years, I've toyed with the idea of writing a book which could double as a text for my students, but it never happened. The only constant in the movie industry is change and I always feared whatever I wrote would become old news in a hurry in addition to wondering whether I was up to the task. I couldn't figure out how to approach it.

Then in June, 2008, I received a call from Harvey Moshman, the producer of First Business, a morning business show syndicated out of Chicago. Harvey was looking for someone with knowledge of the movie business to come in to break down the economics and strategies of the summer movie season. I believe it was supposed to be for just one show but that first appearance led me to becoming a regular contributor for the next 72 weeks. My four to five minute appearances evolved into a branded Movies and Money segment which aired every Friday morning for a year and a half. As the remainder of the 2008 season played out, I started thinking about my weekly appearances in a much broader light and wondering what other opportunities it presented for me. Could this be the hook I was looking for in figuring out how to write about the movie business? What I was doing each week on the air in effect was analyzing the theatrical market-place. Everything I experienced and learned over 35 years was being tested and put to use on the weekly show. This is the world I knew and this is the world I came from.

At the center of the entire history of the movie business lies the theatrical marketplace. For the first 50 years, movie theatres existed alone, had no direct competition and provided 100% of the revenues to the people and companies who made the movies. In the last 60 years, theatres have had a growing number of competitors from the first black and white televisions to today's internet downloading, streaming and premium video on demand. But the movie theatre hasn't gone away, in fact there are as many screens in North America as there has ever been at any point in history, close to 40,000. Movie theatres still enjoy the first exclusive window of play, they still establish the value of a film for all the mediums to follow. They still matter. They remain a strong, effective business model. After over 100 years since the first nickelodeon opened, the theatrical marketplace is still the center of attention and the heart of the industry. Whether a movie plays only for a few weeks or lasts in theatres several months, its significance from a monetary, social and cultural standpoint remains unquestioned. Research and analysis of the theatrical marketplace is still worthy of serious study.

I settled on the central concept for this book. In anticipation to the start of the 2009 season, my idea was to document and follow the entire year as it unfolded. The 2009 theatrical marketplace is the centerpiece and launching point for this book. Each of the 52 weeks is chronicled from the first week in January to the last week of December following my original blog entries that were written as the year unfolded. There have been books full of movie reviews for specific years but I don't know of any that covered the industry in this fashion. I didn't know what to expect or how the year would play out because each year is different, each year has its own personality and dynamic. Each year takes a life of its own. New companies are born, other companies close, some much heralded pictures fail to perform while other movies not even on the radar as the year opens become huge successes, new business models emerge while others are threatened. The challenge was to find fresh story lines tied to either the release of that particular week's opening films, events taking place or industry topics in the news and then trying to wrap them into a larger context. The question would become, can one 52 week calendar season with all of its storylines become not only a record of the movie industry at this particular point in time, but could it become something more, something more universal, something that could stay relevant for years to come? That's the idea, that's the hope. By diving deep into the mechanism of the buying, selling and marketing of movies over the course of a year, what emerged was the inescapable fact that the film industry is built on a core of basic economic principles, fundamentals and practices that have evolved and have been in place for many years. Despite all the changes that have come about in the last decade, there are certain fundamentals of doing business within the movie industry that remain. This book is about those fundamentals and how they work in the context of the multi-billion dollar entertainment industry.

Former studio head and producer Robert Evans once said the movie business is about taking chances. It's a risky, very costly business to operate in and there are always more disappointments than true successes. It's a business that revolves around money; who has it, how to get it, how to spend it wisely, how to divide it up, how to recoup it, how to generate a profit and quite honestly, how it can disappear so quickly. Information, statistics, market research findings are readily available for those working in the industry but information doesn't make decisions, people do, and that's where the real story lies when telling the story of the movie business. It can be found in the decision making of studio executives, theatre owners, film buyers, producers, marketers, agents, independent distributors, the working professionals trying to make things happen. Studios are forced to be risk adverse because of the huge capital involved but distribution and marketing executives still have to make difficult decisions every day just as exhibitors have to do with their businesses. Why did events happen as they did? How did movies become successes or failures and what constituted that? How many screens should be retrofitted with digital 3D? What companies fared the best, what executive decisions and risks paid off and which ones didn't. Who were the people behind the scenes making the decisions? How were the dynamics of the industry changing? What kinds of deals were being structured and what was the rationale behind them? Who had the power and control in certain situations?

Slowly but steadily, the long 52 week season evolved and story lines developed and sprang up to the surface. Just about every topic important to the industry was covered. Release patterns, film festivals, the financial credit crunch, digital 3-D technology, falling DVD numbers, shifting television revenues, exhibitor-distributor film rental deals, copyright issues, sinking star power, film piracy, marketing strategies, the shifting fortunes of Netflix and Redbox, international markets, product placement, viral marketing, the struggles of independent film and much more. Remaining at the core of most discussions was the drama, sweat, and pull of the theatrical market and the distributors, exhibitors and marketers who work in the industry and make it all happen. To acknowledge those professionals who were part of the story of 2009, I conducted interviews during the 2011 season with fifteen executives to allow them to talk about their jobs, their careers, their decision making process, lessons they've learned, and where they think the movie industry is headed in the coming years. The interviews are inserted throughout the book to add valuable context, perspective and updated information on recent developments, such as the continuing battle over Premium Video-On- Demand and the ongoing conversion of theatre screens to all-digital projection systems.

What a year 2009 turned out to be to put under a microscope to study and analyze. When you look back at the years' movies, the release schedules didn't look much different from past years with the usual mixture of blockbusters, sequels, reboots, animation, horror, low brow comedies, suspense thrillers, dramas and art films sprinkled throughout the year. So what made it so special? Well, let's first look at it from an economic standpoint. As 2009 began, the country was in the midst of the deepest recession in more than 70 years, yet the Motion Picture Industry enjoyed a record breaking year in domestic box office, surpassing the $10 billion mark for the first time. Despite audiences having more ways to experience movies than ever before, audiences renewed their love affair once again with the oldest, most durable method of watching movies – outside the home in a movie theatre. Ticket sales jumped more than 5% to over 1.4 billion admissions, stopping a four year slide. Yes, it was helped by more 3-D movies with their higher ticket prices but that only tells half the story. If it was that simple, 2010 and 2011 with even more 3-D releases would have set new records but they didn't; those years fell short in both box office and admissions.

The other half of the story of why 2009 was such a fascinating year to study and write about comes from two distinct areas. The first were all the intriguing story lines that were in play the entire year; the second was the success the various distributors had in maximizing the commercial potential of the movies they were handed to sell and market. Would Digital 3-D be the savior for the industry or would the public eventually tire of it? How about exhibitors? Will they find the money and the desire to convert more of their screens to digital 3-D to keep up with the growing supply from the studios? With some of the studios closing their specialty divisions, what would become of the independent film business which started the year at its lowest, most precarious state in years? With the credit crunch in full swing, where would new film financing come from? After several adult dramas failed for Universal , which led to the firing of its co-heads, will any studios want to continue to make smart movies for the mainstream adult audience anymore? Would Blu-ray grow quick enough to help turn the tide of falling DVD numbers? Was the growing power of Netflix becoming more of a friend or foe for the studios? When will revenue from digital outlets become significant? Will increasing the number of Best Picture candidates from five to ten be a good move for the industry or will it dilute an already slipping institution? And how about James Cameron's end of the year release "Avatar"? Would he be able to not only deliver a blockbuster on the level of "Titanic" with his first feature film in 12 years, but also be able to carry the torch for the entire digital 3-D movement?

The second part of the equation looks at the incredible performance of the movies themselves. From the Martin Luther King weekend becoming the biggest January weekend in history to the last week of December setting the record for the highest weekly gross of all time, it seemed like the box office was on fire all of 2009 and the film business could do no wrong. But it doesn't all happen by chance or blind luck. Sometimes it's easy to forget that the movie industry is not just a science, it's also an art involving real people making decisions every day about how their movies are positioned and perceived in the marketplace. Utilizing their instincts, experience, business savvy, talent and yes, market research too, distributors and exhibitors alike have to make the right calls to insure continued success in a tough, competitive marketplace. This is the final piece of the puzzle that made 2009 such a special year. It was a year of great strategic decision making that turned many of the movies into the successes they became. Fox opening "Taken," a male action thriller, on Super Bowl weekend and making it into a big success, Warner Brothers holding off going wide with "Gran Torino" until mid-January and giving Clint Eastwood his highest grossing movie at the age of 78, Sony's superb viral marketing campaign on "District 9," Paramount's unusual cutting edge release for "Paranormal Activity, Lionsgate taking a black art film with "Precious" and creating blockbuster grosses, and Summit releasing "The Hurt Locker" in the heat of the summer and riding it all the way to the Best Picture of the Year. Even with "The Hurt Locker" winning Best Picture, 2009 proved to be a painful, transitional year for independents who took a backseat to the studios most of the year. It was the studios who often led the way by bucking conventional wisdom, utilizing cutting edge marketing techniques, thinking outside the box and being nimble and creative with their decisions. It was an eye-opening year in that regard.

Week in and week out, lessons from the marketplace emerge, to study and to learn from. Basic information, context and perspective on how the movie industry operates over the course of one 52 week season. Many of the lessons are timeless and could be applied to any year; others are more closely associated to the ongoing changes that are happening in the industry so perspective and updated information from a 2012 vantage point are included following the original weekly chapters.

No single movie year exists in a void as one year rolls into another and yet another after that. But specific years have a significance that can impact and influence years to come. 2009 turned into such a year, a critical turning point for Hollywood and the movie industry that set in motion developments that will be felt for many years, from the rise of digital 3D to the digital conversion of theatres, the upheaval of the independent film industry to emerging new revenue streams, inventive cutting edge release patterns to virtual print fees. Welcome to the wild and woolly movie business world of the 21st century. Enjoy the ride.

David Sikich

July, 15, 2012

A NEW YEAR DAWNS

Week 1: January 2–8, 2009

The movie business always starts out the new year on an odd note.
The first weekend of January is generally the only weekend of the entire year
where there are no new national releases.

Every Friday for the next 52 weeks, I will be chronicling the movie business as it unfolds. As the calendar flips over, it's always exciting to speculate about what is to come and what kind of year the next one will turn out to be. The country is still in the throes of a deep recession, and it appears the 2008 box office will be somewhat flat, matching the previous year's tally of around $9.6 billion. Hanging tough in tough times but showing little to no growth. Can 2009 be the first year to crack the $10 billion mark, or will the business continue to sputter in place or even go backwards? I'll be dissecting the weekly box office results, but the numbers alone never can tell the complete story, so a lot of space will given to the evolving year's story lines and behind-the-scenes strategies and decisions made by all the various industry players, but especially by the distributors and exhibitors, the yin and yang of the theatrical marketplace. Will this be the year that Digital 3-D takes off? Can the studios stop the declining DVD sales? How will the ongoing recession affect movie going? Can the theatrical business be able to withstand the pressure and promise of new ways the public is able to watch movies? Where is the independent film business headed? Those are but a few of the topics we'll be keeping a close eye on, and there will be sure to be many other issues, controversies, deal making and unforeseen happenings to discuss as the year progresses. There always are. Every year is different.

The movie business always starts out the new year on an odd note. The first weekend of the new year is generally the only weekend of the entire year where there are no new national releases. Everything has already opened. When you think about it, it makes perfect sense. What you see on the screen is what you get, and there is certainly enough to see. Most of the Christmas movies are larger budget, important movies from the studios, and the extended holiday playtime with no new competition serves their interests well. New Year's weekend is one of the year's top grossing weekends, and all the business goes to the current attractions, another reason why this period is so lucrative for the movies that have established themselves in the marketplace. Money can add up in a hurry. In addition, there will be plenty of time to open new films beginning next week.

The year is ending on a strong note, and when the holiday films do well and show staying power, they provide more than just momentum for the following year; they can provide the bulk of their grosses that will be counted at the 2009 box office. The end of the year releases thus become part of the new year's story for better or for worse, and once again the movie industry proved that it is both product driven and marketing driven. The studios delivered movies people wanted to see during the most lucrative period of the year, but just as important, backed them up with outstanding marketing. That combination produces big hits. You would think the studios could just put their stars front and center and the dollars would flow, but it isn't as easy as that. The previous week Jim Carrey and Will Smith were plastered on the posters of "Yes Man" and "Seven Pounds" and both movies underperformed. Fox's "Marley and Me" was expected to do well but it was not predicted to beat out Disney's "Bedtime Stories" for the top spot but, $51,000,000 to $38,000,000 over the four-day Christmas weekend wasn't even close.

How did that happen? Putting that big lovable dog front and center in all the marketing materials, including standees and those new digital poster frames, instead of highlighting Jennifer Anniston and Owen Wilson, proved to be a shrewd move. Families and dog lovers flocked to see it. Disney had a strong central marketing image themselves with gumballs falling from the sky and Adam Sandler holding an umbrella over his head, but it couldn't match that cute Marley looking straight at you.

A more stunning surprise was Paramount's "The Curious Case of Benjamin Button" out grossing "Bedtime Stories" for 2nd place over those four days. This is an adult drama, it's 2 hours and 47 minutes long, it gets only four showings a day instead of five and it still grossed $38.7 million. That's a very impressive debut. The film does have Brad Pitt and Cate Blanchett heading the cast, but did that combination turn "Babel" into a big hit? I think the key here is that Paramount was successful in selling the unique concept of the film, the story of a man who ages backwards. Some critics dismissed the concept as a gimmick, but it was a breath of fresh air seeing a studio actually selling the story line of a film for a change. Hollywood is famous for repeating itself over and over again, and this stands out as something original, something people haven't seen before. There's a buzz surrounding it, and the public is responding to that. The suburban theatre I saw it in had a cross section of 400 people riveted to the screen for close to three hours, and I could just feel the emotion of the group movie going experience all around me. It confirmed once again that movie theatres won't be going away anytime soon.

Perhaps the biggest surprise of all the opening films was MGM/UA's "Valkerie" grossing $30 million. No movie had worse buzz going for it. When a movie changes its release date several times, it never bodes well, and then when you add Tom Cruise playing a German with an eye patch, it becomes a recipe for disaster. MGM turned the movie's fate around with its best marketing campaign since the company re-emerged a couple of years ago. Instead of selling it as just another Tom Cruise movie, their television spots sold it as an exciting, historical suspense thriller. They took full advantage of the fact that it was the only thriller in the marketplace and realized many other Christmas movies were going after women and families, so men were available to hook. Cruise was just one of several silhouetted figures in the poster, and the company was discreet in showing him in his eye patch. The distributor knew they had to spend money on marketing, and they did, perhaps as much as $40 million to open it, and all those television ads were able to get its target audience familiar and comfortable with the odd sounding title. When a distributor decides to compete at Christmas, a modest marketing budget is not an option. They are forced to spend big if they want to have a fighting chance. Five movies opened on Christmas Day, and only one of them flopped, Lionsgate's "The Spirit." Lionsgate is normally smart about avoiding head-to-head competition with the studios' biggest movies (they stayed completely out of the summer), so deciding to go out with this movie on Christmas Day proved to be too much for them to overcome. Their strategy of going after the young male gaming audience may have looked good on paper, and they staged an expensive campaign to support it, but the movie just wasn't strong enough to compete at this time and it got lost. Sometimes lessons have to be learned and relearned. For an independent distributor, it's remembering who you are and sticking to the less competitive periods of the year when you can spend less and stand out more.

Historical Perspective: A Sudden Shift in Strategy for New Year's Weekend

I made the point that distributors stay away from scheduling new movies to open ahead of New Year's weekend, but there have been cases where more limited and at times high profile releases have found themselves opening some major markets during this highly competitive period. I was directly involved with one such film. Oliver Stone's "Platoon" was the important end of the year release for Orion Pictures in December, 1986. The initial release strategy was to open in six theatres in New York and Los Angeles on December 19 with the next wave of major cities to launch on January 19. The slow release pattern known as the platform release was and still is the strategy of choice distributors utilize for their high quality films that need to establish credibility and awareness before opening wider. Charles Glenn, Orion's marketing head, told *Variety* at the time, "We're positioning the picture as a class film and opting for a very conservative, near exclusive run; it's too risky to release wide without an education process." As Chicago branch manager, I was still in the process of firming up the Chicago January break when the movie opened on the coasts on December 19. After that weekend, everything started changing. From the first shows on opening day, "Platoon" was a sensation at the box office, selling out the majority of its shows all weekend. In addition, critics were heralding it as the best film of the year. Subsequently, the New York home office wanted more markets and more theatres to open in front of New Year's weekend. I received new marching orders; move the Chicago break up to Tuesday, December 30 and find six top theatres to play it. You would think that theatres would be falling over themselves wanting to play such a hot film, but the average multiplex had only six screens in the mid-80s, and some Christmas films hadn't even opened yet. Theatres had commitments to play other studio films, and no one would dare attempt to open a movie on the Tuesday between Christmas and New Year's.

When a movie has heat, nothing is impossible.

But when a movie has heat, nothing is impossible. We landed the theatres we needed when a few savvy exhibitors found ways to shuffle their bookings around and fit it in at the last moment. "Platoon" went on to become the top grossing film of the holiday season in the markets where it opened, even though it was the last one out of the gate. I still remember the excitement I felt when I experienced the lines around the block on that Tuesday opening. All six theatres sold out their initial shows and continued to sell out the rest of the week. I was on the phone calling exhibitors and shouting, "We caught lightning in a bottle, it's lightning in a bottle," over and over again. The pure thrill of a movie that hits big never gets old. One of the recurring themes in the chapters to follow is the nimbleness that distributors have to have when opportunity presents itself and the willingness and expertise to move fast in order to maximize whatever leverage they have. You have to take advantage of the situation because it just doesn't happen very often. I don't believe I've seen many films attempt a December 30th release on multiple screens since then because if it were a solid film it would have already opened because no one wants to miss out on Christmas Day business. But if a "Platoon" situation came around today, it would be much easier for a distributor to book screens at the last minute between Christmas and New Year's because of the abundance of 16 to 20 screen theatres located in all the major markets. The question then would become less about theatre availability and more about whether it was best for the film and whether or not it was strong enough to compete in an already crowded holiday marketplace.

There will be much more on release patterns throughout these pages because they represent some of the most crucial supply decisions a distributor has to make week in and week out. The questions become whether to go fast or go slow with a film, and then how fast and how slow and at what time of the year? The following two tables clarify more on the logistics and strategy of release patterns:

TOP TEN FACTORS THAT DETERMINE THE PROPER RELEASE PATTERN OF A FILM

1. Quality of the film itself
2. Competitive releases out at the same time
3. Expected gross potential
4. Anticipated word of mouth
5. Anticipated critics' reviews
6. The time of the year
7. Availability of the best theatres for the film
8. Whether it's a national, regional, limited or exclusive release
9. Level of marketing that is available and what needs to be spent to support the film
10. Audience reaction to market research screenings

DESCRIPTIONS OF DIFFERENT TYPES OF RELEASE PATTERNS

► Exclusive run – 1 theatre in each specific market

► Platform – 2 to 50 theatres on a staggered basis

► Limited – 50 to 600 theatres

► Regional – up to several hundred theatres in specific parts of the country

► Wide – 800 to 2800 theatres on a national release

► Super-Wide – 3,000 to 4,500 theatres

THIS WEEK AT THE BOX OFFICE SECTION: *Weekly Attendance: 26,194,257*

Starting with next week's chapter, there will be a "This Week at the Box Office" section listing each of the new movies that opened, their opening weekend gross, their total domestic gross, international gross and worldwide gross. The domestic gross refers to North America, the combined gross of the United States and Canada. For studio movies, the worldwide gross is more of a true barometer of a movie's success or failure. There have been numerous occasions when there has been a rush to judgment on a film with a less than stellar domestic gross only to discover later that very same movie doubled or even tripled its gross in foreign markets. There were 558 films released in 2009 that opened in at least one commercial theatre somewhere in North America. 400 of these movies were non-studio affiliated films, which will be recognized even though the vast majority of them had a very negligible effect on the marketplace. Even in rough economic times, thousands of micro-budgeted films find a way to get made every year, and 400 or so of them achieve some kind of theatrical release. Most of these films do not have an international gross to report because they either didn't have any type of release outside the U.S. or nothing was reported. In addition, when distributors acquire independent films at film festivals, a large percentage of the acquisitions are for domestic rights only. When there is an international gross reported for an independent release, the grosses can be a combined total from a variety of individual distributors scattered throughout the world which can't be attributed to any one distributor.

I wish to thank Doug Stone, box office analyst for Movieline International, for providing me with the bulk of the box office information used in the book. There are also instances when grosses are gathered from either Box Office Mojo or Box Office Guru, and they are duly noted. In addition, Mr. Stone estimates each week's total movie attendance based on the reported total weekly box office figures and average ticket prices. The estimated attendance for the week of January 2-8 was 26,194,257. As we move through the entire year, the attendance figures will fluctuate up and down based on the time of year and the strength of the releases.

MAKING THE CASE FOR MOVIE THEATRES

Week 2: January 9–15, 2009

_The argument can be made that movie theatres, the oldest method
of watching movies for over 100 years, have become the most reliable
and solid component of the movie revenue food chain._

It may be surprising to say, but after seeing the year-end numbers for the theatrical and DVD businesses, the argument can be made that movie theatres, the oldest method of watching movies for over 100 years, have become the most reliable and solid component of the movie revenue food chain. Surprising, because there's been so much talk about how theatres are being threatened by the number of new ways people can view movies, one would think their demise would be just around the corner. The theatrical business doesn't always generate the most dollars for movies, but when you look at how it's trending out, theatres are hanging tough while the crucial DVD market is in decline. The 2008 box office may not have set a new record, but it will land up being very close to the previous year's box office record of $9.6 billion, an impressive figure considering the country has been struggling to climb out of a deep recession. Combined with international's $18 billion, the much maligned theatrical industry represents close to a $28 billion dollar business that deserves respect in this tough economy. Along with a 7% downturn in the DVD market from 2007 to 2008, studios are confronting the prospect of having to accept less revenue from their pay television output deals when their current deals expire which will put added pressure on their bottom line profits. Even with up and coming delivery platforms like video-on-demand, streaming and digital downloads, theatrical, DVD and television revenues still produce the bulk of studio revenues.

The theatrical business is a business model that works very well for both the studios and theatre owners, and each is a profitable business. Neither side takes unfair advantage over the other (well, there are exceptions), nor is there a Walmart among them with disproportionate market size to wield monopolistic power over the other party. Last year studios kept audiences happy with a good mix of movies, and theatre owners kept them comfortable and well fed in their ultramodern megaplexes. You don't hear about theatre chains going out of business, filing for bankruptcy or asking for help. There are more than 39,000 movie theatre screens today, which is consistent with the last several years, and which constitute the largest amount of screens in the history of the industry. In the midst of all the competing technologies inside the home, theatres remain the only option of a social experience outside the home. That's not a bad place to be. New digital technology is in fact a friend of both distributors and exhibitors. 2009 is shaping up to be the most important year for digital 3-D with a dozen 3-D features scheduled to open. As more screens are converted to digital, there are benefits for both parties. Distributors look forward to the day when they won't have to produce and ship 35mm prints to theatres which will save the studios hundreds of millions of dollars a year. For theatre owners, more digital screens will open up more opportunities for alternative programming in off times with simulcast operas, music concerts and sporting events. On average, 25 million people in the U.S. attend movies in theatres each week, and that awareness and word of mouth go on to establish a movie's value in all the markets to follow. The value of theatres run deep and long. Going back to the earliest days of the movie business, theatres existed before production and distribution companies. The vast majority of the first wave of moguls operated nickelodeons before branching out into production and distribution. Movie theatres were the foundation of the motion picture business a hundred years ago, and they still are today. They're hanging tough.

The DVD business remains a big generator, but its days of growth are over. Gross revenues between sales and rentals still total over $20 billion, but 2008 is the third year in a row the numbers have gone down. It's a more volatile business than theatrical and has more direct competition from cable, pay-per-view, video-on-demand, pay television, streaming and digital downloads. For big, popular movies like "The Dark Knight" and "Mama Mia" it's still a very strong business, but average movies are moving a lot fewer units. "The Dark Knight" immediately became the biggest seller of the year with 11 million discs sold in the first week, which generated $200 million for Warner Brothers. Universal's "Mama Mia" continues to amaze, generating $30 million in sales on its street date after grossing $140 million domestically and over $400 million overseas. Unlike the strength of movie theatres, which are the retail outlets of the theatrical business, the DVD retail business has suffered casualties. In the last few years, Tower Records, Musicland and Sam Goody have gone out of business. Virgin Records has closed most of its stores, Hollywood Video and Movie Gallery merged and then contracted and Circuit City filed for bankruptcy and also went out of business. This volatility in the retail sector is a big difference between the theatrical and DVD businesses. All businesses need strong partners and clients, sellers need financially stable buyers and it's true that a company is only as strong as its weakest link. The loss of these retailers has had more of an immediate effect on the smaller, lower grossing films. Independent films are really starting to feel the pinch; the money that used to be there isn't there anymore. A company like Tower Records bought all types of movies. The studios can lean on Walmart, Best Buy, Target and Costco to give them their numbers, but the big box retailers don't even bother carrying a lot of these other movies.

A big question going into 2009 is whether or not Blu-ray will help revive the DVD business and to what extent it can pick up the slack. Blu-ray at this time has a bit of an uncertain future, and it's particularly difficult in a recession to grow a new product. Convincing consumers they need to upgrade to high def when satisfaction with regular DVDs is still high is a challenging proposition. The studios hope that the revenues from Blu-ray will start offsetting the slippage in the regular DVD market by next year. Distributors love Blu-ray because it's a more profitable business with the wholesale price set at $25 compared to $17 for DVDs, without much of a manufacturing cost involved.

A more important question may be how soon is the day coming when physical media like DVDs switches to digital delivery? Well, let's compare it to the music industry where they just announced their 2008 figures. 70% of all music sales came from digital sales in 2008 compared to only about 2% with movies, a very insignificant number. There is really no comparison between the music industry with their two-minute songs and the movie industry with their two-hour movies, which make for much larger files that take longer to download. During the recent Guild negotiations, the unions representing directors and actors fought hard for better deals in the various new media formats, including digital downloads, but the studios persisted in holding them off by claiming there is nothing there yet, that the revenue is inconsequential and that it's an area they'll revisit in three years to see where the business is at then. With the movie industry, people still prefer the physical theatres and to a lesser extent, the physical DVDs over streaming and downloads. Change is coming, but it's happening at its own pace and will arrive in small doses rather than at all at once.

This Week at the Box Office: *Weekly Attendance: 25,496,467*

The first wave of wide national releases of the new year will be hitting the screens with three new movies and Clint Eastwood's "Gran Torino" expanding to 2800 theatres after four weeks of very limited release. For the vast majority of the country, "Gran Torino" will be a fresh release so I am choosing to include it as an opener because in effect it will play as a 2009 film. The new movies are chasing after several different niches as is the norm, and looking at the titles reminds us that we're in January now and the holidays are over. Universal is opening a supernatural thriller "The Unborn," Fox has the wedding comedy "Bride Wars" and Sony is staging a somewhat smaller national release with the African American faith based drama "Not Easily Broke." All three of these movies have their specific audiences. Putting a horror movie in January has been a staple for years after the higher profile films of Christmas, and the 25-and-under crowd should come out to support it; a wedding comedy starring Kate Hudson and Ann Hathaway has a popular concept for women of all ages; and a religious based movie like "Not Easily Broken" should find an audience of older African American women. So where does that put Eastwood's "Gran Torino" this weekend? Considering the business it's done in limited release, "Gran Torino" has a chance to race to the top of the box office charts and put the other openers in its rearview window.

Gran Torino
Warner Brothers
Opening weekend (wide): $29,484,388
Domestic gross: $148,095,302
Foreign gross: $121,862,926
Worldwide gross: $269,958,228
Widest release: 3,045 theatres

The Unborn
Universal
Opening weekend: $19,810,585
Domestic gross: 42,670,410
Foreign gross: $33,843,640
Worldwide gross: $76,514,050
Widest release: 2,359 theatres

Made in the U.S.A.
Rialto
Opening weekend: $11,125
Domestic gross: $95,209
Foreign gross: NA
Widest release: 2 theatres

Bride Wars
20th Century Fox
Opening weekend: $21,058,173
Domestic gross: $58,715,510
Foreign gross: $55,947,951
Worldwide gross: $114,663,461
Widest release: 3,228 theatres

Not Easily Broken
Sony
Opening weekend: $5,314,278
Domestic gross: $10,572,742
Foreign gross: $154,167
Worldwide gross: $10,726,909
Widest release: 725 theatres

Just Another Love Story
Koch Lorber
Opening weekend: $3,470
Domestic gross: $45, 835
Foreign gross: NA
Widest release: 3 theatres

Number of U.S. Theatre Screens
1948–2011

1948 – 18,631

1958 – 16,354

1963 – 12,652

1970 – 13,750

1974 – 15,384

1980 – 17,675

1984 – 19,589

1986 – 22,665

1989 – 22,921

1996 – 29,545

2000 – 37,396

2004 – 36,594

2009 – 39,028

2010 – 39,527

2011 – 39,641

Until 1963, the year the first twin theatre was built by theatre owner Stanley Durwood in Kansas City, all the theatres were single screen buildings. With the vast majority of today's theatres being multi-screen, there are approximately 5,600 theatres that make up the 39,641 screens.

Sources: National Assn. of Theatre Owners, IHS. Screen Digest

Conversations with Industry Professionals

Paul Silk – Senior Vice President, Head Film Buyer, Marcus Theatres, Milwaukee, WI
This interview took place over several sessions during 2011 and 2012.

> *"It's great if everything lines up perfectly to everyone's satisfaction,*
> *but I'm also paid to make and handle trouble when necessary."*
>
> *—Paul Silk*

Q: *How many years have you worked in the film industry?*

PS: It stands at 38 years and counting. My first job was with K-Tel Motion Pictures in Minneapolis in 1974 as their account receivables manager. I came to Chicago in 1975 when I was offered a position as the assistant to the Central Division Manager at Columbia Pictures, again supervising the accounts receivables.

Q: *Beginning your long career in accounts receivables wasn't a bad place to start, was it?*

PS: That's true. It was a chance to learn the movie business from the ground level up. Learning the relative performance of any theatre on your titles is nice to look at, but the full collection of the studio's film rental share of the box office is what mattered most. I was involved in cleaning up some old balances that had been languishing on the books for years, so the research necessary to close those items down exposed me to the collection process of a large studio. Review of the old trial balances gave me a lot of information about how the business worked. In those days they showed the contract terms, any adjustment of terms made to the contract, co-op advertising shares, what had been paid up to that point, and then you closed the items off once they were fully resolved.

Q: *How long were you at Columbia?*

PS: It was a short stint at Columbia because another distributor, Avco Embassy, offered me a job as the Chicago Sales Manager, which quickly turned into a promotion to the Chicago Branch Manager position. It was a great time to break into the movie industry in a large market like Chicago because so many different distributors were represented in the city, affording a wealth of opportunity for movement and advancement in distribution if you demonstrated interest and talent. I left Avco after two or three years to take a job at an independent sub-distributor, Mid-America Releasing, but then Embassy contacted me a few months later and offered me the opportunity to come back as their Midwestern Division Manager, so I rejoined Avco. After another two years at Avco I left, intending to take a similar position with Disney, but instead joining the infamous American International Pictures in the fall of 1979 as their Midwestern Division Manager. It was a good five-year run over there.

Eventually AIP's Sam Arkoff sold the company to Filmways, and they in turn sold to Orion Pictures in 1982. I changed studios three times without leaving my desk in Chicago. Due to lack of titles to distribute immediately following their Filmways purchase, Orion cut their distribution structure from five divisions to three and sent me to Los Angeles as the Western Division Manager. I was out there for a little under a year, but eventually the title count was back on the upswing, and I came back to Chicago when the company structure was restored to five divisions. I stayed at Orion for another couple of years before leaving in 1984 to take a division job at a start- up company, Cannon Releasing. Those were the boom years of the 1980s when there were nearly twenty studio distributors represented in Chicago, all flush with cash from the new home video business.

Q: *Were those good years at Cannon?*

PS: Yes, they were five wild and wooly years. There was constant action as they released a lot of movies. They created an interesting business model with many good genre exploitation movies starring actors like Charles Bronson and Chuck Norris in addition to picking up some worthy art films from film festivals. Cannon reduced the risk of funding a large release schedule with the presale of foreign territorial and domestic ancillary rights, a business model that other specialty companies later adopted.

Q: *Did you have a lot of autonomy at Cannon?*

PS: Yes, I did. One of the advantages of working in the Midwest over placement on either coast was having a greater control of your own shop as opposed to handling New York and Los Angeles where more senior executives were involved in local distribution decisions. Chicago was a challenging market as there was a relatively small screen count in the market at that time to serve a large population base, and the substantial competition from other distributors for space in those theatres kept you on your toes. I had a hand in tailoring the local release patterns, placing the right movies in the right theatres at the right time, and a key negotiating point was that you had some flexibility with the film rental terms. Yes, there was an expectation of delivering a satisfactory bottom line, but I always took the same approach at every studio I represented; that getting the proper theatres was more important than getting a better deal from an inferior theatre. If the movies performed, we collected a higher percentage film rental, and if a title bombed, we adjusted the percentage downward and moved on. Cannon closed down their Chicago office in 1989 after new ownership came in, as they faced some challenging cash flow problems.

Q: *1989 was the year of the big stock market crash which did in a bunch of independent distributors so Cannon's collapse was related to that, wasn't it? There was a big market correction.*

PS: Yes, the crash impaired access to capital for a number of smaller studios. I left film distribution at that point and went into the film transportation business for about a year and a half. In 1991 I was offered the position of film buyer by an old friend at Mid-Continent Theatres in Minneapolis. I had never worked on the exhibition side of the business, liked that possibility, and it meant that I would be going back to my hometown. Moving to film buying and utilizing my experience in film distribution looked like a great way to revive my career. That was November, 1991, and I have been in exhibition ever since. In 1995, the circuit was sold to Carmike Cinemas, and it left me without an employer. I decided to branch out and do some film buying with the outside exhibitors that I represented while at Mid-Continent, and that was the start of my own business.

Q: *So you became an entrepreneur?*

PS: Yes, it was certainly not something that I consciously contemplated, but circumstances forced it, and it was the best thing that ever happened to me. My wife Mary Ann and I built our business into a very viable business, and at the peak we were booking 230 screens in the Midwest, and we enjoyed doing it together. It was hard work and a lot of fun. We represented everything from a first run 21-screen complex down to small town single screens, discount houses and drive-ins; we did a little bit of everything, and the variety made it that much more enjoyable.

Q: *When did Marcus first approach you about going to work for them?*

PS: Marcus first approached me in 2007 to join them as their head film buyer. I was very happy in my existing situation at that time and initially turned them down, but they were very persistent. I knew a lot of the key executives at Marcus from selling them movies over the years, and I knew that the ownership took pride in having a stable management team on the theatre side of the company. Their long time film buyer Mike Kominsky had retired after decades in that role, and his successor Michael Ogrodowski was working toward his retirement after forty plus years with the company. After some very long discussions with Marcus, and with a lot of input and counsel from Mary Ann, we agreed that an opportunity of this stature might never come my way again, and I took the job.

If I had walked away from the offer, I could spend the rest of my career wondering what might have happened had I accepted the job. I started at Marcus in January, 2008.

Q: *How did the transition go from running your own business to becoming a part of a management team again?*

PS: It was a tremendous change, but that was part of the appeal. Getting back to working in an office environment after 13 years working at home and operating within the corporate world within a very different environment has been both jarring and invigorating.

Q: *Marcus Theatres has a long and illustrious history, doesn't it?*

PS: The circuit celebrated its 75th anniversary in 2010. Founder Ben Marcus started the company when he opened the Campus Theatre in Ripon, Wisconsin in 1935, and that single screen theatre remains open to this day. It is still a family run business with Steve Marcus serving as board chairman and with Greg Marcus as our president and CEO. The company operates two separate businesses, our movie theatre business and the hotel business, and both operate with autonomy. It makes for a desirable business mix because it generally seems that if one of the businesses is suffering a bit, the other one is doing better. Each component gives us safety and balance against the potential vagaries of the other. Our hotel business temporarily suffered along with the rest of the travel sector during the recent recession, but a solid performance by our theatre business helped to compensate. When both units are cooking, we're all dancing over at Marcus.

Q: *How many screens and locations does your circuit have?*

PS: Marcus owns and operates 54 theatres and just under 700 screens. All told my department books 71 theatres and over 850 screens when outside management contracts are added to the portfolio. We negotiate for the outside theatres with the same intensity that we do for our owned theatres. Our theatres are located in seven states, and we are currently the sixth largest theatre chain in the country. I supervise five people in the Film Department, and all of them have an active role in buying and booking for some of our theatres. We approve the placement of all studio advertising materials for our theatres, program the trailer placement on individual screens, and we handle some of the customer service issues. As the head buyer, I report directly to Bruce Olsen, the president of Marcus Theatres, while also serving as one of the six members of the theatre division executive committee where we consider our strategic planning, expansion, possible acquisitions, new implementations like the recent rollout of digital screens, food and beverage options, alternative programming, and new media opportunities.

Q: As head film buyer, how are you judged?

PS: Nothing matters more to me and more to Marcus than positioning our theatres to perform at their absolute maximum level while making sure that film costs are as fair and reasonable as possible. At the end of the day, it comes down to how much revenue was delivered to the bottom line. I think that's true for all our different divisions, but since I'm in charge of the film department, there is a lot more focus on what I do because our film box office generates the largest revenues and expense in the theatre division and therefore there is more impact generated by my results. We do set benchmarks and goals to reach based upon our past results and on the anticipated market conditions going forward.

Q: *What kind of autonomy do you have in making your film deals? Do you still get paid for the fair share of haggling you have to do with distributors on a day-to-day basis?*

PS: Yes, cost control for our film product remains my number one priority. With each new release, you must try to assess what the box office results should be for that title, and based on that expectation, you try to determine a fair price for that picture. Marcus generates nearly $150 million a year at the box office, so each percentage point of film cost negotiated in any deal is worth a lot of money.

While I have a lot of autonomy in making those determinations, if I feel that the deal is unfairly priced to anticipated performance and if accepting it would set a bad precedent that could negatively impact our bottom line in the short term or in the long run, I'm not going to go forward and book the picture at an excessive price without having my superiors fully aware of my reservations about the deal in order to let them weigh with their opinion.

I always find that if you have your superiors well informed in advance and everyone is on board, it removes any second guessing and buyer's remorse after the fact that might exist if you did this unilaterally. You don't want to try to hide bad news or expensive news after the fact because you failed to put your problem on the table in advance for a consensus consideration and resolution.

Q: *Have you passed on a major motion picture in the last year?*

PS: Yes, but only as a last resort if I consider a price for that picture to be so unfair that accepting it would set a bad pricing precedent for the circuit or for our clients going forward. I will temper my initial impulse to pass on that picture in order to consult with my superiors and with our clients to say this is a deal that I would not make, but that we also have to consider the potential impact on the relationship with the studio supplier in the future if we decide to pass on the picture.

Q: *Can you talk about the various revenue streams in exhibition?*

PS: The core transaction of the ticket sold to the customer to see the movie remains the primary source of our revenues. As movie attendance has not grown in recent years with the exception of 2009, it is very difficult to expect total attendance growth for the entire industry, but you can concentrate on growing attendance within your specific markets. We have concentrated primarily on the addition of new opportunities to capture additional revenues: new food and beverage options, the addition of alternative programming, and screen advertising.

Q: *It must be a good thing there are a lot more revenue streams for theatres than in the past. However, when we talk revenues, it's not necessarily profits, correct?*

PS: The challenge is to add these new innovations and revenues without any negative impact on our existing areas of profit.

Q: *But concessions have always been the profit center for theatres; I'd imagine that hasn't changed.*

PS: Yes, I was quoted 20 years ago saying that, "If not for popcorn there would be no theatres, if not for DVDs there would be no movies," as they were the core profit centers for exhibitors and studios. Neither of us could survive if the tickets sold were the only revenue stream. There have been some changes over the years; theatres have added a lot of options to what has traditionally been offered at the concession counter, and now the movement is to offer more sophisticated and upscale food items including liquor service in some theatres. In other theatres, we offer in-theatre dining, and we have restaurants attached to some of our theatres.

On the studio side the decline in the DVD market has eroded an important revenue stream that has not yet been fully restored by the steady growth of the foreign box office.

Q: How about your other revenue streams?

PS: Revenue from alternative content programming such as live simulcast or replay of operas, concerts, and other content is growing but remains a relatively small player at this point when compared to film. We have developed a loyal following for our opera and ballet series, and we always hope to find other programming options that will consistently deliver results for us. Negotiating terms for alternative product is challenging as many of the suppliers of that content are relatively new to the game.

Advertising has become a solid revenue source on the screen, in the lobby, and outside of the theatre building, but we have to be very careful about it. The additional revenue is welcome, but we can't go overboard with third party advertising. We have to be careful about the tone and quality of the advertising content that we accept or we risk turning our customers off. We also don't want the marketing that we place in support of upcoming movies to be lost in the overall mix.

Video arcade revenue is a mere blip at this point. The rabid gamers are playing online.

Q: You mentioned you and your staff are involved in trailer placement. When the MPAA introduced the new green band trailer approved for appropriate audiences a couple of years ago, did that make your job more difficult?

PS: In the past it was either a green band trailer approved for all audiences or a red band trailer to be used only with R rated movies. When the MPAA carved out a third trailer option with the designation "for appropriate audiences" it blurred the existing placement standard and shifted the burden to carefully review the trailer content and to determine an appropriate placement of that trailer back to exhibitors. We have always been very careful at Marcus Theatres about our trailer placement; we still review the content of every trailer in order to ensure appropriate placement.

Q: Isn't it difficult to see a difference in a regular green band trailer and one for "appropriate audiences"?

PS: While it is likely that there are some subtle differences in content, it appears that the primary purpose of this change is to expand the scope of our trailer placement to additional features. Generally speaking, we will not place a PG13 film with a G rated picture, for example. We're very careful about how the tone and the content of the trailer matches up with the tone and the content of the feature playing with that trailer regardless of MPAA rating. We want to be confident that all of the trailer footage will be acceptable to the audiences that we expect to see the feature. We continue to strictly adhere to our own guidelines.

As an example, a green band trailer is created for an R rated picture and tagged "for appropriate audiences," and a studio will seek to place that trailer with PG13 titles. As our policy is to place trailers for R rated movies only with R rated pictures, that green band won't get any PG13 placement, so we could just as easily play a red band trailer instead because our trailer placement for that title remains restricted to R rated features. It also means that our R rated features get a lot of trailers for upcoming R rated titles as this is the only placement that we will allow. The restrictions on trailer placement that we impose in our theatres may send the audience to the Internet to view those trailers if they have the interest to do so.

Q: *When you look at a film in advance at a trade screening, what's going through your mind? What are you looking for?*

PS: The first consideration is the relative quality of the picture and its appeal to its intended audience. That being said, I have a lot of screens to book and a lot of seats to fill. Therefore, we are likely to play nearly every wide release that the studios offer us. The key questions become how wide do we go with our support and how much will it cost us to play this picture?

Q: *It's a lot different than it used to be for film buyers when there were fewer screens and competitive bidding for films.*

PS: Today's multiplex business model removes a lot of programming risk that my predecessors faced 25 to 30 years ago. We have larger buildings with bigger screen counts making it far less likely that we will make a critical mistake by playing the wrong picture at the expense of playing the right one. We expect to play almost every title available to us to a varying degree. Today's large complexes are located with sufficient distance between them in so that most cases, nearly every first run theatre in large markets will play the movies simultaneously with each other rather than to compete by bidding for the opportunity to play a title at the exclusion of other theatres in the market. So for a film buyer it is a bit easier knowing that you can draw upon a large pool of pictures, but there are still plenty of other issues that can make the job difficult.

Q: *Are Mondays still the most crucial day of the week for exhibitors and distributors?*

PS: Absolutely. That's game day; nothing has changed there. Our booking plan to determine internally what will play on our screens on Friday is underway first thing on Monday, but the negotiations necessary to reach that outcome can drag on into Tuesday and sometimes even into Wednesday.

Q: *Does it ever happen that you have to tell a distributor you can't open a movie due to holdovers and the number of movies opening on a given week?*

PS: It rarely happens, but there are a couple times of year when there are four or five movies opening into an already crowded market. At that point I have to deliver the bad news to a supplier. Even though the planning and initial negotiating process has evolved to meet a much different contemporary marketplace for exhibitors, we still have the same fights and feel many of the same pressures that we did in the past.

Distributors still fight for every screen and often for the best possible schedule on every screen. In our case since our theatres are large, we want to book multiple prints when appropriate and to maintain those multiple prints as a convenience to our customers as long as they are viable. Our studio suppliers want intelligent use of multiple screens for their titles and may require a minimum shelf life on those additional screens to justify the additional expense that they face to allow expansion of their feature to additional screens.

A current issue is the relatively limited shelf space in some of my theatres for 3D titles. We face an occasional overload of 3D movies, and that's where some of the most frustrating fights have centered. Let me explain it this way. I may be booking a 16-screen theatre, but if within that theatre I have only two 3D screens, it is like booking a twin cinema like back in the day for that 3D component. That's a more difficult dynamic to resolve.

Q: *Take us through a typical Monday morning.*

PS: We start with a look at our internal results and compare them to the national results for all film titles. We evaluate all of the external expert analysis available to us and consider the performance projections for the remaining life of the pictures that are already on the screen as well as the anticipated performance of the titles that we are about to open. We use our technology to acquire and sift through this mass of information, evaluating the overall performance of our theatres, the relative performance of pictures within our theatres, and the relative performance of our competitors in specific markets as compared to what these movies are doing nationally.

It is crucial to have this information as soon as possible to help determine an optimum lineup for each theatre for the upcoming week. You craft your game plan, and then it's a matter of getting on the phone and hashing it out with your suppliers. We try to anticipate what our studio suppliers must deliver to their producers and executives, and we make every effort to deliver what our executives expect of us in our theatres. We negotiate it out, we do some horse trading, and eventually we try to find a compromise to resolve any differences.

That's where I earn my money.

Q: *If Mondays weren't uncomfortable, they wouldn't need the Paul Silks of the world, right?*

PS: You said it. It's great if everything lines up perfectly to everyone's satisfaction, but I am also paid to make and handle trouble when necessary.

Q: *If it was all cut and dried and there were 30 screens and 15 pictures...*

PS: My services are no longer needed.

In our film department, the staff varies in age and in industry experience. The senior members of the team can bring the benefit of their history and perspective to the discussion and will recall what was done in a similar situation or in that particular playing time in the past. We draw upon that experience covering a specific situation to offer guidance to our youngest staff and in order to add to their foundation of experience.

Q: *Are there still conversations that are profanity laden, or is that a thing of the past? Has it become more civil between distributors and exhibitors?*

PS: Let me put it this way, if someone in the office comes over to close your door during a heated discussion, it sometimes means that you're doing your job. Things can still get sticky when suppliers form an unreasonable expectation of what the marketplace can deliver to them and then try to use intimidation to force poor solutions onto situations that don't merit those solutions. You have to demonstrate that you are willing to take the fight on, to go toe to toe with the other party, and to see the fight through to the end because you have a strong belief in the merits of your desired outcome.

The buyer and the seller have differing priorities; some are easily bridged, and some are impossible to bridge. Civility ebbs and flows.

Q: *The rough and tumble world of the movie industry, some things haven't changed.*

PS: Battles keep the adrenaline going. Our professional relationships are such we can conduct those fights, we can finish those fights, and we can still come in to the office the next day and do business together from a neutral starting point. Whatever happened yesterday is now in the past, and we move on. There is still a basic interdependence between the studio seller and the exhibitor buyer. They need us to play their pictures, and we need their pictures for our theatres. If someone threatens to go over my head to complain about me, I would have to believe that whoever is taking that call above me will think that I am doing my job and am not simply rolling over in the negotiation.

Q: *Talking about fights, let's move on to the 800-pound gorilla in the room, Premium Video-on-Demand.*

PS: PVOD is considered to be Armageddon for theatres, pure and simple. The exhibition community has expected a DVD release date at an average of about four months after theatrical release, and we feel that it is crucial to keep that window to maintain the vitality of movie theatres. The studios will seek a varying DVD release date window that may be tied to that picture's performance or to a specific retail season that may be longer or shorter than the four-month average cited earlier. We try to be understanding and reasonable partners in accommodating these variances in windowing to ancillary markets, but there are limits. On occasion, we face a DVD release date that encroaches upon a title that still has some remaining shelf life in theatres, and we feel that we have been shorted if we haven't been given that opportunity to fully realize our revenues.

Now the fight has moved to Premium VOD with the potential for much shorter windows, and that is very troubling. As an industry, we have lived off the natural progression of the traditional windows from media to media at changing price points to the consumer, and if those windows are compressed moving the audience away from our theatres or moving to a cheaper viewing price point at an earlier date, our bottom lines will be greatly impacted. It becomes a threat to our very existence if movie theatre attendance is further eroded by conditions of our own making. By law, exhibitors can't band together to make a collective response to this financial threat, but there is always the possibility that each exhibitor will look at the problem and as individuals reach a common conclusion.

Each exhibitor has their own opinion, and it seems that we rarely agree on anything, but this is such an important issue that it may drive exhibition to a common frustration and then to a purely coincidental common response out of desperation. I can't imagine that this issue will play out in such a hostile fashion or that we can't find a way to agreeably solve this issue with our studio partners instead.

Q: *In the past, the major circuits have protected their turf very well and have been very consistent. Threaten to play a picture day and date anywhere else with theatres and the theatres either pull the dates or don't play the film in the first place.*

PS: This is a very competitive business with some very thin margins for us to protect. We don't want to lose a customer because we have served them poorly, and we don't want to lose a customer because they can now view the picture through pirate sites or other sanctioned media outlets while it is still in our theatres. We still believe that seeing a movie on the big screen with an audience of your friends and family and neighbors is still the best and most enjoyable viewing option.

It seems that even with these very large issues that affect one segment of the industry or another or that may impact the industry collectively, self-interest always seems to trump our mutual interests in the end.

Q: *Has something inherently changed on this issue that is more threatening than ever before?*

PS: Well, distributors keep saying we must try this new revenue option whether you agree with us or not, that it doesn't matter at this point what you think. Many studios are owned by large media conglomerates that must consider the revenues produced by several internal divisions including network and cable stations and their cable systems along with home video. Exhibitors have a much smaller media footprint to worry about.

Q: *Ultra premium priced PVOD initiatives were supposed to happen two different times in 2011 with the latest being Universal with "Tower Heist" and nothing ever happened. Can you recap the particulars of what happened with "Tower Heist"? Is that considered the biggest threat to date and when does the next shoe drop?*

PS: It was widely reported that Universal sought to test a premium priced PVOD offer for "Tower Heist" in two markets three weeks or so after the theatrical opening. Some of the exhibitors in the proposed test markets objected to the encroachment on the theatrical run and objected; that PVOD test was cancelled. As I recall, it was reported that some other theatre circuits were very concerned about that test even though they were not directly impacted. If the test had occurred, the next test could impact a different set of exhibitors directly.

It is difficult to foresee where this issue is headed in the future. Anything that threatens to shift movie viewing interest away from our theatres will always be of concern to us.

Q: *Since that happened, have there been more substantive discussions between the studios and exhibition?*

PS: There hasn't been any grand summit on the subject. Each studio must negotiate individually with theatre circuits, and each exhibitor must also negotiate individually with studios. There may have been some renewed conversation on the topic, but I haven't been involved.

Q: *What's your argument to the speculation that most movies do the majority of their business in the first four weeks so it shouldn't be that big of a deal?*

PS: We have a number of movies that have played for months. We have taken pictures off of our screens prematurely as they were approaching their DVD release date. Perhaps it's only ten movies a year that generate those extended runs with exceptional legs, but that should still be a consideration when determining a reasonable DVD date. One size doesn't fit all when it comes to the DVD window.

The performance of a picture should be also considered before a PVOD date is set. If they announce a PVOD date for a title that is still doing business in theatres, what is our solution? Do we take the picture off the screen? Do we go to our customers and propose that instead of sitting around your flat screen at home, why not come to our theatre instead, and we will match the PVOD price for your family?

These and other potential remedies considered in response aren't under serious consideration yet, but we must consider every possible response as the studios have not seriously discussed with their exhibition partners what considerations might be given to exhibitors to compensate for their potential loss of revenue.

Q: *Considering both 2010 and 2011 have seen drops in attendance and box office; does it strengthen the studios argument and weaken the exhibitors stance that something new has to be attempted to boost their revenues?*

PS: It seems counterintuitive that the studios would put at risk the theatrical revenues that are still very reliable and healthy in order to solve a problem elsewhere in their revenue stream. The domestic theatrical box office will produce $10 billion dollars plus annually. That number is unlikely to rise to $15 billion per year, nor is it likely to fall to $5 billion. Growth in the worldwide box office should improve studio revenues.

Q: *On another subject, I've noticed some of your Chicago area theatres have recently switched to all digital screens. Can you talk about where the Marcus circuit is at the start of 2012 with your conversion from* *film projection to digital projection?*

PS: Our conversion to digital cinema was a four year plus process that was already underway the first week that I joined the company. We met several times over the course of negotiations with every potential supplier as the equipment pricing and the available equipment options improved with the each new innovation over the four years. We met several times with the many financing entities that could help us to fund the digital rollout, and we met many times with the entities that would handle the transactions covering the studio's participation in the funding of our digital conversion.

There were selections to be made for each of these deal components, and the final trick was to pull the whole package together as every piece of the deal impacted all of the other pieces. Every executive in the company was involved in the process.

Digital cinema continues to evolve with the recent introduction of higher image resolutions, higher frame rates, the use of digital options to improve service to our sight and hearing impaired customers, and upcoming improvements to digital sound.

We completed our conversion in the fall of 2011, and my close involvement from the outset was quite an education.

Q: *What's the first skill that comes to your mind that has helped you most in your long movie industry career?*

PS: I think that first and foremost the most important skill that anyone can bring is the ability to listen. Your customers, your suppliers, your associates, and your competitors will all deliberately or inadvertently convey a lot of valuable information and insight to you if you are willing to listen to them. You learn more with your ears and with your eyes than you do with your mouth.

This business moves very quickly, so the ability to effectively process and utilize the information you have acquired through your listening skills into quick and decisive action is a crucial element to this job. Moving that information to a positive result comes from your career experience. It helps greatly to have that foundation of experience to utilize.

Q: *So you use your instinct a lot, your trained memory bank of past experiences and situations you have been involved in before?*

PS: Yes.

Q: *Doesn't that lead to another skill, thinking quick on your feet and being able to have that quick response be the correct one?*

PS: Pulling the trigger and making that right call, that's the leadership question. If you are in a leadership position, get in front and lead. Draw upon your experience, carefully weigh your options, and make the call. That's not to say that a decision can't be changed, but until you put something on the table, you haven't moved the process forward. I can always listen to a contrarian reaction and still reconsider and change my decision.

Q: *Any final lessons you want to share.*

PS: My approach to this job is to honestly look at the marketplace and then to project where it will be in the weeks and months ahead. Chart out what you expect to do in your theatres; chart out how you expect the current and upcoming pictures will perform. Determine what you can easily promise to do, determine which decisions may come down to the last minute, and be certain that you can make good on your promise before giving it. My approach has been very basic; tell the truth, very carefully consider every decision that you make, and deliver on your promises. No one will ever doubt your sincerity, and your good reputation will remain intact. In the end, your success in this business is still tied to your reputation, and that is what truly matters most in an industry with a rather small fraternity of buyers and sellers.

Q: ***Thank you for your time and insight.***

PS: Thank you.

Week 2: Questions for Discussion

1. How can the argument be made that movie theatres are still the foundation of the motion picture industry?

2. Compare the retail portion of the theatrical business to that of the DVD business.

3. How is a film buyer for a movie theatre circuit evaluated by his superiors?

4. Which day is the most crucial day of the week for exhibitors and distributors, and what makes it so? Under what circumstances can it become a very uncomfortable situation for the film buyer?

5. Explain what Premium Video-on-Demand is and why distributors and exhibitors are at odds with this issue. Choose one of the side's arguments and defend that position in terms of what you feel is best for the film industry at this time.

6. How long did it take the Marcus circuit to complete the process of converting to all-digital projection in their theatres? How many parties participated in the discussions, and why did it take so long?

7. What leadership qualities does Paul Silk utilize in his role of head film buyer? Which of the traits of his do you feel would be most important to emulate as you pursue your own passion and career?

REMEMBERING HOOP DREAMS
AND ONE SPECIAL SCREENING

Week 3: January 16–22, 2009

It shows again that Hollywood, even when it seems like it's a cookie cutter business, implements different strategies for different movies.

This weekend is significant for both Hollywood movies and independent films. It marks the first holiday on the calendar with Monday's Martin Luther King, Jr.'s birthday affording Hollywood with one of those four day weekends they love to take advantage of, while in Park City, Utah, the Sundance Film Festival begins its ten day run. When studios set their annual release schedules, the first thing they do after they position their summer and Christmas movies is to look for all the national holidays that provide that extra day to a weekend that can produce a four day weekend gross instead of a three day one. A distributor's job is to maximize a film's gross so whenever kids are off from school, that's where they want to be. The marketplace is on a roll with last weekend being up 14% over the same weekend last year, and this weekend gets crowded in a hurry with six more movies going wide nationally, four new films and two limited ones expanding to over 1,000 runs. Here are the movies hitting the multiplexes:

- ▶ "Paul Blart: Mall Cop" – Sony
- ▶ "Hotel for Dogs" – Paramount
- ▶ "My Bloody Valentine 3D" – Lionsgate
- ▶ "Notorious" – Fox Searchlight
- ▶ "Defiance" – Paramount Vantage (expanding nationally)
- ▶ "Last Chance Harvey" – Overture (expanding nationally)

Six movies going wide in the same week is an unusual occurrence that may happen only two or three times a year. It's a good weekend to open a movie, but six films may be a bit much and will test the strength of a month that is not known for being one of the strongest of the year. There are still plenty of holdovers to contend with, starting with Clint Eastwood's "Gran Torino" which had an outstanding gross last weekend. This has been an interesting movie to follow. It shows again that Hollywood, even when it seems like it's a cookie-cutter business, implements different strategies for different movies. Warners used a platform release with "Gran Torino," a strategy generally used for artier, harder to define films where the interest has to be grown before it attempts to attract a wider audience. The film opened in 19 theatres December 12, and for the next four weeks it only grew to 84 theatres, so most of the county couldn't see it. But what makes this different is "Gran Torino" isn't an art film, it's an accessible mainstream drama with some confrontational action that has Eastwood in his tough guy mode audiences haven't seen in a while. Could "Gran Torino" have gone wide at Christmas and done well? Probably. But the results speak for themselves. Warners waited until January 9 to bust out to 2,800 theatres where it had less competition, and proceeded to gross over $29 million over the three-day weekend, Eastwood's biggest opener of his career. The strategy worked to perfection, building pent up demand for the film by keeping the supply low and allowing word of mouth and interest to build with aggressive television marketing built around another one of Clint's iconic lines delivered to punks, "Get off my lawn."

What's the key to Clint Eastwood's continued success? Even at 78 years old, Eastwood can direct rings around most directors. Last year with "The Changeling" and "Gran Torino," he directed two movies that came out within two months of each other. Who else does that? It's not about age, it's about talent. "Gran Torino" is his 66th film as an actor, 29th as a director. He stays on top of his game because he knows how to tell good stories, makes his movies quickly and cheaply, stays under budget and turns a consistent profit on his films. "Gran Torino" cost less than $30 million, and it has already grossed over $40 million. Eastwood will keep directing more films but he says this may be his last acting role. He is truly one of a kind in today's Hollywood.

Sundance is opening today, and it is the first major film festival since the economic meltdown began on Wall Street last September with the collapse of Lehman Brothers. The filmmakers will be facing a much more challenging landscape. Sundance for years has represented the bellwether for American independent film, the trends, the expectations and the quality of the independent films that will be coming out for the rest of the year. In the past, films like "Hoop Dreams," "Memento," "Blair Witch Project," "Napoleon Dynamite," "March of the Penguins" and "Little Miss Sunshine" have gone on to great acclaim and success. This is where filmmakers hope to get noticed and start careers. It's still the best place to sell American indies, but the economy has meant fewer media making the trek there this year to write about them and fewer distributors left standing to buy them. In 2007 the value of acquisition deals totaled $45 million; in 2008 it dropped off to only $15 million, and no real hits emerged. The worry is that this year that trend will continue and the deal making will be slow.

Robert Redford at the age of 72 has had as an iconic career as Clint Eastwood, but their careers have taken different paths. Redford's lasting legacy will be his singular and unmatched commitment to American independent film as head of the Sundance Film Festival. The growth of Sundance over the last 25 years has mirrored the growth of the entire independent industry that has been built around it. And it's not only the festival but also the yearlong screenwriting and directing workshops that are conducted at the Sundance Institute that help train and nurture future filmmakers. Outside the fact that films that emerge out of Sundance are always some of the best films of the year, they bring the freedom of new ideas, new points of view, new energy and new talent. Without that any business can grow stale and wither away. A number of these young filmmakers have gone on to become very influential figures in Hollywood. Christopher Nolan, Brian Singer, the Coen Brothers, Quentin Tarantino and Steven Soderbergh are just a few of the directors whose first films debuted at Sundance. New talent continues to be discovered, but the opportunities have lessened somewhat with the contraction of the industry, making it harder for filmmakers to break through with what has become a very mature business. The new filmmakers and their films are going through some tough times in today's market, and we may see fewer films being distributed in the next couple of years. With that being said, independent films will find a way to survive and adapt, but whether many of these smaller films will still have a primary theatrical presence remains to be seen.

Remembering "Hoop Dreams"

Fifteen years ago this week I attended my first Sundance Film Festival. Along with my business partner John Iltis, we were the producers' reps for "Hoop Dreams" and this was going to be the first film we ever represented and tried to sell to a distributor. Those ten days in January, 1994 were to prove as exhilarating and tension filled as any I've spent in the 34 years I worked in the movie industry. It was quite a ride that I'll never forget. Sundance was different then. It was more leisurely; the Hollywood agents and random celebrities hadn't invaded Park City, Utah, yet, and there were just a lot fewer people around. It was more of a film festival than a market, and the majority of sales, if they occurred at all, happened after the festival, not during it. The festival had always been separated by the first five days and the last five days (A & B packages), and back then more attention and importance were placed on the back end of the festival rather than the front end. For that reason, I went alone to Sundance as the front man to start the buzz, lay the foundation and cover the first screenings, with the filmmakers and John meeting up with me during the second half. It was a bit intimidating, and I was definitely nervous. It was a good nervous, and I hoped I was up to the task.

What helped was in addition to a stack of press kits in my suitcase, I held a very special transcript in my hands, which was the result of some exceptional work behind the scenes by John Iltis, arguably the top movie publicist in Chicago at the time. This document would prove to be our ace in the hole and, for me, a huge confidence booster as I flew off to

Utah. John had called his old friend Larry Dieckhaus, the producer of the Siskel and Ebert nationally syndicated television show, and pitched him a private screening of "Hoop Dreams" with the idea that Gene and Roger would be the first critics in the country to see this Chicago documentary that was to have its World Premiere at Sundance the following week. We knew they weren't going to Sundance, and it was worth the effort to make the pitch and see what came of it. What made it more problematic was that we had to tell them it was three hours long, it had to be shown in 16mm, and we had to find a place to screen it outside the critics' regular screening room. Even after all of that, they agreed to watch it, and I attended the screening with them in the old spacious Art Institute theatre. It was nerve-wracking sitting in the back of that theatre wondering how they were responding to the film. The professional protocol was that you could never ask them what they thought of it as they departed the screening. This drove the filmmakers crazy, but all I could tell them was that "they looked like they were really into it."

We immediately knew the significance of what was happening; it was
something that never happened before and would never happen again.

We were thinking maybe we could get a good publicity article out of it and never for a minute imagined it would go any further than that. Well, it did. A couple of days later a call came into our office asking for some video clips of the movie at which time our excitement and speculation started growing. They wouldn't, would they? Could it be possible they would put it on their show along with the current releases they were reviewing? A movie without a distributor, without a release date, without ever having been shown in public yet? That's actually what they decided to do, and the show was set to go national during the first weekend of the festival. Was this really happening? I couldn't watch it before I left for Park City, but a transcript of their review was faxed to our office. It began with Gene Siskel saying, "This weekend at Utah's Sundance Film Festival, a premiere showcase for independent film, the movie world will be discovering a very special documentary called "Hoop Dreams"...." All I could say is after I read the full transcript, I figured I didn't need a plane to get to Utah. We immediately knew the significance of what was happening; it was something that never happened before and would never happen again. Gene Siskel and Roger Ebert were at the peak of their careers in 1994 and were the two most influential critics in the country back when critics and newspapers really meant something. We also knew very well that once the show aired any and all of their comments could be used for public consumption, and that transcript could become a blueprint for any future distributor's marketing campaign.

We certainly lucked out, but then again, we put the film and ourselves in a position where good things could happen, and they did. Their rave review on television and the attention it received didn't lead to any immediate offers and a quick sale, but it gave the film a shot of real credibility and momentum as more and more festival attendees and distributors were buzzing about it as the one film everyone had to see. The key to "Hoop Dreams" was the quality of the film itself and the emotional power it had over audiences. Then it won the Audience Award, which just confirmed its audience appeal. But behind the scenes, there were several challenges and negatives we were battling to overcome: The three hour length, the fact it was shot on video, that it was a documentary, that PBS already controlled the first broadcast window, and that the filmmakers had previously agreed to a two week booking of the film at the Film Forum in New York in early March, less than six weeks away. We had a lot of fires to put out, and it took awhile to resolve the various issues. By the time the festival ended, there were distributors circling the film, but the filmmakers and we decided to leave the festival with the movie unsold and continue to screen the film for the distributors and executives who hadn't seen it yet. It was all pretty overwhelming, and we had to figure out the serious bidders from the pretenders as we headed back to Chicago. It took most of February to narrow it down to three distributors before we settled on Fine Line Features, accepting their $400,000 advance and strong back-end profit participation to go along with the president of Fine Line Ira Deutchman's solid marketing and distribution plan. "Hoop Dreams" went on to gross a spectacular $7,800,000 and sold 120,000 videocassettes, so it lived up to all of its buzz and was a complete critical and commercial success for all involved. The word of mouth was so fantastic that there was a theatre in Chicago, the Pipers Alley, that played the film for six months, right up to the video release. And all through the commercial life of "Hoop Dreams," Roger Ebert and Gene Siskel became tireless champions of the film on their show, in print and on various national talk shows. We gave them the opportunity to discover the film, and they ended up setting the tone for all the critics to follow. It was a beautiful thing to witness.

Being a part of "Hoop Dreams" and working with filmmakers Steve James, Fred Marx and Peter Gilbert and producer Gordon Quinn was a career highlight for me and a moment in time I'll never forget. I remember mentioning to John Iltis in the midst of all the excitement that we may not get the chance to be involved in another film like "Hoop Dreams" for another 10 years. I was wrong. We didn't see anything close to "Hoop Dreams" for the next 12 years or as long as we were in business. There is only one "Hoop Dreams."

This Week at the Box Office:

Weekly Attendance: 35,719,886

Paul Blart: Mall Cop
Sony/Columbia
Opening weekend: $31,832,636
Domestic gross: $146,336,178
Foreign gross: $36,956,953
Worldwide gross: $183,293,131
Widest release: 3,206 theatres

My Bloody Valentine 3D
Lionsgate
Opening weekend: $21,241,456
Domestic gross: $51,545,952
Foreign gross: $9,188,766
Worldwide gross: $100,734,718
Widest release: 2,534 theatres

Notorious
Fox Searchlight
Opening weekend: $20,497,596
Domestic gross: $36,843,682
Foreign gross: $3,640,745
Worldwide gross: $40,484,427
Widest release: 1,638 theatres

Hotel for Dogs
Paramount
Opening weekend: $17,012,212
Domestic gross: $73,034,460
Foreign gross: $43,965,738
Worldwide gross: $117,000,198
Widest release: 3,271 theatres

Chandni Chowk to China
Warner Brothers
Opening weekend: $629,921
Domestic gross: $921,738
Foreign gross: $12,517,742
Worldwide gross: $13,439,480
Widest release: 130 theatres

Ballerina
First Run
Opening weekend: $2,656
Domestic gross: $114,507
Foreign gross: $16,953
Worldwide gross: $131,460
Widest release: 5 theatres

Cherry Blossoms
Strand
Opening weekend: $3,322
Domestic gross: $104,012
Foreign gross: $12,751,069
Worldwide gross: $12,751,069
Widest release: 8 theatres

Village Barbershop
Monterey Media
Opening weekend: $89.00
Domestic gross: $4,569
Foreign gross: NA
Widest release: 2 theatres

Owl and the Sparrow
Independent
Opening weekend: $9,474
Domestic gross: $47,071
Foreign gross: $123,253
Worldwide gross: $170,324
Widest release: 4 theatres

2009 Sundance Distribution Deals:

Even though the festival was not the most robust in terms of sales activity, a total of 21 films eventually were sold to distributors. Out of this total, "Precious" and "(500) Days of Summer" were the unqualified hits of the bunch. The following is a list of the films along with their distributors and domestic gross:

- "Precious" (Lionsgate) $47,566,524
- "(500) Days of Summer (Fox Searchlight) $32,391,374
- "An Education" (Sony Pictures Classics) $12,574,914
- "Moon" (Sony Pictures Classic) $5,010,163
- "Good Hair" (Roadside Attractions) $4,157,223
- "The September Issue" (Roadside Attractions) $3,820,067
- "Sin Nombre" (Focus Features) $2,536,665
- "In the Loop" (IFC) $2,388,804
- "Adam" (Fox Searchlight) $2,277,396
- "Rudo y Cursi" (Sony Pictures Classics) $1,827,660
- "Paper Heart" (Overture Films) $1,274,062
- "Cold Souls" (Samuel Goldwyn Films) $905,209
- "Tyson" (Sony Pictures Classics) $887,918
- "The Cove" (Lionsgate) $857,005
- "The Maid" (Elephant Eye Films) $576,608
- "Humpday" (Magnolia Films) $407,377
- "Spread" (Anchor Bay) $250,618
- "Black Dynamite" (Apparition) $242,578
- "Big Fan" (First Independent Pictures) $234,540
- "Arlen Faber" (Magnolia Pictures) n/a
- "The Winning Season" (Lionsgate) n/a

Distribution Rights a Filmmaker Holds on a Completed Film:

When a distributor offers to buy all rights in a movie, the language in a contract may read something like the following copy: "Such rights shall include all world-wide rights to the property, in any languages, in any and all manners or modes of exploitation, media, or technology written known or unknown, discovered or undiscovered at the time of this agreement, including but not limited to …"

Individual Rights

- Domestic theatrical rights
- Domestic DVD rights
- Domestic television rights
- Video-on-Demand rights
- All Internet rights
- Non-theatrical rights (schools, library, army bases, prisons)
- Adaptation, remake and sequel rights
- Airline rights
- Pilot and television series rights
- Merchandising and promotional tie-up rights
- Audiotape rights
- Book and serial publication rights
- Live stage rights
- Music and soundtrack rights
- International rights to all of the above

Advice from Acquisition Executives:

Since there is an almost unlimited supply of independent films made every year that are available to be acquired, distributors can be very choosy and have the upper hand in any negotiations, unless there are multiple suitors involved. The following advice from acquisition executives has been pulled from various sources over the years:

Points to follow when selling a film:

- Have a singular vision and strong point of view
- Have a clearly defined story
- Making a festival run is complex, know what your film is from a sales point of view
- Great films will speak for themselves; make a strong film with integrity
- Director-driven stories tell compelling stories in unique ways
- Get your film accepted by good festivals, win awards
- If you get accepted into a festival, show to some journalists to try to get some buzz going
- Reach for complexity because that's what makes a film and drama memorable
- Make sure you have some elements that will distinguish your film from others, it may be high concept, it may be cast or it may be a twist on a particular genre
- Word of mouth from festivals draws attention
- Do your homework and research some distributors you feel would be good for your film
- Talk to filmmakers who have gone through the process
- Secure a well-known sales agent or publicist who knows the process and has valuable contacts
- Have strong visuals (production stills)

Wrong ways for filmmakers to get attention:

- Narcissistic self-promotion
- Not knowing anything about the distributor and type of movies they distribute
- Excessive hype or gimmicks
- Mailing submissions that say "Requested Material " on the envelope when in fact the distributor never requested it
- Assuming you know more than the distributor and presenting a full marketing plan and evidence that there is an enormous audience for your film
- Telling the buyer you have the next "Saw" or the next "Crash;" your film should stand on its own, and this only comes across as either desperate or naïve
- Sending mass impersonal emails without a compelling subject line
- Sending bad trailers
- Sending memorabilia or bottles of wine
- It bothers buyers when people can't take no for an answer or expect that they owe a filmmaker an in-depth response on why they are passing on a film. So much is instinct and they may not have an in-depth response to give.
- Insisting buyers see their film on the big screen
- Phone calls
- If you don't hear back from them take it as a no.
- Acting like a stalker

Week 3: Questions for Discussion:

1. How has the Sundance Film Festival become the top film festival for American independent films? Is it as important as it used to be for filmmakers and distributors?

2. As a moviegoer or as an aspiring filmmaker, have you paid attention to the films that have emerged from Sundance, or is it something that has been off your radar?

3. Consider the careers and accomplishments of Robert Redford and Clint Eastwood. What has made them special, and why do both of them matter? Name one quality of theirs that you feel would be worthy to follow.

4. What were the challenges David Sikich and John Iltis had in trying to sell "Hoop Dreams"? How did their strategic planning and decision making impact on the final results?

5. Look over the advice from acquisition executives both pro and con. Choose a theme from them, and in your own words write a few sentences about the realities of the marketplace.

WHY SO SERIOUS? A LOOK AT THE OSCAR NOMINATIONS

Week 4: January 23–29, 2009

This year was the perfect time to recognize the significance of how "The Dark Knight" energized the entire industry and popular culture, while also reminding us how a big Hollywood spectacle can still deliver both art and entertainment to the masses.

Heath Ledger's Joker delivers one of his more iconic lines of dialogue in "The Dark Knight" when he sneers, "Why so serious?" a question that is also appropriate to ask after the Motion Picture Academy announced its Oscar nominations this past week. I don't want to belabor the point, but what a missed opportunity by the Academy voters when they failed to nominate "The Dark Knight" for Best Picture. This omission was the biggest surprise and shock of all the nominations. I love serious dramas, but quality comes in all types of genres. Did some voters not even bother seeing the movie because it was a comic book adaptation? What more can a movie do after becoming the second biggest grossing movie of all time while securing tremendous critics' reviews across the board? Following last year's lowest rated Oscar show of all time and now in the midst of such a dour economy, this year was the perfect time to recognize the significance of how "The Dark Knight" energized the entire industry and popular culture, while also reminding us how a big Hollywood spectacle can still deliver both art and entertainment to the masses. I guess the 75 million people who paid to see "The Dark Knight" in theatres don't matter; well, making the time to watch the Academy Awards may not matter much to them either. I understand the academy voters don't really concern themselves with television viewership and approach their choices with artistic integrity, but a little better balance in their choices and a more keen sense of the current zeitgeist wouldn't hurt. Do they know they are turning the Oscars into a more glamorized version of the Independent Spirit Awards? Will this year's show set a new low for viewership? And if it does, will anybody care?

There is an interesting dynamic and a Catch 22 factor involved when it comes to how big of a role box office plays in whether or not a movie is deemed worthy of a Best Picture nomination. On one hand, giant grossing movies may be a turn off for the voters indicating being overly popular is a negative. But that wouldn't be fair to say because many big popcorn movies tend to eliminate themselves anyway by being all sizzle and effects without much substance or story. However, "The Dark Knight" stands out from the pack and deserves recognition as a film that breaks away from the norm. On the lower end of the box office spectrum where the smaller serious films exist, commerce also is part of the equation. The academy wants to see the public respond to a film. A film needs the perception of doing solid business even if it's on a limited basis and hasn't gone wide yet as in the case of both "Frost/Nixon" and "The Reader." If a quality film is rejected by the public and has a short run, it basically has no chance for a Best Picture slot. In addition, other contenders eliminate themselves by not meeting expectations in the marketplace like "Australia," which was never seriously considered as a Best Picture candidate due to indifference by both audiences and the critics.

For some movies, just getting the Best Picture nomination is victory in itself, and that's going to be the case for "Frost/Nixon," "Milk" and "The Reader" because they have no real chance of winning the big prize. There is an immediate box office bump for the nominated films that start this weekend. Excitement is at its highest during the four week stretch between the nominations and Oscar night, and with all the attention, this is really the ultimate sweet spot for these films to ratchet up their numbers at the box office. I used to book a secondary art house, and getting the right films on the screen during this time could make or break the entire first half of the year for the exhibitor. It is the absolute best concentrated four weeks of the year for the art distributors and the theatres playing these specialty films. Just think; it used to be six weeks not too long ago before it was shortened to the current four-week period. How much can actually winning the Best Picture mean to a film's bottom line? There are a lot of variables, and every year it's a little different. How long has it been in theatres? How commercial is the film in the first place? Some films like "Crash" were already out on DVD. I went back and looked at the performance of the previous year's winner "No Country For Old Men" and one of the other nominated films "Juno." What's interesting is that "Juno" had a much better bump at the box office than the eventual winner. At the time of the nominations, "Juno"'s gross stood at $88 million and added $42 million more in the four weeks leading up to the Academy Awards. After the show it added another $13 million to finish with an amazing $143 million. "No Country For Old Men's" gross was $48 million at the time of the nominations and added $16 million in the next four weeks. After it won Best Picture, it only added an additional $10 million to finish with $74 million. "Juno" was a big crossover hit with the teen audience while "No Country For Old Men" was a dark, violent film, which never found too large of a mainstream audience. But box office only tells part of the story. The real value of winning Best Picture of the Year is the ripple effect it has on all the other markets like DVDs, television, international and any future technology that hasn't even been invented yet. The award lives on in perpetuity and keeps on earning money for years to come.

---

*Harvey Weinstein is a fierce competitor who plays to
win and wants it more than anybody else.*

Can a distributor actually buy an Oscar? That argument was most debated during the Harvey Weinstein led Miramax years of the mid-90s to the early 2,000s when Miramax outspent and out foxed the other companies each year and landed up winning the Best Picture three different times during that period. It actually may have come closest to happening the year "Shakespeare in Love" beat out the heavily favored "Saving Private Ryan." What wasn't in dispute was that Harvey Weinstein was the acknowledged master of the Oscar campaign who knew all the rules of the game and stretched a few of them when it would help his cause. He is a fierce competitor who plays to win and wants it more than anybody else. The way he has gone after Oscars is comparable to a top athlete who never quits and does everything in his power to will himself to victory. Whether it's finding every last publicity angle, flaming the winds of controversy or personally calling the media to make a point or pitch a story, no one is more relentless. He has lost a lot of his mojo since he left Miramax and started Weinstein Films with his brother, but guess who's the distributor of "The Reader," the surprise film that managed to squeeze its way into the Best Picture race? None other than Weinstein Films. However, this time Weinstein is just happy to be invited to the big dance. Whereas Weinstein has had the resources to overspend on ads while chasing Oscar nominations and awards, it has hurt smaller distributors in the past when they had a good quality film but just didn't have the money to mount any type of campaign to remind voters that a particular film was worthy. A great film that comes to mind was 2007's "The Devil Knows You're Dead," directed by the legendary Sidney Lumet and distributed by Think Film. Think Film, a company which is no longer in business, was going through major money problems at the time of this film's release and didn't have the resources to give the film the type of release it deserved much less mount an Oscar campaign. Thus it disappeared very quietly and was never a factor in the race.

Who's going to win Best Picture? It's going to be a two horse race between "Slumdog Millionaire" and "The Curious Case of Benjamin Button." "Slumdog" is the hot movie with the momentum after winning Best Picture at the Golden Globes and is definitely the front-runner. But being the front-runner can be precarious, and the tide can still change. I'm a big fan of "The Curious Case of Benjamin Button" and feel it can still win. It's a big classy studio film; it leads all films with 13 nominations, and it's a co-production between Paramount and Warner Brothers. A lot of Academy voters work for the studios, and there is a big difference between 85 foreign journalists voting and 5800 industry workers voting for the Oscars. It's also interesting to note that the last four Golden Globe winners did not go on to win the Oscar for Best Picture.

Box Office for 2007 & 2008 Best Picture Nominees at Time of Oscar Nomination & Final Gross:

		Time of Nom.	Final Gross
2007	Juno	$88m	$143,495,265
	No Country for Old Men	$48m	$74,283,625 (Best Picture)
	Michael Clayton	$39m	$49,033,882
	Atonement	$32m	$50,927,067
	There Will Be Blood	$9m	$40,222,514
2008	The Curious Case of Benjamin Button	$105m	$127,509,326
	Slumdog Millionaire	$45m	$141,319,928 (Best Picture)
	Milk	$21m	$31,841,299
	Frost/Nixon	$9m	$18,622,031
	The Reader	$8m	$34,194,407

This Week at the Box Office:

Weekly Attendance: 27,017,238

The box office continues to sizzle with last weekend becoming the biggest January weekend in history. According to Box Office Guru, all four new movies opened to more than $20 million during the extended four day Martin Luther King Jr. holiday, which performed more like a Memorial Day or Thanksgiving weekend rather than a holiday in mid-January. If this is a harbinger of things to come, 2009 could be a special year, but then again it's still January, so there's a long way to go. But When "Paul Blart: Mall Cop" can open to just under $40 million, and the Top 20 films can gross $185 million over the four-day frame, it puts distributors and exhibitors in a pretty good frame of mind and hopeful the box office can continue to surprise. This week the two new national releases, "Underworld: Rise of the Lycans" and "Inkheart" will probably take a back seat to strong holdovers and the newly minted nominated films.

Underworld: Rise of the Lycans
Sony
Opening weekend: $20,828,511
Domestic gross: $45,802,315 (50.1%)
Foreign gross: $45,551,186 (49.9%)
Worldwide gross: $91,353,501
Widest release: 2,942 theatres

Inkheart
Warner Brothers
Opening weekend: $7,601,379
Domestic gross: $17,231,291 (27.7%)
Foreign gross: $45,146,937 (72.3%)
Worldwide gross: $$62,450,361
Widest release: 2,655 theatres

Outlander
Weinstein
Opening weekend: $59,581
Domestic gross: $166,003 (2.3%)
Worldwide gross: $6,867,680 (97.6%)
Worldwide gross: $7,033,683
Widest release: 81 theatres

Killshot
Weinstein
Opening weekend: $2,148
Domestic gross: $18,643 (0.6%)
Foreign gross: $2,942,350 (99.4%)
Worldwide gross: $2,960,993
Widest release: 5 theatres

Crips and Bloods: Made in America

Argot Pictures

Opening weekend: $10,537

Domestic gross: $83,206

Foreign gross: NA

Widest release: 4 theatres

Of Time and the City

Strand

Opening weekend: $5,595

Domestic gross: $32,667 (6.2%)

Foreign gross: $490,740 (93.8%)

Worldwide gross: $523,417

Widest release: 2 theatres

Dog Eat Dog

IFC

Opening weekend: $80.00

Domestic gross: $80.00

Foreign gross: NA

Widest release: 1 theatre

Week 4: Questions for Discussion

1. In what way does commerce play a part in Oscar nominations? *DISTRIBUTOR SUPPORT*

2. Why are some movies just happy to get nominations, especially if it's for Best Picture? Do you think increasing the Best Picture nominees from five to a maximum of ten films waters the field down and lessens the commercial impact it can have on those films still playing in theatres? With more movies in contention, how important is it for you to see the Best Picture candidates before the night of the Academy Awards?

3. What does it mean when it's said a distributor is trying to buy an Oscar? Is it all about the money?

4. Do some research on the different ways marketing plays a role in securing Oscar nominations and give two examples of how marketing dollars are spent. What disadvantages does a small distributor with a very good film have in trying to secure nominations?

Trade publications
spending money
private screenings

"YES WE CAN." THE PRESIDENT SHOWS MARKETERS HOW IT'S DONE

Week 5: January 30 – February 5, 2009

Axelrod asked Obama early on, "Why are you doing this? What do you wish to accomplish? What is your message going to be? Who will you be speaking to?

I recall during the long Presidential campaign various detractors would take shots at Barack Obama's lack of governing experience or past political accomplishments. One of their favorite arguments was that they dismissed him merely as a former community organizer, as if that carried no weight and had no relevancy in his quest to become president. How misguided that proved to be. That was the first thought that sprang to my mind when I read that the influential *Advertising Age* magazine named the Obama Campaign the Brand Marketer of the Year for 2008, beating out high profile brands like Apple, Nike and Coors and in fact, beating out all the marketing pros at their own game. In their announcement, they went on to honor Obama's campaign for its consistency in delivering its message, its grass roots marketing and its expert use of the Internet and social networking services. In other words, tremendous community organizing, which is another way of defining a successful publicity campaign.

I don't believe this award received much attention inside the world of motion picture marketing, but there are a lot of lessons to be learned here for any filmmakers or marketers who are involved in trying to get the word out about a film with the hope of building a strong base of supporters. Obama had the great fortune of being guided by David Axelrod, one of the top political consultants and strategists in the business. Axelrod has had the luxury of time; he has spent the last 15 years learning, recording and shaping Obama's life story before arriving at his eventual campaign strategy and message. Filmmakers and marketers don't have that kind of time; film marketing happens in a much more concentrated period, but let's look at some basic publicity fundamentals utilized in the Obama campaign that are worth remembering:

- Begin the marketing process as early as possible, preferably in the pre-production stage, when questions like, "why is this movie being made, what is its purpose, what is the point of view and who are we making the movie for" can be addressed. Many independent movies are shot without proper planning and marketing considerations in mind. Axelrod asked Obama early on, "Why are you doing this? What do you wish to accomplish? What is your message going to be? Who will you be speaking to?"

- Filmmakers have to confront the same questions the President had to solve. How to break through all the clutter, how to sound different, how to come across as a new and fresh voice in the vast wilderness of the media universe. The answer often lies in the backstory of the messenger, and with movies, that's the director. The ability to find a compelling story to tell in the bio of the director becomes a key in a movie marketing campaign.

- Develop a central positive theme and image and stick with it. The Obama campaign was honored for its consistency of message, and they were brilliant in that regard, unlike Clinton and McCain who seemed to shift from one message to another. Obama's message of "Change We Can Believe In" and "Yes We Can" held steady throughout the campaign. Even though these two slogans were very general, he kept hammering them home. This is a lot easier said than done for filmmakers because many films have multiple themes and choosing one over another is a difficult challenge, but it's something that has to be done. Whether the film is able to live up to its positive message is another story, but clarity and consistency of message remains a crucial ingredient in any marketing campaign.

▶ Energize your base and have the commitment to work that base with all the drive and determination you can muster. Knowing your audience and knowing whom you are speaking to becomes one of the important steps of the marketing process. A film can't be all things to all people. Barack Obama started his political career on the south side of Chicago knocking on doors and slowly built his base of supporters. The key with films is finding like-minded people who believe in you and the message within the film so they can become supporters who can spread the word to others. It takes time, and it's hard work, and there are no short cuts. When a film is picked up for distribution, distributors usually need a minimum of four to six months to work on a film before it's released, and even then it's a tight schedule.

▶ Become an expert in using new media. Mr. Obama is the first true Internet president, and he travelled a long way from knocking on doors to collecting 13 million personal e-mail addresses. Early in his campaign he posted messages on Facebook and utilized You Tube to transmit his video messages. The big challenge will always be how to create awareness for yourself and your film on the Internet, and that is why it is so important to have a clear, compelling message and a niche audience you know where to find.

In today's ultra-competitive marketplace, movies need to deliver the goods on many levels to stand out from the crowd. By keeping in mind the basic marketing principles the Obama campaign engaged in, filmmakers and movie marketers can put themselves in a better position to get noticed and succeed. Yes You Can.

Hollywood is absolutely thrilled with the new president, which was apparent with the large presence of various stars and directors at the inauguration events. Democratic administrations tend to be more favorable to the arts, which in turn can help create a healthier filmmaking and moviegoing climate in the marketplace. The *Hollywood Reporter* reported an interesting fact. In the last 30 years, box office during the year after a Democrat was elected increased 6.8% compared to 3% with Republicans, with the two worst years coming the year after Reagan and Bush were elected to second terms. The way January has started off, there is a lot of optimism in the air already. The President has a history of being a strong supporter of intellectual property, which should be a positive in the fight against global piracy. He has also pushed hard in the past for a vastly expanded broadband service across the country, an issue that is currently important in Hollywood as Internet and download distribution start to become more prominent. In addition, Obama has been highly critical of Bush's handling of deregulation and anti-trust issues which has led to the media mega-conglomerates of today. We'll see if his administration lands up giving tougher scrutiny to any future takeovers or mergers, but perhaps there won't be as many as there have been in the past. Recently media giants like Viacom and Time Warner have painfully figured out that bigger isn't necessarily better, and those companies have been working to get smaller, either by trying to sell off pieces or breaking up the company by separating divisions and management and giving each one the autonomy to steer its own ship.

Super Bowl Weekend

The $3,000,000 price tag for a 30-second spot on the Super Bowl has scared off some big marketers, but the studios will once again be prominent showing footage from some of their biggest 2009 releases for the first time. Disney has Pixar's "UP," Sony has Tom Hanks in "Angels and Demons" and Paramount is loading up with "Star Trek," "Transformers" and "GI Joe" with other studios still negotiating for lower rates. But the company getting the biggest buzz is DreamWorks Animation debuting the first 3D television commercial ever for "Monster vs. Aliens," their big 3D movie opening March 27. The logistics are formidable to pull this off, and the costs are high, so they have partnered with Pepsi and Intel to defray many of the costs involved. How do you get 125 million pair of free 3D glasses into the hands of the public? The glasses are being distributed through Pepsi displays at retailers across the country and Intel, the creator of the 3D technology, is picking up the $7 million dollar tab for the glasses. The 90-second spot it's being featured on is costing about $8,000,000 in media time, so there is a lot riding on this to pull it off successfully. Jeffrey Katzenburg, the Dreamwork's chief, has been the biggest cheerleader and proponent for 3D movies as the future of the industry, and there will be more than a dozen 3D movies hitting the screens this year. We'll see what kind of wow factor the 3D will have inside the home and whether the glasses get into enough hands to have any kind of impact.

This Week at the Box Office

Weekly Attendance: 22,130,390

I don't know if it's the Obama effect, cabin fever hitting, a good mix of movies, or perhaps it's a combination of all three, but the January box office has been smoking with admissions up 4.5% over last year. What set up the month was the four day Martin Luther King Jr. weekend which was the biggest January weekend of all-time, shockingly bigger than last year's Thanksgiving and Memorial Day weekends. January has never been this strong, but keeping the momentum going into Super Bowl weekend is a tough challenge because this weekend is generally pretty sluggish with 100 million people watching the game at home, which basically turns it into a two-day weekend. For counter programming, distributors usually put out a horror film and a romantic comedy, and this year is no different with "The Uninvited" and Renee Zellweger in "New in Town." The biggest surprise and the one to keep an eye on is Fox's "Taken," an adult male action movie starring Liam Neeson. Fox is definitely bucking traditional wisdom in going after the male audience on Super Bowl weekend.

Taken
20th Century Fox
Opening weekend: $24,717,034
Domestic gross: $145,000,989 63.7%
Foreign gross: $81,829,579 36.1%
Worldwide gross: $226,830,568
Widest release: 3,184 theatres

The Uninvited
Paramount (DreamWorks)
Opening weekend: $10,325,824
Domestic gross: $28,596,818 68.7%
Foreign gross: $13,027,228 31.3%
Worldwide gross: $41,624,046
Widest release: 2,344 theatres

New in Town
Lionsgate
Opening weekend: $6,741,530
Domestic gross: $16,734,283 57.7%
Foreign gross: $12,276,534 42.3%
Worldwide gross: $29,010,817
Widest release: 1,941 theatres

Luck By Chance
Adlabs Films USA
Opening weekend: $217,439
Domestic gross: $356,019
Foreign gross: N/A
Widest release: 57 theatres

Medicine for Melanch
IFC
Opening weekend: $12,265
Domestic gross: $111,551
Foreign gross: N/A
Widest release: 7 theatres

Serbis
Regent
Opening weekend: $12,824
Domestic gross: $64,563 41.6%
Foreign gross: $90,620 58.4%
Worldwide gross: $155,156
Widest release: 4 theatres

Between Love & Goodbye
Emblem Entertainment
Opening weekend: $6,674
Domestic gross: $16,710
Foreign gross: N/A
Widest release: 2 theatres

2012 Update

As strong as President Obama's 2008 marketing campaign was, things haven't quite worked out according to plan. The greatest campaigns in the world can be sidetracked by any number of variables – some that are outside anyone's control, and others that can be self-inflicted. Regardless, in both politics and movies, it's all about delivering results and living up to the hype of the branded message. In politics, results can be judged by any number of things from the health of the economy, the unemployment rate, taxes, new legislation and whether or not the hope promised in the campaign produced the positive change people were expecting. Movies are judged in a more simple way. What did it do at the box office? Ultimately, in both cases word of mouth and the public response will generally trump the marketing message. That doesn't diminish the importance of having a great branding message; all it means is real success happens when someone is able to back up the talk and live up to the expectations that were promised. The President found himself in an intense battle to win re-election in 2012. Even though his branded message of change had been compromised and stymied by a stubborn Congress and a lingering recession, Mr. Obama prevailed and won four more years in the White House. Once again, it came down to his superior organization of supporters and volunteers aided by cutting-edge technology and expert targeting of niche demographics of college age, Hispanic, African American and women voters. The publicity campaign was relentless and it led to the turnout that was needed to succeed. It was yet another confirmation of the power of effective community organizing in the 21st Century.

MARKETING CONSIDERATIONS TO PONDER IN PRE-PRODUCTION

- What are the reasons for making the movie? (art/self-expression, ego, money, entertainment)
- Is there a specific point of view and something to say?
- Is it an original compelling concept?
- Why should the movie be made, and what will make it stand out from the pack?
- Marketing starts with an idea and a title. Is there a strong title that helps to define or describe the film?
- What are the goals in making the film? (film festival, theatrical, DVD, Internet premiere?)
- Is there a subtext to the film with underlying themes?
- Do you have a good idea who your target audience is and how they can be reached?
- Does the film fall into a specific genre?
- Will there be any interesting back stories to pitch the media for publicity purposes?
- What "hooks" will the movie have?
- Do the research. Have an awareness of what else is going on in the industry and how other films, especially those that may be similar to yours, have performed at the box office.
- It's never too early to think of ideas for the right visual image that will be used to market the film. This will help in capturing the right still photos during production.
- Investors, sales agents and distributors have finite time and budgets when looking to finance, represent or buy films. There may be only one chance when making a presentation, so make it look as professional as possible at all times.

Conversations with Industry Professionals

Ziggy Kozlowski – Director of Publicity, Block-Korenbrot Public Relations, Los Angeles, CA

The following interview took place on May 9, 2011.

"Publicity doesn't guarantee box office, it guarantees attention."

—*Ziggy Kozlowski*

Q: *How long have you been a movie publicist?*

ZK: I've been doing film publicity since 1979 when I started at John Iltis Associates in Chicago. In 1987, I moved to Los Angeles where I've worked in publicity for independent films for the last 24 years. I'm currently the Director of Publicity for Block-Korenbrot Public Relations and have been with this company for 15 years. Our primary client is Sony Classics, and we work with a lot of independent distributors on a project by project basis. Our company also has about twelve personal clients among actors and directors, including Alfre Woodard and Paul Haggis. We also work on specific films for the Golden Globe and Academy Award campaigns.

Q: *What is the competitive landscape of working in Los Angeles?*

ZK: Working on specialty films in Los Angeles is quite competitive. We are not in the business of working on mainstream movies; whether it's an art film, foreign film or an independent film, the films we work on would always be considered the underdog. On an average week there are up to 12 independent films opening. Some weeks could have 18 movies opening when you include the commercial movies.

Q: *Are there even enough theatres to play them all?*

ZK: That's part of the problem. It's just not just finding a theatre to open in, it's the following week when a distributor has to try to get the theatre to hold it with a bunch of new movies lined up. It's crazy; most are gone by the following week.

Q: *Talk about your role as a movie publicist and what you are up against In terms of getting press coverage for the films you are working on?*

ZK: The first thing we are up against is what big commercial movie is opening that Friday. That's the biggest obstacle sometimes because that's what the mainstream media is going to focus on with their coverage. You get reminded every week that smaller films don't only compete against each other but also against the big studio films. Fifteen years ago if you had a good quality film, that would place you in good standing among the media, but I don't think that's the case anymore. The mainstream writer may like an independent film a lot, but they still feel they have to concentrate on the bigger movies because they know their readership has more mainstream interests. It's getting tougher and tougher to get attention for our smaller films at the rate we once did. The job of a publicist is harder than it's ever been. The second problem is finding a way to have your film stand out from the other 11 or 12 specialty films opening. The best way to do that is to get some talent in town to do some press, but I have to say, that's even getting harder to do.

Q: *Are there always several movies in effect opening cold with no media coverage?*

ZK: Absolutely, the *L.A. Times* prides itself in reviewing everything that opens, and they still do, but with so many movies opening, the space is not there for every film to get a full review. It's a weekly fight for space. Some of the films get only two paragraphs.

Q: *When you take on outside films, what do you charge for your services?*

ZK: The rates depend on the amount of work involved, so the fees can range from $5,000 up to $12,500 for each film we work on.

Q: *What kind of lead time is best for you?*

ZK: I usually like to get 3 months; we need that time to get long lead publications, which have early deadlines. With only local press, we can do it in one month.

Q: *And you can't guarantee any coverage to the filmmaker or distributor, can you?*

ZK: No, there is an old adage "with advertising you pay, with publicity you pray." You can't control what the media will say about a film. They have to like it before committing to write anything about it. Sometimes they say, "Oh my God, what did you send me?" With so many movies opening, the hard part is getting the important people to see it. It's a time issue, and that's why we have to stage multiple screenings, up to six screenings, to accommodate the critics, and the rental of screening rooms or theatres can add up as an extra expense to be paid by the distributor or filmmaker.

Q: *Do you have individual filmmakers approach you for your services?*

ZK: We get both kinds, distributors and independent producers who are self-distributing their films. Generally it's distributors, and often it's done because an LA opening is required by contract to play a theatrical run before it is able to procure a DVD release. Sometimes these people don't care what the response from critics will be; they are just playing it off. They say whatever the response will be it will be. However, most are hoping for the best and have a legitimate film and release.

Q: *If you can't deliver the media coverage that the party is expecting, can it get a bit testy?*

ZK: Yes, at times it can get to be a bit strained, but that's more the exception than the rule. The important thing is to tell them up front what the deal is. I tell them, "I'll work very hard for you and your film, but I can't guarantee anything." That's the key, delivering sobering news up front and being honest. When you mislead people into thinking everything is going to be great, that's when you have problems. I start off by telling my clients that it's not up to me to consider whether this is a good film or not, it's up to the working press, so I suggest we screen the film for a couple of people to get a response, and then we can react from that.

Q: *I imagine word spreads fast among critics?*

ZK: It does. If I do six screenings on a film, the first two screenings usually don't include the premium critics, but if by the 3rd or 4th screenings I start getting better turnout, higher profile critics, that tells me word is spreading and the reaction is good. It's a ripple effect. The first wave of critics tell others to check it out, it's good, go see it. On the other hand when reaction is bad and you get fewer and fewer critics coming to later screenings, that's when you know you have a problem.

Q: Are bloggers becoming more of a factor in the world of film publicity?

ZK: They have become more of a factor, but it's always hard to know who exactly is reading them, and there's really no way you can count how many readers they have. When I visit their websites, it always seems that it's the same six people commenting. I have my doubts whether these bloggers and websites are that much of a factor in driving audiences to see a film as some in the industry think they are. What remains a factor is opening weekend buzz, especially with young people. By 10:00 pm Friday or Saturday, the country sort of knows if the movie is worth seeing or not, not because of the critics or the websites, but what people are telling each other. Both good and bad news travels very fast today. I see young people texting their friends right in the theatre.

Q: Do you vet bloggers who request to be put on your screening lists?

ZK: Yes we do, and some of them are effective and actually very smart. They write good stories and reviews. Sites like Movie City News and The Wrap are terrific for people who have an interest in movies, but I think what is missing is if you get a story in the *Chicago Tribune*, the hope is that the general public would come across the story and then go see the movie. That's the thing I see that is missing. The general moviegoer doesn't go to those sites; it lacks what newspapers have. Good industry sites don't necessarily translate to wider appeal.

Q: Has newspaper readership been declining in Los Angeles the same way it has been happening across the country? If it has, does that translate to less effectiveness for the reviews and publicity articles?

ZK: Yes, I think it does. I believe people don't pay attention to critics like they used to. The older moviegoers still read the critics and are influenced by them, but younger people could care less. You can see that when mainstream films going after a young teen demo skip ads altogether, and they are fine without them.

Q: If people are paying less attention to newspapers, isn't that scary for independent films? What's replacing the newspaper, if anything?

ZK: That's the scary thing. There is a lot of uncertainty on what is replacing newspapers. When you get a story in the *L.A. Times* 750,000 people still have a chance to see it. I don't know if you get a story on some website how many people are actually reading that and what it means. It's very difficult to measure.

Q: Everyone is living on Facebook, Twitter and other social network sites. How effective are those tools in helping to open a movie?

ZK: Those things seem to come and go. The first couple of movies figure it out, use it as a marketing tool, and it's very effective. Two years later when everyone is doing it, it becomes meaningless. Companies use the Facebook business page because you have to do it because everyone else is. I remember when MTV first came in, movies like "Footloose" and "Flashdance" ran promotions and were huge, others that followed, not so much. The same thing happened with "Blair Witch Project." It took ten years to have another movie use the Internet so effectively and have the same success. When "Blair Witch" hit big, the industry thought that was the answer, but it wasn't. With any new marketing tool the initial rush is great, but after everyone joins the party, it becomes less special and effective in a hurry.

Q: Has anything changed in your job over the last few years when you look at a film and begin the process of working on it?

ZK: It's basically the same. You have to see it yourself, then you have to show it to others, and then you get a reaction to it. If anything has changed, it's fewer critics. The *L.A. Daily News* used to have two full time critics, now they don't have any. The *Daily Breeze* had their own film critic. Now they just buy wire service stuff if they run a review at all. It used to be not so long ago when you opened an art film you could pretty much count on reviews in a lot of different papers in the greater Los Angeles area. That's not the case anymore.

Q: *When Ebert and Siskel were in their prime it was a proven fact they could make little movies into hits like "Hoop Dreams" and "My Dinner with Andre." Can any one critic, including Roger Ebert today, make something into a hit these days?*

ZK: No, those days are gone forever. No one has that kind of power and influence anymore. Aggregate sites like Rotten Tomatoes are popular today; I go to that site myself. It's a product of changing times.

Q: *2009 was the first year when there were ten Oscar nominees for Best Picture. When that was announced in 2009, did you think that was a good decision to increase the field?*

ZK: I was surprised when that happened, and I'm still not sure if it's all a good thing. Even though I work with specialty films and it provides opportunity for more films. Independent films were already doing fine with the Oscars; it was the studios who were getting pissed that films like "The Dark Knight" were being passed over. So I think the change was made more for the studios and mainstream movies.

Q: *Is there a downside to having ten nominees?*

ZK: I think it dilutes the field. If you are one of ten I think it means less than if you are one of five.

The big studios have abandoned the smart adult drama for the most part, and increasing the field is an attempt to get some of their films in the running. The studios are the biggest supporters of the Academy, and I think the studios have recognized that in the last fifteen years independent films have dominated the field and the change is a reaction to that.

Q: *Is your job tougher in the summer than in the winter?*

ZK: Well, to be honest with you, summer tends to be slow for us, and around the time of the Toronto Film Festival things really start picking up. For us, both seasons are tough on different levels. During summer, it's about competing against all the blockbusters for attention; in November and December the competition becomes fierce between all the top specialty films in the marketplace. What I'm saying is it's never really easy. December, January and February are the most intense months of the year because that's the heart of the Oscar season when we're working on campaigns for our clients. That's the bread and butter season for us where we earn our stripes.

Q: *Let me throw some publicity tools at you. Can you tell me how important they still are?*

ZK: The press release. The press release is still a must-have tool, but it probably has lost some of its importance because the dissemination of the media is so fast it can get lost out there in the digital world. It's all done via email now instead of being sent by mail or fax. I don't know if that's the reason that it seems to be a bit diminished from where it once stood, though one of the basics of the press release will always remain the same. Never rush it out and send it out too fast before all the facts are correct. Once the release goes out, it's out, and any mistakes or inaccuracies can cause problems you don't want.

The Press Kit. Always very important. The press kit is the bible for critics and entertainment writers who write about a film. All the information they need from the correct spellings of the names of cast and crew to the production notes that provide pertinent facts and background of the production can be found here. Press kits have gone digital and are also sent by email.

Media Contact List. Very, very valuable. Our media contacts make us valuable. We couldn't be in business without them. It gives us the ability to pick up a phone and call a critic or feature writer at any time. With the Internet, it's much easier to keep contact information up to date. In my earlier years when contact info changed we had to go into our Rolodex, take a card out, get a new index card and type the new information on the card. Now you just go to your computer files and change it very quickly.

Photos. Still very important. One of the problems with photos is once they get out there, they never go away. A star may have approved the use of a photo and then comes back later and says that he or she doesn't like it, or they say they didn't approve a particular photo, but it's too late. Even if you take it off your site, someone has it out there, downloaded it, using it somewhere. Publicists have to be ultra careful with the use of photos and what they send out. We can't control what photos the media uses. A photo can appear in *People* magazine, and a star calls and asks how did that happen?

Q: *How often do you work on films where the still photos supplied are not the greatest quality?*

ZK: All the time. For many small films, filmmakers don't have it in the budget to hire a professional photographer; somebody's cousin is there to take photos. When a distributor acquires a film, they weren't there during production, so they had no control over the quality of photos. It's not the distributor's fault, that's what they were given and have to work with. I talk to newspaper editors all the time, and if there are six movies opening, and they can't find good art for a specific film, they aren't going to ask or seek other photos from that film, they will use something from another film that catches their eye. Unfortunately, producers and filmmakers don't think a year in advance of how certain photos would look in an important movie section or magazine. The bottom line is strong photos get better placement.

Q: *Can you give me an example of a film where strong photos helped get you better placement?*

ZK: "Friends with Money." Jennifer Aniston was one of the nicest persons I've ever worked with considering her stature and was very easy to work with. I think she worked with the unit photographer and helped out with the shots, recommending some things. We received tremendous placement on top of the *L.A. Times* because of the great still art we had for that film. The interview was with the director. They had a great picture of the director, they had a great picture of the four actresses together, a stunning picture of Jennifer Aniston for the inside, and with all those great photos, suddenly you find out that you are the cover story on Sunday. That's what strong still photos can do for you.

Q: *Have you ever devised a publicity campaign from scratch?*

ZK: Most of the time I work in conjunction with an established distributor's strategy, but occasionally a client comes to us and asks, "What would you do with this?" There are questions that have to be asked. Is there an issue that the publicity can be built around? Does the movie have any possibilities of publicity outside the movie section? You start by reading the script or seeing the movie. Does the movie have an initial audience? If it does, you try to target that audience along with thinking how to position it toward the press. With a movie like "Crash," there is a certain way you can go to try to stir up the press, the racial issues, the prejudice stuff. Some movies have more possibilities than others. If it's just another character driven serious drama, the quality of the film may be the only thing we have to work with. The movie itself dictates the direction. The key is try to get stories on the entertainment pages; if you succeed there, then you try to get stories placed in other sections of the paper, editorial, food, sports, but it starts with the movie sections.

Q: *What are some of the more important lessons and fundamentals you have learned?*

ZK: One thing you have to pay attention to is what the media is telling you and what the marketplace is telling you. Pay attention to what the audience is saying; pay attention to what's happening in the screenings. If you don't, you're an idiot. Another rule of the film industry, "No one knows anything." William Goldman was right. You just don't know until the film opens. I worked on "Crouching Tiger, Hidden Dragon" years ago, and I was stunned by the success of the film. I could tell the film was going to be a hit, maybe somewhere between $10 and $20 million, which for a foreign language film would be huge. It goes on to make $128 million. You just don't know what people will take to their hearts. This year's Oscar winner for Best Foreign film was Sony Classic's "In a Better World," but art audiences didn't embrace it, and it didn't perform well at the box office. Two weeks later we opened another Sony Classics movie, "Incendies," that was nominated in the same category but didn't win. That film went on to do excellent business. The two films received comparable reviews. In a weird way, they are almost the same thing. Who knew? Why? I don't know what happened. I remember working on "In the Valley of Elah" for Warner Independent. I had stories on the front page, not on entertainment pages, the front page of the *Wall Street Journal*, half-page coverage in the *New York Times*. The film opens, nothing. That was the first of the Iraq movies back a few years ago, so it wasn't due to viewer fatigue. You didn't know going in or you couldn't predict that no one would be interested in it. It received excellent press, and it was a very good film. Great story, a great performance by Tommy Lee Jones, it had everything but a willing audience. That leads to another very important lesson. Publicity doesn't guarantee box office, it guarantees attention.

Q: *Thank you for your time and insight.*

ZK: Thank you.

Questions for Discussion

1. What form of marketing is closest to community organizing? What do you think are the challenges involved in this aspect of marketing? What would you consider "old school" and "new school" in this area? Has it gotten easier for today's marketers?

2. How did President Obama's campaign win the Brand Marketer of the Year for 2008? There are five lessons that movie marketers can learn from the President's presidential campaign. Put them in order of how you see their importance and discuss them in your words.

3. Should all movie marketing messages be optimistic regardless of the situation? Are there any circumstances that could be the exception?

4. How tough of a job do you think a movie publicist has in today's marketplace? Explain.

5. What is the importance of still photos in movie publicity? What are some of the mistakes made in this area?

6. What message of Ziggy Kozlowski resonates with you the most?

THE UPS AND DOWNS OF THE MARKETPLACE

Week 6: February 6–12, 2009

---

*The marketplace is always in perpetual motion with a combination of good
and bad news, risks that are rewarded, gambles that miss the mark, fortunes
that rise, and disappointment which can deflate the hardiest of industry veterans.*

The first week of February provides an opportunity to discuss an interesting mix of topics affecting the movie industry. The marketplace is always in perpetual motion with a combination of good and bad news, risks that are rewarded, gambles that miss the mark, fortunes that rise, and disappointment which can deflate the hardiest of industry veterans. The following is a look at what's up and what's down in the current marketplace:

UP – The January box office. While getting little fanfare, January has emerged as one of the best months of the year for moviegoing. For the first time ever, the box office reached $1 billion, and perhaps more significantly, attendance rose 16% over last year. Generally, box office increases are due to inflation and higher ticket prices, but that wasn't the case here. The audience actually expanded. January is not necessarily a reliable indicator on how the rest of the year is going to play out, but a fast start can set a pattern for audiences getting out of the house, and momentum is never a bad thing, even though it's impossible to predict how long it will last. Would it be nice to see a billion dollars every month? Sure, but that's pretty much wishful thinking, and that's not going to happen because the industry has never even reached $10 billion for the year. Here are a few reasons why January has become such a favorite time of the year for moviegoers:

> ▶ The sheer variety of films, from lowbrow to highbrow and everything in between. Critics and entertainment writers may see all the Oscar quality films by mid-December, but regular audiences get their first chance to see "The Wrestler," "Milk," "Slumdog Millionaire" and all the other Oscar nominated films during January as they start playing in suburban multiplexes everywhere. How about "Revolutionary Road," "Doubt," and "Frost/Nixon" playing next to "Paul Blart: Mall Cop," "Underworld," "Hotel for Dogs" and "Gran Torino" in the same theatre complex? No other month can match that. If you don't believe me, wait until March and April and see what's on the screen then.

> ▶ The calendar works to January's advantage with Christmas movies heading into the month with a full head of steam, New Year's weekend starting it all off by being one of the biggest movie going holidays of the year and a Martin Luther King Jr. holiday right in the center of the month launching fresh product into the theatres with that extra Monday attached to the weekend.

> ▶ The weather in large sections of the country tends to keep people indoors, so cabin fever can hit at any time. Getting out of the house to see a movie at the local theatre with other like-minded people remains one of life's simple pleasures to escape the winter blues.

Down – Outside producers have to bring more money to the table before the studios and other distributors agree to distribute their movies. P &A, defined as Prints and Advertising costs, used to be fronted by the studios as standard procedure and then deducted as a distribution expense off the top of the distributor gross. There is nothing automatic anymore during this time of tight credit. Production companies are now being asked or forced to raise anywhere between $15,000,000 and $30,000,000 to pay for their own prints and advertising. Why the change? In the past, if a distributor spent $30 million on P & A and the movie tanked and grossed only $20 million, after the theatres took their cut, the studio was $20 million in the hole and chasing money to break even for the next couple of years. In these risk adverse times, the studios have decided not to leverage one cent toward movies they didn't develop and produce themselves, in effect taking the risk out of the equation. They are willing to take a smaller distribution fee of between 7% -15% instead of 30%-35% and pass up ownership in a film in order to have zero risk when dealing with third-party partners. The fact is P & A has become so expensive that it has become the number one consideration for a distributor before they agree to take on any film. They know if they guess wrong it can bury them in red ink. When a distributor is interested in acquiring a smaller film, the filmmaker always hopes there is a nice advance included in their offer, but often a distributor has to pick between offering a sizable P & A commitment or offering an advance.

With "Hoop Dreams," Fine Line offered a $400,000 advance as well as a minimum $500,000 for prints and advertising. So they were out $900,000 before the movie opened. But that was just the beginning. When the film caught on and landed up playing in theatres for six months, they had to keep supporting the film and ran up P & A costs of over $2 million. That's the cost of doing business.

The fact is P & A has become so expensive it has become the number one consideration for a distributor before they agree to take on any film.

UP – 20th Century Fox's gutsy move in opening "Taken" on Super Bowl weekend and making it the number one movie in the country. Whenever someone breaks away from the way things are normally done in Hollywood, there is an inherent risk of failing and then having it rubbed in your face and being held accountable for it. No studio had ever attempted to open a star driven male action movie before on Super Bowl weekend because the thought of giving up the entire Sunday was too much to stomach. I really admire the simple logic and rational reasoning the Fox management team used in making its decision when they reportedly said, "Super Bowl is only one day, not the entire weekend. Why can't we do enough business on Friday and Saturday to make it a success and take advantage of the fact that we would be the only new film going after adult males?" That's exactly what happened, and it could change the way distributors look at future Super Bowl weekends and the movies they choose to put there. "Taken" grossed $24,000,000 over the weekend and over 85% of that gross came on Friday and Saturday. They guessed right. Sometimes it's good to shake things up and try something different for a change, especially when it's backed up by solid rational decision making. It's not as if men have three-day parties leading up to the big game. Time will tell over the next few years if this tactical move becomes a game changer for other studios or if it's merely viewed as a one- time phenomenon.

Down – Super Bowl movie T.V. spots. In *USA Today*'s Ad Meter, year after year the 30-second spots the studios put out there never rank very high compared to the other commercials, and this year was no different. One of the things studios do best is successfully market their big summer blockbusters, so why do they continually fall short when it comes to introducing their upcoming big movies to over a hundred million people? Splashy special effects, quick cut editing and objects flying toward the screen, it's the same old, same old. The benchmark for Super Bowl commercials remains Fox's 1996 "Independence Day." The single image of the White House being blown up by the alien mother ship still resonates today 13 years later. At a $3,000,000 cost for a 30-second commercial, can't the studios do any better? To be fair, many of these movies' special effects have yet to be completed, so they may not have access yet to some of the best images. Perhaps then it's time to really think outside the box. The main purpose for showcasing a movie before the largest home viewership of the year is to create some early awareness and interest in these films. Go the opposite way. Slow things down. Use fewer effects and quick editing. Create something just for the Super Bowl. Most of the movie commercials come across as regular commercials audiences see all the time. Use a star to introduce a film with a well-chosen scene or two. Show a complete scene from beginning to end. And don't forget to include some humor. That's what plays best during the Super Bowl.

Down – The box office for most of the five Best Picture nominees. Other than "Slumdog Millionaire," it's the worst performance by a group of nominees I can remember. There have always been films that didn't get that boost after being nominated, but that's been more the exception than the rule. Several years ago Terrence Malick's "The Thin Red Line" was a terrific film that performed terribly after getting its nomination for Best Picture. However, this may be the first year when only one movie is being helped. "The Reader," and especially "Milk" and "Frost/Nixon," seem to have little to no mainstream appeal with the public turning a cold shoulder to them. "The Curious Case of Benjamin Button" is another story because it has already grossed $116,000,000,but it looks like everyone who wanted to see it already has, and it's limping to the finish line. According to Exhibitor Relations, these four Oscar films are losing a combined 1,953 screens this weekend, only two weeks away from the awards. Theatres are pulling them left and right due to low grosses and to find room for the four new national releases opening February 6th. It doesn't get any worse than that. If you can't do business in the four weeks between the nominations and the awards, something has gone terribly wrong. What this ultimately means for the struggling specialty film market for the rest of the year is up for debate, but there is reason for concern. On the other hand, everything seems to be pointing to a big night for "Slumdog Millionaire" which will be adding 91 screens this weekend for a total of 1,724 theatres, making it at least one specialty film that audiences have embraced.

Down – The 3D "Monsters vs. Aliens" Super Bowl commercial. I don't think the gamble and the $9,000,000 price tag paid off for DreamWorks. The commercial itself was a bit underwhelming and lacked that "wow" factor. Let's face it; the 3D technology for home use is far inferior to what the theatre experience offers. Pairing up with Pepsi may have been a good promotional move for the studio, but the decision to piggyback the movie's commercial with a 3D SoBe's Lifewater commercial with those dancing lizards was confusing and took away from the movie itself. In addition, even with all the promotion and Pepsi's help, it proved how difficult it is for a company to successfully give away something free to the public, especially when it's on a national basis. Many people still simply didn't hear about the stunt nor had the 3D glasses to watch the commercial properly. Does that mean "Monsters vs. Aliens" may have trouble at the box office when it opens at the end of March? Not really. DreamWorks is throwing everything they have at marketing this film, and it will be one of the only options for families and kids in the March /April period. There is plenty of time for the distributor to rebound and get back on track.

UP – Clint Eastwood. A studio head recently was quoted as saying, "If I had my choice of a film doing big business but not getting any Oscar nominations, I'd take the box office every time." With zero Oscar nominations for "Gran Torino," Eastwood and Warner Bros. are laughing all the way to the bank. "Gran Torino" is up to $117,000,000, the biggest gross of Eastwood's career. He's still showing how it's done at the age of 78, and since he already has two Best Picture Oscars on his mantle, the snub is something he can live with. Everyone's happy. Warners and Eastwood will take the box office.

This Week at the Box Office:

Summit Entertainment is opening "Push" this weekend, a sci-fi thriller being marketed to the under 25 audience. This marks the first film for the company since their breakthrough hit "Twilight" took the industry by storm last fall and grossed $360 million worldwide. How much pressure is on Summit to show they can string a couple of hits together? It's not a make or break movie for them by any means; they have bought some time for themselves and have just launched what should be a very lucrative franchise. But they are finding out they're still considered an independent with the exhibitors. With four new wide release movies opening, including Warner Brothers "He's Just Not That Into You," Sony's "Pink Panther II" and Universal Focus's "Coraline, " there is a logjam in the theatres at this time, and Summit couldn't book as many screens as they had hoped. There is a pecking order out there and when things get tight, the established studios still have the muscle, the track record and the relationships to get what they want.

He's Just Not That Into You
Warner Brothers
Opening weekend: $27,785,487
Domestic gross: $93,953,653 52.5%
Foreign gross: $84,893,246 47.5%
Worldwide gross: $178,846,899
Widest release: 3,175 theatres

Coraline
Focus
Opening weekend: $16,849,640
Domestic gross: $75,590,286 60.4%
Foreign gross: $49,310,169 39.6%
Worldwide gross: $124, 596,398
Widest release: 2,340 theatres

Pink Panther II
Sony
Opening weekend: $11,588,150
Domestic gross: $35,922,978 47.3%
Foreign gross: $40,023,637 52.7%
Worldwide gross: $75,946,615
Widest release: 3,245 theatres

Push
Summit
Opening Weekend: $10,079,109
Domestic gross: $31,853,584 65.1%
Foreign gross: $17,047,091 34.9%
Worldwide gross: $48,858,618
Widest release: 2,313 theatres

Fanboys
Weinstein
Opening weekend: $171,533
Domestic gross; $687,609 71.9%
Foreign gross: $272,299 28.3%
Worldwide gross; $960,828
Widest release: 46 theatres

Polytechnique
Independent
Opening weekend: $293,625
Domestic gross: $1,651,101
Foreign gross: N/A
Widest release: 41 theatres

Oscar Nominated Shorts
Opening weekend: $150,203
Domestic gross: $644,635
Foreign gross: N/A
Widest release: 60 theatres

Our City Dreams
First Run
Opening weekend: $4,056
Domestic gross: $34,972
Foreign Gross: N/A
Widest release: 3 theatres

Absurdistan
First Run
Opening weekend: $1,441
Domestic gross; $39,779 35%
Foreign gross: $73,586
Worldwide gross: $113,269
Widest release: 3 theatres

Chocalate
Magnolia
Opening weekend:$1,597
Domestic gross: $14,845 0.5%
Foreign gross: $3,164,169 99.5%
Worldwide gross;: $3,1790,140
Widest release: 7 theatres

Dev D
UTV
Opening weekend: $2,738
Domestic Gross: $18,613 0.5%
Foreign gross: $4,029,356 99.5%
Worldwide gross: $4,047,969
Widest release: 4 theatres

Perspective:
Super Bowl Weekend Openings 2010-2012

After the smash success of "Taken," I posed the question whether "Taken" would become a game changer for other distributors choosing to release action films for the older male audience on Super Bowl weekend, or would it become known as a one-time phenomenon? Let's look at the list of films (and their opening weekend numbers) that opened on Super Bowl weekend from 2010-2012.

2010
"Dear John" ($30 million) female driven romance
"From Paris with Love" ($8.2 million) male action thriller

2011
"Roommate" ($15 million) collegiate thriller targeting young females
"Sanctum" ($9.4 million) Underwater 3D survival film (females 53% of audience)

2012
"Chronicle" ($22 million) high school super heroes
"The Woman in Black" ($20.9 million) horror
"The Big Miracle" ($7.8 million) whale rescue drama for kids and families

It wasn't one of the major studios but Lionsgate who attempted to duplicate the success of "Taken" on Super Bowl weekend the following year. They released "From Paris with Love," a male driven action film starring John Travolta and directed by Pierre Morel, the same French director who directed "Taken," so they were hoping lightening would strike again. Unfortunately the results were quite different, and the movie was dead on arrival with an $8 million opening with both audiences and critics turning a cold shoulder to it. Even when some of the elements seem to match up, it's never a guarantee a distributor will be able to duplicate an earlier success story. In addition, the failure of "From Paris with Love" may have cemented the accomplishments of "Taken," ($145 million domestic gross) into a one-time occurrence. In 2011 and 2012 no distributor came close to putting a similar type of action movie on Super Bowl weekend, instead sticking to the safer genres of horror, romance, teen and family that are usually found on that weekend. What's interesting to note is ever since "Taken," Liam Neeson has turned into a very reliable action star, but that still wasn't enough for a couple of distributors who had the chance to put one of his action movies on Super Bowl weekend but didn't in both 2011 and 2012. In 2011, Warner Brothers released "Unknown" two weeks after the Super Bowl, and in 2012 the new distributor Open Road released "The Grey" a week before it. The doubt still remains. It's looking more and more that "Taken" will continue to be the exception to the rule rather than a game changer.

Week 6: Questions for Discussion

1. What does P & A stand for and how does it impact what independent films are seen by the public? In many cases, what has changed in this area in regards to which party pays for this expense? What's the bottom line truth when it comes to P & A?

2. What decision did 20th Century Fox make with "Taken" that put them at risk? How did they break with tradition and what did they base their decision on which in a way was very rational? In general, how can this decision also act as a lesson in marketing strategy?

3. What was the expense and challenge involved for DreamWorks in attempting a 3D commercial during Super Bowl for "Monsters vs. Aliens"? How did they minimize their cost but at the same time compromise their vision?

4. Search the Internet and find a 30-second television spot for "Gran Torino." After viewing the clip, what single line of dialogue in the ad successfully got the movie's message across to its intended audience?

THE TRICKLE DOWN EFFECT OF FALLING DVD NUMBERS

Week 7: February 13–19, 2009

There is a lot of freaking out by both the studios and independents because the DVD cash cow is not paying out like it used to.

If it was just about box office ticket sales, things would be looking a lot brighter for studios, but the theatrical business is only one part of their film business, and it makes up an even smaller piece of the big media companies who own the studios. These giant global companies are dealing with non-movie businesses such as broadcast media, sagging cable ad sales, theme parks and publishing that are floundering and more than cancelling out the gains being made with theatrical revenues. Even with what looks to be another big box office weekend on tap with both Valentine's Day and President's Day to take advantage of, there is a fair share of fear and uncertainty in Hollywood these days. Free falling DVD sales, big media conglomerates reporting huge 4th quarter losses, Steven Spielberg frantically searching for new financing and yet another "Friday the 13th" hitting the multiplexes each in their own way points to some basic truths and changing realities for the Motion Picture Industry. The movie business turns on DVD sales just as it did in the 1980s and early 1990s with the videocassette business. The vast majority of movies are still in the red before they hit the DVD shelves, and they depend on DVD sales to push them into profit. I saw it first hand with "Hoop Dreams" when the accounting statements were showing a sizable deficit as the film was finishing its theatrical run and immediately shot into a profit after 120,000 videocassettes were shipped. There is a lot of freaking out by both the studios and independents because that cash cow is not paying out like it used to. The numbers from the all important holiday season were plain bad with studios reporting their big titles down 20-25% from the previous year. This precipitous drop in the studios' most dependable and largest revenue source is causing ripple effects throughout the industry in the following ways:

Collapsing Release Windows

The industry has done well with a structured sequence of release windows that have been in place since the early 1980s after the videocassette market was established. Beginning with the theatrical market, these release windows have supplied an exclusive time frame for movies to open in all the various markets such as pay-per-view in hotels and airlines, non-theatrical, home video, Pay-Per-View/Video-on-Demand, pay television, basic cable and syndication. Even with some of these windows narrowing the last several years (DVDs now arrive on average of four months, seventeen days after the theatres instead of six months), the exclusivity for each market had continued to be honored. The softening of the DVD market is starting to change that. Whereas Video-on-Demand has followed the DVD releases by between 30 to 45 days in the past, Warner and Fox have been testing simultaneous releases on both platforms. Look for this to soon become the norm for all the studios as Video-on-Demand becomes a more important slice of revenue at the same time DVD sales continue to lose market share. More than 30 million cable subscribers have access to VOD so this is looked on as a real growth area, though it may take years before it can completely replace the losses in the DVD market.

Film Financing

The lower revenue being generated in the DVD market is making it much harder for producers to find money these days. When the credit crunch with the banks affects even the powerful and commercially reliable Steven Spielberg, you know it's bad out there. It looked like Spielberg and DreamWorks landed on their feet after their split with Paramount when they announced a $500 million financing deal with the Indian entertainment company Reliance along with a new distribution deal with Universal. It all started to unravel last week because the Reliance financing was contingent on getting matching funds from U.S. banks which had become difficult to close on. So they went back to Universal and asked them for $150 million to bridge the gap and help them finalize their deal with Reliance. Universal wasn't interested in this new arrangement because they had signed up to distribute DreamWorks' films not help finance them, so they landed up parting ways with each other. Needless to say, it's been a very rocky several months for Steven Spielberg, but things are starting to look up. After the split with Universal, DreamWorks was able to quickly make a distribution deal with Disney that included a $100 to $150 million loan to be applied toward the Reliance financing deal. The downsized economy led to a downsized deal. DreamWorks has to feel fortunate that Disney decided their current output of 12 movies a year needed to be increased and getting those extra four to six movies a year from a Spielberg-led company fit their needs.

It only took the worst economic downturn in 70 years to force some sanity into the independent film business.

The collapsing DVD market is making a bad economic situation even worse. Budgets are established and approved by figuring out how much each market can safely deliver in revenue, and when the most significant revenue generator can't be depended on like it used to be, investors start looking elsewhere for their investment opportunities. The dollars just don't add up anymore after you factor in all the expenses, including prints and advertising. Falling DVD numbers are having the most effect on independent films. The shakeout has long been overdue in this very crowded, competitive sector, and it only took the worst economic downturn in 70 years to force some sanity into the independent film business. Fewer movies hopefully will mean better quality movies in the marketplace that will then be able to find more breathing room in theatres and make it easier for word of mouth to grow audiences. Having six to eight specialized films open on the same weekend was always a recipe for disaster, which made no rational sense at all. The marketplace just couldn't absorb them all.

Going with the Tried and True

You may scratch your head when you see another "Friday the 13th" open, but actually the business plan behind it is no doubt more solid that the movie itself. Platinum Dunes Production is a production company started in 2001 with the express purpose of reviving old horror franchises, and they have done tremendously well with them. They have produced two new versions of "The Texas Chainsaw Massacre," along with remakes of "Amityville Horror" and "The Hitcher" that have brought in close to $200,000,000 in domestic grosses between them. With the current DVD market softening, a business plan like this makes fiscal sense because they are able to exploit the brand recognition of existing franchises and not start from scratch with new story lines and characters. There have been ten "Friday the 13th" movies between 1980 and 2001. For decades, Disney used to theatrically reissue their animated classics like "Bambi" and "Sleeping Beauty" every seven years because there was a new generation of kids to attract. Well, it's been eight years since the last "Friday the 13th," so there's a new crop of teenagers that have never seen one of these movies in theatres. It works on the same premise. Audiences instantly recognize the titles, and their production costs are under $20 million. OK, so these movies make money, but what's the bigger picture? The danger here is that there may be a lot less daring original films being made in the near future at the expense of more sequels, prequels, remakes, reboots and whatever else you want to call these movies. But wait, isn't that happening already? Yes, but don't jump out of your windows just yet. The business is cyclical, the recession will pass, money will loosen up, new companies will emerge, a new cycle will begin, and producers will start taking more daring chances again. History has shown us it's happened in the past, and it will no doubt happen again.

This Week at the Box Office   *Weekly Attendance: 34,223,092*

Holidays seem to be lining up perfectly for Hollywood this year. Good times should continue to roll at the box office this weekend helped by the rare occurrence when two holidays straddle the same weekend, Valentine's Day on Saturday and President's Day on Monday, giving the industry an extra charge in the midst of an already robust marketplace. On top of that, throw in a Friday the 13th with a movie of the same name opening on that day, and it's almost eerie. What else could align perfectly this year? It's all going to be about the female audience again. Last week saw the romantic comedy "He's Just Not That Into You" capture the number one spot, and with Disney's "Confessions of a Shopaholic" opening alongside "Friday the 13th," women will continue to be a force, with women over 25 supporting Disney's female-lit movie which has built-in awareness from five novels and teen girls flocking to see "Friday the 13th." For similar horror/slasher movies, exit polls always reveal a predominance of teenage girls in the audience. There is some debate over what kind of effect the economy will have on the box office of "Confessions of a Shopaholic" since it's all about a woman who views shopping as sport by racking up huge credit card bills. I have no idea why the movie was in development for eight years, but I'm sure the producers didn't plan on opening their movie in the middle of a deep recession. Will audiences view it as wish fulfillment and take it as fluff, look on it as a cautionary tale, or even view it as another example of crass, cynical Hollywood out of step with the times? The marketplace will figure that out. It always does.

The marketplace will figure that out. It always does.

Friday the 13th
Warner Brothers
Opening weekend: $40,570,365
Domestic gross: $65,002,019 71.1%
Foreign gross: $26,377,032 28.9%
Worldwide gross: $91,379,051
Widest release: 2,364

Confessions of a Shopaholic
Disney
Opening weekend: $15,066,360
Domestic gross: $44,277,350 40.9%
Foreign gross: $64,055,872 59.1%
Worldwide gross; $108,333,872
Widest release: 2,534 theatres

The International
Sony
Opening weekend: $9,331,739
Domestic gross: $25,450,257 42.3%
Foreign gross: $34,710,864 57.7%
Worldwide gross: $60,161,391
Widest release: 2,364 theatres

Under the Sea 3D
Warner Brothers (Imax screens only. 40 min.)
Opening weekend: $661,185
Domestic gross: $27,114,198 95.5%
Foreign gross: $1,415,258 4.5%
Worldwide gross: $28,529,456
Widest release: 108 theatres

Two Lovers
Magnolia
Opening weekend: $117,591
Domestic gross: $3,149,034 19.3%
Foreign gross: $13,154,609 80.7%
Worldwide gross: $16,303,643
Widest release: 148 theatres

Billy Barber
Eros
Opening weekend: $512,124
Domestic gross: $754,928
Foreign gross: N/A
Widest release: 70 theatres

Various Methods of Film Financing

Studios and independents are always on the lookout for the next hottest source of outside money when searching for help with financing their films. Factors are constantly changing, so one year pre-sales to foreign distributors could be the hot thing, but the following year it could be equity investors or state subsidies, hedge funds or wealthy international financers. Everyone is always looking to lay off some risk, and very often it's a combination of many different kinds of money that comes together to make a film possible. It can get very complicated and expensive with lawyers sorting it all out and closing deals with various entities throughout the world. Film financing is a global enterprise just as everything else is in the movie business today. Here are a number of ways films are financed:

- ▶ Traditional studio way of funding their own movies with their annual production budgets, development process and recycled revenues.

- ▶ Studios share costs with large production companies like Legendary Pictures, Mandate, Lake Shore and others.

- ▶ Banks, either through credit lines or financing arrangements with a bank like JP Morgan Chase.

- ▶ Co-studio production deals in which two studios share the cost of production with one taking domestic distribution and the other international.

- ▶ Wall Street investment groups.

- ▶ Studio specialty divisions like Fox Searchlight and Focus Features who have their own annual budgets and at times their own financial partners.

- ▶ Co-production deals with European broadcast stations or foreign distributors.

- ▶ Foreign pre-sales (selling individual foreign territories in advance to cover production costs).

- ▶ Soft money; tax-based incentives from international territories. Other kinds of soft money include tax allowances, loan support, foreign subsidies, and cheap facilities/barter agreements.

- ▶ Private financing with wealthy domestic and international individuals

- ▶ Negative pick-up deal, which is a guarantee from a distributor to cover a specific cost of a film. That guarantee is then taken to a bank and turned into cash by the producer. When film is completed at the approved cost, distributor pays for the film.

- ▶ Tax-based incentives from state film commissions ranging from 15% to 40% deductions from production costs spent in one of the more than 30 states with these types of arrangements.

- ▶ Limited partnerships or limited liability companies with individual investors (through Securities and Trade Commission).

- ▶ Government grants (used mostly for documentaries).

- ▶ Crowd sourcing through Internet websites like Kickstarter.

- ▶ Independent filmmakers producing either a short film, a scene from a movie or a trailer and trying to interest either a distributor, a production company or wealthy investor to finance a feature based on festival success, concept or execution. "Saw" and "Napoleon Dynamite" were both financed in this manner.

- ▶ Doing it yourself through family, friends, savings, credit cards, yard sales, insurance settlements, etc.

Flow of Money from Box Office to Investor

There is a saying in the film business, "first money in, last money out." Over the years, many investors have unfortunately found that out the hard way and have lost their money investing in movies. The only investors who should be approached to invest in a film are the ones who can afford to lose their entire investment. That may be hard to tell someone, but it's a fact, and it's better to get the possible bad news out of the way sooner rather than later. Money flows through a lot of hands, there are a lot of deductions, and it takes time for all the revenue markets to generate income. Generally speaking, investors are content if they can recoup 80% of their investment within two years of release. It takes time, and investors tend to become itchy. Getting back to "first money in, last money out," below is a quick glimpse of how the theatrical flow of money works:

Box office ➝ Exhibitor ➝ Distributor ➝ Producer ➝ Investor

The investors put their money in first and are last to get paid after everyone else keeps their share of the box office and all the distribution costs are recouped. The following unnamed movie from the late 1970s is an example I've used often in class to show how the flow of money works. In this case, the producers saw an ad in *Variety* touting the news that this particular movie had just reached $60 million in world box office gross which got them wondering when they were going to see some money.

The deal was a 50/50 split between the studio and production company after all deductions. This is what they found out when they received the following report:

Movie Earnings Report
- World Box Office Gross – $60 million
- Film Rental (distributor gross) – $30 million
- *Monies actually collected in New York office – $23 million
- 35% Distribution Fee – $8 million
- 30% – U.S. and Canada
- 35% – Great Britain
- 40% – Rest of the world
- Distribution Costs (prints, advertising, shipping) – $9 million
- Cost of Negative – $4 million
- Bank interest – $1 million
- Deferred salaries – $300,000
- Cross collateralization costs of developing other projects from company – $300,000
- Breakeven point; entering profit stage – $400,000
- 50% stays with studio – $200,000
- 50% goes to producer – $200,000

*Point in time when deductions start to be taken and the auditing process begins.

There are a couple of points to be made here. Producers and investors each get paid off the distributor gross (film rental) and not the box office gross, and more specifically, this includes only the dollars that are actually collected from the theatre owners by the distributor. At the point the above earnings report was filed, there was still $7 million in the hands of the exhibitors that wasn't collected yet. Of course, there are not always the same deductions to be taken on every film, but the distribution fees and distribution costs are a staple on most deals unless negotiated otherwise. The above flow of money is perfectly normal and legal in the film business. It's an expensive business, and to make money you have to spend money.

This is an example of how a $60 million starting point can turn into $200,000.

Questions for Discussion:

1. How does the state of the DVD market impact the financing of films?

2. What kind of problems did Steven Spielberg face in finding financing for DreamWorks that involved both production money and distribution services? Do you think Spielberg put any of his personal fortune into financing his own company? Why?

3. Choose one of the methods of financing that is listed and write one paragraph further explaining a specific method and how it works.

4. Describe what "first money in, last money out" means and why it is problematical for both filmmakers and possible investors alike. Do you see any solution to this problem, and how would you handle it if you were involved with a film?

ARTHUR KRIM: THE MAN WITH THE GOLDEN TOUCH

Week 8: February 20–26, 2009

The Motion Picture Academy has been handing out Oscars for 80 years, and there is one man who towers over all others when it comes to winning Best Picture Oscars.

While Fox Searchlight is seemingly on the verge of winning its first Best Picture Oscar, Harvey Weinstein is still insisting that his company's "The Reader" can actually be the one film that can pull off the upset victory. Improbable? Yes, but Weinstein has been down this path before and has won three Best Picture Awards with Miramax. No movie executive in the last two decades has promoted his films more effectively and vigorously than Harvey Weinstein. But this had me thinking about past Oscars and life before Mr. Weinstein, before Miramax, before Fox Searchlight. The Motion Picture Academy has been handing out Oscars for 80 years, and there is one man who towers over all others when it comes to winning Best Picture Oscars. His name is Arthur Krim, and I'd like to talk about the man who oversaw fourteen Best Picture Awards in his long and illustrious career.

Arthur Krim has a firm place in film history books as the lawyer who, along with his law partner Richard Benjamin, bought a dying United Artists from Charlie Chaplin and Mary Pickford in 1951. At the time he took control of the company, the industry was still reeling from the rulings of the government's Paramount Consent Decrees that forced the studios to sell off their movie theatres and outlawed many of their practices that had become anti-competitive and oppressive. Coupled with the growth of television, which sharply dropped box office admissions, Krim entered an industry in turmoil desperately searching for answers. What Krim and his team surmised was if they couldn't afford to run a full-fledged studio, they would become a studio without an actual physical studio to manage and pay for. They would in effect be a pool of money for filmmakers to go out and make the movies they wanted to make after the scripts and budgets were approved, and in return, United Artists would distribute the films and own the rights to them. This may sound like a simple concept, but it was revolutionary in 1951, and their business strategy of extending creative freedom to filmmakers and offering them a percentage of the profits ushered in the independent/producer system that Hollywood enjoys today. This philosophy was the basis of their remarkable success, which spanned two different distribution companies over a period of five decades.

They ran United Artists from 1951 to 1977 and Orion Pictures from 1982-1992. They were able to forge relationships with outstanding filmmakers and production companies, and from this foundation, Oscar quality films emerged. The following is the list of the fourteen films that went on to win Best Picture, ten with United Artists and four with Orion:

United Artists
1955 – "Marty"
1956 – "Around The World In 80 Days"
1960 – "The Apartment"
1961 – "West Side Story"
1963 – "Tom Jones"
1967 – "In the Heat of the Night"
1969 – "Midnight Cowboy"
1975 – "One Flew Over The Cukoo's Nest"

1976 – "Rocky"
1977 – "Annie Hall"

Orion Pictures
1984 – "Amadeus"
1986 – "Platoon"
1990 – "Dances with Wolves"
1991 – "Silence of the Lambs"

Without a doubt, this is a pretty impressive track record and legacy. Now let's compare those 14 wins with the major studios that have been in existence for the entire 80 years the Oscars have been handed out. The following are the number of Best Picture Oscars for each studio:

Columbia – 12
Paramount -9
MGM – 9
Warner Brothers – 7
20th Century Fox – 7
Universal – 6
Disney – 0

Source: *Motion Picture Almanac*

Disney formed their own distribution company in the 1950s after using United Artists as their primary distributor in the 1930s and 1940s. Disney is the only studio to never win a Best Picture Oscar. However, Miramax was a division of Disney when they won their three awards.

When Arthur Krim started Orion Pictures Distribution Corp. in 1982, he was 71 years old and proved he had a strong second act left in him. For the entire 10-year run of Orion, I was fortunate to be the company's Chicago Branch Manager and had the privilege of meeting Mr. Krim at several national sales meetings. For a lover of film history, it was something that meant a lot to me. During an eight-year stretch, the company won four Best Pictures, and Oscar night was always a big night in the Sikich household with my wife Joy and sons Adam and Josh rooting Dad's movies to victory. However the last of the company's triumphs, "Silence of the Lambs," was more bitter than sweet because Orion was forced to file for Chapter 11 bankruptcy protection on December 11, 1991, and closed its distribution offices in May, 1992. The harsh realities of being a stand-alone pure film company eventually caught up with the company. By the time "Dances with Wolves" and "Silence of the Lambs" grossed $300,000,000 between them, Krim had been forced to sell off so many different rights to pay the bills there wasn't much profit left over. Arthur Krim was 81 years old at the time.

The harsh realities of being a stand- alone pure film company eventually caught up with the company.

Harvey Weinstein has had a great run the last 15 years, but he would have to win eleven more Best Picture Oscars to match what Arthur Krim achieved in his career. I would say the record is safe. It's often easy to forget the role history has played in shaping the Motion Picture Industry and all the individuals and pioneers who played a part in its progress and evolution. Arthur Krim is one such man who should not be forgotten, especially now as we approach another Oscar night. While I'm watching the Academy Awards Sunday night, I think I'll toast my old boss and thank him for a lot of great movies and wonderful memories.

Even though the Academy Awards Show on ABC is being promoted as the Movie Event of the Year, there's a distinct lack of buzz in the air, and it all starts with the movies themselves. It's yet another year where a lot of people just aren't interested in the nominees, and there isn't much suspense about which film is going to win. "Slumdog Millionaire" has won every possible award and is being called a "lock." I guess there's still a chance that "The Curious Case of Benjamin Button" can pull an upset, but that's a funny thing to say because it's sort of like a reverse David vs. Goliath; one is the $16 million dollar film from nowhere, and the other is the $150 million dollar studio movie trying to bring it down. Fox Searchlight is in its 15th year as a distributor and is on the verge of winning its first Best Picture Oscar. It's been an impressive run for the company since it began with the 1995 release of Ed Burn's "Brothers McMullen," and they have had three previous Best Picture nominees with "The Full Monty," "Little Miss Sunshine" and last year's "Juno." They not only have an uncanny taste in films and a great instinct in what can do business, but also their ace in the hole is their skill in marketing offbeat films. No company can match them in marketing hip, cutting-edge movies. For "Slumdog Millionaire," they zeroed in on the color, the movement and the fast-paced energy, and made it all seem upbeat, even when parts of the film were harrowing. Searchlight is also doing a great job marketing Mickey Rourke's comeback in "The Wrestler" while not shying away from the grittiness of the film's subject matter. They prove time and time again that independent movies can't just depend on a film's quality and strong critics' reviews; they need to be marketing driven too, and they have certainly been at the top of their game the last few years. Can strong, creative marketing help a small film win awards? Yes, but the film has to be excellent to begin with, and "Slumdog Millionaire" is just that.

With some lackluster ratings the last several years, the Academy is trying to shake up the status quo and inject new life in the show with new producers, a brand new set, a new method of handing out awards, being secretive about who the presenters are and moving away from the comic hosts of the past with a new host in Hugh Jackman. It's anyone's guess if any of these changes will make a difference, but there is a fine line between looking fresh and innovative while at the same time keeping the tradition viewers have come to expect. The other change highlights some of the behind-the-scenes economics of the show. ABC pays about $50 million in license fees to broadcast the Oscars, historically the second most watched show of the year after the Super Bowl, but viewership last year was at an all-time low of 32 million viewers, and selling this year's ad slots have been a challenge with General Motors and other advertisers pulling out. So in a big change for the first time ever, the Oscars will accept ads for movies, which have always been banned from the telecast for a couple of reasons; the Academy wanted to keep the focus on the films being honored, and they also didn't want to give the impression that studio advertising had any influence on the awards. However, there are some restrictions for any studio that wishes to buy ad time during the ceremony such as studios not being allowed to run more than one spot, advertise an entire slate of films or make any reference to the Academy Awards. It's not known how many movies will buy time, but ABC has dropped the price of their 30-second spots from $1.7 million to $1.4 million. But that still seems high because with the Super Bowl getting $3 million a spot with 100 million viewers, ABC is asking half of that amount for delivering only a third of the audience.

The best movie theatre promotion of the year once again goes to AMC Theatres. For the third year in a row, the theatre chain is showing all five Best Picture nominees on one program the Saturday before the show starting in late morning and going all day into the night in select theatres across the country. And what a deal it is. For $30.00, a person can see all five movies with a box of free popcorn thrown in with unlimited refills through the day. So for anyone who has about 11 hours of free time on their hands, loves popcorn and hasn't seen all the movies, a truly unique day of movie watching awaits them.

This Week at the Box Office   *Weekly Attendance: 23,983,867*

The weekend of the Academy Awards is never a huge weekend for the studios or independents to open new movies. For the studios, their attention is more toward the weekend activities and the concern that the Sunday show could cut into the weekend box office. For independent distributors, their major Oscar contenders are already on screen, and with moviegoers only having one last chance to see the nominees, it's too much existing competition to open another high-quality film into. Hence the only two wide national releases are a new Tyler Perry film from Lionsgate and a minor college comedy from Sony called "Fired Up." Tyler Perry's audience will come out in droves as usual on opening weekend and should easily dominate the weekend.

Tyler Perry's Madea Goes to Jail

Lionsgate
Opening weekend: $41,030,947
Domestic Gross: $90,508,336
Foreign gross: 0.00
Worldwide gross; $90,508,336
Widest release: 2,203 theatres

Fired Up

Sony
Opening weekend: $5,483,778
Domestic gross: $17,231,291 92.6%
Foreign gross: $1,367,811 7.4%
Worldwide gross: $18,599,i02
Widest release: 1,811 theatres

Delhi 6

UTV
Opening weekend: $602,850
Domestic gross: $879,913 6.7%
Foreign gross: $12,245,686 93.3%
Worldwide gross: $13,245,666
Widest release: 90 theatres

Stone of Destiny

Independent
Opening weekend: $72,227
Domestic gross: $389,584
Foreign gross; N/A
Widest release: 20 theatres

Katyn

Koch Lorber
Opening weekend: $11,053
Domestic gross: $118,095 0.8%
Foreign Gross: $14,605,218 99.2%
Worldwide Gross: $14,723,313
Widest release: 2 theatres

Three Monkeys

Zeitgeist
Opening weekend: $3,045
Domestic gross: $41,343 2.3%
Foreign gross: $1,898.907 97.9%
Worldwide gross: $1,940,250
Widest release: 3 theatres

Eleven Minutes

Regent
Opening weekend: $3,670
Domestic gross: $7,986
Foreign gross: N/A
Widest release: 4 theatres

2012 Update:

After Weinstein Films won back-to-back Best Picture Oscars in 2010 and 2011 with "The King's Speech" and "The Artist," Harvey Weinstein has narrowed the gap between him and Arthur Krim with his fifth victory. Even though that's still nine short of the record, Mr. Weinstein is enjoying a strong second act of his career with the recent revival of Weinstein Films after a few lackluster years at the helm of his new company.

When the Conglomerates Took Over

As the 1960s began, the moguls who ran the studios were getting old, yes, some of them like Jack Warner were still around, and profits continued to dwindle. The film companies were ripe to be taken over at this point in time, the business was becoming more expensive and risky, and the movie industry has always been glamorous, high profile and cash driven. Something had to happen, and it did. After the stock market was starting to take off in the 1960s, a new type of company emerged, the conglomerate. A conglomerate is the result of large companies buying out smaller unrelated businesses and putting them under the same corporate structure. One after another, conglomerates started gobbling up the studios, including the Arthur Krim led United Artists:

1962 – Universal bought by MCA (Music Corporation of America)

1966 – Paramount taken over by Gulf and Western (steel, plastics, hydraulics)

1967 – United Artists bought by Transamerica (insurance)

1968 – Embassy bought by Avco (insurance)

1969 – Warner Brothers bought by Kinney Services (car rentals, parking lots, funeral parlors)

There are many things that can be said about conglomerates, but an irrefutable fact is that they came in with new-found money and helped stabilize the film industry when it was in pretty bad shape. In 1963, "Cleopatra" was made at a cost of $44 million, which was the most expensive film ever made at that point, and proceeded to flop at the box office. Most of the ancillary markets that are in place today didn't exist, so when a big film died at the theatres, it was a huge loss with little backside protection to help bail it out. Of course, there was a dark side to conglomerates, and much of it had to do with control. In 1977, following three straight Best Picture Awards, Transamerica implemented cost controls and other restrictions on the management team at United Artists, which were too tough for them to stomach. Arthur Krim and his partners decided to leave the company they revived in 1951 to form Orion Pictures, a production company under Warner Brothers that distributed their movies. After four years in that arrangement, they left Warners and returned to distributing their own films so they could once again control all aspects of their films.

Questions for Discussion

1. What significance does Arthur Krim have in the history of the Motion Picture Industry? Why did Orion Pictures have only a 10-year run in the 1980s despite winning four Best Picture Awards?

2. Fox Searchlight releases high-quality films similar to what Orion Pictures did 25 years ago. Discuss at least three differences between the companies and their business models.

3. How did conglomerates first get involved in the movie industry? Discuss what's good and bad about them. Do you think the conglomerate takeover of the film industry was inevitable?

BOX OFFICE MOMENTUM AND THE CHANGING ECONOMICS OF TELEVISION REVENUES

Week 9: February 27–March 5, 2009

Even in the best of times weak product can bring moviegoing to a halt.

Before I get into the topic of theatrical movie sales to television, a few words about the current theatrical marketplace. In baseball, there's an old saying that "momentum is today's starting pitcher." In the Motion Picture Industry, momentum is next weekend's opening movies. It can turn quickly, even with the business doing as well as it is, if new movies don't deliver what audiences are looking for. That's what makes the theatrical marketplace such an unpredictable and challenging business to work in, follow and study. The year has its share of fluctuations, surprises and disappointments, and even the experts can't fully predict where it's all headed.

As we enter the March/April corridor, there is both some concern and optimism about whether or not the 2009 box office can continue on its record-setting pace. Will the troubled economy at some point catch up to the movie business? Right now it looks like it could be a strong year from start to finish. If there are going to be fewer family vacations this year, movie theatres are poised to take advantage of people staying closer to home. Except for higher prices for 3D movies, the price of a movie ticket shouldn't be going up anytime soon, so prices will remain affordable. After factoring in all the theatres in both large and small markets, the national average ticket price is about $7.50. In the immediate future, March and April are two of the lesser profile months, and even in the best of times, weak product can bring moviegoing to a halt. That being said, March looks like it could keep the box office train chugging along. It doesn't hurt to have "The Watchmen" open the month and "Monsters vs. Aliens" close it out, but the performances of all the movies in between will help determine how successful this period will be. The one thing it will lack is the mixture of highbrow, mainstream and lowbrow movies that January and February offered. The marketplace works best when it serves as many audiences as possible, especially this time of year when most movies are going after specific niches. After the Oscar movies fade from view, one niche that will be in short supply is the quality, character-driven adult film that is capable of expanding into suburban multiplexes from the big city art houses. The same thing happens every year. All those quality films are bunched into the last two months of the year when everyone knows they can't all win Oscars and do business, but various pressures, expectations and star/director contracts can dictate otherwise.

A prime example of seasonal booking excess is Overture's "Last Chance Harvey" which opened, played for a while, and is now gone from theatres. Starring Dustin Hoffman and Emma Thompson, this is a good character-driven film with some star power which had no real shot at getting nominations and winning any awards but chose to open limited at the end of the year anyway in the midst of much higher profile competition. It played wider in January and February and did reasonably well with a $13,000,000 gross, but it may have had the potential to gross at least $10 million more if it was held back and opened in either March or April. The film would have stood out a lot more, had more breathing room to stay on screens longer, and would have provided a much needed alternative for the older audience who will be desperately searching for something to see in the next couple of months. Sometimes decisions are either made or forced on the marketplace, which aren't necessarily in the best interests of the film itself, and "Last Chance Harvey" appears to be an example of that.

Sometimes decisions are either made for or forced on the marketplace
that aren't necessarily in the best interests of the film itself.

With "The Curious Case of Benjamin Button" falling to "Slumdog Millionaire" in the Best Picture race, will we be seeing another studio spending $150 million on a prestigious drama? Probably not. This film was made only because Brad Pitt's former production agent, Brad Grey, became the studio head of Paramount and had the power to push it through the system. For the most part, studios will be concentrating their energies and capital on what they do best, producing mainstream moneymakers, whether they be youth comedies, romances, thrillers, action, horror, family movies, animation, 3D, comic book adaptations and of course, plenty of prequels and sequels of hit franchises. As for "Benjamin Button's" bottom line, does it still have a chance to turn a profit? The way Hollywood math works, if a film can gross twice as much as its production, in this case that would be $300 million worldwide, a movie would be able to recoup its production costs from theatrical and then get its marketing expenses and hopefully turn a profit on expected DVD and television sales. "The Curious Case of Benjamin Button" is currently at $156 million international to go along with a domestic gross of $124 million, so the movie will easily gross over $300 million. The problem is with the word "expected." The ancillary markets are not what they used to be, and the studios don't want to be in the business of chasing money for two years in order to make a small profit.

Selling Movies to Television

For the last 30 years, the three main revenue streams for movies have been theatrical, home video and television, and that's still the case today despite advances in Video-on-Demand and streaming movies on the Internet. As it is with the theatrical and DVD businesses, it's two totally different economic realities for studio movies as compared to independent films when it comes to selling movies to television. For studios, there has been a strong foundation in place for years with the three major pay television networks, HBO, Showtime and Starz/Encore. Each of the studios has had exclusive deals with one of the networks that can last for up to seven years, which is a fantastic luxury to have and one that many other distributors can only dream about. These deals guarantee a multimillion payday for each movie based on box office performance that can range from $6 million on the low end to over $20 million for the big hits. The studios have used their economy of size to great advantage in forging these lucrative deals, and these guaranteed television dollars play a crucial role in how they budget and project revenues for each of their movies. Now several of these deals are coming to an end and will have to be renewed, and there has been some posturing that indicates the networks will be trying to downsize their studio output deals in their next negotiations. In the last several years, priorities have changed for pay networks as they continue to produce more original programming (both movies and series) while recognizing that subscribers can see the movies in a variety of formats months before they arrive on pay TV. When the smoke clears, all the studios will no doubt still have some kind of output deal in place, but they will probably have to accept some lower fees and perhaps not have all their movies covered under the blanket deal. The pay networks still want feature films, but they want them for less, and they would like the option not to have to take all of them.

This new reality caused Viacom (which owns Paramount), MGM and Lionsgate not to renew their deals with Showtime when their deals recently expired, and they chose instead to partner in a new Viacom Pay Television Network named Epix to debut later in 2009, creating a fourth pay TV channel. This move by Viacom would have been unthinkable pre-2005 when Paramount and Showtime were sister companies under the Viacom banner, but in 2005 chairman Sumner Redstone divided his Viacom empire into two publicly traded companies, Viacom and CBS, with Showtime and all other television divisions being a part of CBS. Redstone preached total independence for the two new companies, and that has been apparent with both the startup of Epix and CBS later starting their own theatrical distribution company with CBS Films. It was reported in the Hollywood Reporter that Showtime freed up $300 million a year in license fees when those three companies left the fold, which gives you an idea how much money changes hands in these output deals. Weinstein Films jumped in and made their own output deal with Showtime, but it was reported that the distributor had to pay a sizable dollar advance to the pay TV network instead of the other way around just to secure a deal. If that doesn't highlight the changing economic dynamics nothing does. That's the first time I've ever heard of that happening, but Showtime needed some kind of assurance that all the movies being promised to them would actually be made and distributed. Epix's main challenge was getting enough cable and satellite operators to carry their new channel, and as of 2012, Comcast, DirecTV and Time Warner Cable still don't carry Epix, so it remains unavailable in two thirds of cable homes.

The bottom line is that you can't rent a network or
self-distribute your movie on television.

Though the studios may be getting squeezed, they will still have their output deals and still make a very good buck from pay television. What about the vast amount of independent films that get made each year? What has been their success rate in making any kind of television sale? Sad to say, it's not very good. The dirty little secret in the film business is that the majority of independent films are not able to land any type of television deal whether it's basic cable or pay television. A filmmaker can always self-distribute his or her movie, rent a theatre, or hire a professional to book some theatres, and DVDs can be sold at festivals or through a movie's website, but the bottom line is that you can't rent a network or self-distribute your film on television. Unlike with studio movies, independent films are sold on a picture-by-picture basis, and the two main criteria TV programmers look at are who's in the cast and what it grossed at the box office. Without any names in the cast or success in the theatres there is no real chance of making any money from a television sale. It's a simple supply and demand issue. The networks have a certain amount of money budgeted to acquire outside films and a certain number of time slots to fill, and they have hundreds and hundreds of films to choose from. The huge supply has also driven prices down. License fees can be as low as $10,000 to $20,000 on the independent movie channels, IFC and Sundance, which merged in 2008 and made it even tougher when two potential buyers turned into one. Just as it has hurt the studio movies, original programming on all TV channels, especially the abundance of reality shows, is putting the squeeze on feature films. Both IFC channel and Sundance have a number of original shows that fill valuable hours of time and lesson their need for feature films. A good way for any filmmaker to learn what all the channels are playing is to get one of those thick monthly cable guides and study it page by page. It's the same thing as walking into a video store, Best Buy, Walmart or Target and checking to see what's on the shelves. Your eyes don't lie; you can see for yourself what is being bought in the commercial marketplace.

In 1995 when ISA Releasing distributed "Tie-Died: Rock n' Roll's Most Deadicated Fans," the pay television universe provided a somewhat better opportunity for independent films to get a bite at the apple. There were fewer movies being made back then, and the pay networks had more available slots to fill since they weren't producing nearly as much original programming as they are in today's market. In short, they were more dependent on feature films, so they bought more films. Even though "Tie-Died" had a gross of just under $200,000,the music documentary played all the major markets and achieved a bit of notoriety with the untimely death of Jerry Garcia. We actually were able to complete two sales in what is referred to as the first pay window and second pay window. HBO purchased the film for its Cinemax channel, which often played documentaries, for $40,000 for a 16-month exclusive window; nine months later Showtime paid $20,000 for its own 16-month exclusivity in the second pay television window. When we released "Lana's Rain" in 2004, the landscape had changed dramatically when we attempted to procure a television deal, and we were never able to find any takers.

Television is a hard nut to crack for an independent film, and there are no free handouts. A movie has to earn its way by proving it has a good degree of audience appeal or some kind of previous success. It also helps if a film has a specific niche that services a specific channel. There was a Chicago film a few years ago that dealt with true-life crime. The director thought it had theatrical potential, but after a New York film festival showing, the biggest interest came from the A&E Network which offered $250,000 for it to debut on its channel because it was perfect for their brand of showcasing real life crime stories. The director accepted the deal, and the acquisition price covered his production costs by going straight to cable. There are always exceptions to the rule, and making a compelling film for a specific audience is not a bad place to start.

This Week at the Box Office

Weekly Attendance: 18,948,734

Jonas Brothers: 3D Concert Experience

Buena Vista (Disney)
Opening weekend: $12,510,374
Domestic Gross: $19,676,965 82.6%
Foreign gross: $4,024,220 17.4%
Worldwide gross: $23,186,960
Widest release: 1,276 theatres

Street Fighter: the Legend of Chun-Li

20th Century Fox
Opening weekend: $4,721,110
Domestic gross: $8,742,261 68.5%
Foreign gross: $4,021,940 31.5%
Worldwide gross: $12,764,201
Widest release: 1,164 theatres

Echelon Company

After Dark Films
Opening weekend: $500,154
Domestic gross: $666,009 30.5%
Foreign gross: $1,520,773 69.5%
Worldwide gross; $2,186,782
Widest release: 400 theatres

Play the Game

Slowhand Cinema Releasing
Opening weekend: $51,199
Domestic gross: $562,936
Foreign gross: N/A
Widest release: 55 theatres

Crossing Over

Weinstein
Opening weekend: $77,370
Domestic gross: $455,464 12.9%
Foreign gross: $3,074,215 87.1%
Worldwide gross: $3,529,869
Widest release: 42

Bon Heur de Pierre

Alliance
Opening weekend: $103,663
Domestic gross: $372,755
Foreign gross: N/A
Widest release: 44 theatres

Examined Life

Zeitgeist
Opening weekend: $12,085
Domestic gross: $120,712
Foreign gross: N/A
Widest release: 6 theatres

An American Affair

Screen Media
Opening weekend: $11,700
Domestic gross; $28,564
Foreign gross: N/A
Widest release: 2 theatres

Bob Funk

Cinema Epoch
Opening weekend: $4,085
Domestic Gross: $4,085
Foreign Gross; N/A
Widest release: 1 theatre

TELEVISION NETWORKS THAT PURCHASE MOVIES

Pay TV Networks

- ▶ HBO (includes Cinemax) owned by Time Warner
- ▶ Showtime (includes The Movie Channel) owned by CBS, Inc.
- ▶ Starz/Encore owned by Liberty Media
- ▶ Epix owned by Viacom, MGM and Lionsgate

Basic Cable Networks (and their target niches)

- ▶ Spike (young male demo)
- ▶ TNT (brand is drama)
- ▶ TBS (brand is comedy)
- ▶ FX (action, big mainstream movies)
- ▶ Lifetime (women, romance)
- ▶ A&E (true crime)
- ▶ BET (African American)
- ▶ Logo (gay/lesbian)
- ▶ Syfy (science fiction/suspense horror)
- ▶ ESPN Classic (sports movies)
- ▶ VH1 Classic (music)

Independent Film Channels

- ▶ Sundance Channel
- ▶ IFC

- ▶ The major studios have multi-year output deals with one of the pay television networks, which guarantee multi-million license fees per film based on its box office performance. Generally, the fee tops out at about $20 million for the highest grossing films.

- ▶ Sundance and IFC are both owned by AMC Networks and are buying fewer and fewer movies today. These channels have been known to pay between $10,000 and $75,000 per film for an 18-month period. In a way, streaming is quickly replacing the television deal for many independent films, especially for those films and distributors that have an existing deal in place with Netflix.

- ▶ DreamWorks Animation has recently become the first major Hollywood supplier to choose web streaming over pay television by making a deal with Netflix. It is estimated that the deal is worth $30 million per picture over an unspecified period of years.

- ▶ "Busted theatricals" are movies made for theatrical release but are released straight to pay television instead. Prime consideration is strength of cast, and the fee could be as high as one or two million if it has not been released on DVD first.

- ▶ The four broadcast networks (NBC, CBS, ABC & Fox) no longer are in the business of buying feature films. For the first time since 1961, no network has a Movie of the Week slot.

Questions for Discussion

1. How do the studios sell their movies to pay television networks, and what kind of revenue do they get back in return?

2. Was there anything unusual about Paramount's decision to allow its output deal with Showtime to expire in order to partner with two other companies to start their own pay network?

3. What makes it so difficult for independent films to land a television deal?

4. In what ways can an independent film put itself in a better position to land a television sale?

5. When a new pay network is established, what are they at the mercy of?

THE DEVIL IS IN THE DETAILS

Week 10: March 6–12, 2009

Who actually owned the rights to make "The Watchmen"?
The question persisted even after the movie was made.

With the month of February showing a 10% gain at the box office over last year, March is poised to come in like a lion and keep the theatres humming with the release of the year's first true blockbuster, Warner's "The Watchmen." Other distributors are duly impressed and have decided to sit this frame out, giving Warner Brothers the weekend to itself in terms of new wide releases. But whatever is on the screen of this cult comic book adaptation may pale in comparison to the legal disputes and battles that have raged off the screen over copyright ownership of the property itself. It's rare when you have two giant studios like 20th Century Fox and Warner Brothers in such a high profile public battle over a potential blockbuster, but it highlights the complexity of a project that has bounced around Hollywood for over 20 years, and still the question remained, who actually owned the right to make "The Watchmen"? The question persisted even after the movie was made.

The original series of comics came out in 1986, and 20th Century Fox was the original copyright holder. Fox sued Warner Bros. in February, 2008, claiming copyright infringement based on agreements in the contract going back to 1991, the year Fox allowed the rights to pass to another party. Every studio has armies of lawyers looking over each item in a contract, and it seems like it came down to one little clause in the 1991 agreement that is causing Warner Bros. a lot of grief and money. Fox claimed the contract stated that every time the producer came up with a new script, storyline, stars or director, the project had to be resubmitted to them, holding on to the right of still being involved in the movie in some way. Of course, over that long time span elements in the project were bound to change, but Warner Bros. disputed that claim and contended they were the exclusive rights holders. So there was no settlement, and the lawsuit worked its way through the courts.

Any business can get messy, and the movie business is certainly no exception because there is always money involved, and with big movies like "The Watchmen," hundreds of millions of dollars are in play. The behind-the-scenes deal making, power plays, negotiation tactics and legal maneuverings are a huge part of the industry that helps determine what gets made, what gets distributed and who distributes it. The studios are always the biggest targets; they face challenges and lawsuits all the time, and at the heart of it all is control over intellectual property, access to good material that allows them to make the movies to fill out their annual slates. Movies come from a lot of different sources, and most of them have rights holders involved who have to be dealt with properly in order to avoid disputes down the road.

On Christmas Eve, 2008, the judge made the ruling in 20th Century Fox's favor stating the producer who sold the movie to Warner Bros. hadn't secured all the rights from Fox. Often when two studios have a dispute, things get ironed out and bartered behind the scenes, but that wasn't going to happen in this case. Fox was set to go for the jugular; the stakes were too high, and they held all the cards with the release of the movie set to open in ten weeks. Fox began threatening very publicly they were going to get an injunction to block the March 6 release. Once that happened, Warner Bros. knew it was checkmate, game over, and they were forced to make a settlement and get the issue resolved because in no way could they afford facing an injunction blocking the film's release. According to insiders close to negotiations, Warner Bros. agreed to pay Fox $1.5 million for their development costs as well as up to 8.5% of the worldwide distributor gross after the movie breaks even. This was doubly embarrassing for Warner Bros. because they were down this road before in 2005 when a judge issued an injunction blocking the planned release of "Dukes of Hazzard" in a rights dispute. This led to a settlement that had Warner Bros. paying $17 million to a producer who claimed copyright infringement.

Whether "The Watchmen" will prove to be worth all this hassle, litigation, and $130 million in production costs is something that will be determined by the ticket buyers. Many people are hoping it becomes a blockbuster because there are a lot of hands in the pot. Since Warner Bros. actually bought the rights from Paramount. Paramount stayed on as the foreign distributor, so there are three studios sharing in the revenues. There are some commercial risks here. "The Watchmen" is not "Spiderman" or "Batman." It's a cult phenomenon that has rabid fans, but it sits outside the mainstream and is not assured of blockbuster acceptance. The movie is R-rated, not for kids, contains graphic violence and sexuality and clocks in at 161 minutes, perhaps the longest comic book movie ever made. And after all is said and done, if "The Watchmen" hits on all cylinders, Fox may get the last laugh. They hold the sequel rights.

---

*What you don't expect, haven't planned for or didn't see coming
is what can be so aggravating and painful.*

Though seldom as high profile or convoluted as the battle over who had the ultimate right to make "The Watchmen," many producers, filmmakers and distributors often fight their own smaller battles over the issues of copyright ownership. It's not just over copyright registration for the film itself, but it can be for improper use of music, any kind of art work in the background of scenes that weren't cleared or unlawful use of copyrighted products that owners may find exploitative or harmful to their company in some way. The potential list of copyright violations is long and highlights the thorny issue of rights protection that can make an expensive business even more expensive for those who don't protect themselves properly, try to take shortcuts, make bad decisions or don't understand completely what the contracts are saying. Simply put, the movie business is complex, risky and often messy, and when people get a sniff of money or perceive something to have a chance of success, anyone remotely involved in a project can come out of the woodwork claiming rights and looking for their piece of the action. Often problems arise from the fine print of a contract, an added clause, or an error made in defining some right or condition. What you don't expect, haven't planned for or didn't see coming is what can be so aggravating and painful. For that reason, all the studios have an army of lawyers at their disposal to protect their interests, to write their agreements and to pour over the tiniest of details to insure everything is in order to protect against any outside challenges. That still doesn't stop the lawsuits from coming and a situation like "The Watchmen" from happening. There is a lot of finger pointing going on, but someone overlooked one single clause in a 1991 agreement between the original producer and Fox when the chain-of-title report was being done, and that became the basis of the lawsuit which Fox eventually won. It only takes one little clause to cause a lot of grief.

I found out about those devilish details myself while distributing two independent films, "Tie-Died: Rock n' Roll's Most Deadicated Fans" (1995) and "Lana's Rain" (2004). In both cases, problems arose over some of the music used in the films. With "Tie-Died," the producers didn't have properly worded agreements that would cover all the master rights. It was partially my fault that I didn't notice that the agreements only covered mechanical rights, which are not sufficient when inserting a piece of music into a film. It was the first film where I was in a decision making position with the responsibility of overseeing all the details involved with the distribution of the film. Not fully grasping the difference between mechanical, sync and master rights came back to haunt me. I wasn't really worried about the music because this wasn't the Grateful Dead we were talking about. Their music was too expensive for the producers to even consider using. The vast majority of the music came from the fans of the band who made up the parking lot scene profiled by the documentary. There was no initial problem with the theatrical release of the film, which landed up playing in over 125 theatres throughout the country over several months and grossing a disappointing $180,000. The problem arose following the home video release and right in front of our pay television window. A couple of musicians retained lawyers and came looking for money, with the letter from the attorney stating film revenues that were completely wrong, but nevertheless the movie had the perception of being successful since it played across the country, had a video release, and we had made a pay television deal with HBO. Since the proper agreements were not written and their attorney called HBO, they had all the leverage, and we were forced to make a deal to make them go away. I believe we negotiated three $5,000 payments that our Errors and Omission insurance partially paid for.

The situation with "Lana's Rain" was even more aggravating and should have never happened. The producer was good friends with a Chicago band and put a couple of snippets from two of the songs in the film to give them some exposure and to include them in the end credits. They had never published any of their music and signed an agreement that allowed the music to be used in the film for no charge. This was done before I became involved in the film. Everything was fine until after we signed a DVD deal. Soon after that, I received a call from an attorney representing the band claiming his clients had a clause in their agreement that gave them rights to some of the DVD revenues. I brushed him off, but he produced an agreement, which I had never seen, with a clause that stated if ""Lana's Rain" procures a DVD release, a new agreement with the band will be written for an amount to be negotiated or for a percentage of the DVD revenues." I was livid but couldn't do anything about it because it was a valid signed agreement. It was déjà vu again when the attorney called our DVD distributor and told their attorney we didn't have all our music rights cleared. Leverage is a bitch when it's on the other side. I wasn't involved in the film when that clause was added, but the problem came crashing down on me to settle it. The distributor is always targeted, not the producers, because the distributor is on the front lines, has more to lose while the film is still in release, and quite frankly, many independent filmmakers are broke after they complete a film. Just as with the problem with "Tie-Died," we charged our legal costs to the producers, but when a movie isn't in the profit stage, that means very little because it's money out of our pockets. It didn't cost too much to make the band members go away, but having to pay them anything for their music that had no bearing on the film itself was a tough pill to swallow. To throw in that clause was foolish and unnecessary because their music meant nothing to the film and could easily have been removed at any point. Even if it was a friendly gesture, an old boss of mine used to tell me "friends exist to screw you." I'm not nearly as cynical as he was, but I knew what he was trying to say. Things change. Friends drift away. Others can take advantage of you. Greed sets in. Business is business.

The movie industry is full of potential risks and rewards. While chasing the rewards, it's always good business to remember the risks because there are plenty of those lurking in the shadows. Someone once defined risk as meaning that more things can happen than will happen. That's just a fancy way of saying we have no idea what's going to happen. How true that statement is when it comes to movies. And when it comes to securing all the rights it takes to produce a film, a producer can eliminate as much risk as possible by leaving nothing to chance and not throwing in anything in the deal that can become a problem down the road. If it's a deal breaker, sometimes it's better to walk away rather than assuming it won't be a problem or thinking it can be dealt with later. The devil is in the details.

This Week at the Box Office   *Weekly Attendance: 19,937,011*

Though no other studio dared to go up against "The Watchmen," a total of ten independent films opened, mostly in New York and Los Angeles, and none of them registered much interest from art house audiences as detailed below. Week after week, smaller films open and close and are replaced by other titles. 2009 is no different from other years in this regard. Up to this point, no 2009 specialty film has been able to distinguish itself, and as with past years, the first two months of the year has been dominated by the end-of-the-year releases and Oscar nominated films. It wasn't much of a surprise when Warner Bros. chose the first week of March to open "The Watchmen." Warner Bros. had great success with director Zack Snyder's "300" with a release date of March 9, 2007 when it totaled $456,068,181 in worldwide grosses. With the same director, it was a no brainer to try to duplicate that same kind of success. Unfortunately for Warner Bros., Fox and

Paramount, "The Watchmen" fell far short of that total and only grossed $185 million worldwide. With the high cost of production and marketing, it's doubtful the film was able to show a profit to have any revenues to share. Needless to say, there has been no talk of a sequel.

The Watchmen
Warner Brothers
Opening weekend: $55,214,334
Domestic gross: $107,509,799 58%
Foreign gross: $77,749,184 42%
Worldwide gross: $185,258,983
Widest release: 3,611 theatres

Tokyo!
Liberation Entertainment
Opening weekend: $23,030
Domestic gross: $351,059 29.5%
Foreign gross: $838,803 70.5%
Worldwide gross: $1,189,862
Widest release: 18 theatres

12
Sony Classics
Opening weekend: $12,042
Domestic gross: $125,120 1.7%
Foreign gross: $7,412,333 98.3%
Worldwide gross; $7,537,453
Widest release: 20 theatres

Phoebe in Wonderland
Think Film
Opening weekend: $29,766
Domestic gross: $72,979
Foreign gross: N/A
Widest release: 11 theatres

Explicit Ills
Peach Art
Opening weekend: $9,125
Domestic gross: $25,627
Foreign gross: N/A
Widest release: 2 theatres

Yaaurum Nalam
Ad Labs
Opening weekend: $11,056
Domestic gross; $36,594
Foreign gross: N/A
Widest release: 6 theatres

Sherman's Way
International
Opening weekend: $2,789
Domestic gross: $13,282
Foreign gross: N/A
Widest release: 4 theatres

Nightwatching
Film Circuit Alliance
Opening weekend: $5,665
Domestic gross: $15,219
Foreign gross: N/A
Widest release: 1 theatre

Reunion
Abramorama
Opening weekend: 6,542
Domestic gross: $8,030
Foreign gross: N/A
Widest release: 2 theatres

13B
Ad Labs
Opening weekend: $6,752
Domestic gross: $49,043 2%
Foreign gross; $2,445,478 98%
Worldwide gross: $2,494,521
Widest release: 10 theatres

Shuttle
Truly Indie
Opening weekend: $1,925
Domestic gross: $1,925
Foreign gross: N/A
Widest release: 1 theatre

WHAT DOES A PRODUCER DO?

The Producers Guild defines a producer as an individual who has exercised decision-making authority over a number, but not necessarily all, of the following duties:

- Conceiving of the underlying concept of the story, or selecting and securing the rights to the material on which the story is based
- Selecting the writer(s)
- Supervising the development of the script
- Securing initial financing and serving as the point of contact with the financial entity/studio network

- Preparing (or supervising the preparation of) the preliminary budget
- Selecting the director and the key technical personnel (e.g., production designer, cinematographer, editor, etc.)
- Selecting the principal cast
- Approving the shooting schedule
- Providing in-person, on-set consultation with the director, cast, and department heads
- Supervising the day-to-day operations of the shooting company, both on location and in studio
- Viewing dailies and providing in-person consultation on them
- Consulting with the editor and director on initial cut(s)
- Selecting the composer and supervising scoring and recording sessions
- Supervising all titles, optical, and visual effects
- Delivering answer print or edited master to distribution
- Consulting with distributor/studio/network on marketing and publicity plans

The Option Agreement

The option deal in the entertainment industry is widely used to purchase a literary property within a specified period of time for a specific price. That property can be a book, a newspaper or magazine article, a short story, a written play, a comic book, an essay, even a blog. Unless a producer absolutely knows he or she is working with an original story or script, one of the crucial responsibilities of a producer is to conduct a chain-of-title report to track the history of who has controlled the property over the years. Many literary properties can change hands multiple times as different producers attempt and then fail to either find the right script, the right cast, the financing or specific rights like music licensing which then provides an opening for another set of producers to take a swing at making something happen with that same property after the option period expires.

Whether it's a small producer or one of the major studios, utilizing the option process is generally a cost efficient way to control an author's original work while working toward making a film based on the property a reality. As is the case with many other facets of the film business, there are misconceptions in regards to the option agreement. Perhaps one of the more important points to note is that during the first step of the process, little or no money could change hands between the two parties when making an agreement. The following are some of the key terms and items that are considered during the negotiation process:

- The Option Fee. If it's an independent producer negotiating the rights to something, he or she is usually using his or her own money and so will try to negotiate the lowest fee possible, from $0 to $1,000. In return, the producer usually stresses his passion for the material and convinces the writer that he will work hard in trying to bring all the elements together necessary to make a film out of the material. If it's a studio deal, the option fee can be about 10% of what the actual purchase price is going to be if the deal is ultimately completed and the movie moves forward and is made. For example, the option fee could be $50,000 on a purchase price of $500,000.

- The Option Period. Everything is always negotiable, but the standard length for an initial option period is one year to eighteen months. It can be shorter, but it takes time for a producer to bring everything together. During the option period, the producer exclusively controls the property, but then again, if it doesn't work out, the rights revert back to the writer where it's available again on the open market. That's how a literary property can change hands multiple times.

- The Option Extension. Generally, an extension is worked into the agreement because getting the financing is always a difficult process to complete. The extension can be the same length as the original time frame, and the writer retains the right to keep the fee where it is or to request a higher fee for the extension.

► The Purchase Price. Purchase prices for literary properties can range from a few thousand dollars for an unknown writer's work to several millions of dollars for a hot property from a well-known author. The projected budget of the film serves as an effective starting point in determining the purchase price, which can range between 2% and 5% of the final budget.

► Exercising The Option. The actual act that results in the transfer of the rights from the writer to the producer. This involves the payment of cash to the writer and is usually paid before the applicable option period expires.

Source: www.medialawyer.com

Questions for Discussion

1. Was there more than one party at fault in "The Watchmen" copyright ownership case between Warner Bros. and 20th Century Fox? Was a lawsuit inevitable, or could it have been avoided?

2. What is a producer's responsibility in regards to the use of intellectual property? What are some of the things that can go wrong that can lead to conflicts and threats of litigation?

3. How can movie companies protect their self-interests when one of their film properties changes hands?

4. When an independent distributor acquires a film from a producer and a legal issue arises over some of the rights, who is ultimately responsible from a legal and monetary standpoint?

5. How can a literary property have a number of different producers attached to it at various periods of its life? In an option agreement, describe the difference between an option fee and the purchase price and why one of them is higher than the other.

THE LAW OF DIMINISHING RETURNS

Week 11: March 13–19, 2009

---

*Invariably investors discover two basic truths about film financing:
the return is less than what they expected, and it takes longer
than they thought to see any real money.*

I'm often reminded of how basic economic principles are so applicable to what is happening in the Motion Picture Industry. Three principles stand out the most:

► Market Equilibrium – Only at equilibrium is the quantity demanded equal to the quantity supplied.

► The Invisible Hand – The market behaves as if some unseen force were examining each company's supply or demand schedule, then selecting an amount that ensures a correct balance.

► The Law of Diminishing Returns – When output continues to increase at a steady rate, any factor of production or demand will begin to diminish at some point.

To put it more simply, the bubble will burst when there is too much of a good thing, and the market itself will let you know when that happens. We've seen it with housing, the stock market, and even with donuts. There was a time when Krispy Kreme Donuts was the hottest thing going, and people were willing to drive miles to pick up a dozen of those warm tasty treats. Then seemingly overnight you could find them in every grocery store and gas station, and for some reason they didn't seem special anymore. Soon after, their stock price began falling, and the company found itself in trouble. Some similar things have occurred in the movie industry. Too much outside money in the period between 2003 and 2007 flooded the market, which led to too many movies. That led to more competition and clutter and too little return for the hedge fund operators and other financiers who gambled on putting their money into film production. Invariably investors discover two basic truths about film financing: the return is less than what they expected, and it takes longer than they thought to see any real money. It's not surprising that the hedge funds, backed by the major banks, have come to this conclusion in such a down market. The flow of money through various hands always takes its time, and profits on many films come from the after-markets several years after a film's initial theatrical release. As I tell my students, money sticks to whoever has it at the time. It's a tough business, especially for those who are looking to make a quick buck.

The current credit crunch is forcing some changes in the financial landscape, which will be impacting studios down the road. From 2005-2007, hedge funds partnered with all the major banks to pump literally billions of dollars into helping to finance entire slates of studio movies over a period of years, taking on the risks of Hollywood production in return for the share of future profits. But that's when money flowed freely. Banks don't have the luxury in recessionary times to wait around for future profits, especially after some box office duds. Banks need money now and have been forced to write down securities that are backed by film assets. Some are even trying to sell off their positions with the film companies at discounts from 30% to 50% of their investment values and a few of them are finding willing buyers in experienced investors who are able to take a longer term view on returns. One such investor is Mark Cuban who is already deeply invested in the movie business as owner of the Landmark Theatre chain and distributor Magnolia Pictures. Cuban has already purchased 34 films and over 200 hours of television through his Content Partners Company. The studios have enough financing through these deals through the next couple of years but look for continued market correction.

The six major studios have the game figured out pretty well when it comes to finding outside financing and choosing the right number of movies to make and distribute. All that extra hedge fund money did lead to an increase in production and a much more competitive landscape which the studios had to live with. When you take all that money, you have to put it to use. However, conditions are starting to change, and the market is starting to correct itself. There will be fewer movies in 2009 than in 2008, and 2010 will even see more of a decrease in releases. What won't change so much is how the studios strategize their releases. On any given week, there is an average of three wide national releases, some weeks a little more and other weeks a little less. The problem is when there are four or more films battling it out, and that's when over supply rears its ugly head. The studios were well aware of this and realized a market correction was needed. That's why Warner Brothers eliminated three of their independent distribution divisions, and Paramount all but eliminated their own Paramount Vantage to help contain their costs and control the output that hits the screens.

But getting the screens is only half the battle, making a movie work is always the much tougher challenge.

How does this affect the other independents and those producers and investors who want to jump in to take advantage of the studios' credit crunch and a less crowded field of distributors? With opportunity also comes risk. Companies like Summit Entertainment and Overture Films are filling in some of the holes, and there is probably room for other new players. I like to track the number of wide releases and specialty releases that open in Chicago each week, and for a number of years, independent films more than doubled the studio releases. Most weeks were a blood bath with too many art films competing for the same limited audience. At least in Chicago, the numbers tell a different story in 2009. The first 10 weeks brought 28 wide release movies compared to only 15 specialty films being released in commercial theatres. There are always many more films released in New York and Los Angeles than in Chicago, so the numbers can be skewed. Will it stay that way for the rest of the year? No, with the Oscar films ending their runs, there will be an increase of independent films looking to take their screens and carve out some box office for themselves. March, April and May are good months to debut new independent films, and the opportunity will be there to get the screens. But getting the screens is only half the battle, making a movie work is always the much tougher challenge. In past years, movies like "My Big Fat Greek Wedding," "Memento," "Crash," "Namesake," "Waitress" and "Thank You For Smoking" became indie hits during this period.

Whereas studios are able to utilize all twelve months of the year to release their movies, the majority of independent films that are not festival winners or Oscar contenders don't have much of a chance during certain parts of the year. January and February are taken over by the Oscar films, sucking up most of the available screens and attention from the art audience. Once the big blockbusters start hitting the screens and hot summer weather arrives, it always becomes more difficult for serious, heavy art films to find audiences who are in the mood for lighter fare. Starting in mid-August and going through October is prime time to open independent films, but then when November hits, the best and strongest of the independent films start rolling out for the rest of the year, which makes it difficult for lesser films to find respect from both exhibitors and audiences alike. The law of diminishing returns kicks in again. Getting back to the current situation, it's hard to say whether any specialty films will be able to break away from the pack this spring and connect with audiences the way those other films did. As the studio movies continue to dominate the box office, the pressure is on the independent film business to show they can muscle up some hits outside Oscar season. The marketplace is wide open. There should be no excuses. The future is now.

---

*It's not about critics or even advertising campaigns, in the later weeks it is
purely word of mouth. You can call it the invisible hand of the public at work.*

The key to the big uptick at the box office in the first two months of 2009 has been the fact that a number of movies have been going strong for weeks. I've always loved the industry term and speculation of whether a movie will "have legs." It's a very appropriate term that refers to a movie getting its footing, showing endurance, being able to play week after week simply because people fall in love with a movie, talk about it and convince others to go see it. It's not about critics or even advertising campaigns; in the later weeks it's pure word of mouth. You can call it the invisible hand of the public at work. Word of mouth can't be bought or spit out of a computer, but it truly remains the holy grail for big success and even bigger profits for distributors, their financial partners and their shareholders. And movies like "Paul Blart," "Gran Torino," "Taken," and "He's Just Not That Into You" have accomplished that. Even "Confessions of a Shopaholic," which got off to a rocky start, has found some legs and has fallen less than 35% the last two weeks. Then you have the champ "Slumdog Millionaire" entering its 18th week, passing the $125 million mark and still going strong. On the other end of the spectrum, it remains a very quick take-the-money-and-run business for movies that burn out quickly. Two recent flameouts have had two of the biggest second week drops in history, "Friday the 13th" with an 81% drop and "Jonas Brothers" last weekend off 78% from its opening weekend. One last note here. Warner has finally stopped tracking the grosses for "The Dark Knight" after 231 days and 33 weeks. The blockbuster officially ended its run with a $533,300,000 gross, second only to "Titantic's" box office of $600 million.

This Week at the Box Office   *Weekly Attendance: 18,245,018*

The upcoming weekend doesn't look too exciting and shouldn't add to the list of long running movies with staying power. Universal is releasing yet another remake of a horror classic. This time it's "Last House on the Left," and it's a good bet some horror fatigue in the marketplace will limit its prospects. 20th Century Fox has a new sex comedy called "Miss March," and I don't know what it is about sex comedies, but they never seem to ever gross much. This one doesn't look to change the pattern. The best of the bunch will be Disney's "Race to Witch Mountain" for the kids and families, but overall the mid-March doldrums seem to be inflicting the marketplace. The most interesting thing to keep an eye on is how the second weekend of "The Watchmen" holds up. Will it find its legs to build on or will it begin to fall apart from its $55 million dollar first weekend? If the drop can stay around 50% it could be okay. If it's closer to 65% to 70%, it will be in deep trouble. With so many financial partners involved with "The Watchmen," that would not be good news.

The March 13th weekend became the busiest of the year so far in the number of total movies opening. In addition to the already mentioned three wide national releases, there were an astounding thirteen independent films vying for attention. Only one of them found any real success; Overture's "Sunshine Cleaning" became the first indie hit of 2009 with a gross of over $12 million.

Race to Witch Mountain	*Last House on the Left*	*Miss March*
Disney	Universal	Fox Searchlight
Opening weekend: $24,402,214	Opening weekend: $14,118,685	Opening weekend: $2,409,156
Domestic gross: $67,172,594 63.1%	Domestic gross: $32,752,215 72.3%	Domestic gross: $4,543,320 98.9%
Foreign gross: $39,214,547 36.9%	Foreign gross: $12,534,013 27.7%	Foreign gross: $48,309 1.1%
Worldwide gross: $106,387,141	Worldwide gross: $45,286,228	Worldwide gross: $4,591,629
Widest release: 3,268 theatres	Widest release: 2,402 theatres	Widest release: 1,742 theatres

Sunshine Cleaning

Overture
Opening weekend: $219,190
Domestic gross; $12,062,558 72.8%
Foreign gross: $4,517,692 27.2%
Worldwide gross: $16,580,250
Widest release: 642 theatres

Throw Down Your Heart

Argot
Opening weekend: $7,283
Domestic gross: $115,778
Foreign gross: N/A
Widest release: 3 theatres

Edge of Love

Capitol films
Opening weekend: $3,944
Domestic gross: $28,635
Foreign gross: N/A
Widest release: 5 theatres

The Perfect Sleep

Cinema Epoch
Opening weekend: $4,680
Domestic gross: $6,224
Foreign gross: N/A
Widest release: 1 theatre

Dédé, à travers les blumes

TVA Films
Opening weekend: N/A
Domestic gross: $1,620,589
Foreign gross: N/A
Widest release: 72 theatres

Tokyo Sonata

Regent
Opening weekend: $28,345
Domestic gross: $278,356 29.6%
Foreign gross: $662,074 70.4%
Worldwide gross: $940,430
Widest release: 10 theatres

Severed Ways

Magnolia
Opening weekend: $7,686
Domestic gross: $18,154
Foreign gross: N/A
Widest release: 1 theatre

Carmen and Geoffrey

First Run
Opening weekend: $5,656
Domestic gross: $14,130
Foreign gross: N/A
Widest release: 1 theatre

Hope & Redemption

B.D. Fox Independent
Opening weekend: $18,125
Domestic gross: $18,125
Foreign gross: N/A
Widest release: 1 theatre

Brothers at War

IDP/Samuel Goldwyn
Opening weekend: $33,142
Domestic gross: $153,148
Foreign gross: N/A
Widest release: 18 theatres

Z (40th Anniversary Reissue)

Rialto
Opening weekend: $10,144
Domestic gross: $83,305
Foreign gross: N/A
Widest release: 2 theatres

Waiting for Dublin

Cinema Libre
Opening weekend: $4,184
Domestic gross: $5,925
Foreign gross: N/A
Widest release: 4 theatres

The Cake Eaters

7-57 Releasing
Opening weekend: N/A
Domestic gross: $35,817
Foreign gross: N/A
Widest release: 9 theatres

Conversations with Industry Professionals

Ira Deutchman – Managing Partner of Emerging Pictures and Chair of Film Department, Columbia University, New York

The following interview took place on June 16, 2011 and October 15, 2011

> *"Right now, the key to any of the new business models is to make movies for next to nothing, because next to nothing is exactly what the potential is unless someone gets incredibly lucky."*
>
> —*Ira Deutchman*

Q: Ira, you have been involved with independent film since 1974 as a producer, distributor and marketer. Look back at the year 2009; was this the year it all came crashing down?

ID: To be honest with you, I don't see 2009 as a watershed year in that way. In reality, all the doom and gloom and angst that has been going on during the last decade has been very misplaced. From my perspective, the specialty business has always had its ups and downs, but the reality is it has never been an enormous business. Whenever it feels like it's an enormous business, it's usually been some kind of a bubble. One can say there was a long indie bubble that lasted from the mid-80s to the late 90s, but the reality is it rarely has been a consistent business. Even when there have been what looked like big grosses, many of those cases were because there was so much money being spent, so they were not profitable ventures. That's why studios have gone in and out of the business; they like the idea of it and wake up one morning and look at the numbers and realize it's not really much of a business.

Q: But you can't discount the effects of the Great Recession, can you? Companies were going out of business, movies were going unsold, there was a lot of hurt going around.

ID: The downturn in the economy certainly didn't help because a huge amount of money being put into the equity of films disappeared. During the period before the crash, investment money in independent films followed a formulaic business plan with name actors in the cast who theoretically had some value in the DVD and television markets, and their spreadsheets were telling them they couldn't lose. Investors and producers alike were ignoring the fact that most of these films didn't have a distributor in place, which always presents an inherent risk. When all these movies flooded the market, it just so happened the DVD market was starting to collapse at the same time, and you ended up with a glut of failed theatricals, movies designed for theatrical release that no one was interested in acquiring. Their back up formulas just didn't work, and it took a long time for all that product to flow through the marketplace and disappear. Once they did disappear, there was no equity money left, and at that point the marketplace collapsed. Over the years, many different formulas have been followed until they don't work anymore. This turned into another bubble that crashed and burned.

Q: If the life cycle of the independent film business is birth, growth, maturity and decline, where would you put the business today?

ID: Rebirth.

Q: What stage of rebirth?

ID: Embryonic. (laughter)

Q: So much of the independent business has been tied to the growth of home video, first in the 80s with VHS, then in the late 90s with DVD. What do you see emerging as new revenue sources?

ID: Old business models are under threat because of new technology, and these are all things just beginning to gestate to the point of figuring it out on what it all means. There is a lot of experimentation going on that pokes at some possible solutions, but I don't think I know anyone who has a grasp of exactly knowing where things are going or how it's going to play out. The things that do emerge will play a part in another resurgence. I believe that will happen. I also think that the major studios getting out of the independent business is probably the best thing that has happened. These studio independent films were cluttering up the marketplace in ways that were drawing away the art audience from the smaller films, which then didn't have much of a chance. Now that three studios have removed themselves from the marketplace, it's a lot less cluttered, and we are starting to see some smaller films emerge that wouldn't have had a chance three or four years ago.

Q: Has there ever been a point of time when there haven't been 8 to 12 movies a week opening in New York? Are there fewer movies being released in 2011?

ID: On average in New York, there are still a large number of movies opening each week. However, I think the biggest difference is that for a lot of those movies there is a different set of expectations. It's clear that many of the films are limited runs for small niche audiences and not a deluge of terrible movies coming out because they have P&A commitments or something like that.

Q: What do see as some of the new business models for independent filmmakers?

ID: The key to any of the new business models is to make movies for next to nothing because next to nothing is exactly what the potential is unless someone gets incredibly lucky. There are indications that the market will eventually mature and become more profitable. For starters, the IFC model of using theatrical as sort of an advertising promotion model that leads to real sales on cable Video-on-Demand has found some success. You have to keep in mind the cable model is in a large percentage of American homes, and it's a way to get the films on the big screens in their living rooms. So right now, even though the numbers aren't huge for this, at least we know that there is something of a market. The problem with cable VOD is there are too many middlemen, and as a result, not a whole lot of money trickles back to the filmmakers. Being able to release something directly digitally in one form or another is probably going to be a way to make some real money, but right now there is a lot of confusion in that market. Until there is a standard with one box being able to get movies on to peoples' television sets, accessing independent movies will remain somewhat difficult and confusing for large groups of consumers. The other obstacle right this second, even in the Internet space, is a few very powerful players are controlling the marketplace. It's not as if the power of the big companies are going to disappear and everyone will be able to publish their stuff on the Internet, whether it's Apple, Amazon, I-Tunes or Netflix. These are companies that are making their money on being enormous aggregators of product, and they have no interest whatsoever in dealing one on one with individuals. There is an enormous amount of business left on the table for smaller filmmakers that can't get access to those things unless they go through an established company.

Q: Are film festivals still the best way for independent films to get noticed?

ID: I would say that the film festival model is not necessarily the best thing for each film anymore; the film festivals themselves don't have enough slots to handle all the movies that are being made. That's why some of the festivals are getting involved with VOD distribution. Tribeca, Sundance, even the New York Film Festival are offering some form of distribution for a select number of their selections. The idea of making a movie, taking it to a film festival and selling it there is as much of a lottery ticket than it ever was.

Q: *You are not painting too pretty of a picture, are you?*

ID: I'm a believer in that there have been only two types of businesses for movies. One side is the studio blockbuster business where mass amounts of resources are spent with a realistic justification of those movies becoming global blockbusters. The other end of the business is the art end of the business. Filmmakers who are serious about using the medium as an artist should not have as their major concern whether or not they make a profit. Since the art business has proved to be terribly inconsistent over the years, it's the only rational way of approaching it. When you get outside the United States, art films are supported by government money. We don't have such a thing. Independent filmmakers have been clever and entrepreneurial about figuring out how to get investors involved with their movies with the hope that somehow they would break through and earn a profit. The way this has been done is pointing at a recent film's success, showing it was possible for these type of films to be successful and saying that you have the next big thing. But if you really look at some actuary tables and see how often that has happened, it always has been a tiny, tiny percentage of the number of films that have been made. I look at it like I'm looking through a telescope. If you are there to create art, commerce is secondary, so forget about the mainstream marketplace and start making your movies for a lot less money and figure out ways to sell directly to a specific audience on a modest level that can support you and keep you going. That's what folks like Ed Burns are doing, bypassing theatrical and selling directly to the Internet. It's comparable to other artists who go to street fairs and galleries trying to sell their work, and at the end of the day you try to cover your overhead. Many of these artists have other means of support, and they get by somehow. That's a class of filmmaker that hasn't existed before, and it can open the door to a new business model.

Q -– Has there been any hard numbers showing how Ed Burns has done in the digital field?

ID -– We don't know because he's not sharing his numbers, but he's made noise that it's been working for him, and we don't know if that's because he's making money doing other stuff along with his low budget movies.

Q: *When there are no figures being touted I always think there is not much there. Should someone like Ed Burns, who started out as a struggling filmmaker himself, make this information known?*

ID: The information is too fragmented at the moment. Someone doesn't want to share the information because they are either embarrassed by it or they are concerned about making promises to other people they can't keep.

Q: *Let's shift gears and talk about your company, Emerging Pictures. What was the basic idea behind the company when it was launched in 2002? Include the number of current venues.*

ID: Emerging Pictures was partially a direct result of my own frustration with a marketplace in which I thought there was very little imagination being exhibited. I went to the 2001 Sundance Film Festival and ran into Barry Rebo, a pioneer of high-definition video, and someone I had known for a long time. He told me that he and a partner were looking at the idea of putting high-end digital projectors into alternative spaces to create an alternative distribution network. I thought the idea was really interesting, and it got my imagination flowing in terms of the potential repercussion for theatrical release of indie films. I merged my distribution services company with theirs, and that's how the company was born. Now we have over 130 independent theatres on the network, showing films from all the smaller independent distributors, plus special events that we put together – cultural events like opera, ballet and concerts, but also special documentary events and curated thematic festivals.

Q: Nine years later, what are you most proud of in regards to your company?

ID: Nine years ago, there was so much resistance to what we were trying to do. There were the film purists, the business model purists, and the just plain doubters. Now all that resistance is gone. We are fulfilling a real need since we offer a cost effective solution that is an alternative to the studio digital standard, which is far too expensive for most of the independent theatres. For distributors, we put up a great picture on the screen without having to ship any physical object, while also making sure that the files are secure and can't be pirated. For filmmakers, we help to bring down the cost of theatrical exhibition, opening up new ways of looking at theatrical release. And did I say that digital distribution is ecologically green?

Q: In a sense, it seems like you and your partners have created a new business model, which has helped art films earn extra revenue with having more potential theatres to play their films in. Weren't you ahead of the curve because mainstream theatres have just been converting their screens to digital in the last three or four years?

ID: When we started, there were other companies doing the same thing. Everyone knew this was coming. Our triumph is that we're still here. I can't even remember the names of those other companies.

Q: Who came up with the proprietary server technology that is installed in the projection booths of these venues? What was the cost to the venues to install the digital projection systems? It isn't the same $75,000 to $100,000 cost per screen that the mainstream theatres have to cope with, is it?

ID: We used open source tools and off-the-shelf hardware and licensed some additional tools to make it work. Our system costs 1/5 of the studio servers, and the projectors that most of our theatres use cost ¼ to 1/3 of a studio system.

Q: The old business model for an independent film was they would be booked for a seven-day run and would play every showtime during the week. The problem was that many small films weren't strong enough to warrant that many shows. With your digital model, don't these venues play multiple films and other events that still work fine for all involved?

ID: The entire theatrical model of 7-day runs of 4 shows per day is built on the notion that the 35mm print was so expensive to manufacture and ship that distributors wanted to get as much play out of the valuable asset as possible. Once you remove the cost of a physical print, you can begin to think about programming a theatre in day parts like a network. The truth is that the old system most often left a lot of empty seats on the table. We're trying to fill those seats.

Q: How does Emerging Pictures make its money?

ID: We make our money on a percentage of box office. This is more palatable than fixed fees since we are taking the risk side-by-side with the distributors. If the film doesn't gross, we don't make any money.

Q: Do you see social networking sites helping smaller, independent films?

ID: I've seen social networking used most effectively in two different ways. The first is with issue-oriented documentaries that go after specific audience groups that have interest in particular topics and causes. The other way is when alternative filmmakers choose to forge a career by working to create their own fan base as Kevin Smith has been successful in doing. The strategy here is trying to create a consistency in content and style with people who share in the same interests and ideology. John Sayles was one of the first independent filmmakers who became a brand name before there was social networking. In those days John would be sitting with all these email addresses of fans that helped him consistently gross $3 to $5 million on his movies. Ed Burns may be working on that same kind of model with his fans, and other people are out there trying to create their own databases of supporters that they can count on no matter what. That kind of effective use of social media can become one of those new business models we've been talking about.

Q: *What's an important lesson you have learned through the years about the film business?*

ID: For me, it's always been about the fact that I'm a consumer of my own product, and if I can figure out a way to convince myself what could get me out of the house and into the theatre, then I believe I have the hook to get other people in. It's always been that way with me. If I'm not part of that individual niche then I need somebody else that is who can give me guidance about who those people are and realistically whether we can get them to go see it in a theatre. I'm full of stories of filmmakers who were convinced that a certain niche was there for their films, and then when we scratched under the surface, we found out those people didn't go to the movies, and that becomes a problem. So I think it's about being realistic. Filmmakers for the most part are a little too naïve on how difficult it is to actually get people to go to a movie theatre, and that equation is only getting harder, not easier. With the advent of all the new technology making so much available in your home at a moment's notice, these are things that are creating bigger obstacles in getting people off their butts and into the seats. The bottom line is that you always have to keep in mind how difficult it is and try to approach it from a personal point of view. If you are someone who doesn't go to the movies, then you have no business trying to get other people to go to the movies.

Q: *What continues to stoke your passion for independent films?*

ID: I hate it when someone tells me that something is impossible, and that motivates me to prove them wrong.

Q: *Thank you for your time.*

ID: Thank you.

Questions for Discussion:

1. Name the three economic principles that help govern the Motion Picture Industry. Define what they are in your own words and rank them in how you perceive their importance.

2. "Money sticks to whoever has it at the time." What basic truths about movie financing are tied to this adage that makes it tough on investors?

3. What changes have the economic downturn of the last several years brought to the film financing world? Is it different for the independents than it is for the studios? What does Ira Deutchman say about this topic?

4. Why are "failed theatricals" never a good thing, and what results from them?

5. Discuss Ira Deutchman's view of the future for independent film? Do you feel he is more optimistic or pessimistic of where things are headed? Give your reasons why.

6. Describe the business model of Emerging Pictures and how it is helping filmmakers who make quality micro-budgeted films.

STARS ARE ONLY ONE PART OF THE EQUATION

Week 12: March 20–26, 2009

How important are the big stars in the ultimate success of any movie?

With Julia Roberts and Nicolas Cage opening new movies this weekend, the question pops up again, how important are the big stars in the ultimate success of any movie? The value of developing a movie and basing the marketing strategy around a star goes back to the earliest days of Hollywood with popular actors like Douglas Fairbanks, Jr. and Mary Pickford. Put their names and faces on a poster, and their fans will pay to see them. Stars are the human capital for the film companies, the collateral, the insurance policy used to stem off a possible box office disaster. Brand names are able to stand out from the crowd and demand attention. But do all stars earn their salary? Are some stars overpaid? All the studios are grappling with this issue, and they are using the economic downturn to their advantage by asking even some of the biggest stars to drop their going rates by up to half their usual rates. Tighter credit and falling DVD sales certainly gives them good cause to look at every possible way to cut costs. What adds fuel to their argument is the number of movies that have become hits in 2009 without the studios having to pay those big upfront salaries to stars. Movies like "Taken" and "Paul Blart" have either been story-driven or high-concept films starring medium range actors without a history of being box office draws. Clint Eastwood has been the lone big star to carry a movie to great success this year, and even then "Gran Torino" had a strong story that matched Eastwood's strength and audience appeal.

Ah. The story. That gets the conversation going. Yes, stars are important, but it's far from being the only part of the equation. Even the biggest names need some help. What's the story about? Is it a subject matter audiences will want to see? Is the marketing campaign able to take full advantage of the star and sell the movie's premise in a clear, concise manner? What are the critics saying? Is it getting good word of mouth? With "Duplicity," Julia Roberts has her first starring role in about five years. She's being paid $15,000,000 in the hope that her fans will flock to see her headline a movie again. Maybe she still has the magic, maybe not; we'll find out soon enough. What I find surprising is how tepid Universal's marketing campaign is. The heart of every studio's campaign is the 30-second television spot, and after seeing the commercials multiple times, I still have no idea what the actual storyline is. It's a sexy spy caper, but what's the damn story? I guess the studio figures the presence of Julia Roberts is enough, but the posters and ads don't really take full advantage of her star power. She's hidden behind sunglasses in a narrow shot of her face. I just don't get it. If the movie underperforms, the blame game will start with the marketing department. Nicolas Cage's movie "Knowing" has some of the same problems. He's being asked to carry this movie, but it's being sold as just another sci-fi special effects disaster movie saddled with a terrible title. Look for a decent opening weekend followed by a big drop off. Isn't it about time that Nicolas Cage rediscovers himself again in a challenging independent film? It has been 13 years since Cage won his Best Actor Oscar for "Leaving Las Vegas." That could be a smart move at this stage of his career. "Bangkok Dangerous" should have told him that.

Speaking of independent films, how important are stars to independent films, and how much do they contribute to a film's bottom line? The business models, costs and expectations for studio movies and independent movies are different from each other and are meant to be different. Ever since the birth of film, independent films have sprung up outside the mainstream and whatever studio system there was at the time. Only in the last 25 years or so have studios moved in and out of the independent business whenever they thought there was a buck to be made. The problems between the studios and their independent divisions always begin when the business model starts changing and the two types of movies start looking the same with bigger budgets, more stars and higher expectations attached. One thing that has been proven over time is that stars and big advertising campaigns are a totally different animal for studio films than they are for independent films. There is an old saying, "You can't buy a gross for an art film," meaning the art audience is looking toward publicity, festival awareness and strong critics' reviews rather than star power and a huge television campaign for their signals whether to support a film or not.

You can't buy a gross for an art film

It's a curious thing about stars in independent films. They certainly can help in raising money to finance a film, particularly with foreign investors where much of the financing for independent films comes from. There is an annual list of actors that is compiled based on their drawing power in markets around the world that is used when films are being developed and packaged. Sometimes even a secondary star can have enough of a following in a single territory like France or Japan to convince a distributor in that territory to kick in some production coin in return for distribution rights. When selling a film, having a star or two in the cast is seldom a bad thing. As a producer's rep, with any film I was selling I was always asked, "Who's in it?" so I'm not going to say stars don't matter with small films. On the other hand, there have been plenty of star driven independent films that have never been sold or perhaps sold direct to cable or DVD. Also, if the movie is a mess and the reviews are bad, having a star in the cast won't get people to pay to see it in a theatre. After four decades of blockbuster hits, Harrison Ford has finally made an independent film, "Crossing Over," which has received mediocre reviews and is tanking at the box office. It's disappearing as quickly as it's opening and will be lucky to gross $500,000. Where stars still show their value is in the DVD, pay television and international markets where a Harrison Ford film will be able to generate much stronger revenues than the average $500,000 grosser with no names attached to it. Whether that's enough to recoup all the costs is another matter, especially with the DVD market slumping so badly. Then there is "Slumdog Millionaire," a film with no stars but will gross ten times its cost just in the U.S. and bring in real profits to Warner Brothers and Fox Searchlight.

There are fewer dependable rules to follow in the independent world when it comes to star power and many more surprises, both good and bad. Even with the surprise hit, the major studios have come to question and doubt the viability of their specialty divisions and the stress and uncertainty it brings them. As profits continue to get squeezed from all directions, there may be more studios tempted to throw in the towel and abandon the independent film business as Warner Bros. has and apparently Paramount is now doing. If that happens, it may not be all that bad of a thing and actually would be welcome by those who believe the studios have done more harm than good to the independent field by overspending, blurring the line between what constitutes an independent film, rushing films out into the marketplace too quickly and helping to kill off the smaller, traditional independent film which can't compete with the more expensive studio hybrid films. Independent filmmakers started without studio assistance, and with or without the studios, they will find ways to survive. Then again, it's difficult to erase the past and put the genie back in the bottle once it has been out.

This Week at the Box Office   *Weekly Attendance: 19,346,125*

Nicolas Cage proved his worth, Julia Roberts didn't. With an estimated production cost of $50 million, "Knowing" landed up grossing $183,593,586 worldwide and was a profitable film for Summit Entertainment, whose experience in the international markets certainly shows they understood Cage's drawing power in various foreign territories. The beleaguered actor came through for them. On the other hand, "Duplicity," which is estimated to cost $60 million to produce, only grossed $78,146,652 worldwide despite its use of international locations, is considered a big disappointment for Universal. Julia Roberts was once the top-grossing actress in the world, but her time away from the big screen obviously has dimmed her popularity with audiences. Clive Owen wasn't the strongest co-star, but when Roberts was going strong that wouldn't have meant much of a difference.

Knowing
Summit
Opening weekend: $24,604,751
Domestic gross; $79,957,634 43.6%
Foreign gross: $103,635,952 56.4%
Worldwide gross: $183,593,586
Widest release: 3,337 theatres

Duplicity
Universal
Opening weekend: $13,965,110
Domestic gross: $40,687,642 51.9%
Foreign gross: $37,573,823 48.1%
Worldwide gross: $78,146,652
Widest release: 2,579 theatres

Sin Nombre
Focus
Opening weekend: $81,446
Domestic gross: $2,536,665 49.7%
Foreign gross: $2,565,091 50.3%
Worldwide gross: $5,101,756
Widest release: 87 theatres

Valentino: the Last Emperor
Vitagraph
Opening weekend: $21,762
Domestic gross: $1,755,134 79.7%
Foreign gross; $448,269 20.3%
Worldwide gross: $2,203,403
Widest release: 38 theatres

Great Buck Howard
Magnolia
Opening weekend: $115,004
Domestic gross: $750,857 83.3%
Foreign gross: $150,102 16.7%
Worldwide gross: $900,689
Widest release: 76 theatres

Skills Like This
Shadow Distribution
Opening weekend: $9,413
Domestic gross: $62,408
Foreign gross: N/A
Widest release: 7 theatres

Super Capers
Roadside Attractions
Opening weekend: $21,559
Domestic gross: $30,995
Foreign gross: N/A
Widest release: 80 theatres

The New Twenty
Argot
Opening weekend: $6,272
Domestic gross: $17,652
Foreign gross: N/A
Widest release: 1 theatre

Coyote County Loser
Roebuck
Opening weekend: 4,724
Domestic gross: $16,204
Foreign gross: N/A
Widest release: 2 theatres

Perestroika
Strand
Opening weekend: $3,532
Domestic gross: $26,054
Foreign gross: N/A
Widest release: 1 theatre

Mancora
Maya Releasing
Opening weekend: $7,675
Domestic gross: $29,967
Foreign gross: $166,372
Worldwide gross: $196,069
Widest release: 2 theatres

TOP TEN HIGHEST PAID ACTORS AND ACTRESSES
IN HOLLYWOOD ON AN ANNUAL BASIS

June 2009 to June 2010	May 2011 to May 2012
Johnny Depp - $75 million	Tom Cruise - $75 million
Ben Stiller - $53 million	Leonardo DiCaprio - $37 million
Tom Hanks - $45 million	Adam Sandler - $37 million
Adam Sandler - $40 million	Dwayne Johnson - $36 million
Leonardo DiCaprio - $28 million	Ben Stiller - $33 million
Daniel Radcliffe - $25 million	Sacha Baron Cohen - $30 million
Robert Downey Jr. - $22 million	Johnny Depp - $30 million
Tom Cruise - $22 million	Will Smith - $30 million
Brad Pitt - $20 million	Mark Wahlberg - $27 million
George Clooney - $19 million	Taylor Lautner, Robert Pattinson - $26 million

June 2009 to June 2010	May 2011 to May 2012
Sandra Bullock - $56 million	Kristen Stewart - $34.5 million
Reese Witherspoon - $32 million	Cameron Diaz - $34 million
Cameron Diaz - $32 million	Sandra Bullock - $25 million
Jennifer Aniston - $27 million	Angelina Jolie - $20 million
Sarah Jessica Parker - $25 million	Charlize Theron - $18 million
Julia Roberts - $20 million	Julia Roberts - $16 million
Angelina Jolie - $20 million	Sarah Jessica Parker - $15 million
Drew Barrymore - $15 million	Merryl Streep - $12 million
Merryl Streep - $13 million	Kristen Wiig - $12 million
Kristen Stewart - $12 million	Jennifer Aniston - $11 million

Source: *Forbes* magazine

Forbes comes out with a top ten list of stars' earnings each year after researching and compiling all the information they can get their hands on in regards to upfront pay, profit participation, residuals, endorsements and advertising work. So in that regard, it goes beyond movie salaries. A couple of things jump out at you when looking at the two periods. Men continue to earn significantly more than women, and the money being paid to the top tier of stars has remained pretty consistent even though some of the names may change. What the studios have tried to control is giving the stars their demands on both the front end and the back end. In the past when a big star received a $20 million upfront fee for a movie, he may also have been able to get 10% gross participation of the revenues, a situation that can drain most of the profits away. Much of Sandra Bullock's $56 million in earnings in 2009 stemmed from her taking a smaller upfront salary on "The Blind Side" in return for a generous back end participation. When "The Blind Side" became a huge success, Bullock enjoyed a giant payday the old fashioned way – she earned it.

Week 12: Questions for Discussion

1. In your opinion, what movie stars earn their salaries and get you to buy tickets to their movies regardless of reviews and word of mouth?

2. After looking at the lists compiled by *Forbes*, what impressions or reactions do you have concerning Hollywood and its star system?

3. What are the pros and cons to having name actors in the cast of an independent film?

4. What does the expression "You can't buy a gross for an independent film" refer to?

CAN 3D SAVE WEAK PLOTS, MUCH LESS THE ENTIRE MOVIE INDUSTRY?

Week 13: March 27–April 2, 2009

---

*Hollywood is rolling the dice and placing its bet squarely
on the back of Digital 3D as its savior of all things.*

This is a watershed moment for Hollywood. Even though the box office has been red hot this year, the country's economic crisis has led to cutbacks, layoffs and a fair share of fear among those left with jobs in the Motion Picture Industry. Everyone knows a lot more change is coming, but it's always good to recall what screenwriter William Goldman said years ago about Hollywood, "Nobody knows anything." He was referring to the fact that no one can predict popular taste or what the future will bring, and because he hit on such a basic truth, that quote will live on as long as movies do.

What I find intriguing is that in the midst of this fear and uncertainty, Hollywood is rolling the dice and placing its bet squarely on the back of Digital 3D as its savior of all things, something that will transform movies in the same way as when silent movies converted to sound and black and white switched to color. Those heady proclamations come from Jeffrey Katzenberg, the CEO of DreamWorks Animation, who through his position in the industry and his sheer will and passion, has become the leading advocate and spokesman for the entire global 3D movement. This is show business, and Katzenberg is a great showman, but at this point in time, he's dealing in as much hype as he is in reality. There is nothing wrong with that since the movie business is built on large degrees of hype in the first place, but it's instructive to take a closer look at the situation and try to make a little more sense out of it. Can 3D save weak plots much less the entire movie industry? That's only one question, but it's not a bad place to start the discussion. Personally, I still think of 3D as a gimmick, and regardless of how far the technology has come, you still have to wear those annoying glasses and pay three extra dollars a ticket for the privilege to do so. From time to time that could be fine, but the thought of the industry flooding the screens with forty-five 3D titles in the next two-and-a-half years is both astonishing and depressing to me. History has shown us with 3D that the technology seems to always take precedence, and the actual story and characters are sacrificed for flying objects thrown at you. That can get old fast, and with so many of these movies coming down the pike, how soon will audiences begin to tire of the experience as they did in past decades?

No one would disagree that the quality of 3D today is vastly superior to what was playing on the screens in the 50s and 60s during the format's first cycle before it eventually lost favor with both filmmakers and audiences. Another reality is that 3D is a hot commodity right now in a variety of entertainment platforms including gaming systems, webcams and television, so it's not surprising to see a big push in the movie industry as well. Hollywood is right about looking to the future and trying to grow the business by differentiating the theatrical experience after many flat years at the box office. The fact is Digital 3D increases revenues. 3D theatres have been known to out gross regular theatres playing the same movie 4-1 while distributors collect more film rental from theatres through higher ticket prices. But on the other hand, claiming 3D is going to be both the savior and the future of the industry is a bit of a reach at this time. Some problems such as falling DVD revenues will require more than a quick fix to solve its various complexities. Also, the fact of the matter is that growth in 3D screens has been much slower than expected. Katzenberg had earlier predicted there would be 4,000 3D screens for "Monsters vs. Aliens," but there are only 2,000 available as of this weekend, 5% of the total U.S. screens. Even though DreamWorks Animation has announced that all their future movies will be in 3-D, "Monsters" is their only release in 2009, with their next film being "Shrek 4" in May, 2010. That's a big gap.

One studio executive recently posed the question,
"What comes first, the content or the screens?"

Many theatre owners are being cautious in converting more screens to Digital 3D because they first have to convert existing screens to digital projection, an expensive ordeal costing up to $75,000 per screen. With the country still in a recession, the credit crunch with the banks is not helping matters any either. Katzenberg was also trying to convince exhibitors to charge $5.00 more a ticket for their 3D screens, but all he could do was suggest a price. No distributor can force a theatre to charge a specific amount; that would be considered price fixing. Theatres decide what admission prices to charge, and since they are concerned about raising prices during these tough times, the average increase has been in the $3.00 range. One studio executive recently posed the question, "What comes first, the content or the screens?" That's a great question, so let's look at the breakdown of screens and theatres that are playing "Monsters vs. Aliens."

- ▶ 7,000 total screens (counting multiple screens in theatres playing movie)

- ▶ 4,104 locations (actual theatres playing movie)

- ▶ 1,550 3D sites (number of individual theatres playing movie in digital 3D)

- ▶ 2,000 3D screens (counting multiple screens in each theatre playing movie in 3D)

- ▶ 5,000 2D screens (number of regular screens playing movie)

To answer the above question, the content has arrived before the screens. Only 29% of the total screens playing "Monsters" are in 3D, not quite what Katzenberg had expected. Distributors would like to see at least three 3D screens in each theatre, but many have only one, so that's going to pose a big problem as more 3D movies are released. Even though it's trending upward in terms of more and more theatres converting more screens to digital 3D, a number of theatre owners are being cautious and not buying into all the hype just yet. That's a rational way of sizing up the situation because unless movies other than animation and teen flicks show they can attract other audience segments, it's not worth the cost and hassle. How can this technology be the future of the industry if it's catering to only kids and teens? A survey taken after DreamWorks ran the first ever 3D commercial for "Monsters" during the Super Bowl, revealed that the largest segment of voters (41%) never bothered to pick up the glasses to begin with. There's a lot of work to be done. One other thing, I wonder if any exhibitors took offense at the comment Katzenberg made that theatres have not done anything to change the theatrical experience in many years. That dismisses the hundreds of millions of dollars theatre circuits have spent in the last decade building new deluxe cinemas with stadium seating, larger screens and more amenities, including dining options, which have made moviegoing a much more comfortable experience for audiences. I hope someone called him on that because it was a thoughtless and misguided remark to make. There's plenty of other ways to improve the theatre experience other than having to put funny glasses on.

Will Digital 3D be a fad or the wave of the future? It's way too early to say, but the rest of 2009 will tell us a lot. Starting with "Monsters vs. Aliens," there will be ten movies released, which comes out to about one a month. Surprisingly, none of the future films will be a DreamWorks film, so Katzenberg will be put in the position of a cheerleader, hoping the other companies with their 3-D films will be able to grow the technology. The two I'm looking forward to seeing are Pixar's first 3-D movie "UP," which has just been selected to open the Cannes Film Festival and James Cameron's "Avatar," which will close out the year at Christmas. "UP" being selected as the first animated film to ever be selected to open Cannes is a pretty impressive feat and well deserved for Disney/Pixar. What has separated Pixar from other animated films is their great storytelling, and I'm excited to see how they combine the special effects with the story. "Avatar" is on a different level altogether and could prove to be a game changer for the industry. James Cameron hasn't made a feature film for 12 years, ever since he was the self-proclaimed King of the World with "Titanic." What does a director do after he wins Best Picture of the Year and his movie grosses $600,000,000? What he didn't do was rush into his next project. The expectation and buzz for this film will be off the charts. The production cost has been reported at $300,000,000 with over 1,000 people working on it at one time or another. It is a futuristic sci-fi spectacle and will be in live-action digital 3-D. If the film delivers on its potential and early hype, it has the potential to gross in "The Dark Knight" and "Titanic" range and give a tremendous boost to the new 3D technology. We will certainly know a lot more after the entire year plays out.

On a marketing side note, DreamWorks has signed Bank of America to run a promotional ad for "Monsters vs. Aliens" to run on 18,000 ATM machines at more than 6,000 branches. The bank will give away free ticket upgrades online to whoever wants to see it in 3D at the regular 2D prices. After receiving $45 billion in government aid, Bank of America has decided to pass on some savings to their customers and figures the promotion will cost them $175,000. What a great country we live in. Now if they can only start reworking more of those delinquent mortgages.

This Week at the Box Office
Weekly Attendance: 24,713,731

The week belonged to "Monsters vs. Aliens," but two of the smaller films below are prime examples of films not being helped at all with stars in the cast. "The Education of Charlie Banks" had Jesse Eisenberg and Jason Ritter in the cast, and the film grossed a total of $15,078. "Spinning Into Butter" had Sarah Jessica Parker, Miranda Richardson and Beau Bridges in the cast and grossed only $8,064 for its entire run.

Monsters vs. Aliens
Paramount (DreamWorks)
Opening weekend: $59,321,095
Domestic gross: $198,351,526 52.0%
Foreign gross: $183,158,344 48.0%
Worldwide gross: $381,509,870
Widest release: 4,136 theatres

Haunting in Connecticut
Lionsgate
Opening weekend: $23,004,765
Domestic gross: $55,389,516 71.4%
Foreign gross: $22,138,216 28.6%
Worldwide gross: $77,527,732
Widest release: 2,732 theaters

12 Rounds
20th Century Fox
Opening weekend: $5,329,240
Domestic gross: $12,234,994
Foreign gross: $5,045,632 29.2%
Worldwide gross: $17,280,326
Widest release: 2,331 theatres

Goodbye Solo
Roadside Attractions
Opening weekend: $38,032
Domestic gross: $871,445 92.4%
Foreign gross: $71,428 7.6%
Worldwide gross: $942,209
Widest release: 33 theatres

Shall We Kiss?
Music Box Films
Opening weekend: $28,680
Domestic gross: $535,499 18.2%
Foreign gross: $2,400,938 81.8%
Worldwide gross: $2,936,437
Widest release: 33 theatres

The Cross: The Arthur Blessit Story
8X Entertainment
Opening weekend: $309,455
Domestic gross: $741,557
Foreign gross: N/A
Widest release: 221 theatres

Education of Charlie Banks
Anchor Bay
Opening weekend: $8,537
Domestic gross: $15,078
Foreign gross: N/A
Widest release: 3 theatres

America Betrayed
First Run
Opening weekend: $245
Domestic gross: $1,311
Foreign gross: N/A
Widest release: 1 theatre

American Swing
Magnolia
Opening weekend: $10,174
Domestic gross: $30,156
Foreign gross: N/A
Widest Release: 2 theatres

Guest of Cindy Sherman
Treza Media
Opening weekend: $7,685
Domestic gross: $27,052
Foreign gross: N/A
Widest release: 1 theatre

Spinning Into Butter
Screen Media
Opening weekend: $5,534
Domestic gross: $8,064
Foreign gross: N/A
Widest release: 4 theatres

Mysteries of Pittsburgh
Peace Arch
Opening weekend: $37,572
Domestic gross: $80,283
Foreign gross: N/A
Widest release: 20 theatres

The Country Teacher
Film Movement
Opening weekend: $8,192
Domestic gross: $50,072
Foreign gross: N/A
Widest release: 3 theatres

Conversations with Industry Professionals

Chris Johnson – Vice President of Classic Cinemas, Downers Grove, IL

The following interview took place July 13, 2011.

> *"Of course, we have to fight for every dollar. Even when you lose an argument you feel good about it after you do it because you have to stand up for your business."*
>
> —*Chris Johnson*

Q: *What was the genesis of Classic Cinemas, and how did you begin in the family business?*

CJ: The roots of our business began when my father and uncle purchased the Tivoli Theatre property in Downers Grove, IL in 1977 for investment purposes, and an exhibitor named Oscar Brotman had a general lease to operate the theatre. In 1978, a message on the marquee appeared that read, Closed for Remodeling, and in the middle of the night, trucks showed up in the parking lot trying to remove the equipment from the theatre, which didn't belong to the exhibitor. My dad didn't know what to do. He had a lease until 1992, and he bought it as a passive property. The manager at the time, Ed Doherty, had managed the theatre for a number of years and said he could keep the theatre running. My father decided to give it a shot, and that became our first entry into the movie theatre market with a one-screen theatre. The first movie was from Disney, "Hot Lead Cold Feet," and the admission price was $3.00. The next movie we played we charged $1.25, and we stayed with that price for quite some time playing second run films. The first film that really took off was Columbia's "China Syndrome" in 1979, and from that point on the theatre started making money. My first job was cleaning out the basement of the Tivoli and doing some maintenance work, and then in 1980, I became an usher at the theatre. In 1982, we picked up our second theatre, the Park Forest, with the Lake and York theatres following soon after. I started managing theatres in 1984 when we had four theatres, and then in December 1984 we opened our first single screen first run theatre, the Lindo in Freeport, IL. We turned it into a three-screen first run theatre, and that's how the circuit started forming in the late 70s and early 80s. Jumping forward to a number of years, we were still mainly a bargain operation. Around 1990 we bought a five-screen first run theatre from General Cinema in Carpentersville, IL, which was a competitive zone, so we started learning the challenges of booking first run films, which is much different from the second run business in terms of film cost and competitiveness. In the 90s we saw the handwriting on the wall that the future wasn't going to be in second run theatres with low priced video rentals and second run availability knocking into each other, and that's when we started converting as many theatres that we could to first run theatres. During the 90s we were up to 20 locations, the economy was going good, but toward the late 90s a number of theatres were struggling, including some of ours, and we decided that if a theatre wasn't making it we should close them. We went from twenty locations to twelve, and this was in 1999 and 2000 when much of the exhibition industry was in turmoil with bankruptcies and consolidation.

Q: *That period proved to be one of the most perilous times for theatre owners in the entire history of the movie business.*

CJ: It was very tough because the economy was doing so well until the Dot Com crash, and that actually became a blessing in disguise because of all the over building going on including building theatres too close to other theatres. If somebody built an 18-screen theatre next to one of your theatres, it effectively could chop your business in half.

All the money available in the financial markets made it too easy for theatre owners to build too quickly. I think the biggest mistake was that people built theatres in a vacuum with the thought process being if they built this new theatre, everyone would come to them, and the theatres in the area wouldn't have any impact, and they will just go away. That didn't happen. As it turned out, people still go to the theatre that's nearest to them provided the theatre still supplies a good experience at a reasonable price. First and foremost, people go to the movies to see the movie they want to see, and second, [they go] to a theatre that's close to them that makes sense. Not everybody was willing to pay top dollar for the extra amenities the new theatres were offering. In 1995, I went to grad school for the sole purpose of learning more about financing because we were planning to do an IPO because the 1990s was a great decade for the economy, and we figured with an IPO we would be able to expand the circuit and float more money out there. But when we started analyzing it, the exhibition business in the late 1990s was considered an industry to stay away from because of the problems it was facing, so we decided to not go forward with the IPO. It turned out to be the best thing that could have happened because we were able to dodge bankruptcy that pulled down about nine major and regional circuits.

Q: *How many locations and screens do you have in 2011?*

CJ: We have 99 screens in 13 locations. We are actually building our 100th screen as we speak. We started it July 5th in our York Theatre in Elmhurst. There are nine screens now, which began as a single screen. We opened the York as single screen bargain house, then we went to three screens, then to five, then to seven, then to nine, and now will hit ten screens. We kept buying properties next to it for expansion purposes, and all the theatres are stadium seating except for three of them. It's a digital theatre, and it's one of the coolest theatres because it has the same façade from years ago but with a digital marquee with all the theatres tucked behind the retail we own, and it goes far back, and our patrons are blown away with what we did. The Theatre Historical Society is on the upper level of the theatre, which adds a nice touch. In hindsight it perhaps would have been nice to go up to 10 screens all at once, but that's not how it works. We wanted to build up the business first and keep adding on to keep up with the growing demand. The York is one of our older downtown suburban theatres, and downtowns were out of favor for a time as people flocked to the malls. Everything has come full circle with habits and trends changing with the retro feeling of downtown areas back in vogue, and that has definitely helped us. It's something that you can't predict, how people will go back to things they once walked away from.

Q: *Your circuit still has a couple lower priced theatres, but they aren't considered in the same way as the older sub-run theatres were. Can you talk about theatres as intermediate or move over runs?*

CJ: Yes, we just raised the Ogden from $3 to $4 and the Tivoli from $4 to $5 after 5:30pm. A lot of it had to do with increased cost, but some of it had to do with the availability of product and how we are treated differently. In order to play certain film companies and not be treated as a sub-run, you have to have a certain price.

Q: *Is that price in Chicago four or five dollars rather than three dollars? Does that mean that per capita is not in play anymore?*

CJ: With the price increase of that extra dollar it makes it easier for us to get movies faster. But per capita still is used by some companies. For instance Fox has a $7.00 per capita that is figured by every adult admission taken in at the theatre. We will play Fox films in 3-D because we will match their price with the 3-D up charge, and the per capita is only for adults after 6:00pm. We could do that because not that many tickets would be affected. The point of it is there are certain cases when we make the decision to get picture early and pay the extra per capita ticket charge. That's what kind of messed us up with the Tivoli when we played "Avatar" pretty quickly. I think it was three or four weeks into the run. It was horribly expensive for us because we had to pay the per capita, we paid the high terms, we were using Master Image so we had to pay for the 3-D glasses, then the up charge. It was the highest film rental I ever paid in my life. But even after that, "Avatar" was tremendously successful, but then an area theatre, became upset and sent letters to all the distributors that it was a mistake and they don't play with us, and there should be clearance between the two theatres, and that taking our theatre hurt them.

Q: *How many miles is it between the theatres?*

CJ: About four miles. This theatre misrepresented the situation saying it was a mistake they played with us, but we had played with them all the time. The studios took note of the complaint, and that hurt the Tivoli because clearance wasn't granted before. But what happened was that we matched what that theatre grossed in their first three weeks in our first five days we played it. Their total gross of their engagement before we started playing it was about $35,000. We did that the first weekend and went on to gross over $100,000. They felt we impacted their gross, but my point was they didn't have 3-D at the time, and they were behind the ball, and they weren't that successful with it because just about everyone needed to see "Avatar" in 3-D. So generally speaking you have to price your theatre according to the market you are in to get the full range of product. Even with theatres playing with everyone else these days, you can still have those skirmishes with competitors from time to time, though not nearly as much as in the past.

Q: *So some studios include the per capita clause and others don't?*

CJ: Several companies are enforcing them to various degrees, not on sub-runs but with first runs, they are setting them from market to market, and they are raising the bar to really press the need to keep your price at a certain level. Per capita is usually set at $7.50 to $8.50 in the Chicago market for the adult evening price for a standard 35mm 2D print. Sometimes a company will have a weighted per capita where they factor in all your prices, students, matinee, passes, and you divide it into the number of people, and the concept there is if you charge more on weekends and less on weekdays you better be doing enough to cover that. There were theatres doing five buck clubs and five dollar nights, and the film companies were not happy about that because the film companies don't want you discounting their product, and if you do, they will bill you up. They have people in the back rooms analyzing box office reports to determine who is doing a lot of special deals, and they are coming back and doing everything they can to discourage discounting of their product.

Q: *College students are always complaining about lack of student discounts available to them.*

CJ: We used to have student discounts everywhere, but now we have them in only one theatre because of the pressure we're getting from studios. The thing is, a theatre has to have all the movies at a consistent price or else you will lose your audience. We can't have one admission policy for films from a couple of studios and a different one for the others; it would confuse the public too much.

Q: *But no distributor can dictate what a theatre has to charge at the box office. Don't they say charge whatever you want, but if you play our first run film, this is the level we expect, and if you aren't there, we will bill you up and get our money through the per capita clause?*

CJ: Absolutely. That's correct. But studios can do certain things to influence you to do things you have to do, and if your price is too low, they can choose not to service you and make you wait for a later run. I was on a panel with Jeffrey Katzenberg in 2007, and he was really pushing exhibitors to have a $5.00 up charge on 3-D films, and this was very early in the 3-D movement when we were having a discussion. I was saying when we started off we were charging a $1.00 extra, then we went to $2.00, but he was beside me holding up five fingers. The point he made is that it is very expensive, it takes a lot of extra money to do 3-D right, and people will pay for a premium experience. I get that, and early on that was correct. But what happened was when you go from a handful of theatres that have it to every theatre on the corner having it, then it gets diluted, and it's not a big deal anymore. Things are only special until everyone has the same thing. You can't charge that amount on an extended basis and expect the public to keep paying it. Our circuit had been getting an extra $2.50 for 3-D, but we have dropped the price to $2.00. I did a survey and received 6,000 responses, and the price for 3-D was an issue but not the only issue. Some people liked the 3-D experience while others hated it; 35% of the respondents really didn't like 3-D at all, but only half of those who didn't like it said it was the price. So we landed up dropping the price to $2.00 extra, which is less than what our competitors charge, and we told our patrons we would always try to have both 3-D and 2-D for every film. You have to listen to your customers, and they want an option; more of our patrons are choosing to go see movies in 2-D rather than 3-D.

Q: *How do you position your theatres in the Chicago market in relation to the larger national circuits that make up your competition?*

CJ: The first thing we want to do is to take away the idea we are a nickel and dime operation. We try to be the folksy alternative with our older theatres, offer a little lesser admission price, give a mint to everyone on the way out so we can say goodnight, offer free refills on all sodas and popcorns sizes, a thirty-minute guarantee, if you don't like the show we give you your money back, we have loyalty programs, do a lot in the community, we are a little something different. We do keep up with the technology; we have the highest percentage of digital and 3D screens among all the circuits, so we were on the forefront of that. Most of all we want to be perceived as the hometown theatre by playing up our Chicago roots.

Q: *How expensive has been the digital conversion for your company?*

CJ: It's been an expensive ordeal. Up to this point we have converted 26 screens to digital with all of them having 3-D capability, and we we have paid for all of them out of own pocket except for three of them. Originally, we had just a few digital screens because we felt that it would be a selling point for certain films and for some people to see it in a digital presentation, but that meant nothing to the public. If you had a nice presentation, you had a nice presentation; people didn't care if it was digital or not. We have spent roughly $70,000 plus on converting individual screens, though it has come down some for some of our smaller screens, but what everybody forgets is that's not the only cost involved. When you have a digital projector, you then have to have a digital server, your management system, you have to have a network operations system to monitor everything, you have to have all these Internet connections, satellite connections; it's not all as cut and dried as everybody thinks. It comes down to the studio either sending a hard drive of the movie or a theatre receiving the film via satellite. We are hooked up with Technicolor, and the movies come over satellite. Eventually I think it will all go over to satellite, but the problem is there are two different satellite providers, and they don't share their satellite with others. If you wanted to have everything delivered on satellite, you would have to sign up with both providers, so it's a bit complicated now. First and foremost, the digital era will benefit the studios because they are going to save a lot of money not having to print 35 mm copies and then have the expense of shipping the prints. There are more things an exhibitor can do with digital screens, and I hope the advances will eventually drift down to the exhibitors. It will probably happen, but at the same time film rental keeps going up, so every bit of savings will be taken back out.

Q: *Would you say exhibitors were fine with 35mm prints?*

CJ: Yes.

Q: *I guess Katzenberg pushing for more digital 3-D screens as the industry's top cheerleader really pushed exhibitors to convert their screens because before they could play 3-D, digital conversions had to come first. Is that what happened?*

CJ: That was pretty much the case. If digital 3-D movies didn't have that early success, and if "Avatar" didn't come out when it did, I think the deals would have looked a lot different for the digital conversion. Exhibitors would have said make it attractive to us or else we will stay with what we have.

The tail wagged the dog so to speak. The studios are now saying that they will begin to phase out 35mm prints in 2013 because most of the deals with outside companies to help in the conversion cost will expire September 30, 2012. After that date, if you are not fully 100% digital in a specific complex, an exhibitor will not be eligible for the deduction of virtual print fees with the studios. We will make the deal and be all converted by that date.

Q: *Do you get involved with the film rental deals, or do you allow your film buyer to handle those transactions with the distributors?*

CJ: Some distributors give us a choice of scale, aggregate or terms. Aggregate is the same percentage for every week you play; the scale is based on the final domestic gross. If there is a choice to make, I make the call. For "Horrible Bosses," I took the scale because the aggregate was too high, and based on its opening, I made the right choice unless it keeps going and going. I blow it sometimes. I took the scale on the first "Hangover," and I got killed because it was such a surprise hit and grossed so much.

Q: *Even though the deals have changed over the years has one thing stayed the same? When a distributor has a hot film, a pre-sold commodity, is that company going to get what it wants?*

CJ: Yes. One of the studio heads had an epiphany that they should make three types of movie deals; a standard movie should be about 60%, a B movie should be 58 or 59%, and a big tentpole should be in the low to mid 60%, and that should be it. The part that they don't realize is that you can do that, but I just won't play it. That would make it super easy. So when you come around with your piece of crap I'll just pass on it. You can't pass on the "Harry Potters" because if you do, you might as well get out of the business because you have to serve your market. Whether or not you play a movie like "Friends with Benefits," it's not going to impact your life one way or another.

Q: *Sometimes you have to push back, don't you?*

CJ: Of course, we have to fight for every dollar. Even when you lose an argument, you feel good about it after you do it because you have to stand up for your business. The studios switched to aggregates and scale deals before the movie opens for one reason; if you take the negotiation out of the equation you can eliminate a lot of time and personnel.

Q: *Does anyone offer you 90/10 deals anymore?*

CJ: A couple of studios still offer it as an option on some films, but the traditional deals come more from the specialty companies with their independent films. Sony Classics had a more traditional deal on "Midnight in Paris," and it played to their advantage to keep it on the screens longer in the summer. If one movie has to go, and the grosses are in the same ballpark, and one is at 35% for their later weeks and the other is a 59% scale deal, I am going to hold the 35% film. It's more like the old days when a lower deal got you the dates, and if it did business, it kept holding.

Q: *Do you think film rental deals are too expensive?*

CJ: Absolutely they are too expensive. I would kill for a 50/50 deal, but now I have to accrue film rental across the board at a minimum of 55%. One film company is the worst as far as terms go. They take the position, if you want to play the film, pay these terms or don't play it, but they don't really mean that. They are saying you have to play this film and you have to pay this price.

Q: *How important has alternative programming been for your theatres? Any money there?*

CJ: The majority of alternative content up to this date has not worked. We just played "The Company," which was pretty good, and it had an $18.00 ticket price.

Q: *What do you keep of that $18.00?*

CJ: What happens is the distributor splits it 50/50 with the talent, and then you are splitting the $9.00 and not the 18.00 with the distributor. So if you look at it from a percentage basis, it's horrible.

Q: *Can you comment on the year of 2009 and how your theatres did?*

CJ: Checking back on my records, it was the absolute best start of the year we ever had. We could do no wrong; it seemed like everything was doing business. Out of the first 17 weeks of the year, we set circuit records for 12 of those 17 weeks, so the start of that year was very special. Our January was up 25%, our February was up 24%, March was down 13%, but April was up 46%. Contributing to that was "Slumdog Millionaire" which was released in November, 2008 but made most of its money in 2009. Another thing about 2009 that was gravy is that we anticipated this 3D thing, and we jumped in and had 3D in most of our theatres, and we did big business. We were a little ahead of the curve. I remember doing huge business with "My Bloody Valentine," and "Coraline" did much better than we thought it would do. The spread of 3D was almost perfect, one a month if I recall. It was just a fabulous year for the industry in general and for our circuit.

Q: *How important is the theatre manager in the success of a movie theatre?*

CJ: Most of our managers have come up through the ranks. They are first and foremost the most important part of the organization because they are the face of the company. They have face-to-face contact with our guests. They are important for setting the culture of that location: showing and teaching how the staff should act, how people should be treated, how to resolve problems when they arise. We set parameters and rules, but it's only as good as the managers themselves. Managers are at times treated very badly by patrons. The majority of people just go to the show, enjoy the movie and walk out, but there are always those people who are never satisfied, make an issue bigger than it has to be, and it's up to the manager to diffuse the situation and not take it personally and do it in an effective way. It makes all the difference in the world.

Q: *Is being diplomatic the most important skill for a theatre manager to have?*

CJ: Probably the most important skill is being able to manage the employees and lead them and set the proper atmosphere of how to act and how to treat our guests. To get everyone on board to make our guests feel important and [that] we appreciate them.

Q: *The potential of theatre managers to move into other industry jobs is much more limited than it used to be. Do a lot of managers look on this as their career now? What are the opportunities?*

CJ: When we got into the business, we hired kids to be managers and gave them kid wages, but we realized at some point we have to get more seasoned people who can really manage and not just be key holders. We have managers that range from the ages of 25 to 60 managing, some who have been with us for years, and we pay them accordingly. Typically the starting salary for managers is in the $30,000 to $40,000 range, but based on high performance and service years it can go much higher than that after factoring in bonuses. We offer bonuses if they can increase sales and keep profit margins up starting from a base we present to them. We used to give bonuses off concession numbers, but that can be skewed if too many concession workers are on duty, which cuts into the overall profits. They were working for their bonus, and they didn't care about how many workers it took to deliver higher numbers.

Now we keep it simple: here's the margin, here's the sales, see what you can do. We're paying much more to managers than we used to. We have former General Cinema managers, AMC managers, and people through our system. We have people who have started as ushers and concession workers, some moving up to work in our office. We get college graduates coming in. The pool of talent has gone way up. In 2008 at North Riverside Mall we had a two-day job fair, and within a couple of hours we had long lines and had the cream of the crop to choose from. We canceled the next day. We haven't had to put a help wanted ad in years. People come to us.

Q: How do you handle risk with your theatres?

CJ: You have to be honest with yourself and ask what is the long term projection for this theatre, what are the long term sales for this location, and if you can say it's going to grow if we do this or this or this, great stay there. But in good faith if you can't see the theatre improving, you have to cut your losses and run. You can't produce sales out of nothing. If it's not there, it's not there. The worst situation we had to deal with was the theatre in Park Forest, IL where we had over a million dollars into it after buying and renovating it, but it just wasn't responding. We landed up selling it for $50,000 and biting the bullet.

Q: Are all your locations profitable now despite the high cost of digital conversion and high film costs?

CJ: Yes, there are a couple blips now and then, but we have no theatres we are looking to close, so they are doing good enough.

Q: What's an important lesson you have learned about operating movie theatres?

CJ: There are going to be some people who are going to rip you off and lie and things like that, but you have to remember the majority of people are honest and reasonable, so those two to three percent may get away with things, but don't lose sleep over that, don't make sweeping rules because of a few oddballs, and never get into an argument with a guest because you are not going to win. There is no winning an argument with your guests. The other thing is it's a pretty fun job when you really come down to it. People go out to have a good time, to enjoy themselves, so you don't want to screw that up. So spend the extra time, the extra money to get a team who gets that. The movie theatre is a commodity, everyone has the same picture, everyone has similar seats, most theatres have done a nice job upgrading their facilities, and the way you differentiate yourself from others is flat out taking care of servicing your guests. It sounds so basic, but I think it is really lost on a lot of people. Don't just focus on every expense because watch out for what you wish for. You'll cut your expenses, but in doing so you won't be doing everything you should be doing. I guess the little things are the most basic things that you have to remember if you are to be successful.

Q: Thank you for your time.

CJ: Thank you.

Week 13: Questions for Discussion:

1. What is your feeling about the studios putting their money on 3D technology as the key to their future?

2. Why were theatre owners still being cautious in 2009 about converting more of their screens to digital 3D?

3. According to Chris Johnson, how did the digital conversion of screens happen? What does he mean when he says, "The tail wagged the dog," in this instance?

4. Give the reasons for all the troubles and bankruptcies movie theatres faced in 1999 and 2000.

5. Define 'per capita' and how it affects movie theatres and the admission prices they charge.

6. How can specialty distributors like Sony Classics keep their successful films on screens for longer periods?

7. How does Classic Cinemas position itself to compete with the larger theatre circuits?

A LOVE-HATE RELATIONSHIP THROUGH THE YEARS

Week 14: April 3–9, 2009

---

*Threats, accusations, shouting matches and lawsuits litter the
history books and the memories of long time industry veterans.*

Going back to the earliest days of the movie business, distributors and exhibitors have often had an adversarial relationship. The movie industry has always been a rough and tumble business with the two sides seemingly always at odds with each other over one thing or another. From the days of bidding and anti-bidding laws to product splitting and unfair treatment toward independent theatre owners, conflicts were common occurrences. Threats, accusations, shouting matches and lawsuits litter the history books and the memories of long time industry veterans. That's just the way it was, and to a lesser extent, the way it still is at times. Even though they may be on better working terms than perhaps any time in history, that doesn't mean there still aren't problems and conflicts the two sides have to deal with. They know they need each other, and at times have been referred to as "partners," but the fact of the matter is they operate different businesses with different business models, and that leads to conflicts. Other than how to split up the box office pie, which will always be a tug of war match, two of the most hotly contested issues that distributors and exhibitors haven't seen eye to eye on in recent years are the timetable for converting more screens from 35mm to digital and the constant threat of encroachment on their theatrical window. With the theatre digital conversion set to be completed by 2013, the biggest problem between the two parties shifts to the threat of Premium Video On Demand and the studios' push for a much shorter period between the theatrical release of a film and its home availability.

These issues won't be going away anytime soon. The studios have put a whole lot of 3D movies into either production or the planning stages despite the fact there are only 2,500 of the close to 40,000 screens in the U.S. capable of playing them. The theatres don't work for the studios and don't really like to be bullied into rushing into something that costs so much money and has very questionable return to their bottom lines. It's a tough economy, and no distributor, not even Jeffrey Katzenberg, can guarantee that digital 3D will have lasting power for years to come. So why rush into it too quickly? The two sides are looking at the risk/reward factor in different ways. The studios would like to see all the screens convert to digital so they can eliminate making film prints altogether, but the exhibitors are the ones who have to fork over the dough to convert perfectly fine 2D screens, which are producing steady revenues for them now. 3D adds an extra middleman to the mix in the form of the 3D supplier who gets a cut of the action, and the biggest piece of the higher admission price charged to the public goes back to the distributor. When in doubt, follow the money. On top of that, 20th Century Fox has been telling exhibitors this week not to expect any financial support for costs associated with the use of special glasses when their 3D pictures play later in the year. The lines are being drawn.

With DVDs, the average time from the theatrical launch to the shelves at Walmart is four months and thirteen days, but often it's closer to three months. What skews the figures are when the early summer movies are held back to take advantage of the end of the year holiday season. The rest of the year tells a different story. With many Christmas Day releases out already, the window between theatrical and DVD continues to narrow, and that is a big concern for exhibition. It doesn't matter if the theatres aren't playing a movie anymore, it's more about the perception the public has that the time they have to wait is getting shorter and shorter. What's the breaking point? Two-and-a-half months? Two months? Theatres are very good at protecting their turf and love to remind the studios that the movie theatres are still the ones driving the revenue train. They have to be vocal about protecting their businesses because if they don't, who will? "Slumdog Millionaire" came out on DVD this week when it was still playing on 2,000 screens the week before, and most theatre circuits pulled the picture because they didn't want to set the precedent of playing day-and-date with DVD. As with the digital screen issue, the shrinking DVD window and other home encroachments will remain a thorny issue between the two sides.

ShowWest Convention

There was an interesting announcement from ShowWest, the annual gathering of theatre owners that took place in Las Vegas this past week. Industry statistics from the previous year are always presented by the head of the Motion Picture Association of America, but this year one set of statistics was left out. The MPAA has decided to discontinue announcing the average annual production and marketing costs for all the movies from the studios and their independent divisions. They said it's getting harder and harder to obtain reliable data, and they didn't want to put out any misleading information. I always wondered about the accuracy of the figures, and I was especially suspicious last year when I saw the numbers. Here were the stats from the 2007 movies:

Studio Releases
- $70.8 million – average production cost
- $35.9 million – average marketing cost
- For a total of $106.6 million per picture

Studio Independent Releases
- $49.2 million – average production cost
- $25.7 million – average marketing cost
- For a total of $74.8 million per picture

I didn't question the studio costs, but I remember being stunned at those independent film figures. Almost $50 million to make the average indie and another $25 million to market it? Those numbers seemed way too high, even though there have been more larger budget films coming out of the studio divisions such as "There Will Be No Blood" and "The Painted Veil." None of the independent divisions finance and produce all the films they release, and I doubt the statistics took into account the films that were acquired at film festivals at costs ranging from $1 million to $10 million. When someone else produces and finances a movie and sells it to a distributor, the acquisition cost becomes in effect the substitute cost of production for the studio and is much less than an in-house production. Also, Sony Classics is an example of a studio division that distributes traditional art films, and their costs are in no way near the above averages. So I'm not surprised they've stopped trying to figure out these costs because somebody must have started to question the validity of them and perhaps even the repercussions of giving out uncertain information. I have to wonder if Warner and Paramount looked at those figures and were reminded of how expensive the independent business was becoming when they decided to eliminate their own divisions last year. I hope that wasn't the case, but perception has a way of becoming reality.

With 2009's first quarter numbers in the history books, the industry set a blistering pace for the rest of the year to keep up with. Ten of the twelve weeks were stronger than last year, $2.4 billion was taken in at the box-office, and there was a double-digit increase in paid admissions. This was all done with fewer movies. The first quarter saw 36 movies open in wide release, which was down 16% from the 43 movies released over the same period in 2008. Less has definitely meant more. Fewer movies not only give movies more breathing room, but it also allows marketing departments more time to concentrate on each feature. DreamWorks Animation took this to the extreme with "Monsters vs. Aliens" being the company's only 2009 release. They put everything they had into this movie and couldn't afford to fail. That's why they chose the end of March as their release date because there would be very little to compete against for the family audience. With a $59.3 million weekend, DreamWorks delivered for themselves and for the exhibitors.

Obviously after a huge weekend, there is an even bigger push on the exhibition community for more 3D screens. Only 30% of the screens for "Monsters vs. Aliens" were 3D, yet those screens produced 58% of the business with reports of many sellouts and people being turned away. Actually, that's not too surprising because all the marketing was geared for 3D, which creates a demand at the expense of the screens playing it in regular theatres. You can say the message to the other theatres is to get on board or continue to be left behind.

But on another front, the real profit for theatres has always been at the concession counter, and even though audiences continue to line up at the ticket windows, they're spending less on snacks and drinks to save some money. In response to somewhat lower demand, more and more theatre chains are starting to roll out value menus, dropping their popcorn and soda prices, especially during mid-week. Since there is already a big profit margin on these items, theatres have wiggle room to offer more enticing deals at the concession counter without touching their admission prices.

> *" … It will take hundreds of thousands of 3D admissions*
> *per screen to cover the total conversion cost."*

Except for the 3D screens of course. Being able to raise ticket prices on the back of 3D technology is a significant piece of the 3D movement. In most major markets, there is a three-tier pricing structure in place. In Chicago for example, Imax 3D was charging $15.00, digital 3D screens $13.00 and regular theatres $10.00. What are the economics for the theatres that install digital 3D? After speaking to a high-ranking theatre executive, the numbers aren't adding up too well. Per screen installations run between $75,000 and $110,000 depending on servers, booth alterations and silver screens. Other expenses include film rental payment to the distributor on the up charge, either a royalty payment to the 3D supplier of glasses purchased, or the labor costs to handle and clean the glasses. Costs add up in a hurry, and there isn't much left at the end of the run. The exec said it will take hundreds of thousands of 3D admissions per screen to cover the total conversion cost. At this point, it's a better deal for the studios than it is for the exhibitors, but when taking the long view, things may even out.

"Slumdog Millionaire" is hitting the DVD market only five weeks after the Academy Awards, whereas 15 to 20 years ago Best Picture winners would play into summer. There is no real surprise there since today's industry has a more concentrated business model. Fox Searchlight may be leaving some money on the floor, but since they've grossed $140 million on a $15 million production cost, the distributor is moving to the next revenue stream with no regrets.

This Week at the Box Office   *Weekly Attendance: 28,025,291*

This weekend sees two new wide releases and a national expansion of the first independent hit of the year. Universal will be opening the latest version of their "Fast and Furious" franchise, and Miramax has the teen comedy "Adventureland," from the director of "Superbad," as this specialty distributor continues to veer toward low budget to mid-range mainstream movies and away from art films. Is this a new beginning for Miramax or the beginning of the end for the iconic company made famous by the Weinstein brothers? Speaking of specialty films, Overture's "Sunshine Cleaning" expands to 500 screens and will continue to try to take advantage of a rather barren landscape for commercially viable independent films.

Fast and Furious
Universal
Opening weekend: $70,950,500
Domestic gross: $155,152,411 42.7%
Foreign gross: $208,100,000 57.3%
Worldwide gross: $363,164,265
Widest release: 3,674 theatres

Paris 36
Sony Pictures Classics
Opening weekend: $44,690
Domestic gross: $846,294 6.6%
Foreign gross: $11,974,783 93.4%
Worldwide gross: $12,821,077
Widest release: 52 theatres

Songs of Sparrows
Regent
Opening weekend: $7,863
Domestic gross: $116,372 52.8%
Foreign gross: $103,988 47.2%
Worldwide gross: $220,360
Widest release: 5 theatres

Bart Got a Room
Anchor Bay
Opening weekend: $32,763
Domestic gross: $53,760
Foreign gross: N/A
Widest release: 11 theatres

Adventureland
Miramax
Opening weekend: $5,722,039
Domestic gross: $16,044,025 93.5%
Foreign gross: $1,120,352 6.5%
Worldwide gross: $17,164,377
Widest release: 1,876 theatres

Anvil! The Story of Anvil
Abramorama Ent.
Opening weekend: $34,651
Domestic gross: $667,911 70.2%
Foreign gross: $283,469 29.8%
Worldwide gross: $951,380
Widest Release: 27 theatres

Alien Trespass
Roadside Attractions
Opening weekend: $43,437
Domestic gross: $104,526
Foreign gross: N/A
Widest release: 40 theatres

Gigantic
First Independent
Opening weekend: $10,294
Domestic gross: $102,704 61.9%
Foreign gross: $63,184 38.1%
Worldwide gross: $165,888
Widest release: 11 theatres

Sugar
Sony Pictures Classics
Opening weekend: $60,140
Domestic gross: $1,082,124 94.6%
Foreign gross: $62,314 5.4%
Worldwide gross: $1,144,438
Widest Release: 51 theatres

Tulpan
Zeitgeist
Opening weekend: $8,620
Domestic gross: $158,174
Foreign gross: $1,007,603 86.4%
Worldwide gross: $1,166,344
Widest release: 4 theatres

Rolling
Indican
Opening weekend: $10,935
Domestic gross: $103,318
Foreign gross: N/A
Widest release: 4 theatres

The Escapist
IFC
Opening weekend: $3,075
Domestic gross: $13,439 3.5%
Foreign gross: $374,735 96.5%
Worldwide gross: $388,174
Widest release: 2 theatres

There are several truisms to point out when looking at the above movies and their total grosses:

▶ "Fast and Furious" was a worldwide success with a global gross of $363 million. This big action franchise movie performed as many other blockbusters do, grossing significantly more in foreign territories than it does in North America. Action and special effects play well to audiences everywhere and need no translation.

▶ A movie like "Adventureland" is one of the toughest to distribute and market. It's more conventional than an art film and smaller than the average studio wide release film, so it's caught in the middle when it goes out in 1,000 theatres. This is a good example of why several studios have lost faith in the independent business. "Adventureland" grossed $16 million domestically, but only $1 million in the rest of the world where the real growth in the industry is occurring.

▶ Sony Classics acquired two of the movies that opened this week, "Sugar" and "Paris 36." "Sugar" grossed slightly over $1 million in worldwide grosses, "Paris 36" grossed over $12 million, and they performed completely differently from each other. "Sugar" was an English language minor league baseball film set in the United States, and 94.6% of the box office occurred in North America. The film only grossed $62,000 overseas. "Paris 36" was a foreign language film that Sony Classics acquired for domestic rights only after it grossed $11 million internationally. It went on to gross $846,294 domestically, which constituted only 6.6% of the worldwide gross.

2012 Update:
The Industry Conversion to Digital

In regards to digital and digital 3D screens, the landscape has significantly changed since the time I wrote this particular chapter. Digital screens continue to grow rapidly, and over half of the world's screens are now digital. The following tables show the growth since 2009 in the domestic market:

Digital Screens (U.S./Canada)
- 2009 – 7,736
- 2010 – 15,483
- 2011 – 27,469

Digital 3D Screens (U.S./Canada)
- 2009 – 3,538
- 2010 – 8,505
- 2011 – 13,695

Source: MPAA.org

As of June 2012, close to two thirds of the nearly 40,000 movie screens in the domestic marketplace have switched from 35mm projection to all-digital projection with about 50% of those screens also having digital 3D capabilities. That type of change has seldom happened so quickly in the movie industry, but it's also misleading in the sense that the transition to digital has been in play for well over a decade. It's been a very complex, expensive ordeal to pull off, with the biggest hurdle being how it was going to be paid for. The exhibitors never felt that motivated to take on such an expense since they were fine with their 35mm projectors. The main cost all along was converting screens to digital ($75,000 – $100,000 each) with some additional smaller costs needed to make them 3D compatible. Do the math – with a 14-screen complex that amounts to well over a million dollars per theatre. As the interview with exhibitor Chris Johnson in the previous chapter indicated, distributors attacked the issue from the digital 3D angle. If distributors made successful 3D movies that the public embraced, those theatres without digital 3D screens would be left on the sidelines and miss out on the latest trend and the higher ticket prices that the public would be willing to spend for the new technology. The phenomenal success of "Avatar" at the end of 2009 sealed the deal for the entire 3D technology movement and convinced masses of exhibitors they needed to find ways to start converting their screens to digital.

It was a circuitous route to an all-digital world for theatre owners, but it did get the industry where it needed to be to best compete and stay relevant in the 21st century. The most antiquated part of the movie business, shipping 35mm prints in metal cans via trucks and planes to theatres, is coming to an end. The announced phase out of 35mm prints is on schedule to begin in 2013. It took a combination of studios, manufacturing technology companies and the theatres themselves to work together in financing the massive industry change from analog to digital projection systems. The financing was made possible through what are called Virtual Print Fees (VPF), a program in which the major studios agreed to help subsidize the conversion costs by paying an $850 fee for each booking over a set period of time, which can last up to ten years. These fees are sent to the manufacturing companies that supplied the digital equipment. The studios knew they had to contribute toward the cost of equipment for theatres, and it made perfect sense for them to do so because of the hundreds of millions of dollars they would save over time with the elimination of 35mm prints. Even though smaller distributors were not part of the discussion, they too have to pay the $850 VPF for theatres they book to play their films that are part of the program, an additional expense that is squeezing their already small margins.

It has diminished the argument about having enough 3D screens because there are more than 13,000 of them now, and that figure is still rising. Digital 3D is part of the industry and should remain so for years, but since it has become so common, the specialness of 3D has waned for many people, especially when the extra admission surcharge is factored in. What has been established is that often more than half of the movie going audience chooses to see a 3D movie in 2D, so exhibitors will continue to offer both versions to the public.

Conversations with Industry Professionals

Clark Woods – Vice President Film, iPic Theatres

The following interview took place on March 29, 2011 in Las Vegas during the CinemaCon convention.

> *"The business between exhibitors and distributors is not a business of contracts, it's a business of handshake deals, and in order to survive and prosper in the business your word has to be good"*
>
> —Clark Woods

Q: *Clark, you spent many years in distribution. Can you talk about those years?*

CW: I was at Paramount for 27 years working my way up through the company until I was the Executive Vice President & General Sales Manager, the number two job in distribution. When DreamWorks was bought in 2006 by Viacom, our parent company, a strange thing happened. All our jobs were thrown out; it was almost like a reverse takeover. Rick Sands was the CEO of DreamWorks at the time of the purchase. I knew Rick for years, and I called him to ask what was going on, and he told me I was going to get fired. He said he was going to MGM and offered me a job. I drove off the Paramount lot and went to MGM. When MGM folded, life got tougher because I had to scramble a little bit.

Q: *How long were you at MGM?*

CW: I was at MGM for three years, 2006 to 2009. MGM's basic business model was a bad deal. Sony was going to make Blu-ray DVDs; the larger the library you can control, the more you can force the format. It made sense for Sony to purchase MGM for $500 million so they could sell all the "Rockys" and "Rain Mans" again in this new format. MGM's business plan was to spend minimal money on new productions because they had an existing pay television Showtime deal, and they would attract third party producers and even other distributors who craved that guaranteed ancillary income. So MGM returned to being a theatrical distributor, and that idea proved true as outside producers with finished films and even Harvey Weinstein wanted their films to be released through MGM to take advantage of our Showtime arrangement. But a basic problem immediately arose, and that was the company could not service its $3.5 billion in debt with the cash flow we were going to have; I don't think anyone could. Some very smart, astute people somehow bought into the premise that inherently doesn't make sense. We made enough money to make the distribution group a profitable enterprise. The whole operation cost $5 to 6 million in distribution and marketing to run the company annually with employees, expenses, offices, and we were taking a minimum $2 million dollar distribution fees for every film we distributed. It was a nice $40 to 50 million dollar net business; without the debt we would have been fine.

Q: *So the outside companies paid for their own print and advertising costs, and MGM made their money on distribution fees with no risk of losing marketing dollars but no chance of much of an upside either?*

CW: Yes, but then we needed our own productions, and we could only make two to three movies out of the cash flow. At the end of the day if the DVD business was flat, we were dead. It had to grow. The business had to have another explosion of profits with the creation of Blu-ray, and not only didn't Blu-ray take off, but all of a sudden consumer taste changed from an ownership model to more of a rental model. Studios used to net about $12.00 out of a $19.99 DVD after deducting some expenses and royalties, but the bottom line, it was a pile of money that was $12.00, and it was yours. But the DVD sales business crashed, and the peak was at the beginning of the MGM sale, so it was terrible timing. Like I said, the business model was shaky from the start, and it couldn't sustain itself as a viable entity, too much debt and too little revenue coming in.

Q: *What about the all important film library?*

CW: We also saw the value of the library drop in value. In the early part of the 2,000s, it was like a license to print money. First VHS provided an opportunity for people to start owning the movies they thought were important to them, then DVDs came out with movies presented in a fancier format with better quality and more features, and the business skyrocketed. What that meant for our industry was lots of product in the marketplace. It was pretty simple, make the movie, do some business, the DVD will cover our butts, make more movies, and add to our library.

Q: *Would you agree the studios were smart and never went too crazy making more movies to keep up with exhibitor growth when the circuits were building all those megaplexes?*

CW: Exhibitors hurt their own businesses when they overbuilt. They really did. Back in the day in Chicago, a man like Richard Rosenfield had real power because he had highly coveted theatres, and he could make a decision; he didn't have to play all the movies. He played the companies and the movies he wanted to play, and he had long term strategic planning because he looked down the road. He would be friends of certain companies and do them favors and basically could write his own deals.

Q: *I remember it well. In those days it was a buyer's market, and strong regional circuits like M & R held the power.*

CW: Correct, when the big circuits started building all those 20 screen theatres in closer proximity to other theatres, the studios understood what was happening. Theatres were no longer competitive, and they had all those screens to feed, so film rental went through the roof. They could basically pick any number. What could the exhibitor pass up? The exhibitor couldn't pass anything. It wasn't like he could pick a fight with one distributor and switch over to another guy; he needed to play everything. From that point on, the basic dynamic between exhibition and distribution was changed forever.

Q: *Distributors had different priorities 20 years ago, didn't they?*

CW: In competitive markets the two most important things were being in the best theatres and having the ability to hold on to the screens. When Paramount was negotiating film and Wayne Lewellen was president of distribution, he had the strongest relationships, both positive and negative with exhibitors. We weren't shopping our movies to the theatres across the street; he told them to go away. However, he drew a line in the sand. You had to hold the movie, whatever he wanted them to do, the customer would be required to do, and that was the basic premise of the sale, and in a competitive environment it worked brilliantly. I remember an exhibitor once asked me if a two-theatre zone was the best for us. Actually the best was a three-player zone where you gave 50/50 to two players and nothing to the third because everyone knew where they could be in this equation. They could be the guy with nothing.

Q: *Are there many competitive zones in the country right now?*

CW: Very few, about 40 perhaps. For many years exhibitors were smart and built their theatres six to eight miles from the closest theatres, and customers became accustomed to driving that distance to see a movie. This is what created zones. Now theatres are two to three miles from each other, and everyone plays with everyone else.

Q: *What were you doing in 2009?*

CW: By 2009, I was gone from MGM; all their money collapsed and there wasn't much of a revenue stream to support a distribution organization without any movies to distribute. I think there was only one release, "Fame," and it didn't work, but by that time it really didn't matter because there was too much debt weighing on everything. For the first time in my career I took a job in exhibition and became a film buyer for Marquee, a West Virginia circuit with over 140 screens. I was able to stay in Los Angeles and book all the screens from there.

Q: *How was the transition for you from distribution to exhibition?*

CW: It wasn't so bad, but I was a distributor for my entire career, so it was something I didn't envision doing. Working on the other side I found most distributors are indifferent toward most of their customers, so it's like "take it or leave it and move on; however, we will feel insulted if you treat us the same way."

Q: *Were they acting like you may have acted at times as a distributor?*

CW: I'd like to think I wasn't as bad as that and worked more in the middle in my dealings with exhibitors. Some of the distributors are very difficult to work with. They come to work and are just happy to have a job.

Q: *2009 was a record breaking year at the box office. What's your take on that year?*

CW: The quality of the product was extraordinarily good in 2009. The exhibitors had the quality venues and enough 3D screens to handle the good product the studios were putting out. People who hadn't been going to movies were returning and enjoying what they were seeing. When you look back to 2009, there was a broad audience being reached. All the segments were responding, and they kept coming back. It was the first year in a while where attendance increased, and the exhibitors played a part in that resurgence because they provided a satisfying experience for their patrons. It was a great year for distributors because they did very well with unproven stars in movies like "Paul Blart," "Taken" and "Paranormal Activity" where they didn't have to pay much for talent. Plus, they also hit with their tentpoles, so doing both is not an easy thing to pull off.

Q: *I'd like to talk to you about film rental deals from that year and how you determine which deal to take from a distributor when you are given a choice. What kind of deal did Fox offer on "Avatar"?*

CW: It was a very expensive deal, which is probably fitting since it became the biggest grossing movie of all time. Some exhibitors paid more for "Avatar" than any other movie they ever paid for in their careers, but only if they took the scale deal. They offered a choice between an aggregate deal in the low 60% range, which would be paid each week of the engagement, or a scale deal based on the ultimate North American box office gross, which would rise on a huge gross. It was a tough choice for exhibitors to make because even the aggregate deal seemed high, but when you looked at the point where the scale met the aggregate, a gross of $275 million was the breakeven point. The exhibitors who took the scale were betting the under, thinking it would be big but maybe only $250 million or so.

Q: *Did you see the movie in 3D before you chose what deal to take?*

CW: No, I don't like to see a movie before I make the deal because it can often influence me in the wrong way. I'd rather see the tracking. I want to see the advertising, what the experts are saying about it. The movie often leaves me in a positive or negative direction I don't want to be in because if I like a movie, I would say this movie should really work, and that could cloud my judgment.

Q: If you had seen the movie would you have locked in the aggregate deal?

CW: I did take the aggregate. This is what I did. I did a real simple equation. I asked myself what was the worst I thought it could do, and I thought it would do at least $250 million. It may have cost me a point that would have been a bit higher on the scale. Did I want insurance, which were the firm terms, or was I willing to gamble that it wasn't going to go over $300 million? I had no reason to believe that is was going to be what it was, the biggest movie of all time over $700 million. No one alive could have predicted that. Was it going to be $250,275 or $300 million? That was the area most people were wondering about. If you were the guys to take the under, you paid more. I didn't think it was a smart play because I believed it was going to be very close to the $275 million breakeven point, so I just locked in the aggregate price.

Q: That's how a film buyer can save their client a lot of money. Can you go through another deal on a high profile movie? Also, what was the aggregate you paid for the entire year combining all the movies the circuit played in 2009?

CW: It came out to 54.1% for the year. All owners always think it should be less, but it's tough to get the circuit wide aggregate down because none of the summer blockbusters will be less than 57% and some will probably be as high as 62%, and those big movies will constitute 70%-80% of the summer box office. An interesting movie in 2009 was "The Blind Side" which was a huge hit for Warner Brothers and a strong film for our circuit. I did see this movie, and I look at November from a distributor's viewpoint that some November movie is going to play through Christmas and New Year's and into the following year. I thought the movie that had the best chance of playing through was "The Blind Side." If it plays through, you throw out all the rules on what it could gross. In that case, we were offered either a scale deal or an aggregate deal, and since I had already put my faith in "The Blind Side" in having great legs and playing into the following year, I took the aggregate firm terms based on what I thought it would gross. Since the movie did have a very long run and grossed $250 million, those who took the scale deal paid more, just like they did with "Avatar," because the higher the gross, the more expensive a scale deal becomes. My decision turned out to be right again because we landed up paying several percentage points less than what we would have with the other deal. I'm not always right. I definitely missed on "Despicable Me," but this gives you an idea of the thought process that goes into choosing film deals.

Q: Do distributors still ask for guarantees and advances from exhibitors?

CW: No, back at Paramount when we had "Godfather 3," we collected more in guarantees, $47 million, than what the movie grossed, and that presented a problem with exhibitors asking for some of the money back. Going down that road the distributor was asking for trouble, and with the high terms today, they don't need to ask for money upfront.

Q: Can you talk about your new job as film buyer for iPic Theatres?

CW: It's a much smaller and more exclusive circuit than the previous one I worked for. iPic only has eight locations in the country with 62 screens, and they are referred to in the industry as premium theatres. It's a small but growing trend in the industry. There are 450 premium screens in the United States, and the number will keep rising. Our circuit has plans to open two or three more high-end complexes every year for the next three or four years.

Q: What are the distinct differences between these theatres and regular theatres?

CW: These theatres are true destinations in their own right with fine-dining restaurants and bars in central areas within the theatre. Admission prices are much higher and can go as high as $29 in our top locations to $22 in others. They give the moviegoer the most comfortable viewing you could ever imagine to watch a movie, and that includes home. It includes recliners, blankets, pillows, food and drink service brought right to your seat, bar and food service at the table. There are no commercials shown before the movies, and another big difference is with the concession per capita. The average concession income in a major movie theatre is $3.50 per person. Our theatres are often in excess of $20 to $25. In addition we have only 40 to 80 seats in each of our screens, so it is a different type of business model than the average theatre.

Q: *Obviously this theatre experience wouldn't be for everyone, especially with the high ticket price.*

CW: It's not for everybody. We choose locations very carefully, and we are looking for customers who don't have a problem dropping $150 to buy dinner, drinks and a movie. We have those people in Scottsdale, we have them in Pasadena, and the patrons are loyal. Some come back every week. It attracts a different kind of customer that the studios haven't been getting. The bottom line is that every place our theatres have opened they have proven to be incremental income to the closest existing theatre. The closest existing theatre does not see any decline at all. It's just added revenue into the marketplace.

Q: *What is your opinion of digital 3D?*

CW: I think the industry has to look at 3D very closely and ask why we get the up charge for 3D. The consumer pays ten bucks to see a movie. Whether it costs $200 million or $1 million, theatres don't charge more to cover higher distribution costs. The public has a choice whether or not to see a movie in 3D or not, and at best only half the audience chooses 3D. A good percentage of people want to pay the normal price; they don't see the value of 3D. Families think it's too expensive and don't like shelling out the extra dough.

Q: *What is a basic fundamental of the business that hasn't changed and one that has changed?*

CW: The one thing that hasn't changed is you live by your word. The business between exhibitors and distributors is not a business of contracts, it's a business of handshake deals, and in order to survive and prosper in the business your word has to be good. Anybody whose word isn't good has a short tenure in the film business. What has changed is the concept of relationships. There are still some, and I have some, but relationships between important distributors and exhibitors have really changed. Relationships guided the business and shaped the fortunes of both individuals and film companies. The concept of the regional exhibitor began after the Paramount Consent Decree ruling when the studios sold their theatres to local theatre owners and they became the king of that market. What happened was that those guys went all the way to the end of their business careers, and they controlled their towns and gave up very little ground. The change in the business can be traced to the end of those people's estates or them cashing out which started the trend toward huge national circuits like Regal, AMC and Cinemark. Old exhibitors would love to fight over film prices. It was sport to them, and you would have to match them with wit and guile. We don't have that at all anymore.

Q: *What's the theatrical business going to look like in 20 years?*

CW: What's the best 20-year-old movie theatre in the country? I don't know what it is, but I bet it isn't a very good theatre. If you think about important theatres from the 1980s like the Grand in Dallas, they don't exist anymore. In 1985, the Grand changed the business by being the first complex with more than 20 screens, but it didn't survive, and it's gone. Even in 10 years the theatres that are driving the business now won't be driving the business in 10 years. When you look back every 20 years back to the 1950s, every 20 years there was a new crop of theatres, so theatres tend to have a viable life span of less than 20 years. The exhibition community will always need to keep regenerating itself.

Q: *The big question will be how the studios will be dealing with the movie theatres of the future. Will theatres still enjoy the first position of exclusivity over all other formats in 10 or 20 years?*

CW: Movies and filmed entertainment are different in theatres than they are in the home. That's not going to change, and theatres are not going away. That being said, I see the studios pushing new concepts on the theatres that will not go over well, and the theatres will not be afraid to push back. Four studios just tested Premium VOD, and I didn't really understand what they were doing. You can go to the movie theatre today and see a movie for $10 or $12 depending on where you live. With Premium VOD you can wait 60 days and pay to see the same movie at home for 30 bucks. But if a consumer waits 90 days, they can get it for a dollar in some cases. What product goes from $30 to $1 in 30 days? I understand the studios have to try something to try to rescue the home video business, but I'm not sure this is the answer. Perhaps something more worrisome is lurking in the weeds. Theatrical distribution companies have always been headed by film people coming out of either distribution or exhibition who were lifers who loved the theatrical business and who understood the business like the back of their hands. At Disney, one of those lifers Chuck Viane just retired, and Disney replaced him with executives from their home video and digital interactive divisions. That's a scary development, and that will have to be watched if other companies follow suit because those other executives don't have the loyalty and allegiances to the theatrical business, and that's a dangerous thought because it's all about the bottom line, so anything can happen.

Q: *Thank you for your time and insight.*

CW: Thank you

Week 14: Questions for Discussion

1. Distributors and exhibitors both need each other to conduct their businesses, but there has been much conflict between the two parties over the years. What are some of the issues that have caused this conflict in the past, and what are the biggest current problems that exist between them?

2. On paper, why is the 3D conversion seemingly better for the studios than it is for movie theatres?

3. How is a movie like "Adventureland" challenging for both the distributor and the theatres that play the film?

4. Define what a VPF is and the role it has played in converting the nation's screens to an all-digital projection system.

5. Describe the difference between a scale deal and an aggregate deal from an exhibitor's viewpoint. What criteria did Clark Woods use to determine which deal to take on "Avatar?" Did he make the right decision? Why?

6. Describe the business model for iPic Theatres. Have you ever attended a premium theatre with dining and drink options? If yes, how was your experience, and would you do it again?

CAUSE AND EFFECT

Week 15: April 10–16, 2009

It always comes down to the executives who make the decisions and map the strategy along the way, which makes it possible to have that kind of success.

Audiences continue to flock to the movies even though some people may feel there is really nothing for them to see. Isn't that always the case? Different strokes for different folks. Many divergent demographics make up the vast audience pool, and that is the beauty and strength of the Motion Picture Marketplace, which keeps chugging along as other industries continue to feel the sting of the recession. After a record-breaking 1ˢᵗ quarter, the question was what would April bring, another notoriously slow month, which acts as the final bridge to the start of the big summer season? Well, how about a $71,000,000 weekend gross for the fourth installment of "Fast and Furious"? Now it's easy to scoff and criticize macho action pictures like "Fast and Furious," and I'm not a fan myself. But I've found that it's always more instructive to look at the bigger picture and see what that kind of runaway success means for the studio involved, the audience and the industry at large. In addition, a movie commands respect when it exceeds the previous one in the franchise by $45,000,000 and out grosses the all time previous April opening by $29 million, achieved by "Anger Management" in 2003. In a year of very successful movies, those are crazy numbers. That's not easy to do. A lot of things have to go right for that to happen, and it always comes down to the executives who make the decisions and map the strategy along the way, which makes it possible to have that kind of success.

Universal is the studio behind "Fast and Furious," and they did a great job on all fronts, from bringing back the original cast, to staging a very strong marketing campaign, and then moving the release date from June to April to take advantage of the weaker competition. Obviously, Universal will benefit the most with huge profits, but audiences benefit also because profits from genre movies are channeled into financing more ambitious, quality films from Universal like "Duplicity" and next week's upscale thriller "State of Play," starring Russell Crowe and Helen Mirren. It takes all kinds of movies to make an annual release schedule, and sometimes what is considered mindless entertainment makes good movies possible. With a built-in audience, sequels are much easier to market than original films, where the pressure to perform often comes down to the first three days. Studios have to make these movies in order to stay alive. It only becomes problematic and disappointing when it's the only type of movie they decide to make. Universal highlighted the power and simplicity of high concept with "Fast and Furious" by successfully narrowing its marketing message down to only four words "NEW MODEL ORIGINAL PARTS." It's much more challenging to market a film like "Duplicity," and Universal stumbled on this one. Even so, it's certainly possible to go high concept with a star like Julia Roberts. Perhaps they could have gone with its own four word sell JULIA ROBERTS IS BACK, borrowing from the memorable tagline for 1945's "Adventure" which marked the return of Clark Gable from the military, "Gable's Back and Garbo's Got Him!"

On the other hand, the release schedule is a giant chess match between competing studios, all looking for that perfect date to open, trying to take advantage of any sign of weakness and playing to the strengths of the movie itself and the calendar. It's only conjecture now, but the perception is that when Universal moved "Fast and Furious" out of its original June 12ᵗʰ date, it may have left the important month of June lacking in big pictures. Each move in the marketplace has a cause and effect, and with fewer movies in the pipeline this year, filling each week in the summer with a proven hit gets more difficult. The month of May has heavy hitters every week with "X-Men: Wolverine," "Star Trek," "Angels and Demons," "Terminator Salvation," "The Night at the Museum" sequel and Disney/Pixar's "UP." Wow, that's an impressive lineup. July has Johnny Depp and Christian Bale in "Public Enemies" and the new "Harry Potter" to anchor the month.

Even though June has a number of movies on tap, only "Transformers: Revenge of the Fallen" at the end of June is a guaranteed certified blockbuster. There seems to be an abundance of mid-range comedies like "The Proposal" and "The Hangover," and the month could still turn out fine if at least one of those films breaks out or if some of the May movies show strong legs to carry over into June. June is too important of a month to just get by. Perhaps there is another move by a distributor still to be made, but it's probably too late for that to happen.

Each move in the marketplace has a cause and effect, and with fewer movies in the pipeline this year, filling each week in the summer with a proven hit gets more difficult.

DVD Release Patterns

The DVD market remains much more challenging than the theatrical market, even when considering the 3D issue that's being worked out. The various studios have different opinions on whether the recent downturn in DVD sales is more cyclical or a fundamental shift in consumer behavior, so they are playing around with different ways to release their product and also looking at the rental market with fresh eyes to see if they can lean on that side of the business for any good news. Well, one out of two isn't bad. Tuesday has been the traditional day of release used by distributors to release their DVD titles, but they have decided to mix it up and start using other days of the week to launch movies. Summit had great success with choosing Saturday night to come out with "Twilight," creating a lot of buzz and excitement with midnight screening parties and sold three million copies the first week. Disney is releasing "Bedtime Stories" on a Friday, and other studios are experimenting with their own titles. Will this have any long lasting positive effect on sales? So far this year, DVD revenues have shown a little improvement over the 4th quarter losses, but it's still too early to call. Whether the studios can depend on rental income more heavily, there are doubts because of some basic problems with rental that are hard to overlook.

Looking at the business models of Blockbuster, Netflix and the fast-charging Redbox point to three different sets of problems for the studios to deal with. Blockbuster, the old brick and mortar power house, is hanging on for dear life with a stock price under $1.00 and no guarantee they will be able to survive. They've cut back on their DVD orders to preserve cash, and that's not a good thing. Netflix has been wildly successful and continues to grow with its stock price up nearly 50% this year. That has to be good news for the studios, right? What's great for Netflix isn't necessarily great for film distributors. Netflix has been tremendous in coming up with new ways to add value to their subscribers, offering them features like streaming capabilities for no additional charge, but that doesn't aid the studios. Studios make the most money on individual transactions while Netflix makes theirs on a huge monthly subscription base. Studios will have to raise their upfront prices to squeeze more money out of Netflix, but for the time being Netflix has a great business model. They are making money, and they have a tremendous CEO in Reed Hastings who is always thinking of innovative ways to grow the company. Yet another growth area is with the discount rental business, and Redbox is leading the way with $1.00 vending machine kiosks in front of grocery stores and drug stores. This business was actually started by McDonalds and is growing fast with 13,000 kiosks in the U.S. The studios aren't too thrilled with this business model either because it undermines their long time economics that have propped up the movie industry for decades. The studios' fear is that the cheap price is giving the movies away and will give consumers another reason not to buy DVDs, which of course is the real moneymaker. Universal has already battled with Redbox by refusing to offer them their biggest titles on the day of release, and Redbox has filed suit against them for restraint of trade. Three different rental businesses, three different sets of positives and negatives for the studios to deal with.

> *Studios will have to raise their upfront prices to squeeze more money out of Netflix, but for the time being, Netflix has a great business model.*

Yet another bit of news on the Universal front. Their July release, "Bruno," Sacha Baron Cohen's follow up to "Borat," has been rated NC17 by the MPAA Ratings Board. Right now they are taking advantage of the publicity and showing a racy trailer on the Internet. However, there is no way this movie will keep this rating. It will be re-edited and re-submitted and will be released with an R rating. Universal has invested too much money to acquire this project to limit their audience with the box office killer NC17 rating.

This Week at the Box Office   *Weekly Attendance: 24,443,990*

Speaking of release schedules, where does Easter rank with the rest of the year's holidays in terms of importance and box office performance? All you have to do is look at the three wide movies that are opening this weekend to get the answer, "Hannah Montana," "Observe and Protect," and the martial arts "Dragonball: Evolution." Some potential niche hits but not too awe-inspiring. Easter has never been one of the stronger holidays for movies for several reasons:

- ▶ The holiday always jumps around and falls on a different week each year.

- ▶ It's a more religious holiday, which starts off with the solemn Good Friday and ends with Easter Day family gatherings.

- ▶ Spring break school vacations are scattered around the country on different weeks, so national releases can't take advantage of everybody being off at the same time.

- ▶ Studios are holding off on opening their bigger movies until May.

Only four independent films chose to open over Easter weekend, much fewer than the double-digit openings of prior weeks. Fewer films did not lead to stronger grosses as none of them created much of a ripple in the marketplace.

Hannah Montana The Movie
Disney
Opening weekend: $32,324,487
Domestic gross: $79,576,189 51.2%
Foreign gross: $75,969,090 48.8%
Worldwide gross: $155,545,279
Widest release: 3,231 theatres

Observe And Report
Warner Brothers
Opening weekend: $11,017,334
Domestic gross: $24,007,324 89%
Foreign gross: $2,966,230 11%
Worldwide gross: $26,973,554
Widest release: 2,727 theatres

Dragonball Evolution
20th Century Fox
Opening weekend: $4,756,488
Domestic gross: $9,362,785 16.3%
Foreign gross: $48,134,914 83.7%
Worldwide gross: $57,497,699
Widest release: 2,181 theatres

Lymelife
Screen Media
Opening weekend: $27,758
Domestic gross: $421,307 80.1%
Foreign gross: $104,938 19.9%
Worldwide gross: $526,245
Widest release: 35 theatres

Monster Beach Party
Indican
Opening weekend: $3,730
Domestic gross: $112,791
Foreign gross: N/A
Widest release: 8 theatres

Winter of Frozen Dreams
Monterey Media
Opening weekend: $5,750
Domestic gross: $8,321
Foreign gross: N/A
Widest release: 1 theatre

Terra Mera ki Rishta

Eros

Opening weekend : $130,324

Domestic gross: $271,942 78.8%

Foreign gross: $73,121 21.2%

Worldwide gross: $345,063

Widest release: 17 theatres

2009 Studio Release Schedules

Universal
1. Unborn – January 9
2. Last House on the Left – March 13
3. Duplicity – March 20
4. Fast and Furious – April 3
5. State of Play – April 17
6. Fighting – April 24
7. Drag Me to Hell – May 29
8. Land of the Lost – June 5
9. Public Enemies – July 1
10. Bruno – July 8
11. Funny People – July 31
12. A Perfect Getaway – August 7
13. Love Happens – September 18
14. Couples Retreat – October 9
15. The Vampire's Assistant – October 23
16. The Fourth Kind – November 6
17. It's Complicated – December 25

Paramount
1. Hotel for Dogs – January 16
2. The Uninvited – January 30
3. Friday the 13th – February 13
4. I Love You Man – March 20
5. Monsters vs. Aliens – March 27
6. The Soloist – April 24
7. Star Trek – May 8
8. Dance Flick – May 22
9. Imagine That – June 12
10. Transformers: Revenge of the Fallen – June 24
11. G.I. Joe: The Rise of Cobra – August 7
12. The Goods – August 14
13. Paranormal Activity – September 25
14. Up in the Air – December 4

20th Century Fox

1. Bride Wars – January 9
2. Taken – January 30
3. Street Fighter: Legend of Chuli – February 27
4. Miss March – March 13
5. 12 Rounds – March 27
6. X-Men Origins: Wolverine – May 1
7. Night at the Museum: Battle of the Smithsonian – May 22
8. My Life in Ruins – June 5
9. Ice Age: Dawn of the Dinosaurs – July 1
10. I Love You Beth Cooper – July 10
11. Aliens in the Attic – July 31
12. Post Grad – August 21
13. All about Steve – September 4
14. Jennifer's Body – September 18
15. Fantastic Mr. Fox – November 27
16. Avatar – December 16
17. Alvin & the Chipmunks: The Squeakquel – December 23

Sony

1. Not Easily Broken – January 9
2. Paul Blart: Mall Cop – January 16
3. Underworld – January 23
4. Fired Up – February 20
5. Dragon Ball: Revolution – April 10
6. Obsessed – April 24
7. Angels and Demons – May 15
8. Taking of Pelham 123 – June 12
9. Year One – June 19
10. The Ugly Truth – July 24
11. Julie and Julia – August 7
12. District 9 – August 14
13. Cloudy with a Chance of Meatballs – September 18
14. Zombieland – October 2
15. The Stepfather – October 16
16. This Is It – October 30
17. 2012 – November 13
18. Planet 51 – November 20
19. Armored – December 4
20. Did You Hear About the Morgans? – December 18

Warner Brothers

1. Gran Torino – January 9 (following four weeks limited release)
2. Inkheart – January 23
3. He's Just Not That Into You – February 6

4. Watchmen – March 6
5. Observe & Protect – April 10
6. 17 Again – April 17
7. Ghosts of Girlfriends Past – May 1
8. Terminator Salvation – May 22
9. The Hangover – June 5
10. My Sister's Keeper – June 26
11. Harry Potter and the Half Blood Prince – July 17
12. Orphan – July 24
13. Time Traveler's Wife – August 14
14. Shorts – August 21
15. The Final Destination – August 28
16. Whiteout – September 11
17. The Informant – September 18
18. The Invention of Lying – October 2
19. Where the Wild Things Are – October 16
20. The Box – November 6
21. The Blind Side – November 20
22. Ninja Assassin – November 27
23. Invictus – December 11
24. Sherlock Holmes – December 25

Disney
1. Confessions of a Shopaholic – February 13
2. Jonas Brothers 3D – February 27
3. Race to Witch Mountain – March 13
4. Hannah Montana the Movie – April 10
5. Earth – April 24
6. UP – May 29
7. The Proposal – June 19
8. G-Force – July 24
9. Ponyo – August 14
10. Surrogates – September 25
11. Walt & Gropo – October 23
12. Toy Story/Toy Story 2 in 3D – October 2
13. The Christmas Carol – November 6
14. Old Dogs – November 27
15. Princess and the Frog – December 11

2012 Update:
On Blockbuster, Netflix and Redbox

Any business that is dealing with changing digital technology as much as the movie rental business has had to contend with the last several years is certainly not going to be in the same position as it was in 2009. Blockbuster was feeling a lot of pain and trying to hold on for dear life when it was forced to file for bankruptcy in September 2010. They continued to operate but began to furiously close thousands of underperforming stores in a last ditch effort to stave off total liquidation. In April 2011, satellite television provider Dish Network acquired Blockbuster at auction for $233 million and assumption of millions in liabilities and other obligations. From its peak of 4,000 stores in 2009, the company is down to less than 1,000 traditional stores, but Dish is moving Blockbuster into new directions with the opening of portable Express Kiosks in locations across the country as well as working to expand its digital business with Blockbuster On Demand.

Netflix has gone through some big changes itself and is evolving into a different type of company. Its meteoric rise in stature, subscriptions and stock price to over $300 a share (from a price in the $40 range in early 2009) was nothing short of mind-boggling. Just when it seemed that Netflix could do no wrong, it started crashing down to earth in August 2011, when Reed Hastings announced the DVD-by -mail business was being separated from the streaming business and that subscribers would have to start paying for each service separately. The announcement was a publicity disaster, which led to a few million subscribers dropping their subscriptions and the stock price starting to free-fall all the way down to the $60 range. In addition, the company's deals with the various studios were expiring, and the new arrangements for content became much more expensive. By the summer of 2012, the company started rebounding with their emphasis clearly on their Internet streaming service, which had 26.5 million worldwide subscribers. Even though they are trying to wean people off their DVD mail service because that end of the business is much more expensive, physical DVDs may still survive another ten years because it's still a popular service for millions of people. Netflix is also becoming a producer of its own shows, an original series, "House of Cards," starring Kevin Spacey, as well as producing new shows of the cult favorite "Arrested Development." Both sets of shows are being created for its streaming service. After Reed Hastings announced that Netflix subscribers watched more than 1 billion hours of online video in June 2012, the stock price rose over 13% in two days to $80. Though Netflix is here to stay and should remain a profitable company, it's doubtful it will ever reach the heights the company enjoyed when it monopolized the DVD-by-mail business because there is much more competition in the streaming business from the likes of Amazon, Comcast, Verizon and others. Redbox has changed the least of the three companies and remains the leader in the kiosk business, though its owner Coinstar is also getting involved in the streaming business. There is much more on the developments of Redbox in chapter/week 32.

Week 15: Questions for Discussion

1. Describe the business models of Blockbuster, Netflix and Redbox. If you are a renter of movies, which of the three businesses have you preferred? Give your reasons why.

2. Why was Netflix a better business for them than it was for distributors? It's not easy to get the upper hand on the studios, so how did they do it, and how has that dynamic now changed?

3. What kind of company does Reed Hastings want Netflix to become? And what is it starting to be compared to, based on strategies currently being implemented? Do you think they will find success in this area?

THE CLOCK IS TICKING

Week 16: April 17–23, 2009

---

*Whenever someone protects his downside,
his upside is equally affected.*

With only two weeks to go before the summer movie season begins, my mind wanders about what is to come and about some missed opportunities along the way. With big blockbusters scheduled to open each week in May, screens across the country are going to get awful crowded as movies like "Wolverine," "Star Trek," and "Angels and Demons" open on multiple screens and smaller, lower grossing titles either get pushed out or find they have no place to grow. That's why I'm surprised that there were so few attempts by distributors in March and April to open more independent films that had the potential to have an impact and crossover to play in the more commercial, upscale suburban theatres. Now that window is closing fast. I live in the suburbs and don't frequent the art theatres in Chicago as often as I once did, so I've been depending more and more on the upscale theatres closer to home for my art house fix. Unfortunately, only one film in this period has been able to widen out to the suburbs, Overture's "Sunshine Cleaning," which originally opened in four theatres a couple of months ago and is currently playing in about 600 theatres across the country. With a $7 million gross, it's a small blip in the marketplace, but it's still considered a success because it has been the only specialty film to emerge and to be able to compete on a wider release. Is there room for more independents to play in commercial theatres? Of course, but it's not an easy proposition to pull off. Getting the screens is not the main problem; making the movies work and keeping them on the screens is the real battle. Movies have to have the right commercial hook either with concept, story or a little star power to have the capability to escape what is referred to crudely as "the art house ghetto." Just as important, a distributor is needed with the marketing muscle and moxie to support the release over an extended period of time with increased print and ad buys. There have been plenty of good art films like "Two Lovers," "Sin Nombre," "Gomorrah" and "Tokyo Sonata" playing on an exclusive basis in big city art houses, but those movies are too small and specialized to even be considered for wider play. However, there are two reasons for some optimism, one in the immediate future and one down the road.

While looking over the release schedule for the next couple of months, there are a number of notable specialty films listed to open as counter programming to the blockbusters, hoping to break through and find an audience beyond the art house. Hope is in the air with these films:

- April 25: "The Soloist," with Jamie Foxx And Robert Downey Jr.
- May 1: "The Limits of Control," directed by Jim Jarmush, starring Bill Murray
- May 15: "The Brothers Bloom," with Adrian Brody and Mark Ruffalo
- May 22: "My Girlfriend Experience," directed by Steven Soderbergh
- June 12: "Moon," starring Sam Rockwell
- June 19: "Whatever Works," Woody Allen's new film with Larry David
- June 26: "Cheri," starring Michelle Pfeiffer
- June 26: "The Hurt Locker," directed by Kathryn Bigelow with Guy Pearce

There are some good directors and actors involved with these films so they all have a fighting chance to succeed. Whether they do or not depends, as always, on a combination of critics' reviews, smart marketing, competition, good word of mouth and the fickleness of public taste and timing. If four of the eight films find their footing along with an audience, that would be a welcome sight for lovers of offbeat, quality cinema who happen to live outside the major cities.

Is market share the definitive factor of what constitutes success in the movie industry? No, but it can still be an effective indicator of what kind of year a distributor is having.

One of the reasons for fewer breakthrough indies is fewer well-financed distributors to handle them. Help is on the way as Bob Berney, one of the most successful and respected distribution and marketing executives in the business, is poised to announce soon a new distribution company he will be heading. You may not have heard of him, but you've heard of the movies he has marketed and distributed: "Memento," "My Big Fat Greek Wedding," "Pan's Labyrinth," "Whale Rider," "Y Tu Mama Tambien" and "The Passion of the Christ," among many others. Berney has been out of action ever since Warner Brothers axed Picturehouse last year. He has been a master at making hits out of unlikely films, and in today's marketplace, a man like him is needed back in distribution. There's an old adage that every film has an audience. That may be debatable, but if there is an audience to find, Bob Berney has a pretty good chance of finding it.

The clock is also ticking for Lionsgate, the industry's largest independent distributor, which is in a battle with billionaire corporate raider Carl Icahn for control of the company. Anyone who has worked in the movie business or has followed it closely over the years knows there is as much intrigue and action off the screen as there is on it. When you look at it, it's not surprising to see Lionsgate in play. The mini-major is the largest stand-alone independent studio and has been a solid company for a number of years, which also happens to have a vast library of 12,000 movies and television shows. That key asset is the company's crown jewel that Icahn has his eye on. Looking at the studio market share rankings for the first four months of 2009, Lionsgate is having a strong year and is even ahead of Disney (7.7% to 7%), but that's misleading because their violent action movie "Crank" could be their last movie until Labor Day. Lionsgate generally stays out of the summer competition of studio blockbusters and instead concentrates on building their market share in off times. Over the last five years, their annual market share is between 3.5% and 4.5%. Market share is a way distributors are ranked based on each company's annual box office gross in relation to the total industry gross of all the released movies. Is market share the definitive factor of what constitutes success in the movie industry? No, but it can still be an effective indicator of what kind of year a distributor is having. Without a doubt, the studios that release the most movies every year, like Warner Bros., have a better chance of finishing on top. The companies that release fewer movies use the argument that profitability matters more than market share, and you can't fault that logic either.

Getting back to Lionsgate, is a 3% or 4% market share good enough for the largest independent in the industry? Can it or should it be better? Their business plan of going after singles and doubles is smart on paper as it protects their downside. It has been said that Lionsgate has never lost more than $10 million on any movie. But whenever someone protects their downside, the upside is equally affected, and for Lionsgate that means not having the capability of earning hundreds of millions in profits that the studios are able to do on their biggest blockbusters. No one knows Icahn's ultimate intentions in wanting control of Lionsgate. There has been speculation that Icahn may even include Yahoo, a company he has a big stake in, pushing Yahoo to buy Lionsgate and leveraging all those titles into a viable online distribution business.

This is an intriguing story line, and it will be interesting to see what happens, but it's hard for me to get too worked up about it one way or another. I have no rooting interest in either side. Lionsgate specializes in releasing hard-edged genre movies and introduced what has become known as "torture porn" to the masses with their "Saw" and "Hostel" franchises. They used to sprinkle in some art films from time to time but have mostly abandoned that end of the business to concentrate on their bread-and-butter genre movies. In fact, it was only four years ago when Lionsgate won the Oscar for Best Picture of the Year with "Crash," the first film acquired at a film festival that went on to be honored as Best Film. But what comes around goes around. A couple of years ago, Lionsgate was in the role of corporate raider trying to wrest control over DVD distributor Image Entertainment but was rebuked and lost that battle. The big swallows the small, and the bigger swallows the big. On the other hand, I have no sympathy or support for Carl Icahn, the billionaire bully who relishes striking fear and chaos in companies with the hope of moving the stock price and making even more millions. No, I don't care who wins this battle. Lionsgate will continue to operate no matter who runs the studio, and the only other sure thing is that another "Saw" will open at Halloween.

This Week at the Box Office   *Weekly Attendance: 19,077,368*

The teen market is doing just fine with Warner Brothers set to open "17 Again" this weekend following last week's success of "Hannah Montana" from Disney. Teen films have a big audience base to draw from; the last two "Hannah Montana" movies have opened to over $30 million each, and with Zac Efron from "High School Musical" fame starring in "17 Again," the teen market should enjoy another number one hit this weekend. Studios love them for their low production costs, the absence of any gross participants, the ability to open on 3,000 screens and the potential of high profits. Miramax, a traditional art distributor, attempted to combine a little independent quirkiness with a younger audience with "Adventureland" a couple of weeks ago, but it failed to catch on. There have been some successes in the past that married independent film to the teen film, "Napoleon Dynamite" and "Juno" spring to mind, and when that happens, a movie can explode into the mainstream even though it remains a tricky thing to find the right balance to satisfy both audiences. Switching over to Universal, the studio is releasing "State of Play" over the weekend, which is a counterpunch to their own "Fast and Furious," going from mindless entertainment to an adult drama for smart audiences. With summer movies opening soon, it's an opportune time to take advantage of a good quality film opening in over 2700 theatres. "State of Play" cost $60 million and is without a doubt the most challenging type of movie studios green light, hence it's also on the most endangered list. The $50 to $70 million adult drama depends on audiences to think a little while also hoping for adults to come out and support it on its opening weekend, not an easy thing to pull off. The film has an all-star cast led by two former Oscar winners in Russell Crowe and Helen Mirren, but that doesn't guarantee a big weekend gross. What's becoming more apparent with each passing year is that any movie that isn't high concept in today's marketplace is a risk, pure and simple, and "State of Play's" story of a congressman and a news reporter and some seemingly unrelated murders in Washington D.C. certainly wouldn't qualify as high concept. But it doesn't hurt an adult drama to have thriller, suspense, and murder mystery elements thrown into the mix to make the drama more appealing to audiences, though that still doesn't mean it will be able to recoup P&A costs on top of a $60 million production budget.

17 Again
Warner Brothers
Opening weekend: $23,722,310
Domestic gross: $64,167,069 47.1%
Foreign gross: $72,100,407 52.9%
Worldwide gross: $136,267,476
Widest release: 3,255 theatres

Is Anybody There?
Stony Island
Opening weekend: $46,209
Domestic gross: $2,026,765 60.2%
Foreign gross: $1,341,544 39.8%
Worldwide gross: $3,368,300
Widest release: 165 theatres

The Golden Boys
Roadside
Opening weekend: $18,366
Domestic gross: $184,169
Foreign gross: N/A
Widest release: 20 theatres

Gooby
Monterey Media
Opening weekend: $1,552
Domestic gross: $3,564
Foreign gross: N/A
Widest release: 5 theatres

State of Play
Universal
Opening weekend: $14,071,280
Domestic gross: $37,211,783 42.2%
Foreign gross: $50,794,416 57.8%
Worldwide gross: $87,812,371
Widest release: 2,807 theatres

Lemon Tree
IFC
Opening weekend: $14,602
Domestic gross: $569,672 7.7%
Foreign gross: $6,817,816 92.3%
Worldwide gross: $7,387,488
Widest release: 29 theatres

Leon Morin, Priest
Rialto
Opening weekend: $9,515
Domestic gross: $27,567
Foreign gross: N/A
Widest release: 1 theatre

Oblivion
Icarus
Opening weekend: $5,061
Domestic gross: $10,857
Foreign gross: N/A
Widest release: 1 theatre

Crank High Voltage
Lionsgate
Opening weekend: $6,963,565
Domestic gross: $13,684,249 39.6%
Foreign gross: $20,876,328 60.4%
Worldwide gross: $34,560,577
Widest release: 2,223 theatres

American Violet
IDP/Samuel Goldwyn
Opening weekend: $243,162
Domestic gross: $554,434
Foreign gross: N/A
Widest release: 279 theatres

Sleep Dealer
Maya Releasing
Opening weekend: $35,050
Domestic gross: $80,136 74.5%
Foreign gross: $27,423 25.5%
Worldwide gross: $107,559
Widest release: 18 theatres

2012 Update: Lionsgate

After several years of Carl Icahn feuding with Lionsgate that resulted in lawsuits and counter suits, Icahn parted ways with the distributor in August 2011 and sold off all his shares of the company. The reason for the departure or any type of agreement between the two parties was not revealed, though Lionsgate had to be thrilled to be rid of their main adversary. It freed them to concentrate on their movie slate, and 2012 proved to be a breakthrough year for the longtime independent distributor. "The Hunger Games" was released on March 23, 2012, and the single/doubles distributor finally hit it out of the park with its first true homerun blockbuster, grossing $404 million in the domestic market and totaling $618 million in worldwide grosses. Being able to secure the rights for the three books in the series showed foresight and aggressiveness, which has strengthened their standing in Hollywood and will no doubt increase their industry market share which has fallen off in recent years. Another huge development in 2012 was the company's acquisition of Summit Entertainment, a strategic move that brings together two of the largest independent distributors under one roof. There is one more "Twilight" film, which will be released in November 2012 that Lionsgate will be distributing. What a difference a year makes. Lionsgate was always a distributor that had to stay away from summer and holiday playtime because they didn't have the firepower to compete with the majors. Now they will be a guaranteed major player in the crucial Thanksgiving holiday period for the next four years. The company has scheduled the second picture, "Catching Fire," for November 22, 2013 and will split the final book into two films, "The Hunger Games: Mockingjay Part 1" to be released on November 21, 2014 and "Mockingjay Part 2" for November 22, 2015.

Hierarchy of Motion Picture Distribution Companies (2012)

Major Studios
- Walt Disney Pictures owned by Walt Disney Corp.
- Warner Bros. owned by Time Warner
- Paramount owned by Viacom
- Universal owned by Comcast
- Sony/Columbia owned by Sony Corp.
- 20th Century Fox owned by New Corp.

Studio Affiliated Specialty Distributors
- Sony Classics owned by Sony
- Fox Searchlight owned by 20th Century Fox
- Focus Features owned by Universal

Top Stand-Alone Independent Distributors
- Lionsgate
- Weinstein Company
- Relativity
- Film District
- Roadside Attractions
- CBS Films

Independent Distributors (Cont.)
- IFC
- Open Road Films
- Magnolia
- Samuel Goldwyn
- Music Box Films
- Eros
- Reliance Big Pictures
- National Geographic
- Freestyle Releasing
- Zeitgeist
- ATO Pictures
- Oscilloscope
- Strand
- First Run
- Anchor Bay Films
- Abramorama
- Millennium

STUDIO MARKET SHARE RANKINGS 2009 - 2011

January 1-December 31, 2009	*January 1-December 31, 2010*	*January 1-December 31, 2011*
Domestic Gross: $10.619 billion	*Domestic Gross: $10.567 billion*	*Domestic Gross: $10.174 billion*
Warner Brothers – 19.8%	Warner Brothers – 18.2%	Paramount – 19.2%
Paramount – 13.9%	Paramount – 16.2%	Warner Brothers – 17.9%
Sony / Columbia – 13.7%	20th Century Fox – 14.0%	Sony/Columbia – 12.5%
20th Century Fox – 13.1%	Disney – 13.8%	Disney – 12.2%
Disney – 11.6%	Sony / Columbia – 12.1%	Universal – 10.2%
Universal – 8.4%	Universal – 8.3%	20th Century Fox – 9.6%
Summit – 4.5%	Summit – 5.0%	Summit – 4.0%
Lionsgate – 3.8%	Lionsgate – 4.98%	Weinstein Co. – 2.9%
Fox Searchlight – 2.4%	Fox Searchlight – 1.4%	Relativity – 2.2%
Weinstein Co. – 1.9%	Overture Films – 0.8%	Lionsgate – 1.8%
Focus Features – 1.5%	Weinstein Co. – 0.8%	Fox Searchlight – 1.55
Overture Films – 1.5%	Focus Features – 0.7%	Focus Features – 1.2%
Paramount Vantage – 0.6%	CBS Films – 0.7%	FilmDistrict – 1.2%
MGM/UA – 0.6%	Sony Classics – 0.6%	Sony Classics – 0.9%
Miramax – 0.6%	MGM/UA – 0.5%	CBS Films – 0.6%
Sony Classics – 0.5%	Miramax – 0.3%	Roadside Attractions – 0.3%
Apparition – 0.2%	Music Box Films – 0.2%	Open Road – 0.2%
Freestyle Releasing – 0.1%	Apparition – 0.1%	IFC – 0.2%
Magnolia – 0.1%	Anchor Bay – 0.1%	Magnolia – 0.1%
Roadside Attractions – 0.1%	Samuel Goldwyn – 0.1%	Samuel Goldwyn – 0.1%
IFC – 0.1%	IFC – 0.1%	Reliance Big Pictures – 0.1%

There were approximately 100 other distributors on the charts for each of the years that were listed with 0.0% market share when their annual total gross was added up.

Source: Box Office Mojo

Week 16: Questions for Discussion

1. Who was the parent company for Overture Films in 2009? Supply a little history of the company and some of the movies they released. In July 2010, the company was sold. Research the details of the transaction and name the company that bought Overture.

2. Where does Lionsgate fit in the hierarchy of film companies? Why did billionaire Carl Icahn stalk the distributor for several years? Does Lionsgate's market share from 2009 to 2011 indicate anything to you? What does "Hunger Games" do for the company, and do you think it assures them continued success even when that series of movies end?

3. What is the difference between a distributor of specialty films and a distributor of genre movies, and can one company partake in both types of films?

4. Total up the combined market share of the six major studios for each of the years between 2009 and 2011. Draw some conclusions. What does it tell you about the makeup of the motion picture industry? What about all the other distributors below them?

FILM PIRACY: NO LONGER A VICTIMLESS CRIME

Week 17: April 24–30, 2009

It's too bad that some people feel it's their right to get anything
they want whenever they want it whether it's legal or not...
There is right and there is wrong. Film piracy is dead wrong.

The Internet leak of an unfinished print of "Wolverine" at the beginning of April and the subsequent mass illegal down-loading of the film just weeks before the kickoff of the summer movie season brought the huge problem of film piracy to the forefront once again. I'm going to come out and say it and not mince any words. Anyone who participates in any kind of film piracy, whether it's illegal downloading of movies on the Internet, buying pirated copies of DVDs on the street, even accepting pirated copies from friends or co-workers while they're still playing in theatres, is breaking the law and should take a big step back to consider what kind of activities they're actually participating in. Even if they believe they aren't doing anything wrong, they are, in both a legal and moral sense, and those activities can have larger repercussions in today's world than ever before. As a film industry lifer and teacher, I'm hard-nosed about this issue and give no quarter to anyone who tries to rationalize his or her position on why they are doing whatever they are doing. There is right and there is wrong. Film piracy is dead wrong.

When I refer to film piracy as no longer being a victimless crime, I need to clarify that statement because I don't want to imply there haven't been victims in the past, because there have been. It's just now there is a new face to film piracy. The stakes have risen to new heights, and the new victims lie far outside the movie industry and can impact any number of unsuspecting, innocent people wherever they live. When people use the rationalization that the Hollywood studios are making enough money, why should they care about piracy, they're using a misguided, uninformed judgment because the collateral damage runs deep as piracy has led to:

- ▶ The stealing of intellectual property.

- ▶ The denigration of the director's creative process through unauthorized, often inferior copies of his creation. Even if it's a good copy, the artist's work is being stolen and he or she isn't being compensated for it.

- ▶ Loss of revenues to the distributors of pirated films.

- ▶ The drop in revenues due to piracy leading to job loss within the industry when studios cut back spending and are forced to contain costs and make fewer movies.

- ▶ Job loss to all the ancillary businesses that feed off the movie industry when less production takes place, having an impact on many regular working class people such as hair dressers, set-builders and limo drivers.

- ▶ The reduction of independent movies being able to be financed through foreign pre-sales due to the rise of global copyright piracy.

Yes, there have been victims, but the recently released study from the RAND Corporation titled "Film Piracy: Organized Crime and Terrorism" takes it to an entirely new level. The findings in the report are stunning as 14 case studies connect the dots and follow the money to show how organized crime is increasingly playing a more active role in film piracy by controlling the entire supply chain from manufacture to street sales of pirated movies. The report also profiles three cases that even link terrorists to piracy profits. I'm surprised how little discussion this extensive report has received in the press, including movie trade publications. There were some initial stories immediately following the release of the report in March without much fanfare, commentary or reaction, and I haven't seen much of anything since then. In some quarters, the content of the report seemed to be dismissed either as a bit farfetched or too partisan because the MPAA supplied a grant for the study. That's weak reasoning and discounts the body of work and reputation the RAND Corporation has established for itself over the last 60 years as the leading, nonpartisan research company in the United States. The high caliber of their researchers is well known throughout the corporate and political worlds with many former Nobel Laureates having worked for RAND either as employees, consultants or in an advisory capacity. Their initial mission statement in 1948 simply said, "To further and promote scientific, educational and charitable purposes, all for the public welfare and security of the United States of America."

By the 1960s RAND was bringing its trademark method of experienced independent analysis to the study of many vital domestic social and economic problems such as the health care system, affordable housing, national defense, space systems and digital computing. RAND's research agenda has always been shaped by the priorities of the nation, so its research into worldwide film piracy should not be taken lightly. The research is based on 2,000 pages of documents and interviews with more than 120 law enforcement and intelligence agents from more than 20 countries. Their data and analysis should be taken seriously based on its decades' worth of invaluable research, work which has benefitted countless American institutions. RAND stands for quality and integrity, and their reputation is unmatched. The full report is available at www.rand.org.

Just as the film industry is a global business, film piracy is a global problem. As well as documenting cases in North America and Europe, the report outlines the involvement of organized crime with film piracy in South America, Russia and many parts of Asia. In one instance, a simple arrest at a UPS store for shipping illegal DVDs led to the exposure of a large-scale human trafficking ring. In New York City, Yi Ging, a gang based in Chinatown, terrorized local merchants through their activities. They would receive DVDs manufactured in China that would be smuggled into New York, and their strong-arm tactics extended into cities like Columbus, Ohio and Detroit. Another case involved the tri-border area of Brazil, Argentina and Paraguay that has emerged as the most important financing center for Islamic terrorism outside the Middle East, channeling $20 million annually to Hezbollah. At least one transfer of $3.5 million was made to Hezbollah by known DVD pirate Assad Ahmad Barakat, who was labeled a "specially designated global terrorist" by the U.S. government in 2004. Greg Treverton, the RAND report's lead author and director of the Center for Global Risk and Security said, "If you buy pirated DVDs, there is a good chance that at least part of the money will go to organized crime, and those proceeds fund more dangerous criminal activities, possibly terrorism."

94% of those surveyed believed that stealing a CD from a store is wrong in all instances, whereas only 36% felt that taking intellectual property online is wrong in all instances.

The Internet leak of "Wolverine" four weeks ahead of its release underscores the difficulty of controlling and keeping up with technology, even when it happens so close to Hollywood with an alleged vendor or postproduction house being the suspected source. It will continue to be an ongoing battle that will probably never be completely won. As much as it is a technology problem, it's also an attitude and perception problem inherent in a lot of people. A global study a couple of years ago showed 94% of those surveyed believed that stealing a CD from a store is wrong in all instances, whereas only 36% felt that taking intellectual property online is wrong in all instances. A more concerted effort will have to be made to reach school age kids from grade school age on through high school and college with the right message and facts on the impact and dangers of film piracy. It's not easy to change people's minds, but if the industry starts early and often with a widespread educational outreach program, perhaps it could make a difference in young peoples' minds that will stay with them for the rest of their lives. Changing human behavior can turn technology into the studios' ally instead of enemy.

In terms of confronting the issue of demand, the studios are doing what they can to accommodate consumers by adding free digital copies of movies to the regular DVD packaging, offering consumers more ways to utilize technology legally rather than downloading illegally. They are also showcasing more of their films online through sites like Hulu, and that area will continue to show growth. Still, some say, why not release movies in theatres and DVDs at the same time. That will solve the problem of piracy. That's not going to happen. The studios aren't going to allow thieves to dictate a change in the fundamental way the movie business operates. For starters, a day and date release would kill off close to 40,000 theatre screens. That shortsighted hypothesis fails to grasp that not all movies have instantaneous awareness and demand; interest has to be allowed to build over time, and that's why the current system of staggered release windows has worked so well over the last 30 years. It's too bad that some people feel it's their right to get anything they want whenever they want it whether it's legal or not. They'll find out in time, many things in life don't work that way, and for every action taken there are consequences, both known and unknown.

This Week at the Box Office   *Weekly Attendance: 19,164,782*

For the final weekend before the much-anticipated start of the summer movie season, there will be four new movies trying to establish their footprint before blockbusters start flooding the screens:

- ▶ "Obsessed," a romantic thriller starring the popular singer Beyonce
- ▶ "Fighting," a drama starring Channing Tatum
- ▶ "Earth," the animal documentary from Disney
- ▶ "The Soloist," the upscale drama starring Robert Downey, Jr. and Jamie Foxx

Obsessed
Sony
Opening weekend: $28,612,730
Domestic gross: $68,261,644 92.5%
Foreign gross: $5,568,696 7.5%
Worldwide gross: $73,830,340
Widest release: 2,312 theatres

Earth
Disney
Opening weekend: $8,825,760
Domestic gross: $32,011,576 29.4%
Foreign gross: $76,963,584 70.6%
Worldwide gross: $108,975,160
Widest release: 1,804 theatres

The Soloist
Paramount
Opening weekend: $9,716,458
Domestic gross: $31,853,584 82.7%
Foreign gross: $6,612,836 17.3%
Worldwide gross: $38,332,994
Widest release: 2,090 theatres

Fighting
Universal
Opening weekend: $11,024,370
Domestic gross: $23,302,410 71.1%
Foreign gross; $9,383,110 28.9%
Worldwide gross: $32,474,120
Widest release: 2,312 theatres

Tyson
Sony Pictures Classics
Opening weekend: $85,046
Domestic gross: $887,918 92%
Foreign gross: $77,002 8%
Worldwide gross: $964,920
Widest release: 2,312 theatres

Treeless Mountain
Oscilloscope
Opening weekend: $5,014
Domestic gross: $60,332 48.6%
Foreign gross: $63,687 51.4%
Worldwide gross: $124,023
Widest release: 4 theatres

Il Divo

Music Box Films

Opening weekend: $13,867

Domestic gross: $240,159

Foreign gross: N/A

Widest release: 7 theatres

Nursery University

Variance

Opening weekend: $11,307

Domestic gross: $26,047

Foreign gross: N/A

Widest Release: 6 theatres

The Garden

Oscilloscope

Opening weekend: $4,114

Domestic gross: $26,930

Foreign gross: N/A

Widest release: 4 theatres

Jazz in the Diamond District

Trulie Indie

Opening weekend: $5,107

Domestic gross: $7,634

Foreign gross: N/A

Widest release: 1 theatre

2012 Update:
"Wolverine" Pirate Gets Prison Time

When the Internet leak of an unfinished print of "Wolverine" was first discovered, one of the theories was that it might have been an inside job originating from a vendor or postproduction house. That wasn't the case. Gilberto Sanchez, a 49 year old from New York, pleaded guilty in March 2011 to uploading a "workprint" copy of the film to the site Megaupload.com about a month before the film's release. He further made the upload known by posting links on two sites to provide easier access. Sanchez was brought to justice as the result of an investigation by the F.B.I. He was subsequently sentenced to one year in federal prison, plus one year of supervised release, along with various computer restrictions. United States Attorney Andre Birotte Jr. said that Sanchez's sentencing "sends a strong message of deterrence to would-be Internet pirates ... The Justice Department will pursue and prosecute persons who seek to steal the intellectual property of this nation."

Source: thewrap.com

Covert Filming Yields Jail Term

In June 2011, a 37-year-old man was caught recording the movie "Easy A" at a Joliet, Illinois theatre, using a camera hidden in sunglasses. The man was sentenced to 60 days in jail after pleading guilty to illegally recording about 45 minutes of the movie. The man was being tracked after he was identified by the Motion Picture Association of America after allegedly posting just-released films to two websites that illegally offered them to paying customers. Illegal recordings of movies in theatres are the single largest source of fake DVDs sold on the street and unauthorized copies of movies distributed on the Internet. For this reason, camcording is a serious offence and a federal felony in the United States. The MPAA has a reward program in place that awards $500 to any theatre employee who discovers and reports anyone recording a movie illegally in his theatre. Forty-one states have anti-camcording laws to further safeguard creative works.

Sources: Chicago Tribune, mpaa.org

TOP 10 MOST PIRATED MOVIES OF 2011

TorrentFreak released its list of the ten most pirated movies of 2011. Though it has always been difficult to make any kind of direct correlation between illegal downloads and movie revenue, DVD sales figures in 2011 compared to 2010 are much more pronounced than they have been in recent years. In 2010, seven movies exceeded $100 million in DVD sales, led by "Avatar," which pulled in more than $183 million. In 2011, no DVD did $100 million in sales; Disney's Tangled was the highest-grossing DVD of the year with $96 million in sales. The following is the complete list of the most pirated movies of 2011 along with torrent download totals. The sheer amount of illegal Internet downloads is staggering and points to how serious of an issue movie piracy continues to be. When you look at the close to seven million illegal downloads for the independent film "127 Hours," it would be difficult to believe that amount of illegal activity wouldn't have an effect on the film's revenue.

1. Fast Five – 9,260,000 illegal downloads
2. The Hangover II – 8,840,000 illegal downloads
3. Thor – 8,330,000 illegal downloads
4. Source Code – 7,910,000 illegal downloads
5. I Am Number Four – 7,670,000 illegal downloads
6. Sucker Punch – 7,200,000 illegal downloads
7. 127 Hours – 6,910,000 illegal downloads
8. Rango – 6,480,000 illegal downloads
9. The King's Speech – 6,250,000 illegal downloads
10. Harry Potter and the Deathly Hallows Part 2 – 6,030,000 illegal downloads

Source: Zach Epstein, bgr.com, 12/29/11

Week 17: Questions for Discussion

1. What are your personal feelings on film piracy? Whatever it is, explain your reasoning and beliefs on the topic.

2. Have you ever seen or known anyone that participated in film piracy? If you did, what was your reaction to it, and did you let your feelings be known at the time?

3. As alternative distribution methods move toward the Internet, what are some ways film piracy can affect the work of independent filmmakers? Do you feel that the notion of the Internet being "free" adds to the problems of illegal behavior on the Internet?

4. In regards to the findings of the Rand Corporation, does it change your thinking to read that organized crime and perhaps even terrorist activities are behind some aspects of film piracy?

"WE'RE GOING TO NEED A BIGGER BOAT"

Week 18: May 1–7, 2009

_It's fun to look back at the summer of 1975 when 409 theatres
was considered a very wide release and when the term summer
blockbuster was as foreign as hot chocolate on the 4ᵗʰ of July._

When Roy Scheider's character in Universal's "Jaws" uttered, "We're going to need a bigger boat," he could have in fact also been saying, "We're going to need a bigger summer." The date was June 20, 1975, the day Steven Spielberg's "Jaws" opened in 409 theatres across the United States. The day summer changed forever for both Hollywood and its audience. As another summer movie season gets under way with "X-Men Origins: Wolverine" opening in 4,000 theatres, it's fun to look back at the summer of 1975 when 409 theatres was considered a very wide release and when the term summer blockbuster was as foreign as hot chocolate on the 4ᵗʰ of July. The phrase hadn't been invented yet, not until "Jaws" came along. Before that, summer was an odd combination of, well, just regular movies, westerns, comedies, dramas, action, drive-in fare, foreign films from Fellini and Bergman, a little bit of everything. "Jaws" ushered in the modern era of the summer blockbuster, and it had that summer of 1975 all to itself. There is a very telling scene in the excellent documentary "The Last Mogul," which speaks to how much the industry has changed. The film profiled the career of Lew Wasserman, who was the head of Universal when "Jaws" was released. Following a rousing test screening of the movie in Hollywood, Wasserman called all his executives into the theatre manager's office for a meeting. The head of distribution very proudly said, "Lew, it's a record, we booked more than 600 theatres!" Lew looked back at him and said, "Lose half of them. I don't want people to get into it; I want lines around the block." It became the number one movie at the box office for 14 weeks in a row as it went on to gross $260 million, a new all-time record, with an average ticket price of $2.00. Adjusted to today's dollars, that would translate to a domestic gross of over $800 million.

When I think of it, even 34 years later, has there ever been a more perfect summer movie? It didn't take too long for the other studios to catch on. "Star Wars" followed two years later and became the first film to gross over $300 million, then came "Alien," "Return of the Jedi," "ET," "Raiders of the Lost Ark" and countless summer hits too many to count and remember. Perhaps because Spielberg and George Lucas are still such seminal figures, it doesn't seem that long ago when one movie was able to transform the entire industry in so many different ways from television saturation campaigns to national release patterns, to merchandising, to cross promotions, to the reliance on summer movies to pull in 40% of the year's annual take. Some detractors over the years have actually blamed Spielberg and Lucas for ruining the movies with this blockbuster mentality at the expense of quality cinema, but that misses the point. In fact, when the studios started shifting their business model to these bigger franchise movies, it supplied an opening in the marketplace for independent film to emerge, and that's exactly what happened starting in the late 70s and early 80s. There are some points in history that are just ready for change to occur, and the movie business was more than ready to be kick started into a new era in the summer of 1975.

It took a lot of years for Hollywood to perfect the blockbuster release and learn how to take full advantage of the summer calendar. The business has gone from one blockbuster in an entire summer to six potential blockbusters in one month as we are seeing this May. It presents a compelling scenario. Cramming so many big movies into a single month may excite moviegoers, but it also poses some real risks for the distributors involved. One of two things can happen. Either the marketplace can expand and all these movies will find their audience and succeed, or they will step on each other's toes, there will be some casualties, and it won't be pretty. The studios do a great job of spreading out their blockbusters, but there will be no breathing room in May. There's going to be a lot of nervous executives with their fingers crossed watching the numbers come in. It was just two years ago in May 2007 when three big franchise movies opened within a few weeks of each other. When the smoke cleared, "Spider-Man 3," "Shrek The Third," and "Pirates of the Caribbean: At World's End," each grossed over $300 million, proving how potent the month of May has become. With twice as many blockbusters this May, helped by a quirk in the calendar which gives the month five weekends, each of the movies has its fan base and could do well, though it's doubtful any of them will be able to gross $300 million with the increased competition.

May 1 – "X-Men Origins: Wolverine"

May 8 – "Star Trek"

May 15 – "Angels and Demons"

May 22 – "Night at the Museum: Battle of the Smithsonian," "Terminator Salvation"

May 29 – "UP"

I've been discussing how summer has evolved, but it had me thinking about how Hollywood has also come to master the full 12-month calendar with their releases. It took many years for the industry to settle on the first weekend of May as the official start of the summer movie season, moving up from the traditional June when more schools were closed for the year. What they've done is to break down the year into four parts, four months of summer from May to August, two months of holiday releases in November and December, the January to April period and finally, September/October. So six months of the year is blockbuster season with the thinking if they can hold their own during the other times, they're sitting pretty. That is, if all their movies do the business they're supposed to do, which they don't all do. There are always failures and disappointments scattered through the year for every distributor; they just don't know which ones they are going to be.

Every Monday morning following a movie's opening, there are tough decisions studios have to make regarding how they will continue to support each of their movies.

With a record-setting first four months of 2009, the studios have done more than hold their own, and how they've accomplished this is to scatter summer type movies into these months like "Monsters vs. Aliens," "The Watchmen" and "Fast and Furious." But what's good for the studios and movie theatres is not necessarily good for other types of films. There has been some collateral damage, and it's being felt the most with mainstream adult dramas and basically a good portion of the independent films that have been coming out. The marketplace works best when it has balance, and too many blockbusters have been known to drown out the smaller fish in the pond, though the quality and commerciality of the other films have to also be considered. Can "State of Play" be considered small with a $60 million dollar budget with star power to boot? After a solid opening, the second week tumbled with a 51% drop, which was disappointing to see. This is a good movie, and I thought it had a chance to hang in a lot stronger than that, but I wonder, did Universal drop the ball with their marketing after the first weekend? Every Monday morning following a movie's opening, there are tough decisions studios have to make regarding how they will continue to support each of their movies. In the case of "State of Play," it would seem the decision was to pull back and not really keep pouring money into the campaign to keep the title fresh in audiences' minds. That's a shame, but it's the reality of the times when the vast majority of the marketing on many movies is spent before a film opens. With falling DVD numbers, no studio can afford to overspend on marketing, especially on a drama, when the ancillary revenues are not as dependable as they used to be. Still, I would have liked to have seen a better effort from Universal on this one. Even a bigger casualty was "The Soloist." Jamie Foxx came out and blasted Paramount for moving the film from an end-of-the-year release to the last week of April, and he has a point. Why open the film a week before the summer movie season begins when there are already three other new wide releases fighting for attention the same week? Coming in fourth place is never a good thing, which is what happened to "The Soloist." Paramount had all of March and April to play with, so I don't understand their thinking. How much attention can they focus on it now with "Star Trek" set to open next week? The answer couldn't be easier to see. Not very much.

Speaking of falling DVD numbers, The Digital Entertainment Group, a trade association of home entertainment companies, reported that sell-through DVDs to consumers fell 14% in the first quarter of 2009. I've always maintained you can learn much about the movie business by going out and being attentive when you visit a movie theatre, walk into a video store or flip through your cable guide. The proof is in what you see. So when I walked into my neighborhood Best Buy this week and noticed the DVD section has been relocated farther back in the store, that spoke volumes about the changing consumer buying habits the industry is facing in this economic downturn.

One last note. I see where Fox has announced they are going to make a sequel to the 1988 "Wall Street" with Michael Douglas returning as Gordon Gekko. For years Oliver Stone was on record saying he wasn't interested in doing another "Wall Street" movie, but after seeing the latest script he has signed on to direct. I'm a fan of "Wall Street," and the movie perfectly mirrored the slick go-go 80s with the mantra of "greed is good," so I'm very intrigued what kind of tone Stone will strike with this one. Will he go for all out satire, or will he do a scathing social commentary on the self-proclaimed masters of the universe who helped lead the country into such a deep recession? Either way, it will be a much-needed film for these times because audiences need more than a steady diet of blockbusters.

This Week at the Box Office   *Weekly Attendance: 26,174,457*

While "X-Men Origins: Wolverine" is set to kick off the summer blockbuster season, two other movies are going wide as counter programming. Warner Brothers is opening "Ghosts of Girlfriends Past," a romantic comedy starring Matthew McConaughey and Jennifer Garner, which should be able to find its target audience of young women. The other movie is much more problematic. Lionsgate is releasing a non-descript animated film called "Battle for Terra" which has close to zero awareness among the family audience and should disappear quickly without much of a whimper.

X-Men Origins: Wolverine
20th Century Fox
Opening weekend: $85,058,003
Domestic gross: $179,883,157 48.2%
Foreign gross: $193,179,707 51.8%
Worldwide gross: $373,062,864
Widest release: 4,102 theatres

Ghosts of Girlfriends Past
Warner Brothers
Opening weekend: $15,411,434
Domestic gross: $55,250,026 54%
Foreign gross: $46,973,243 46%
Worldwide gross: $102,223,269
Widest release: 3,008 theatres

Battle for Terra
Roadside Attractions
Opening weekend: $1,082,064
Domestic gross: $1,647,083 26.9%
Foreign gross: $4,482,446 73.1%
Worldwide gross: $6,129,529
Widest release: 1,159 theatres

The Limits of Control
Focus
Opening weekend: $55,250,026
Domestic gross: $426,688 21.7%
Foreign gross: $1,539,883 78.3%
Worldwide gross: $1,966,571
Widest release: 27 theatres

The Merry Gentleman
IDP/Samuel Goldwyn
Opening weekend: $74,981
Domestic gross: $347,977
Foreign Gross: N/A
Widest release: 33 theatres

Revanche
Janus
Opening weekend: $16,330
Domestic gross: $308,686
Foreign gross: N/A
Widest release: 8 theatres

A Wink and a Smile
First Run
Opening weekend: $2,346
Domestic gross: $20,169
Foreign gross: N/A
Widest release: 3 theatres

The Skeptic
IFC
Opening weekend: $1,553
Domestic gross: $6,671 6.3%
Foreign gross: $99,457 93.7%
Worldwide gross: $106,128
Widest release: 2 theatres

Home
Monterey Media
Opening weekend: $1,587
Domestic gross: $10,405 57.5%
Foreign gross: $7,704 42.5%
Worldwide gross: $18,109
Widest release: 3 theatres

Eldorado
Film Movement
Opening weekend: $3,372
Domestic gross; $10,443
Foreign gross: N/A
Widest release: 1 theatre

Break
Cinema Epoch
Opening weekend: $1,191
Domestic gross: $1,191
Foreign gross; N/A
Widest release: 1 theatre

Week 18: Questions for Discussion

1. What is the biggest change "Jaws" brought to the movie industry that still resonates today? What statistic is tied to its release that is impossible to duplicate today?

2. How do the studios break down their 12-month release schedules? Are all the weeks equal, or are there strong and weak points during the year?

3. When does the summer movie season begin for the studios, and how has that evolved?

4. Was there a danger of having six potential blockbusters open in the same month as they did in May 2009? What was the result of placing so many big movies in one month? Analyze the actual opening weekend numbers and final grosses for these movies, including what they did worldwide. Do you think any of them suffered from too much competition?

TOP GROSSING MOVIES BY DECADE (NOMINAL GROSSES, DOMESTIC MARKET)

TEENS AND 1920'S
1. Big Parade (1925) $5.5 million
2. Birth of a Nation (1915) $5 million
3. Ben-Hur (1926) $4 million

1930's
1. Gone With the Wind (1939) $76.7 million (not including reissues)
2. Snow White & the Seven Dwarves (1937) $26.7 million (not including reissues)
3. King Kong (1933) $5 million

1940's
1. Bambi (1942) $18.7 million (includes some reissues)
2. Fantasia (1940) $15.5 million (includes some reissues)
3. Pinocchio (1940) $13 million (includes some reissues)

1950's
1. The Ten Commandments (1956) $43 million
2. Ben-Hur (1959) $36.7 million
3. Around the World in 80 Days (1956) $23.1 million

1960's
1. Sound of Music (1965) $79 million (not including reissues)
2. The Graduate (1968) $49.1 million
3. Dr. Zhivago (1965) $46.6 million (not including reissues)

1970's
1. Star Wars (1977) $322.7 million (not including 1997 Special Edition reissue)
2. Jaws (1975) $260 million
3. Grease (1978) $153.1 million

1980's
1. E.T. (1982) $399.8 million (not including 2002 reissue)
2. Return of the Jedi (1983) $263.7 (not including later reissue)
3. Batman (1989) $252.2 million

1990's
1. Titanic (1997) $600.7 million (not including 2012 3D reissue)
2. Star Wars 1 Phantom Menace (1999) $431.1 million (not including 2012 3D reissue)
3. Jurassic Park (1993) $357.1 million

2000's
1. Avatar (2009) $760.5 million
2. Marvel's The Avengers (2012) $623.3 million
3. The Dark Knight (2008) $533 million

Source: gathered from various publications through the years

LIVE LONG AND PROSPER

Week 19: May 8–14, 2009

> *It's a testament to the power of marketing and the movies themselves. Movies matter to people. They are an escape, and audiences continue to find a way to fit them into their busy lives.*

The blockbusters this month are like planes on a runway, one after another waiting to take off. "X-Men Origins: Wolverine" opened the summer movie season with an $85 million gross, and even though it was $13 million less than last year's "Iron Man," it's still a very respectable figure and a strong start for Hollywood considering some of the obstacles the movie was facing: mediocre reviews, the piracy issue of the leaked print, the flu scare (originating in Mexico) and the year's first beautiful weather weekend in the Midwest and other parts of the country. It's always hard to quantify the immediate effect on the box office from any individual outside factor, but when there are several in play, there can be a cumulative effect that can take its toll. That being said, it was a good showing, and industry insiders are optimistic that the summer will keep pumping out consistently strong numbers. There is never a total guarantee that the movie that launches the season will be an unqualified blockbuster. You only have to look back to 2006 when "Mission Impossible 3" opened to only $47 million, leading to the messy departure of Tom Cruise from his Paramount contract.

Speaking of Paramount, they're the next studio on the bubble as they have the $130 million challenge of trying to re-vive their "Star Trek" franchise, all but left for dead after 10 movies and countless television spin-offs. Will it live long and prosper? The studio would like to make a new series of "Star Trek" features, but they have to make this one work first, and that's where the pressure lies. There is some definite overlap with "Wolverine's" audience, and placing it only one week later is a gutsy move that provides no buffer zone of comfort. Will the market absorb both films fine, or will they take a bite out of each other's gross? That will be a pivotal question each week as more and more big films muscle their way into the marketplace and the summer gets more and more crowded. Wherever the studios place their event movies, they believe they have the goods, and they're not afraid of the competition. Often they're right; other times they guess wrong and have to pay the price. With "Star Trek" they might actually be right, and their secret weapon looks to be the quality of the movie itself. The advanced word and early reviews have been terrific, and *Newsweek* even had it as its cover story, though I found it a stretch comparing Spock to President Obama as both being interracial, as if that could somehow have any type of effect on the film itself. To be frank, a lot of summer blockbusters do huge business without being very good, while getting blasted by the critics, so aren't these popcorn movies supposed to be critic proof? For the most part they are, but it never hurts to get strong reviews because those reviews can expand the audience and help convince people on the fence to check it out. Especially when a movie like "Star Trek" has a bunch of young, unknown actors in the cast. Do you think "Iron Man," a lesser comic book character, could have grossed over $300 million domestic without those great reviews and positive word of mouth? No way. When the reviews are describing "Star Trek" as the perfect summer movie, fun, thrilling and action packed, audiences tend to take notice. What people are also going to notice is a cross pro-motional campaign valued at $50 million with partners like Kellogg's, Burger King, Verizon and Nokia spreading extra awareness with their own product tie-ins and campaigns. With Tony the Tiger flashing the "live long and prosper "sign on cereal boxes, Paramount is going after a slightly younger audience than "Wolverine," even though both movies have PG-13 ratings, and their campaign harkens the big summer promotion deals to follow. For the movie itself, Paramount is using the same strategy that helped turn around the James Bond and Batman franchises by re-booting everything, start-ing from scratch and reinventing the series by telling an origin story. It's proven to be a smart way to go, but where those earlier movies went dark and edgy to find their success, "Star Trek" stays true to its roots by being lighter, more optimistic and fun. In these times, that's not a bad commodity to sell. Live long and prosper indeed.

With all the attention the blockbusters receive, it seems like they are the only movies that open in the summer, when in fact there are just as many, if not more, regular type movies from both the studios and independents that will be released throughout the next four months. The problem with the smaller films lies in creating enough noise to get noticed and being able to hook a particular target audience to show up at the theatres. With the media attention focused on big budget spectaculars and the theatres supplying multiple screens to them, it's a challenge to gain traction, both in getting the press and proper number of screens and then being able to hold on to them. The popular term that is used in the summer when distributors choose to open their films against the pre-sold franchises is counter-programming – offering up alternative choices to moviegoers who have different tastes and preferences. Probably the most common counter-programming in the summer is films geared toward women, but other demos include the upscale specialty audience, African Americans and older males. In the past, independent films like "Little Miss Sunshine," "Blair Witch Project," "March of the Penguins" and "Napoleon Dynamite" have become big summer hits, but there have been fewer of them able to break through in the last couple of years. It's funny to think of Meryl Streep as the queen of summer counter-programming, but that's what she has become with "The Devil Wears Prada," "Mamma Mia" and this summer's "Julia & Julia" where she plays Julia Child. She has become a summer force and has a big following of fans. But counter-programming not only happens in the summer. It goes on 52 weeks of the year where distributors are constantly sizing up the competition and placing their movies on weeks where they are going after different audiences than their rivals. It has become standard industry policy and plain old good business strategy.

It's amazing to think of how much of a powerhouse the month of May has become, because the circumstances that made distributors avoid the month in the past still exist. I mentioned the great weather last weekend for the mid-section of the country, and that still comes into play with people wanting to be outdoors after six months of being stuck inside. The old thinking went something like this. In early May, the adults are working on their lawns and gardens, high school kids are in the middle of prom season, and college students are finishing up their semesters buried deep with their final projects and exams. That all still happens, yet the box office delivers the big numbers in spite of these seasonal activities. It's a testament to the power of marketing and the movies themselves. Movies matter to people. They are an escape, and audiences continue to find a way to fit them into their busy lives.

This Week at the Box Office
Weekly Attendance:26,925,745

The only wide release movie that dared to go up against "Star Trek" was "Next Day Air," an urban comedy released by Summit Entertainment. Obviously, the movie had a much different audience than "Star Trek," but looking at the gross below, not all counter-programming proves effective.

Star Trek
Paramount
Opening weekend: $79,204,289
Domestic gross: $257,730,019 66.8%
Foreign gross: $127,950,427 33.2%
Worldwide gross: $385,680,446
Widest release: 4,053 theatres

Next Day Air
Summit
Opening weekend: $4,111,043
Domestic gross: $10,027,047 98.6%
Foreign gross: $145,472 1.4%
Worldwide gross: $10,172,579
Widest release: 1,139 theatres

Rudi y Cursi
Sony Classics
Opening weekend: $211,460

Little Ashes
Regent
Opening weekend: $73,394

Domestic gross: $1,827,660 16.4%
Foreign gross: $9,341,572 83.6%
Worldwide gross: $11,169,232
Widest release: 219 theatres

Adoration
Sony Classics
Opening weekend: $39,358
Domestic gross: $294,244 76.5%
Foreign gross: $90,415 23.5%
Worldwide gross: $384,659
Widest release: 20 theatres

Objectified
Independent
Opening weekend: $8,668
Domestic gross: $134,981
Foreign gross; N/A
Widest release: 1 theatre

The Window
Film Movement
Opening weekend: $2,771
Domestic gross: $11,840
Foreign gross: N/A
Widest release: 2 theatres

Domestic gross: $481,586 62.7%
Foreign gross: $285,981 37.3%
Worldwide gross: $767,567
Widest release: 15 theatres

Julia
Magnolia
Opening weekend: $12,524
Domestic gross: $65,108 4.9%
Foreign gross: $1,268,133 95.1%
Worldwide gross: $1,333,241
Widest release: 4 theatres

Kabei
Strand
Opening weekend: $3,072
Domestic gross: $14,416
Foreign gross: N/A
Widest release: 1 theatre

The History of the Star Trek Franchise

- Star Trek: The Motion Picture - $82,258,456 12/7/79
- Star Trek II: The Wrath of Khan - $78,912,963 6/4/82
- Star Trek III: The Search for Spock - $76,471,046 6/1/84
- Star Trek IV: The Voyage Home - $109,713,132 11/26/86
- Star Trek V: The Final Frontier - $52,210,049 6/9/89
- Star Trek VI: The Undiscovered Country - $74,888,996 12/6/91
- Star Trek: First Contact - $92,027,888 11/22/96
- Star Trek: Generations - $75,671,125 11/18/94
- Star Trek: Insurrection - $70,187,658 12/11/98
- Star Trek: Nemesis - $43,254,000 12/12/2002
- Star Trek - $257,730,019 5/8/2009

Source: Box Office Mojo (Domestic gross only). All films distributed by Paramount.

Conversations with Industry Professionals

Vinnie Bruzzese – President Ipsos MediaCT, World Wide Motion Picture Group, Culver City, CA

The following interview took place on March 29, 2011 in Las Vegas during the CinemaCon convention.

> *"The moment someone is trying to spin you into thinking that their story is going to be bigger than "Avatar," and it's a documentary on rabbits, they should be sent far, far away to the land where Nobody Knows Anything, because there are actually some things you can know."*
>
> —Vinnie Bruzzese

Q: *The thing I've always heard about OTX is that it was the first market research company to do on-line surveys for Hollywood film companies. Tell me about your company and yourself.*

VB: Ipsos is a multibillion-dollar research company with offices in over 65 countries. I head the movie division. I started in at OTX in 2002; we were purchased by Ipsos in 2010 and have worked here for a little over 10 years. It's true we were the first research company in Hollywood to conduct surveys online, and that began in about two years before I joined. There are over 35 full-time employees and 150 part-time and freelance staff who primarily work out of the Culver City and New York City offices; however, our clients and projects are global. Our clients include studios, production companies, financial institutions, individuals, mini-majors, exhibition, and just about any organization that is involved in the movie making process.

Q: *You've just come from heading a panel on non-mainstream audiences. Is there a concerted effort to do more work on independent films in addition to the work you do with studio films?*

VB: We really changed the philosophy of our group in a lot of ways, and one of the things we did was put special attention on independent films, to try to work more with independent filmmakers and small production companies. I always felt that the independent film market kind of got the shaft because they weren't able to get access to the information that the majors were able to get access to because they couldn't afford it; it wasn't in their budget. We decided to create a specialized part of our company with reduced rates. For instance if someone makes a film for under $5 million or purchases a film for less than that, we give them 75% off our regular rates. Normally hosting a research screening costs about $13,000 in addition to renting out a theatre, which averages out to $7,000, so the total price is in the $20,000 range. By renting out smaller screens for independent films, we can offer a full test screening for $5,000, which includes all the survey cards and a focus group discussion.

Q: *That sounds like a fair deal, but don't a lot of independent filmmakers think they know who their audience is already, the typical art house audience?*

VB: That's a narrow way of looking at it because there are all different kinds of lower budget films, not just art films. Producers spend their money to make these films, and often they find themselves without distribution, or without the type of distribution they wanted. In addition to providing them with valuable screening results and other pertinent information, we have taken it to the next level, actually helping films to get noticed and find distribution. If a film coming out of Sundance is looking for distribution and wants to have the movie screened for other distributors, having strong test scores from one of our screenings can help motivate important heads of companies to take a look at it. In today's market, it's difficult to get the right people to see your film unless you have the scores. We have found that the independent audience is only 10% of the film going audience, so independent producers should pursue any advantage they can to get to that audience and win it over.

Q: *How do the distributor screenings work?*

VB: All the results of the screenings are confidential until our clients say otherwise. If the film screens great, they may ask us if we can send it out to distributors. We can set up distributor screenings in Los Angeles and/or New York, which would include a VIP list of thirty distributors and agencies to sit among regular moviegoers, which we also would have arranged to be at the screening. Ideally the movie will screen through the roof, and then, in the best-case scenario, the bidding begins.

Q: *If a distributor of an already acquired film requests a test screening in another city, how does that work?*

VB: We can have people in place in any city the next day whether it's in Chicago or in the middle of Ohio. We have relationships all around the country, well-trained staffs, connections with focus groups, e-train recruiters etc. We can recommend theatres matching up action or art films with the right theatre and audience. We have film specialists and recruiters working just on movies to insure the right audiences. Regardless of where the screening is held, studios and other distributors and producers insist on secrecy. You have to make sure the people recruited have no association with the film industry; you don't want a theatre filled with writers, actors or other insiders. You want a real audience. In Los Angeles, we can replicate a Middle America audience by going down to Orange County. Having this infrastructure is the benefit of being the market leader in this area.

Q: *On your audience surveys, are the first two questions the same as they've been for the last 25 years, "How would you rate this movie?" and "Would you recommend this movie to your friends?"*

VB: This is a problem. The world has changed so much, the audience has changed, but the questions we ask have not changed.

Q: *Is that because of the reference with all the past databases, which include historical scores of every type of movie genre?*

VB: Right, but what we have tried to do is to change these questions and build new norms. For example, the money question on each survey is, "Will you recommend ... ?" That can't predict what a movie will open to because that refers to playability; it gives you an idea about the legs of a film. I also don't know what it means when someone says they will probably recommend a film. That tells me nothing, so we go deeper in the focus groups and ask people how they will go about recommending it. On paper, two people can both be definite recommends, but one person can say they will text friends right out of the screening praising the film and calling it the greatest, while another person may wait until someone asks about it and say, "Yes I saw it. It was good." The key here is what is the level of enthusiasm; that's what our company is trying to accomplish, and that's what separates us from other research firms.

Q: *What would be your second choice after definite recommend on the survey?*

VB: It would be how would you recommend it and how soon would you do it?

Q: *How about the first question, "How Would You Rate This Movie?"*

VB: It's not simply how people are rating the movie, but what's the context? Are they rating it on the movie itself or on the architects of the genre? Are they rating a romantic comedy as compared to "When Harry Met Sally?" So we ask how it would rate with other movies of its genre. That way, you get a better feeling where that rating is coming from.

Q: *So you dig deeper than what the usual questions uncover?*

VB: We try to get behind the words, reasons and behavior. We try to get to the truth. What really matters today is urgency. Our most lucrative form of research is testing trailers and television spots, and we do the same thing with these vital tools. We ask if you are interested, how interested are you? Will you be first in line on opening day, or will you go see it if nothing else is playing? That makes a big difference. [With] Everyone I talked to, there was equal interest in "Salt" and "Inception" before they opened, and "Inception" landed up blowing it away. The definite interest in "Salt" did not have the intensity that "Inception" did. I use the "Animal Farm" quote, "All answers are equal, but some answers are more equal than others." If you can't get to the bottom of someone's interest and how soon they will do something, claiming they're interested or will recommend a movie only has so much meaning.

Q: *What are some of the problems you run into when trying to do more extensive testing?*

VB: The biggest problem is that we get called in too late in the process. We have thousands of screenings, and some of the bigger problems are conceptual. Take a movie like "Mars Needs Moms," one of the biggest flops in history. I'm sorry, but it's a movie about aliens kidnapping moms. Conceptually, that's not a movie a child wants to see. Kids were crying in the theatre I saw it in.

Q: *How early in the process do you want to get involved, the script stage?*

VB: Yes, we do script assessment, and no one else is doing it because you need a database of about ten years to do this kind of work. The way we were able to sell this to writers and producers is telling them the truth, which is right now they have the most power over their vision, but soon there will be 50 people in a room all suggesting changes to their "baby," and since it always gets changed anyway, and wouldn't it be better if they could change it right now with their own vision instead of allowing someone who wasn't involved with the film change it later. We provide the information they need to do that. My message to them is here is the information up front, here are the issues and scenes distributors and audiences are going to have problems with, this is what marketing people will have a problem with. We are doing work on $100 million dollar scripts as well as smaller independent scripts. This process is different when it comes to the financial world though, where it is more about mitigating risk. What is the required opening and playability needed to hit an ultimate? It depends on the correct genre identification and likelihood of profit.

Q: *Can you give me any specifics of how your script assessment works?*

VB: We get scripts sent to us asking us what we think of the script. We have formed a genre committee who meets once a week to discuss the architects of genres. We have a huge database, and we can go back to check screening results of R-rated raunchy comedies or horror movies or even superhero movies and analyze how and why they worked or didn't work and what trends exist. We discover some things like every time the best friend of the lead character in a R-rated comedy isn't there to support the lead at his most crucial point, the heartbreak scene, it affects the pacing of the film, and the audience is going to reject it. Or if you have a horror movie, and you have multiple killers in it, the killers have to be insane. It's the insanity that breeds the fear in horror movies. Then we started creating our own sub-genres of existing prototypes to dig even deeper to see what works and what audiences respond to. The vigilante superhero that becomes more for the people is oddly enough always rich like Bruce Wayne. Audiences respond to billionaires being altruistic and giving back. We have found out it's an additional way to assess scripts and completed films, and we have even expanded it to the marketability side by cross-checking trailers we've worked on to see if the right scenes are included. Another value of our script assessment service is we can estimate a film's box office potential. We may say if you want to do the movie lower the budget. It can do $60 million; don't spend $90 million to make it.

Q: How important are movie titles?

VB: It's hard to come up with the perfect title for every film. More than 100 years of titles have been used. The quality of a film is always more important than the title of a film. That being said, there are some titles in certain genres that are going to hurt you if you choose them. "Snakes on a Plane" screamed out campy. When you call it that, it's a campy movie, nothing more, nothing less, and people are probably going to make fun of it, which they did. But a movie title that perhaps people don't understand at first is not automatically a negative. In a couple of weeks they can get used to it and it will be fine. The important question to ask is, "Can the title hurt you in any way?" If the answer is yes, then you need to change it.

Q: From what your research is telling you, what type of movie has been most consistent for the studios and what type is faring the worst?

VB: The big studio tentpole movies have been the most consistent in their box office performance. The average gross of the top ten highest grossing movies each year, when adjusted for inflation, is around $300 million. That's why the blockbuster is the foundation for every studio. The erosion of ticket sales has come from the bottom up, mostly the independent films that rank from 151 to 200 and then the middle films that rank from 100 to 150. The middle is disappearing, and it's a huge problem created by the industry. The ripple effect is felt by the large multiplexes when they have to depend so much on playing multiple screens on the bigger movies. When any of these movies flop, the theatres don't have anything to cover it. Today's shorter runs don't help. The multiple on a film in the 1970s was 8 or 9, which means if you opened to $4 million you could figure on grossing $36 million. In the 80s the multiple was 5, so if you opened to 10 million you would gross $50 million. Now the multiple is only 2.7%. Movies are not staying around too long, and that's for both mainstream and independent films, the exception being the end of the year Oscar films, which can still enjoy long engagements.

Q: What can the industry be doing better to improve the overall health of the movie business?

VB: During my meetings at this convention, the focus is all on the sensory experience. What the MPAA and NATO, the two large trade groups representing distributors and exhibitors, should be promoting is the joy of moviegoing itself. Remind people that seeing a comedy in a movie theatre surrounded by people laughing with you can't be duplicated in your living room. Create a marketing campaign, "Make a Memory, Go See a Movie," something like that. Remind them to get out, socialize, and smell the popcorn. But the business is so busy pushing digital 3D and other technology that they are losing sight of a basic truth. All our data shows it's the emotional experience moviegoers love, and they are not being reminded of that. The studios own the networks, and they could easily do promotional spots, but they don't. They are missing out on a big opportunity.

Oh, and ban "spin." The moment someone is trying to spin you into thinking that their story is going to be bigger than Avatar, and it is a documentary on rabbits, they should be sent far, far away to the land where Nobody Knows Anything, because there are actually some things you can know.

Q: Where is social networking fitting into the mix?

VB: The studios are constantly trying to figure out how to reach more moviegoers through Facebook and Twitter and other sites. My question to the industry would be if the multiples were so much greater in the 70s and 80s, and multiples are driven by word of mouth, and the multiples keep falling, why is that happening? The rotary phone was the big driver of word of mouth back then, and supposedly more people are communicating today through social networking, so there is a disconnect somewhere. There are a couple of different scenarios; either the industry is putting out horrible product and the word of mouth is bad or they are not utilizing the word of mouth correctly.

Q: Are you saying online buzz isn't reliable?

VB: I have yet to see a steady stream of accurate predictions based on social networking and Twitter. There is no evidence right now that online buzz, however you define it, is indicative of anything. You can notice a movie is getting a lot of activity on Twitter but what does that ultimately mean? I can tell four people about a movie; person A, it doesn't matter, they weren't going to see it anyway; person B is not going to see it because I told him, so he doesn't count; person C was on the fence. They were going to be exposed to the campaign whether I told him or not and they were going to decide then. The only person who counts is the one who wants to go see the movie because I told him. It caused him to find out more about it, or I convinced him somehow to go see the movie. Only in that instance did my recommendation work.

Q: The old tracking was calling people at home to see what their first and second choices of movies for the weekend were. Does anyone do that anymore?

VB: That's not being done anymore. People don't answer their phones, and 20 % don't even have a landline anymore. All the surveys are being done online now. Our company has 65 different quantitative samples. We are constantly doing surveys on any number of topics such as 3D, DVR use, red band trailers, streaming, income and concession preference to name just a few. We have the U.S. Census Department come in and audit our samples, and they gave us an award for the most comprehensive samples among research companies.

Q: What is the incentive for people to fill out online surveys?

VB: People like movies and enjoy sharing their thoughts. Sometimes there are incentives like being entered into a sweepstakes, and other times we partner up with a company that offers something. It takes about 15 minutes to fill out a survey, and older females are the easiest to get with younger males being the hardest.

Q: What are some of the basic lessons you have learned over the years?

VB: Like I mentioned before, the biggest lesson I've learned is a philosophical one; don't give in to the spin. As a researcher, stay true to the numbers because in this industry you have the greatest salespeople in the world. Everyone thinks their movie is amazing, and if it's not, they don't want to hear it's not marketable or it has holes. At the end of the day being a patsy doesn't help anyone. When someone is sitting there spinning their movie, calling it fantastic and saying the screening reports have got to be wrong or the script assessment is wrong, it's very easy to give in to spin. We've all done it, get pumped up on box office projections and ignore the reports. We have to be able listen to what the people are saying and be aware of when we are spinning ourselves. Our job is talking to moviegoers. We are the interpreters of the audience, and their opinions can be whatever it is. All we can do is to say this is what the people are telling us about your film, and this is what we think you should do. There is art and there is commerce and there is ignoring the audience, and if someone wants to make art and put it on their wall they can do it with their own money. But using someone else's money is commerce, and we are here to tell them what the consumer wants, and the less spin the better.

Q: Any last words of wisdom?

VB: I have never seen a movie that's both playable and marketable not do well. If you make a quality product that is easily marketable to your audience, you will make money. Quality product is key to everything.

Q: How many filmmakers set out to make a bad movie?

VB: None of them do. They all think they made a good movie

Q: Thank you for your time and your insight. I appreciate it.

VB: Thank you.

In April, 2013, Ipsos announced that it was selling its theatrical research division, the Motion Picture Group, to a private investment group led by Vinnie Bruzzese. Both parties agreed to a three year partnership that was structured to ensure a seamless transition for clients.

HISTORICAL PERSPECTIVE: STAGING A MARKET RESEARCH SCREENING

In 1998, I was asked to do a market research screening in Chicago for a small independent film that had played at the Slamdance Film Festival in Park City, Utah. A Midwest-based distribution company acquired the film and had a disagreement with the filmmakers who thought they had a movie that could play to suburban audiences as well as it would be able to play to art audiences. In other words they were spinning their own film, so the distributor wanted a test screening in a commercial 1st run suburban theatre to see firsthand how it would play in the suburbs. After picking a theatre and working out the rental price for the screening, the challenge was to fill a 200-seat theatre with an unknown film with a no name cast. For an independent film like this, it's much harder to fill a theatre, so common practice is to hand out flyers/invitations eight to ten times greater than the seating capacity of the theatre. So for a 200-seat auditorium, there were 1,000 invitations handed out, each good for two admissions. The best way to get the flyers into the hands of people who may actually turn out for a free screening is to hang out at the theatre playing the film and get the invites into the hands of active moviegoers who attend that given theatre. The screening was on a Tuesday evening, so the bulk of the invitations were handed out the weekend before.

Perhaps the easiest part of the process was to design the movie survey that the attendees would complete when the screening was over. I had saved many past surveys from my Orion days when there were multiple films tested in the Chicago area which I was present for. The basic format of a research survey hadn't changed much over the years. Whatever experience a person has in his or her career, it's always smart to take notes, pay close attention and learn from it because you never know when you may called on to do something similar. Then when you are asked if you could do something that you never actually did before, you can say, "Sure, I could do that." Without revealing the actual name of the movie, the following is the list of questions on the movie survey that I used:

How would you rate this movie? (Mark One)
- Excellent
- Very Good
- Good
- Fair

Would you recommend this movie to a friend? (Mark One)
► Definitely
► Probably
► Probably Not
► Definitely Not

Would you see this movie again?
► Yes
► No

Which of the following describe your reasons for coming to this preview?
(Mark as many as apply)
► The movie sounded interesting
► I liked the title
► The image on the flyer looked interesting
► A friend invited me
► Other (Specify)_____

Had you heard about (name of film) before you were invited to this preview?
► Yes
► No
► If yes, where did you hear about it? _____

Which of the follow words or phrases best describe (name of film)
(Check as many as apply)
► Entertaining Different/unusual
► Action packed Interesting characters
► Funny Fast paced
► Too silly Has a good story
► Good music Slow/boring

Please list what one or two things you enjoyed most and enjoyed the least about the movie.

_____

_____

Did (name of film) remind you of any past movies you have seen? Yes_____No_____
If yes, please name them.

What single thing stands out the most in your mind about (name of film)?

_____

Generally speaking, how do you feel about the way the movie ended? (Mark one)
- ▸ Primarily liked it
- ▸ Primarily disliked it
- ▸ Liked it and disliked it in parts

Please indicate your age? What was the last grade of school you completed?
- ▸ Under 12 (Check one)
- ▸ 12-17 Some high school or less
- ▸ 18-20 Completed high school
- ▸ 21-24 Trade school
- ▸ 25-34 Some college
- ▸ 35-49 College or more
- ▸ 50 and over

Please indicate your sex:
Male _____ Female_____

To say the screening didn't go over well with the suburban audience would be an understatement. People were fleeing early and had to be corralled to complete the survey. The first two questions are always the most important ones and are judged by the number of respondents who mark the top two boxes of each question. A film company would like to see between 55% - 60% of the audience choose the first two boxes of the first question and 75-80% for the second question. Anything less and the movie is considered suspect. With this screening, 9% of the respondents marked either of the first two boxes of the first question and 19% did so on the second question. A terrible score.

The movie was too slight, offbeat and weird for the suburban audience, but the poor reaction didn't surprise the distributor who pretty much knew what he had on his hands. At times research screenings are held to prove a point with filmmakers who have an unrealistic view of their own movie. This was the case here. Each research screening includes a focus group following the movie with ten to fifteen audience members sticking around and discussing the movie, which I led and moderated. Whereas many of the questions on the survey are considered quantitative with their one-word responses, the focus group becomes a qualitative experience, which explores feelings and more open-ended questions. This part of the process didn't go any better for the film.

That was the only time I ever conducted a market research screening. It was an interesting process to go through, and I'm glad I did it, but it was a lot of hard work to pull off, and I still wasn't able to fill the entire 200-seat theatre. I wrote a full report and analysis of the screening, and after the filmmakers read it (they did not attend the screening because they were in Los Angeles), they were still in denial and didn't believe that so many people could dislike their movie. When the film actually opened, it had a very short life in some art houses and never did make it out to the suburbs.

For filmmakers who can't afford to hire a professional researcher, it's possible to do a variation of a test screening following the above order of questions. The important thing to remember is to get the right demographic mix that the movie deserves without inviting anyone you know to the screening so you can get objective responses. I seem to recall I charged $3,500 as a fee to conduct the screening, but unlike Vinnie Bruzzese and Ipsos, had no infrastructure and past database of films to back me up. With Ipsos now offering a full test screening for $5,000 for smaller independent films, it provides low-budget filmmakers with access to the top research professionals in the field at a very affordable price.

Week 19: Questions for Discussion

1. What has Ipsos Media done to better their relations with independent films in the area of market research? Name at least three different ways a research screening can help one of these films.

2. Do you think there is any downside to conducting a market research screening for a smaller film?

3. Vinnie Bruzzese refers to the infrastructure of his company as a benefit. Discuss what that infrastructure is and what he sees as his company's advantages and strengths?

4. When it comes to getting as accurate a response as possible to figuring out a person's words and behavior, what is the one word that matters most? Discuss and provide an example of what this means.

5. Define what the statement "don't give in to the spin" means. What makes it so difficult for people in the industry to accomplish that?

6. After reading the above interview, what are your feelings toward market research and the need for it in today's movie marketplace?

7. Discuss if you have ever been involved in a market research screening or have completed any kind of movie survey and what that experience was like.

8. How important do you think a movie's title is to the ultimate success of the film? Do you remember either going to see a movie or staying away from one based on its title? Look at all the movies currently playing in your market and choose what you feel is the best title and the worst title. Discuss.

LOOKING FOR POSITION AND FINDING IT

Week 20: May 15–21, 2009

You need nerves of steel and deep pockets to sit at the big table, and that's why there are only six chairs, one each for the six major studios.

In the holy game of poker the smart players always play for position. When it comes their way, they know how to take advantage of the situation, whether to be aggressive from the start, lie in the weeds, bluff like hell or take that final raise. You can think of the Motion Picture Marketplace as a giant poker game, and distributors have to decide when to hold them, when to fold them and when to go all in. It's an expensive game, especially in the summer, with hundreds of millions of dollars in the pot. You need nerves of steel and deep pockets to sit at the big table, and that's why there are only six chairs, one each for the six major studios.

Position is one of those key concepts in the movie business that can't be overstated. It can be the deciding factor between success and failure, whether it's choosing the correct release date or marketing a movie in a specific way to either a mass or niche audience. The executives who make those decisions get paid a lot of money to make the right calls. It certainly looks like Paramount made all the right calls with "Star Trek" after it grossed $79 million in its opening weekend and made believers out of a lot of people, both fans and non-fans alike. More importantly, they find themselves in great position. Putting the movie between "Wolverine" and "Angels and Demons" took guts, and they won the bet by wrestling away the position "Wolverine" enjoyed by being the first summer movie out of the blocks. With "Wolverine" losing a massive 70% of its audience, "Star Trek" stripped it of all of its mojo, basically making it a non-factor in the weeks to come. By guessing that "Wolverine" would not be as formidable of a foe with its story focus on only one of the X-Men's characters and knowing that "Angels and Demons" was going after an older, adult audience, placing "Star Trek" on May 8th proved to be a great move, and now it's poised to build on its opening numbers. That is, at least for another week or until the sequels of "Night at the Museum" and "Terminator" open on back-to-back days. It's never easy to achieve, but if "Star Trek" can go into its 3rd weekend with a head of steam, it has a chance to hold its own and blast past $200 million at the box office.

That is, $200 million in the domestic market. With the big summer blockbusters, it's not a choice of either doing business at home or abroad, it has become a necessity to be able to gross well throughout the world in order to recoup the huge production and marketing costs that the studios have riding on their bets. Paramount realized the "Star Trek" series had never done particularly well overseas, and they knew they had to go to work to change that. The most recent "Star Trek" film was released seven years ago and did an anemic $27 million overseas. The studio put their publicity machine to work by sending director J.J. Abrams on a tour of several important countries months ahead of release to show footage to theatre owners and journalists and to talk the movie up. Then Paramount hosted a number of special Premiere screenings before opening day to seal the deal. All that extra marketing paid off with an opening international weekend gross of $35 million with many more territories yet to open.

Sony's "Angels and Demons" isn't in too bad of a position itself. No one is opening a wide national release against it, which is the ultimate compliment from rival distributors. The movie also stands out as the only one of the big May releases geared to an adult audience, and with Tom Hanks heading the cast, has the most star power of the bunch. From all indications, it's a much better film than ""The Da Vinci Code," which pretty much got critically panned and left audiences somewhat cold, but still grossed a staggering $758 million in worldwide grosses. Sony is positioning "Angels and

Demons" as an action-packed conspiracy thriller and not going out of their way to market it to the Christian audience, which is a smart move. And why not? It's a mass appeal film with a ready-made world audience, and the studio really doesn't have to do much niche marketing to find its audience. Sony is aware that many Catholic moviegoers are going to see it anyway, despite some mild protests from the Catholic Church. It's a piece of fiction. It's entertainment, and a little controversy never hurts. After "The Da Vinci Code" brought in $540 million in overseas grosses, "Angels and Demons" is in position to do it again and be one of the more potent international grossers of 2009.

There are close to 40,000 screens in the country, and
80% of them show paid ads before movies.

In-Theatre Advertising

Just as studios depend on international revenues to support their business model, movie theatres look for additional revenue streams to support their businesses. It's expensive to open your doors 365 days a year, and any additional revenue helps to keep those doors open. That's why you see ads on the big screen before the movies begin. I've never been a fan of them myself, but I've come to tolerate them in the context of today's economic realities. For theatre owners, it's not a primary source of revenue, but it has become a dependable side revenue, and if it wasn't there, it would be missed, especially with concession income taking a hit during the recession. There are close to 40,000 screens in the country, and 80% of them show paid ads before movies. Pre-show advertising has become more than a $500 million industry and one of North America's fastest growing advertising media segments. Pre-show advertising started creeping into the industry in the late 1970s and early 1980s when it was a hot button issue. Several of the studios and portions of the moviegoing audience were fiercely opposed to this invasion of screen space. Walt Disney Pictures fought against it the hardest and for years wouldn't book films in theatres that ran commercials before features. Eventually all the studios relented, and bans were lifted as it became harder and harder to enforce them. It seems that moviegoers more or less accept the ads now as standard practice with fewer complaints and protests. However, there were a couple of nuisance lawsuits a few years ago by moviegoers suing individual theatres for displaying incorrect movie showtimes and being forced to sit through ads before they got to the feature. They wanted the price of a ticket as well as their time wasted back. At least they received some publicity for their efforts. But for that very reason, having a captured audience in a darkened theatre watching a huge screen has made screen advertising such a lucrative business for the companies selling the advertising and for the theatres themselves.

Two companies dominate the pre-show advertising business, NCM Network, co-owned by the three largest theatre circuits AMC Theatres, Regal Entertainment and Carmike Cinemas, and the privately owned Screenvision. NCM controls ads for 19,000 screens, and Screenvision services 15,000 screens. Since the national advertising is based on the amount of people viewing the ads, the biggest grossing theatres with the most screens generate the most ad revenues and can earn up to $250,000 a year in extra income. Pre-show advertising is here to stay because of those simple economics. The money is too easy to pass up, and it helps the bottom line. However, there is one type of theatre that is going the opposite way in which pre-show advertising does not fit into its business model, and that is the upscale in-theatre dining cinemas that are starting to pop up around the country. There are only a few hundred of these plush theatres, but it is an emerging trend, and we'll be seeing more of them in the coming years. These theatres offer an upscale experience for adults, and one of the tradeoffs of higher admission prices is a policy of no ads shown before the movies. It becomes more of a pure movie going experience with perks like a gourmet burger and a salad with a glass of wine to wash it down.

Movie theatres have proven to be a strong cash generating business over the years and are now creating new ways to increase revenues for themselves. Is this the time for studios to think about getting back into the theatre business like they did in the 1980s and 90s when government policies eased anti-trust laws to allow studios to once again own movie theatres? Don't count on it. It didn't take too long for studios such as Sony and Universal to realize theatres can become a cash drain in a hurry when business slows down, eventually deciding to cash in their chips and leave exhibition to the exhibitors. They wanted to concentrate on only one game of poker at a time, the one they know best, with the market power to go all in whenever they saw fit.

This Week at the Box Office   *Weekly Attendance: 26,002,489*

With all the attention turning to blockbusters, smaller films continue to struggle, and another independent film with a major star flopped over the weekend. "Management," starring Jennifer Aniston, opened on 212 screens in limited runs and averaged only $1,700 a screen for the three-day weekend. That figures out to less than 200 people a screen over the weekend, and even though the distributor said exit polls reported that people liked the movie, there weren't enough of them to help future word of mouth. On a limited release, distributors hope they can attract at least 600 to 800 patrons per screen, which would give a film enough traction in the marketplace to have a chance for an extended run and to allow any good word of mouth to spread. Aniston has appeared on annual lists of top paid actresses for her drawing power and popularity, but there are certain films where that doesn't matter. "Management" is one such film. Saddled with a weak title, a muddled story line and sketchy marketing, the movie never had much of a chance to succeed in theatres, regardless of who starred in it. With some theatrical awareness however, there's always Netflix and Redbox down the road.

Angels and Demons
Sony
Opening weekend: $46,204,168
Domestic gross: $133,375,846 27.4%
Foreign gross: $352,554,970 72.6%
Worldwide gross: $485,930,816
Widest release: 3,527 theatres

The Brothers Bloom
Summit
Opening weekend: $90,400
Domestic gross: $3,531,756 63.9%
Foreign gross: $1,999,088 36.1%
Worldwide gross: $5,530,764
Widest release: 209 theatres

Summer Hours
IFC
Opening weekend: $49,484
Domestic gross: $1,647,083 21.6%
Foreign gross: $6,002,257 78.4%
Worldwide gross: $7,659,258
Widest release: 50 theatres

Management
IDP/Samuel Goldwyn
Opening weekend: $375,916
Domestic gross: $934,658 38.9%
Foreign gross: $1,467,085 61.1%
Worldwide gross: $2,401,743
Widest release: 212 theatres

Jerichow
Cinema Guild
Opening weekend: $8,042
Domestic gross: $60,105 6.7%
Foreign gross: $845,221 93.3%
Worldwide gross: $905,600
Widest release: 3 theatres

Not Forgotten
Anchor Bay
Opening weekend: $18,468
Domestic gross: $53,744 37.8%
Foreign gross: $88,311 62.2%
Worldwide gross: $142,055
Widest release: 4 theatres

Big Man Japan

Magnolia

Opening weekend: $7,133

Domestic gross: $40,257 0.4%

Foreign gross: $9,722,448 99.6%

Worldwide gross: $9,763,244

Widest release: 5 theatres

Death Factory Bloodletting

Nocturnal Features

Opening weekend: $3,822

Domestic gross: $4,638

Foreign gross: N/A

Widest release: 1 theatre

Week 20: Questions for Discussion

1. What are the main criteria used to determine the amount of revenue movie theatres can earn playing paid advertising before their trailers and features begin?

2. What is your feeling toward seeing ads on the big screen? Have you ever been influenced to purchase any product you saw from any of the ads?

MEMORIAL DAY WEEKEND AND THE CANNES FILM FESTIVAL

Week 21: May 22–28, 2009

---

*In any business, the lowest barrier of entry tends to be the
most competitive, and the movie business is no different.*

As the Memorial Day weekend gets under way with two more big studio movies hitting the screens in North America, the Cannes Film Festival and Film Market in the south of France begin to wind down their ten-day runs. The dynamics, cultures and business models of the three events could not be more different from each other. Yet, if you take a closer look at them and recognize what is happening, basic truths and realities spring forward. That says a lot about where the movie business is today and points to where it's headed toward in at least the near future. Three different types of films are on display that represent the full spectrum of budgets, styles and expectations:

- ▸ The big budget studio franchise movie
- ▸ The character-driven, high-end art film
- ▸ The cheaply-made B movie genre

At this particular moment in time, only one of the three types of films is on firm ground, and that of course is the studio franchise movie. What the studios are selling in these tough economic times is the same thing they have been producing for years, familiar larger-than-life entertainment that resonates and plays throughout the world, the safest of safe bets for both the studios and audiences alike. If audiences are going to pluck down their hard-earned money, they want to know what they're going to get in return. So we get another "Terminator" and another "Night at the Museum" because an important holiday weekend like Memorial Day demands big movies with proven track records that can deliver. How the studios are selling these two movies says everything you need to know about the selling of summer blockbusters. Warner Bros. is touting "Terminator Salvation" as "The Summer's Biggest Thrill Ride" before summer has officially arrived, and Fox is marketing "Night at the Museum: Battle of the Smithsonian" with "The Biggest Comedy in History Starts Friday." Hollywood knows too well that subtlety has no place in the summer. What's a bit surprising is to see two large tentpole movies opening against each other, though the audiences for the two movies are completely different and shouldn't interfere with each other – the male action sci-fi audience for one and the PG family-friendly audience for the other. On paper, there should be room for both movies to potentially gross between $60 and $80 million over the extended weekend (including Thursday evening and Monday grosses), and if they can accomplish that, it will be five out of five for the May blockbusters with one more to go on May 29th, Disney/Pixar's "UP."

For the most part, these pre-sold blockbusters take film critics out of the equation, and the critics realize that. Summer is far from their favorite season to review films, and they look forward to the fall when the serious film season begins. Famed critic Pauline Kael used to take the summer off for that very reason. Even though I said last week that strong reviews can only help the big summer movies, there are certain movies that play better with audiences than with critics and don't really need that critical support to do well. "Night at the Museum" is one such franchise. I've already seen several two star reviews for "Battle of the Smithsonian," but that shouldn't have much effect on the performance of the film. In its own way, it's a franchise that has presented a positive message about how fun and exciting museums can be. The first film in the series has already inspired museums around the country to host all night events for families to tour the museums with flashlights, which sounds very cool. The films may be silly, but people from the ages of 8 to 80 love these movies, and what's wrong with that? We can all probably use a little more silly in our lives.

The critics are much more at home at the Cannes Film Festival where their views on the latest art films carry much more weight, though not as much as they used to. The business for high-end art films continues to be challenged by a variety of factors that when taken together presents an alarming landscape:

▶ The credit crunch brought on by the worldwide recession is squeezing margins for the financiers, distributors and exhibitors alike, where margins were small to begin with.

▶ Studios like Warner Bros. and Paramount retreating from the specialty film market. The studios' deep pockets in the past helped independent movies cross over into the mainstream, led by Miramax using Disney's money so well in the 90s when they turned a challenging film like "The Crying Game" into a $60,000,000 hit. We're not seeing that kind of support now.

▶ Critics themselves being on the endangered list with newspapers continuing to struggle to stay alive. Critical support has always been a vital component in the success of art films, but a number of important critics have lost their jobs and fewer people are reading newspapers, so a backbone of this market is getting shakier every day.

▶ Theatrical distribution is getting harder to come by with fewer viable distributors, coupled with the decline in the DVD market, which has taken away an all-important safety net and revenue source. The money doesn't add up like it used to.

There continues to be more of a shift to watching art movies at home rather than in movie theatres with Video-on-Demand being at the forefront of the movement. Led by distributors IFC and Magnolia, companies which have a cable component in place through their ownerships, their specialty films have been either going out day and date with the theatrical release or even premiering on cable before theatres play them. More and more business models are being rolled out, but they're still in the early stages, so the jury is still out on how lucrative this business can be for both distributors and filmmakers. Any distribution is better than no distribution, but will the dollars add up? Looking back at the last four decades of the modern-day American independent art film business show that it follows the classic arc of a traditional business cycle that is often experienced by either a specific company or industry:

▶ 1970s – The latter part of the decade starts putting the infrastructure in place for a new independent business to emerge.

▶ 1980s – The actual birth and growth period, fueled by new talent, access, demand and home video.

▶ 1990s – The maturity, when it peaked with the financial support from the studios and multiple Academy Award wins.

▶ 2000s – The decline, for reasons stated above, in addition to the entire scene becoming overheated, too commercialized and too expensive.

Business cycles have peaks and valleys, and some businesses bounce back while others wither away. The art film business still has a future and should bounce back during the next few years, but it may take some time, and it's sure to look different than it does now.

While the traditional art films at Cannes are hoping to find viable distribution, another kind of movie is screening at the Market portion of the event. These are the so-called B movies, and there are 1,500 completed genre movies being shown to buyers representing all the major territories in the world. Horror, crime, action movies, erotic thrillers, zombies, serial killers – basically the bottom feeders that constitute the lowest barrier of entry into the movie business. Movies with titles like "Stripped Naked," "House of the Devil," "Vigilante" and "The Invisible Woman" to name just a few.

In the past, there has been a business model for these movies consisting of DVD and international television sales, but those avenues have dried up considerably with the worldwide recession and changing audience and buyers' preferences. The DVD business has slowed everywhere with some countries hurt more than others due to film piracy, and television money has seen a downturn with falling ad sales which has led to fewer film acquisitions. The international buyers are looking for higher budgeted product with a little star power now. In any business, the lowest barrier of entry tends to be the most competitive, and the movie business is no different. There is a tremendous over supply of cheaply made genre movies in every corner of the globe with nowhere to go and no one to sell to. Why is this fact important, and who should care about this? Well, for starters, how about anyone with a camera, whether coming out of film school or not, with a dream of making that $100,000 horror or crime thriller and selling it for big bucks? Going lowbrow has never been more risky regardless of the cost. There are just too many of them already. Come to think of it, it's the same situation with the very low-budget, character-driven art film competing in the highbrow film festival circuit. Due to very affordable digital cameras that have brought down the cost of making an entry-level film, the glut of films runs deep. There will always be filmmakers who will need to make their movies to fulfill their artistic ambitions and to express themselves without any concern for commercial realities. I respect that, but having a sense of where the marketplace is and how it operates can make a big difference. A little knowledge can go a long way. Even with the smaller movies costing less these days, someone still has to come up with the money, and filmmakers should respect that too.

This Week at the Box Office

Weekly Attendance: 34,917,000

Night at the Museum: Battle of the Smithsonian

20th Century Fox
Opening weekend: $54,173,286
Domestic gross: $177,243,721 42.9%
Foreign gross: $235,862,449 57.1%
Worldwide gross: $413,106,170
Widest release: 4,101 theatres

Terminator Salvation

Warner Brothers
Opening weekend: $42,558,390
Domestic gross: $125,322,469 33.7%
Foreign gross: $246,030,532 66.3%
Worldwide gross: $371,353,001
Widest release: 3,602 theatres

Dance Flick

Paramount
Opening weekend: $10,643,536
Domestic gross: $25,794,018 81.6%
Foreign gross: $5,776,985 18.4%
Worldwide gross: $31,439,140
Widest release: 2,459 theatres

Easy Virtue

Sony Classics
Opening weekend: $110,443
Domestic gross: $2,656,784 14.4%
Foreign gross: $15,807,009 85.6%
Worldwide gross: $18,463,793
Wide release: 255 theatres

The Girlfriend Experience

Magnolia
Opening weekend: $202,965
Domestic gross: $695,840 69.0%
Foreign gross: $312,122 31.0%
Worldwide gross: $1,007,962
Widest release: 48 theatres

O' Horten

Sony Classics
Opening weekend: $24,938
Domestic gross: $302,232 17%
Foreign gross: $1,476,559 83%
Worldwide gross: $1,778,791
Widest release: 23 theatres

The Boys: The Sherman Brothers' Story
Buena Vista
Opening weekend: $14,632
Domestic gross: $55,513
Foreign gross: N/A
Widest release: 5 theatres

Burma VJ
Oscilloscope
Opening weekend: $5,554
Domestic gross: $51,674 41.8%
Foreign gross: $71,805 58.2%
Worldwide gross: $123,477
Widest release: 3 theatres

Week 21: Questions for Discussion

1. How do business cycles affect specific industries and their overall performance? Why is it important for filmmakers and managers alike to understand at what point in the cycle the independent film industry is at any given time?

2. Discuss the differences between the Cannes Film Festival and the Cannes Film Market. What types of activities occur at the two events?

3. Explain the terms "bottom feeders" and "low barrier to entry" as it applies to film markets. Is this a good business to be in, and how has the world of genre movies changed?

Lana's Rain: The 10-Year Timeline of an Independent Film

▶ 1996 – Michael Ojeda, Joel Goodman and Jeff Dillard form Reigning Pictures, Ojeda begins writing script for "Lana's Rain."

▶ 1997–98 – Limited Partnership created to raise production financing. Script goes through five different drafts.

▶ July 1999 – Production begins on a $215,000 budget. The actual shooting takes seven weeks but is spread out over six months to take advantage of Chicago's changing seasons.

▶ March 2000 – Michael Ojeda begins editing movie.

▶ January 2001 – David Sikich and John Iltis sign on as producer reps/publicists.

▶ February 2001 – Interviews with director and producers conducted; press kit created.

▶ March 2001 – Actors called back for filming two additional scenes; unit photographer hired to gather more photos.

▶ April 2001 – Distributor screenings held in Los Angeles and New York. A video cut is projected.

▶ May 2001 – No offers for distribution are made. Consensus is movie is too long at 120 minutes. Ojeda starts editing to shorten film by 15 to 20 minutes.

▶ June to Sept. 2001 – Submitted to following festivals: Montreal, Toronto, Venice, Telluride, Sundance & Slamdance. Rejected by all of them.

▶ October 2001 – Editing continues; new music composer hired.

▶ November 2001 – Search for international distributor to help in funding postproduction.

▶ December 2001 – Submitted to 2002 South by Southwest Film Festival and is rejected.

- February 2002 – Harmony Gold signs on as international distributor and commits $20,000 to pay for finishing funds. Submitted to and rejected by Tribeca and Cannes Film Festivals.

- March 2002 – Covitek Technicolor Lab in Montreal is hired to do the postproduction work, including cutting the Super 16mm negative and producing a 35mm answer print.

- May 2002 – Still unhappy about the music in the film, Michael Ojeda hires composer William Brown, and his score becomes the dominant music in the film.

- July 2002 – Submitted to Chicago International Film Festival and is accepted.

- September 2002 – Harmony Gold amends International contract by agreeing to increase their finishing funds to $50,000 upon delivery of all materials.

- October 2002 – "Lana's Rain" has its World Premiere at the Chicago International Film Festival with a newly created 35mm print. *Chicago Tribune* mini-review produces a strong quote, which will eventually land up on the theatrical poster.

- Nov. 2002–Jan. 2003 – "Lana's Rain" print is sent to L.A. and starts screening in distributor screening rooms in search of a distributor.

- February 2003 – Harmony Gold hosts a screening at the American Film Market in Los Angeles for additional foreign distributors.

- April 2003 – Harmony Gold terminates international agreement on grounds that all delivery materials were not delivered on time. $50,000 in finishing funds never paid.

- Summer 2003 – The long search for distribution continues with individual screenings for smaller distributors who haven't seen the film yet.

- September 2003 – David Sikich decides to distribute "Lana's Rain" through ISA Releasing and proceeds to form a Limited Partnership to raise P&A money.

- October 2003 – The Music Box theatre in Chicago is dated for the theatrical launch set for February 27, 2004. Work begins on creating the poster and trailers as vendors are hired.

- November 2003 – "Lana's Rain" has its international debut at the Milan international Film Festival. Oksana Orlenko, star of "Lana's Rain," is awarded Best Actress.

- December 2003 – Word-of-mouth screenings are held in Eastern European communities. Movie website is introduced.

- February 2004 – "Lana's Rain" opens at the Music Box with an opening week gross of $17,000.

- April to June 2004 – Chicago success can't be duplicated in Los Angeles, Washington, D.C. and San Diego, and theatrical runs end with a total gross of $44,000.

- July 2004 – DVD deal is completed with Image Entertainment with a $75,000 advance.

- January 2005 – DVD is released with 18,000 units shipped.

- January 2006 – Limited Partnership is dissolved with little hope of additional revenues. Each of the eleven P&A investors recoup 50% of their invested amount from the DVD advance. Film is returned to Reigning Pictures.

Conversations with Industry Professionals

Steven Friedlander – Executive Vice President of Theatrical Distribution, CBS Films, Los Angeles, CA

The following interview took place on March 30, 2011 in Las Vegas during the CinemaCon convention and updated in 2012.

"You have to fight every day, every week, for your films and try to maximize the value of every screen you play. Failure isn't an option."

Steven Friedlander

Q: *CBS Films is a new distributor. Can you talk about the process of getting the company up and running?*

SF: I was hired in 2008, and 2009 was a year of putting together a distribution company, looking for office space, hiring a sales staff; these things take a while. DreamWorks took almost three years setting up their company before their first film was released.

Q: *I imagine it's a lot easier to start up a new company in today's world compared to years ago when a distributor needed to also open branch offices?*

SF: No question about it. The barrier to entry is a lot lower, cheaper and more manageable. Everything is done out of one office in Los Angeles, and we cover the entire country with seven sales people including a general sales manager and two division managers. There are two cashiers and an operations person and also a marketing staff to round out the staff.

Q: *You have a lot of experience with independent film companies after having worked for Fine Line Features and Warner Independent. How big of a blow was it when Warner Brothers announced the closing of New Line, Warner Independent and Picturehouse, all their affiliated independent divisions?*

SF: New Line was first to be closed in the early part of 2008, we were next, and we saw the handwriting on the wall. It's never a good thing when a division is axed. Warner Independent had some nice successes like "March of the Penguins" which grossed $77 million after the film was bought for $500,000 at Sundance. Morgan Freeman was brought on to be the narrator, and the music was re-done, but that film was highly profitable. Warner Brothers just didn't feel good about the independent business anymore and made the decision to get out. The irony was the last film we developed and were set to release was "Slumdog Millionaire." I pushed hard for them to keep that film, we tried everything we could to persuade them, and it's not like they didn't understand what we were saying, it's just their final decision was made, and it wasn't their business model anymore. We made the call to Fox Searchlight, who had seen the film, and sold the film to them while keeping a piece of the film for Warner Bros. But we could have had the whole thing. We bought North American rights for $4 million, and the movie went on to gross $141 million and win Best Picture of the Year.

Q: *Do you think studio involvement was ultimately bad for independent films?*

SF: There is something to the fact that they overspent and drove up acquisition prices at festivals. It's a fact you can't throw a movie on 2,000 screens and try to force it to gross $40 to $60 million instead of allowing it to grow organically for eight to ten weeks. Then again, studios helped out their independent divisions with their clout and larger presence in the marketplace. Warner Brothers really helped "March of the Penguins" when it attached its trailer to the prints of "Charlie and the Chocolate Factory," which put the trailer in front of a large mainstream audience. For that advantage to work you have to have an excellent trailer, and "March of the Penguins" had a terrific one. But the truth of the matter is that it's not a bottom line business for studios; there are no sequels, no merchandising, no guaranteed revenue streams running through it. It takes as much work to do a trailer and poster for a film going out on two screens as it does for "Harry Potter," so the studio felt they could use their resources in other ways. But there were important intangibles for the studio to be involved with independent filmmakers as a way to find new talent. Many directors behind big Warner movies were discovered out of Sundance, David Fincher, Brian Singer, Darren Aronofsky and Steven Soderbergh all started as art house guys.

Q: *What's the business model for CBS Films?*

SF: It' similar to Summit Entertainment and Relativity where you have to do more commercial films than the smaller films. Small films alone can't cut it anymore unless you are Sony Classics. They have it down to a science because they have been doing art films for so many years. Having a strong pay TV deal with Showtime is a position of strength because pay deals are harder to come by these days. We get a lot of added value with CBS, which hopefully will help us as a theatrical distributor. An interesting statistic I saw is that 90% of Americans see something on CBS every day of their lives. We are very fortunate to receive extra promotional help from CBS radio, CBS outdoor and from CBS Internet sites.

Q: *Where is the money coming from to finance the movies?*

SF: The company is doing some retooling now, and there has been a change with a new COO. The business model is changing, and we have a target of around six films a year. Originally we were set up to take a worldwide risk, and the company was putting up all the financing while having another studio handle international distribution for a fee. That's a dangerous and expensive game to play. You need a significant amount to do it that way with a full slate of pictures. Our new model is more flexible – split rights, domestic only, foreign pre-sales – all different ways to minimize risk while protecting our potential upside.

Q: *Is it a little worrisome that you don't have much coming out for the rest of the year?*

SF: Exhibitors would like a steadier flow of product from us and in turn that would help us out in gaining more strength in the marketplace. We have some lag time with movies in development and will focus more on strategic acquisitions. We bought "The Mechanic" last year, and it grossed $30 million, so that was a great purchase. While there is a lull I'll be sending my sales people on the road to meet exhibitors, look at theatres and cross train some people to learn each other's territories. Later in 2011, CBS Films acquired the supernatural thriller "The Woman in Black" which accumulated over $54 million at the domestic marketplace and became the highest grossing film in our company's history.

Q: *The industry has moved to firm terms with exhibitors. Are you able to get the same type of deals?*

SF: Exhibitors don't mind firm terms as long as they are reasonable and fair. Each movie has to be priced individually, and we can't just ram terms down their throats and say take it or leave it.

Q: *Have the main revenue generators changed for today's movies?*

SF: The three main revenue generators are still theatrical, DVD and television, but they are all fluctuating from where they have been. Streaming, VOD and downloading haven't produced any significant revenue yet, so distributors are basically saying they are going to make fewer films. Marketing costs haven't gone down, and audiences are splintered more, so we have to be more innovative with our money. The answer is to take fewer risks and more sure bets, and the result is what we see in the theatres each week. So if an exhibitor has a 30-screen theatre and depended on 200 films a year to play, and all of a sudden there are only 140 films to play instead, that theatre is forced to hold movies longer and play more double prints of movies. There are hundreds of theatres playing movies on multiple screens because they need to fill screens, not that certain movies actually need them. That's why you can walk into a theatre during the first week of a successful movie and find ten people in a particular auditorium. It's either show new movies on extra screens or else hold an $80 gross of an older movie.

Q: What's your take on digital 3D and how it has been handled by the industry?

SF: We have always been an industry that has been successful in creating a need in people whether it's a need to see a particular movie by creating a brand or introducing new technology, bigger and wider pictures, better sound, whatever it's been. However with 3D, it seems like we are pushing it down the public's throat by making so many 3D movies before we have seen if it's a long-term need of the consumer. Now we are seeing a leveling off; we forced this technology into the marketplace, and we're surprised to see a number of consumers rejected it. People who don't like wearing glasses when watching a movie, or it makes them dizzy, or the price is too high. It doesn't make a lot of movies special and produces a darker image. Digital 3D has its share of issues. With admissions either flat or down, I'm all for working to build a bigger pie for distributors and exhibitors to share in. The industry is looking at several things, and I think Lionsgate did a very interesting thing with "Lincoln Lawyer" when they ran a promotion with Groupon for reduced $5.00 tickets on opening weekend. Research revealed most of the people who used the tickets would not have seen the film otherwise, and those people loved the movie and spread such positive word of mouth that the movie had one of the best second weekend holds of the year. A promotion like that helped grow the audience, but questions still remain concerning long-term profitability and growth.

Q: Is marketing much more front loaded than it used to be?

SF: Yes, and we did it to ourselves. As an industry we created a need to be number one each weekend. A few years ago, 75% of the advertising budget was spent pre-opening day and 25% after. Now it can be 97% before, 3% after, so marketing dollars are dropped very quickly because after the first weekend you know what you have.

Q: In five or ten years do you think the dominant advertising cost will still be on network and cable television?

SF: It will be more interstitials, stuff audiences have to find, things that are worked into programming. New kinds of on-site movie theatre advertising will be more prevalent. Countries like Spain are already doing some things we haven't seen yet in America. When you walk up to a theatre like the Cinema 17 in Madrid, your mobile device picks up a signal and it welcomes you. While you are waiting, you will be able to watch trailers or perhaps see behind-the-scenes footage of the movie you will be seeing, those types of things.

Q: How are you judged by the job you do?

SF: Dating our movies is most important. There are a myriad of factors we take into account when determining the best date for a movie to open whether it is a wide release or a platform release. In regards to domestic distribution, how many screens did we get, how many of those theatres are among the top 10 or 20 screens in the country such as the Grove, Archlight or Lincoln Square, and how many screens we hold on to. The third thing is trailer placement, which is a huge priority that will get only bigger in the next couple of years. With Regal and AMC getting into film distribution, trailer space will get intense. We will be judged on how we adjust to these new realities.

Q: *Can you share some of the lessons you have learned over the years?*

SF: You have to make a movie for somebody. There has to be an identifiable audience that you can reach effectively and reach time and time again, and that audience has to want to see that movie. You have to give them a reason to get out of the house to go see it. As a distributor, you have to have strong relationships with exhibitors and supply them with a steady flow of product. You have to treat each of your films separately and effectively and give them what they deserve. You have to fight every day, every week, for your films and try to maximize the value of every screen you play. Failure isn't an option.

Q: *Thank you for sharing your insight, and good luck with your company.*

SF: Thank you.

Historical Perspective: The Distribution Branch Office

In the early years of film distribution companies as they were growing their businesses, regional sales offices started sprouting up around the country to service the theatre owners in the various local markets. A structure evolved over time that divided the country into designated territories, which were distinguished by two practical sets of factors. The first factor was the location of the most important theatres in each state along with the offices of the exhibitors who owned them, and the second factor was the practicality and distance of shipping the physical film prints to those theatres. Many of these offices included shipping facilities in the back rooms. Sales offices, also known as branch offices, were established and staffed by distributors in the following 30 cities which became known as territories within the film industry:

New York	Buffalo	Omaha	Dallas
Los Angeles	Cleveland	Detroit	Kansas City
Chicago	Indianapolis	Milwaukee	Seattle
Boston	Pittsburgh	Atlanta	Portland
San Francisco	St. Louis	Charlotte	Denver
Washington, D.C.	Des Moines	Jacksonville	Salt Lake City
Philadelphia	Minneapolis	New Orleans	
Cincinnati	Baltimore	Memphis	

Branch offices remained in each of these cities through at least 1960 at which time some consolidation took place, and smaller offices were rolled into the larger markets. When I started my first distribution job in Chicago in 1976 with Avco Embassy, the company had 17 branch offices throughout the country; some of the major studios still had over 20 offices. The branch system was both the learning ground and the feeding ground for distribution companies. This is where people learned the film business, living in the trenches, learning individual markets and its theatres, building relationships along with experience and expertise. There was often movement between branch and division offices, with the better salesmen, branch managers and division managers being transferred and promoted to larger territories, and for the chosen few, perhaps landing up in the home office with a top level national job. It was a fun business, but it was also hard work that could be disruptive to families when forced to relocate. This movement between branches continued somewhat into the 1990s but more consolidation brought fewer branch offices, which left a core of 8 markets with branch offices left standing in 1990.

Distribution Organizations in 1990

► New York
► Los Angeles
► Chicago
► Boston
► Washington, D.C.
► Dallas
► Atlanta
► Kansas City

The original branch sales office structure worked effectively for decades as long as there was a strong core of vital local exhibitors in those markets to service and maintain relationships with. Business was conducted face-to-face over lunches, dinners, Variety Club meetings, golf outings and sporting events. As more and more local theatre chains were being bought by larger national circuits like AMC and Cineplex Odeon in the 1980s and 1990s and moving central booking offices to the coasts, the die was cast. There was less and less need for film companies to continue to maintain multiple sales offices, even in a large market like Chicago, because the big local exhibitors were no longer there.

Location of Studio Distribution Branch Offices in North America in 2012

- ▶ New York
- ▶ Los Angeles
- ▶ Dallas
- ▶ Toronto

In the United States three super branches survived, New York, Los Angeles and Dallas. Dallas survived over Chicago because there were several important national theatre circuits with central booking offices in the south, and it was a lot cheaper and practical to maintain a sales operation there. Times continue to change, and there are only two remaining studios with offices in Dallas, Sony and Universal; the rest have consolidated to Los Angeles. In 2011, it was very surprising, if not shocking, to read the announcement that Paramount was closing its New York office and would run the entire country from its L.A. office. The film industry began on the east coast, and the New York territory, especially Manhattan, to this day is the number one, most lucrative and important market in the country. Into the 1970s, New York was the home office for all film distribution and marketing operations with production staffs based in Los Angeles. All of the other five major studios continue to maintain a sales office in New York. A Canadian office remains in place for the studios since it is a separate country with its own currency, customs and procedures.

The territories that were established 100 years ago basically remain the same; the only difference is that film companies now cover the country from one or two offices. As Steve Friedlander said in his interview, the barrier to entry to start a distribution company is much cheaper and doable in the 21st century, with CBS Films being able to run the entire operation out of one office with seven salespeople. It's interesting to note that those seven people are veterans of the industry who came out of the branch system and know their stuff. The branch system may now be a relic of the past, but for all those who built their careers and professional lives around them, there was no better way to learn the film business than from the ground level up.

UP, UP AND AWAY: THE VALUE OF QUALITY

Week 22: May 29–June 4, 2009

---

*Pixar continues to stretch themselves to create the most unconventional stories
anyone could imagine … It's a business model that keeps paying off for them.*

In tough economic times, does the actual quality of a Hollywood blockbuster matter more for the consumer than ever before? That question is reverberating throughout the movie industry, and there are some interesting findings emerging that are causing headaches for studio executives. Even though the month of May has seen the launch of five successful franchise films, there are troubling signs ahead for those big movies that have been disappointing audiences and not quite delivering on their promise. However, one company that doesn't have to worry about the issue of quality is Pixar Animation because they have set the gold standard in delivering the highest form of entertainment to audiences year after year. Today, Pixar's 10th film, "Up," opens in 3,800 theatres, and it's fitting they will be able to cap an historic month at the box office with their special brand of quality motion picture, unmatched in the industry.

The timeline of Pixar is one for the history books. It all began with George Lucas and his small computer graphics division, which he sold to Steve Jobs for $10 million in 1986, and then Jobs changed the name of the company to Pixar. As part of the deal, he inherited a key creative executive in John Lassiter who has been the unequaled leader and force of the company ever since. The string of successes began with "Toy Story" in 1995, and in 2006 Steve Jobs sold the company to the Walt Disney Company for $7.4 billion. Not too shabby for a $10 million investment. You can almost say the other shoe finally fell on Mr. Lucas who 30 years earlier made one of the all-time best deals when he negotiated to retain merchandising rights for all the "Star Wars" movies. Disney has distributed all of Pixar's films but until 2006 only acted as the distributor. In addition to John Lassiter continuing to run Pixar, he is also the CEO of Disney's entire animation division. John Lassiter once revealed in an interview with Esquire magazine that all Steve Jobs ever said to him about making that first "Toy Story" was "to make it great."

Pixar continues to make it great and to stretch themselves to create the most unconventional stories anyone could imagine. "UP" has a 78-year-old man as its star. In today's youth-obsessed culture and merchandising-dominated summer landscape, that would be the kiss of death in anyone else's hands. Who would even attempt to make it? You could say the same thing about the story of a rat who dreams of becoming a chef in a French restaurant or the tale of a small waste-collecting robot who falls in love in a film that has no dialogue in its first 30 minutes. With the Pixar team, it's business as usual; that's what they do, create movies that no one would touch or even dream of doing, delivering original stories and grade A quality to the masses. It has been a business model that keeps paying off for them. All of their previous nine movies have been huge hits with both the critics and public. They are batting a thousand, which should be impossible to do. How do they keep doing it? How do they avoid the occasional clunker? Are they smarter than the rest of Hollywood? Are their filmmakers the best directors? Is there a formula to follow? Is there a secret to achieving the quality that their films have and seem to enjoy so effortlessly?

If only there was a secret formula or magic pixie dust that could be spread over all the blockbusters that get put into production. Producers all over Hollywood would take that dust and hope that the Pixar magic would rub off on their own films. Just think if all the summer blockbusters were also great movies. That's a nice thought; if only it was that easy, but it doesn't work that way. The reality is that many blockbusters are mediocre, living off their brand names, star power and massive marketing campaigns. For years, that has been enough for big profits, both in the theatres and in the all-important DVD market. Only half that equation is working now, and it's causing panic throughout the studios. The business continues to be booming at the theatres, but in the last six months or so, many of the big movies are selling a lot fewer DVDs, and that's where the ultimate profits are found. This is where the panic sets in. What's happening? Is it the economy? Do people already own too may DVDs? Is it affecting all movies? Is there a common denominator? A recent article in the *L.A. Times* shed some light on the situation, and it was very revealing. Consumers are becoming more quality conscious and much more discriminating in their DVD purchases. Quality has taken on a whole new value in Hollywood. Movies that were disappointing, didn't deliver what the marketing promised and had poor word of mouth have been selling fewer DVDs, even if they grossed $200 or $300 million at the box office. Movies like the last "Indiana Jones," "Hancock," "Quantum of Solace," "Yes Man" and "Seven Pounds" fall into this category; whereas movies with more quality and better word of mouth like "Iron Man," "Dark Knight," "Wall-E" and "Twilight" have held up much better in the DVD market. Continuing that line of reasoning with the current May releases, the eventual DVD performance could see "Star Trek," "UP" and perhaps "Night at the Museum" on the plus side and "Wolverine," "Terminator Salvation" and "Angels and Demons" on the negative side based on the perceived quality of the productions and the current word of mouth hitting the streets.

If the studios can find a way to make more of their blockbusters into better films, the sky's the limit in the profits they would achieve.

Blockbusters have long been marketing driven rather than critic or story driven, and they have been able to thrive. But the tide is changing. Fool people once at the box office but not twice at the video store. The reliable DVD numbers aren't so reliable anymore. Studio executives can react to this development in one of two ways. Some are saying they will have to be more cautious in what they green light, but how much more cautious can they be? They are green lighting movies based on comic books, video games, toys and even board games and continue to churn out prequels and sequels by the dozen. The other way is the complete opposite, the Pixar way. Dream big and create more original movies people haven't seen before and above all else, concentrate on telling good stories that can connect emotionally with audiences. Certainly other studios and producers practice some of the same principles Pixar follows such as scrapping a movie before it starts if the script isn't right or not being afraid to switch directors in production if problems arise, but they still fail to duplicate Pixar's unblemished success rate. Why can't Hollywood movies be better? No one goes out and tries to make just an average movie or give people something they won't like. But it happens too many times. The script had problems or was never finished. The story was weak and made no sense. The director was in over his head. The production was rushed to meet a release date. Too many cooks in the kitchen. Bad decisions. Star vanity projects. Going to the well once too often. Retread material. Not enough control over creative decisions. There are countless ways movies can fall off the track. Sometimes there isn't enough top talent to go around. Regardless of the reasons, studios need to take a good hard look at what's happening and realize moviegoers are becoming more quality conscious and demanding of how they spend their money.

At least they are still showing up at the theatres opening weekend. What if that starts to erode if the public gets tired of being disappointed? If there's panic now, what would happen then? If the studios can find a way to make more of their blockbusters into better films, the sky is the limit in the profits they would achieve. Saturation marketing and familiar franchises get them in the door, but it's the quality that keeps them coming back for more, whether it's repeat viewings at the theatres, paying for Video-on-Demand or buying the DVD. I saw "Star Trek" and "Terminator Salvation" in the last week, and the differences in the two franchise films and my reaction to them couldn't be more different. "Star Trek" received strong reviews and was getting tremendous word of mouth before I went to see it, and it lived up to its laurels.

While I was watching all the characters being introduced and the story line being established, I was thinking to myself this is a character driven film above all else; J.J. Abrams got it right. The movie had it all, exciting action sequences, a story you could follow, witty dialogue, some humor and most importantly, characters you got to know and care about. Bingo. Quality through and through. On the other hand, "Terminator Salvation" was everything that is going wrong with today's blockbusters. I saw it in a state-of-the-art theatre with a massive screen and tremendous sound system, and I felt I was beaten up in the process and left with a headache. Overly loud. Full of explosions. Plenty of carnage. Non-stop action. No time to think. Little or no character development. Not much of a story. These two movies should be studied for what to do right and what to avoid when making a blockbuster. Maybe some of the studios have taken audiences too much for granted with their franchise films. Falling profits for mediocre summer spectaculars may actually prove to be a good thing for audiences down the road if studios start concentrating more on character and story and less on explosions and special effects. It doesn't have to be a choice between one or the other, but more balance between the two, less noise and more substance, could go a long way in improving the situation.

Studios may not have a choice in the matter if they want to continue making those $150 to $200 million dollar blockbusters and wish to keep their profit margins up at the levels they have come to expect. They need to look no further than Pixar to see how a business model built on originality and Grade "A" quality can lead to such consistent success. Look up to the sky, watch those balloons float way, and those can be profits rising along with them.

This Week at the Box Office   *Weekly Attendance: 30,611,102*

Even though "UP" is Pixar's first film in 3D, it's interesting to note that the 3D angle is not front and center in Disney's marketing campaign. They are still selling the story first with the 3D information more toward the bottom in the ads and posters. The campaign is totally different in comparison to how Paramount and DreamWorks marketed "Monsters vs. Aliens." That entire campaign was built around 3D, starting with the 3D Super Bowl ad and the glasses giveaway. The movie proved to be very successful, but their marketing push tended to marginalize the theatres that played it on regular 2D screens. Disney doesn't have to go that route and is supremely confident with the Pixar brand name and its track record and also realize that half of the screens playing the picture won't be in 3D. However way audiences choose to see the movie, Disney believes they have another big hit on their hands. The only other wide release this weekend comes from Universal, and instead of looking up, well, they are looking down with Sam Raimi's "Drag Me To Hell." This is a return for the director to his earlier horror roots, and his fan base should be there for him. With a budget of only $25 million, Universal is in a decent position to carve out a profit on this one.

UP
Disney
Opening weekend: $68,108,790
Domestic gross: $293,004,164 40.1%
Foreign gross: $438,338,580 59.1%
Worldwide gross: $731,342,744
Widest release: 3,886 theatres

Drag Me to Hell
Universal
Opening weekend: $15,825,480
Domestic gross; $42,100,625 46.3%
Foreign gross: $48,742,021 53.7%
Worldwide gross: $90,842,646
Widest release: 2,510 theatres

Departures
Regent
Opening weekend: $74,945
Domestic weekend: $1,543,346 2.1%
Foreign gross: $68,434,177 97.9%
Worldwide gross: $69,932,387
Widest release: 27 theatres

Laila's Birthday
Kino
Opening weekend: $92.00
Domestic gross: $13,689 66.6%
Foreign gross: $6,852 33.4%
Worldwide gross: $20,541
Widest release: 3 theatres

Pressure Cooker

Bev Pictures

Opening weekend: $8,151

Domestic gross: $44,802

Foreign gross: N/A

Widest release: 3 theatres

Pontypool

IFC

Opening weekend: $1,541

Domestic gross: $3,865 12.0%

Foreign gross: $28,253 88.0%

Widest release: 1 theatre

Rashomon (Reissue)

Janus Films

Opening weekend: $6,152

Domestic gross: $96,568

Foreign gross: N/A

Widest release: 4 theatres

Munyuran Gabo

Film Movement

Opening weekend: $1,703

Domestic gross: $8,055

Foreign gross: N/A

Widest release: 1 theatre

2012 Update: Inside Pixar's Numbers

The string of number one hits and unqualified successes for Pixar now stands at thirteen. After "Up" opened to $68 million and grossed $293 million domestically, it was followed by three more winners in 2010, 2011 and 2012. In 2010 and 2011, Pixar retuned with sequels, "Toy Story 3" and "Cars 2" with "Toy Story 3" becoming the company's biggest film ever with a $110 million opening weekend, $415 million in domestic gross and over one billion in worldwide grosses. "Cars 2" came back to earth but still grossed over $500 million in worldwide grosses. In the summer of 2012, Pixar returned with an original story, "Brave," starring its first female lead, which went on to gross $237 million domestically and $298 million in international markets. For all thirteen Pixar films, the average opening weekend gross is $62 million, the domestic gross is $226 million, and the worldwide gross is $537 million. The beat goes on for this singular company.

The 22 Rules of Storytelling by a Pixar Insider

In the summer of 2012, Pixar's storyboard artist Emma Coats shared the following free advice with her readers on Twitter:

1. You admire a character for trying more than for their successes.
2. You have to keep in mind what's interesting to you as an audience, not what's fun to do as a writer. They can be very different.
3. Trying for theme is important, but you won't see what the story is actually about until you're at the end of it. Now rewrite.
4. Once upon a time there was _____. Every day,____. One day_____. Because of that,_____. Because of that,_____. Until finally_____.
5. Simplify. Focus. Combine characters. Hop over detours. You'll feel like you're losing valuable stuff, but it sets you free.
6. What s your character good at, comfortable with? Throw the polar opposite at them. Challenge them. How do they deal?
7. Come up with your ending before you figure out your middle. Seriously. Endings are hard, get yours working up front.
8. Finish your story; let go even if it's not perfect. In an ideal world you have both, but move on. Do better next time.
9. When you're stuck, make a list of what WOULDN'T happen next. Lots of times the material to get you unstuck will show up.
10. Pull apart the stories you like. What you like in them is a part of you; you've got to recognize it before you can use it.
11. Putting it on paper let's you start fixing it. If it stays in your head, a perfect idea, you'll never share it with anyone.
12. Discount the 1st thing that comes to mind. And the 2nd, 3rd, 4th, 5th – get the obvious out of the way. Surprise yourself.
13. Give your characters opinions. Passive/malleable might seem likable to you as you write, but it's poison to the audience.
14. Why must you tell THIS story? What's the belief burning within you that your story feeds off of? That's the heart of it.
15. If you were your character, in this situation, how would you feel? Honesty lends credibility to un-believable situations.
16. What are the stakes? Give us reason to root for the character. What happens if they don't succeed? Stack the odds against the character.
17. No work is ever wasted. If it's not working, let go and move on – it'll come back around to be useful later.
18. You have to know yourself: the difference between doing your best & fussing. Story is testing, not refining.
19. Coincidences to get characters into trouble are great; coincidences to get them out of it are cheating.
20. Exercise: take the building blocks of a movie you dislike. How do you rearrange them into what you DO like?
21. You have to identify with your situation/characters, can't just write, "cool." What would make YOU act that way?
22. What's the essence of your story? Most economical telling of it? If you know that, you can build out from there.

Week 22: Questions for Discussion

1. Why do you think a large percentage of Hollywood movies end up being mediocre at best? Is it a studio problem, a producer problem or a screenwriter problem? Discuss.

2. What do you think separates Pixar's successful business model from other companies? What has been the key to Pixar's success? Do you think it's possible for another production company to duplicate Pixar's perfect record of high quality and huge box office?

3. What can film producers do to insure better finished movies?

4. In your opinion, rank what you feel are the five best pieces of advice from Emma Coats to follow when writing a story.

A GIFT FROM THE GODS OR A BURDEN OF EXPECTATIONS?

Week 23: June 5–11, 2009

When a movie is made for everyone, it runs the risk of being for no one.

Movies that become a true phenomenon are few and far between. They can't be predicted, explained or duplicated, but when they happen, it can seem like a gift from the gods for the director or star involved that can soon turn into a burden of expectations. Orson Welles was only 25 years old when he directed "Citizen Kane" in 1941. The film is still hailed as the Best American Film ever made, and Welles was never able to match that pinnacle achievement and carried the burden of unfulfilled promise for the rest of his life, though he didn't get much support from the studio system of that era. Quentin Tarantino's "Pulp Fiction" took the world by storm in 1994, winning both tremendous critical acclaim and huge commercial success, going on to become the first independent film to gross over $100 million. For years after that, Tarantino struggled with the burden of that huge burst of glory, directed only a couple of films for the rest of the decade and never has come close to matching "Pulp Fiction's" magic. James Cameron has taken 11 years since "Titanic" became the world's biggest grossing film and winning the Oscar for Best Picture to attempt another feature and finally has his new movie "Avatar" scheduled to open at Christmas. "Blair Witch Project" became the phenomenon of the summer of 1999 when that ultra low-budget feature became the first sensation for the Internet generation, but the filmmakers for the most part have been missing in action since then.

My thoughts have turned to phenomenons with the release this week of "My Life in Ruins," starring Nia Vardalos. You may ask who is Nia Vardalos? Well, she was the writer and star of "My Big Fat Greek Wedding" which, make no mistake about it, became a genuine phenomenon in 2002. It was a classic case of a movie coming out of nowhere, a movie no distributor wanted to distribute, and a movie that was written off as film not having enough quality to play as a specialty film and not being commercial enough to go mainstream. So much for the experts. The $5,000,000 feature opened in 108 theatres in April of 2002 and played in theatres for the next 10 months, grossing a staggering $241,000,000 while never being number one at the box office. Even though it was expertly distributed, and Tom Hanks's production company was involved, there is no real explanation of how and why it was able to do what it did in the marketplace, having the staying power to play through the summer and fall and still be on first run screens at Christmas. That just doesn't happen in the modern-day movie business. It wasn't a great film, it didn't break any new ground, and many critics dismissed it as a glorified sitcom. It didn't even make it as sitcom the following year as it immediately bombed on television with Vardalos reprising her same role on the small screen. No matter. With all things considered, "My Big Fat Greek Wedding" could very well be the most surprising movie phenomenon of all time.

So getting back to Nia Vardalos, what has she been up to in the last seven years, and is it possible that "My Big Fat Greek Wedding" could still have any carry over impact on "My Life in Ruins," especially since it's another Greek themed movie? She is facing several giant hurdles, and it won't be easy. The thing about Nia Vardalos is she may have become famous with her one iconic role, but she never became a star. She is not Meryl Streep; she is not Sarah Jessica Parker; she's not Sandra Bullock who is opening her own romantic comedy "The Proposal" in two weeks. Her only starring movie was "Connie and Carla" in 2004, which landed up bombing at the box office. She has been writing scripts and has had a few guest spots on television shows, but her career momentum has stalled. I'm very curious to see how her new film opens and how much of her earlier fan base (including the Greek audience) will be there for her. Since she has already been in a movie that defied all odds, it's possible for her to surprise again, but the distributor, Fox Searchlight, will have more to say about how the movie performs than Vardalos herself. Fox Searchlight is one of the best in the business in guiding small to mid-sized films to success, but I'm scratching my head in trying to figure out what they are doing with this film. Choosing to open in June in over 1,000 theatres leaves no margin for error, so the movie needs strong support right out of the gate for it to have any chance at all and to be able to hold on to its screens for more than two weeks. I don't know if Searchlight has been screening the movie in advance extensively, creating awareness and building the audience, but we'll find out soon enough with the weekend numbers. I'm rooting for the film to do well because so few movies around the edges of the marketplace have been able to emerge this year, and it's always more satisfying to recognize and analyze success rather than talk about why the latest film failed. I would also like to see Nia Vardalos have a second act and be able to get her acting career back on track. At this point in time, no one expects anything close to another "My Big Fat Greek Wedding," so having much lower expectations may be the best thing going for it.

The five-year period between 1999 and 2004 was an incredible period for breakthrough independent films. The following three films and their total domestic grosses highlight a boom time for non-Hollywood fare:

- ▶ 1999: Blair Witch Project - $140,539,099
- ▶ 2002: My Big Fat Greek Wedding - $241,438,208
- ▶ 2004: Passion of the Christ - $370,274,604

Each of these films set benchmarks as the all-time highest grossing independent film at the time, and they couldn't be more different from each other. It showed the vibrancy of the marketplace where such diverse movies could capture large specific segments of the population and ride them to phenomenal heights. Young high school and college students, the Greek audience and women, and the Christian/religious audience were the demographics that drove the train for these immense hits. After "My Big Fat Greek Wedding" demolished the "Blair Witch" record, I thought it would stand alone for many years with that $241,000,000 figure. Then Mel Gibson came along two years later, financed the film himself, had it independently distributed, and rewrote the record books again with a gross that has a chance to last for many years to come. Considering the current struggles of independent films, those numbers seem unfathomable and unreachable. But the marketplace always has its peaks and valleys, and surprises can strike at any time from any source. Perhaps there is another gift from the gods being planned for some filmmaker out there who will deliver the right film at the right time for the right audience that will become the next phenomenon. We're due for another one, and the marketplace will be ready and willing to embrace it when it arrives.

The studios hope to survive the month of June with fewer blockbusters then they had in May. The fact is there are a finite number of blockbusters that can be produced, so there aren't enough of them to fill every week of the summer. It's strange that June will feel a bit barren of big movies, and the industry runs the risk of not being able to keep up with last June when hits like "Kung Fu Panda," "Wanted," "Wall-E" and "Get Smart" opened to huge grosses. Some weeks may be down, but all those May blockbusters are still playing, so the overall numbers may even out, especially if a movie like "The Hangover" helps the cause and hits pay dirt in a big way. The marketplace is catching its breath a little, but the blockbusters will return in late June and July starting with "Transformers" on June 24th, which is tracking like it could be the biggest movie of the summer.

This Week at the Box Office
Weekly Attendance: 32,790,774

One thing "My Life in Ruins" will have going for it is that it will have little competition for the female audience this weekend. Whereas Warner Bros.' "The Hangover" is poised to become a sleeper summer hit on a modest $30,000,000 budget, grabbing men from 18 to 40 as its core audience. The other new wide release, Universal's "Land of the Lost" just seems lost. With a budget close to $100,000,000, it has a blockbuster cost without the blockbuster status. It looks like it could be the first real money loser of the summer. Universal's head honchos have to be worried they may have another "Evan Almighty" on their hands, a big-budget, special effects comedy made for a wide general audience that failed to have a core niche audience to build from. When a movie is made for everyone, it runs the risk of being for no one.

When filmmakers try to throw in a little something for many different age groups and miss the mark, it falls to the level of pandering, and they're not completely satisfying anybody. The PG-13 movie's main marketing hook seems to be Will Farrell being chased by a bunch of dinosaurs, which would seem to appeal to families and young teenage boys. The early reviews indicate the movie contains a rather large amount of crude, bathroom humor which will not go over too well with parents, so that may leave young teenage boys as its only audience. It's ironic that the director of "The Hangover" also directed "Old School," one of Will Farrell's most popular movies with the same male audience that will be going out in droves to see "The Hangover" on opening weekend. There seems to be a disconnect here with the two movies opening on the same weekend. The question begs to be asked, is Will Ferrell in the wrong film?

Getting back to "The Hangover," where is all that positive buzz coming from? Warner Bros. is doing a great job generating buzz from two separate fronts. With an R-rated comedy, cutting a very funny, raunchy trailer is one of the first steps a distributor can take in getting the young male audience to take notice and start spreading the word, and with "Hangover" they certainly have a funny one out there. Since R-rated red band trailers have disappeared for the most part from being shown in theatres, Internet sites like YouTube have been a godsend for studios and have become the 24/7 go-to destinations for movie fans to sample upcoming movies. This is where the buzz started for "The Hangover," but for the buzz to really kick in, a distributor needs to start showing the finished movie to audiences. That's exactly what Warner Bros. has done. Going after that young male audience, screenings were scheduled on college campuses in 80 cities and on multiple military bases to go along with the traditional radio promotion screenings in all major cities. That is one of the first rules in marketing movies; when a distributor loves a movie and feels it has the goods, get it out there in front of your target audiences as much as possible. There is an expense involved in renting theatres, shipping prints, promotional costs and giveaway items, but the financial return on a movie that clicks with audiences makes it all worthwhile. It's simply the cost of doing business.

The Hangover

Warner Brothers
Opening weekend: $44,979,319
Domestic gross: $277,322,503 59.3%
Foreign gross: $190,161,409 40.7%
Worldwide gross: $467,483,912
Widest release: 3,545 theatres

Land of the Lost

Universal
Opening weekend: $18,837,350
Domestic gross: $49,452,120 71.9%
Foreign gross: $19,339,184 28.1%
Worldwide gross: $68,791,304
Widest release: 3,534 theatres

My Life in Ruins

Fox Searchlight
Opening weekend: $3,223,161
Domestic gross: $8,677,425 42.4%
Foreign gross: $11,790,070 57.6%
Worldwide gross: $20,455,276
Widest release: 1,165 theatres

Away We Go

Focus
Opening weekend: $130,411
Domestic gross: $9,451,946 63.4%
Foreign gross: $5,447,471 36.6%
Worldwide gross: $14,899,457
Widest release: 506 theatres

Seraphine

Music Box Films
Opening weekend: $38,637
Domestic gross: $884,613 9.7%
Foreign gross: $8,263,264 90.3%
Worldwide gross: $9,147,877
Widest release: 41 theatres

Unmistaken Child

Oscilloscope
Opening weekend: $6,293
Domestic gross: $306,140 84.4%
Foreign gross: $56,750 15.6%
Worldwide gross: $362,890
Widest release: 11 theatres

24 City
Cinema Guild
Opening weekend: $6,082
Domestic gross: $30,799 7.9%
Foreign gross: $360,273 92.1%
Worldwide gross: $391,073
Widest release: 2 theatres

Herb & Dorothy
Arthouse Films
Opening weekend: $9,272
Domestic gross: $194,271
Foreign gross: N/A
Widest release: 2 theatres

Downloading Nancy
Strand
Opening weekend: $10,324
Domestic gross: $22,282
Foreign gross: N/A
Widest release: 5 theatres

Art of Being Straight
Regent
Opening weekend: $3,778
Domestic gross: $12,831
Foreign gross: N/A
Widest release: 2 theatres

Week 23: Questions for Discussion

1. When thinking about a movie phenomenon like "Blair Witch Project" or "My Big Fat Greek Wedding," do you think there is anything the principles involved with such an unexpected success could have done differently that would have helped keep their momentum going?

2. Discuss what you think the following statement means. "When a movie is made for everyone, it runs the risk of being for nobody." Do you agree with this concept? Can you remember a recent movie, which you believe was made for everyone, that was wildly successful?

3. Where do you experience or hear buzz on a new movie? Provide examples. Have you ever gone to a word-of-mouth screening for a movie before it opens? Do you remember if you gave it good word of mouth or bad word of mouth?

DIVIDING UP THE BOX OFFICE:
THE SHIFTING SANDS OF SUPPLY AND DEMAND

Week 24: June 12–18, 2009

Sometimes the only way to get your share of the pie is through persistence, pressure, leverage and pure doggedness. That's the way the movie business works, fighting for every dollar.

As the summer movie season continues to kick in with more and more new films entering the marketplace, the battle to open on as many screens as possible for the biggest movies will only heat up.

The majority of the most promising wide releases generally open in between 3,000 to 4,000 theatres (locations). Though the theatre count remains the official release number, that only tells half the story. To produce those giant opening weekend grosses, the studios need to be on as many additional screens as possible, and often the blockbusters are on 7,000 to 8,000 total screens. That's why it's not unusual when you see your local 14-screen complex showing only seven or eight movies playing on multiple screens. The key to record-breaking grosses is having as many showtimes as possible to make moviegoing as convenient as possible for people on the go. What isn't widely known is how a shift to a more streamlined way distributors and exhibitors split up the box office has made it easier for both parties to add as many additional screens as a movie demands, and theatres can absorb right up to opening day. This is what happened with "The Hangover," when Warner Bros. decided to add extra screens on the Monday before release when their tracking showed that interest for their movie was rising and that the positive buzz demanded more seats. They proved to be right when "The Hangover" became the surprise number one hit in the country, grossing $45 million.

The late A.D. Murphy, the legendary financial reporter for Variety, once wrote "the realization that an exhibitor's overall film costs are composed of various percentage splits of the box office with the distributors on thousands of different runs of hundreds of different films is the beginning of wisdom in understanding the film business." To put it more simply, he was saying to be able to understand how the movie business works you have to first understand all the various ways the box office is divided up and who keeps what and who gets what. The box office gross is the sexy number that gets reported by the media, but the more important figure for the distributors has always been the film rental they collect from theatres, also known as the distributor gross. This figure is the starting point in the entire revenue stream a movie generates that goes toward paying production costs, star salaries and investors. On the other side of the table sits the exhibitor, who fights to retain as much of the box office as he can. One advantage the exhibitor has wielded over the years is the fact that theatres have possession of the money first and like to keep as much of it as they can. There is an old adage that goes "money sticks to whoever has it at the time." Sometimes the only way to get your share of the pie is through persistence, pressure, leverage and pure doggedness. That's the way the movie business works, fighting for every dollar.

Like A.D. Murphy said, this is where the action is, in the trenches dividing up those box office dollars and understanding the process in how and why the economics are what they are. This is the world I come from and where I came to learn the basic fundamentals of how the movie industry works. The various financial deals had names like 90/10s, four-walling, split percentages, minimum floors, firm bids, percentage with review, sliding scales and flat prices. When I started in the business in the early 1970s, the theatrical marketplace towered in importance because pay television was in its infancy and video cassettes were still five to ten years away. Getting every last dollar out of theatrical was of prime importance, and film salesmen, branch managers, division managers, film buyers and bookers were paid by their ability to do just that. All the above financial deals came into play at one point or another because movies played in theatres for a much longer time, and there were many creative ways to keep them going on the screens through double features, sub-runs, reissues, drive-in second features and whatever other way we could squeeze extra revenue for the distributors or theatre circuits we worked for. It was fun, and this is where I learned that there was an art and creativity to the film business that I found invigorating and challenging.

Since the studios need to get their biggest movies on the largest number of screens, they in essence become the demand while the theatres with all their screens become the supply.

Time marches on, and things are much different today. The theatrical market is a much shortened window, and the philosophy for most movies now is to get the money as fast as you can before handing it over to the ancillary markets of DVD, VOD, streaming and other digital forms of delivery. Don't get me wrong, splitting up the theatrical pie is just as important, and each side still fights for the best deal, but the negotiation process is a lot less exotic and complex than it used to be. And like many things in the world of business transactions, it comes down to the basic economic principles of supply and demand. Simply put, the studios have the supply and the theatres represent the demand and the power, and leverage has shifted between the distributors and exhibitors over the years, depending on the number of movies in circulation and the number of available screens available to play them. With studios releasing only about three wide release movies a week on the average, and with close to 40,000 screens needing to play all the top product, distribution has held the upper hand in the last decade when leasing their movies to exhibitors. However, when it comes down to the biggest, most expensive studio movies, supply and demand has a curious way of switching sides and balancing out the equation. Since the studios need to get their biggest movies on the largest number of screens, they in essence become the demand while the theatres with all their screens become the supply.

This reality has led to a new type of deal brought on by the needs and wants of both distributors and exhibitors. For about 40 years starting in 1965, the primary financial deal between distributors and exhibitors was the 90/10 deal, built on a computation of weekly box office grosses based on a theatre's house allowance and sliding minimum floor percentages starting at 70%. This deal worked fine for both sides for many years until a couple of factors forced change in the basic way a movie is licensed. On the distribution side, the focus was to streamline the process and move away from having to compute the film rental on a weekly basis because the number of sales offices and staff had greatly shrunk and settling film rental the old way was too labor intensive. In addition, the studios settled many engagements following the run, and they wanted to set a firm price before the movie opened rather than wait until after it played. On the exhibition front, theatre owners also wanted to move away from the 90/10 deals because film grosses had become too front loaded with movies opening big and falling off fast, which led to exhibitors paying inordinately high percentages in the first couple of weeks and left them with high bills when most movies failed to have much staying power in today's marketplace. Theatres just couldn't make up the difference in the later weeks anymore with smaller grosses to divvy up.

This brings us back to the summer blockbusters and the new type of deal that has emerged from all of this, the aggregate deal. The aggregate deal is a deal that assigns a specific percentage to cover the entire engagement of a film's run rather than negotiating percentages on a weekly basis. The aggregate deal has become the new primary way movies are sold today, and it has made it much easier for distributors to add as many screens as they can get for their blockbusters while eliminating the exhibitor's concern that they will be paying higher film rental in the early weeks by supplying those additional screens. Before the aggregate deal became the new norm, some theatres would gross so much on the old 90/10 deal, they would be forced to pay as high as 80% of the box office in the first week, and by the 3rd or 4th week the movie would be dead. This was not acceptable, and exhibitors pushed for change and got it. The majority of aggregate deals average around 55%, which is paid each week of the run regardless of the weekly gross. The majority of the biggest films get higher aggregates, and some of the weaker films get lower ones. Other variations can include aggregates that can rise based on the eventual domestic gross of a film and companies that offer a choice between an aggregate deal and a terms deal. The aggregate deal is also used with studio divisions like Fox Searchlight and Focus Films, but many of the smaller distributors still use the 90/10 as their primary deal with exhibitors. With the independent film business providing fewer hits and more box office failures, exhibitors pay much less than they pay for studio films, averaging more in the area of 45% and lower. For drive-ins, which play two first run movies, special considerations are made. The top feature playing in its first week may pay a straight 50%, and the second feature, which may be in its third week of release, may accept as little as 10%. Ten percent may seem like a paltry percentage, but some of the drive-ins can produce big numbers, and their seasonal status begs for special consideration.

Behind every deal is a cause and effect, which reverberates and reflects the current state of where the movie business is at any given time.

The financial deals are not as complex as in years past, but the aggregate deal is much more functional for this day and age based on the needs and demands of the marketplace. Without those extra screens added at the last minute on "The Hangover," it no doubt would have had trouble beating out "UP" as the top grossing movie of the weekend. Most veterans of the business lament that it just isn't as fun as it used to be when you could wheel and deal more freely and that the industry culture has become much more corporate and stifling. That may be the case, but what hasn't changed is A.D. Murphy's belief that the beginning of wisdom in understanding the film business lies in the different ways the box office is split. What was true back then is still true now. Behind every deal is a cause and effect that reverberates and reflects the current state of where the movie business is at any given time.

HISTORICAL PERSPECTIVE: Financial Deals between Distributors and Exhibitors

In the early years of the film industry, movies were sold for flat fees. They were sold by the foot in standard lengths of 1,000-foot reels at rates based on theatre size rather than the quality of the films themselves. During the first decade movies were basically short films averaging 15 to 20 minutes in length, so selling them this way made sense by using a quick and easy transaction. In 1915, D.W. Griffith's "Birth of a Nation" changed everything when it was the first feature length movie to become a major box office draw, which spurred changes in how movies were sold to theatres. One year later Adolph Zukor from Paramount introduced two new policies that were to be in place for years to come. The first change involved moving away from a flat sales price to offering films on a percentage basis based on the quality of the film and its box office potential, and second was a policy that became known as block booking. This policy insisted that if an exhibitor wanted any of its pictures, they would have to take all of them without even having a chance to see them first. If this sounds like a predatory, unfair practice that took advantage of theatre owners, well it was. The amazing thing is that block booking was able to stay in place for over 30 years or until it was ruled illegal and put a stop to by the U. S. government in the Paramount Consent Decrees of 1948. For over 30 years, Paramount, along with other major studios, was assured of steady outlets for all of its pictures regardless of their quality or demand. The studios shoved movies down the exhibitors' throats, in effect selling bundles of movies without titles.

The studios shoved movies down the exhibitors' throats, in effect selling bundles of movies without titles.

By the mid-20s, the studios started to assume the vertically integrated shape that would dominate the industry for the next three decades. Theatre owners were acquiring production and distribution organizations; producers and distributors in turn were buying theatres so consolidation of control was made possible by putting production, distribution and exhibition under the same roof. An example of this was in 1924 when theatre owner Marcus Loew bought Goldwyn Pictures and Louis B. Mayer Productions and merged it with his Metro Pictures (a studio he bought in 1919) to form MGM. What eventually emerged was a hierarchy of eight major companies referred to as the Big Five and the Little Three.

THE BIG FIVE

(Controlled Production, Distribution and Exhibition)

- ► Warner Brothers
- ► Paramount
- ► 20th Century Fox
- ► MGM
- ► RKO

THE LITTLE THREE

(Controlled Production and Distribution only)

- ► Universal
- ► Columbia
- ► United Artists

These eight companies controlled 95% of the industry and pretty much had their way with things, but film rental percentages were one area that prices didn't change much. One of the reasons for this is that the Big Five studios owned the vast majority of the important first run theatres in the country, which earned a large chunk of a film's revenues. They were in effect selling to themselves with money going out one pocket and going into the other pocket. That made the film rental percentage a minor point. In the 1920s, films were rented to exhibitors for less than 20% of the box office receipts and in the next couple of decades only rose to an average of 25-30%. Of course these percentages represented the average film rental taken in by distributors for any given film that covered sometimes thousands of different play dates that were sold at various price points depending on when a theatre was able to get the film. The later runs and double features could be flat prices as low as $35 or split percentages of 10% or 15%. The point here is that for many decades theatres kept the majority of the box office. Even as the Big Five studios were forced to sell off their theatres as ruled in The Paramount Consent Decrees, exhibitors still were able to retain the larger portion of the box office. As the 1960s started, the average film rental paid to distributors was still lower than 35%. It was part past practice and precedent and partly due to the rather still limited supply of large grossing theatres that all the studios desired to play and competed for against each other. It was still a buyers' market instead of a sellers' market where the exhibitors held the upper hand in negotiations.

1965 proved to be a major turning point in financial deal making between distributors and exhibitors. The introduction of the 90/10 deal is generally accredited to 20th Century Fox for "Sound of Music." This deal from the very start was created to establish a higher ceiling of earnings for distributors, especially for those films that became huge hits. The timing was perfect since there was no bigger movie than "Sound of Music," which dethroned "Gone With The Wind" as the top grossing film of all time after the iconic Civil War drama spent 26 years at the top of the charts. The new deal became so popular with distributors that the 90/10 became the primary deal in the industry for first run films for the next 35 to 40 years. How does the deal work, and why did it become perhaps the least understood deal in all of Hollywood, especially among the media but even among some who worked in the business? The misconception always started with that number 90. I don't know how many times over the years I saw something written to the effect that distributors collected 90% of the box office from the poor theatre owners who were left with scraps and their popcorn money. The truth of the matter is that it was a pretty fair deal for both parties; it wouldn't have lasted as long as it did if it was as one sided as it sounded or looked on paper.

The new deal became so popular with distributors that the 90/10 became the primary deal in the industry for the next 35 to 40 years.

The key point in a 90/10 deal is the distributor negotiates a weekly house allowance for each theatre screen playing one of its movies. This figure is not a true factual amount of how much it costs to operate a theatre; it's none of the distributor's business to know what a theatre's true operating expense is, just as it is none of the exhibitor's business in knowing the details and costs of film production. The house allowance is determined by several factors including size and number of seats in an auditorium, the theatre's grossing potential, past performance and finally its ability to earn on a 90/10 deal. High grossing big city and suburban theatres could be allowed $10,000 to $15,000 per screen as a weekly house allowance whereas a small low grossing theatre could have $1,500 as its figure. This figure is important because after the weekly seven-day gross is tabulated, the first thing that is deducted from the gross is the approved house allowance, after that 90% of the subtracted amount is calculated to get the 90/10 figure. Let's look at an example and see how it's done:

Roxy Theatre 2, Springfield, USA
Terms: 90/10 over $10,000 House Allowance

Weekly Gross:	$28,575.00
Less House Allowance:	-$10,000.00
	$18,575.00
90% of $18,575.00	= $16,717.50

$16,717.50 is the 90/10 figure. In order to determine the earnings on a 90/10 deal, the gross is divided into the film rental.

$16717.00 / $28,575 = .5850

The distributor earned 58.5% of the gross. The subtraction of the house allowance off the top of the gross is the great equalizer in a 90/10 deal. As you can see in this example, the theatre would be paying only a rounded off 59% and not 90% as it would if it was paying off on a pure 90/10 basis.

Let's look at another example in which there is no 90/10 earning because the film grossed less at the box office. We will use the same $10,000 house allowance.

Weekly Gross:	$12,340.00
Less House Allowance:	-$10,000.00
	$ 2,340.00
90% of 2,340.00	= $2,106.00

In this case when you do the division, the 90% film rental figure amounts to only 17% of the gross, which would not be an adequate figure for the distributor to earn. To counter against when there are minimal or no earnings on a 90/10 (when a movie flops, the gross could be less than the house allowance), the studios include in each 90/10 deal sliding minimum floor percentages for each week a movie plays. First run movies are contracted to play multiple weeks, and often the deals are written for 8 weeks in the large cities. The percentage floors start at 70% and decrease at 10% intervals. Let's use the same figures we previously used for the fictional Roxy Theatre and work in the accompanying floors in our new deal.

Terms: 90/10 over $10,000 vs. the following floors:

1st & 2nd weeks:	70%
3rd week:	60%
4th week:	50%
5th week:	40%
6th, 7th, 8th weeks:	35%
If held over, all additional weeks:	35%

The percentage floors are the distributors' insurance policy if a movie underperforms or even when a movie does well. In a 90/10 deal, a 90/10 earning can be looked upon as the base or starting point in a negotiation. A distributor has the flexibility of taking whatever figure is greater. If that Roxy's gross of $28,575.00 occurred in the first week of the run, the distributor would bypass the 90/10 formula and settle for a straight 70% of the gross, which increases the film rental due from $16,717 to $20,002. Good for the distributor, not so good for the exhibitor. If that same gross was earned in the third week of the engagement, the 90/10 earnings of 59% would just about match the 60% floor, and it would be a negligible difference in that week's payment.

A crucial point of every financial deal between distributors and exhibitors through the years has been whether or not the terms listed in the contract were firm terms or adjustable terms. All 90/10 deals looked very similar throughout the industry, starting with 70% or 60% floors in the early weeks and ending with 35% in the final weeks. A fact of life in the film business is that many movies fail or underperform at the box office, and distributors had to be flexible in their deals in order to procure the necessary play dates from exhibitors. If your deal was too rich, theatres could just pass and play other films instead. Personally, I never worked for a distributor that was able to command firm terms. Every film I ever sold for Avco Embassy Pictures and Orion Pictures in a regular oral negotiation were deals that contained adjustable terms. Those companies were leading independent distributors of their day, perhaps even mini-majors, but still didn't have the clout or consistently high grossing movies to warrant firm term contracts. The deals were written one way, but the exhibitors were told, "We will look to see how the film performs and settle it at the end of engagement. This is not set in stone." This is how the industry operated for years when there was far fewer supply of theatre screens available. The haggling was done at the end of run. In all these deals, the 90/10 formula was in place, so if a film really took off, even a non-major distributor could reap the benefits and collect high terms. But a film had to perform and deserve it. Nothing was handed to you.

A fact of life in the film business is that many movies fail or underperform at the box office, and distributors had to be flexible in their deals

The best example I have from my Orion days of a film that performed fantastically and led to very high film rental settlements based on 90/10 earnings was Oliver Stone's "Platoon" in 1986. As Chicago Branch manager, I booked six theatres to open between Christmas and New Year's Day based on the film's tremendous New York debut earlier in the month. The Chicago runs were spectacular with the six theatres combining for a $400,000 cumulative gross after seven days which returned $300,000 to the company in film rental, averaging out to a 75% return. I recall we spent about $100,000 in advertising to open the film so after only one week there was a $200,000 profit in Chicago. "Platoon" was probably the most exciting film I ever distributed, and it played into June the following year after it won Best Picture of the Year. Having the 90/10 in place meant never having to undersell your picture. If it hit, you collected.

To further your understanding of these type of deals, please work out the following two 90/10 situations based on actual grosses and deals from the first week of "Platoon" in Chicago.

1. Gross: $89,582.00
    H.Allw.: $10,900
    90% Fig. =
    Percentage of gross =

2. Gross: $66,500
    H.Allw.:$10,750
    90% Fig. =
    Percentage of Gross =

Through the 1970s and 1980s, Universal was known as the only distributor that had a firm term policy for all their films. They did however have special grandfather type deals for the established big city theatres throughout the country that had been playing all their films for years. These deals generally started with 50% or 40% floors attached to the traditional 90/10 formula. During this period of the 1970s and 1980s, there was a method for distributors to get firm terms from exhibitors even when the movies didn't fare too well at the box office. The method was called bidding. Bidding was the process in which a distributor sent out written invitations to all of the first run theatres in a given market inviting them to send in a written offer if they wished to play the film. They were given seven to ten days to reply, and after that date, if there were multiple offers, the distributor would choose the winning bids based on the terms offered and the grossing history and potential of the theatre. Bidding worked best when there was true competition between several different exhibitors in a specific geographic area (known in the film industry as a zone) and they all wanted the same picture. With the bidding process, a distributor just let the competitors slug it out and told them to "give me your best offer." Bidding really helped distributors in this era to get stronger and firm terms for their films. By 1990, the average film rental paid throughout the industry crept closer to 50%.

Formal bidding of films slowly faded away due to a variety of reasons:

1. The bidding process included a lot of paperwork, and with the closing of regional sales offices and fewer office staff, work became more streamlined.
2. The passing of anti-blind bidding laws in 26 states placed more obstacles on distributors.
3. The consolidation of the exhibition community into fewer circuits with many once formidable regional circuits being bought out by larger competitors and others going out of business.
4. With the rise of the megaplexes and an abundance of screens to choose from, distributors don't need bidding to guarantee higher terms anymore. They get firm terms now anyway.

The history of financial terms between distributors and exhibitors has been the uphill struggle for distributors to control the largest share of the box office for their films. Whether it has been the theatres controlling the money first, sweetheart deals with dominant theatre chains, periods with it being a buyers' market (more movies available than good screens), discount and sub-run houses bringing down the average or a steady diet of underperforming films that called for adjustments, even the studios struggled to get their film rental averages consistently over 50%. That was in the past.

In today's world, the studios wield the upper hand. In many ways, the larger megaplexes and abundance of screens the theatres have to fill have played to the studios' advantage. Only the six studios can consistently provide the product and marketing power to fill those screens, but while the theatres expanded their capacity, distributors kept their release schedules either at the same level or actually reduced the number of films they released. This has produced a huge sellers market for the studios. With the move to aggregate terms, shorter theatrical runs and much fewer discount engagements, the studios are averaging their highest film rental retention ever – 55% and higher. With the high grossing blockbusters, aggregates can average over 60%. Whereas the haggling used to be after the engagement, now it takes place before the movie opens where both sides fight for every percent of the deal. All studio negotiations are final with firm terms so each distributor and exhibitor has to set a price in their own minds in what they are willing to offer and accept. Sometimes negotiations are continuing until the day before a movie opens, even with the prints shipped and advertising set, two strong adversaries fighting right to the end for every dollar on the table and future dollar to be earned.

This Week at the Box Office:

Weekly Attendance: 28,148,274

Taking of Pelham 123
Sony
Opening weekend: $23,373,102
Domestic gross: $65,370,585 43.6%
Foreign gross: $84,713,814 56.4%
Worldwide gross: $150,166,126
Widest release: 3,074 theatres

Imagine That
Paramount
Opening weekend: $5,503,519
Domestic gross: $16,222,392 70.1%
Foreign gross: $6,861,871 29.9%
Worldwide gross: $22,985,194
Widest release: 3,011 theatres

Moon
Sony Classics
Opening weekend: $136,046
Domestic gross: $5,010,163 51.3%
Foreign gross: $4,749,941 48.7%
Worldwide gross: $9,760,104
Widest release: 252 theatres

Tetro
American Zoetrope
Opening weekend: $37,334
Domestic gross: $518,522 18.2%
Foreign gross: $2,334,393 81.8%
Worldwide gross: $2,852,915
Widest release: 16 theatres

Youssou N'Dour: I Bring What I Love
Shadow Distribution
Opening weekend: $32,598
Domestic gross: $172,226
Foreign gross: N/A
Widest release: 7 theatres

Combat Dans L'ile
Film Desk
Opening weekend: $10,217
Domestic gross: $45,256
Foreign gross: N/A
Widest release: 1 theatre

Call of the Wild 3D
Vivendi Reliance
Opening weekend: $10,713
Domestic gross: $28,682 10.6%
Foreign gross: $241,528 89.4%
Worldwide gross: $270,210
Widest release: 14 theatres

Kal Kissne Dekha
Big Entertainment
Opening weekend: $13,681
Domestic gross: $24,625 45.6%
Foreign gross: $29,423 54.4%
Worldwide gross: $54,048
Widest release: 18 theatres

Sex Positive

Regent

Opening weekend: $3,408

Domestic gross: $12,069

Foreign gross: N/A

Widest release: 1 theatre

Death of a Ghost Hunter

Nocturnal

Opening weekend: $3,648

Domestic gross: $4,490

Foreign gross: N/A

Widest release: 1 theatre

Betty Blue: The Director's Cut

Cinema Libre

Opening weekend: $2,438

Domestic gross: $13,029 (reissue)

Widest release: 1 theatre

Week 24: Questions for Discussion

1. When a studio released one of their big movies, there was a distinction between the number of prints, locations and screens that were utilized. Explain what each of the three items was and how digital technology has altered the equation. Which figure still gets announced to the media and public as the official release number?

2. What role does supply and demand play in the way the box office gets divided up? In what ways do supply and demand shift between exhibitors and distributors, and how does that affect negotiations on the price of any individual movie?

3. When did the movie business start turning into more of a seller's market rather than a buyer's market for distributors and exhibitors? What does this mean? Do you think it's possible it may change back to a buyer's market sometime in the future? Why?

4. What was bidding, and how did it produce higher film rental for distributors?

5. What is a 90/10 deal, and why has it been replaced by the aggregate deal as the most widely used studio negotiation between distributors and exhibitors? Figure out the below deal using the following numbers and compute the film rental, first using the 90/10 model and then the aggregate model.

1ˢᵗ Deal:

90/10 over H.E. of $8,500 vs. 70%, 60%, 50%, 40% (four-week engagement)

1ˢᵗ week gross: $34,350

2ⁿᵈ week gross: $16,000

3ʳᵈ week gross: $8,542

4ᵗʰ week gross: $3,850

2ⁿᵈ Deal: Aggregate deal, 55% each week

Which deal works out best for either the distributor or exhibitor?

SNEAK PREVIEWS, STRONG LEGS AND THE LURE OF SUMMER

Week 25: June 19–25, 2009

That's what the lure of summer can do to a lot of mid-level
movies, leave them for road kill on the side of the road.

For some time now, the summer movie season has evolved into a predictable revolving door of new number one movies every week. Come to think of it, most of the year is like that too. That's a testament to the studios doing a good job of having just about every week covered with an attractive new release to go along with saturation marketing that hooks moviegoers to show up on opening weekend. So what happened last weekend was a rare occurrence when two holdover films, "The Hangover" and "UP," sat on top of the box office, in mid-June no less. There are two ways to look at this. It's refreshing to see two movies at the same time with tremendous staying power and great word of mouth do so well and buck the trend of summer movies opening big and falling fast. On the other hand, what made that possible were weaker than expected new movies which has led to the overall box office falling behind last year for the third week in the row. No two years are ever the same in terms of releases, economic conditions and other unpredictable factors, so seasonal fluctuations in the box office are to be expected. However, when it happens in June it catches everybody's attention, and people start to wonder if this is the start of a downward cycle that will play out for the rest of the summer. There are some bigger movies just around the corner set to open, and it remains to be seen how they will perform and stack up to last year's hits. But what makes a tough business even tougher is the fact that economic numbers are published and reported on every week of the year, and the pressure to produce is right out in the open for everyone to see. There is no other industry in America that endures that kind of scrutiny and analysis. To keep matters in perspective, year to date revenues are still running 9% higher than last year, so things are still looking pretty good for Hollywood. Is this an official June swoon? I'll call it a market correction instead and wait and see how the rest of the month plays out.

Is there anything to point to for why June is so weak this year? There are several things to point to. Last week would have been much been stronger if "Fast and Furious" stayed on its June 12th date and didn't move to April where it set a new record for that month. The labor strike from last year and the threat of additional ones disrupted production, and June may be feeling that now with fewer movies. In addition, the economy comes into play with its credit crunch. Six studios are the main suppliers for close to 40,000 screens in the summer. When the studios have fewer movies, the impact is felt because the industry is getting no help from movies from outside distributors. There are no DreamWorks' movies, no MGM, no Weinstein, no Summit, no Miramax, no Lionsgate, no Warner Independent. These companies are either restructuring their financing, sitting on the sidelines or out of business altogether, and this is the sector that produced past early summer hits like "Fahrenheit 9/11" and "March of the Penguins," which were able to provide a lift to the overall box office. The competition is fierce, and it's getting harder to find any non-studio movies trying to carve out some business for themselves by going after a commercial audience in the summer. The way summer movies have evolved, movies have to be a certain size, scope or air of importance to get noticed and find success. A good example of a recent movie that tried and failed is "My Life in Ruins." It didn't get good reviews, it seemed a bit inconsequential, and Fox Searchlight went a little light on the marketing. Those three factors are always a recipe for disaster.

Another reason the June box office is down is because studios continue to bankroll Eddie Murphy movies and believe he still has enough appeal to carry a summer movie. For the second June in a row, Murphy failed to produce even a $6,000,000 opening weekend gross; last year it was "Meet Dave" and last weekend was "Imagine That." According to Boxoffice Mojo, those two movies rank in the top five of the worst wide openings of over 3,000 theatres of all-time. I wanted to think that his salary had fallen in recent years to coincide with his box office failures, but then I looked at the latest *Forbes* Hollywood earners list. In 4th place, tied with Nicolas Cage, was good old Eddie who earned $39 million for two movies in the last 12 months. Do the math. The man is still pulling in $20 million a picture. The studios talk about how they need to reign in star salaries, but as long as fallen stars like Eddie Murphy continue to rake in that kind of coin, it just remains a lot of empty talk.

The way blockbusters dominate the landscape, some companies are smart to avoid the summer and wait it out to the fall season. When I worked for Orion Pictures in the 1980s, the thinking back then was that in order to get the full respect and support from exhibitors, a distributor had to be a supplier of films 12 months of the year, and that's what we did. So each summer the company scheduled one June movie, one July movie and one August movie. At times it worked out fine when we had a "Bull Durham" or "Robocop," but often the company was left with substantial losses from movies that weren't strong enough or good enough to compete with the big boys. Looking back in my files, I came across the summer of 1989, which was particularly devastating and was what proved to be the beginning of the end for Orion as it filed for bankruptcy only two years later. This was the summer of "Batman," "Indiana Jones the Last Crusade," "Ghostbusters II," "Lethal Weapon II" and "Honey I Shrunk the Kids." Orion's three summer movies that year were "Great Balls of Fire," "UHF" and "Rude Awakening," starring either Cheech or Chong and a smoking fish. That trio of movies grossed a total of $22,000,000 between them and has to be considered one of the weakest summer slates of all time. That's too bad because Orion was a much better company than that, and their strength was in upscale films better suited for the fall and winter. But that's what the lure of summer can do to a lot of mid-level movies – leave them for roadkill on the side of the road.

This Week at the Box Office   *Weekly Attendance: 41,419,549*

It's been proven time and again that the two-minute movie trailer is the centerpiece of every marketing campaign, and if a distributor has a strong one, a movie has at least a chance for breakout success. That was the case for "The Hangover," and it looks like it may be the case for Disney's "The Proposal" which is opening this weekend. The trailer has a lot of energy to it; it's funny, sexy, Sandra Bullock looks great, and the movie has a real screwball comedy feel to it. The success of that trailer and the positive response to it by audiences was a factor in Disney's decision to conduct an old-fashioned sneak preview at 1,100 of the highest grossing theatres in the U.S. last Saturday night. I refer to the sneak preview as old-fashioned because it looks like it has gone out of style, and there have been very few of them in recent years. This is not an easy decision for distribution execs to make, and they have to consider the following factors before setting it in place:

► Are they absolutely confident that audiences will love the film and spread positive word of mouth to their friends? No studio would risk conducting a national sneak if they thought audience reaction could work against the film. Sneaks should only be held for certified crowd pleasers, so there is pressure to make the right call.

► All studios look at research tracking numbers, which indicate the level of awareness and want to see for upcoming movies as they approach their opening dates. If a studio sees the level of awareness is lacking for a movie they feel will have a lot of playability, sneaking a movie in advance is a viable method that can be used to increase awareness, buzz and water cooler talk during the entire week before a movie opens.

► Are there extra marketing dollars to add to the budget? To properly conduct a national sneak preview, a distributor has to spend an additional $2,000,000 to $5,000,000 on extra television and newspaper ads to make sure audiences know it's happening.

► The decision has to be made which day and which weekend to conduct the sneak. There have been Friday night, Saturday night and even Sunday afternoon sneaks for family films, though Saturday night remains the most popular with it being the top movie going day of the week. The vast majority of sneaks occur the week before opening, but there have been sneak previews placed two weeks before opening date and, depending on the results, repeated again the following week at different theatres.

► Finally, distributors must decide and negotiate which current movie they wish to play with and replace on the night of the sneak. The thing with sneak previews is that the box office revenue taken in for the sneak goes to the current movie that's playing and being replaced, not to the movie that is sneaking. Even though the prime motive for a sneak is to create extra awareness and buzz, distributors would prefer to pair it with one of their own movies so the company can keep the box office generated by the sneak and have it applied to their other movie. If a distributor doesn't have either an appropriate movie to pair it with or no movie in the marketplace at the time, they have no other choice but to try to match it up with another company's films and get their permission to do so.

Disney's only movie in the marketplace was "UP," entering its third week of playtime. They made the decision to go with "UP" so all the box office collected for "The Proposal" stayed in house. What made the decision easier for Disney were the multiple screens "UP" was playing on in these theatres, so taking away a single 7:00 or 7:30 p.m. showtime still left early evening shows for families who were not inclined to see the romantic comedy.

On Monday morning, Disney reported the sneaks were filled to 88% capacity and audiences loved the movie. That prompted the distributor to add additional screens for the opening and date more small towns that were not included in the original release strategy. So far, their decision to go with the sneak preview has worked to perfection. The only thing left for them to do now is to stand back, see how the weekend plays out and hope all their work pays off with a strong opening weekend gross and a long run in the theatres.

The Proposal
Disney
Opening weekend: $33,627,598
Domestic gross: $163,958,031 51.7%
Foreign gross: $153,417,000 48.3%
Worldwide gross: $317,375,031
Widest release: 3,099 theatres

Year One
Sony
Opening weekend: $19,610,304
Domestic gross: $43,337,279 69.5%
Foreign gross: $19,020,621 30.5%
Worldwide gross: $62,357,900
Widest release: 3,022 theatres

Whatever Works
Sony Classics
Opening weekend: $266,162
Domestic gross: $5,306,706 15.1%
Foreign gross: $29,791,109 84.9%
Worldwide gross: $35,097,815
Widest release: 353 theatres

Dead Snow
IFC
Opening weekend: $5,663
Domestic gross: $46,742 2.4%
Foreign gross: $1,937,920 97.6
Worldwide gross: $1,984,662
Widest release: 4 theatres

The Windmill Movie
Film Desk
Opening weekend: $3,832
Domestic gross: $30,050
Foreign gross: N/A
Widest release: 4 theatres

Brighton Rock (re-release)
Rialto
Opening weekend: $10,626
Domestic gross: $49,466 81.2%
Foreign gross: $11,484 18.8%
Worldwide gross: $60,950
Widest release: 1 theatre

Worst Wide Opening Weekends (3,000+ Theatres)
1982 – Present

1. Hoot (New Line, 2006) $3,368,197
2. The Seeker: The Dark is Rising (Fox, 2007) $3,745,315
3. Meet Dave (Fox, 2008) $5,251,918
4. Imagine That (Paramount, 2009) $5,503,519
5. New York Minute (Warner Bros., 2004) $5,962,106

Source: Boxoffice Mojo

Conversations with Industry Professionals

Chuck Viane – President of Distribution, Walt Disney Studios

The following interview took place on June 2, 2011, a month before Mr. Viane retired on July 1, 2011 after 25 years with Disney. In October 2011, Mr. Viane was hired by DreamWorks Animation as a distribution consultant.

> *"If you don't do it as a team, if you do it as a lone wolf, there can be a a lot of hiccups along the way which can lead to big problems."*
>
> —*Chuck Viane*

Q: *You started on the exhibition side of the business with General Cinema in Chicago in the 1970s and went to work for Disney in Los Angeles in 1985 on the distribution side. Did you have a career strategy to move to the West Coast to get closer to where the center of the industry was?*

CV: My sights were never set on going to the West Coast. But as the 1980s evolved, there was never a doubt, whether you were in distribution or exhibition, that regional offices would be closing. It wasn't a matter of if branch offices would close, it was a matter of when. When I was in exhibition, I don't think I realized just how much consolidation would happen because many circuits were owned by individual moguls, not public companies. So everyone had to anticipate that reality and keep their eyes and ears open. So when Disney offered me a job in distribution, I accepted it and moved to Los Angeles.

Q: *Speaking of consolidation, give me a quick capsule of the size of Disney's theatrical distribution organization from when you started with the company and where it is in 2011.*

CV: When I started at Disney in 1985 there were 34 satellite offices, and today there are three sales offices in New York, Los Angeles and Toronto. There are less than 50 people in the sales organization today compared to around 200 back then. Technology has put us in the situation where we can be much leaner. We used to have 8 to 10 cashiers, and now we share four cashiers with home video. Our deals are firm and exhibitors pay accordingly, many of them electronically, which has made a huge difference. We don't touch any checks; they go straight to the banks. It's a very clean process. In addition, Rentrak gets all our grosses. Algorithms show you the 200 missing theatres and what they would do. We don't have to have someone on the phone all day chasing after missing grosses. In addition, when it's reported in the trades that more layoffs are coming out of domestic distribution, it depends how you define domestic distribution. In our company, distribution encompasses theatrical, home video and television, so it's a much bigger area than just theatrical.

Q: *Over the years it hasn't been that unusual for distribution and exhibition executives to cross over to the other side and take high-ranking jobs. Did your experience in exhibition help you in your transition?*

CV: I believe that was a key in my success when I got the distribution opportunity with my not too distant exhibition past. That was a common thread with myself and my associates Chris Leroy and Tom Sherak who also came out of exhibition. That made us unique for a while because we could see both sides of the argument to try to make it a win/win for both sides. That definitely helped our success as distributors.

Q: *When you began at Disney in the mid-80s, the company was going through its own changes, wasn't it?*

CV: Yes, that was when Michael Eisner and Jeffrey Katzenberg were bringing new energy and ideas to Disney with movies like "Down and Out in Beverly Hills" and "Ruthless People," comedies made for an adult audience, which landed up being very successful. That created the kind of atmosphere where the industry realized that Disney could do live action as well as animation. It's been a very exciting ride ever since.

Q: *In January 2010, your duties were expanded when you became President of Global Distribution. How has that worked out for you overseeing the international market as well as the domestic market?*

CV: When I took over international, I had the opportunity to travel to many countries, and it was a great experience. I loved every minute of it because it allowed me to be energized again, to play a part in making digital 3D a major part of our global business, to watch the digital revolution flourish. Having the opportunity to absorb new things so late in my career was invigorating. I'll tell you I've learned as much in the last two years as I've had any time in my career. You always think that you are confident, but every day something new comes up that needs a decision, and you can't be afraid to make an error because that's part of the learning curve. When you work with people who run the home video arm or the consumer products division and see firsthand what the global impact is, it changes everything. It's been documented often how the international gross dominates domestic, and having the ability to oversee everything gives me the opportunity to place films worldwide. Not every film should be day and date because when it's summer here it's winter somewhere else in the world. You have to understand the differentials in each country, one territory compared to another, matching up with any local holidays, things like that. It's that learning curve that's so much fun.

Q: *Do you have a specific lesson that you have learned that you can share that deals with a particular territory?*

CV: Some of the things may seem obvious, but when you don't deal with it on a day-to-day basis it's not front and center in your mind. South Korea is a country in which literally the home video business doesn't exist. The reason it doesn't exist is that there is so much piracy that by the time you get to the third week of a film's release, the movie is being sold in every black market situation there is. So it's tough to try to do anything because the product is already on the street, which forces us to play off movies very quickly. We look at situations from the context of all our divisions and how it impacts the entire life cycle of a movie. We can figure out where the profit will come in. In Korea we're missing a major component, so before we go into that market we have to figure out if it makes economic sense to release a movie in that country. You can never allow Korea to go out before other parts of the world because some of the quickest growing countries like Russia, China, India and Brazil have their own piracy problems, but they are not quite as bad as in Korea.

Q: *What are your main responsibilities as president of distribution?*

CV: As president, I'm more of an overseer with everyone reporting to me rather than actually doing specific duties, but one duty I've retained is choosing the release dates for our films in the domestic market. My job is to bring my managers the best type of information and make my suggestions and to get them to sign off on it. At Disney we are big with team consensus. There is a lot of collaborative involvement with the heads of the various divisions during our meetings. You look at the leader of that specific team, whether it's in distribution, home video, marketing, consumer products, media buying, and you collaborate as a group, and then you look at the person who has to make the decision. You can take teamwork too far sometimes, but overall I think we've done a remarkably good job with our group. When you put the five or so leaders together, regularly there are no surprises and the rest of it sort of works. With a great production team you talk to them on how to build a schedule so distribution will have pictures for 12 months of the year, and they have to figure out how that can happen with production schedules, post production, special effects work that needs to get done. And we in distribution know the more expensive films have to be coddled in different ways. If you don't do it as a team, if you do it as a lone wolf, there can be a lot of hiccups along the way, which can lead to big problems. I also want to stress that marketing people have never told me what theatres to play, and I've never told the marketing department how to market the movies. We are all collaborative, but we know the jobs we have to do and the decisions we have to make on our own.

Q: *Can you talk more about release date strategy?*

CV: One of the components of a successful year is to have a release schedule that compliments itself, having an ebb and flow, which works best on the exhibition side, and what's best for the film. If we have a claim to fame we've done a pretty good job with counter-programming. In 2009, when we can go with a "Hanna Montana" in April and "The Proposal" against all the heavy hitters in June and walk away with doing the business we did with those two movies, those are the fun days when you pick the right dates and the films are very successful.

Q: *On the flip side, when a movie doesn't work, how often does the release date get blamed?*

CV: It's a convenient excuse when a movie underperforms, but I don't see release dates being blamed very often. Typically the public is so good at figuring out what they want to see and what they don't want to see, all you have to do is put the right creative materials in front of them, and they will make that choice. There are exceptions when great movies don't do well, and I believe you can't use a bad release date as a crutch unless you put something out on a date when a similar type of movie is opening. In the entire year there are only two weeks when I would not want to release a movie, the week after Labor Day and the week after Thanksgiving.

Q: *But no studio has ever released an important tentpole on the Friday before Labor Day. How about Labor Day?*

CV: I think someone should do it.

Q: *But it's not going to be you, right, and wouldn't it be risky for someone to be the first one to try it?*

CV: It could be if I had the right picture and I was still working, but what I would probably do is open the movie two Fridays before Labor Day where you could have a strong opening and strong second week, and since nobody would release much the week after, you automatically get a third week. Product doesn't rebuild until the end of September, so you would have a diminished marketplace to yourself, a four to five week stretch where your competition would be minimal.

Q: *In 2009, Disney had an 11.8% market share and was ranked fifth among the major studios. How important is studio market share at Disney?*

CV: We have never been in the market share business; we are in the profitability business. We don't release 25 to 30 films a year; we are in the 13 to 16 range, so we would never be able to compete just on market share, but we can certainly be one of the more profitable studios. You can find out more about profits by looking at the stock price and reading the quarterly reports of the companies.

Q: *I'd like to have you talk about two of your most successful films of 2009. First, Pixar's "UP." You have been there for all the Pixar films, and they all have been big hits. What does that mean for you to have* *guaranteed hits that can be placed on a release schedule for you and the exhibitors? That must be special.*

CV: It really is special, but you have to realize that nothing is totally guaranteed before it opens. When you read the storylines of some of the Pixar movies years before they open, the pitch lines of movies like "Wall-E" or "Ratatouille," it was an unbelievable challenge to make them work. Whoever you talk to, everyone would say the most important aspect of a film is the story. The Pixar filmmakers make extremely engaging stories; they never forget who they make their movies for and how to make them as enjoyable as possible for audiences. I think their commitment to such detail is why people look forward to them. Pixar's movies are made for everyone and not just for any particular demographic, and that is rare today and why their movies are so unique. Our marketing campaigns play a major role in motivating audiences to choose our films. Being a Pixar film makes that choice a little easier.

Q: *"Up" opened on May 29, 2009 following five other blockbusters that opened in the same month. It was one of the more competitive months that I've ever seen. Did that play a part in placing it after all the others?*

CV: It really is what's right for the movie. In that month we were following some major-league talent on the screen and they all had their unique audiences. Coming last didn't change anything because our audience was more readily available to us being closer to more schools being out for the summer.

Q: *I'd say it worked out pretty well for you because "UP" landed up with a worldwide gross of $731 million, making it the biggest of those May blockbusters. Let's switch to "The Proposal," which was another big success for Disney. The interesting thing for me with that film is the rare national sneak preview that you held the Saturday before it opened on June 19, 2009. Holding sneak previews was once a common practice but not anymore. You rarely see one anymore. Talk about your decision to do 1,100 sneaks the week before "The Proposal" opened.*

CV: I don't know why no other companies have been doing it, but I believe in the sneak preview approach when you have the right movie. If you have a movie which is getting good word of mouth, you should consider it, but you also have to consider how to do it, when to do it and why are you doing it. You may remember there was a very competitive space at the time of "The Proposal," yet other movies seemed to have bigger profiles than we did. So distribution thought holding sneak previews would be a smart move, and marketing thought it would be very easy to promote the sneaks, so it went forward. It worked to perfection, and the public loved the movie. The theatres that played the sneaks had an 88% capacity; so when you have that kind of capacity you have to ask yourself did we need to do it because that's a really strong capacity. The answer to that, whether you needed it or not, it did not hurt the film, as a matter of fact it put out one of the greatest word-of-mouth campaigns ever, and it went on to be Sandra Bullock's biggest opening up to that time. Just a tremendous success.

Q: *A lesser success story that year was "Confessions of a Shopaholic" which was your January release in 2009. That was still during the recession. Was the subject matter wrong for that particular time?*

CV: That movie was in development for several years, so the timing may not have been the greatest when it finally came out. In hindsight, people can look at things and make pronouncements on how something performed, but then again, this movie had a lot going for it. If it had a little more comedy it could have perhaps done better at the box office. I don't know, but like I said before, the public is the only one that determines if the decisions we are making are the right ones.

Q: *Over the years one of your roles has been as the spokesman for Disney commenting to the media on the weekend business when you open a new movie. Can you address the process of estimating weekend grosses to the media before the weekend is over?*

CV: On a big weekend I'm talking to 10 or 12 media outlets. We service some of them via fax with grosses and highlighted information with a quote, but most of them are direct conversations on Sunday morning. Estimating a weekend gross can be tricky but estimates have become a lot more accurate based on track records and gross retrieval. A larger number of theatres are able to supply grosses to us because of sophisticated tools, so we are actually receiving Friday and Saturday grosses from 92 to 93% of all the theatres playing a movie. It used to be that we had to estimate 500-600 theatres; now it's only about 200 theatres, and you play the law of averages and balance it out. I don't want to underestimate the value of a movie, but at the same time I don't want to be overly aggressive because if you miss that figure you actually disappoint some people. I'm not just talking to media over the weekend but to producers and directors too. It's always nice to talk to talent and hear their perspective; for some of them it's good news and it's nice to hear their excitement. When it's bad news you hate to deliver it, but reality is reality, and you have to tell it like it is. When something performs better than expected, it's much more of a pleasant weekend, but in this business there are probably more rainy days than sunny days. You have to make sure the sunny days are strong enough to protect you against the rainy days.

Q: *With massive releases and the disappearance of clearances and zones, has the art of distribution taken a hit when everyone basically plays the same movies?*

CV: You know, I would turn that question around. For me, it's taken the art of film buying away. In the old days you had certain film buyers who could make a movie into a hit by saying "Butch Cassidy" will be a big picture or "Love Story" or the exhibitors who picked "Star Wars" instead of "The Other Side of Midnight" when there were A & B tracks to choose from. Those were decisions where guys made their careers on the decisions they made. You have to remember film buyers were booking single screens or 2 or 4 plexes. Those were tough business decisions to pull the trigger on in the bidding era. That's why I say the art of film buying is gone. In distribution you can still decide for yourself whether you platform or go exclusive or go out with 600 runs or 3,200 runs and still be able to choose the specific week to open.

Q: *3D movies seem to be losing some steam with the public. How big of a concern is that?*

CV: Disney distributed "Chicken Little" in digital 3D in 2004. We were the originators when there were no 3D screens. We partnered with Dolby and Real D and did a 100 day road trip trying to convince exhibitors that 3D was something they should invest in. Our goal was to get 100 3D screens, and we delivered 84 of them because we couldn't get enough 3D projectors. It was a huge success for those theatres that showed it in the new format, but what we painstakingly did was give the public what they anticipated. And that is something that would jump off the screen, end up on their laps or make them reach out and have them touch something like a snowflake. We did an extremely good job on that film. The dip in excitement for 3D that we are seeing now is a combination of issues. The economy can be playing a part, the pricing could be an issue, and there is the simple fact the industry is making some 3D movies that should have never been made – cheater films which are hurting the perception that 3D is not worth the higher admission price. Last but not least, we forget why the public is willing to pay a premium, to get something they can't get anywhere else in a 2D auditorium. At this moment, foreign theatres are hanging in better than domestic. On the latest "Pirates," $213 million of our opening worldwide grosses were in 3D. That is substantial.

Q: *Can an argument be made at this point in time that theatrical is the most solid and steadiest component*

in the life cycle of a film?

CV: Theatrical is performing well, and it would be a good argument to make. Nothing happens without theatrical; it's still the engine that drives everything. On a big film, substantial money flows in very quickly from theatres around the world, but you also have to remember that the studios have hundreds of millions of dollars that has already been spent with high production and marketing costs. Very few movies, there are some definite exceptions, turn a profit just from theatrical. It needs the entire life cycle of a film to create the profits.

Q: Do you think the United States has enough screens?

CV: It could be the correct amount of theatres at around 39,000, but I believe the number of theatres in certain cities is really exaggerated. Many cities can do with a lot less screens, and some cities could use several more. So the number would probably be the same, but they could be shifted around some. Do we really need 120 to 125 runs in New York City? I doubt it.

Q: Will theatres still have a decent exclusive window in ten years?

CV: That's a difficult question. It's hard to tell because ten years ago if you would have asked me about where the digital conversion would be, I would have told you the whole world would be digital by now. That didn't happen. There were financial issues due to the cost of conversion, and then the financial meltdown in the county hit which slowed things down. I know in ten years I'll still be seeing my movies in theatres. Nothing can beat the communal experience of a theatre.

Q: How much longer do you see 35mm prints being struck?

CV: Physical prints will start getting phased out in 2013. The obvious answer for the switch to digital is that the savings will be substantial, but part of going through all this wasn't purely a cost savings, it was a quality issue also. If you went into a theatre in the third week of a 35mm print compared to a digital print in its third week, you know there was a huge difference in quality. A film print can break down after the very first screening and continue to break down every showing thereafter. Oil is a component of striking a film print; silver is a component; those costs have skyrocketed. Whoever we use for our prints, Kodak or Fuji, they pass on their costs to distributors, and it will get to the point where it won't be economically feasible to continue down that road.

Q: Hasn't the cost of prints gone down to about $1,000 per print when you do a bulk run of 4,000 prints?

CV: 4,000 prints wouldn't be a problem if that's all there was. Some studios have struck 10,000 prints in the U.S. alone, and then when you factor in the rest of the world, it could be 30,000 prints. That is why whether it's satellite delivery or sending digital cards to the theatres, the delivery cost of prints will go down to a reasonable level so when you go anywhere you will believe there is an economic chance of breaking even. In today's world you don't get to use a print over and over again in different locations because the smaller theaters don't want to wait. We have to adjust to that. After the initial runs are over we have thousands of prints shipped back to us just sitting there.

Q: Will the switch to digital mean the end of the small town theatre?

CV: I totally disagree with everyone on this point. Why would it cause the death of small towns? Digital projection will add life to their theatres because they will be able to secure prints much sooner, near or on availability because the cost of delivery will be at a price that is affordable for a studio to supply them. If I was small town America, I would consider expanding, not contracting.

Q: *I've always heard that foreign theatres pay less film rental to distributors than domestic theatres. Is that true?*

CV: Let me put it this way. There are over 100 markets, and there are probably at least 101 different deals out there. Some markets pay more. Some markets pay less. Lower film rental could have been the case years ago, but the theory that all markets pay less is not true. All negotiations are done market by market. Some countries used to be legislated in terms of what we could get out of them, but that's not an issue anymore. The one country that is a lot less is China. China not only has a quota of how many U.S. films they play a year, but they also pay the least amount of film rental to distributors at this time. We're hoping with the negotiations going on that will be changing for the better in the future.

Q: *But the studios are doing better than ever in their film deals with U.S. exhibitors, correct?*

CV: It took many decades for film rental deals to get to the point of where they are now. Yes, splits have become more equitable for the studios. Film rental deals are far removed than they used to be because past deals like 90/10s out-lived their usefulness, and other deals like the Manhattan deal or the Chicago deal went away because they didn't work for distributors anymore. I can't talk about our film terms on any specific basis, but things are going well for us in being able to procure a larger share of the box office revenue.

Q: *Can you talk to me about the impact the falling DVD market has had on decisions that are being made at Disney?*

CV: The home video market was the profit center for Disney and all the other studios. This is where the profits kicked in. DVD revenue delivered huge sums of money, and in the last few years it's been on a downward spiral, severely hampering cash flow and operating income. The risks are multiplying because we don't have the same safety net anymore, so the studios are less healthy now despite the growth we are seeing in international. Everyone is trying to figure out where the next revenue stream is going to come from, and that's going to be interesting to watch. The public loves movies, and we have to figure out how to serve them, where they want to see them, when they want to see them, how they want to see them.

Q: *Hasn't everyone been waiting for Video-on Demand, downloading and streaming to show some life? They have all remained minor revenue streams. When is something going to jump up and become a serious revenue generator?*

CV: It's a very simple question with a very simple answer. Nothing has emerged yet.

Q: *I guess that leads to the topic of Premium VOD, which four studios are now experimenting with, but your company is not one of them. This strategy is all about making movies available inside the home much quicker for a higher price, and it has caused a lot of anxiety among exhibitors who feel their livelihood is being threatened. What's your take on this?*

CV: I'm of the belief that no technology will take the first level of distribution out of the business. The reason is the social intertwining of the public when they go to a movie theatre to get that communal effect; a comedy is a lot funnier when you are laughing with 300 people. I don't think the theatrical experience can be duplicated other than inside a theatre; that's just the way it is. I don't believe distribution will make it too close to jeopardize the theatrical window. These are smart people, and the question is when the two sides will get together and work it out properly. Shouldn't studios be allowed to test something new? People should not make assumptions that it will kill the business. If it's to anyone's detriment, don't pursue it. If it doesn't hurt, the industry has to move forward because thinking the DVD business will bounce back, it won't; it's over.

Q: *Why haven't there been any numbers released on how Premium VOD has been doing?*

CV: Well, they are just dipping their toes into it now. Like I said, it would be good if all the partners could get together to talk it out. There should not be any sacred cows anymore. It's a great industry, and both sides have to work together to give the public what they want. People won't buy something just because you tell them to wait 90 days. Think of piracy. A movie comes out and plays in theatres less than four weeks; then you have to wait to the 120-day mark before it shows up on DVD, which gives people 90 days to pirate and download illegal files. That being said, I don't have the answer.

Q: *What skills and talents have made you successful in the movie industry?*

CV: I think when you understand your partner's pain, it's easier to forge a model to move forward rather than being an adversary. At Disney I put tons of effort into being a good partner; we didn't do anything just because that's how it was done before. I once read something that I adhere to. There are three traits you need to be successful, patience, commitment and resiliency, and there is no question that the hardest part for me was having patience. Over the years when I became a more patient leader I became a much better executive. I had commitment from day one; that one was pretty easy, and resiliency, well you better have it in the movie industry because you have to bounce back from a lot of releases that don't land up where you think they are going to be.

Q: *Is it patience with those working under you or with exhibitors?*

CV: It's both. It's patience to make the proper decision, to be truly knowledgeable about a situation and not make rash judgments. There were times when we would think something or someone was going to harm the company, but when you slow down the process and analyze it, you find out it was meant to help you. That's what patience allows, to do some fact finding, not letting your temper become a hair trigger. These types of things can make a huge difference. We have all made a decision too quickly, and then you have to rectify the mistake, which is never fun. You can't let egos get in the way. You may have to say you're sorry or seek someone's council because they may know something you don't know.

Q: *Do you learn more from failure?*

CV: The failure is in not trying. It isn't in not succeeding.

Q: *Anything else about leadership you would like to share?*

CV: Listening. Too many people don't listen. One party has a point of view, and they are intent in getting it across. They don't listen to anyone. When you rebut something with a reasonable argument and nobody learns from it, that is a disappointment. Listening is a very important factor in good leadership. My parting word of wisdom is that both sides of the fence have got to work together, to listen to each other. We have a successful industry, everyone is making money, but we have to sit down at a table to honestly work out the problems facing distribution and exhibition.

Q: *It has been a love/hate relationship for 100 years.*

CV: It has to be that way because it starts with a simple premise – both sides want to make the most money they can – one side wants to pay less, and one side wants you to pay more and therein starts the battle.

Q: What's a basic fundamental of the movie industry that has been in place for years?

CV: It's not about us; it's about the consumer, the customer. If you don't take care of the customer, the rest of these plans don't work. Everything the public has asked for they have been given; stadium seating, larger screens. Every time we have come up with innovations the industry has gotten healthier. We can't lose sight of what the main driver is, making the theatrical experience very special so that the public is willing to pay for distributors providing the best possible films with good stories and exhibitors having clean and modern theatres, well-run with great projection.

Q: Looking ahead, is it a concern that younger audiences may not have the same passion for movies that the older generations have had?

CV: We have to hope that we can hook the younger generation to become loyal moviegoers in whatever way they want to see it. We can look at the baby boomers who remain strong moviegoers after 50 years of going to movies. We need that from the next generation to keep the movie industry healthy for many years to come.

Q: Thank you for your time and insight and good luck in the future

CV: Thank you.

Week 25: Questions for Discussion

1. Why can't all films play successfully in the summer months? What are the challenges involved in marketing a movie in the summer? Can smaller films survive the crunch and find an audience? Provide at least two examples of smaller films that found success in past summers and relate how they did it.

2. Discuss the strategy of sneak previews and the expense and risk involved for a distributor that chooses to do one.

3. With an 88% capacity for the sneak preview of "The Proposal," Chuck Viane mentioned that they had to ask themselves if they needed to do it. What does he mean when he says that?

4. From an exhibitor's standpoint, what could be the pros and cons of agreeing to hold a sneak preview on a Saturday night at one of their theatres?

5. Describe the difference between market share and profitability of a studio. What's a valid point in why Disney prefers to concentrate on profitability over market share?

6. Pixar has never had a losing film and makes it look easy. In actuality, is it as easy as it looks?

7. What three traits does Chuck Viane adhere to that has helped make him be successful in the movie industry? What has been the hardest for him to master? Looking at those same three traits, how would you rate yourself in those qualities?

BIG ROBOTS, BIG MONEY AND BIG PROMOTIONS

Week 26: June 26–July 2, 2009

> *You can almost say "Transformers" is the best
> and worst the studios have to offer.*

Wednesday, June 24, 2009 turned out to be a memorable day for Hollywood. On the same day that "Transformers: Revenge of the Fallen" opened and grossed $60,000,000 to set a new box office record for a Wednesday opening day, the Motion Picture Academy announced that the Best Picture category would double from five nominated films to ten films starting with this year's crop of movies. I'm as surprised as everyone else with the announcement from the Academy because there was no hint that it was coming, but I applaud them for it, and it will be great fun to speculate on all the possibilities it presents for a wider range of films the rest of the year. But more on the Oscar change at a later date, it's "Transformers" and summer movie promotions that I'm going to explore today. A movie like this can easily become the poster child of everything that is wrong with movies becoming a mere commodity and one big commercial, but every movie in essence becomes a product to be marketed and sold if it wishes to be seen by the public. "Transformers" is at the extreme end of that equation, but speaking from personal experience, seeking out promotional partners and commercial tie-ins is not something to be derided and dismissed so easily. Any experienced producer or distributor would agree that finding promotional partners to help create awareness is a good thing, not a bad thing. It's just that size matters, and the most effective movie promotions generally have a massive amount of money backing them, and no one can match up to the size and deep pockets of the Hollywood studios.

"Transformers" is not about Oscar nominations. It's about big robots, big money and big promotions. The first one in the series surprised the industry when it grossed $700 million worldwide in 2007, so I shouldn't be shocked when the sequel does $60 million on its first day. But I am. That's crazy money. Only when we approach it more as a marketing event than a mere movie, a combination of advertising, promotions and products that it starts making more sense. This is the state of today's Hollywood summer blockbuster. You can almost say "Transformers" is the best and worst the studios have to offer. It is the best being from an economic business model standpoint, which shows Hollywood's ability to gross hundreds of millions of dollars throughout the world in a very short period of time. The worst of it being that it epitomizes ear-splitting mindless entertainment at its most excruciating level.

To call a movie "branded entertainment" should not be perceived as an immediate negative because marketing is part of the essential DNA of every movie, from the smallest art film to the most expensive blockbuster. Branding is just another term for giving a movie a specific identity, and all movies need an identity. It always comes down to a film's quality and needs. A delicate art film may be able to get by with publicity and strong critics' reviews, but when a movie costs over $200 million like "Transformers: Revenge of the Fallen," a studio needs to look for promotional partners and product placement opportunities to help offset the huge production costs. That's exactly what Paramount did. The latest "Transformers" is certainly one of the biggest promotional movies of the summer, and whatever the movie achieves has a lot to do with the multitude of cross promotions the studio has lined up for its new tentpole.

You may think that after the first "Transformers" became a monster hit, Paramount could ease up and not have to worry as much about outside promotional partners, but the exact opposite is true. When you have it, you flaunt it and push for more. When you are a success, you want to become a bigger success. When you have about $350,000,000 riding on production and worldwide marketing and distribution expenses, a distributor needs to have as many promotions and additional marketing support as they can get to insure they get their investment back and secure the highest profits possible. Aiding in that goal, when a movie has already established itself in the marketplace, more companies become interested in getting involved in it. Helping to connect studios and advertisers are more than 40 companies in the Los Angeles area that specialize in setting up promotions and product placement opportunities. Companies have long relied on movies to help promote their products, and the following are several different ways deals can be structured:

► Companies that have their brands appear in films with no money exchanging hands and no product placement fee involved. This is the deal General Motors has with Paramount on the Transformer movies as they showcase five new vehicles in "Revenge of the Fallen." Their only expense is in the manufacturing costs of the cars themselves. Money doesn't change hands, but the products and services are showcased, which can save the production company money in the long run. Generally, it's a product that fits well into a specific scene and works for both parties. With the bigger films and larger companies in this type of deal, the companies can also agree to spend marketing dollars to help promote the film's release. A bankruptcy filing forced GM not to spend money on an expensive advertising campaign this time around as they did for the 2007 movie, so they are getting the benefit of exposure without any additional expense.

► A straight product placement deal for a product to appear in a movie in a cash transaction. Over the years, beer companies have paid to have their brands on screen. Years after its release, I still recall the scene in "The Firm" when Gene Hackman reaches in the fridge and hands Tom Cruise a Red Stripe beer.

► Tradeoff deals. In the James Bond film "Quantum of Solace," Ocean Sky, a British private jet company, lent the production five of its jets which are valued at $100 million each which were used to fly the cast and crew out to Panama for a week's worth of filming. They usually charge $5,000 an hour, and the total cost of the deal was $600,000, but instead of a cash exchange, Ocean Sky was featured five times in the movie.

► Cross-promotional tie-ins where companies may not be featured in the movie but get involved with marketing their products and associating themselves with a hot Hollywood movie. This is a very common type of deal for blockbusters in which companies agree to spend millions of dollars in advertising support by becoming official marketing partners on a specific film. For "Revenge of the Fallen," Paramount's partners include Burger King, Mars Candies, Kmart, Verizon Wireless and Hasbro. These companies in return generally spend between $10 and $20 million to promote the movie with their own advertising campaigns on television, in print and on the Internet. Michael Bay, the movie's director, directed many of the television commercials for the above companies, incorporating scenes from the movie with the individual brands. Often, companies use these opportunities to introduce new products or limited edition items, as is the case with Mars introducing M&M's Strawberried Peanut Butter Chocolate Candies and Snickers Nougabot as part of the movie promotion.

► Straight merchandising deals with apparel, toys and games, household products and other categories where a percentage split and guaranteed minimums are negotiated between the two parties.

► Stunts and gimmicks: Creating and pulling off stunts to help promote your film is only limited by one's imagination and marketing budget. In the old days when downtown theatres had exclusive engagements, stunts could be as simple as putting an employee in a gorilla suit and walking around the crowded downtown streets passing out fliers, to more complicated ones like closing down streets and staging a parade. That was when local exhibitors were the main promoters of a movie rather than the distributor. Nowadays the major stunts and gimmicks are pulled off by the distributors as when DreamWorks had Jerry Seinfeld fly over the Cannes Film Festival in a flying harness to promote the animated feature "Bee." One of the most memorable gimmicks of the last decade was when 20th Century Fox turned a limited number of 7-Eleven convenience stores around the country into Kwik-E-Mart stores for "The Simpsons Movie." This was an ingenious idea that received tons of coverage, which is the goal of any staged promotion, turning your promotion into free publicity gold. I remember visiting one of these converted stores in a Chicago suburb where there was a huge line just to get in. It was just a great promotion, and everyone had a lot of fun with it.

> *An old friend of mine working for a studio told me one of the most brutally honest things anyone ever said to me, "Dave, awareness is a national television campaign and a 1,000 print theatre release."*

So the latest "Transformers" movie has been aided greatly by all the additional marketing dollars being spent on its behalf, but what if a filmmaker has an independent movie with no stars and a limited budget to work with. Are setting up promotions possible? Always. They will be on a much more modest scale, but opportunities are out there. Promotions are all about making deals with 3rd party partners, and one can be as creative as possible thinking of cross promotions and trade-offs. Promotions can involve screening passes, two-for-one ads in local newspapers, a restaurant tie-in, radio station screenings with free mentions on the air, t-shirt giveaways, a promotional stunt which leads to media coverage, opening night parties, the list goes on and on. Promotions are fun, but they can also cost money to pull off, so the proper strategy along with realistic expectations is recommended. I've been personally involved with a couple of independent films where the expectations and attempt at a promotional campaign didn't live up to the reality of the situations. In both cases, it came down to lack of money, the restraints of limited distribution and lack of awareness by the public. As a producer's rep for "Hoop Dreams," my partner and I held back merchandising rights for the filmmakers to keep when we made the distribution deal with Fine Line Features. With a great brand name and the basketball theme, we thought this could be a lucrative angle to pursue. What we discovered was the difficulty all specialized films encounter when there are a limited number of prints and cities playing a film; not enough awareness and money being spent on the release to interest merchandisers to get involved. We actually found a Florida apparel company willing to produce a variety of "Hoop Dreams" t-shirts and procured a modest advance. The company actually came out with a line of compelling designs and made a deal with J.C. Penney. There were a couple of problems. For about 10 days, the shirts were displayed in selected stores, and it was exciting to see the shirts on the racks. Unfortunately, the Florida manufacturer turned out to be financially strapped and basically had no resources for much of an advertising campaign, so the public didn't know about the shirts, and they were sent back when they didn't sell. It was a noble attempt, but it was a fruitless effort that failed to produce any merchandising profits for the filmmakers.

The other stab at a big promotional push involved our distribution of the movie "Tie Died: Rock n' Roll's Most Deadicated Fans," the documentary about Grateful Dead fans. I knew it was a very promotable movie where we could create colorful tie-dyed t-shirts, work with classic rock radio stations, do promotional tie-ins with head shops and funky bars and have a lot of fun along the way. We were also able to tie-in with the publisher of the book "Dictionary for Deadheads" and received complimentary copies of the book to hand out at radio screenings and even made a deal with Ben & Jerry's for free coupons for their peace pops. We had fun all right and did a lot of good things but were again hindered by both a limited budget and a limited release. We thought we were creating enough awareness for the film, but an old friend of mine working for a studio told me one of the most brutally honest things anyone ever said to me, "Dave, awareness is a national television campaign and a 1,000 print theatre release."

Indeed. There are constant lessons that are learned while working in the motion picture marketplace; some are harder lessons than others. "Transformers" and "Tie-Died" are on the extreme ends of the movie industry. The only thing they share was the attempt to turn over every rock and pursue every promotional opportunity humanly possible to make the movies into the biggest successes they could be. One was successful; one wasn't. But if you don't try, you don't get.

As independent films face a very struggling time, hope for the future will come from that kind of concerted effort, pushing, prodding, overturning those rocks, making smart decisions and never giving up. No one said success in the movie industry would ever be easy.

This Week at the Box Office

Weekly Attendance: 46,419,549

Transformers: Revenge of the Fallen
Paramount
Opening weekend: $108,966,307
Domestic gross: $402,111,870 48.1%
Foreign gross: $434,185,358 51.9%
Worldwide gross: $836,297,228
Widest release: 4,293 theatres

The Hurt Locker
Summit
Opening weekend: $145,352
Domestic gross: $17,017,811 34.6%
Foreign gross: $32,212,961 65.4%
Worldwide gross: $49,230,772
Widest release: 535 theatres

New York
Yash Raj
Opening weekend: $467,694
Domestic gross: $947,694 51.4%
Foreign gross: $938,383 48.5%
Worldwide gross: $1,935,820
Widest release: 60 theatres

Surveillance
Magnolia
Opening weekend: $4,590
Domestic gross: $27,349 2.5%
Foreign gross: $1,088,144 97.5%
Worldwide gross: $1,115,493
Widest release: 3 theatres

Afghan Star
Zeitgeist
Opening weekend: $3,671
Domestic gross: $102,115
Foreign gross: N/A
Widest release: 1 theatre

My Sister's Keeper
Warner Brothers
Opening weekend: $12,442,212
Domestic gross: $49,200,230 51.4%
Foreign gross: $46,514,645 48.6%
Worldwide gross: $95,714,875
Widest release: 2,606 theatres

Cheri
Miramax
Opening weekend: $405,741
Domestic gross: $2,715,657 29.0%
Foreign gross: $6,650,570 71.0%
Worldwide gross: $9,366,277
Widest release: 191 theatres

Stoning of Soraya M.
Roadside
Opening weekend: $115,503
Domestic gross: $637,421 58.5%
Foreign gross: $452,839 41.5%
Worldwide gross: $1,090,260
Widest release: 34 theatres

Quiet Chaos
IFC
Opening weekend: $3,190
Domestic gross: $11,434 0.1%
Foreign gross: $11,313,102 99.9%
Worldwide gross: $11,324,536
Widest release: 2 theatres

Week 26: Questions for Discussion

1. Do you believe that every movie in essence, including art films, is a product to be marketed and sold to the public? Do you have a problem with that?

2. Discuss the different ways promotional deals can be structured. Put them in order of what you believe is most valued by the studios that gives them their biggest bang for the buck.

3. Recall a past movie promotion that grabbed your interest and made you purchase an item or buy a ticket to a movie.

4. Name at least five 3rd party partners that even filmmakers and distributors with smaller films can make promotional deals with.

5. What are some of the things that can go wrong when setting up promotions on an independent film?

AT THE HALFWAY POINT OF THE YEAR, UNIVERSAL TAKES A CALCULATED RISK

Week 27: July 3–9, 2009

_The quest to simplify and perfect the marketing message
lies at the heart of the high-concept era._

As July begins, the 2009 box office has been nothing sort of spectacularly consistent. It started out strong, and for the first 26 weeks of the year, it has stayed strong. Despite the deep recession, moviegoers continue to flock to their local theatres week after week. After "Transformers: Revenge of the Fallen" grossed $200,000,000 in its first five days to close out June, the year-to-date gross stands at $5.16 billion, a sturdy 10.7% increase over 2008 according to industry tracker Exhibitor Relations. The 4th of July holiday is always a benchmark for the industry as it falls right in the center of both the year itself and the summer movie season, and it has always been considered one of the top moviegoing holidays of the year. For that reason, studios have generally placed their most expensive, big budget movies here to take full advantage of the playtime. Recent July 4th releases have been "Spiderman II," "War of the Worlds," "Pirates of the Caribbean," "Transformers" and last year's "Hancock," starring Will Smith, an actor who has become synonymous with the holiday with prior hits "Independence Day" and "Men in Black."

This year the 4th of July provides an extra challenge and a new wrinkle. The challenge is the holiday falls on Saturday, already the biggest moviegoing day of the week, and with fireworks celebrations and family activities, the question is always on how that will affect business. The wrinkle is Universal's decision to buck conventional wisdom by opening "Public Enemies," a Depression-era gangster movie, on this all-important holiday. Since it's not a prequel, sequel or franchise, certainly there's risk involved because it's not a pre-sold brand name or your typical light popcorn fare usually found on July 4th. I love Universal's decision to go out on the 4th with "Public Enemies." It's good to see a studio go against the grain and gamble a bit. Yes, it's risky, but it's a totally calculated risk that was deliberately planned and carefully considered. Universal announced the July 1st release well back in 2008, knowing full well they would be in the middle of fighting robots and flying wizards but feeling they would be able to stand out more in the midst of all the youth-oriented product. Adults want to go to the movies in the summer too, and that makes perfect sense on paper, but what's on paper doesn't always prove true at the box office, and therein lies the risk. It's not that Universal hasn't been down this road before and felt the sting of a failed counter-programming decision. Just four years ago in the summer of 2005, Universal opened the Depression-era boxing drama, "Cinderella Man," starring Russell Crowe and Renee Zellweger, and it blew up in their face with an underperforming gross and a highly publicized war of words with producer Brian Grazer over the early summer date. A couple of factors that were different with that film was the June 3rd release date, probably too early in the summer to try a serious film, and the fact it was a boxing movie coming close on the heels of "Million Dollar Baby's" Oscar Best Picture win which played well into May that year. Even though there is a new distribution team in place at Universal, it takes nerve for the company to attempt to go down the same road twice in the span of five years. What they realize is that there are a set of new dynamics with each film, and what happened in the past shouldn't automatically dictate what you do in the future. There are times it pays to be bold and fearless; success isn't always with the tried and true. Audiences often want to embrace the familiar, but other times they look for something different and wish to be taken out of their element by experiencing something fresh and new.

"Public Enemies" should prove to be a much easier sell and a better gamble for Universal than "Cinderella Man" was. It never hurts to have Johnny Depp as the star, as the three "Pirates" movies have made him into a global sensation.

A recent ranking of stars ranked him the number 2 actor in the world after Will Smith. With that kind of success comes the extra pressure of delivering a big audience. Depp is being asked to carry "Public Enemies" on his back in a year and in a summer where many stars have underperformed at the box office. The entire campaign is built around him and him alone, not even a mention of co-star Christian Bale, Batman himself. Universal is keeping it simple, high concept simple, one single image, Depp as Dillinger wearing a fedora and brandishing a machine gun. It's everywhere, posters, lobby standees, bus shelters, on top of taxicabs, newspaper ads, magazine articles. No tag line, no clutter. Smart, when you have a stud, ride him all the way to the finish line. But almost just as important is the director, Michael Mann, raised on the north side of Chicago who has always felt he was the man to make this movie. He has been a top movie director for close to 20 years and has directed some true classics like "Heat," "Last of the Mohicans," "Collateral," "Ali" and "Insider," has worked with some of the biggest actors in the world but somehow has yet to produce a real blockbuster at the box office. Universal is hoping this could be the one and quite frankly, "Public Enemies" has a chance to become his most successful film, beating out the $100 million that "Collateral" grossed.

Even though the marketing campaign is built around Depp, Michael Mann is also playing a crucial role in the selling of "Public Enemies." Last week was all about movie promotions with "Transformers." This week is all about the power of publicity. Even though Depp appeared on David Letterman and did a few other shows, the publicity campaign has revolved around Michael Mann, and well it should be because the director is always the perfect spokesman for a film. The media wants to talk to the director, hear about his vision, talk about the message he wants to get across, provide the context and spin the story in a way only a director can do it. Good old-fashioned publicity articles have been the backbone for more serious, adult movies being able to connect with their audiences for decades, but with the decline of newspapers and shrinking readership, this important component of the marketing process has taken a big hit, especially with the smaller art films. "Public Enemies" has no such problem getting the press. Taking advantage of a marketplace lacking in interesting films geared to an adult audience, Universal and its field publicists had interviews and articles with Mann talking about his movie in seemingly every newspaper in the country, and he has done an outstanding job talking about the long journey he had in making the movie, the reason he chose to shoot the film in hi-def digital instead of film and especially his passion for historical accuracy and his use of the actual locations Dillinger encountered 75 years ago. The message he delivered was one of authenticity, wanting to make moviegoers feel not just like they were watching a movie set in 1933, but also feel what it was like to be living in 1933. Only a director can deliver a message like that, and Michael Mann has delivered it masterfully. That's the power of publicity, firing up readers' imaginations, positioning the film in the most compelling way in peoples' minds and inspiring them to go to the theatre and buy a ticket.

STATE TAX INCENTIVE PROGRAMS

Producing an historically based film in an authentic way is never a cheap enterprise, and " Public Enemies" was no exception to the rule as its production budget is reported to be in the $100 million range. To keep production costs down, studios are always on the lookout for additional ways to reduce their productions costs, and one of the more popular ways in recent years to do that is through the tax incentive programs offered by individual states to lure productions to their states. Nearly two-thirds of the states offer some kind of tax relief/rebate programs for television and film production crews. In regards to "Public Enemies," the movie depicts the last 13 months of Dillinger's life which took place in Illinois, Wisconsin and Indiana, and Mann wanted to shoot as many scenes as he could at the actual locations the events of Dillinger's life occurred. Hence the entire film was shot on location in those states with the most being done in Illinois, where $47 million in revenue was generated. The Chicago Film Office reported that the production spent $25 million in the city, creating a wide range of jobs and giving a boost to local casting agencies, film scouts, film crews, prop rental stores and catering services. It has become very competitive between states in pitching to the studios and production crews to come and shoot their productions in their home states. Illinois initially began their program with a 20% tax credit on feature productions that spent a minimum of $100,000 within the state and a 20% credit on Illinois salaries up to $100,000 per worker. Both figures have since been increased to 30% to stay competitive with states like Michigan, which offers a 42% credit. Refundable tax credits are transferable, and how it works in a state like Illinois is that the production company, after all the dollars spent are added up and confirmed, sells its credit amount to an Illinois firm, such as a large utility, which uses the credit to reduce their own tax liabilities. This transaction in turn reduces the production cost of the film. Other state programs can offer tax rebates, grants or exemptions. In these tight economic times when many states are struggling with unbalanced budgets, the benefits of these tax incentive programs have been hotly debated in state legislatures where some programs have been ended while others have been maintained or even increased.

Source: Illinois Film Production Services Tax Credit Act, Chicago Film Office

This Week at the Box Office   *Weekly Attendance: 34,515,314*

The other major wide release is more of a traditional summer holiday attraction from 20th Century Fox, the third installment of their very successful "Ice Age" movies, "Ice Age: Dawn of the Dinosaurs." Produced by their own computer animation company, Blue Sky Animation, the two earlier films from this franchise grossed a combined $1 billion in worldwide grosses. Before the opening of the latest 3D film, Fox angered theatre owners by announcing they were not going to share in the cost of 3D glasses, which the studios have done in the past, and that led to a war of words on both sides. Some of the largest theatre chains told Fox they would play it in regular 2D theatres and keep "UP" on their 3D screens if they indeed were going to change their policy on the glasses. Eventually, Fox gave in to the demands of the exhibitors, order was restored, and the distributor received their full complement of 3D screens.

Public Enemies
Universal
Opening weekend: $25,271,675
Domestic gross: $97,104,620 45.4%
Foreign gross: $117,000,000 54.6%
Worldwide gross: $214,104,620
Widest release: 3,334 theatres

Ice Age: Dawn of the Dinosaurs
20th Century Fox
Opening weekend: $41,690,382
Domestic gross: $196,573,705 22.8%
Foreign gross: $690,113,112 77.8%
Worldwide gross: $886,686,817
Widest release: 4,120 theatres

The Girl from Monaco
Magnolia
Opening weekend: $83,755
Domestic gross: $602,992 8.0%
Foreign gross: $6,950,168 92.0%
Worldwide gross: $7,553,160
Widest release: 31 theatres

Kambakkat Ishq
Eros
Opening weekend: $768,542
Domestic gross: $1,445,739 48.2%
Foreign gross: $1,553,201 5.2%
Worldwide gross: $2,998,201
Widest release: 100 theatres

Lion's Den
Strand
Opening weekend: $3,484
Domestic gross: $14,739
Foreign Gross: N/A
Widest release: 1 theatre

I Hate Valentine's Day
IFC
Opening weekend: $2,448
Domestic gross: $11,004 0.3%
Foreign gross: $3,499,693 99.3%
Worldwide gross: $3,510,643
Widest release: 3 theatres

The Beaches of Agnes
Cinema Guild
Opening weekend: N/A
Domestic gross: $239,711 97.0%
Foreign gross: $7,392 3.0%
Worldwide gross: $247,103
Widest release: 7 theatres

Local Color
Monterey Media
Opening weekend: $7,183
Domestic gross: $49,939
Foreign gross: N/A
Widest release: 7 theatres

The Selling of High Concept – The Power of the Single Image:

When discussing high concept in today's Hollywood, the starting point is always the movie poster and the key art that is created that accompanies it. Along with the movie trailer, creating the poster and the key art that defines the movie remain the two most important marketing tools in a distributor's arsenal. Even though the present time is far from the greatest period for inventive, classic posters, the choice of what ultimately goes on the posters is still a crucial decision. The poster image gets plastered everywhere on billboards, bus shelters, magazines and newspapers, the Internet, promotional items and then on DVD covers and other ancillary products. In effect, that single image can live for forever. The quest to simplify and perfect the marketing message lies at the heart of the high-concept era. Though high concept started taking prominence in the 1980s to coincide with the increased love affair with market research, "Jaws" in 1975 showed the way again, as it has proven in so many different areas, why it's considered one of the most influential movies of the last 40 years. For my money, it is the most influential movie without exception. It's easy to recall the "Jaws" poster because we have seen it so many times from posters to advertisements to DVD covers. The giant, sharp-toothed shark – its mouth wide open – approaching a lone female swimmer. That poster was the work of Tony Seiniger, a graphic artist in his first year running his agency, who has gone on to become perhaps the most successful poster creator of his time. That iconic image didn't come easy as his agency spent a then unheard-of six months developing the poster. As he told *USA Today* in a 2003 interview, "No matter what we did, it didn't look scary enough. The sharks in the test posters kept looking more like dolphins." Then a simple idea hit him that changed his life and made his career. "You had to actually go under the water and underneath the shark so you could see his teeth," he said. The rest is history. The business of creating Hollywood's movie posters is now a $250 million industry, and Seiniger is still at it. In that same article he talked about how complex and costly it is to create posters for big-budget blockbusters. His agency created the poster for the first "Hulk" movie and created 691 different poster looks before the final one was chosen, an image of an angry, green creature mostly hidden by his own enormous hand. What was Seiniger paid for the "The Hulk" work: a cool $500,000.

There are specific elements in a movie campaign that help define the features of high concept. The more a movie contains, the stronger it is, at least on paper.

►   Instant identity. The recognition of titles epitomized by sequels, prequels, reboots, series and remakes.

►   The ability to describe a movie in 10 words or less.

►   Being able to sell the movie with one single image.

►   Star power.

►   Bankable directors and/or big name producers.

►   Belonging to a specific genre (action, comedy, horror, 3D computer family animation, etc.).

►   Other recognizable elements like popular music or best-selling books.

►   Cutting edge special effects/technology.

Not all high-concept films are on equal footing. They can come in all shapes and sizes. "Public Enemies" is not the same as "Transformers" or "Harry Potter." "Public Enemies" has a big star and a single image on its poster, but its Depression-era theme isn't exactly typical summer escapist fare or a pre-sold commodity. One of the values of high concept is that even independent films can borrow elements from it. The quest to break any film down to its essence and to understand what individual images may be able to effectively get the film's message across is never a bad thing. It's just smart marketing. The problem is that many indie films have complex or multiple themes that are difficult to market, in effect being low concept films. I don't think the filmmakers thought of high concept when they came up with "Hoop

Dreams" as the title for their documentary, but it certainly is a terrific high-concept title. However, the process of creating the poster was challenging, and there was no single image available to be able to sell it in a traditional high-concept manner. No problem, the title alone has become iconic, and it became a film that will always be remembered. For other films, you do the best you can and work with what you have and aspire to be great. That's all anybody can ask for.

Week 27: Questions for Discussion

1. Define the term "high concept" in relation to movie marketing. Why has Hollywood embraced this concept?

2. Why is the marketing on "Public Enemies" considered high concept, and how does it differ from other summer blockbusters?

3. When you are deciding whether to see a film, is it the publicity campaign or the advertising that usually wins you over?

4. Take a look at current posters and identify one that you feel would be considered high concept and another that would be considered low concept. Discuss the elements that differentiate the two posters.

A SHADOW COMPANY AND THE IRONCLAD CONSENT FORM

Week 28: July 10–16, 2009

> *No one remembers any case in which a consent form*
> *was deemed invalid. Studios never lose.*

The marketplace is in the middle of what is referred to as a bridge week between the 4th of July weekend and the opening of the new Harry Potter movie on Wednesday, July 15th. Everyone knows that movie is going to be huge, and competing studios have to figure out how to play this week with a narrow five-day window before "Potter" storms into theatres. Universal and Fox have turned to the comedies "Bruno" and "I Love You Beth Cooper" to carve out some niche business, but only "Bruno" has a chance to break through, and as it so happens, this is the movie with the interesting back story to really get into and discuss. Universal has had a tough year up to this point, but perhaps with the back-to-back releases of "Public Enemies" and "Bruno," they may be starting to turn things around. No two movies could be more different from each other, and for that reason Universal put them on back-to-back weeks so they could each find their audience without stepping on each other's toes. The studio's gamble in deciding to release "Public Enemies" during the 4th of July weekend paid off with a $40,000,000 five-day gross, and it's now in good position to have a lengthy run with nothing remotely like it opening against it anytime soon.

Now Universal's attention turns to making Sacha Baron Cohen's "Bruno" into a hit. It has been three years since "Borat" was a sensation for 20th Century Fox and three years since Universal won a bidding war for the rights to distribute "Bruno." At about the same time "Borat" opened, the Endeavor talent agency, the agency that represents Cohen, struck when the buzz was at its peak and put the rights to "Bruno" up for auction, and Universal won with a $42.5 million guaranteed offer. That's a huge number for a film not even made at the time, but it just goes to show how hot the property was. How the deal went down was somewhat controversial. Endeavor had created a separate financing entity called Media Rights Capital a few years ago to help raise financing for their clients' movies, and MRC ultimately financed the movie through Universal's winning bid offer. This raised eyebrows because it has been illegal for talent agencies to produce movies and television shows ever since the government cracked down on Lew Wasserman and MCA more than four decades ago when they dominated the industry by doing that same thing. Endeavor insists MRC is a separate entity run by a former partner in the company and that MRC is a financier and not a producer. What exactly did Universal get for their $42 million? Distribution rights in all English speaking countries for 15 years with no ownership stake in the movie since they weren't involved in actually financing the film, even if their pool of money was used toward that purpose. That's not the type of deal Universal or any studio likes to make, but when a creative artist like Cohen creates his own fictional characters that become very popular, the artist and his representatives basically can call all the shots and control the deal. With the $42.5 million price tag and the limited term deal, Universal carries some real risk and has to hope for the same kind of success for "Bruno" that "Borat" achieved. You may think that it's still a slam dunk deal for Universal, but Bruno is a different type of character than Borat, more divisive and less likable, an over-the-top gay fashion show presenter who already has parts of the gay community upset with the film because of perceived gay stereotypes. There is no guarantee that a big mainstream audience will warm up to the character either.

The person who received the best deal out of it all is Sacha Baron Cohen, the creator and star. He received a $15,000,000 salary for the film, the lion's share of the profits, total creative control and in the end, ownership of the negative. That's the type of deal that can make a studio shudder. But Universal also realizes Cohen is their secret weapon and the movie's selling point, who may after all is said and done, still turn the movie into a nice moneymaker for the studio.

The man is simply one of the greatest self-promoters in the industry and the master of the publicity stunt who stops at nothing when promoting his movies. The promotion is part of the entire package which adds to his value and allows Universal to contain their marketing costs because Cohen is doing all the heavy lifting, constantly creating awareness and increasing interest and want-to-see in the movie. After detailing the rich deal he has for himself, you can see where his motivation comes from in working to make "Bruno" into the biggest success possible for himself and to a lesser extent for Universal.

On another front, movies like "Borat" and "Bruno" are not your average movies and carry a lot of baggage, hassles and legal concerns with them. This of course stems from the very nature of the movies themselves, using ordinary people who are put into embarrassing situations and then making fools out of them. This isn't a new concept that was invented by Sacha Baron Cohen. It's been a staple in television for years going back to "Candid Camera" and continuing with shows like "Punked." But it is still a bit of a dicey way to make a movie and carries a lot of liability when it comes to getting people angry about how they are ultimately portrayed on screen. It's always prudent for the companies involved with movies like this to put additional funds aside for legal defense. Even though Universal is acting only as the distributor, they are on the front lines of any lawsuit because the distributor is always the first one any unhappy party goes after. Universal has already been served papers on one lawsuit before the movie even opened, and no doubt there will be others to follow. Is there anyone more at fault in these cases, either the production company gathering unwitting people to participate in the filming or the people themselves who agree to participate? There are definitely issues on both sides of the debate. Regular people are being used with their own permission. No one is being forced to participate. Perhaps it touches on human nature, in this era of "American Idol" and all the other reality shows where ordinary folks get their fifteen minutes of fame, individuals can be enticed to get in front of a camera because they figure they can control what they say and enjoy seeing themselves on screen. On the flip side, production personnel have been accused of not being totally honest with these people and misleading them into thinking it's a smaller production than it actually is. On "Borat," some participants were allegedly told the movie wouldn't even be shown in the United States. That's when people become upset and feel they were deceived, and then when a movie becomes successful, let the litigation begin. A curious thing happened on the way to the courthouse. I believe 20th Century Fox won every single case brought against them on "Borat," and what it comes down to is always the signed consent form. When a person signs a standard consent agreement allowing producers to use their real identities on screen, they also sign away their right to complain about it. If people feel they were publicly humiliated, it's still not, from a legal standpoint, sufficient grounds for a lawsuit. What was proven with some of the unhappy people who came forward on "Borat" was that they didn't even bother reading what they signed. They just signed off on it and later complained they didn't know it was going to be such a big hit. Either these people were naïve, foolish or very trusting individuals. In these types of negotiations, a signed document always trumps an oral understanding, and movie industry consent forms are considered ironclad defenses. No one remembers any case in which a consent form was deemed invalid. Studios never lose.

Generalized terminology strengthens these agreements, and the wording I've come across over the years while working in distribution goes something like this in a nutshell:

> BLANK PRODUCTION COMPANY SHALL EXCLUSIVELY BE ENTITLED TO USE OR LICENSE RECORDED MATERIAL THAT INCLUDES THE PARTICIPANT "WITHOUT RESTRICTION IN THE MEDIA THROUGHOUT THE UNIVERSE IN PERPETUITY AND WILL SUPERCEDE ANY OTHER PRIOR OR IMPLIED AGREEMENT BETWEEN THE PARTIES."

In layman's terms it says:

▶ We can use your image worldwide.

- ► We can use it forever.

- ► We can use it in every known media format that exists or is yet to exist including theatrical, DVD, television, Internet streaming, Video-on-Demand, etc.

- ► This is a legal document that states the contract supersedes the oral representation relayed.

- ► As long as participant agrees to a consent form and signs it, it doesn't matter whether that person has a copy of it or not in their possession.

As previously stated, the movie industry consent form is ironclad. That doesn't mean film companies need to be arrogant and misleading when working with average people off the street. An expert on deception-as-entertainment model, Eric Nelson, whose company produced various television shows such as "Busted on the Job: Caught on Tape," talked to Hollywood Reporter after "Borat" was in the news and had some interesting things to say about how he conducted business. Nelson said, "Even if people sign a release, they can still claim after the fact that they didn't know what they were getting into. That's why when you do this kind of entertainment, you have to go one step further and that is to bring back the 'marks' to screen the final product. I believe we needed to get a final sign off when they saw how dubious we made them look. Without exception," Nelson adds, "every single one of our victims signed off on a second release despite some serious character flaw about them." As cynical as Cohen and company were at the venality of Americans, they weren't cynical enough. "I believe everyone in the film would have signed off on their pre-release appearance no matter how they came off, because they always think they look good." Nelson submits that those behind "Borat" had a responsibility to reveal the truth to those who had been duped once filming was completed and should have offered each a cash payout, an invite to watch a cut of the film with a chortling audience and presented a second release to sign. "Not only would they have gotten every airtight release they needed, they also could have slept better at night."

It sounds to me like some pretty good advice on how to conduct business. Any person who gets involved in a production of this kind should be smarter about reading everything thoroughly before signing it. Likewise, any production personnel involved in gathering unsuspecting people to film should be more forthright and honest with them, realizing that past precedent shows that they will get what they need anyway. Have the guts and professionalism to do it the right way. The final outcome may not change, but it would certainly help to diffuse even any thought of litigation and save a lot of time, worry and expense along the way. In addition, you can never underestimate the value of a good night's sleep.

This Week at the Box Office   *Weekly Attendance: 39,127,012*

Bruno
Universal
Opening weekend: $30,619,130
Domestic gross: $60,054,530 43.3%
Foreign gross: $78,751,301 56.7%
Worldwide gross: $138,805,831
Widest release: 2,759 theatres

I Love You, Beth Cooper
20th Century Fox
Opening weekend: $4,919,433
Domestic gross: $14,800,725 93.5%
Foreign gross: $1,021,182 6.5%
Worldwide gross: $15,821,907
Widest release: 1,872 theatres

Yoo-Hoo, Mrs. Goldberg
International Film Group
Opening weekend: $19,302

Weather Girl
New American Vision
Opening weekend: $5,772

Domestic gross: $1,134,623

Foreign gross: N/A

Widest release: 25 theatres

Humpday

Magnolia

Opening weekend: $28,737

Domestic gross: $407,377 85.9%

Foreign gross: $66,603 14.1%

Worldwide gross: $473,980

Widest release: 105 theatres

Soul Power

Sony Classics

Opening weekend: $23,893

Domestic gross: $207,121 81.4%

Foreign gross: $47,461 18.6%

Worldwide gross: $254,582

Widest release: 23 theatres

The Vanished Empire

Kino

Opening weekend: $3,328

Domestic gross: $10,289

Foreign gross: N/A

Widest release: 1 theatre

Domestic gross: $20,519

Foreign gross: N/A

Widest release: 2 theatres

Blood: The Last Vampire

IDP/ Samuel Goldwyn

Opening weekend: $110,029

Domestic gross: $257,413 4.4%

Foreign gross: $5,617,118 95.6%

Worldwide gross: $5,874,530

Widest release: 20 theatres

Mississippi Mermaid (re-issue)

Film Desk

Opening weekend: $3,668

Domestic gross: $26,893

Foreign gross: N/A

Widest release: 1 theatre

Lake Tahoe

Film Movement

Opening weekend: $1,822

Domestic gross: $5,959

Foreign gross: N/A

Widest release: 2 theatres

2012 Update: "Bruno" Lawsuits Dismissed

As was the case with "Borat," there were lawsuits filed against "Bruno" that were ultimately dismissed by the courts. In one case, a woman claimed she was physically injured during a scene in a bingo parlor in which she attempted to pull the microphone away from Cohen and during a struggle lost consciousness when she hit her head on the concrete floor. The court ruled that "Cohen's exchange with the woman aided in Cohen's effort to obtain a reaction ... for subsequent use in the film," and thus was ruled free speech. In another case, a federal judge dismissed a copyright claim by a writer who said a scene in "Bruno" was very similar to his own original script. The particular scene in dispute involved the lead character being stuck in a Velcro suit, but the court ruled that the idea of a man in a Velcro suit was not subject to copyright and that the two works were not that similar. Another suit that was still pending involved a Palestinian man claiming he was misrepresented and defamed when he was characterized as a terrorist in the film. In the final box office tally, "Bruno's domestic gross of $60 million was less than half of "Borat's" $128 million.

On a related front, the Endeavor talent agency has further separated itself from Media Rights Capital and is no longer an investor in the company. Media Rights Capital continues to grow and in 2011 finalized a deal with Universal to distribute 20 of their films over a five-year period, including Seth MacFarlane's 2012 summer hit comedy, "Ted." Flying under the radar, MRC has also become a leading supplier of primetime television programming.

Sources: *Hollywood Reporter, New York Times*

Week 28: Questions for Discussion

1. What did Universal get for their $42.5 million purchase of "Bruno"? Do you think it was a good deal for the studio? Who acted as the executive producer, and who was the producer in this project?

2. Why is the movie industry consent form considered an ironclad agreement? Even so, where does the gray area exist for a producer when dealing with getting clearances from people that can lead to conflicts and litigation?

3. As a producer, what is a good rule of thumb in trying to diffuse any chance of litigation down the road?

THE TWO EXTREMES OF THE MARKETPLACE COME TOGETHER IN JULY

Week 29: July 17–23, 2009

---

*Summit is not only fighting an anti-Iraq bias but the summer mindset as well,
coupled with the fact that it's awfully difficult to expand outside the art houses
in the summer when the studios have control of the suburban screens.*

The pull between mainstream Hollywood movies and challenging independent films has been a fascinating component of the industry for some time now. They may be two separate industries and work under different business models, but they are interconnected in many ways. The two businesses coexist, compete and sometimes crossover in their attempts for money, stars, distribution deals, movie screens and audience approval. Up until last year, all six studios had independent art divisions, but Warner Bros. and Paramount have since abandoned this end of the business, and the independent sector has been on a downward trajectory. When once all kinds of money was chasing after independent films, now it's the exact opposite; money is running away from it as quickly as possible. The demand has fallen with investors, distributors, exhibitors, audiences and DVD companies. You name it, the shine is off. With the 2009 box office on a record-breaking pace, someone forgot to invite the independents to the party. It has been all about studio movies this year, and summer has driven that point home with a vengeance; it's one of the weakest in years at the box office for specialized product.

With this dynamic in place, mid-July has brought two movies into the spotlight from the extreme ends of the marketplace, Warner Brother's "Harry Potter and the Half Blood Prince" and Summit Entertainment's "The Hurt Locker." Not that they're converging and competing against each other. One is on 4,200 screens and the other is on 69 screens, but it's what they signify; the powerhouse studio franchise that is stronger than ever, and the acclaimed, serious independent feature set during the Iraq War looking for commercial success in a crowded, light-hearted marketplace. It's interesting how both these movies landed up on movie screens in July. "Harry Potter" was scheduled to be released last November, but Warner Bros. moved it to July because the studio had more of a need for a big blockbuster in mid-2009 than they did in 2008 because "The Dark Knight" had already grossed over $500 million for them last year. When they saw that no other movie was booked into the July 17th week and it just happened to be the same exact week "Dark Knight" opened on, it was a move they felt they had to make. After opening to a record $22 million on their opening night midnight shows, beating "The Dark Knight's" previous record of $18.5 million, Warner Bros. is poised to make more on "Potter's" sixth installment than they did on any of the others. It's a move that is immediately paying off. Summer is better playing time, and the delay just heightened the demand for the film. One of the biggest decisions a distributor has to make is deciding the release dates for their movies. Many millions of dollars ride on these decisions.

I've said before that when one company makes a release date change, it can put other changes in motion that can alter the fates of any number of movies and companies. Summit Entertainment was helped a great deal when "Harry Potter" was moved out of November because it provided an opening in the marketplace and less competition for their own "Twilight," a would-be franchise with a similar audience of young female fans that went on to become a smash hit and now the start of a lucrative series of movies, which is soon to become a significant franchise, for the new distributor. It's funny how things happen and how the big success of "Twilight" perhaps helped pave the way for Summit's acquisition of "The Hurt Locker." When money flies into the coffers of a company, those funds can provide a financial cushion to stretch into other areas and take a risk or two along the way. When "The Hurt Locker" started drawing attention at film festivals last fall, Summit decided to buy the distribution rights and plunge into the prestige business. The film was financed by foreign investors, and though the acquisition price hasn't been revealed, I wouldn't think Summit paid more than a $1 million or $2 million advance for the rights, so their risk in this film may not be too high, although future print and advertising costs always add to a distributor's financial liability. On the other end of the spectrum, the same could also be said about Warner Brothers $250 million investment in the latest "Harry Potter." The risk is minimized by the historical success of the franchise and the almost guaranteed results and profits that will follow.

Whatever the business model and money that is at risk for a distributor, making the right call on when to release a film is the same for the major studios and smaller independents alike. The pressure is the same to guess correctly. Whereas Warner Brother's strategy to open "Potter" in July has already been discussed and validated, will Summit's decision to release "The Hurt Locker" in mid-summer rather than in the fall, which would have been a more traditional safer bet, prove to be as smart of a move? This is where things get tricky and much harder to forecast. Regardless of what release date they chose, Summit must have realized all the hurdles they confronted when they chose to distribute the latest movie set during the Iraq War. Every single Iraq movie that has been released in the last couple of years has either been a disappointment or an all out disaster at the box office. It has been proven over and over again that audiences have not been interested or willing to see these movies while the war is still going on. It's instructive to note the comparison between six Iraq movies and six Vietnam movies and how they performed at the box office. The Vietnam War was as unpopular at the time as the Iraq War is today, but the big difference between the two is that all the following Vietnam movies were made well after that war ended in 1975.

Iraq Movies:

- Lions for Lambs - $15,000,000
- Stop-Loss - $10,900,000
- Rendition - $9,700,000
- In the Valley of Elah - $6,700,000
- Redacted - $65,385
- Grace is Gone - $50,899

Vietnam Movies:

- Coming Home (1978) - $32,000,000
- Deer Hunter (1979) - $49,000,000
- Apocalypse Now (1979) - $83,000,000
- Platoon (1986) - $137,000,000
- Full Metal Jacket (1987) - $46,000,000
- Born on the Fourth of July (1989) - $70,000,000

Looking at those Vietnam titles, I shake my head in awe. The majority of them are classics that are some of the best films of their day. It didn't hurt to have directors like Oliver Stone, Francis Ford Coppola, Stanley Kubrick, Hal Ashby and Michael Cimino at the helm of these movies. The list of Iraq movies pales in comparison. Maybe Summit Entertainment saw the same thing and figured "The Hurt Locker" could be the exception to the rule. Fighting history and past precedent is never easy, but distributors sometimes like to think they can be the one to buck a trend and be the first one to accomplish something that no other distributor has yet to do. What Summit has going for them are the best reviews of the year for any picture other than "UP" and no doubt the best reviews for any Iraq movie up to this point. Yes, reviews are crucial for this type of film, but it's still only one factor in the strategic launch of a film. The easy move would have been to nestle it in at the end of the year to take advantage of the top ten lists and any Golden Globe or Oscar nominations. But that's what every specialized distributor does, and the competition is fierce for both awards and attention. However, audiences are ready and primed for serious films then unlike in the summer months when lighter fare rules the day. Summit is not only fighting an anti-Iraq bias but the summer mindset as well, coupled with the fact that it's awfully difficult to expand outside the art houses in the summer when the studios have control of the suburban screens.

So why did they choose to go out with such an acclaimed film in the middle of the summer? It's another attempt at summer counter-programming, but in this case they run the risk of killing the film off very quickly in the unforgiving summer marketplace. Summit's decision now is whether to let the movie sit in the art theatres and hope that great word of mouth can slowly expand the audience base and not attempt to move into the suburbs too quickly. That's what I would have figured they would do, but in the Chicago market the distributor is increasing its run from three theatres to ten theatres in the second week, so they are wasting no time and being very aggressive. To run a successful platform release is a delicate work of business that requires patience, experience and impeccable timing. Going out in the heat of the summer was risky to begin with; increasing the theatres too quickly heightens that risk. The next two weekends bring five or six new wide releases to the multiplexes. If "The Hurt Locker" doesn't perform immediately in the new runs, it can find itself on the outside looking in, losing screens very quickly.

Summit is doing all they can to convince audiences to go see the movie, stressing that it's action packed and suspense filled and not a preachy message movie full of political ideology. In addition, they are promoting the film as the first Iraq movie since the American troops have pulled out of Baghdad. I find that a questionable strength because people know the war is still going on, and from the people I've talked to, they're either not interested in seeing the movie or not quite ready yet. It's still too soon. Summit is trying to make the movie sound as mainstream as possible despite the subject matter and the fact that the title of the movie is ambiguous and art house sounding. What is a hurt locker? Like I've said, they are working hard to make the movie work, but changing a specific mind-set can prove to be an impossible task, and choosing to launch it in the summer and moving too quickly with it only makes it more difficult to pull off. If the movie fails, its distribution strategy will be questioned and pointed to as one of the main culprits, even though no one will be able to know for sure if an end of the year release would have produced different results.

Returning to Warner Bros. and "Harry Potter", it's pretty impressive how they have handled this franchise. There are a total of seven books in the series, and "Harry Potter and the Half-Blood Prince" is the sixth movie. The seventh book is being filmed now, and it's being split into two final movies; Warner Bros. has already set the release dates for them, one on November 19,2010 and the final movie on July 15, 2011.

After it's wrapped, it will be a nice eight movie, eleven-year, seven billion dollar franchise that will keep generating money for Warner Brothers for years to come. Not all blockbusters become franchises, think Will Smith's "Hancock," which was one and done, and not all franchises become all-time classics, think "Rambo" and "Pink Panther" and many others. Only movies that evolve into cultural touchstones like "Star Wars," "James Bond," and perhaps a few others have achieved that kind of status. The "Harry Potter" series can certainly be added to that short list.

This Week at the Box Office: *Weekly Attendance – 32,954,637*

Harry Potter and the Half-Blood Prince
Warner Brothers
Opening weekend: $77,835,727
Domestic gross: $301,969,197 32.3%
Foreign gross: $632,000,000 67.7%
Worldwide gross: $933,959,197
Widest release: 4,455 theatres

(500) Days of Summer
Fox Searchlight
Opening weekend: $834,501
Domestic gross: $32,391,374 53.3%
Foreign gross: $28,331,360 46.7%
Worldwide gross: $60,772,734
Widest release: 1,048 theatres

The Wonder of It All

Indican

Opening weekend: $18,988

Domestic gross: $781,139

Foreign gross: N/A

Widest release: 39 theatres

A Woman in Berlin

Strand

Opening weekend: $12,439

Domestic gross: $292,014

Foreign gross: N/A

Widest release: 9 theatres

The Way We Get By

International Film Circuit

Opening weekend: $7,149

Domestic gross: $106,542

Foreign gross: N/A

Widest release: 7 theatres

Somers Town

Film Movement

Opening weekend: $7,452

Domestic gross: $54,526

Foreign gross: N/A

Widest release: 4 theatres

Death in Love

Screen Media

Opening weekend: $14,296

Domestic gross: $23,412

Foreign gross: N/A

Widest release: 4 theatres

Homecoming

Independent

Opening weekend: N/A

Domestic gross: $973

Foreign gross: N/A

Widest release: 3 theatres

Week 29: Questions for Discussion

1. There is no single bigger decision a distributor has to make than deciding the release date for their movies. Go through what the decision making process is and how the actual release dates are chosen by distributors.

2. Is the decision of when to release a movie the same for independent distributors as it is for the studios? Name at least two similarities and two differences.

3. What is the term used when a distributor goes against common practice when picking a film's release date? What is the risk factor involved? Can you think of an example in another industry that utilizes a similar strategy?

"THE GEEKS HAVE INHERITED THE EARTH, AND THAT'S GOOD NEWS FOR US"

Week 30: July 24–30, 2009

---

*That's the movie business, where for better or worse, no matter
the size or budget, studio or independent, a movie can be judged
either a success or failure based on one weekend.*

As the summer movie season rolls into the final third of the season and starts winding down with last week's "Harry Potter and the Half-Blood Prince" being the last of the traditional summer blockbusters of 2009, it's a good time to look into the phenomenon of the opening weekend which drives the entire blockbuster industry. Friday. Saturday. Sunday. The three most important days of the week for distributors, producers, investors and exhibitors. But what about audiences, the moviegoers who either show up at the theatres on opening weekend or decide to stay away? Without them, it can't happen. There is an undeniable aura, mystery and yes, terror, to opening a movie, and when people show up in good numbers on opening day, it's a little bit of magic, but when the opposite happens and a movie fails to deliver that expected audience, it is pure heartbreak for all those involved. There have been some famous directors over the years who have decided to leave the country, vacation on an island, get as far away as possible, so they wouldn't have to feel the pressure of opening weekend. That's the movie business, where for better or worse, no matter the size of budget, studio or independent, a movie can be judged either a success or failure based on one weekend.

It's fitting that this weekend in San Diego the annual Comic-Con convention is being held, and at the heart of this pop culture event is the recognition and the celebration of the passionate, devoted fans who are the ones who buy the tickets on opening weekend and make the blockbusters possible for the studios. What started out as a small gathering of comic book fans buying and trading rare comic books has evolved into a huge event for Hollywood where studios introduce and promote their upcoming sci-fi, fantasy and comic book movies – the movie genres that dominate the blockbuster landscape. 125,000 fans gobble up the tickets; 300 media representatives attend. The annual event has become a marketing goldmine because the studios realize this is where the buzz starts, that these diehard fans are the buzz generators who start the advanced word in blogs, Internet chat rooms and social networking sites. The studios cater to these fan's needs and make them feel important because they are important. They can make or break a movie, and that's why a director like James Cameron has chosen to show 20 minutes of his highly anticipated "Avatar" to these fans immediately after he showed it to 200 top theatre owners last week. Jon Favreau, the director of "Iron Man" and "Iron Man II," which is being promoted at this year's convention, was quoted as saying, "The geeks have inherited the earth, and that's good news for us."

Comic-Con also happens at the perfect time for the studios because all their summer blockbusters have opened, and it's time to look ahead, plan and promote the next wave of tentpoles that will be opening in the coming year. If you think of the studios as manufacturing plants and the movie theatres as retail outlets, it's no different for movies than it is for a new clothing line or next year's car models. Obviously, the studios need to know that these loyal and passionate fans are on board for their upcoming expensive and important franchise movies, but I also want to get into the importance of the opening weekend for all movies and some of the strategies smaller films have utilized in the past to get their audience to show up that first weekend. But before that, I want to look back at the summer so far and see how the various opening weekends have played out.

The twelve weekends since May 1st have yielded 22 wide release movies, which averages out to about two movies a week. That is an indication that the biggest, most pre-sold movies generally open against the fewest number of new releases, which just adds to their dominance and huge opening grosses. The first list of opening weekend grosses will include ten movies, eight established franchise films plus Disney/Pixar's "UP" and Universal's "Bruno," movies that enjoyed established fan bases:

- ▶ Transformers: $109 million (Wed. opening, 5-day gross $200 million)
- ▶ X-Men Origins: Wolverine: $85 million
- ▶ Harry Potter: $77 million (Wed. opening, 5-day gross $158 million)
- ▶ Star Trek: $75 million
- ▶ UP: $68 million
- ▶ Night at the Museum: $54 million (Thur. opening, 4-day gross $70 million)
- ▶ Angels and Demons: $46 million
- ▶ Terminator Salvation: $42 million (Wed. opening, 5-day gross $65 million)
- ▶ Ice Age: $42 million (Wed. opening, 5-day gross $66 million)
- ▶ Bruno: $30 million

For the most part, all of the above established franchises delivered strong opening numbers, and that's all marketing departments can do, make sure the movies open big and the expected audience comes out; after that, word of mouth will determine their staying power. The twelve other movies that have opened wide are listed below:

- ▶ The Hangover: $45 million
- ▶ The Proposal: $33 million
- ▶ Public Enemies: $25 million (Wed. opening, 5-day gross $40 million)
- ▶ The Taking of Pelham 123: $23 million
- ▶ Year One: $19.6 million
- ▶ Land of the Lost: $18.8 million
- ▶ Drag Me to Hell: $15.8 million
- ▶ Ghosts of Girlfriends Past: $15.4 million
- ▶ My Sister's Keeper: $12 million
- ▶ Imagine That: $5.5 million
- ▶ I Love You, Beth Cooper: $4.9 million
- ▶ Next Day Air: $4 million

There's definitely more misses than hits among this group, and generating big opening weekend audiences proved elusive, even in the summer when there were only at most two national releases a week opening. There were a few exceptions starting with the amazing "The Hangover," which has sailed past the $235 million mark and has become a blockbuster in its own right. Sandra Bullock's "The Proposal" has also grossed over $100 million and "Public Enemies" could reach that figure in the next few weeks. Other than that, the rest of this group has been pretty disappointing and points to the reason why it's so difficult to open a lesser movie in the summer and why there are so few of them, it's too easy to become a sacrificial lamb and roadkill left in the shadows of the big blockbusters.

---

*Filmmakers dismiss the audience at their own peril. If they
don't worry about who would most likely see their film, who will?*

Unfortunately, most movies are not helped by the buzz at the Comic-Con convention, but the need and wish for a solid opening exists for all movies. Let's start off with a few questions:

- Should all filmmakers be concerned about who the audience will be that will show up for their films on opening weekend?

- Do all films necessarily have an audience?

- What are some ways that have been used to strengthen the odds of pulling in an opening weekend audience?

Well, filmmakers dismiss the audience at their own peril. If they don't worry about who would be most likely to see their film, who will? A distributor? Distributors reject the vast majority of films for that very reason; they don't see an audience for them. Film is an art form, and for some filmmakers they approach it as an art rather than as a commercial venture. That's fine, but filmmaking is not painting or writing poetry; it's an expensive art form which often involves getting money from outside sources, so there is a responsibility in trying to understand how the marketplace works. There is nothing wrong about considering the audience in advance, and doing so can actually improve the film itself by tweaking the concept, story line, plot developments or casting choices that would appeal more to an intended audience. Sometimes all a filmmaker may have to do is research a subject matter more thoroughly and make smarter decisions in the pre-production stage.

To answer the second question about whether or not all films have an audience to begin with is a thorny one. Perhaps a better way to frame the question is whether they have the potential for a commercial audience or not? The problem with so many low-budget movies, whether they are art films or genre movies, is that there is not much of an audience for most of them due to their size and modest means. Other limitations can be poor production values, derivative story line, obscure or downbeat subject matter, unknown cast and often, they are just not good enough to compete in the marketplace. But that doesn't stop filmmakers from trying to reach an audience, which leads us to the third question in regards to ways that have been used to improve the odds of reaching and motivating a specific audience to attend a movie on opening weekend. Here are three paths that have been utilized successfully:

- Film Festivals
- First weekend clubs
- Advance ticket sales

For an arty, character-driven film, getting selected to play in film festivals has been the traditional first step in creating interest and buzz among smart audiences. It's the closest comparison to what happens at Comic-Con, even though it happens on a totally different scale. It's all about reaching an intended audience and media (film critics, entertainment reporters, bloggers) interested in quality art films. With fewer acquisitions occurring at festivals, filmmakers are becoming more savvy and having DVDs of their films for sale right at the fests or taking advantage of the local communities they play in to forge plans for a theatrical release at a later date, employing volunteers who are fans of the film to help in the effort. In addition, there are websites such as withoutabox.com, which help filmmakers in all aspects of film festival activities from the application process to connecting with audiences.

First weekend clubs have been around for the last couple of decades and involve volunteer e-mail organizations that let their members know when and where a niche film is opening and then remind them not only to get out the first weekend but to keep going and bring friends along with them. There are clubs for African Americans, gay and lesbians, Latino and Asian-American groups. The motivation behind these groups is to show Hollywood that there is enough support for those films and that more of them should be made. The organizers involved in forming the groups recognized that movies are judged on their opening weekend grosses, so one of their top missions is to continually remind and encourage their members not to wait for the second or third week but to attend the movie on the first Friday or Saturday because if they don't, it will be taken off the screen before they get a chance to see it. These clubs have helped movies in the past like "Barbershop," "Better Luck Tomorrow," "Bend It Like Beckham" and "Blair Witch Project." The concept is a sound economic strategy that can work if there is a large enough specific fan base to reach and organizers passionate enough to rally the troops, motivate others to join the cause and be willing to get their hands dirty and do whatever it takes to get the job done.

The motivation to sell advance tickets for "Lana's Rain's" opening weekend came from not wanting to go through the excruciating pain of wondering if anyone would show up opening night.

Advance ticket sales don't immediately come to mind when thinking of independent films, but it's something to consider when opening a movie on an exclusive run, especially in a city one lives in.

I was involved in this strategy myself when ISA Releasing launched "Lana's Rain" in Chicago several years ago. Years earlier, when we distributed "Tie-Died: Rock n' Roll's Most Deadicated Fans," I felt the sting of a terrible opening weekend on a multiple city release which basically sealed its fate from the first night on. Yes, it can all be over that quickly. I've had filmmakers I've worked with wonder if the audience was waiting for Saturday to see the film and whether business could improve substantially the next night. It would be nice to say that can happen, but the movie business doesn't work that way. A disappointing Friday gross establishes the level of business for the rest of the weekend. The motivation to sell advance tickets for "Lana's Rain's" opening weekend came from not wanting to go through the excruciating pain of wondering if anyone would show up opening night. Anyone who has ever tried to open a film, or even a theatre owner who is taking a chance on an unproven film, understands how nervous one can get counting heads between 5:00 and 8:00pm on Friday night praying for people to show up at the theatre. But before we could even think about pre-selling tickets, I had to change the traditional 90/10 percentage deal that was made with the Music Box Theatre that kept the selling of all tickets in their control. What I wanted was the flexibility of selling tickets outside the theatre box office and its website at a price we chose rather than what the theatre mandated.

There is only one financial deal that allows distributors and filmmakers to have control over how tickets are sold in advance for their movie, and that is the four-wall deal. In this deal, the theatre is in effect purchased for the week for a flat price that is paid in advance to the theatre, and then every single dollar taken in at the box office goes to the distributor or filmmaker who made the deal. This allows much more control over pricing and strategy. The wrinkle is, along with more control and potential upside comes some very real risk. In a standard percentage deal, the box office is split between the two parties, and most of the time no money changes hands before the movie opens. When we switched to a four-wall deal, I negotiated a price of $7,500, which had to be paid to the theatre before the movie opened. This was not in the budget and made my partner John Iltis angry because there is always the possibility of burying yourself deeper and losing additional money. I just felt strongly that this was the way to go, and the pressure was squarely on my shoulders to deliver positive results and make sure enough tickets were sold to cover the additional expense. There have been numerous occasions when someone who was self-distributing a movie got burned by taking in much less at the box office than what was paid out as a rental price. But sometimes you have to take a calculated risk and back it up with a solid strategy and action plan to make it work.

This goes back to understanding who your target audiences are and how to reach them. Without that knowledge, there is little chance for success. We targeted the following audience groups:

- Friends and family (not a demographic group but selling tickets to those closest to you is a nice starting point)
- The art audience
- Women's groups
- Columbia College students, faculty, alumni (filmmakers were alumni)
- Chicago area Eastern European communities)

The plan was to utilize as many people as we could get who were involved with the film to help sell tickets starting three weeks before the opening date. The tickets we were selling were only for the Friday, Saturday and Sunday of the opening weekend with special events and appearances by the stars and director creating an extra added value. The regular Music Box ticket price at the time was $8.75, and we decided to sell tickets for $6.00 for both groups and individuals who were price sensitive. For those who could afford it, we sold the tickets at the theatre price. The goal was to sell a minimum $7,500 worth of tickets to cover the rental price, which would in effect remove the angst of the possibility of a disappointing turnout. This would also put us in a good position of keeping every additional ticket sale for ourselves. By opening day, we exceeded our goal by selling $8,500 worth of tickets and then went on to sell an additional $9,000 at the box office to finish the first full week with an excellent gross of over $17,500.

This strategy is definitely a possibility for anyone who is self-distributing a film and is confident of being able to reach an audience. A theatre would always be interested in making a four-wall deal with an independent distributor or filmmaker because it takes away the risk of playing an unproven movie and gives them cash in advance. These deals generally work better with a local independent exhibitor who can be more agreeable in working out a fair rental price than what you would be able to get with a more corporate chain theatre. The whole idea is to get people to come out the first weekend, whatever it takes.

This Week at the Box Office: *Weekly Attendance 31,438,826*

Starting with the July 24th weekend, there will be more releases each week leading up to Labor Day trying to take advantage of a more level playing field full of more regular type movies instead of the established franchise movies. In fact, for the first time this summer there will be three new releases opening that will be directed toward specific audiences, kids and families for Disney's "G-Force," women for Sony's romantic comedy "The Ugly Truth" and teens for the Warner Bros. horror film "Orphan." For the rest of the summer things will get more crowded at the multiplexes, which on one hand gives hope to a greater amount of movies becoming successes, but on the other hand there will be more competition for those films and diminishing audiences in August due to many schools opening earlier and earlier. When more movies open, more movies have to be taken off the screen to make room for them, which can lead to little battles between distributors and exhibitors about which movies are ready to be tossed out. Of course, distributors would love all their films to hold onto their screens, hence the fights. More independent films will be hitting the screens with the hope of finding a late summer audience, and there are two interesting films that are profiled on the next page that are going about it in two different ways.

G-Force	*The Ugly Truth*
Disney	Sony
Opening weekend: $31,706,934	Opening weekend: $27,605,576
Domestic gross: $119,436,770 40.8%	Domestic gross: $88,915,214 43.3%
Foreign gross: $173,381,071 59.2%	Foreign gross: $116,383,693 56.7%
Worldwide gross: $292,817,841	Worldwide gross: $205,298,907
Widest release: 3,697 theatres	Widest release: 2,975 theatres

Orphan

Warner Brothers

Opening weekend: $12,871,483

Domestic gross: $41,596,251 54.2%

Foreign gross: $35,103,381 45.8%

Worldwide gross: $76,699,632

Widest release: 2,750 theatres

Shrink

Roadside

Opening weekend: $16,443

Domestic gross: $189,621 62.5%

Foreign gross: $113,810 37.5%

Worldwide gross: $303,431

Widest release: 27 theatres

If I Die Tonight

Indican

Opening weekend: $9,646

Domestic gross: $20,519

Foreign gross: N/A

Widest release: 2 theatres

How to Be a Serial Killer

Monterey

Opening weekend: $899

Domestic gross: $899

Foreign gross: N/A

Widest release: 1 theatre

In The Loop

IFC

Opening weekend: $191,866

Domestic gross: $2,388,804 30.7%

Foreign gross: $5,398,683 69.3%

Worldwide gross: $7,787,487

Widest release: 92 theatres

The Answer Man

Magnolia

Opening weekend: $12,998

Domestic gross: $25,589

Foreign gross: N/A

Widest release: 6 theatres

Loren Cass

Kino

Opening weekend: $2,135

Domestic gross: $8,125

Foreign gross: N/A

Widest release: 2 theatres

Shadowland

Independent

Opening weekend: $5,420

Domestic gross: $8,221

Foreign gross: N/A

Widest release: 1 theatre

Week 30: Questions for Discussion

1. What's the underlying message the studios send at the annual Comic-Con convention?

2. What is the mystery and excitement of a movie's opening weekend? Discuss a past movie you went to see on opening day and why you just couldn't wait to see it. What kind of experience did you have and did it meet your expectations?

3. What have independent filmmakers done in the past to improve their chances of drawing a sizable audience to their films on opening weekend? List the pros and cons of each method. Are there any other methods that weren't mentioned that you feel could also be effective?

4. In what way can a small film debuting at the Sundance Film Festival be comparable to what happens at the Comic-Con convention? On the other hand, what are the differences between the two events in relation to the promotional opportunities they offer to the movies themselves?

HISTORICAL PERSPECTIVE – THE FOUR-WALL DEAL

The four-wall deal is a deal born out of the ingenuity and perhaps the desperation of the independent producer. When someone makes a film, the idea is to find someone else to take it off your hands and do the heavy lifting to get it released. But what happens when distributors show no interest, when a movie is considered too slight, too off the beaten path, too non-commercial to bother with it? Or when filmmakers feel the deals being offered aren't strong enough and believe they can do something with it themselves and go out and do it? Perhaps that's what was going through the minds of the people behind the production of some Alaskan hunting films back in 1965 who began renting out hunting lodges and high school auditoriums in Salt Lake City to play their nature film. After finding that enough hunters, outdoor enthusiasts and families were enjoying the movie and telling others about it, they gave it the title of "Alaska Safari" and started renting out movie theatres in outlying towns. The producers kept opening it in new towns, state by state, taking three years to go around the country and eventually grossing $15 million dollars, an incredible achievement for its day. Legend has it that this is the first account of a movie that successfully used the four-wall technique on such a broad scale. If it wasn't "Alaska Safari" that paved the way, then it was probably something pretty close to it because the four-wall template that followed was to have a very similar look to it.

The 1970s and early 1980s were the golden age of four-walling, and two companies emerged to dominate this end of the business during this period. The dominant company was Sunn Classic Pictures, a Mormon organization in Park City, Utah, and the other company was Pacific International Enterprises based in Medford, Oregon. These companies developed the following strict rules and created a template that they never wavered from when utilizing their four-wall strategy:

▶ By utilizing sophisticated computer technology, they designed movies based on extensive research and test-marketing.

▶ They identified their main target audience as working-class families who only saw one or two movies a year.

▶ They chose two distinct types of movies to produce: low-budget family nature films like "Grizzly Adams" and "The Adventure of Frontier Fremont," or low-budget pseudoscientific docu-dramas like "Beyond and Back" and "In Search of Historic Jesus."

▶ Only make G rated or PG rated movies in order to have access to the greatest number of people and access to all times of day and night with their television advertising.

▶ Create the television commercials first, and then build the actual picture around them. As many as 14 different commercials for each film were developed.

▶ Distribute movies in one territory at a time to save on prints and personnel, and then move those prints to the next market at the completion of the run. A territory like Wisconsin would have several distinct local television orbit areas like Milwaukee, Green Bay, Madison and Lacrosse, which would all play at the same time.

▶ Rent maximum number of theatres in each television market, concentrating on neighborhood and low-cost theatres to keep expenses down.

▶ Start the distribution in the smallest, most unsophisticated markets first in order to test market results in case changes had to be made in the advertising, and then move to larger markets later. In a complete reversal from the studios, the two most sophisticated, expensive markets of New York and Los Angeles either played last or not at all.

▶ Saturate the airwaves in each market with a barrage of television advertising, hooking viewers with a variety of different spots.

- ▸ Concentrate distributing movies in the winter months when television viewership is at its highest. The best months became November, January and February.

- ▸ Book the movies to play for only two weeks, fill the theatres, and then move the prints to the next territory.

The four-wall movies during this era had nothing to do with art and everything to do with science. Critics blasted the simplistic, derivative story lines, and Hollywood scoffed at their use of computers in creating movies, but it didn't stop these movies from being very popular with a lot of people. From 1974 to the end of the decade, Sunn had hit after hit with "In Search of Noah's Ark" leading the way with a $28 million dollar gross on a $360,000 production budget. Credit also has to be given to director/star Tom Laughlin and the role he played in popularizing the use of the four-wall method. After Warner Brothers failed to find an audience for Laughlin's film "Billy Jack" in 1971, Laughlin convinced the company to allow him to rerelease the movie in California through his own company. He proceeded to rent as many theatres as he could, created fresh television commercials and used saturation marketing well before it became the norm for studios. "Billy Jack" became one of the biggest hits of the year. Billy Graham's organization also found success four-walling some of their religious films. Studios were so impressed with the results that some of them started to reissue hit films like "Blazing Saddles" and "Jeremiah Johnson" by renting theatres outright, but exhibitors weren't too happy with this arrangement because these movies were proven hits, and they felt the studios were taking advantage of them by eliminating their upside profit potential. Their complaints were heard by the Justice Department, which stepped in and told the studios to cool it on this practice and to return to selling their movies on the usual percentage basis. As with many popular trends and styles, these four-wall movies eventually ran their course by the mid-1980s, and the era of the wide release saturated four-wall movie gradually came to an end. They became less and less profitable for several reasons:

- ▸ Advertising costs kept getting higher and higher.

- ▸ Their bread and butter neighborhood and city theatres were going out of business, being squeezed out by newer chain multiplexes.

- ▸ Theatres demanding higher rental costs.

- ▸ Audiences tiring of the same formulas and story lines.

Regardless of the poor quality of many of the movies, no one can argue that these movies represented a very successful business model. In their day, it was something to see and marvel at. When these movies hit the Chicago market, the distributors easily had hundreds of thousands of dollars spent on theatre rentals and television advertising before the doors of the theatres even opened. You have to know what you are doing when you have that kind of money on the line. While the era of the wide release four-wall movie is dead and gone, the legacy and formula of this unique deal lives on for any enterprising filmmaker to attempt who has a movie, a dream and a target audience to reach.

Week 30: Questions for Discussion

5. If you think of the studios as manufacturing plants and movie theatres as retail outlets, who dictates the price of purchase for the product and the price the public will pay for it? Does the four-wall deal change that dynamic? If yes, in what way?

6. What are the pros and cons of a distributor having a four-wall deal instead of a percentage deal with a movie theatre?

7. On "Lana's Rain," ISA Releasing changed the deal from a 90/10 deal to a four-wall deal 4 weeks before the movie was set to open. The following are the specifics of each deal:

First deal:
90/10 over house expense of $10,000 (750 seats)
Specific conditions agreed upon for first week of engagement:
1st week gross under $10,000 will net 40% film rental
1st week gross between $10,000 and $16,999 will net 50% film rental
1st week gross over $17,000 will net 60% film rental
1st week gross over $30,000 will be governed by the 90/10 formula

Revised Deal:
$7,500 four-wall rental to be paid by ISA Releasing seven days before opening date. Distributor will retain 100% of box office to be paid within 7 days of completion of 1st week by Music Box Theatre. Any additional weeks of playtime will be negotiated separately between the parties.

Results:
The first week gross on "Lana's Rain" was $17,738. Please compute both deals and arrive at what the film rental paid to ISA would be in each case. Do you think ISA was right to change the deal before the film opened? Then consider whether the box office gross would have been the same regardless of how the financial deal was written. Give your reasons for your answer. (Refer back to week 24, June 12-18, on how the 90/10 deal is calculated.)

THE NOT SO FUNNY BUSINESS OF TAKING RISKS

Week 31: July 31–August 6, 2009

When the numbers are crunched and they don't add up, studio heads are paid to walk away from the deal rather than throw their money in on a wing and a prayer.

Judd Apatow's "Funny People" is opening this weekend, and there really isn't anything funny about what's at stake for Universal and its co-heads Marc Shmuger and David Linde. They need a hit movie, preferably a big hit movie, and they need it sooner rather than later. It has been a bad year. They're last in market share among the six studios, and they're starting to feel the heat from their bosses at General Electric. Universal has been taking more risks than the other studios this year with adult-driven films like "Duplicity," "State of Play" and "Public Enemies," and GE wants to start seeing some of these risks turn into profits.

Will "Funny People" be funny enough to become that elusive hit Universal has been looking for? So far Apatow has been good for the studio with "40 Year Old Virgin" and "Knocked Up" grossing a combined $400 million in worldwide box office. It would seem another movie from the director couldn't be coming at a more opportune time, but Universal can't seem to catch a break because Apatow is breaking away from his usual winning formula, adding some serious issues of illness and mortality to the comedy mix and saddling it with a long running time of 146 minutes. Inserting Adam Sandler as the star should help, but with him in the cast the budget sits at $70 million, double the cost of his previous films. Put it all together and Universal is staring at another risky investment on its hands. Directors have done this type of thing in the past. They deliver several hit films for a studio and make them a lot of money, and then they push for doing something more serious, perhaps more personal, a little different from their sweet spot, and it's tough for the studio to say no. It's just happening at the wrong time for Universal.

Taking risks in today's Hollywood is not something the studios like doing, especially with DVD sales down double digits for the second year in a row. Their profit machine has slowed down, and that is making the decision-making process on what movies to green light even more conservative than it was before. When the numbers are crunched and they don't add up, studio heads are paid to walk away from the deal rather than throw their money in on a wing and a prayer. That's what happened recently when Sony walked away from Steven Soderbergh's "Moneyball" script with Brad Pitt attached after they previously approved the project. Sony felt Soderbergh made changes to the script that would have made the film more risky, so they walked. If Universal's risks continue to not pay off, one of two things will happen, GE will make a change at the top and move in another direction, or the current chiefs will be forced to make fewer ambitious films and more cookie cutter ones that will start looking like everyone else's release schedules. Either way, it would be bad news for moviegoers. When people complain about the overall quality of studio movies they have a point. The annual studio output leaves a lot of to be desired for the mainstream adult moviegoer, but movies have come to cost so much to produce and market, and profit margins are so slight, what are they supposed to do? When you are making a majority of your movies for a global audience, it's not the easiest question to answer.

I've always been fascinated with the concept of risk/reward and how movie distributors and exhibitors have dealt with it over the years. It has always been a very expensive business to operate in, and when push comes to shove, when one side or another gets squeezed, when someone gets desperate and looks to get the upper hand or when greed sets in, it usually comes down to people looking to maintain more money, power and control. Sometimes the ploys they have used have been legal, other times illegal.

Two historic court cases involving litigation between distributors and exhibitors have helped define and govern the movie industry when one side, then the other side, have attempted to lower their risk and improve their odds for reward through illegal practices, The Paramount Consent Decrees in 1948 and the Product Splitting case of 1981. The Golden Age of Hollywood between 1930 and 1950 produced many great screen classics, but those years were not golden for everyone in the industry. The studios had an iron grip control over both distribution and exhibition, as they owned and operated many of the most important theatres in the country in addition to producing and distributing their own movies. They controlled the whole shooting match, all three facets of the industry, production, distribution and exhibition, and sold their movies to their own theatres, actively working to keep competition out and denying independent theatres access to their top films. Not surprisingly, this led to a class action lawsuit against the studios, which evolved into a government anti-trust case that took ten years to work its way through the federal courts and finally up to the Supreme Court. The major producers-distributors-exhibitors were eventually found guilty of restraint of trade, conspiracy, price-fixing and depriving independent theatre owners of top 1st run movies and were forced to sell their theatres and adhere to a set of new sale procedures that are still in place to this day. It came to be known as the Paramount Consent Decrees, and it did more to influence the structure of the contemporary film industry than any other occurrence in the industry's first 50 years.

It was an early form of a fantasy sports league, but instead of picking ball players, they were picking movies, in effect becoming both the distributor and exhibitor.

In 1981, it was the exhibitors' turn to face the music in a government court case and it was directly tied to a dubious sales practice utilized by distributors in the 1970s call blind bidding. After the Consent Decrees, the studios were forced to bid out their movies and make them available to all theatres, giving them an opportunity to send in a written bid if they were interested in playing a specific movie. As the 1970s proceeded, the studios began asking for bids on more and more movies before the movies were actually finished, putting the exhibitors at a disadvantage by having to commit to films and guaranteed money purely based on star power, glossy brochures or ten minute product reels. The movies were still in production, and the studios wanted to firm up the theatres as early as possible. As more and more movies failed to pan out and losses mounted for exhibitors who guessed wrong in this bidding process, exhibitors became angrier and angrier. This led the exhibitors down two roads, one legal and the other that proved to be illegal. The legal method was pushing for anti-blind bidding laws in individual states which would prevent distributors from asking for offers on movies before they were completely finished. After all was said and done, about 30 states eventually passed laws outlawing the blind bidding process. The other method was theatre owners calling each other up in various markets and agreeing within the group not to bid against each other. What they did was meet in secret and work out a system of dividing up all the movies among themselves each quarter and supplying the booking dates to distributors while bypassing the blind bidding process. It was an early from of a fantasy sports league, but instead of multiple rounds of picking ball players, they were picking movies, in effect becoming both the distributor and exhibitor. The practice was called Product Splitting, and this time the government was on the side of distributors when the anti-trust case was staged against exhibitors in 1981. The ruling was a per se victory for distributors because it made product splitting an illegal criminal act anywhere in the country. With the bidding process long since abandoned, there has been no need for exhibitors to even think about engaging in this activity for many years, but nevertheless it was a major ruling in its day.

What these two cases have in common, and what is a guideline for any business in an openly competitive marketplace to avoid, is the simple word and concept of collusion. When it comes to trying to eliminate risk and getting an edge, no like-minded businesses can ever conspire together to make group decisions that would give unfair advantage to themselves at the expense of others. Collusion is blatantly illegal. Each company has to compete on its own, making its own decisions, deciding on its own path and staying away from getting too close to competitors in discussing specific business practices and competitive situations.

One of the perfectly legal ways studios use to eliminate some risk is to cut costs, readjust their budgets and lower their expenses. It makes sense they would look closely at their marketing budgets to see what they could trim. Newspaper advertising has been an area where cost reductions have been made across the board by all the film companies. It personally pains me to look at Friday movie sections to see how small the ads have become and how quickly ads are dropped in the second or third weeks of a run, no matter how successful the movie is. Is this an example of studios getting together and agreeing to all run smaller ads in the hope of driving down rates? No, that's not the case. It's companies coming to the same conclusion that fewer moviegoers are reading newspapers and that they are getting more of their information from the Internet. The studios are working independently of each other and don't have an ulterior motive other than trying to trim dollars wherever they can and move more of their ad budget into the digital and interactive realm. Most newspapers are more than willing to cut deals with distributors to either run larger ads or make two for one deals on color ads and keep their rates very reasonable, but distributors aren't being swayed and say they don't have anything left in their budget. That's why Universal has stopped running newspaper ads for "Public Enemies" and "Bruno." There's nothing illegal about that. It's perhaps somewhat shortsighted, because there are still a good number of people who are reading newspapers, and newspaper ads can still be an effective reminder, especially on an adult driven movie like "Public Enemies" which continues to do business in large cities like Chicago.

Another example of studios going their own way and making their own decisions is in the area of DVDs and what to do with Redbox, the company that is becoming more popular by renting DVDs overnight for $1.00. Each studio is grappling with a fundamental choice of how this business model will affect long-term growth measured against short-term gain and how their risk factor will play out. Every day, every week, every month, every year, decisions like this have to be made. Much more on this topic in next week's chapter.

This Week at the Box Office: *Weekly Attendance: $26,043,956*

"Funny People" did indeed have problems at the ticket window, both in the domestic and international markets, and grossed significantly less than the previous two Apatow Universal comedies. Whereas "Funny People" only grossed $71 million in worldwide grosses, "Knocked Up" grossed $219 million, and "40 Year Old Virgin" totaled $177 million.

Funny People
Universal
Opening weekend: $22,657,780
Domestic gross: $51,855,045 72.4%
Foreign gross: $19,730,190 27.6%
Worldwide gross: $71,585,235
Widest release: 3,008 theatres

Aliens in the Attic
20th Century Fox
Opening weekend: $8,008,423
Domestic gross: $25,200,412 43.5%
Foreign gross: $32,680,644 56.5%
Worldwide gross: $57,881,056
Widest release: 3,108 theatres

The Collector
Freestyle
Opening weekend: $3,576,296
Domestic gross: $7,712,114 81.7%
Foreign gross: $1,731,904 18.3%
Worldwide gross: $9,444,018
Widest release: 1,325 theatres

Love Aaj Kal
Eros
Opening weekend: $1,241,762
Domestic gross: $2,430,083 11.7%
Foreign gross: $18,364,902 88.3%
Worldwide gross: $20,794,985
Widest release: 102 theatres

Adam
Fox Searchlight
Opening weekend: $68,377
Domestic gross: $2,283,291 89.3%
Foreign gross: $272,209 10.7%
Worldwide gross: $2,549,605
Widest release: 177 theatres

The Cove
Roadside
Opening weekend; $57,640
Domestic gross: $857,005 73.7%
Foreign gross: $305,417 26.3%
Worldwide gross: $1,162,422
Widest release: 57 theatres

Lorna's Silence

Sony Classics
Opening weekend: $34,411
Domestic gross: $338,795 6.6%
Foreign gross: $4,784,881 93.4%
Worldwide gross: $5,123,676
Widest release: 23 theatres

Thirst

Focus
Opening weekend: $55,889
Domestic gross: $318,574 2.4%
Foreign gross: $12,690,363 97.6%
Worldwide gross: $13,008,937
Widest release: 17 theatres

Flame & Citron

IFC
Opening weekend: $15,254
Domestic gross: $148,089 1.5%
Foreign gross: $10,037,995 98.5%
Worldwide gross: $10,186,084
Widest release: 8 theatres

Not Quite Hollywood

Magnolia
Opening weekend: $4,694
Domestic gross: $21,152
Foreign gross; $159,805
Worldwide gross: $180,957
Widest release: 6 theatres

You, the Living

Palisades
Opening weekend: $6,924
Domestic gross: $15,696
Foreign gross: N/A
Widest release: 1 theatre

Act of God

Zeitgeist
Opening weekend: $522
Domestic gross: $9,995
Foreign gross: N/A
Widest release: 1 theatre

Ghosted

First Run
Opening weekend: $980
Domestic gross: $1,780
Foreign gross: N/A
Widest release: 1 theatre

2012 Update:
"Moneyball" Resurfaces as a Solid Hit

When Sony made the decision to shut down "Moneyball" due to script problems, it appeared there was a decent chance the movie was never going to get made. Thanks to a script by Aaron Sorkin and, perhaps more importantly, Brad Pitt's refusal to allow the project to wither away, the film was made with new director Bennett Miller and released in September, 2011. This is a good example of a studio making a tough decision to temporarily shut down a film project which had a top director and star attached. That the movie resurfaced with the same star but with a different director and screenwriter is a testament to how Sony managed their risk with this project along with everyone else involved in the process. The movie was a critical and box office success for Sony, grossing a solid $75 million in the domestic market and being nominated for Best Picture of the Year. The movie became an instant baseball classic and ranks second to all baseball films at the box office. Surprisingly, it trails only Sony's 1992 "A League of Their Own," the only baseball movie to gross over $100 million at $107 million.

Week 31: Questions for Discussion

1. Why are studios so risk adverse in today's corporate climate? With Universal taking multiple risks in 2009, what became of the fate of co-heads Marc Shmuger and David Linde?

2. Describe what the Paramount Consent Decrees and the Product Splitting legal cases were and which one had more of an impact on the structure of the film industry. In what way did it provide an opening for new companies to enter the industry?

3. What is the main factor that distinguishes hard-nosed fair competition from collusion?

BATTLE LINES ARE DRAWN AT A THEATRE AND KIOSK NEAR YOU

Week 32: August 7–13, 2009

---

*Whenever one revenue source is impacted in any way, the results
are felt throughout the industry in the number and type of movies
that are made, distributed and seen by the public.*

There are two interesting battles raging this weekend. The first one is inside the nation's movie theatres, where it's really not much of a contest but more about the adult audience, specifically women in this case, attempting to show some box office mettle against those omnipotent fan boys. The other one is a behind-the-scenes power struggle within the home entertainment industry where studios are fighting to maintain value for their films and a sequential order to their distribution. It's easy to fixate on the week-to-week theatrical business, but it's also instructive to explore the happenings in the DVD, television or international markets from time to time to see how everything is connected. Whenever one revenue source is impacted in any way, the results are felt throughout the industry in the number and type of movies that are made, distributed and seen by the public.

At the theatres this weekend, Columbia's "Julie & Julia" opens against Paramount's "GI Joe: The Rise of the Cobra," and even though "GI Joe" is in no danger of not finishing number one at the box office, it would be nice to see the adult audience turn out in force for the latest Meryl Streep summer counter-programmer. It's amazing to think that at the age of 60, Streep is now considered one of the most bankable actresses in Hollywood and a big reason "Julie & Julia" was made in the first place. In two of the last three summers, she has had huge $100 million dollar plus hits with "The Devil Wears Prada" and Mama Mia" which has transformed this Oscar winning actress into more of a box office draw than she has ever been in her 30-year career. The importance of a good showing this weekend stems from the fact there have been so few wide releases geared for the adult audience this summer; the industry needs to be reminded there is still a pulse in the 35 and over demographic. We are now beginning the fourth month of the summer movie season, and there have only been a handful of movies that could be considered made for the adult audience, "Angels and Demons," "Public Enemies," "Taking of Pelham 123," "The Proposal" and "The Hangover," which was geared for a slightly younger audience of under 30 year olds but nevertheless has attracted adults of all ages. That's a sad statement, but that's what the summer movie season has evolved into.

With the national box office in a bit of a rut for the last four weeks, the combination of adult women and young males flocking to see their particular movies this weekend should prove to be a winning tonic. Hollywood always seems to be shocked when a female-driven movie opens strong, and it will be no different Monday morning when "Julie & Julia's" weekend gross comes in higher than what was projected. Women make up a gigantic audience, but they get very little respect in the male dominated industry. With Meryl Streep playing Julia Child, it got me thinking about cooking and food themed movies, which have always seemed to do well in the independent arena. Numerous movies such as "Big Night," "Like Water for Chocolate," "Eat Drink Man Women," Mostly Martha," "Babette's Feast" and "Waitress" have all proven to be popular with audiences. The specialty audience seems to be drawn to cooking themed films while being helped by the fact that every newspaper has a weekly food section which generously provides publicity stories for them, making it easier to reach its intended audience than with your average independent release. For independent films, publicity still reigns supreme. But I was surprised to notice that very few wide releases have dealt specifically with cooking. In the modern era, Warner Brother's "No Reservations," a remake of the foreign hit "Mostly Martha," is the highest live action grosser with $43 million. Disney/Pixar's "Ratatouille," with a gross of $206 million leads the field. It won't take long for

"Julie & Julia" to surpass "No Reservations" and become the highest grossing live action cooking movie of all time. In regards to "GI Joe," it's the last big summer action movie, and even with some questionable buzz, it should gross at least $50 million over the weekend with no problem.

With a $175 million dollar budget, Paramount better hope it does at least that amount. I'm not the least interested in seeing toys turned into movies, but I understand the thinking behind it. But after reading that Hasbro announced movie deals for the Ouija Board and board games Battleship, Candyland and Monopoly, a strange sense of gloom swept over me.

The theatrical business continues to set the awareness and value for movies, but the profits still kick in with the DVD release, and there have been fewer profits this year. It can't be overstated how important DVD revenues are to a film's bottom line. Before a studio puts a movie into production, they first have to project how that movie will perform throughout its various stages of distribution. If they have to adjust downward their DVD projections, they try to either find ways to lower the budget or scrap the film altogether. Taking a look at the statistics of Home Entertainment's performance for the first half of 2009 is schizophrenic to say the least:

January 1 to June 30, 2009
- ▶ Total U.S. Home Entertainment – down 3.9%
- ▶ DVD and Blu-Ray Rentals – up 8.3%
- ▶ DVD Sales – down 17%
- ▶ Digital Sales and Rentals – up 21%

Source: The Digital Entertainment Group

Home entertainment is going through a transitional phase with new formats such as high-def digital downloads, streaming and more emphasis being put on Video-on-Demand, but times of change tend to drag revenues down as the new ways of generating income take a while to kick in. That's what's happening with the current DVD market. The new formats are showing growth, but they pale in comparison to the studios' core DVD sales business, which is falling for the second year in a row. Nothing can make up for the 17% drop in DVD sales in the first half of the year. From the time DVDs entered the market in 1997, it was a license to print money for the studios as the business changed from a predominantly rental market ($65 wholesale, $90 retail price) to a sales market with consumers gobbling up $19.99 DVDs, rushing to build personal film libraries as well as buying them as gifts for friends and families. DVDs became the fastest rising home technology in history and for ten years in a row showed incredible growth. Sales of DVDs brought in more revenue and profits than rentals, and the money flowed into the distributors more quickly. Everyone was happy, but things never stay exactly the same. With consumers looking to save money in this recession and realizing they may own more DVDs than they can ever watch, the business is shifting back to more of a rental business, which is not something the studios prefer but have to deal with nonetheless. Not all categories of movies are showing the effect of the recession and changing consumer habits. Studios report that R-rated comedies, action-adventure films and cult fan titles have been holding up the best. It's interesting to note that family and kid movies were not mentioned, so parents must also be deciding they have enough titles on hand to keep the kids happy.

With Blockbuster and other brick-and-mortar video stores either forced to close in recent years or battling to turn around their businesses, the growth in rental is mainly coming from Netflix (up 22% in revenues in the 2nd quarter) and Redbox, the company with those red kiosks in front of grocery and drugstores throughout the country. Redbox is the dominant player in the dollar-a-night rental kiosk business and has shown incredible growth from being in 600 locations four years ago to over 17,000 locations today with a projection of 22,000 by 2010. This is where the real growth is coming from, so why aren't the studios jumping for joy with this growing revenue source? It comes down to the pricing pure and simple. The dollar-a-night rentals do not thrill the studios which have been living off selling DVDs to big box retailers at $17.00 a unit wholesale and pocketing over $12.00 profit on each DVD sold, after manufacturing, shipping and marketing costs were factored in. For studios, they have multiple concerns, starting with the precedent of the dirt-cheap rental price, the prospect of more low-priced used DVDs flooding the market and the all-important perception of maintaining value for their product. For independent distributors, especially for those outside the studio specialty divisions, the rise of Redbox is even more dire because, due to its limited kiosk space, only the most popular movies tend to be carried. Most independent films, which tend to have low grosses and limited releases to begin with, will have very little shot in getting any piece of the kiosk revenue stream.

How much can the studios risk in devaluing their product in the home market?

The studios are on their own in figuring out how to deal with the Redbox issue. Some are fighting it while others are making deals with the company. It's a tough situation for the studios. It's hard to avoid selling to companies that sell product for such a low price, especially when a company such as Redbox is growing so rapidly and in a way in which the public is embracing. But a few crucial questions arise. How much can the studios risk in devaluing their product in the home market? How could it affect long-term industry growth? Legally, do the studios have to service all retail outlets at the same time, regardless of the price they charge? These are tricky questions, and different studios are responding in different ways. The two studios at the extreme ends of the spectrum are Universal, which is currently being sued by Redbox, and Columbia, which has just announced a five-year distribution deal with the company.

Let's look at Universal first. Several months ago, Universal made the decision to withhold their first run films from Redbox for 45 days, which led to Redbox filing an anti-trust lawsuit against the studio. What Universal was saying is that they will sell their films to Redbox but not on first run availability. They will have to wait their turn. The precedent is in the theatrical marketplace where historically there has been a pecking order of a sequential release pattern servicing a wide range of theatres with various operational and pricing policies. Even though the majority of screens in the United States have first run policies, there is still a range of theatres with the following policies:

- First run theatres
- Large format theatres
- Drive-in theatres
- Art theatres
- Calendar theatres
- Repertory theatres
- Intermediate theatres
- Discount theatres
- Draft house cinemas

I'm not sure if that precedent will be applicable in the DVD market, but bargain priced theatres have never been able to play movies at the same time as first run theatres. They have had to wait their turn and play a few months later or after all the first theatres in a given market completed their runs. Redbox has filed an anti-trust suit against Universal, but the studio's attorneys understand what they can and can't do and are guided by the general anti-trust rules that have been in place for 60 years. Studios understand they have a lot of latitude when selling their movies to customers. They don't have to sell to everyone who requests a film; they can sell to those who they believe will return the most revenue back to them, and they are entitled to release a picture on an exclusive or selected number of runs. There have been many cases where distributors have made DVD deals with specific retailers like Blockbuster or Best Buy for an exclusive period before the other retailers could get their hands on it. That still doesn't guarantee Universal will win the lawsuit (if it isn't settled first), but those are the factors they weighed before they instituted their 45-day policy. 20th Century Fox Home Entertainment also announced this week that they are seeking to impose a 30-day delay on the availability of its DVD titles for all dollar-per-night rental kiosks.

Fox said in a statement that the studio "supports the vending machine business in a 30-day window following our initial home video street date. The basis of this position is to continue to provide the consumer with broad title choice and access to Fox movies while maintaining the quality image and value perception of Fox movies. Our desire is to maintain for Fox movies a thriving network of distribution serving all types of consumer preferences, on reasonable business terms for Fox as well as our distribution partners."

Other studios are choosing to make deals with Redbox rather than confront them on the price issue, even though that may hurt the industry in the long term. In effect, they are looking for short-term growth for their own companies. The most high profile deal was announced by Columbia after they signed a five-year deal worth a reported $460 million. Columbia will receive preferential treatment and increase their depth of copies with Redbox from 14% to 20% and made Redbox agree they would send back the used DVDs instead of releasing them into the general marketplace to be sold at drastically discounted prices. So they made a good deal for themselves. It goes to show again that studios can't and will not work in unison when it comes to how their movies are sold.

The only constant in the Motion Picture Industry has always been change, and there's plenty of that for all the industry heads and their management to deal with. What's different about the situation with Redbox is that this is one instance where the Internet is not in the middle of the equation when it comes to change or smaller revenue returns. This time the battle is with the old-fashioned, very physical vending machine. That doesn't make it any less stressful; it just points to the fact that business conflicts and opportunities come in all shapes, sizes and formats. One way or another, with millions of dollars at stake, they have to be dealt with while considering the past, present and future. Did Universal or Columbia make the right decision with Redbox? Time will tell.

This Week at the Box Office:

Weekly Attendance: 29,568,701

GI Joe: The Rise of Cobra
Paramount
Opening weekend: $54,713,046
Domestic gross: $150,201,498 49.7%
Foreign gross: $152,267,519 50.3%
Worldwide gross: $302,469,017
Widest release: 4,007 theatres

Julia & Julia
Sony
Opening weekend: $20,027,956
Domestic gross: $94,125,426 72.7%
Foreign gross: $35,415,073 27.3%
Worldwide gross: $129,540,499
Widest release: 2,528 theatres

A Perfect Getaway
Universal
Opening weekend: $5,948,555
Domestic gross: $15,514,460 67.9%
Foreign gross: $7,337,178 32.1%
Worldwide gross: $22,852,638
Widest release: 2,159 theatres

Paper Heart
Overture
Opening weekend: $219,494
Domestic gross: $1,274,062 98.2%
Foreign gross: $22,909 2.8%
Worldwide gross: $1,296,971
Widest release: 96 theatres

Cold Souls

IDP/Samuel Goldwyn

Opening weekend: $63,302

Domestic gross: $905,209 80.1%

Foreign gross: $224,944 19.9%

Worldwide gross: $1,130,153

Widest release: 52 theatres

Bliss

First Run

Opening weekend: $7,039

Domestic gross: $40,349

Foreign gross: N/A

Widest release: 14 theatres

Mugabe and the White African

First Run

Opening weekend: $1,907

Domestic gross: $7,986

Foreign gross: N/A

Widest release: 1 theatre

Beeswax

Cinema Guild

Opening weekend: $5,844

Domestic gross: $46,590

Foreign gross: N/A

Widest release: 3 theatres

I Sell the Dead

IFC

Opening weekend: $3,529

Domestic gross: $8,050

Foreign gross: N/A

Widest release: 2 theatres

2012 Update:

Disney, 20th Century Fox, Warner Bros. and Universal imposed waiting periods averaging about one month on all their releases to rental services like Redbox and Netflix. Paramount, Sony and Lionsgate continue to service these retailers without restriction.

Conversations with Industry Professionals

Mitch Lowe – President of Redbox, Oakbrook, IL

The following interview took place on June 21, 2011. Mr. Lowe has since left the company to pursue entrepreneurial and other interests.

> *"We figured out how to get movies out of the warehouse and into consumers' hands very quickly, earning money all the time"*
>
> Mitch Lowe

Q: *You've been in the video business from its earliest days and ran your own video store chain for 14 years. You sold it in 1998 as the business model was changing from rental to sell-through. Was that a calculated move on your part?*

ML: The video rental stores were a lot of fun if you were a movie lover like I was. Being able to be behind the counter and talk to customers about movies, trying to figure out how to drive demand face to face, it was really exciting for me, and I loved every minute of it. Moving out from running the stores was really more about the demand Netflix started drawing from me. Actually, my family still owned those stores up to a couple of years ago through my brother who I had sold them to. My brother still is operating three of those stores in Northern California. I would have never left that business if my time wasn't being pulled away from it first by Netflix and then by Redbox.

Q: *You were in on the ground floor with Netflix?*

ML: Yes, out of the whole group that really got Netflix going was a man named Mark Randolph, who was funded by Reed Hastings, who ran a software tools company, and it was really Mark's and Reed's vision to get into the DVD business. They had no domain experience in the rental business, so I was the guy who brought the experience of renting movies.

Q: *How did your experience at Netflix prepare you for what was to come at Redbox? They share the same rental business with each other but are there also a lot of differences between the two companies?*

ML: The interesting part is that both companies succeeded because we developed unique business models and solved a lot of the puzzles that consumers had in renting movies. I started at Netflix in 1997, and the company rented out its first movie in 1998. At that time, Netflix was trying to be the Amazon of DVDS and rented movies out for a week at a time for $4.00, but there was clearly this business issue where consumers didn't want all the anxiety of returning movies within a specific time frame. There was a lot of experimentation done to get to where Netflix is today. With Redbox, we had to solve the issue of affordability and convenience, trying to get the movies to a point of pure impulse and a no-brainer for people to bring a movie home, then bring more movies home and watch more movies than they did under the existing model. Customers had to be more selective because the original cost of a rental was $4.00, and they were forced to have to return it to the same place they bought it from. That wasn't convenient for a lot of people, so both businesses fought really hard to solve big problems for consumers in renting movies.

Q: *You became president of Redbox in 2009, correct?*

ML: Yes, in April, 2009.

Q: *When you arrived you inherited a lot of industry problems to deal with. How challenging was that year for you and the decisions you had to make?*

ML: You are right; it was a very challenging year, mostly because half of our suppliers (major studios) essentially didn't want to provide product for us at the same terms they were providing to our competitors. You know the movie business, every film is essentially a monopoly for that film, and you can't live without "Avatar" or the latest "Harry Potter." You just can't find a replacement for those types of movies in this business. So having half of your suppliers not wanting to work with you was incredibly challenging. The hardest challenge I had to deal with was just the clear unfairness of how we were being treated. Here we were providing a great service to our customers, making it incredibly affordable to rent a movie while the economy was going through some rough times with many families feeling the pinch, and the studios wanted to crater this innovation we had come up with. We were perfectly happy paying the same wholesale price as Blockbuster, Netflix and all the other retailers were paying, but the studios had other things in mind. It was about trying to stay calm in the midst of such unfair treatment by your suppliers. My other challenge was keeping the organization focused on the solution. We could solve this if we focused on our customers, and one of the most gratifying things I saw was the people in our company figured out how to serve our customers despite the fact some studios were trying to do everything they could to stop us.

Q: *What did you do to get product?*

ML: My staff figured out how they could go out and buy hundreds of thousands of copies of a single title by going to Walmart, Target and Best Buys throughout the country, buying five copies at a time. We were creating some big market shares for Walmart, but it was more complicated than just buying them; we had to take the shrink-wrap off, get them into the system, make sure we didn't lose any and follow our plan of how many copies we needed for each location. It was a crazy way to get DVDs, but it was very gratifying to watch what an organization is capable of doing when it focuses on the customers' needs.

Q: *When a few of the studios refused to supply you with product on availability it reminded me of the bargain theatres that had to wait to play first run movies in the theatrical marketplace. Did you see the similarities between the two situations?*

ML: There is a big difference between what we were doing and what the dollar theatres were doing. Those bargain theatres were never prepared to pay the same cost of goods as the theatres that were charging first run admission prices. The innovation that Redbox developed was to deliver the film at a lot lower cost, yet it's not just the innovation of the equipment, but it's really the velocity rate of the title. Think about Blockbuster at the time. They were charging four dollars a rental, and some of them were five-day rentals, and others were for seven days which comes to less than a dollar a night. We are charging a dollar a night and keeping our product in customers' hands, earning money both for us and the studios at about the same rate or even more than what Blockbuster was doing. This is the magic of the models that both Netflix and Redbox have created. We figured out how to get movies out of the can or out of the warehouse and into consumers' hands very quickly, earning money all the time. In fact when we came up with the whole subscription idea with Netflix, it was the leadership team walking into a warehouse with millions of DVDs, row after row after row sitting there not earning anybody any money. And the thought was "why don't we make it so affordable that they're actually sitting in people's homes?" Maybe it's not so much per day, but it's at least earning more than they are sitting in a warehouse. With Redbox we did the same exact thing. The majority of our inventory is out inside people's homes or at the kiosk. It's so affordable, and they're in such convenient locations.

The minute it gets back to the kiosk it rents out very quickly again to another customer. That's the magic of those two models.

Q: *In 2009, Redbox sued the three studios, Universal, Warner Brothers and Fox, which were denying you product on availability, filing anti-trust suits against them. Did you actually feel you had a chance to win these cases, or was it more about doing something to grab their attention to get the impasse resolved?*

ML: I didn't think the lawsuits would go all the way to trial, and they didn't. No company likes to get sued, and we felt we had some very strong arguments, and the lawsuits indeed grabbed their attention. The result was that it moved the conversations forward and eventually some agreements and compromises were worked out with the studios, and the lawsuits were dropped.

Q: *Do you look back at 2009 as a pivotal year?*

ML: Yes, everything has changed since then. I think it was the beginning of a new world. We are not at the end of the transition; things continue to evolve, but I think it was the beginning of the end of bricks-and-mortar. It was clear at that point; whether it was Blockbuster or Hollywood Video or an independent store, they had kind of lost touch with the consumer.

Q: *Would you describe your relationships with all the studios as better now than they were in 2009?*

ML: Yes, it's much better. There is more of a common understanding, a mutual respect for each other. We are working hard to understand and compromise to solve both our customer issues and the studio issues. I want to say that the studios are not as comfortable with these new innovations as we are. They are more about risk reduction or risk prevention than they are about new ways to serve the customer, but I've seen some improvements in this area.

Q: *Are you still fighting the belief that $1.00 rentals are costing the movie industry a lot of lost revenue?*

ML: Not anywhere near what we had to do deal with a couple of years ago. Many people in the business missed the big consumer shift away from collecting, and we were the easy target to blame for that. We were really the by-product of that change instead of the culprit. Consumers got to the point where libraries at home were big, they weren't watching them as often, and more importantly, and I think this is the true cause for this issue, you can just access so much entertainment, whether it's movies or television, on the Internet, whatever you want and whenever you want it. Why would you collect anymore? At Netflix there are tens of thousands of titles available at all the times. People are streaming more and more. There are so many hours in the day. There is no reason like there was five or six years ago to buy DVDs.

Q: *I know what you're saying. I was one of those collectors.*

ML: Then you have the issue of what technology will be coming next, and you don't want to be investing in something that may not be around. We are not getting the same push back from studios in that regard. In fact, every single studio did their own analysis, and it was pretty funny because their sales reps would tell me, "Just between us, our data doesn't tell us you are affecting sales, but our bosses tell us to tell you that you do because we believe you must be because your product is so cheap."

Q: *I read somewhere that you were behind the concept of $1.00 rentals. Is that true, and how was*

McDonald's involved?

ML: McDonald's was the first owner of Redbox. That was back in 2003, and I was kind of the leader of the analytics to figure out a price point. In 2002, McDonald's had their first year of declining store sales, and that was when I started there. We were looking at all the different ways to drive traffic in the restaurant, and at the time they believed, and they were right, renting a movie would be a great way to increase traffic. Their idea was a video store in a box. Patrons would pick up a video and would have to make a return trip and most likely it would be in the evening when the restaurants were a little light. Their main traffic was breakfast and lunch business, so in the evening parking lots would be more open, and people would return a movie and smell the burgers and hopefully pick up some food and another movie. They had this huge selection and essentially video store pricing, $3.00 for a three-night rental. On paper it made sense, but it was not the way a consumer thought about a vending experience. They didn't want to browse for 10 or 15 minutes, and you also knew there were video stores everywhere, so there had to be something compelling about it. When I came on I spent the first six months testing a lot of different concepts, small selection, low price, large selection, low price on different days, quantity of days, many different scenarios. The one thing I learned at Netflix, and Reed Hastings taught me this, was when you find the right business model, it's not a 5 or 10% improvement, it's a doubling or tripling of the business even if you tested it in a funky way, and you didn't get everything exactly right. You will know it's the right one when it really takes off, and that's exactly what happened. Suddenly when we got the selections down to the hit titles that everyone wanted, and when we brought the price point to a dollar, business exploded. It was like wow, kiosks were doing six or seven times the business of other kiosks, and that's what led to the policy. It was really the result of testing and learning.

Q: How many Redboxes are still in front of McDonald's?

ML: They're still in about 2,800 locations out of 14,000 locations nationwide, so less than a fourth of their sites.

Q: All combined, how many locations are you at across the country?

ML: 27,000

Q: What business model do you think is better, the video store of the '80s and '90s or the kiosk business today?

ML: The best one for the consumer is the one we have today because it's at a super affordable price in front of locations people shop at every day. It really does allow people to try films they wouldn't normally try because of the low price. It works now because there are other ways the consumer can get to the deeper catalogue, whether its online or with Netflix. Many customers compliment their Redbox usage with Hulu for television shows or Netflix for their documentaries and harder to find titles. I think for the consumer today getting their big hits from Redbox and deep catalogue titles from Netflix is the optimum way to go.

Q: What is the makeup of your average customer?

ML: Early on, our customer was really skewed more toward younger people, middle to lower income, but as we have grown, that has changed, and it can touch every demographic. We do know that our average household has lots of kids, between three and four, and a $66,000 annual family income. Age wise, it's between 25 and 54, so it really comes close to what the average American household is. When we look at the various retail customers we work with, our customers skew to the type of location it is. When we are in front of a grocery store, women are our largest customers. When it's outside a 7/11, it's a young adult male.

Q: How product driven is your business?

ML: Hollywood has to keep making good movies for us to continue to do well, and for the most part they are doing that. For us the titles our customers love are the titles they didn't get a chance to see in the theatres or the ones they loved and want to see again. It's not necessarily the $100 million plus blockbusters; it's more the $20 to $50 million dollar titles. When the studios make a lot of good medium sized movies, that's great for us. It's always been a fact in the video industry that 60% of the customers do not have a specific movie in mind when they go looking for something to rent. They are coming up to one of our boxes and want to find a good movie they will like and look at us to make a recommendation to get through all the clutter of all the different titles available out there, so it comes down to our ability to stock the kiosks in the best way possible. It boils down to once a customer trusts you, and they do because we continue to deliver value, then they look to us to help them discover new titles. We can't completely control demand, but we do have a lot of impact on what the customers rent based on the merchandise we stock. We actually are able to take independent product and drive awareness. If a movie does $3 million in theatrical, we are able to drive awareness and get a lot of turns on it.

Q: There are still a lot of the smaller independents that say they can't get their movies into your kiosks. What are the criteria you use to choose titles?

ML: We are always looking for what our customers want to rent and what we can drive demand to. A lot of it is based on historical performance on comparable titles. However, we are constrained by the capacity of the kiosk. We have 620 slots, and the way we can afford to pay the same amount as our competitors and rent it for much less is to keep the titles moving at all times. That creates a challenge for your more obscure independent titles; we are not in the business of waiting for a title to take off. That's why having a centralized inventory like Netflix where you can mail it out to a huge geographic area works for those titles, but when you are filling a slot in a kiosk, we have about a five mile radius at the most. We might have 50 people who like independent films, but you can put a title in, and only one person in five miles may want to rent it. Whereas when you have a centralized library, you can send smaller titles out to thousands of locations and have enough people to support those titles to use them as a supplement.

Q: Can you take me inside a kiosk? How many DVDs can actually fit into one?

ML: Even though a kiosk has only 620 slots and we have to keep enough space for returns, on a Thursday for example, there are always more returns than rentals, so we have to keep enough space for that. Despite all that, there are more than 620 DVDs often associated with a single kiosk. You might have two to three hundred rented out in customers' hands all the time, so when one comes back another one goes out, so we're able to keep that inventory available for each individual kiosk high, and the way we do it is we have our own field team of merchandisers at least once a week [who] are putting new product in and pulling old product out. It's all based on demand, which is different across the nation. Different movies are going in and others are taken out in different quantities simply based on how well they are doing.

Q: Do you utilize your size and exclusivity when you buy non-studio titles?

ML: What's interesting is that filmmakers would love for us to pre-fund the making of a film because we land up buying so many copies, but we are in a pretty enviable position with the studios releasing fewer and fewer theatrical titles because movies are still being made with big stars and big budgets, so we are able to, especially those with big names in them that didn't do that well at the box office like "The Company Men" or "Stone" with Robert DeNiro, support them almost as if they did $50 million box office. What's great for these distributors is now there is much more awareness for their films for their television or international sales. We work closely with these independent companies, especially with the independent divisions of the major studios, to increase awareness for their films, and we do that even with some of the smaller film companies.

Q: *How difficult is it to guess right on the amounts of copies to order on each movie?*

ML: If every single title came out by itself and had 100% of the audience without any competition, it would be easy, but of course that's not the case. It's really about understanding the interplay among titles and how they compete with different audiences. A customer will probably watch only two movies a week even if there are four great titles out there. This conflict with competing titles is the interesting dynamic that is always challenging.

Q: *Is Saturday your biggest night of the week, similar to movie theatres?*

ML: It's almost equal between Friday and Saturday with Saturday being a little bigger, but it generally follows tradition with Friday, Saturday, Sunday and Tuesday, when the new releases come out; those are the busiest days. To be really successful in the business you have to figure out how to get people to rent Monday, Wednesday and Thursday.

Q: *Whom do you consider your main competitors?*

ML: It's just about anybody who provides movies, so Netflix I would say is one of our primary competitors. That goes for cable television too. Even with all their financial problems, Blockbuster is still a competitor. They are going to do more than a billion in rental revenue this year.

Q: *I find it interesting that two very old-fashioned ways of consuming movies, movie theatres and vending machines, are continuing to do well in the midst of all this new technology. Do you feel a kindred spirit with movie theatres?*

ML: I do feel a kindred spirit with movie theatres. I feel a kindred spirit with anyone who is working with getting entertainment out to consumers because we are all facing the same issues, how do we deal with our suppliers and how do we get our consumers to consume more. I love going to movie theatres; I love independent films, so I'm at the Landmark theatre at least twice a month.

Q: *How many people do you have on staff to purchase films for the country, and are there any significant differences in titles bought in different parts of the country?*

ML: There are about a dozen film buyers for the company, and there isn't a big geographic focus. It's more of a focus on studio and independent product, children's product, that sort of thing. The way we buy is based on the demand per kiosk. We have kiosks that do exceptionally well with children's films or in direct to video titles, action films, even Spanish language films, so we customize the inventory and the quantity based on the performance of previous titles that look the same or share the same genre.

Q: *With the biggest titles can you give me an estimate of how many units you would buy?*

ML: I can't get into any specific numbers, but we order many hundreds of thousands, 500,000 and over on the biggest titles. The biggest titles seem to be the mass appeal comedies that people want to see over and over again. Comedies make people feel good. "Paul Blart: Mall Cop" was our biggest title in 2009.

Q: *How long do you think your current business model will last?*

ML: I think it has a really long future as one of the premier ways to get movies. There's definitely going to be growing competition from other ways to get movies, but it's a pie that can continue to get bigger. As long as we can continue to provide a very affordable and easy way to get movies, I think this business can stay very strong. It's definitely moving away from a collectors' business. It's more try before you buy, and with the studios who do work very closely with us making their product available day and date, they see when our customers rent a movie and like it, they often go out to buy it. So the more we can work closely with the studios and encourage our customers to try before they buy, they'll feel like they're getting value for their money instead of sitting there with a collection of movies at home where they may watch it once and never want to watch it again.

Q: Do you have a global presence?

ML: No, our business is just in the United States.

Q: Can you reveal one or two of the most important lessons you have learned in your career?

ML: Something I've learned over and over again is if you use your own taste in films to make decisions as opposed to understanding what the consumer wants, you are going to miss a lot of opportunities. So the more you can understand your customer, the more you can research them, and I know it sounds pretty obvious, but often we can let our own tastes and beliefs get in the way of truly understanding our customer. A perfect example is a film like "Paul Blart." That is just a fun film that people in the film business or critics can dismiss pretty easily, but you have to understand that customers want to have a break from their daily lives; they want to escape from reality and enjoy some good laughs. The other foundation that keeps ringing true is that a good movie with good acting and a good story will continue to pay off over and over again. A movie with a good story like "The King's Speech" can always make money and be the type of film you can count on. That's what troubles me about Hollywood; they just are not making enough unique, original good story movies and [are] doing too many sequels and rehashing the same stories over and over again. If they keep doing that more people will move away from long-form filmed entertainment.

Q: Studios try to go after the sure thing, but sure things aren't always sure, and often the films that have the most difficulty getting made become the movies that people come to love the most.

ML: That's true. I count my blessings being in the home portion of the business because we can at least see what the demand was in theatres first. I admire the people who make the films because there is always a big risk involved, and for no reason a movie can either flop or do incredibly well.

Q: Thank you for your time and insight.

ML: Thank you.

2012 Update:

Redbox has since raised the price of a daily rental to $1.20 with seemingly little resistance from their customers.

Week 32: Questions for Discussion

1. Why has the DVD business been shifting back to more of a rental market? Which of the two markets produce more revenue for distributors?

2. How much can the studios, or any distributor, risk in devaluing their product in the home market? What's at stake?

3. What were some of the challenges Mitch Lowe faced when he became president of Redbox in 2009? How did he get around the fact that several studios refused to sell the company first run product on availability? Did his solution to the problem surprise you?

4. How are Redbox and Netflix similar to each other? How did they perfect their business models? Was it instant success for either of the companies?

5. What did you learn about Redbox that you didn't know before that you found meaningful?

DISTRICT 9: THINKING SMALL WHILE DREAMING BIG

Week 33: August 14–20, 2009

> *The old adage is that talent will rise to the top and eventually get recognized. There is too much mediocrity around for that not to happen; if you have the goods, you will stand out.*

It happens every year around this time, as the summer starts winding down and schools start getting ready to open, more movies flood the screens in a mad dash to get a chunk out of the summer box office. Some distributors may have to live up to a contractual agreement stating a film has to open in the summer months, other movies may have been pushed back from earlier time periods to escape stronger competition, and still others are there because the distributor has had previous success in mid-August with a certain type of film and hopes lightening can strike again. Whatever the reason, five new movies are opening wide across the country this week, the most of any summer week by far, and generally speaking, that many movies are usually not a good thing. Think of it this way, these movies aren't the strongest on any-one's release schedule, and the heightened competition only makes it tougher to get noticed and find an audience. It may not seem fair, but the biggest, most pre-sold movies have the least competition going against them; with weaker movies, it's the exact opposite. No one ever said the movie business was fair, did they? Looking at the five movies more closely, to their credit, they each have a marketing hook or two as they chase after their specific audiences:

▸ Warner Bros. "The Time Traveler's Wife," a sweeping time travel romance for women based on the 2003 best-selling book and starring two attractive leads, Eric Bana and Rachel McAdams.

▸ Paramount's raunchy R-rated comedy, "The Goods: Live Hard, Sell Hard" for the young male/college audi-ence, starring Jeremy Piven and two actors from "The Hangover" and produced by Will Ferrel, who also makes a cameo appearance. Can the "cash for clunkers" program somehow help the weak used car salesmen storyline? Don't bet on it.

▸ Summit Entertainment's wholesome PG movie for young teens, "Bandslam," a battle of the bands movie star-ring the popular Vanessa Hudgens from "High School Musical 3." As an extra marketing ploy, Summit is show-ing exclusive new footage of "New Moon," the next film in the "Twilight" series before the feature.

▸ Disney is releasing the Japanese animated movie "Ponyo" in a dubbed version after the movie grossed $169 million overseas. Obviously, they're going after kids and families and hoping that the voices of Miley Cyrus's younger sister and the youngest Jonas brother will be a draw. This has the fewest runs of any of the new openers and is a far cry from the usual Disney or Pixar film.

▸ Sony's "District 9," the under the radar sci-fi movie, which isn't so under the radar anymore with this week's _Entertainment Weekly's_ cover story calling it "The Must See Movie of the Summer." It tells the story of a group of aliens who landed in South Africa some years ago and have been confined to a specific area, segregated from the rest of the city's population.

Nothing against the other movies, but the most interesting movie of the entire bunch and the one with the most intrigue and upside is "District 9," and that's the movie I want to take a closer look at this week. In a week full of very wide releases, including that of "District 9," I want to go in the opposite direction and discuss the concept of starting small, being small, thinking small while dreaming big, specifically in the areas of beginning filmmakers and viral marketing campaigns. The back story and business model for "District 9" are enlightening and perhaps shines a light on what it will take for filmmakers, producers, investors and distributors to work together in the future with a common goal of making good, profitable movies that all parties can share in and benefit from. Filmmakers make movies and need distributors to buy and distribute them. Distributors are always on the lookout for movies to pick up and distribute, so why are people either saying there's too many movies being made or there's not much out there to acquire? The issue is never one of quantity, but one of quality. There are too many bad to mediocre feature length movies being made that will never have any real chance of finding viable distribution. In addition, we're in the middle of a period where there are fewer deep pocket distributors capable of financing a decent release. Too many filmmakers make the rash decision of making a feature length movie with little idea of their own talents and with no sense of the needs and wants of the marketplace. A much smarter strategy is to concentrate on making short films instead, which have the following benefits:

- ► Shorts are much cheaper to make than features.
- ► There are plenty of outlets and film festivals to showcase them in.
- ► Filmmakers can hone their craft and prove their mettle.
- ► Filmmakers can show their story-telling skills and style of filmmaking.
- ► Short films become a part of a filmmaker's video portfolio.

This was the path "District 9" took. "District 9" had its beginnings as a six-minute short by director Neill Blomkamp. Blomkamp has an interesting backstory, growing up in Johannesburg, South Africa and then moving to Vancouver, Canada where he made a living shooting music videos and television commercials. In his spare time he made short films, pouring in as much as 40% of his annual salary financing these films. One of these short films, the six minute "Alive in Joburg," caught the eye of both Universal and Peter Jackson when they were looking for a fresh, new director for the high budget "Halo," and he was selected to direct. When that project was eventually scrapped due to budgetary and profit participation concerns, Jackson wanted to continue to work with the director on something else, and that something else became taking his short film, "Alive in Joburg" and expanding it into what would become "District 9."

Thinking small while dreaming big. Blomkamp didn't necessarily make this short for the sole purpose of someday turning it into a feature, but an experienced producer like Peter Jackson saw the potential in it. Making a compelling short film with a strong story that can be expanded out is not the easiest thing to pull off, but it's certainly a way for filmmakers to test themselves and see what kind of talent is actually there. If the talent isn't there a person can always choose a different career, sometimes even staying in the film business. This is a path I've been advocating to film students for years, and there have been enough success stories to validate that short films can be an entry into the film industry. One of the more high-profile films in recent years that began as a short film was "Napoleon Dynamite." The short was a very low-budget film shot in black and white, and it was selected to premiere at the Slamdance Film Festival where it was seen by an investor who eventually gave the filmmakers $400,000 to turn it into a feature. The feature length version premiered at the 2004 Sundance Film Festival, was acquired by Fox Searchlight and went on to gross $44 million that summer. The short film had some different actors in supporting roles, but star Jon Heder was showcased, and the sly deadpan humor of the film came through loud and clear enough to convince someone with money to take a gamble on some young filmmakers. This short can be found on the two-disc "Napoleon Dynamite" DVD, and it's fun to see the genesis of this iconic high school movie. A term was coined some years ago that referred to short films as "calling cards" for bigger and better things to come. That can be still true, but there is a right way and a wrong way to go about it. The wrong way is to spoof a popular movie and put it on You Tube waiting to be discovered. There are countless numbers of spoofs on this site, and they all start running together. The right way is the way Neill Blomkamp went about it, crafting a story based on his life experiences and layering it with substance and allegory. Blomkamp grew up with apartheid in South Africa and used the aliens to comment on this social, economic and cultural problem. Being able to infuse that into a six-minute short is pure talent and harkens back to sci-fi movies of the '50s such as "Invasion of the Body Snatchers" which used the genre to comment on the political news of the day such as the rise of the McCarthy era in America.

The old adage is that talent will rise to the top and eventually get recognized. There is too much mediocrity around for that not to happen. If you have the goods, you will stand out. It certainly doesn't hurt when a filmmaker has a mentor like Peter Jackson to help pave the way. There have been numerous instances in the past couple of decades where famous directors like Martin Scorsese, Quentin Tarantino, Spike Lee, Steven Spielberg and others have lent their names and support to independent filmmakers with varying degrees of success. "Spike Lee Presents" or "Quentin Tarantino Presents" on the top of a poster or trailer doesn't automatically turn something into a guaranteed success, but that kind of support is always welcome and can help open doors. However, Peter Jackson Presents "District 9" is the real deal, and its impact has been tremendous even before the first ticket has been sold at the box office. Jackson's handprint is all over "District 9" as he spent $500,000 of his own money on its development, handpicked the director, produced the movie, used his own effects house to create the special effects and arranged for the $30 million in financing. Jackson jumped at the opportunity to make a true independent film and control its own destiny far away from the Hollywood studio system, and it sure looks like he and the director pulled it off. He put his money where his mouth was.

Even the most talented of filmmakers and the most powerful of producers still need the power and expertise of a Hollywood studio to release a movie throughout the world. After Sony Pictures bought the distribution rights for North America, all other English-language territories and Korea, Italy, Russia and Portugal, they have been at the center of creating and managing a very effective multi-faceted marketing campaign for "District 9." Sony is doing what studios do best, utilizing their extensive marketing and distribution organizations to full advantage. When all is said and done, their marketing expenditures will no doubt exceed the $30 million dollar production cost of the movie itself, but that's a non-factor in the equation. They are doing what they have to do to get the word out and insure that their investment in the movie is maximized to the fullest. Controlling all media rights in multiple territories could turn into a very lucrative venture for the studio if the apparent upside is reached.

To reach that upside, Sony also embraced the concept of small by starting their marketing by creating a viral campaign on the Internet, the place where these campaigns usually spring up. A viral campaign is very organic, spreading word of mouth over a period of time from person to person. It allows interest to build at its own pace, and the longer the lead time, generally better the results. Sony was smart to take their cue from the movie itself and the mystery surrounding the title, the production and the story line. In the sci-fi/horror genre, there have been two hugely successful movies that have gone this route, "The Blair Witch Project" and "Cloverfield." I'm a big believer in high-concept movie titles, even in smaller art films if it's appropriate, that can help define or describe what a specific movie is about. For a serious, critically acclaimed documentary, "Hoop Dreams" had a very high-concept title. Usually ambiguous or overly arty titles work against a film rather than help it. But in the case of sci-fi films, that's really not the case at all. "Blair Witch Project," Cloverfield," "District 9." All three titles are a bit open ended and vague, a bit mysterious and not revealing much of anything about the films themselves. It is evolving into its own template with these types of films and their campaigns:

- ▶ Leave people guessing.
- ▶ Don't reveal too much.
- ▶ Create multiple websites and links.
- ▶ Develop problem-solving puzzles that include secret codes to decipher.
- ▶ Have some dark secrets and a hidden agenda.
- ▶ Create either a fictitious organization or events.
- ▶ Film it in a real-life documentary-like fashion.

This is what Sony has done, which became the strategic marketing plan for everything to follow. Not all movies have proved to be successful when trying to manage their viral campaigns. Remember when "Snakes on a Plane" came out several summers ago? When I heard about it, I said wow, this epitomizes high concept. You can hold the story in your hand, and it sounds like fun. Well, that supposed strength became perhaps its big weakness. The title turned out to be too literal and left nothing to the imagination. There was initial excitement on the Internet, but instead of that interest building, it slowly diminished, and by the time the movie was released, the fans were busy mocking the title and creating their own homemade spoofs. Maybe the original title wasn't so bad after all, "Pacific Air 21."

It takes time, patience and professional expertise to forge an Internet campaign and allow it to percolate at its own pace. But that's only the start of a movie campaign. On May 1, the teaser trailer for "District 9" was officially released online and also attached to "X-Men Origins: Wolverine" on thousands of movie screens, and the full length trailer was released to the Internet on July 8 and alongside the film "Bruno." Starting in June, signs on bus benches, bus shelters and on the side of buses themselves began appearing in major cities reading, "Bus Benches for Humans Only" and "This Bus is for Humans Only," which provoked more mystery and conversation. In the last few weeks, Sony has sealed the deal with an aggressive television campaign, and in the past week, publicity stories have popped up in various newspapers and magazines right in time for the opening. All the work has been done, and the movie is set to open in about 2,700 theatres. Will it be number one at the box office? All indications point to "District 9" being successful, but a movie still has to open and prove itself. In a summer of pre-sold commodities, loads of prequels and sequels, movies about old television shows and toys, "District 9" has the look and feel of something original, something intelligent, something new and fresh that audiences are ready for. This is one to keep an eye on to see if it emerges as a genuine late summer sleeper.

This Week at the Box Office: *Weekly Attendance: 28,480,911*

As already discussed, mid-August is a period in which movies flood the market for better or for worse. For independent films, it's often for the worse. There were a total of 15 films which opened in at least one theatre in the country on Friday, August 14, 2009. If you take a good look at the full list of movies below, out of the 10 smaller films that opened, seven of them grossed less than $100,000 domestically. The theatrical marketplace is a tough nut to crack, and that's proven every week of the year, more so when there are so many new films opening. It's a jungle out there.

District 9

Sony
Opening weekend: $37,354,308
Domestic gross: $115,646,235 54.9%
Foreign gross: $95,173,376 45.1%
Worldwide gross: $210,819,611
Widest release: 3,180 theatres

Time Traveler's Wife

Warner Brothers
Opening weekend: $18,623,171
Domestic gross: $63,414,846 62.6%
Foreign gross: $37,929,566 37.4%
Worldwide gross: $101,344,412
Widest release: 2,988 theatres

The Goods: Live Hard, Sell Hard

Paramount
Opening weekend: $5,642,137
Domestic gross: $15,122,676 98.9%
Foreign gross: $172,234 1.1%
Worldwide gross: $15,294,910
Widest release: 1,849 theatres

Ponyo

Disney
Opening weekend: $3,585,852
Domestic gross: $15,090,399 7.5%
Foreign gross: $186,660,538 92.5%
Worldwide gross: $201,750,937
Widest release: 927 theatres

Bandslam

Summit
Opening weekend: $2,231,273
Domestic gross: $5,210,988 42.6%
Foreign gross: $7,014,035 57.4%
Worldwide gross: $12,225,023
Widest release: 2,121 theatres

It Might Get Loud

Sony Classics
Opening weekend: $92,679
Domestic gross: $1,610,163 84.9%
Foreign gross: $286,081 15.1%
Worldwide gross: $1,896,244
Widest release: 75 theatres

Kaminey

UTV
Opening weekend: $726,834
Domestic gross: $1,286,143 69.1%
Foreign gross: $577,153 30.9%
Worldwide gross: $1,868,980
Widest release: 84 theatres

Spread

Anchor Bay
Opening weekend: $122,948
Domestic gross: $250,617 2.1%
Foreign gross: $11,782,365 97.9%
Worldwide gross: $12,032,983
Widest release: 103 theatres

Cloud 9

Music Box
Opening weekend: $6,617
Domestic gross: $91,675 1.9%
Foreign gross: $4,759,548 98.1%
Worldwide gross: $4,851,223
Widest release: 8 theatres

My Fuhrer

First Run
Opening weekend: $1,197
Domestic gross: $2,465 0.0%
Foreign gross: $7,693,278 100%
Worldwide gross: $7,693,278
Widest release: 1 theatre

Patrick, Age 1.5

Regent
Opening weekend: $408
Domestic gross: $57,468
Foreign gross: N/A
Widest release: 9 theatres

American Casino

Argot
Opening weekend: $1,397
Domestic gross: $47,149
Foreign gross: N/A
Widest release: 3 theatres

Earth Days

Zeitgeist
Opening weekend: $2,408
Domestic gross: $26,748
Foreign gross: N/A
Widest release: 5 theatres

Taxidermia

Regent
Opening weekend: $4,472
Domestic gross: $11,408
Foreign gross: N/A
Widest release: 3 theatres

Grace

Anchor Bay
Opening weekend: $6,174
Domestic gross: $8,297
Foreign gross: N/A
Widest release: 2 theatres

Week 33: Questions for Discussion

1. Discuss any viral campaigns that you have been involved in, have been impressed with, or have influenced you to see a movie. What aspect of a viral campaign do you think is most effective in driving moviegoers to actually go to a theatre to see the film itself?

2. Name all the key marketing elements that went into the selling of "District 9? What part did the viral campaign play in the success of the film? Do you feel the film still could have been successful without the internet campaign? Could it have been as successful without the traditional television support and only the viral campaign?

3. How can short films be a smart marketing strategy for filmmakers? Do you think there's any way a viral campaign could help a short film? Discuss.

4. What does the term "calling card" mean in regards to movies and also what does it mean in the broader sense?

SHOWMANSHIP ALIVE AND WELL ON
MOVIE SCREENS BIG AND SMALL

Week 34: August 21–27, 2009

When you think you have the goods, when you know you have the goods,
be fearless, go for it all, and shout it out for the whole world to hear.

Showmanship and movies go together like water and air, essential elements to the mix that have been alive within the movie industry for as long as celluloid has been run through the earliest projectors at the start of the 20th century. Friday, August 21st was supposed to be all about the opening of "Inglourious Basterds" until 20th Century Fox announced August 21 "Avatar Day" as they show 16 minutes of footage in Imax theatres around the world for a movie that won't even be opening for another four months. Perhaps that move won't have any effect on the performance of "Basterds" this weekend, but I think it does signify possible trouble ahead and shifting tides for two seminal figures in the Motion Picture Industry.

Both Harvey Weinstein and Quentin Tarantino have been great showmen and talk big games, but they haven't delivered in a while. They both need "Inglourious Basterds" to be a big hit, Tarantino for the sake of his career and Weinstein to help keep his company afloat as he stares at mounting debt and shrinking financial resources. The two have been in business together since 1992 when Miramax distributed Tarantino's first film "Reservoir Dogs," but it wasn't until two years later in 1994 when the cult of Tarantino really took hold with the release of "Pulp Fiction," the first independent film to gross over $100,000,000. If that somehow seems like a century ago, it is a century ago. Fifteen years is a long time ago when we consider where the American Independent Film industry was in 1994 and where it is today in 2009. Tarantino and Weinstein were superstars in the go-go '90s, Tarantino for his one monster hit and his potential for more to come and Weinstein for being the dominant independent distributor as co-head of Miramax Films with his brother Bob. The decade of the 1990s was truly one of growth for the independent film business. Every year there were new directors being discovered and new distribution companies being formed. In 1992 alone, Tarantino and Robert Rodriguez each debuted with their first films, "Reservoir Dogs" and "El Mariachi," and in a quirk in the release schedule, both directors open movies in 3,100 theatres this weekend, Rodriguez with the family film "Shorts." But this is 2009, and things are much different now. Looking back, Tarantino has never really been able to build on the success and artistic quality of "Pulp Fiction," only directing four full-length features since then including the current one. Weinstein is far from being the mogul he was while working under the Disney banner, running Weinstein Films along with his brother as the invisible man. He's released only four movies in 2009, all on very limited runs and none since February. Weinstein has been a complete non-factor in the marketplace garnering a pitiful ½% market share while contributing to the overall malaise the independent sector has felt this year.

The investors who put money into his company can't be too thrilled about that kind of performance. In 2005, the Goldman Sachs Group raised $700 million in loans and over $400 million in equity to finance the newly minted Weinstein Company following their departure from Disney. It no doubt made sense at the time considering the excellent track record of proven hit films that Harvey and Bob Weinstein produced over the years as well as how easily available money flowed on Wall Street in the pre-recession days. Four years later with no $100 million dollar hits to show for all that money and some failed ventures outside the film business in an online social networking site and in the fashion industry, the Weinstein Company has been left reeling and vulnerable with an abundance of debt and a paucity of commercial films. Will it be able to survive, or will it wither away like countless other film companies have done over the years? Other than the six major studios, all distribution companies eventually come to an end for one reason or another. The only question is will it be sooner rather than later? Harvey Weinstein is 57 years old, and this is his fourth decade running film companies. He has weathered a lot of battles and experienced the highest highs the movie industry has to offer. The ego looks to be still there, but what about the passion, the focus, the drive, the hard work and the attention to detail that have always been a part of his DNA? When you battle and scratch for so many years, accomplish so much, and amass a personal fortune, the passion and drive perhaps isn't quite there like it used to be. It's tough to run an independent company today and operate between wide mainstream and limited art houses releases. Combine that with the recession and the general downturn in core revenue streams like DVDs, and it doesn't paint a pretty picture. His company has burned through a lot of money in four years, and it will be much tougher to raise new financing in the current environment. Harvey Weinstein was the face of independent film for many years; now all his struggles seem to epitomize its many problems.

Harvey Weinstein was the face of independent film for many years;
now all his struggles seem to epitomize its many problems.

That being said, Harvey Weinstein and Quentin Tarantino are showmen, fantastic self-promoters who have been very good for the film business and have done very well for themselves. They are both skilled at drawing attention to themselves and to their films. They understand themselves; they understand their roles in helping to sell their films, and they're not afraid of the media. In fact they embrace the media, certainly one of the personality traits all showmen share. They know what buttons to push to create interest. Other directors who also have been effective self-promoters like Kevin Smith, Michael Moore and Robert Rodriguez have often worked for Harvey Weinstein too. Whether it's a coincidence or the environment that encourages directors to create their own brands and legacies, this brand of filmmaking and promotion has gone a long way in generating buzz, box office hits and creating identities for countless number of independent films in the last two decades.

Which brings us back to "Inglourious Basterds." Can this movie prove be a game changer for both men? Can Weinstein Films use this strange hybrid of a war film as a springboard back to prominence and profitability? I have my doubts, but I may be wrong. Tarantino still has a fan base among filmgoers (predominantly men) and critics, so the movie will no doubt be on top of the box office charts this week with an opening projected to be around $25 to $35 million. A gross in that area would still be about $10 million less than last week's "District 9," a movie with a first-time director and unknown actors, which cost $40 million less than Tarantino's film. What will also aid the film is the incredibly weak competition going up against it, "Shorts," "Post Grad" and "X Games 3D: The Movie." Ugh. Another reason it will be difficult for "Basterds" to have a huge impact for Weinstein is that they sold half the film to Universal, so they will reap only half the profits the movie generates. Weinstein would have a much better upside if they kept all the rights, but their financial situation dictated otherwise. They needed the Universal money to help pay for the $35 million marketing campaign. I don't know if it's just me, but has anyone else fallen off the Tarantino bandwagon? Ever since I read about this movie being his next film with the title misspelled, it rubbed me the wrong way and seemed overly pretentious. I guess just because his movie was somewhat based on the 1978 Italian war film "The Inglorious Bastards," which no one saw in the first place, we were supposed to be impressed by his unmatched knowledge of long forgotten exploitation movies. Tarantino elevated "Pulp Fiction" to the realm of art, but in reality he is a self-proclaimed lover of exploitation movies, which seem to be his greatest influence as a director. He made so much money for Weinstein with "Pulp Fiction," Tarantino was even able to persuade Harvey to let him create his own offshoot company restoring and distributing old drive-in titles like "Switchblade Sisters." Since the only drive-ins around today play first-run movies, the only place to play them were in art houses under "Quentin Tarantino Presents." Needless to say, this venture was an unmitigated disaster, and after many $300.00 opening weekends, the plug was pulled on this division in no time. Whatever Quentin wanted, Harvey gave him, but what Harvey Weinstein wanted most was another "Pulp Fiction" blockbuster, which never came. From the "Basterds" title to the over-the-top Southern accent of Brad Pitt in the trailer to the main conceit of the fantasy of having Jewish soldiers hunting down Nazis and scalping them, it just seems very unappealing to me. But it's not about what I think but how the audiences will react, so we will see how it all plays out on the screen and what effect it will have, if any, on the financial future of the Weinstein Company.

20th Century Fox has a reported $240 million riding on James Cameron's "Avatar," which will be opening in theatres on December 18. Their marketing decision to show 16 minutes of footage on 100 Imax screens around the world on the evening of August 21 for two separate showings is an unprecedented and unusual type of sneak preview, especially for a movie that won't open for another four months. Tickets were free, and so many people went to the movie's website for tickets it crashed the site on the first day tickets were made available. How big of a risk is Fox taking with this sneak peek? The risk would seem to be minimal since the same footage was recently shown at Comic-Con and it went over well, but the truth is, every decision you make when you have a quarter of a billion dollars on the line has to be carefully thought out. The expectations are huge, so Fox and Cameron would not want to risk any potential negative word or mouth with four months to go to opening day. I like what Greg Foster, the president of Imax Filmed Entertainment was quoted as saying, "I think there's not enough understanding of what show business means. You can't have business without show-manship, and what this sneak preview is, is showmanship. We're calling August 21st "Avatar Day." That says it all. When you think you have the goods, when you know you have the goods, be fearless, go for it all and shout it out for the whole world to hear.

This Week at the Box Office: *Weekly Attendance: 24,042,449*

Inglourious Basterds
Weinstein
Opening weekend: $38,054,676
Domestic Gross: $120,540,719 37.5%
Foreign Gross: $200,914,970 62.5%
Worldwide Gross: $321,455,689
Widest release: 3,358 theatres

Shorts
Warner Brothers
Opening weekend: $6,410,339
Domestic gross: $420,919,166 72.2%
Foreign gross: $8,053,342 27.8%
Worldwide gross: $28,972,508
Widest release: 3,105 theatres

Post Grad
Fox Searchlight
Opening weekend: $2,651,996
Domestic gross: $6,382,178 99.5%
Foreign gross: $34,710 0.5%
Worldwide gross: $6,414,729
Widest release: 1,959 theatres

My One and Only
Freestyle
Opening weekend: $58,692
Domestic gross: $2,479,538 81.9%
Foreign gross: $546,734 18.1%
Worldwide gross: $3,026,272
Widest release: 256 theatres

X Games 3D: The Movie
Disney
Opening weekend: $837,216
Domestic gross: $1,391,434 94.5%

Baader Meinhof Complex
Vitagraph
Opening weekend: $17,348
Domestic gross: $478,746

Foreign gross: $81,313 5.5%

Worldwide gross: $1,472,747

Widest release: 1,399 theatres

World's Greatest Dad

Magnolia

Opening weekend: $4,675

Domestic gross: $221,805

Foreign gross: N/A

Widest release: 30 theatres

The Headless Woman

Strand

Opening weekend: $14,778

Domestic gross: $100,177

Foreign gross: N/A

Widest release: 3 theatres

Street Ballers

MSK

Opening weekend: $11,581

Domestic gross: $21,442

Foreign gross: N/A

Widest release: 2 theatres

Confessions of a Ex-Doofus-ItchyFooted Mutha

Yeah

Opening weekend: $604

Domestic gross: $2,310

Foreign gross: N/A

Widest release: 2 theatres

Foreign gross: N/A

Widest release: 38 theatres

Art & Copy

Seventh Art

Opening weekend: $20,559

Domestic gross: $139,418

Foreign gross: N/A

Widest release: 5 theatres

Casi Divas

Maya

Opening weekend: $27,491

Domestic gross: $46,612

Foreign gross: N/A

Widest release: 22 theatres

Five Minutes of Heaven

IFC

Opening weekend: $5,364

Domestic gross: $15,676 17.8%

Foreign gross: $72,230 82.2%

Worldwide gross: $87,906

Widest release: 2 theatres

The Marc Pease Experience

Paramount Vantage

Opening weekend: $2,641

Domestic gross: $4,033 1.0%

Foreign gross: $386,551 99.0%

Worldwide gross; $390,584

Widest release: 10 theatres

2012 Update:
Weinstein Co. Rebounds with New Financing

"Inglourious Basterds" did indeed begin a comeback of sorts for both the Weinstein Co. and Quentin Tarantino. The film was very successful, grossing $120 million domestically and another $200 million in foreign markets. In the reconfigured Best Picture category, it was one of the 10 nominees, and Christopher Waltz won the Oscar for Best Supporting Actor. The film seemed to get the company back on track even as it continued to have major cash flow problems. The $700 million in loans from Goldman Sachs was the albatross for Weinstein, which could have easily bankrupted the company. As a stopgap measure, Goldman Sacs was allowed to take control of over 200 films from Weinstein's library as collateral for the money owed to the investment firm. This bought the company some time, and eventually they started buying back groups of their films as their situation improved. "The King's Speech" in 2010 further put the company in better financial position when it became a smash hit ($139 million domestic) and won Best Picture of the Year, following it up in 2011 with another Best Picture Oscar for "The Artist." It became clear what Weinstein's strategy was. They have not been a 12-month a year distributor for several years now. Far from it. They have been conserving money, cutting back on mainstream, family and even genre productions and concentrating on the high-brow end of the year releases which win Oscars, their bread and butter and the films they know the best. In 2012, this renewed focus led to a new financing arrangement with two banks, giving the distributor a revolving credit line totaling $225 million to use as the need arises. Are they out of the woods yet? Is this the second coming of the Weinstein Co.? Could be, but $225 million can be used up in a hurry in today's Hollywood, so the pressure is always there for the brothers to continue to make the right choices when it comes to what films to distribute, when to release them and how best to market them. As for Quentin Tarantino, Weinstein has slotted his next film, "Django Unchained," a revenge western starring Leonardo DiCaprio, Jamie Foxx and Christopher Waltz, to open on Christmas Day, 2012. Harvey Weinstein once again is putting his money on his star director to deliver for him and his company, this time on the most coveted and lucrative week of the year.

2012 Update: Imax

Imax continues to be an incredible growth engine for itself and for the Hollywood blockbusters it plays on its screens. "The Dark Knight Rises" shattered box office records for Imax, grossing $50 million on its screens in the first two weeks of release. It has become a brand name that is known worldwide. The only negative for the studios is that there are only 383 Imax screens in North America and 280 screens internationally. That means that many big movies can't get access to their screens when their movies are released. It has definitely become a factor when distributors decide on release dates for their most important movies. On the other hand, its limited supply of screens is an important part of its appeal and demand.

Source: The Wrap

Week 34: Questions for Discussion

1. If the director is the main spokesman for a film, how important do you think being a showman is a part of the equation? How would you describe showmanship?

2. Harvey Weinstein as a movie executive and Quentin Tarantino as a director are both considered showmen. Think about that for a moment. Put yourself in the role of an executive and also in the role of a director of the same movie and come up with different ways they could go about promoting both themselves and the movie.

3. Can you think of other directors, either past or present, who were great showman? Give examples.

4. Do you think if 20th Century Fox decided to show 16 minutes of "Avatar" footage in 2,000 regular theatres rather than in 100 Imax theatres, would it have been more effective, less effective or have no difference from a publicity standpoint? How about from a financial standpoint?

HOW "WOODSTOCK" HELPED USHER IN THE NEW HOLLYWOOD

Week 35: August 28–September 3, 2009

_The studios were bleeding cash, and when a movie flopped in theatres
it was almost a total loss; there wasn't much ancillary revenue to tap into._

With the 40th anniversary of Woodstock, there has been a lot of discussion about the importance of that singular event from a cultural and generational standpoint, and it was certainly a watershed moment in time that still resonates today. As the new movie from Ang Lee, "Taking Woodstock," opens this weekend, I'm not here to add to that dialogue; instead I'm going to take a look back at the precarious situation the movie industry found itself in during that tumultuous period and how "Woodstock" the movie played an important role in helping the industry get back its financial footing and usher in the New Hollywood.

Between 1969 and 1971, the seven studios were in the worst three-year slump the movie business had ever experienced, even surpassing their struggles of the Depression years. The Motion Picture Industry found itself with one foot firmly in the past while at the same time trying to dangle its other foot into a future they didn't quite fully understand. Several of the earlier moguls were still hanging around the boardrooms and stubbornly conducting business as if it was still the 1950s. The country was changing, the Vietnam War was raging, but old Hollywood continued to churn out big-budget traditional war movies and musicals such as "Tora, Tora, Tora," "Darling Lili," "Chitty Chitty Bang Bang" and "Paint Your Wagon" that simply weren't working anymore. An independent company, Embassy Pictures, had a huge hit with "The Graduate" in 1967-1968, which hinted at the influence of a new young audience, and Columbia picked up the rights to "Easy Rider," which was a smash, in 1969, but it was far from a changing of the guard. The studios fell on their faces trying to cater to this young audience by making clunkers like "The Strawberry Statement," "Getting Straight" and "R.P.M.," a would-be radical campus film starring Ann Margaret as a revolutionary student and Anthony Quinn as the president of the university. The studios just couldn't get it right; whatever they tried didn't work. The year 1971 reached the absolute low point of the industry's 25-year decline from the apex of 1946's four billion annual admissions to a paltry 820 million admissions in 1971. The Academy Awards epitomized the schism of tastes and styles in the films that were being made and honored. In 1968, the old-fashioned G-rated "Oliver" won Best Picture of the Year. The following year, "Midnight Cowboy" won, the only X-rated movie to ever win Best Picture. All the studios were on the ropes, a few were selling their back lots to raise cash; their futures were up in the air. The studios were bleeding cash, and when a movie flopped in the theatres it was almost a total loss, there wasn't much ancillary revenue to tap into.

This was the state of the industry in the summer of 1969 as the Woodstock festival approached, and the concert promoters found themselves running out of money. They approached Warner Brothers with the idea of making a movie, and Ted Ashley, who was running the studio for conglomerate Kinney National at the time, figured they didn't have much to lose, and things couldn't get much worse than they already were, so Ashley signed on for Warner Bros. to produce and distribute the documentary. That decision turned into one of the sweetest deals in history. For a supposed $50,000, Warner's purchased all movie and soundtrack rights and spent an additional $600,000 to actually make the film. When the documentary opened in the summer of 1970, it became an instant hit and played for months to packed houses. It became one of the top grossing movies of the year when it topped out at $50 million, which would translate to more than $200 million in today's dollars. This one movie probably saved the Warner Bros. film division from being closed down. That's how dire the situation was. Impressive as the gross was, that didn't begin to tell the story of how influential "Woodstock" became in helping to pave a new way for the studios to unlock the potential of its various film properties.

255

It not only showed Warner Bros. the value of cross-marketing and merchandising, but it reminded all the studios of the huge potential and upside that movies had if they were able to make the right movies that audiences actually wanted to see. With the huge success of "Woodstock," Warner Bros. pursued other opportunities, and a few years later became the first studio to get into the pay television business when they bought HBO, and after that, they purchased their own cable network to show HBO on. One by one over the years the other studios followed Warner Brothers' lead, buying various television stations, networks and cable stations, eventually becoming the global media giants they are today.

Change didn't come overnight because as the 1970s started, the Motion Picture Industry had more of its share of problems to figure out. Patterns of distribution were evolving away from the big downtown theatres, and the industry needed new theatres in the suburbs to play movies closer to where moviegoers lived. The invention of the enclosed shopping mall with free parking played a crucial role in growing the business as various theatre circuits like General Cinema and AMC leased out space in these malls to build new multiplexes. Finding outside methods of film financing to lower the risk for the studios also became a priority, and when a tax loophole was discovered by a Chicago attorney in the early 1970s, private investors flocked to invest in movies which in turn helped stabilize the studios' bottom lines. This development brought even more interest from larger companies and wealthy individuals who wanted to get a piece of the glamorous movie industry. Finally, the industry needed new blood, new directors to connect with the growing young audience for entertainment that they could relate to. "Woodstock" showed the way here too. After Ashley purchased the rights to make the movie, he went out and hired as many film students as he could find from NYU and Columbia film schools who could work a camera or edit the thousands of feet of film footage they had of the concert. One of the editors was a young Martin Scorsese. The '70s saw the first wave of film school graduates take advantage of the industry's need for new talent, and directors like Scorsese, Coppola, Lucas, DePalma and others seized the opportunity and became powerful forces when their movies proved to be successful with audiences. However, the director who didn't graduate from film school became the most successful one of them all, Steven Spielberg.

That brings us back to "Taking Woodstock." In no way, shape or form will this movie be comparable to "Woodstock" in its gross or influence. It's a modest movie with modest expectations. With a $30,000,000 production budget, it actually looks fairly risky for a distributor to take on such a low-key period movie about the festival without any of the music acts in it. But Focus Features is not just any distributor. Focus is a division of Universal and is on firm ground, and along with Fox Searchlight and Sony Classics, they are the three remaining studio specialty divisions. The company has a couple of aspects that really distinguish them. They have a very strong international distribution organization, which serves them well with distribution partners strategically placed throughout the world, and they have a CEO in James Shamus who is a filmmaker himself. Shamus is the longtime filmmaking partner of Ang Lee who has written his last eleven screenplays with Lee, including "Taking Woodstock." That is how the movie got made. A movie like this is tricky to market and tough to predict. The company is hoping to attract an audience of older baby boomers feeling nostalgic and younger moviegoers who are interested in either young comedy star Dimitri Martin or discovering more about an event they have heard so much about. Grabbing either niche isn't a certainty. When you go down the route of not being able to sell the music but instead tell a backstory of how the festival came together, it is inherently a risky venture. I learned that myself when I distributed "Tie-Died: Rock n' Roll's Most Deadicated Fans" in 1995. This documentary was about Grateful Dead fans and the parking lot sub-culture during a summer tour that didn't include any music from the band itself. The music rights were too expensive, and the filmmakers couldn't afford the expense. I overestimated the appeal of the film, and I was wrong to believe Grateful Dead fans would be interested in watching other fans do their thing and talk about the band without being able to actually see or hear their music. The music was the reason for the entire movement of Deadheads, and without the music, something was lacking at its core, and the movie failed. As a Grateful Dead fan myself, I was moved by passion as much as anything when I decided to get involved in distributing the film, but I learned that passion and hard work can take a distributor only so far in the movie business. You need the right film at the right time for the right audience with the right campaign and the marketing dollars to back it all up. That's a tall order.

"Tie-Died" wasn't the right film and had too many limitations to succeed. Jerry Garcia dying a month before release also threw an unexpected wrench into our overall strategy for the film.

"Taking Woodstock" won't be breaking any box office records this weekend, but I don't think Focus Features is too concerned about it. "Taking Woodstock" is as much a passion project as "Tie-Died" was to its filmmakers and myself. I'm happy this movie was made, and I plan to see it wearing one of my old tie-dyed t-shirts to the theatre. In a bottom-line movie business where numbers are crunched every which way before movies are approved, it's nice to be reminded that the passion to tell a story still means something, even when the numbers may not add up completely. However, the other reminder is it's smart to hedge your bet and not lose too much money going down that road.

This Week at the Box Office: *Weekly Attendance: 21,996,054*

Distributors have done well in recent years turning to more R-rated movies in mid to late August as children head back to school and the summer starts winding down. The two previous weekends had the R-rated "District 9" and "Inglourious Basterds" top their respective weekends with $37,000,000 grosses. This weekend was unusual when two horror movies faced off against each other, which generally is not a smart decision because no distributor wants to split the weekend with another movie that shares a similar audience. Looking at the results, it was Weinstein's "Halloween II" which was hurt the most and would have been better off with a different release date. It proved to be a bad decision to go up against "The Final Destination," which had an extra advantage of being in 3D. With a worldwide gross of $186 million to "Halloween's" $39 million, the Warner Brothers' film carved up Weinstein's "Halloween" into little pieces. The duel was pretty one-sided.

The Final Destination
Warner Brothers
Opening weekend: $27,408,309
Domestic gross: $66,477,700 35.7%
Foreign gross: $119,689,439 64.3%
Worldwide gross: $186,167,139
Widest release: 3,121 theatres

Halloween II
Weinstein
Opening weekend: $16,349,565
Domestic gross: $33,862,903 84.7%
Foreign gross: $6,028,494 15.3%
Worldwide gross: $39,421,467
Widest release: 3,088 theatres

Taking Woodstock
Focus
Opening weekend: $3,457,760
Domestic gross: $7,712,114 74.8%
Foreign gross: $2,515,533 25.2%
Worldwide gross: $9,975,737
Widest release: 1,395 theatres

The September Issue
Roadside
Opening weekend: $220,663
Domestic gross: $3,820,700 59.3%
Foreign gross: $2,622,233 40.7%
Worldwide gross: $6,442,300
Widest release: 143 theatres

Big Fan
First Independent
Opening weekend: $24,266
Domestic gross: $234,422
Foreign gross: N/A
Widest release: 15 theatres

Still Walking
IFC
Opening weekend: $20,298
Domestic gross: $167,047 5.1%
Foreign gross: $3,091,257 94.9%
Worldwide gross: $3,258,304
Widest release: 13 theatres

Into Temptation
Independent
Opening weekend: $10,916
Domestic gross: $99,090
Foreign gross: N/A
Widest release: 2 theatres

We Live in Public
Abramorama
Opening weekend: $7,325
Domestic gross: $44,344
Foreign gross: N/A
Widest release: 2 theatres

Open Road
Anchor Bay
Opening weekend: $13,323
Domestic gross: $19,716
Foreign gross: N/A
Widest release: 14 theatres

Daddy Cool
Adlabs
Opening weekend: $14,319
Domestic gross: $14,319 75.1%
Foreign gross: $4,750 24.9%
Widest release: 18 theatres

Creating the Coming Attraction Trailer: "Tie-Died: Rock n' Roll's Most Deadicated Fans"

For any film distributor, the process of creating the coming attraction trailer becomes one of the most crucial, if not the most crucial, aspect of a film's marketing campaign. The first film I was involved with as a distributor in a decision-making role was "Tie-Died" in 1995. As soon as we made the decision to distribute the film in May of that year, the thought immediately turned to getting the trailer made. We had decided on a late September release, so there were four months to complete the entire marketing campaign. That four-month lead time is about the minimum needed to get the job done properly after a distributor acquires a film to distribute. All I know is that we needed every one of those days and then some. Decisions have to be made constantly, and when you're facing a deadline, days tend to slip by very quickly.

The first decision was to hire an outside vendor/trailer maker to do the job. The trailer industry is a very competitive industry with over two dozen boutiques in Los Angeles that cater to the studios and a number of smaller firms in New York with more reasonable prices who primarily work with independent films. We chose a Los Angeles firm to create the trailer for "Tie-Died," and the cost was set at $24,000. What we received for our money were creative services including concept development, script, script revisions, rough cut, up to three revisions, editorial services including picture conform, cut tracks, direction of narrator, services of narrator, optical negative, optical track negative, direction and supervision. My job was to give them an idea of what we were looking for and what we wanted to emphasize, more of a feeling than anything else, concepts like colorful, good times, communal, blue sky, positive vibes. We were already in the process of creating the poster and settled on the tag line of "It's more than just the music; it's a way of life," so that was something else they could work with. With up to three revisions being the norm in the trailer business, it is a process that often takes a while to get to a finished version that all parties are satisfied with. That's why you need time. It was enlightening to see how the process unfolded, and it started the same way all films do, with a script, about twenty short lines of copy to try to get to the heart of the story. The script also serves a couple of different purposes; the copy is a good way to break up the images and supply some needed pacing, and if the decision is made to use a narrator, that's the copy that will be read. If you watch closely, you'll notice most trailers either use copy with or without a narrator or perhaps narration minus the copy. Our trailer combined both copy and narration.

I remember the morning of August 9, 1995 as if it was yesterday. I was flying to Los Angeles to meet with exhibitors and to also sign off on the final version of the trailer. Before we decided to distribute "Tie-Died," my partner John Iltis asked me a simple question, "What if Jerry Garcia dies before we release the movie?" Garcia, the leader of the Grateful Dead and its heart and soul had been battling health and drug problems for a number of years, but I looked at John and said he wasn't going to die. What did I know? As I was getting off the plane in Los Angeles, the phone started ringing, and it was the office back in Chicago with the news that Jerry had died in his sleep that morning. It was sad news; I was a huge Dead fan and had seen about 30 of their concerts, but now I had a job to do. I went directly to the trailer shop, and we went to work writing a tribute/eulogy that would go at the head of the trailer. If he died a week later, the trailer would have been completed and already either on its way to theatres or already on the screens. Within the week, we had the newly finished trailer with the fresh, up-to-date copy in some theatres about five weeks before release. I was happy with how the trailer turned out; the firm we hired did a great job, and we did as well as we could with what we had to work with. A strong trailer is important, but it's still only one part of the equation. The movie didn't do well when it opened, just as "Taking Woodstock" couldn't find an audience either. Two different movies dealing with the '60s counterculture vibe telling backstories without the main event, the music itself. A tough hurdle to overcome, especially in this case when combined with the unforeseen death of a rock n' roll icon who symbolized an era and way of life for countless number of fans.

The following are additional points on trailers:

▶ A trailer is a selling tool, pure and simple. The one and only goal is to motivate people to go see the movie, preferably on opening weekend.

▶ Trailers are not sustained narratives that build to a climax. Many times, less can be more. A trailer should be more of a tease, leaving more to the imagination, which hopefully will make people check it out. Again, it's best to go for feeling rather than worrying about explaining the movie in two minutes.

▶ There are two basic lengths of trailers, the teaser trailer 90 seconds or less, which is normally the first trailer created that comes out six months to a year in advance, and the regular length trailer at two and a half minutes, a length that is regulated by the MPAA. There is a waiver that allows each studio one film a year to surpass the 2:30 length.

▶ Choosing the right music for the trailer is very important since a trailer is not about plot, it's about feeling, and music conveys feeling better than anything else. That is why some trailers include music that isn't even in the film. It's all about finding something that helps create the mood and feeling you want the viewers to have when watching it.

▶ Every trailer should start with a point of view and central idea that the rest of the piece is built around.

▶ When you look at most trailers, it's a series of very quick cuts. One trailer maker described it this way, "I watch purely from the standpoint of single moments, someone turning his head quickly, a fast camera sweep, lines with compressed emotion. I live in fractions of a second; one second is an eternity."

▶ Studios can spend more than $500,000 on one trailer, and they often outsource the work to several different firms to see which one comes up with the best version. Sometimes they even combine elements from the different companies in the final version, which is referred to as "Frankensteining."

▶ A trailer often debuts on the Internet before it hits the theatres. Distributors go through a trailer holding company to post the trailer, and then they are sent out to as many as 180 websites. It's a paid service that reports back every site it's playing on. Some independent films make deals to have a trailer run exclusively for a week on sites like The New York Times or Barnes and Noble if it fit the needs of the individual film.

▶ The theatres themselves decide what trailers go on their screens. There is a lot of politicking and badgering by the distributors to get top placement on the best screens with the hottest films. Trailer placement has been a hot button issue for years and no doubt will continue to be so.

Week 35: Questions for Discussion

1. What made "Taking Woodstock" tricky to market for distributor Focus Features? In general, how do you react to any movie that attempts to depict or recreate the 1960's era?

2. From a marketing standpoint, how do you think the death of Jerry Garcia six weeks before the release of "Tie-Died: Rock n' Roll's Most Deadicated Fans" affected the interest, buzz and performance of the movie? Do you think a performer's death ahead of a movie is generally a positive or negative development for a movie's distributor to deal with?

3. Name a current trailer that has caught your interest and makes you want to see the film. Explain why it is effective for you. What do you look for in a trailer? Is it the music, plot, genre, style, images, stars, other?

4. What is the first thing that should be done when creating a trailer, and what should it aspire to accomplish?

LABOR DAY BLUES: THE BOX OFFICE SLOWS DOWN

Week 36: September 4–10, 2009

> *Yes, $100 million still means something, especially*
> *for those movies that can't quite get there.*

Throughout the year, I've written about the ebb and flow of the Motion Picture Marketplace as if it's a living, breathing organism that can take on a life of its own. I believe that to be true, and those who have worked in the day-to-day business of making, distributing and exhibiting movies know what I mean. 365 days, 52 weeks, 12 months, 7 days a week, movies light up the close to 40,000 screens throughout the country. Day in and day out, week in and week out, month in and month out, the movies bring life to the marketplace, but it's a fact not all movies are created equal and not all playing time is either. Some have argued that a good movie could do business anytime of the year, but that isn't quite the case, and it isn't that simple of an equation. If it was, we would see a big important expensive film be released on Labor Day weekend one of these years, but that has never happened. Why?

After four months of another record-breaking summer movie season, the marketplace is about to take a breather and slow down. As the leaves start to fall, the business falls along with it. It happens every year at this time. Just as September is historically the worst month of the year for the stock market, it's also the weakest month at the box office, and it starts with Labor Day weekend and the usual less than stellar slate of releases. This year is no different when you look at the three movies opening wide nationally, Lionsgate's "Gamer," Fox's "All About Steve" and Miramax's "Extract." Labor Day never gets respect as a weekend to open a movie, and it's not only about the weekend itself but the entire month that follows. It's tough to buck historical trends, and numbers and enough data exists that show moviegoing levels drop dramatically in September for a variety of reasons from kids going back to school, family budgets being tighter, vacations being over, moviegoers being spent after four months of big movies, people taking advantage of being outdoors or even competition from the new television season beginning. Whatever the reasons, it's tough to change a historical pattern. Other times of the year we have seen distributors take a chance and try something different, but I don't see anyone bold or perhaps foolish enough to open a big blockbuster on Labor Day weekend anytime soon. It would be just too damn risky to go against the percentages. Would someone put their job on the line to be the first movie to prove the entire industry wrong? No way. High-level distribution positions are too valuable these days. Out of about twelve national holidays in the year, Labor Day will continue to be the one studios either avoid or use as a dumping ground.

Labor Day signifies more of an end than a beginning, and it takes awhile for the marketplace to rev up again, and when it does, it takes on a different look and feel with smarter films and smaller films better able to compete in the months ahead. I recall a movie I was very fond of when I worked for Orion, John Sayles's baseball movie "Eight Men Out." It was the summer of 1988, and Orion already had a big hit with the Kevin Costner baseball movie "Bull Durham," which was released in the prime June period and grossed $50 million. We all knew "Eight Men Out" wasn't going to be as commercial as "Bull Durham," but slotting two baseball movies into the same season was a tricky proposition for the company. The best seasons to release a baseball movie are spring and summer; even though the playoffs and World Series are in the fall, fans are more into football by then. So when we got the word to book "Eight Men Out" for Labor Day weekend on a wide release, I knew that wasn't good news for the movie, and it wasn't. It only grossed $6,000,000. Later I found out it was in the contract that the movie had to be released in the summer, and since Labor Day is considered the last weekend of the summer movie season, the movie lived up to its contract. Was it best for the movie? No, but those type of compromises and decisions happen in the movie industry from time to time, and those unfortunately caught in the middle of those decisions can feel the pain.

Looking back at the summer movie season the studios relearn some of the same lessons every year. It's the season for big action tentpoles, animation and comedies. On the other hand, dramas, independent releases and more gentle fare seem to struggle to get a foothold a little more with each passing year. Focus Features found that again last weekend when "Taking Woodstock" only opened to $3.7 million. Their hope that the younger generation would show up didn't materialize, and not enough baby boomers supported it. It has been another bad summer for the independents. Fox Searchlight's "(500) Days of Summer" is the lone standout with a $25 million gross, and it's still playing in theatres. Another film I'd like to give a shout out to is Summit's Iraq drama "The Hurt Locker," which is closing in on $12 million. I'm surprised at how well this film has held on to its theatres in the heat of the summer. Its core art audience is spreading good word of mouth and the distributor has done a solid job marketing it. The gross isn't a world beater, but considering Summit acquired the film for $1.5 million, it will be profitable for them, and it will be heard from again at Oscar time. It's difficult to conjecture whether "The Hurt Locker" could have grossed more at the end of the year when it would have faced stiffer competition for the specialty dollar, but needless to say, they held their own in the summer, didn't get buried and made the movie stand out. That's no easy task in today's climate.

Would someone put their job on the line to be the first
movie to prove the entire industry wrong?

Getting back to Hollywood's mainstream releases, the critics didn't much care for many of the top grossing movies, but summer isn't for the critics, it's for the audiences, and they certainly didn't seem to mind the studios' choices. Even though no movie could match "The Dark Knight," there were many more hits than misses. There have been about a dozen movies that have passed $100 million at the box office, and it got me thinking whether this financial benchmark is even still relevant for many of the big budget releases. The industry has been acknowledging this standard for four decades as a beacon of success, but does it carry the same relevance and magic as in years past? One thing the industry has discontinued is the Golden Spokes Award for each movie passing the $100 million mark. There have just been too many to hit that mark lately. Of course a film's budget plays a huge role in determining how significant reaching $100 million is. It's certainly a different equation for the $30 million "The Hangover" than it is for the $175 million "G.I. Joe." But that being said, the figure still carries a fair share of magic, and that's why it has survived. Just think of all the movies that never get close to it. Let's look at some of the summer disappointments. Don't you think "Bruno," ($60 million) "Funny People," ($51 million) "Land of the Lost," ($49 million) and "Year One" ($43 million) would have been thrilled to join the club? And how about "Public Enemies" sitting at $97 million with a dwindling number of theatres playing it. Universal would be much happier at $100 million than finishing at $98 million. $100 million is such a round definitive number with a much better ring to it; it's a little like a hitter in baseball finishing with a career batting average of 299 instead of 300. Yes, $100 million still means something, especially for those movies that can't quite get there.

3D continues to solidify itself as a force at the nation's theatres and is playing a part in helping the business grow. Whether it's kids, families, or teens, the grosses for the 3D screens are impressive. Last week's "Final Destination" saw 70% of its $28,000,000 gross come from its 3D screens. The majority of theatres playing 3D also offer regular showings of the same film, but moviegoers invariably choose to pay more for the 3D experience, at least for now when it's still a bit of a novelty. That fact alone can't be overstated; as prices are going down in all kinds of retail businesses to entice consumers, theatres are charging more and getting it. Is this a short-term blip? Will audiences eventually tire of the process, or is it here to stay as Jeffrey Katzenberg keeps preaching? Everyone is looking at James Cameron's "Avatar," opening at Christmas, to supply some of the answers. What I'll be keeping my eye on in the next few months is the number of new screens theatre owners will be converting to 3D in anticipation of "Avatar." The confidence level among exhibitors will be a telling sign of things to come. Unfortunately, the opposite is happening in the DVD market as prices continue to drop along with demand. This applies to both regular DVDs and high-def Blu-ray. The studios have come to the conclusion that the best way to grow the high-def market is to drop prices from the high $20 range to the low $20 range, even as low as $19.99. The overall problem for the studios as they move forward is that the DVD business is more down than what the theatrical market is up. For the theatrical market to stay strong, the DVD market needs to be strong; the bottom line profitability of movies is too interconnected for it to slip anymore than it already has. If the slide continues, it will affect the number and types of movies that get released and also impact the studios' ability to spend the huge dollars needed to market their movies in a way that will keep moviegoers flocking to the theatres.

The big news of the week was Disney announcing a deal to acquire Marvel Entertainment for $4 billion in cash and stock. For Marvel, it's a great move immediately for their stock price and their future prospects. In the past year, Marvel had taken control of their own destiny by raising their own cash and changing the deals they had with distributors like Paramount so they would be able to keep more of the profits on movies like "Iron Man." What Marvel didn't like so much was having to be responsible for the $80 million or so that it takes to market their superhero movies to a worldwide audience. With this deal, they not only will have Disney's cash, but Disney will be the one spending the production and marketing dollars through their international marketing and distribution channels. That suits Marvel fine. For Disney, they're looking at the deal more long term, 10 to 20 years in the future, because they will have to honor existing contracts and won't take control of all the characters and movies for several years. The stock market tends to look at deals more short term, and the day after the deal was announced, Disney's stock took an immediate hit and lost $1.5 billion in value. But this deal looks great for Disney when you look a little down the road and imagine the value of acquiring 5,000 characters in the Marvel family. There is gold to mine in merchandising, theme parks, as well as in movies, and Disney is in a much better position to take full advantage of all the opportunities than Marvel ever did. Along with last year's deal to distribute future DreamWorks' movies, this deal will also fortify their annual release schedules. What I'm wondering is if this deal will have any impact on Disney's Miramax division. The art distributor has been pretty quiet with releases in 2009, and with last year's contraction of Warner Independent and Paramount Vantage, there is a distinct possibility that the fate of Miramax could be in question. With the independent business having another down year, anything is possible.

This Week at the Box Office:

Weekly Attendance: 19,565,734

All About Steve

20th Century Fox

Opening weekend: $11,241,214

Domestic gross: $33,862,903 84.4%

Foreign gross: $6,242,639 15.6%

Worldwide gross: $40,105,542

Widest release: 2,265 theatres

Gamer

Lionsgate

Opening weekend: $9,156,057

Domestic gross: $20,534,907 50.3%

Foreign gross: $20,293,633 49.7%

Worldwide gross: $40,828,540

Widest release: 2,502 theatres

Extract

Miramax

Opening weekend: $4,340,108

Domestic gross: $10,823,158 99.8%

Foreign gross: $25,625 0.2%

Worldwide gross: $10,848,783

Widest release: 1,614 theatres

Amreeka

National Geographic

Opening weekend: $71,548

Domestic gross: $627,436 29.8%

Foreign gross: $1,548,868 71.2%

Worldwide gross: $2,176,304

Widest release: 40 theatres

Carriers

Paramount Vantage

Opening weekend: $71,694

Domestic gross: $120,866 1.8%

Foreign gross: $5,698,070 98.2%

Worldwide gross: $5,802,422

Widest release: 100 theatres

Sandstorm

Independent

Opening weekend: $1,744

Domestic gross: $3,444

Widest release: 1 theatre

The 25 Highest Grossing Limited Releases of Summer 2009

1. (500) Days of Summer (Fox Searchlight) - $25,409,711
2. The Hurt Locker (Summit Entertainment) - $11,626,061
3. Away We Go (Focus Features) - $9,451,946
4. Whatever Works (Sony Pictures Classics) - $5,220,351
5. Moon (Sony Pictures Classics) - $4,652,960
6. Food, Inc. (Magnolia Pictures) - $4,098,279
7. The Brothers Bloom (Summit Entertainment) - $3,531,756
8. Cheri (Miramax) - $2,715,657
9. Easy Virtue (Sony Pictures Classics) - $2,631,543
10. Rudo y Cursi (Sony Pictures Classics) - $1,827,660
11. In the Loop (IFC) - $1,779,340
12. Summer Hours (IFC) - $1,657,001
13. Adam (Fox Searchlight) - $1,393,329
14. Departures (Regent Releasing) - $1,279,245
15. Paper Heart (Overture) - $951,473
16. Management (Samuel Goldwyn) - $934,658
17. The Wonder of It All (Indican) - $707,537
18. The Girlfriend Experience (Magnolia) - $695,417
19. Seraphine (Music Box Films) - $655,388
20. Yoo-Hoo, Mrs. Goldberg (International Film Circuit) - $641,811
21. The Story of Soraya M. (Roadside Attractions) - $621,676
22. The Cove (Roadside Attractions) - $619,467
23. The Girl From Monaco (Magnolia) - $554,905
24. Cold Souls (Samuel Goldwyn) - $475,615
25. Little Ashes (Regent Releasing) - $472,680

Includes limited-release films released between May 1-August 31. Grosses as of August 31st.

Source: Indiewire

Week 36: Questions for Discussion

1. Why doesn't the month of September get the respect that other months do when a distributor chooses its release dates? Do you agree with the reasoning given? What distinction does the Labor Day holiday hold in the film industry?

2. Has there ever been a September release to gross $100 million? Do some research on your own to complete the question and discuss your findings.

FEWER MOVIES, A NEW INTERNATIONAL RECORD AND THE MOST UNLIKELY TYCOON IN HOLLYWOOD

Week 37: September 11–17, 2009

> *For Tyler Perry, it wasn't about who he knew*
> *because he didn't know anybody in Hollywood.*

There's no shortage of story lines as the industry slinks into what is historically the slowest week of the year at the box-office, the weekend following Labor Day. Earlier in the year, I had made a point about how the studios break down the twelve-month release schedule into four parts; January-April, May-August, September-October and November-December. So far, so good, the first two four-month blocks have more than held their own, and the overall box office is still running around 5% over the same period in 2008. The last four months of the year are always trickier to figure out. When publications like *Entertainment Weekly* do their seasonal forecasts of upcoming movies, they always group the September to December films into one huge category of fall releases, and I can see why they do it that way, but the reality is that September/October and November/December are two totally different animals. September and October are two of the slowest months on the release schedule with numerous genre, mid-range commercial and art films fighting for attention. Not that there won't be some very good films out there, several box office successes and a few unexpected surprises, but studios won't be putting too many of their heavy hitters into this period. They wait to put those in November and December, which is now considered the eight-week holiday season leading up to Thanksgiving and Christmas, two of the more lucrative moviegoing holidays of the year.

According to research done by Jeff Bock of Exhibitor Relations, a box-office tracking firm, the last four months of the year will definitely be different from years past in regards to the number of releases hitting the theatres. Everyone in the industry has been waiting for a real shakeout from the glut of films that have jammed the theatres during this decade, due to the easy money that has flowed from Wall Street and private investors, but that party is over for now. Last fall's economic collapse and credit crunch took care of that, and finding film financing has become much more difficult which, needless to say, leads to fewer movies. If Mr. Bock's math is correct, a dramatic fall off of movies is about to occur. His research shows that there will be 135 movies released this year from September to December compared to 199 in 2008, down a whopping 32%. Even though the numbers can be misleading because many of those films can very well be smaller art films that get minimal releases in a few markets, it's a remarkable drop-off nevertheless. Many of those films found their way into the month of October, which has crowded that month with specialty films like no other month of the year. Back in 2005, I remember a three-week stretch in Chicago that saw 38 movies being released. The critics didn't have the time or space to review them all, and it was complete insanity. The vast majority of those films never had much of a chance and disappeared as quickly as they arrived.

On paper, fewer movies will give more breathing room to the films that get distributed, and that should be a good thing. But will it produce more successes at the box office due to less competition and more available screen time? Will the drop-off in releases be felt only in the independent arena, or will it be also felt with studio releases, and what would that do to the weekend box office tabulations? The one studio that has announced a retraction of releases in the fall is Paramount, which will be moving two films out of this period into next year so they can shift the marketing costs of the two films to the next fiscal year. That's how closely studios are looking at their bottom lines these days. One of the films being pushed back is the high profile "Shutter Island," directed by Martin Scorsese. I wonder what Scorsese thinks about that. His film looked like it could have been one of October's bigger releases while it also takes him out of this year's expanded Oscar derby. It's going to be very interesting to track the releases in the next few months to see if in fact there will be fewer movies and how that will impact the marketplace one way or another. The marketplace doesn't operate on paper. The movies that do open still have to prove to be the right movies at the right time with the right marketing that moviegoers are motivated to go to see.

The International Marketplace

Summer not only set a new domestic box office record with about $4.3 billion, but also a new international record with $5.8 billion, which gives the studios more than a $10 billion summer in worldwide grosses. Pretty impressive numbers when you consider where the economy has been this year in many countries and that the exchange rate hasn't been as favorable for U.S currency as it has been in the past. Those numbers reinforce a few facts. The theatrical business is not only hanging in like a rock in North America, but it remains the foundation of the business throughout the world. The international market remains the largest and fastest growing revenue stream that Hollywood has. People everywhere still love watching movies in movie theatres despite all the new ways they can see them. Another indisputable fact is that big Hollywood movies continue to dominate the world's screens as they have done since the 1920s. Despite dealing with territorial quotas for local films, studios are still able to carve out a 60-65% market share in many countries. No other country on earth produces blockbusters like Hollywood, and foreign audiences can't get enough of them. Looking at the top grossing summer movies in the following list tells the global story:

TITLE	INTERNATIONAL	DOMESTIC	WORLDWIDE
Harry Potter	$613 million	$295 million	$908 million
Ice Age	$640 million	$193 million	$833 million
Transformers	$429 million	$400 million	$829 million
Angles & Demons	$351 million	$133 million	$484 million
Up	$156 million	$289 million	$466 million
The Hangover	$160 million	$270 million	$430 million
Night at the Museum	$233 million	$176 million	$409 million
Star Trek	$126 million	$256 million	$382 million
Terminator	$246 million	$125 million	$371 million
X Men: Wolverine	$166 million	$180 million	$346 million

Source: Variety

There are close to 40,000 screens in North America and close to 110,000 screens in the rest of the world. The number of screens in America isn't expected to change much, but internationally is a different story where countries like Russia and China are on the rise, and other countries are modernizing and building new screens. What a contrast between the U.S. market share in foreign countries and foreign film market share in America where they enjoy less than 1% of the market. It's similar to the situation the majority of smaller American art films face when trying to crack the overseas market; there's not that much room or interest for these films. International territories are interested in the mainstream studio movies and only the largest of the independents; the rest of the screens are filled with locally made films. Just like in this country, it's a tale of two distinct business models that produce two distinct revenue streams that are worlds apart from each other.

The Unlikely Tycoon

The most unlikely tycoon in Hollywood has to be Tyler Perry, who is opening another movie this weekend through his distribution partner Lionsgate, "Tyler Perry's I Can Do Bad All By Myself." This will be his seventh movie since 2005, and they have all been successful hits. I haven't seen any of them, but that doesn't mean anything because I'm not his target audience. Here's a man who epitomizes the entrepreneurial spirit and proves how far a person can go in life and what can be achieved in the movie business through hard work, perseverance, talent and perhaps most importantly, finding a niche Hollywood leaves alone, which now he has come to own. That niche is the African American audience and more specifically older, church going black women. For Perry, it wasn't about who he knew because he didn't know anybody in Hollywood. It was about starting with nothing, scratching out a living and paying his dues. He's the classic rags to riches story, homeless and living in his car when he started putting on plays with his Madea character in churches throughout the South, slowly building up a strong base of middle class African American women and churchgoers which kept growing and growing when he sold DVDs of his plays. That is called creating an authenticity over time that money can't buy. When he moved to films using the same characters and stories, he had a target audience he could count on and knew how to reach. Now he is a very rich individual who is said to have made $75 million last year, owns all his movies and became the first African American to open his own studio, which isn't located in Hollywood but in Atlanta. He has not only become a force in movies, but he has conquered television with "House of Payne" and "Meet The Browns." Perry has done a few very smart things beginning with branding all his work by inserting his name in the titles, staying within his niche and staying away from opening against the big Hollywood blockbusters. It's easier to dominate and be number one at the box office in September or February than it is in July or December. Blacks make up only 12% of the population but 20% of the moviegoing audience, so Mr. Perry has a little goldmine on his hands. Over the years, I've come to understand how difficult it is to achieve success in the marketplace with independent projects. To achieve not only success on his own terms but to also become a brand name in the process is a life and career achievement that is rare indeed.

This Week at the Box Office: *Weekly Attendance: 15,593,041* **(lowest of year)**

There is another brand name behind one of the movies that's opening this week and that's Tim Burton, who is the producer of the animated sci-fi fantasy "9." Name recognition certainly helped Tyler Perry and Burton since they had the only movies out of the fifteen that opened that registered any kind of gross. If the week after Labor Day is the worst week of the year, you may wonder why so many movies chose to open this week. Generally three different scenarios play out:

▶ Movies that have a shot at success open against weak competition.

▶ Distributors use the date as a dumping ground for their lesser releases such as "Sorority Row" And "Whiteout."

▶ Those involved with smaller, independent films take advantage of the "hole" in the marketplace and are just happy to find theatres to play their films.

Tyler Perry's I Can Do Bad All by Myself
Lionsgate
Opening weekend: $23,446,785
Domestic gross: $51,733,921
Foreign gross: $0.00
Widest release: 2,255 theatres

9
Focus
Opening weekend: $10,079,109
Domestic gross: $31,749,894 65.6%
Foreign gross: $16,678,169 34.4%
Worldwide gross: $48,428,063
Widest release: 2,060 theatres

Sorority Row
Summit
Opening weekend: $5059,802
Domestic gross: $11,965,282 44.0%
Foreign gross: $15,240,838 56.0%
Worldwide gross: $27,206,120
Widest release: 2,665 theatres

Whiteout
Warner Brothers
Opening weekend: $4,915,104
Domestic gross: $10,275,638 57.6%
Foreign gross: $7,565,229 42.4%
Worldwide gross: $17,840,867
Widest release: 2,745 theatres

Crude
First Run
Opening weekend: $16,595
Domestic gross: $170,295 91.6%
Foreign gross: $15,585 8.4%
Worldwide gross: $185,881
Widest release: 7 theatres

The Other Man
Image
Opening weekend: $51,909
Domestic gross: $149,530 13.1%
Foreign gross: $994,328 86.9%
Worldwide gross: $1,143,856
Widest release: 11 theatres

White on Rice
Variance
Opening weekend: $8,079
Domestic gross: $69,171
Foreign gross: N/A
Widest release: 7 theatres

Beyond a Reasonable Doubt
Anchor Bay
Opening weekend: $17,164
Domestic gross: $32,917 0.8%
Foreign gross: $4,355,646 99.2%
Worldwide gross: $4,388,563
Widest release: 5 theatres

Walt & El Groupo
Disney
Opening weekend: $6,059
Domestic gross: $20,251
Foreign gross: N/A
Widest release: 4 theatres

Gogol Bordello Non-Stop
Lorber
Opening weekend: $2,793
Domestic Gross: $5,532
Foreign Gross: N/A
Widest release: 2 theatres

The Horse Boy
Zeitgeist
Opening weekend: N/A
Domestic gross: $156,612
Foreign gross: N/A
Widest release: 10 theatres

No Impact Man
Oscilloscope
Opening weekend: $15,215
Domestic gross: $100,028 86.0%
Foreign gross: $16,321 14.0%
Worldwide gross: $116,349
Widest release: 8 theatres

Broken Hill
Audience Alliance
Opening weekend: $32,140
Domestic gross: $50,076
Foreign gross: N/A
Widest release: 48 theatres

The Big Gay Musical
Embrem
Opening weekend: $8,053
Domestic gross: $24,140
Foreign gross: N/A
Widest release: 1 theatre

Give Me Your Hand
Strand
Opening weekend: $2,434
Domestic gross: $3,601
Foreign gross: N/A
Widest release: 1 theatre

2012 Update: Worldwide Box Office

Worldwide box office for all films reached $29.9 billion in 2009. International box office (19.3 billion) made up 64% of the worldwide total, while U.S. and Canada (10.6 billion) made up 36%, a proportion consistent with the last several years. When we jump ahead and look at the statistics from 2011, international growth continues to lead the way in an even more impressive fashion. Global box office reached $32.6 billion in 2011, an increase that was totally due to international box office, which totaled $22.4 billion, an increase from 2009 of 15%, whereas the domestic box office fell 4% to $10.2 billion in 2011.

2011 Top 10 International Box Office Markets – All Films (US$ Billions)
1. Japan - $2.3
2. China - $2.0
3. France - $2.0
4. U.K. - $1.7
5. India - $1.4
6. Germany - $1.3
7. Russia - $1.2
8. Australia - $1.1
9. South Korea - $1.1
10. Italy - $0.9

Sources: *IHS Screen Digest*, MPAA

No Global Coin for Tyler Perry

Historically, black themed and black cast movies have always had a rough time translating successfully to international audiences and doing any significant business outside the United States. It is no different for Tyler Perry, the most successful African American director working today. In his seven-year career as a director from 2005 to 2012, the numbers speak for themselves. The following is a complete list of his films and their grosses. With his first four films, there is a very minimal foreign gross averaging less than 1% of the total gross and starting in 2008 there are no foreign grosses even listed for many of the films according to Box Office Mojo. That means one of two things. The international numbers are so inconsequential that they are not being reported or Lionsgate doesn't even attempt to sell Perry's films in foreign markets anymore. To make money you have to spend money, and when marketing and print costs become more than what the generated revenues are, then the rational decision may be to just forget it and be satisfied with the domestic market. Since Lionsgate and Perry split the cost of the movies between them, there is no foreign component involved that would make an international release necessary, as in pre-sales. While sticking to modest production costs and enjoying a built-in loyal audience in the domestic theatrical, DVD and television markets, they are in the enviable position of not needing international revenues to turn a tidy profit on each of the films. Why chase business that just isn't there to begin with?

"Diary of a Mad Black Woman" (2005)
Domestic gross: $50,633,099 100%
International gross: $19,104 0.0%

"Tyler Perry's Madea's Family Reunion" (2006)
Domestic gross: $63,257,940 99.9%
International gross: $50,939 0.1%

"Tyler Perry's Daddy's Little Girls" (2007)
Domestic gross: $31,366,978 99.2%
International gross: $242,265 0.8%

"Tyler Perry's Why Did I Get Married?" (2007)
Domestic gross: $55,204,525 98.8%
International gross: $658,361 1.2%

"Tyler Perry's Meet The Browns" (2008)

Domestic gross: $41,975,388 100%

International gross: $0.0

"Tyler Perry's Madea Goes to Jail" (2009)

Domestic Gross: $90,508,336 100%

International gross: $0.0

"Tyler Perry's Why Did I Get Married Too?" (2010)

Domestic gross: $60,095,852 99.0%

International gross: $578,120 1.0%

"Tyler Perry's Good Deeds" (2012)

Domestic gross: $34,025,791 100%

International gross: $0.0

"Tyler Perry's The Family That Preys" (2008)

Domestic gross: $37,105,289 100%

International gross: $0.0

"Tyler Perry's I Can Do Bad All by Myself" (2009)

Domestic gross: $51,733,921 100%

International gross: $0.0

"Tyler Perry's Madea's Big Happy Family" (2011)

Domestic gross: $53,013,000 100%

International gross: $0.0

Week 37: Questions for Discussion

1. Is having too many or too few movies in the marketplace at the same time a good or bad thing? Make a case for how either of the dynamics can be viewed as both having positives and negatives.

2. Is the booming international market a fair market for all films? Discuss. When putting together a business plan for an independent art film, what should a producer include in regards to the international potential of that film?

3. What is the secret of success for Tyler Perry? In what ways can his success be a template for other filmmakers? What's the lesson here?

FILM FESTIVAL SEASON USHERS IN HOPE AND QUESTION MARKS

Week 38: September 18–24, 2009

How can movies continue getting financing, even with stars attached, if distributors aren't willing to distribute them?

The fall moviegoing season is going to be a crucial bellwether for quality adult films, from the smaller American independents to foreign films to the higher budget upscale prestige films. It's always refreshing when fall arrives and brings with it a mix of better quality films for audiences to enjoy, but the big question is will discerning moviegoers flip on the switch and start supporting these films better than what they've been doing. The box office performance for adult dramas and upscale films in general has been dismal this year, and you can almost call it a make or break time for the specialty business to start showing a pulse and turn its fortunes around. There's no better time to do it than beginning right now. The overall economy is showing signs of picking up, there's more confidence and optimism in the air, and the six-month stretch of great playing time leading to the Oscars in late February has begun.

Going hand in hand with the smart movie season are the film festivals. It's hard to imagine one without the other. Over the last 30 years, festivals have become a vital cog in the independent film business, providing a tremendous cultural experience for people in cities large and small, introducing art films to cities without an art house, building new art audiences where there previously were none, creating a networking hub for filmmakers to meet fellow filmmakers and industry professionals, getting their films noticed and buzz started. Taking all that into account, there are still two roles the top festivals play that loom larger than all others:

▸ They act as a commercial launching pad for prestige films that already have distributors.

▸ They double as a marketplace where unsold films are looking to sell their films to distributors

In the fall, there is a trio of important festivals that set the tone and establish what films are going to be the ones to watch out for, which ones are going to be the Oscar contenders. The ball gets rolling at the Venice Film Festival in late August, shifts to the Telluride Film Festival over Labor Day weekend and kicks into high gear with the Toronto Film Festival that begins the second week of September and is now headed into its final weekend completing its ten-day run. So in less than a month, three of the most important festivals of the year take place that will define the pecking order of the best films of the year for the next six months. Powerful stuff. What makes the best festivals so influential is the fact that all the important gatekeepers are there. The leaders of the industry, the power brokers, the decision makers who help filter the good from the bad:

▸ Festival programmers
▸ Acquisition executives
▸ Distributors
▸ Sales agents
▸ Theatre owners
▸ Film critics
▸ The media
▸ Cable programmers
▸ DVD distributors

▶ Audiences

Toronto as a launching pad for films getting ready to open commercially is as important as ever. This weekend we'll be seeing the first of the bunch with Steven Soderbergh's "The Informant" opening nationally and arriving with strong buzz. Other films from Toronto that will be opening in the next couple of months that will be Oscar contenders are Jason Reitman's "Up in the Air," starring George Clooney, the new Coen Brothers movie "A Serious Man," Michael Moore's "Capitalism: A Love Story" and smaller titles like "Bright Star," "Precious" and "An Education" which may not be too well known now, but will gain prominence after they open. But there is a cloud hanging over Toronto that is the same one that has been hanging over the independent business for more than a year, and it has to do with tighter money, lower revenues, too many flops and fewer viable distributors. This is putting a crimp into the business of selling movies at festivals like Toronto. More than 130 movies debuting at Toronto are unsold and looking for distribution deals, including some with stars like Bill Murray, Michael Douglas, Demi Moore, Robert DeNiro and Edward Norton. The question is, how many of them will find buyers? Up to this point, there hasn't been much action, and distributors are being very cautious with their money. It's strictly a buyers market and distributors can afford to wait until asking prices come down. It's pretty much a crisis for anyone involved in trying to sell a film today, and much has changed in the last two years.

Following on the heels of the huge success of "Little Miss Sunshine," the 2007 Sundance Film Festival was a seller's paradise where 15 films were sold for $50 million in advances. Distributors were spending money like drunken sailors on a weekend leave. Looking back at that festival and the sales prices paid for individual films is a lesson in irresponsible spending and miscalculation of the marketplace which led to the downsizing of the specialty market and much tighter distributor purse strings. One can say that some of the individual buys made at that festival no doubt played a part in the eventual shuttering of several distributors. Three distributors no longer in existence had big buys, which proved to be disastrous; Warner Independent paid $4 million for "Clubland," a movie I don't recall even being released, Paramount Vantage paid $6 million for "Son of Rambow," and Think film paid $2 million for the documentary "In the Shadow of the Moon," which didn't find much of an audience. In addition, this was the same festival that Harvey Weinstein bought "Grace is Gone," starring John Cusack, for $4 million and went on to gross a grand total of $52,000 in its theatrical release. Those spending days are long gone, and it's much tougher to sell any kind of film in today's downsized and changing marketplace. One of the problems in selling a film is that there are so few proven ways to make a sale outside of trying to get into one of the top film festivals. Other methods are staging group distributor screenings in Los Angeles and New York, arranging screenings for individual distributors in their private screening rooms and the most desperate of all, sending DVD screeners in the mail to theatrical distributors, DVD distributors and cable television outlets hoping for a response. It's hard to sell a film. If most of the movies go unsold at Toronto, I wouldn't be surprised if there is even more downsizing in distribution and production. How can movies continue to get financing, even with stars attached, if distributors aren't willing to distribute them?

Best Picture Candidates
With talk of Oscar candidates coming out of Toronto, it got me thinking about how the Best Picture category is going to play out this year with the field expanded to ten nominees. One of the reasons floated for expanding the field was to be able to recognize the more quality commercial movies that the general public was familiar with to go along with the art films that have recently dominated the competition. A funny thing may happen on the way to the Academy Awards; it could look a lot like the most recent shows, only with even more specialty titles in the running. There have been over eight months of 2009 releases, and I've seen some early lists of possible Best Picture candidates, and the only two movies that have actually opened that show up on the lists are "UP" and "The Hurt Locker." The mainstream movies that have received strong reviews like "Star Trek," "Harry Potter," "Public Enemies" and "The Hangover" are nowhere to be found. The only one of those films that I would consider worthy of a nomination is "Public Enemies," but there are enough mixed reviews and detractors that it doesn't seem to be getting much respect at this time. Why expand the field to honor

more art films? They're already being honored the day before the Oscars at the Independent Spirit Awards. The Academy voters not only have to consider good reviews and commercial acceptance when compiling their candidates, but they also have to look deeper into the substance of a film, whether it has layered themes, deeper meaning, important subject matter, is it groundbreaking, emotionally powerful, timely, does it speak to the zeitgeist? Most Hollywood studio movies lack those components. Will it come down to whether or not James Cameron's "Avatar" can bridge the commercial and Academy gap as his "Titanic" did 11 years ago in order for a big studio release to be part of the Best Picture race? Either way, the race is tilting toward specialty films like it has for a number of years. The hard truth is that the studios aren't in the business of chasing Oscars; they're in the business of chasing box office. You can't squeeze a square peg into a round hole.

Declining Newspaper Fortunes

The struggles newspapers are going through in trying to keep their businesses afloat while maintaining their audience base is similar to the struggles the independent film business is experiencing with their theatrical operations. Even though blockbusters could live without newspapers, quality films have always counted on papers for support and promotion, so the shrinking fortunes of newspapers are adding to the pain and hardship of specialty films. Local movie critics are being laid off, movie sections are being downsized, less space and interest for publicity articles have all been affecting the marketing of upscale films and the Internet, bloggers and websites aren't offering the same payoff. On top of that, the two largest national theatre circuits, Regal Entertainment and AMC Theatres, have eliminated running movie show times in local papers in some major markets, looking to cut costs while following the lead of studios that have drastically cut back their own newspaper budgets, down 50% from what they spent five years ago. The time when distributors used newspaper advertising to help turn their films into events with full-page ads and even double truck ads (side-by-side full pages of the same movie) are over, and that loss of revenue for newspapers cuts deep. Distributors have experimented going with smaller ads and budgeting fewer weeks for news ads and have found out it has had little effect on how a film performs. They are going where the eyeballs are going, and that's more on the Internet and social networking sites. Newspapers and independent films are fighting the good fight, but it seems like if it's not one thing it's another in their battle to stay profitable and relevant in a changing world.

This Week at the Box Office: *Weekly Attendance: 17,164,001*

Cloudy with a Chance of Meatballs
Sony
Opening weekend: $30,304,648
Domestic gross: $124,870,275 51.4%
Foreign gross: $118,135,851 48.6%
Worldwide gross: $243,006,126
Widest release: 3,119 theatres

The Informant!
Warner Brothers
Opening weekend: $10,464,314
Domestic gross: $33,316,821 79.8%
Foreign gross: $8,454,347 20.2%
Worldwide gross: $41,771,168
Widest release: 2,505 theatres

Love Happens
Universal
Opening weekend: $8,057,010
Domestic gross: $22,965,110 63.6%
Foreign gross: $13,122, 918 36.4%
Worldwide gross: $36,088,028
Widest release: 1,922 theatres

Jennifer's Body
20th Century Fox
Opening weekend: $6,868,397
Domestic gross: $16,204,793 51.4%
Foreign gross: $15,351,268 48.6%
Worldwide gross: $31,556,061
Widest release: 2,738 theatres

The Secrets of Jonathan Sperry
Five & Two Pictures
Opening weekend: $258,400
Domestic gross: $1,355,079
Foreign gross: N/A
Widest release: 18 theatres

Paris
IFC
Opening weekend: $46,518
Domestic gross: $1,010,194 4.3%
Foreign gross: $22,318,324 95.7%
Worldwide gross: $23,328.518
Widest release: 34 theatres

My Heart Goes Hooray

Yash Raj

Opening weekend: $351,457

Domestic gross: $644,046 57.1%

Foreign gross: $484,165 42.9%

Worldwide gross: $1,128,211

Widest release: 54 theatres

35 Shots of Rum

Cinema Guild

Opening weekend: $9,576

Domestic gross: $177,511

Foreign gross: N/A

Widest release: 5 theatres

Pretty Ugly People

Independent

Opening weekend: $2,523

Domestic gross: $6,537

Foreign gross: N/A

Widest release: 3 theatres

Wanted

Eros

Opening weekend: $217,432

Domestic gross: $349,637 86.5%

Foreign gross: $54,462 13.5%

Worldwide gross: $404,099

Widest release: 71 theatres

Disgrace

Paladin

Opening weekend: $12,615

Domestic gross: $69,705 3.3%

Foreign gross: $2,052,869 96.7%

Worldwide gross: $2,112,574

Widest release: 9 theatres

The Burning Plain

Magnolia

Opening weekend: $58,749

Domestic gross: $200,730 3.7%

Foreign gross: $5,267,917 96.3%

Worldwide gross: $5,468,647

Widest release: 26 theatres

Teza

Mypheouh

Opening weekend: $8,908

Domestic gross: $30,071 83.3%

Foreign gross: $6,029 16.7%

Worldwide gross: $36,099

Widest release: 1 theatre

As it worked out, the ten nominees for Best Picture in 2009 split down the middle between mainstream studio movies and independent films with no distributor getting more than one Best Picture nomination:

- ▸ Avatar – 20th Century Fox
- ▸ The Blind Side – Warner Brothers
- ▸ Up – Disney/Pixar
- ▸ District 9 – Sony
- ▸ Up in the Air – Paramount
- ▸ Inglorious Basterds - Weinstein
- ▸ An Education – Sony Classics
- ▸ The Hurt Locker – Summit
- ▸ A Serious Man – Focus
- ▸ Precious – Lionsgate

Week 38: Questions for Discussion

1. What six months of the year make up what is referred to as "the smart season," and what role do film festivals play in this time period?

2. What are the options for the filmmaker who is trying to sell a completed movie to a distributor? How does supply and demand enter into the equation?

3. Research the films that debuted at the 2009 Toronto Film Festival and separate them into the following three categories: films that had distributors, films that were sold to distributors and films that went unsold. You should list at least several examples for each category. After compiling the list, what conclusions can you draw?

Conversations with Industry Professionals

Burt Rast – Advertising Account Executive, *Chicago Sun-Times*, Chicago, IL
The following interview took place on August 12, 2011.

> *"There have to be ads before we even think about doing any promotions for a distributor. We have drawn that line in the sand, and we're not crossing it."*
>
> *Burt Rast*

Q: *You have been in charge of motion picture advertising for the Sun-Times for eleven years or so. How did things change from the start of the decade until the end of it (2001-2010)?*

BR: I think we can talk in pretty broad strokes because from the beginning of the decade until about 2007, it was pretty much a status quo thing, nothing much was changing, nothing much was evolving. We didn't realize the importance of it. The Internet of course was coming along, but it was still kind of considered for young people only, very much a niche advertising tool, but some of the studios began developing their databases and realizing this was a way to communicate with potential moviegoers. That didn't develop overnight, but when it did it really took off, and that was around 2007 or so. I think as much as any single thing, the ability to see trailers on the Internet, one sheets being put up six to nine months in advance, all of a sudden it caught the fancy of people online, and we didn't know it, but it buried us. It's the same as when you think of it as television. It's motion, it's movement; it's color; it's sound; it's excitement. It's not just lying there on paper.

Q: *So the studios were creating so much awareness online, they felt they could start cutting back on their newspaper presence?*

BR: I don't think smaller and smaller ads were part of their thinking at first. It became evident to the studios that they could reach their most important demo, the young kids, the high school kids, the 18-24, the 18-29, those are the people who want to see a movie opening weekend. Those are the ones who will go more than once, and little by little as the decade unfolded, they started to realize there were better ways than newspapers to reach these people. Now they're in a place where they don't think they can reach this audience with newspapers. A perfect example is a goofy movie called "30 Minutes Or Less." It's kind of a major picture, and it's opening today, and the only newspaper ad is in Red Eye, the free daily. Otherwise, all their marketing is either online or cable television.

Q: *That's the one with Jesse Eisenberg from Sony. I guess they figure they're going only for the younger audience whereas Sony's "The Social Network" with the same star had a different demographic and a good presence in newspapers.*

BR: That was a very good one for us. We built nicely with that and had ads for weeks and weeks and weeks. You know what I was thinking about; do you remember "My Big Fat Greek Wedding"? John Iltis bought newspaper ads 39 straight weeks for the distributor. That movie was made by newspaper readers.

Q: *That was in 2002, and it was distributed by an independent distributor; I guess it's hard to imagine something like that happening again. During that decade as the Internet was slowly creeping up in importance, what was happening with the circulation numbers of the newspaper?*

BR: We were bubbling right at 400,000, and now it's in the area of 260,000 to 270,000 daily newspapers.

Q: So that decline happened over ten years?

BR: Yes, but during that time we acquired some suburban newspapers in Elgin, Joliet, areas like that and have created what's known as Sun-Times Media, which is all of our daily papers lumped together. When we lump them all together we are back up to 400,000 covering the same geography, the same large Chicago market. The benefit to the film companies is the following. We only work with these papers on Fridays, and what we do is we take the entire broadsheet weekend movie section that appears in the *Sun-Times*; we print extra copies and insert them into all the suburban papers. The section is intact; the reviews from Roger Ebert are intact. Everything you see in the *Sun-Times* is the same in the suburban papers. The only thing different is the cover page. Instead of saying Chicago *Sun-Times* on top it says Naperville Sun or the Joliet Herald for example. For the studios especially, and the agencies, they jump on board because they know it's important, it's all about environment. Instead of saying we will throw in an extra ad for Joliet to reach those 40,000 additional people, they don't care if the environment isn't right. They want movie editorials, and on Fridays they want reviews, and that's what we give them intact and within their own movie section.

Q: So the bottom line is that they get their 400,000 editions, and when distributors buy their ads they get all these suburban papers as part of the package.

BR: Yes, the studios get the benefit of reaching the outlying suburban audiences, but think about the benefit to the readers also. People buy the Naperville Sun and get this movie section with Ebert and Zwecker and our other writers. How do you do any better than that?

Q: How do you determine the actual readership, and do you use that as an argument with your clients?

BR: Yes, we have readership figures, and at the beginning of the decade we had 1.6 million readers, and today we are at almost 1.1 million. And that's total readers of an issue of the *Sun-Times*. Researchers ask "Did you read a newspaper yesterday?" and if they answered yes, they ask them which one.

Q: So there's over a million people a day reading your paper?

BR: Yes, these are actual readers, not buyers or paid circulation; these are adults 18+ who reported they read a paper yesterday. When you think about that, that's still a significant number.

Q: I'm sure that's part of your argument to distributors on why it still pays to advertise in the Sun-Times, but is it falling on deaf ears?

BR: Sometimes. There is still money set aside for print, but there are exceptions like "Transformers" and "30 Minutes Or Less" where they know they are going to attract such a young audience, and that audience already knows about the movie. They don't need a newspaper ad on Friday to remind them it's opening today.

Q: When the smart movie season starts in the fall and goes to Oscar night, that could be close to a six-month stretch. Is this your sweet spot where newspapers become more important?

BR: Absolutely. We still show strength during that period, and a lot of those films that come out, especially in December, are made to generate Oscar nominations, and newspapers become a primary need to getting the word out. It becomes the smart thing to do for distributors of these films. "The King's Speech" did not spend a fortune for no reason.

Q: *That was Harvey Weinstein, and he was spending like he was back in his Miramax days. My movie marketing class was going on at the time, and some students were shocked to see the size of the ads in the later weeks and would ask, "Hasn't this movie been out for months already?"*

BR: It didn't work out too bad for him or his film, did it?

Q: *You don't see much of Weinstein for most of the year, and then he shows up every year at the end of the year with at least a couple Oscar worthy films ready to spend. You have to love that. When you make your argument to distributors that they should increase their ads on specific movies, how often do you win those arguments?*

BR: I'd love it more if Weinstein had more of a consistent release schedule throughout the year where he was buying ads. In terms of my arguments, I'd say it's about a 50/50 success rate. Sometimes we know we are being bated when someone orders a 2" by 5"ad for Friday and a 2" by 3" for Sunday, and what we do is come back and propose make that Friday a 14" or even a 21" ad, and for an extra $1,500 we will give you a 6" ad for both Saturday and Sunday. Bump your ad on Friday and we will contribute a little the rest of the weekend. It's a way for us make to some more money, and for the movie it creates more impressions. We remind them Saturday night is the biggest night for movies, so you shouldn't be in the paper only Friday and Sunday. But what we are seeing more and more now is we are only getting Fridays only, and that is worrisome.

Q: *I have to ask you about the news that the two largest advertising agencies in the country that handle movie publicity, promotion and advertising in local markets, Allied Advertising and Terry Hines & Associates, have merged. What's your take on this, and will it affect the Sun-Times in any way?*

BR: What you have to remember about those two agencies is that almost everything about them was print. The graphic houses, the trailer companies, none of those companies are merging, but the decline in the print business is having a tremendous ripple effect. Think of those two companies with their offices across the country with all those employees, and those offices have been doing mostly publicity lately, and they were billing it up thinking they could get by with just publicity. Things have changed dramatically, but the one constant is that print billings are decreasing, and the merger was surely out of necessity. Terry Hines lost more quickly, and of course they are the ones being absorbed. It had to come. There just wasn't enough billing to maintain the business model that worked for them for many years. What's going to follow, and it could come as soon as right after the end of 2011, you will see some of the offices closing and some of the media buyers being let go.

Q: *This won't change much for you then?*

BR: No, we will be working with the same people with different phone numbers.

Q: *Legend has it that newspapers always charged more for movie ads because they were stiffed by shady operators in its early years. Any truth to that?*

BR: That surprises me, we never did that. Our amusement rates for the movie studios have always been halfway between our retail rate and our national rate. The *Tribune* on the other hand I believe always charged them national, the same as their computer ads or anything else because I know the *Tribune* rates were always 20% to 30% higher than us even when our circulations were more close together. But I do know now the *Tribune* is wheeling and dealing more enthusiastically than we are.

Q: *Today's movie ad rates are a little like the Fed's interest rates, aren't they, never going up?*

BR: We haven't issued a rate card for movies since 2008. We're just keeping them the same, and when we make deals it's based on the 2008 rates. We used to do annual increases of 3%-5%, so there were never any big jumps like in New York or Los Angeles. Our current rate is $225 per column inch seven days a week. So companies could actually get ads in for less than the 2008 column inch rates if they are willing to do some moving and grooving and shaking some things up. Another thing we will do is when somebody runs color, and especially if it's for Friday only and if they buy either a Saturday or Sunday ad, it doesn't have to be the same size ad, we will throw in color for that ad at no charge. The people here have given me the autonomy and flexibility to do what I have to do to increase ad spending.

Q: *Since the Sun-Times has gone to a broadsheet, the era of the full-page ad looks like it's over. When you were the tabloid size, the 70" ad was the full-page advertisement.*

BR: You know what our deal for that is? If you order up a 70" ad, we'll offer you a broadsheet full-page ad at the same price. And you know why you don't see them anymore? They don't even prepare ads that size anymore. Ads just aren't that big anymore.

Q: *How about the Sunday New York Times? I see a full-page ad from time to time, and they of course have a broadsheet.*

BR: Yes, but the New York market is considered an AA market along with Los Angeles, and those size ads are prepared only for those papers.

Q: *Chicago is an A market. If the ads are prepared already, why can't they use them in Chicago? Rejecting that type of offer, which would showcase a movie so dramatically, would seem to be the result of either corporate indifference or pure laziness.*

BR: They are not willing to do it, and I don't have the answer why. An important thing to note is that all the movie ads used to be done directly by the Chicago agencies, and now they are all prepared on the west coast, so that probably comes into play. Let me give you an example of a creative use of a full-page space this year. Fox had the animated "Rio," and they wanted to do something different; they didn't want traditional ads. They wanted to reach families. They wanted to reach parents who wanted to drop the kids off at the multiplex, and they had to use newspapers. Fox called what they wanted to do a "stair step." I'm not sure where that term came from, but it was an ad that stretched from top to bottom in a twisty fashion, but the page included some editorial content too. They didn't want just the ad by itself, they wanted a more organic use of space, so they bought space for a full-page ad in color, and there are two different film stories or reviews on the same page. It was pretty eye catching, and the movie did tremendous, and everyone was happy, and we're trying to work with Fox on a couple of other things because that's sort of a template. They proved that you can still make the newspapers an important part of your marketing campaign, and movies like that are what have made my job fun over the years. Several years ago Fox pulled off another highly creative use of space with "The Simpsons Movie" where they had a horizontal line of all the many, many characters that have shown up on the show waiting in line to buy tickets at the box office, and it stretched over two pages. I think it was the first time a film company had newspapers writing the copy around the creative.

Q: *What is the demographic of the average reader of the Sun-Times?*

BR: The demos are remaining constant. The one thing that is changing is that the average age of the reader is increasing, which is in the upper 40s, and that's not good news. The lowest I remember it being was 42 years old in the last decade. We have loyal readers, but we are having trouble attracting new readers. We are slightly more predominantly male than female; we are much younger than the *Tribune*'s readership and more urban than the *Trib*'s readership. Their suburban readership is almost double ours, and I'm talking about percent of total readers. They are by far a suburban entity whereas we are more Chicago. That was another reason for buying all those suburban papers and creating a network, because we were underrepresented out there.

Q: *Do you think you are reaching new readers online?*

BR: There is an online *Sun-Times*, there is an iPad *Sun-Times*, there is a Kindle *Sun-Times*. There are lots and lots of ways to read this newspaper every day.

Q: *Are there statistics available for all those different devices?*

BR: Not yet. The numbers haven't been big enough.

Q: *Do you think newspapers made a mistake for offering all their online versions for free? Now you see some of the bigger ones putting their content behind pay walls. Was that a mistake in strategy?*

BR: I don't know if it as much of a mistake as it was the recognition that we were underestimating the importance of online; we were underestimating the potential.

Q: *The potential to really damage the physical newspaper with people saying they can read it free now?*

BR: When I come downtown on the train I always see a few people with their iPads reading the dailies or the Wall Street Journal, so little by little it's evolving from a print product, but having said that I'm a believer that we will always put out a print edition. We may put out only 100,000 of them, but there will always be people who will want to hold the paper in their hands and physically turn the pages of a newspaper.

Q: *Just like there are always going to be movie theatres. But isn't it a reality that everybody is having the same problem with the digital realm, it just isn't returning the revenue that physical products did?*

BR: That's correct.

Q: *With newspaper ads and promotions through the paper, are you tying ad support having to be there before you run any promotions such as advance screenings or run of the engagement passes?*

BR: Absolutely. There have to be ads before we even think about doing any promotions for a distributor. We have drawn a line in the sand, and we're not crossing it.

Q: *Some large newspapers like the Washington Post list free movie showtimes for all the theatres in the market? How does that pay off for them, and has the Sun-Times ever considered doing that? What is the upside and downside to that?*

BR: To be very honest, when AMC made the decision to pull all their ads from the *Sun-Times*, and that was a big chunk of money going away, we discussed it because we didn't quite know, because it's hard to quantify, how many people were relying on newspapers to get show times. All of sudden the 500 pound gorilla, meaning AMC, wasn't in the paper, and all the rest of the theatre ads combined that were still in the paper didn't do the box office that the AMC theatres were doing that were pulling out. We didn't know the importance to our readers, so we decided to go 30 days monitoring every phone call or email from every irate reader saying, "Hey, what's up with this?" We talked them off the ledge if we could, or if we missed their calls, we would call them back. There were three of us doing it, and we made it our business to call everyone back and talk to our readers, just trying to get a sense of how important it was. Is it one of the reasons people buy the paper, because we sure weren't willing to lose any subscribers? But enough of the theatres hung in there, and the furor eventually calmed down, and the decision was made to stay the course and not switch to the free listings. If you run the theatre clock for all the theatres, there is no revenue, and even without AMC we were still getting substantial revenue from the theatres and circuits that were still buying display ads with us. So we would be kissing that money completely goodbye, and then we would have to pay money out of our own pocket to donate our own newsprint to run the same exact listings for nothing. A great example of a theatre owner who still believes in print is Tony Kerasotes and his Showplace Icon in the south Loop, now in its second full year of operation, who runs a significant newspaper ad 365 days a year in both the *Sun-Times* and *Tribune* and has recently surpassed the AMC River East as the top grossing theatre in the Chicago market. I don't think that's a coincidence. Tony recognizes the value of what that daily newspaper presence has meant to his theatre. We keep working on AMC with new ideas to do some things with us as they add Imax screens to various theatres and other stuff they are doing while also keep coming at them about the Icon Theatre, saying we can't be absolutely sure, but the theatre that has an ad in the paper every day has just surpassed your flagship theatre as number one in the market.

Q: *What effect, if any, have the financial troubles and corporate shenanigans of past ownership groups had on your end of the business?*

BR: Well, keep in mind that the *Sun-Times*, in the middle of the last decade, was discovered to be manipulating circulation figures and misrepresenting what our daily and Sunday circulation was. And those figures didn't come from our department or any other department, they came from the highest levels of the company, and that's not easy to get wrong because you're messing with the ABC's of your own circulation.

Q: *Was that the one thing that really hurt the most, people coming back to you and complaining that the figures that were being given to them weren't even true?*

BR: It hurt us from a credibility standpoint, and absolutely it hurt us from a bottom line standpoint because we had to give companies their money back. We couldn't charge them for service that we weren't delivering, and that became provable. We had to send a lot of rebate checks to both distributors and exhibitors. It was just a real mess, and don't forget it just wasn't the movies; it was Marshall Fields, Carson's all the retailers. Past ownership took the *Sun-Times* to the cleaners.

Q: *What is the importance of Chicago remaining a two-paper town?*

BR: First of all the most important thing to keep in mind is that each paper reaches over a million people a day. There are over seven million adults 18 and over in the Chicago metropolitan area, so both papers combined are still getting 25% to 30% of grownups as readers, and I think those boxcar numbers make people glad two strong daily newspapers are here. Certainly the agencies like it because they get to prepare two sets of ads. They're with us and I think they keep the studios' focus on the fact that both papers reach a mainstream audience, and as things get more fragmented every single day, the word millions still has some meaning. We can bemoan the fact that we are getting a lot of 10" ads, but that's probably the reason we're still getting them.

Q: *Would you want to be the only newspaper in Chicago?*

BR: Only if I was a real lazy man. Seriously, without competition you don't work as hard, and you start to go to hell. With competition you stay on top of your game, and if we play that game right we want to be a little better than the other guy, to be thought of more highly and hence do a little better for the distributor and the agency.

Q: *The year 2009 was a record-breaking year at the box office. What do you recall from that year?*

BR: For those of us who worked in newspapers, 2009 was the continuation of a declining trend, and it was nothing more than that. The box office exploded to its best year ever, and it had some incredible films. Fox spent week after week with ads on "Avatar" and Warner's spent well on "The Hangover," but the point of it is the spending was already going down, and none of those films altered it, at least not enough to make any quarter of 2009 better than it was in 2008. Disney was starting to cut way back, and even in the mid-2000s, they were spending well over a million dollars a year on ads just in the *Sun-Times*. They were starting to release fewer films, and for a time they were trying to figure out what was happening in the marketplace. At our highpoint we were billing $18 to $19 million a year. I don't have the numbers from 2009, but this year we are struggling to get to $6 million in movie advertising buys.

Q: *I guess that really puts it into perspective. You are saying your business is down 65% from its heyday, which wasn't all that long ago.*

BR: And a lot of that drop-off came from exhibitors, don't forget. AMC used to spend well over million a year; Loews spent more than a million a year; even Crown spent a quarter of a million a year on only two theatres. We don't get to exclusively place the blame on distributors because exhibitors have cut back on print dramatically too.

Q: *How is your performance judged by your superiors in this age of declining business?*

BR: We definitely have goals to reach. They know the market is declining, and they set the goals based on what was achieved the previous year. Even though they probably know that we will probably not match last year's numbers, they don't come down on me if we don't. The only way to answer your question is to say I'm still here.

Q: *What's an important lesson you have learned about the movie business and the job you do?*

BR: It's just nothing more than some basic things. Be there for the clients. Try your hardest to come up with deals for them, think of creative things for them. It obviously comes down to putting butts in the seats, and I try to continuously come up with fresh ideas on how to get people to go to the movies. I think my people see that in me, and I even get a compliment now and then when they notice something and say they hadn't thought of that. That's all I can do for my clients, keep helping them and keep trying to get people to see their movies. I have to be proactive. If I just sit here and wait for them to call us or wait for them to place business, you know what happens? Little by little those calls are less and less frequent. You have to be supplying them with something all the time and keep the lines of communication constantly going.

Q: *What's a basic fundamental that never changes?*

BR: There's a right way to do things, and there is wrong way to do things. Get it right, and do it correctly, and move forward. Don't let things slip through the cracks or be forgotten about. Part of that mentality comes from the fact that the *Sun-Times* has always been the number two paper, and we have always had to try harder. There is no such thing as not being able to do something. We'll make it happen.

Q: *Look into your crystal ball. What will the movie sections be like in five or ten years?*

BR: In either five years or ten years things are going to be about the same. It's going to bottom out fairly soon, and what that means is we will have a movie section on Friday, but it won't be any bigger than it is now. We're going to do four to six pages on Friday; Saturday and Sunday will become almost non-existent. The films that run the full weekend will be those targeting adults. There will never be three to four pages of movie ads in the Sunday paper anymore. I'm a believer that there will always be people who want to hold a physical newspaper in their hands, and I think newspapers and movie sections will continue to be there.

[Author's note: In 2012, the *Sun-Times* changed the size of their movie section from broadsheet to tabloid. Also in 2012, the Showplace Icon stopped running daily ads in both the *Chicago Sun-Times* and *Chicago Tribune*.]

Week 38: Questions for Discussion

5. What are some of the ways the Chicago *Sun-Times* is trying to counter the drop in newspaper movie advertising?

6. What is the upside and downside of a local newspaper choosing to list all the movie theatre showtimes free of charge?

7. Burt Rast discusses several changes that have been occurring over the past five to ten years that have led to declining news advertising by the studios. From your perspective, list those changes in order of how destructive they have been to newspapers and explain your reasoning. Do you ever use a newspaper for your movie information?

8. When does credibility really count in the newspaper business, and what dire effects can result when there is a breech in that credibility?

CHANGING ECONOMICS COMES DOWN
TO WHO'S IN CONTROL

Week 39: September 25–October 1, 2009

---

*What's lost in the translation in this new hybrid type deal is how
much it's going to cost filmmakers to keep control of their movies.*

The matter of control hovers over everything that happens in the Motion Picture Industry, who has it, how to get it, how it's used, when to fight for it and how to co-exist with it. Events in the last week have crystallized the issue of control both at the box office and what happened (or didn't happen) at the Toronto Film Festival. The economics in the industry for both the biggest and smallest players has been changing for some time now due to the recession, evolving market trends and new technology, so it's helpful to take a closer look at what happened in the last week to figure out how the various players are managing those changes. First the studios: The studios are managing very well for themselves and have decades of experience, in good times and bad, of being in power and being in control of their own destinies. It was very telling when three different studios spun similar storylines after their movies all opened rather softly on the weekend of September 18, Warner Bros. with "The Informant," Universal with "Love Happens" and Fox with "Jennifer's Body." Each were proclaiming positive results and predicting profitable outcomes for their movies despite the mundane grosses. Take a look at the results:

- ▶ The Informant: Production cost - $22 million: Opening weekend gross - $10 million
- ▶ Love Happens: Production cost - $18 million: Opening weekend gross - $8.5 million
- ▶ Jennifer's Body: Production cost - $16 million: Opening weekend gross - $6.5 million

It's always suspect when a studio proclaims that they are happy with a weekend gross that is under $10 million because anything under that figure is usually a disaster. But outside of their very expensive blockbusters that are made for a wide global audience, the studios are showing better fiscal restraint with the more modest movies that fill out their release schedules. In fact, they are using the economic downturn to their advantage by keeping their production costs down, taking on partners to lower their risk and getting stars to take lower salaries as Universal did with Jennifer Aniston on "Love Happens." Universal is having an off year but was confident enough following the weekend to proclaim "Love Happens" already profitable because their exposure was covered by foreign pre-sales. The studios remain firmly in control of their businesses. Fewer movies being made and tough economic times have increased their leverage with the stars, especially in a year where concept and story are trumping star power at the box office. Weekend box office numbers often don't tell the whole story, especially in a month like September when lower grosses can still lead to profits by containing costs and allowing others to share the risk.

Speaking of control, the most interesting storyline this coming weekend is the return of MGM as both a producer and distributor with a remake of their 1980 hit movie "Fame." Their film distribution operation has been dormant all year; for the last couple of years they had been distributing movies from outside companies like the Weinstein Company, which took advantage of MGM's existing pay television deal with Showtime. MGM is once again attempting to reinvent itself and become relevant again by going back into production. This is a company that hasn't been in control of their own destiny in quite some time, and quite frankly, it's surprising to see them still out there fighting. MGM was once the largest most successful Hollywood studio, but that was some 50 years ago. In the last 40 years, the studio has been sold too many times to count, picked apart for its famed library and other assets and left to wither away time and time again by the likes of Kirk Kerkorian, (several times) Ted Turner in the mid-'80s, Italian financiers in the early '90s who landed up going bankrupt, and a consortium led by Sony Pictures several years ago. Their independence from the Sony deal was improbable to say the least and came with a lot of financial baggage. MGM is saddled with $3.5 billion in debt, the company has about 150 lenders, the CEO has recently been ousted, and a turnaround specialist has been hired to figure it all out and try to keep MGM out of bankruptcy. "Fame" will be their only release of 2009, and it could have a respectable showing at the box office, but MGM will need much more than that to become a significant industry player again. Several movies are on their 2010 release schedule, including a February movie called "The Hot Tub Time Machine," a steep fall from its glory days of "Wizard of Oz," Grand Hotel," "Ben-Hur" and Doctor Zhivago." It would look a lot better if they still controlled their library classics with this week's 70th anniversary of "Wizard of Oz" and all the hoopla involved with the one-day theatre showings in 400 cities and the newly restored high-def DVD and Blu-ray editions hitting the stores. But those rights were bought by Ted Turner 25 years ago and later absorbed by Warner Bros., so Warner Home Video is in control of the rights, the release and all the subsequent profits.

Living down to its low expectations, market activity at the Toronto Film Festival was dismal. Out of the 130 movies up for sale, only a couple of deals were completed. More than ever, it's an undeniable fact that filmmakers and their investors who make movies with no guarantee of distribution, are partaking in a total crapshoot of wish fulfillment if they are counting on receiving a traditional all-rights deal from an established distributor. It doesn't seem to matter if the movie has fantastic production values, has a great script, has critical support, tells a compelling story and even has some name actors attached; it's still left to the whims and pocketbooks of the distributors, and right now they're not buying much of anything. The buyers have all the control, and the sellers have very little. The high stakes poker type deals this decade that led to bidding wars at festivals is officially over for now. Festival deal making is harkening back to the mid-'90s when most deals happened weeks and months after festivals instead of during them. That was what happened at the 1994 Sundance Film Festival when I was one of the producer's reps for "Hoop Dreams." "Hoop Dreams" had a slow build up of interest during the ten-day fest and won the Audience Award on the last day, but it took another month of negotiations with interested parties to finally complete the deal with eventual distributor Fine Line Features. There will be more deals made for some of the Toronto films, but it will be for lesser amounts than hoped for and based more on the distributors' terms than on the sales agents' asking prices. That's not the scenario in which top talent agencies like William Morris and Creative Artists became involved in representing films in the first place. They live for the action, the bidding wars, so it will be interesting to see how long they stay with selling films in this climate. When top independent films today can easily cost in the ten to fifteen million-dollar range, it makes for a pretty tough negotiation and sale. Whereas a sales rep may be looking in the area of a $5 million advance and a $5 million print and advertising commitment, a distributor would be staring at $10 million in spending before the movie even opens. With so many independent films grossing less than $5 million this year, that kind of risk is too much to stomach.

Despite the tough sales market, some independent film mavens and consultants are cheering on and championing the arrival of hybrid distribution, a new state-of-the-art business model where filmmakers maintain control of their own movies by splitting up the various rights and selling them off separately. Instead of an all-rights deal with one distributor which can tie up rights for 15 to 20 years, filmmakers look to sell specific rights like Video-on-Demand, DVD rights and digital download to distribution partners who can handle those rights well. This type of deal will be become more common in future years, but for now it's best suited for lower budget films that don't have much to recoup. There wouldn't have been 130 films at Toronto willing and able to sell their movies to one distributor for all rights if that type of deal was so bad to begin with. What forces filmmakers to consider alternatives is when there are either no traditional offers on the table or when distributors lowball filmmakers with little or no front money but still want to control the film's rights for an extended number of years. If that doesn't seem fair, well, it isn't, but it's also a lot to ask of a filmmaker to steer his or her film in its commercial release. Filmmakers make movies. Distributors distribute them. The same consultants who are heralding the hybrid deal also warn filmmakers it's important to hire a distribution team made up of the following professionals to help make all this happen:

- A producer's rep
- Foreign sales agent
- Webmaster
- A publicist
- Theatrical booking agent
- Outreach coordinator
- Online aggregator
- Print fulfillment company

The big problem with any type of self-distribution is that many filmmakers are broke after they complete their films. What's lost in the translation in this new hybrid type deal is how much it's going to cost filmmakers to keep control of their movies and the time and effort it will take to generate revenues. Nothing is easy right now, and it would be best for filmmakers to keep their eyes wide open, watch out for any potholes on the road to the new hybrid deals and figure out in advance how much keeping control of their movies will actually cost. Going out and having to raise additional funds can be a costly and painful experience, especially since there are no guarantees that any future revenues will be able to pay for those extra costs, much less the cost of the production itself.

This Week at the Box Office: *Weekly Attendance: 16,460,320*

After detailing how many September films have modest production costs that don't require huge grosses to recoup their expenses, this weekend brought Disney's "Surrogates" starring Bruce Willis with a reported budget of $80 million. The disappointing performance of the film, especially its domestic gross, played a part in Disney's decision to change course and go only with branded entertainment in the future. "Pandorum" is yet another horror film to underachieve in the last few weeks following "Sorority Row" and "Jennifer's Body," proving once again the modestly budgeted horror film is the most overworked genre in Hollywood, and October hasn't even arrived yet. Two films which have begun with very limited runs, "Paranormal Activity" and "Capitalism: A Love Story" will be discussed in full in the coming weeks.

Paranormal Activity
Paramount
Opening weekend: $77,873
Domestic gross: $107,918,810 55.8%
Foreign gross: $85,436,990 44.2%
Worldwide gross: $193,355,800
Widest release: 2,712 theatres

Surrogates
Disney
Opening weekend: $14,902,692
Domestic gross: $38,517,772 31.5%
Foreign gross: $83,867,000 68.5%
Worldwide gross: $122,444,772
Widest release: 2,902 theatres

Fame
MGM
Opening weekend: $10,011,682
Domestic gross: $22,455,510 29.1%
Foreign gross: $54,756,326 70.9%
Worldwide gross: $77,211,836
Widest release: 3,133 theatres

Pandorum
Overture
Opening weekend: $4,424,126
Domestic gross: $10,330,853 50.0%
Foreign gross: $10,314,474 50.0%
Worldwide gross: $20,645,327
Widest release: 25,06 theatres

Capitalism: A Love Story

Overture

Opening weekend: $231,964

Domestic gross: $14,363,397 82.4%

Foreign gross: $3,073,112 17.6%

Worldwide gross: $17,436,509

Widest release: 995 theatres

I Hope they Serve Beer in Hell

Freestyle

Opening weekend: $366,909

Domestic gross: $1,429,299

Foreign gross: N/A

Widest release: 266 theatres

The Boys Are Back

Miramax

Opening weekend: $49,342

Domestic gross: $809,752 25%

Foreign gross: $2,424,953 75%

Worldwide gross: $3,421,953

Widest release: 2 theatres

Trailer Park Boys 2

Independent

Opening weekend: $1,396,229

Domestic gross: $2,944,096

Foreign gross: N/A

Widest release: 199 theatres

The Blue Tooth Virgin

Regent

Opening weekend: $1,926

Domestic gross: $2,762

Foreign gross: N/A

Widest release: 2 theatres

Coco Before Chanel

Sony Classics

Opening weekend: $177,339

Domestic gross: $6,113,834 12%

Foreign gross: $44,649,100 88%

Worldwide gross: $50,812,934

Widest release: 307 theatres

Brief Interviews with the Hideous Men

IFC

Opening weekend: $18,510

Domestic gross: $33,745

Foreign gross: N/A

Widest release: 2 theatres

What's Your Rashee?

UTV

Opening weekend: $169,005

Domestic gross: $257,413 81.9%

Foreign gross: $57,013 18.1%

Worldwide gross: $314,881

Widest release: 78 theatres

Blind Date

Variance

Opening weekend: $2,787

Domestic gross: $8,449

Foreign gross: N/A

Widest release: 1 theatre

Conversations with Industry Professionals

Richard Abramowitz – Independent Film Distributor – President of Abramorama Films, New York

This interview took place on August 17, 2011.

> *"If you start thinking about your audience, you've already adjusted your vision, but on the other hand, you're not painting watercolors in your attic."*
>
> *Richard Abramowitz*

Q: *How many years have you worked in the film business, and can you tell me about your current company?*

RA: I started in 1981 with United Artists, which quickly became MGM/UA after the two companies merged. I worked the college sales in the non-theatrical division of the company until 1983 when I left to go work for the independent distributor Cinecom, which lasted until 1991. I then set up RKO Distribution for a couple of years until I went out on my own producing and consulting with New York distributors. From 1997 to 2000 I ran a distribution company, Stratosphere, for Carl Ichon, and from that point on I was back out on my own. Today I distribute films through two companies, Abramorama Films and Area 23A, in addition to consulting and service deals with outside producers and filmmakers where I do the work for them. I collect fees for my services based on the amount of work a particular project needs. There are a lot of films looking for help, so I stay pretty busy most of the time.

Q: *I would say 30 years qualifies you as a lifer in the independent film business.*

RA: No doubt about it. I don't think I have any other transferable skills.

Q: *Are you a one-man operation?*

RA: I have a home office with one employee and a network of specialists who I can call on at any time. I have a designer, a field publicist, a couple of different bookers I use on larger releases. I have a lot of flexibility and function as a contractor with a series of subcontractors.

Q: *How many films do you see in the average month while looking for films to get involved in?*

RA: There are times I watch two a day, and there are times when I don't watch any in a month. That's when I'm consumed with distributing a film and giving all my energies to that given film. At any given time, there are 10 to 20 screeners in my office just waiting for me to find the time to watch them.

Q: *Are there the same number of films being made today as in years past, and where are all they coming from?*

RA: Technology affords a lot more access for a lot less money than it used to, so that means anyone can make a film, not that everyone should make a film, but everyone can make a film. Because of the economy of digital filmmaking and the access to high-quality equipment, it doesn't really cost much to make a movie anymore. The filmmakers today are doing it on their own with their own savings or family assistance, so there is a constant stream of ultra low-budget films trying to get attention. It's not like it used to be when you had to max out your credit cards to do something. The truth is all the money in the world won't necessarily make a good movie, or the lack of financial resources doesn't dictate that you are going to have a bad movie. It comes down to talent. More money does give someone additional flexibility if they have to reshoot a scene or use multiple locations, but you don't need a ton of money to make a good film if you have the talent.

Q: *Were you at the Sundance Film Festival in 2009?*

RA: That's the one year in the last twenty that I wasn't able to go because I was producing an inaugural gala for the Creative Coalition organization.

Q: *What do you remember from that year as it began in regards to the condition of the independent film business? Was it as dire as some industry insiders were saying it was?*

RA: It was bad out there with distributors dropping like flies; perhaps half of the meaningful distributors were going out of business, but I have a totally different perspective on what was happening due to the nature of my business. When companies were going out of business, that meant a couple of things. There were fewer options for filmmakers, and because there were fewer options, there was less competition for each picture. The deals that were being offered to producers for completed films weren't as enticing as in previous years. Let's say a movie cost two million to make; instead of getting an offer for a million or a million and a half, they would only get one for $250,000 for all rights in North America for 15 to 20 years or something similar to that. So if they're two million into it, and they get an offer for $250,000, they can look around and see what alternatives are out there. If they can raise an additional $250,000 for prints and advertising funds, they can hire someone like my company, Abramorama, to distribute their film, and they can actively participate in its release. They also can see accelerated payments because my company can pay them weekly as receipts come in and not have to wait for quarterly payments. We can segregate the rights and make deals with Netflix (which was possible at the time), I-Tunes, a DVD company. We can make those deals at a lower fee than what a larger distributor would take, and suddenly this type of deal looks more attractive even though the producers have to dig deeper for more cash to get the ball rolling. At the risk of sounding like I'm dancing on the graves of my friends and colleagues, when it got bad at large it got better for me.

Q: *Let me ask you about a couple of films you distributed in 2009 through Abramorama, "We Live in Public" and "Anvil: The Story of Anvil." "We Live in Public" won the Grand Jury Prize: Documentary at Sundance, and the reported box office gross was $42,000. Can you talk about the performance of that film and its modest gross?*

RA: Let me rephrase the context with you. To suggest that "We Live in Public" didn't do well is not to understand what the agenda was. That was an Oscar-qualifying run. I was hired to make that film eligible for the Academy Awards, and for a documentary that meant opening it in New York and Los Angeles according to the Academy's regulations. The producers had an investor who put up $40,000 for the marketing, and I booked the theatres and handled the limited distribution. This is the business I'm in. Producers put up the money for prints and advertising, and I'm hired in a service arrangement.

Q: *The point you make about not rushing to judgment on a film based on just the gross is an important one. You're saying each film has its own agenda, which most people often aren't aware of.*

RA: That's correct. With this film that's all the producers were looking for. There wasn't much money available for any wider theatrical distribution, though I ended up opening 8 or 10 additional markets where it didn't cost much to open. It can't be termed as a disappointment because there were no commercial expectations to begin with. They got their qualifying runs, though it failed to receive an Oscar nomination for Best Documentary. The producers did have a DVD and a VOD deal set up, so no one expected any revenue from theatrical. In addition to becoming Oscar eligible, the limited theatrical exposure created attention and some very strong critics' reviews. From that context, the film was very successful.

Q: *Is having even a small theatrical run still as important for independent films as in years past?*

RA: When you ask if it's still important, important to what? Theatrical is still the place where you can get the most attention for a film and qualify for Oscars, so in that regard the importance remains the same as it ever was. But important to producing revenues and profits and good ancillary deals? That's up to each individual film, and the vagaries of the quality of the film and the needs of the marketplace at any given time.

Q: *"Anvil: The Story of Anvil" grossed over $600,000, which has to be considered a pretty good success for a documentary. Can you talk about that film?*

RA: Again, that was another case where we didn't spend that much money, but the success came from the huge amount of media coverage it received. I think the perception of that film was much greater than the action at the box office would indicate. There were over 100,000 DVDs shipped, which was a phenomenal number. The movie premiered on VH1, and the real level of success in my view was what happened to the band itself. That band was basically invisible for almost 25 years, and since that film came out, the band has not stopped touring the world.

Q: *The film kick-started their career again. I guess this is another example of a film's success stretching a lot further than merely it's theatrical performance?*

RA: Absolutely. They came back from oblivion, and they now tour nonstop.

Q: *Do you recall how much money was spent on prints and advertising to get that $600,000 gross? And in regards to prints, was that still mostly 35mm prints or a mixture of digital and film prints?*

RA: P&A was probably around $500,000 or a bit less than that. All the theatres that played the film were almost exclusively 35mm. Even though the largest circuit for art films, Landmark Theatres, has digital capacities in a lot of their theatres, they were still playing predominantly 35mm in 2009.

Q: *What kind of deals did you use when selling "Anvil" to theatre owners, and do you recall what the aggregate percentage was for all the engagements?*

RA: Generally I go in with open terms, and we settle the engagements after the results are in. It's a fair deal based on how a film performs and how long it plays. If a film plays a theatre for multiple weeks, the aggregate price is surely to go down; plus New York has a 25% floor, which can skew the percentages lower. In "Anvil's" case, we earned 90/10 in its early weeks and 25% in the later weeks in New York because it played in Manhattan for 16 weeks. For a film that had long engagements like "Anvil," it's fair to speculate the aggregate for all theatres combined probably came in between and 40% and 42%.

Q: *Manhattan has historically been the best market for art films but also the market that's most expensive to open and where the deals with theatres are the toughest. Doesn't that put a burden on small films with small marketing budgets?*

RA: Yes, it's expensive to open a film in New York, and bad reviews can kill an independent film very quickly. The key is being good enough to find an audience so you can enjoy an extended run. If a film can hold theatres after the advertising spending has ended, it can start netting money in the later weeks to recoup some of earlier money spent.

Q: It has always been tough to clear a profit just from theatrical, right? In "Anvil's" case, the profit obviously came in from the very successful DVD release.

RA: It often comes down to how much money is spent to get that gross. Frankly, if I had more control over the marketing campaign, I would have spent less. One of the characteristics of the work I do is the collaboration I have with the producers because generally it's their money, so the final determination of how that money is spent is not mine. If I say I don't want to spend $10,000 on radio in Portland, but if they say they do, then I spend it. I would have spent a little less money, but it's their money, and I try to do the best I can with it.

Q: I saw where "Anvil" grossed $200,000 in foreign territories. Were you involved with foreign?

RA: No, I wasn't. I just stick to the domestic market.

Q: What are the top cities for independent films?

RA: New York, Boston, Chicago, Seattle, San Francisco. I reluctantly include Los Angeles because it isn't a particularly strong market for independents, but roughly speaking it's better than a lot of others. You can look at where Landmark has theatres; Minneapolis is a good market, Phoenix is very good. If you have a film for older audiences, Florida can be very strong. When you consider theatres and different markets you have to include not-for-profit theatres and film societies because they supply the backbone for independent films outside the large urban markets. There are dozens of these theatres around the country, which do real well and have loyal customers and large mailing lists. Without them, that's half your specialized gross for a lot of independent films. We can pick up a lot of money in these situations because there is little or no expense involved. They have strong programming with a steady and dependable customer base cultivated over many years. They do quite well.

Q: Would you agree with the statement that art audiences don't do independent films any favors by waiting for Netflix to see a film instead of paying to see the film in a theatre?

RA: Well, Netflix can make substantial contributions to producers, and I don't think people who go to theatres and people who use Netflix are totally exclusive from each other. There is a lot of overlap. People who go to theatres go to be part of the experience, and it's our jobs as distributors and marketers to present a compelling argument to moviegoers to go see movies in theatres rather than sit home and wait for them. I started this company a couple of years ago called Area 23A, and the idea behind it is to create an experience that you can't have on a flat screen in your living room or a lap top in your dorm room. What we do is structure movie events. It might be a lecture, a panel discussion, a party, in the case of "Anvil" it was live performances. We've done quite well with music films. We toured "Anvil" with the movie; after the movie finished and the lights came up, the band started to play, and it was a euphoric experience for everyone involved. It wasn't just that the performance was enjoyable but it created word of mouth for the rest of the run, and because of social media, it spread out throughout the country and created buzz for future engagements. The movies that work best in this area are social issue films, music films, films that start off with a strong audience base.

Q: It sounds like you've created a great niche business. Let me get back to Netflix. You made a statement about "when you could sell directly to Netflix and how Netflix makes substantial contributions to producers." Can you go more in detail about what kind of deals Netflix can do for an independent film?

RA: Netflix now offers flat fees for films. It could be $30,000 or $50,000 or $250,000 or higher; it depends on the movie, it's gross, whether it has name actors in it, critics' reviews, awards, those types of considerations.

Q: *I didn't know Netflix had moved from buying a set number of DVD units from a distributor to offering flat fees like a broadcaster. That's a big change in their policy.*

RA: Netflix subscribers are movie lovers; that's how they got started. Netflix is transitioning now and becoming more like a pay cable service, but one of the things that drove that the company in the first place was the depth of their catalogue, so they will always be interested in acquiring all types of films including the smaller art films. For that one flat price, that includes all streaming rights, which is becoming more and more important for Netflix.

Q: *Correct me if I'm wrong. A filmmaker can't sell a film directly to Netflix; it has to go through an established distributor?*

RA: That's correct. I'm a service distributor, but I don't have a deal with Netflix at this time, but I think it will happen in the not too distant future. Netflix has assigned aggregating powers to a variety of different companies, so it's important for me to have an agreement with them. I have a relationship with a lot of different DVD companies, and it would enable me to provide access to them for my clients and make those types of home video deals in addition to the theatrical work I do.

Q: *What does it take for an independent film to get a television deal these days?*

RA: It's very hard to get any kind of television deal now, but that loss is being minimized with the growing streaming business, which is starting to generate more money to the independents than what the cable companies were willing to pay. The Sundance channel and IFC channel used to be two different outlets which would be potential buyers for independent films, and now they are a part of the same company, so that situation is not as good as it used to be. It's not like they could be depended to buy a lot of new films anyway, but it was better when they were totally separate from each other. There are only so many available slots, and all cable channels produce more of their own original programming these days. Most of the cable channels have their own niches, and if your film is geared to a specific niche audience as "Anvil" was as a classic hard-rock film, a station like VH1 would more likely be interested in acquiring it.

Q: *There is a lot of talk about Video-on-Demand becoming an important revenue source, but how can that be depended on when it's so difficult to judge the potential of it or to get any reliable numbers on specific movies?*

RA: It's hard to project what VOD is going to become because there is so much mystery surrounding it. Speaking to some of my friends who have had films involved with VOD, they tell me certain genre movies can do very well, and I think there has been some success with going out day and date with theatrical and VOD. But getting any numbers publicized is not something that any company seems to be willing to go public with.

Q: *That has to be worrisome for both filmmakers and distributors. Why the big secret? Where's the money? How much money is coming in? How many hands are touching it? With the large cable companies, it's a tough situation when you have no idea of what to expect.*

RA: I'm not going to disagree with that argument.

Q: *There has been so much written on the new hybrid deal where a filmmaker keeps control of his film by making separate deals with theatrical, DVD, VOD, Internet rights, etc. Very little is talked about on what the price of maintaining that control costs? Can't if get very expensive to hire many different specialists to do the work?*

RA: Yes, I've been telling filmmakers for 20 years that when you raise your money to make the film, also raise additional funds for P&A. Any responsible investor would respect that. You may not have to use it, but it provides you with an option. That message seems to be sinking in as more filmmakers are doing just that, which makes these hybrid deals possible. They know they have to have some extra money put on the side when a traditional distribution deal is not in the cards.

Q: *That's good to hear that independent producers recognize this sea change. Do you see any difference in the independent business in general in the last couple of years? Is it on firmer ground?*

RA: This business has never been easy. In the mid-'80s the debate was do we release the film this weekend when there are three or four films opening or the following week when there are three or four films opening. You used to be able to avoid direct competition for the demographic you were trying to reach. Now there are always eight to fifteen movies opening in New York and Los Angeles on any given week, so you can't do that anymore. Not that many films ever open in other cities, but distributors have to deal with this weekly glut when they launch their films, so in that regard not much has changed since 2009 when it comes to the number of movies still hitting the marketplace.

Q: *It seems like there is a big change going on in 2011 with many theatre complexes switching all their screens to digital and getting rid of 35mm. Is that starting to affect your way of doing business?*

RA: The change to digital has been staggering. I have a particularly acute sense of outrage at this because when theatres utilize the virtual print deals with the equipment companies and studios, they are basically retrofitting their theatres on all the distributors' backs, including small ones like mine which were not part of those deals where the studios agreed to help subsidize the theatres' huge expense of purchasing digital projectors. The big difference is that every time I move a digital print to a participating theatre with a VPD agreement, I'm charged an $850 licensing fee by the equipment company to be on the new screen in addition to a $150 shipping charge to ship the digital drive. The cost of theatrical distribution has skyrocketed in this regard. For me, I'm used to having between five and fifty prints and moving them around the county from theatre to theatre. On "Exit in a Gift Shop," there were no digital prints, just 35mm, and there were probably 250 to 350 engagements on that film. I did that with 50 prints where shipping charges were between $40 and $150 depending on the situation. Imagine if they were all DCPs (digital cinema package) with virtual print deals and I had 300 engagements. That would add over $200,000 in distribution and shipping costs to my bottom line. On service deals, that's significant additional money filmmakers have to absorb.

Q: *With those extra fees, do you have to look more closely at what kind of digital setup a theatre has and whether or not they can earn enough film rental to warrant a print?*

RA: Definitely. Getting minimum guarantees sometimes is the answer to insure you don't lose any money on the engagement. I try to do business with people who will honor their commitments and avoid those who I don't trust. In that way, it's the same as it has always been. A bad pay is a bad pay whether it's digital or not. There are still exhibitors who don't pay and I don't deal with them anymore. Some of them are bad people. The majority are great people to work with, and then there are the scumbags. Slow pay is one thing; we all understand cash flow problems. It's when a guy pays 18 months later, and I tell the producer it's been taken care of, and he tells me the check bounced. I thought it was covered, and I find out I'm still owed $4,000.

Q: *When the smaller theatres you service don't have a virtual print deal arrangement, I imagine it's a much better situation for you.*

RA: Yes it is. When I play with the theatres under the Emerging Pictures circuit there is an initial cost of $1,000 to transfer a film to their hard drive, and thereafter there is no additional cost, which works out great. Then there are the smaller theatres that are playing Blu-ray, and that's a big savings for us. It hardly costs anything to make a copy and almost nothing to ship them. Moving forward, it's getting more complicated very quickly.

Q: *What are a couple more lessons or fundamentals you have learned over the years?*

RA: From my perspective in the theatrical world, the essentials still apply. You have to have a film where you can define an audience and determine an effective and cost efficient way of bringing the film to that audience. The basics haven't changed. What has changed is how you go about it, and new tools like social media can play a big part of the marketing mix if used properly, and you can get like-minded audiences spreading the word for you. I teach, and the conversation I have all the time with my students is if you start thinking about your audience, you've already adjusted your vision, but on the other hand you're not painting watercolors in your attic. If you want people to see your movie, you want to figure out in advance how you are going to appeal to them, understand who they are and how you are going to reach them. It doesn't mean that you have to adjust your vision to accommodate them, but I work in the commercial film business. Even though it is the art film business, it still is a commercial enterprise. My job is to get people into the theatre and in effect monetize the creation of the artist. It's not for me to tell a filmmaker how to make his movie. It's for me to come in and say this is the movie you made, this is who I believe your audience is and who we can appeal to and get inside a theatre. When I produce a movie it's a different dynamic, but when I'm a distributor I'm there to maximize the commercial viability of a film. If I ask filmmakers who their audience is and they say they don't know, I tell them you might want to begin thinking about that. If there is an economic equation involved, than an essential part of that equation is where the ultimate revenue is coming from. And if you don't know who your audience is, it may be helpful to define that so that you can understand what your vision is. I see movies that are made for a family audience that have profanity in them. Now that doesn't show much foresight and consciousness of the audience.

Q: *What keeps you in the game? You've been at this a long time.*

RA - What keeps me in the game is I wouldn't know what else to do. This is what I've always done. I was an usher in a movie theatre [during] high school. I managed a theatre in college. I transferred where I was studying Spanish and Archeology at a state school to the Film Department because the best teacher I had was a film teacher. I transferred to the NYU film school, and while I was there I was a manager of a movie theatre, and I worked at a Film Center where I cleaned and organized their 16mm film library. I graduated from that and then I went right into the film business. What the hell else can I do other than be a bartender?

Q: *Thank you for your time and insight.*

RA: Thank you.

Week 39: Questions for Discussion

1. Even though 2009 was a dreadful year for independent films, in what ways did it benefit an independent distributor like Richard Abramowitz?

2. Explain what a hybrid distribution deal is and how it's different from a traditional deal with an established distributor.

3. What do you feel is the biggest advantage and biggest disadvantage for filmmakers as they look for distribution in this changed climate?

4. Why is the domestic gross for a small film not always a good indicator of whether or not a film could be labeled a success? What are other considerations that play a part in this equation? In your opinion, if you were ever involved with a feature-length film, what would constitute success for that film?

5. How has the exhibitor switch to digital screens made theatrical distribution more complex for small distributors and filmmakers alike? Explain why moving prints from theatre to theatre has become more expensive?

CAPITALISM: THE BEDROCK OF THE MOTION PICTURE INDUSTRY AND MICHAEL MOORE'S CAREER

Week 40: October 2–8, 2009

Just because Moore is calling capitalism evil doesn't mean he won't be monitoring all the box office numbers over the weekend and adding up the grosses as they come in.

As we enter the month of October, the finishing line to the 2009 movie season can start to be seen in the distance. Friday, October 2nd starts the 40th week of the year, twelve weeks to go, the crucial final quarter, which will determine whether this year will be one for the record books. Ticket sales have just passed a billion admissions, and year-to-date revenues are still running 7% over last year. From the start of January the entire year has shown tremendous resiliency and strength in the midst of a soft economy and high unemployment. Talk of fewer movies for the rest of the year hasn't materialized yet with five more movies hitting the screens on wide national breaks. Picking a storyline this week among the openers was easy. Michael Moore's "Capitalism: A Love Story" is the one to focus on.

The American Film Industry from its very beginning at the start of the 20th century has celebrated and embraced the idea of capitalism. The Eastern European Jewish immigrants, who were the first movie moguls and basically built the movie industry from scratch, seized the opportunity through their hard work, talent, passion and drive to make themselves rich and successful while creating and shaping the film industry we know today. America is not Europe or any other socialist country that helps subsidize their local film industries. The American Film Industry has always had only one primary goal, to make the highest profits through the production, distribution and exhibition of films. About 100 years later, Michael Moore is following in the footsteps of the first moguls and has forged a very successful and lucrative career making movies. The free enterprise system has served him well.

With that being said, I'm not here to knock Michael Moore and call him a hypocrite for attacking capitalism in his latest film or saying it should be replaced. We have come to expect contradictions involving Moore's films, and that's why he elicits such passionate responses in people, both positive and negative. That's also one of the reasons for his success. The worst thing for any artist or entertainer is to be ignored. Michael Moore doesn't have to worry about that. Just because he's calling capitalism evil doesn't mean he won't be monitoring all the box office numbers over the weekend and adding up the grosses as they come in. The opening weekend gross will be as important for him as it is for Sony with "Zombieland." For better or for worse that's the way success is measured in the film business today. Looking at who is distributing "Capitalism" is also a head scratcher. Overture Films is a division of Liberty Media and is owned by John Malone, a staunch conservative who has run into problems in the past for his Wall Street dealings and has amassed some fines for questionable activities he's allegedly been involved with. Nevertheless, love him or hate him, Moore is the only filmmaker, fiction or non-fiction, who makes timely, controversial political/economic films on a regular basis for a mainstream audience. For that we should be thankful. All anyone has to do is to take a close look at the movies playing at the typical suburban multiplex this weekend:

- ► Zombieland
- ► Fame
- ► Surrogates
- ► Pandorum
- ► Capitalism: A Love Story

- ▶ Whip It
- ▶ Love Happens
- ▶ Jennifer's Body
- ▶ The Invention of Lying
- ▶ Sorority Row
- ▶ Cloudy with a Chance of Meatballs
- ▶ The Informant
- ▶ Toy Story 1 & 2 combo in 3D

Michael Moore brings a dose of reality to the big screen, some real bite that stands out from the clutter of studio releases. In economics that's referred to as a distinct advantage. For what he does, he has no competition on a national basis. Other wide releases have no interest in tackling the important issues of our time, and the documentaries that have confronted similar subject matter in the last few years are relegated to opening in a couple of art houses, and thus most moviegoers never hear of them. Last weekend "Capitalism: A Love Story" opened in four theatres in New York and Los Angeles and averaged $57,991 per theatre, a tremendous debut. Does that insure a great weekend coming up when the movie widens out to close to 1,000 theatres? Not necessarily, but opening in that many theatres puts his film on a national stage, and that's no small feat. In a free enterprise system the cream rises to the top, and supply and demand for any product works itself out. Moore has helped create demand for his movies, and he deserves all the credit in the world for that. His career started 20 years ago with "Roger and Me," and over the years he has become his own brand, not an easy thing for a documentary filmmaker to accomplish. He is simply a great promoter, and marketing is a large part of his arsenal. Over the last two weeks he has been everywhere on television from *Jay Leno* to *Larry King* to *The View* to Bill *Maher* on HBO, night after night selling his movie and his message on mainstream outlets. Where some would call him a showman, others would call him a grandstander. He's a populist, able to combine humor with tough facts and commentary, and his ability to make his documentaries entertaining while working tirelessly to promote them is the key to his success in the theatrical marketplace.

In the niche world we live in, you can say the majority of movies preach to the converted.

Moore's critics have said "he's preaching to the converted" used in a dismissive fashion as if that automatically makes an effort less than successful. There is another way to look at that when thinking about marketing movies or really marketing any kind of art or entertainment. In the niche world we live in, you can say the majority of movies preach to the converted; they have a target audience and go after it and count on that base to show up and support it. Whether it's Tyler Perry, horror movies, upscale dramas, teen comedies or female romances, specific audiences are enough to turn a film into a profitable success, especially when the budget is reasonable in relation to its commercial potential. If you are able to motivate your core audience and at the same time be able to attract a percentage of people outside the core, a film is in good shape. "Capitalism" will no doubt attract mostly a liberal audience, but it should also get the curious and even some conservatives to check it out too. There aren't too many "Titanic's" anymore that reach out and attract everyone. The real problem for many independent films is that they fail to attract even their niche audience, or worse yet, they failed to even identify who their audience could be and thus are doomed from the start. Michael Moore doesn't have to worry about that. He has built a dedicated audience who he can count on to show up for his films.

The budget and financing for "Capitalism: A Love Story" has been pretty secretive, and I don't know if that's because of the film's subject matter or not. Since he's attacking capitalism, perhaps he has been extra sensitive about the money part and would prefer to not have the movie's financial information become part of the dialogue. When you come down to it, a film's budget is nobody's business except for the filmmakers, the financiers, the accountants and the distributor. Revealing budgets are tricky and can be part of the strategy of whether to reveal it or not or even to float a misleading figure that's higher or lower than it actually is. What serves a film the best in terms of whether to float a film's production budget or not is another one of those crucial decisions producers and filmmakers make. It used to be in the independent world it was a badge of honor to reveal how low a film's budget was, but nowadays that can be labeled as too low budget and small to distribute and not worthy of even a small advance. It almost became a cliché at film festival Q & As when filmmakers would say their films cost "a little less than a million." Sometimes it's best to keep them guessing. If I had to guess Moore's budget, it probably falls in the area between $10 and $15 million. It was a very long 16-month production schedule, a lot of people worked on it, and there was extensive traveling involved and many music rights and other copyrighted material to clear. In regards to financing, there are three companies over the title, Overture, Paramount Vantage and Weinstein, so no doubt the financing came from several sources. Michael Moore does not have trouble raising financing. The bottom line is his movies make money. Worldwide, his movies are popular with foreign audiences, and that just seals the deal for him even more.

This Week at the Box Office: *Weekly Attendance: 18,120,929*

With five movies either opening wide or going wide this weekend, there may be something for everyone playing at their local theatre. Sony has the horror spoof "Zombieland" for young males, Warner Bros. has the comedy "Invention of Lying" for couples and mainstream audiences, Disney is bringing back "Toy Story and "Toy Story 2" as a double feature in 3D for families, Fox Searchlight has "Whip It" for the female audience, and then there is "Capitalism: A Love Story." This is a weekend in which the two most interesting releases come from independents, Moore's film and Fox Searchlight's "Whip It," a coming of age woman's roller derby movie directed by Drew Barrymore, her first time behind the camera. As I've chronicled all year, it has been a tough year for independents as only one release has been able to gross $30 million, and that also came from Searchlight, "(500) Days of Summer." Buzz has been building with "Whip It." Sneak previews were held last weekend, and the girl power, sisterhood and female empowerment themes are firing up the young female audience. Perhaps the biggest thing it has going for it is having Fox Searchlight as its distributor because no company is better at marketing this type of film, and they have an exciting colorful campaign underway. This is no disrespect for the movie itself, Drew Barrymore, the roller derby subject matter or any of the actors, who includes Ellen Page from "Juno" fame. What it points out to is the absolute importance of having the right distributor for the right film, and having that distributor passionate and skillful enough to totally get behind it and to be able to create a marketing and distribution campaign to take it as high as it can go. In an off year for independents, we could be seeing the two biggest independent movies of the year opening wide on the same weekend.

Zombieland

Sony
Opening weekend: $24,733,155
Domestic gross: $75,590,286 73.8%
Foreign gross: $26,801,254 26.2%
Worldwide gross: $102,391,540
Widest release: 3,171 theatres

Invention of Lying

Warner Brothers
Opening weekend: $7,027,472
Domestic gross: $18,451,251 56.95
Foreign gross: $13,955,256 43.1%
Worldwide gross: $32,406,507
Widest release: 1,743 theatres

Toy Story Combo 3D

Disney
Opening weekend: $12,491,789
Domestic gross: $30,702,446 95.1%
Foreign gross: $1,582,154 4.9%
Worldwide gross: $32,284,600
Widest release: 1,752 theatres

Whip It

Fox Searchlight
Opening weekend: $4,650,812
Domestic gross: $13,077,184 78.4%

A Serious Man

Focus
Opening weekend: $251,337
Domestic gross: $9,228,788 29.4%

More Than a Game

Lionsgate
Opening weekend: $182,943
Domestic gross: $950,675 99.0%

Foreign gross: $3,589,672 21.6%
Worldwide gross: $16,633,035
Widest release: 1,738 theatres

Foreign gross: $22,201,566 70.6%
Worldwide gross: $31,430,334
Widest release: 262 theatres

Foreign gross: $9,712 1.0%
Worldwide gross: $960,387
Widest release: 111 theatres

Wake Up Sid
UTV
Opening weekend: $355,532
Domestic gross: $718,766 16.8%
Foreign gross: $3,559,315 83.2%
Worldwide gross: $4,278,081
Widest release: 79 theatres

Do Knot Disturb
Reliance
Opening weekend: $124,591
Domestic gross: $213,525 90.5%
Foreign gross: $22,452 9.5%
Worldwide gross: $235,977
Widest release: 57 theatres

Afterschool
IFC
Opening weekend: $2,606
Domestic gross: $3,911
Foreign gross: N/A
Widest release: 1 theatre

Chelsea on the Rocks
Independent
Opening weekend: $4,286
Domestic gross: $11,799 77.9%
Foreign gross: $3,349 22.1%
Worldwide gross: $15,148
Widest release: 3 theatres

Fallen Idol: The Yuri Gagarin Conspiracy
Indican
Opening weekend: $2,546
Domestic gross: $14,471
Foreign gross: N/A
Widest release: 2 theatres

Week 40: Questions for Discussion

1. Define the term "preaching to the converted" in the world of marketing. Does this limit your audience if this is all a marketer attempts to do?

2. Do you feel there is a commercial paying audience for every film? Discuss. If you said there isn't, what are the implications involved in this dynamic, and how should independent filmmakers approach this potential reality?

3. Should a filmmaker attempt to make a feature film without first knowing who would be interested in seeing it?

AN EVENTFUL WEEK OFF THE SCREEN IS A HARBINGER OF TROUBLE AHEAD

Week 41: October 9–15, 2009

_There simply is not a strong enough alternative at this time to
match the dollars that Walmart and other retailers have produced
for the studios by directly selling DVDs to their customers._

The weekly box office is only one barometer of the industry's health. Though it's certainly important as a bellwether of the continued strength of the theatrical marketplace, the decisions made off the screen, inside the boardrooms of the distributors and exhibitors, the buyers and sellers, the retailers and media outlets, dictate the direction of where the business is today and where it is headed in the coming years. Looking over the events of the past week point to some rocky days ahead for both the studios and independents. Over the past 15 years or so, a solid foundation had been built based on the growing success in the independent sector, the studios' involvement with them, and DVDs as the guaranteed revenue generator where the actual film profits kicked in. That foundation has been showing serious cracks.

First, in a move that many in the industry could see coming, Disney has all but thrown in the towel on their Miramax division. Miramax has been awfully quiet this year while producing no hits, and their latest film, "The Boys Are Back," starring Clive Owen, just opened to very mediocre business. Disney announced Miramax will be down to three films a year, the staff has been cut to 20 employees, and the studio will now take over its marketing and distribution duties. With those kinds of marching orders, what's the purpose of even keeping it a going concern? To put it in proper perspective, when Harvey Weinstein ran Miramax under Michael Eisner, the company had 500 employees. Specialty films aren't performing like they used to, and it's just another indication that the studios are abandoning the independent business, joining Warner Bros. and Paramount, which in the past 18 months have discarded their own specialty divisions. In another boardroom across town, Universal's terrible year has led to the firing of the two co-heads of production. The new replacement wasted no time in announcing the company will focus on "reasonable risks" in choosing what movies to produce, implying there will be fewer adult dramas like "State of Play" and "Public Enemies" and more cookie cutter branded entertainment for families and kids. The deals Universal has made recently with toy companies provide a glimpse of what to expect from the studio in coming years, movies based on the board games "Battleship," "Monopoly," "Candyland" and other properties. Taken together, the news from Disney and Universal presents a sobering reality for lovers of character-driven quality films. There will be fewer of them down the road. With several companies like Comcast kicking the tires of NBC Universal as possible suitors, its parent company General Electric might have had enough with their entertainment division and may be looking to get out. There have been a minimum of six major studios in Hollywood for over 80 years, but it's possible that number could shrink in the next five to ten years as the media landscape and reliable distribution channels continue to experience seismic shifts. Who knows, another studio may even buy Universal.

Talk about seismic shifts, the other shoe dropped in a boardroom in Arkansas when Walmart announced they are cutting back on their DVD presence in their stores across the country, stating they will even do away with display cases used to promote the hot new titles. I have no idea if any of the studios saw this one coming, but that announcement coming in the fourth quarter ahead of the holiday season has had to send shock waves throughout Hollywood. The falling DVD business has been a major storyline all year, and Walmart is responding to the decline in consumer demand among their customers in buying DVDs with the same frequency they did in the past. Walmart is not totally abandoning the DVD business, but any contraction from them will have a significant effect on the bottom lines of all the studios since the company accounts for more than a third of all the retail DVDs sold in the country. Where can the studios pick up the slack from the revenues they will lose at Walmart? Rental revenues are up due to Blu-ray's growth and Redbox popularity, but rental revenue doesn't return the same kind of profit that sell-through does. There simply is not a strong enough alternative at this time to match the dollars that Walmart and other retailers have produced for the studios by directly selling DVDs to their customers. It has to really burn the studios to see Walmart allowing Redbox to put kiosks in front of their stores. Even though the connection between $1.00 rentals and declining DVD sales is still up for debate, everyone would agree the situation is not good. However, in many ways everything is connected. The recent decisions and change of direction made at Universal and Disney were not all caused by the problems in the DVD market, but certainly it has played a part.

Speaking of Redbox, 20th Century Fox is one of three studios that are being sued by Redbox, and last week Fox filed a motion to dismiss the suit. The following is part of what the court documents stated:

> "Antitrust law does not require a seller to provide its product through the distribution channel that the buyer demands, on the date that the buyer demands, or at the price that the buyer demands. To the contrary, sellers have considerable freedom under the law to sell (or not to sell) to whomever they want, how they want and when they want. To this end, a seller's distribution policies do not violate (antitrust law) unless the plaintiff proves a contract, combination or conspiracy that injures competition. Redbox cannot meet any of these elements."

20th Century Fox is stating what all film distributors know to be true. Distributors have a good amount of leeway on how and to whom they sell their movies to. Conspiracy of collusion certainly would be difficult prove since three studios have gone ahead and cut their own deals with the kiosk company. I believe the suit will either be dismissed or dropped, but the damage may have already been done. Will the studios that made their deals with Redbox to serve them on availability be proven to have misplayed their hands? Fox, along with Warner Bros. and Universal, never said they wouldn't sell to Redbox, they just wanted to delay it for 30 days or so. I've conducted my own survey with the people I know who rent movies from Redbox. Every single person said if they had to wait 30 days to rent the latest titles that would not be a problem for them, and they would rent them when they became available. Did the studios do any surveys on this issue?

Studios also can get lucky, and it sure looks like Paramount hit the jackpot with the independent horror sensation "Paranormal Activity," a movie they're distributing and widening out to 159 theatres this weekend following two weekends of sellout shows. The backstories of movies that seemingly come out of nowhere are usually fascinating, and the story behind "Paranormal Activity" is no exception. It's the stuff Hollywood dreams are made of, especially independent movies made on a reported shoestring budget of $15,000 like this one. The first question I had was why isn't an independent distributor involved in this? How can Paramount be distributing this tiny movie after they got rid of their own indie distribution division? It has been such a bad year for independents, and all the distributors are always on the lookout for the next big thing. This movie was made in 2006 by a video game designer named Oren Peli, and it has been kicking around film festivals and Hollywood looking for a distributor for three years. What happened? Did every independent distributor drop the ball and fail to see the movie's potential? This movie could be in the hands of an independent distributor, but it isn't, so it looks like a lot of acquisition executives may have missed out on what looks like a real sleeper hit. When the sales agent was peddling it around, the only interest came from someone at DreamWorks, where it eventually found its way to Steven Spielberg's desk. The story gets pretty unusual and funny from this point on. According to a Paramount spokesperson, Spielberg watched the movie at his home, became freaked out with it and thought his house was haunted when his bedroom door locked from the inside, and he had to call a locksmith to get it opened. He then reportedly called a messenger to take the screener back to the studio in a garbage bag, not wanting to touch the damn thing. Whether this actually happened or not, it made for a good publicity story. However, he was so impressed with the power of the film, his company bought the rights with the thought of possibly remaking it with a larger budget. When

DreamWorks later split from Paramount, the movie's rights, along with other movies, remained in Paramount's possession where they eventually decided to release the original film after having it tweaked a bit. Two weeks ago, Paramount opened it at midnight in eleven college towns where it did great business, and last weekend they expanded to 30 larger cities where the movie grossed over $500,000, and audiences went nuts for it.

Can it become the next "Blair Witch Project"? Well it has about $139 million to go to match that gross, and this weekend will determine an awful lot. Paramount deserves credit up to this point because they have created a frenzy for this film without spending much traditional advertising money. It's been a viral campaign that has been growing on the Internet and through twitter users. This weekend is a game changer because Paramount is opening it on regular runs with full daily show times and on multiple screens. This is where Paramount may be stumbling. In Chicago, it's going from one theatre playing midnight shows for three nights to eight theatres playing the movie every half hour from morning to night. One area theatre is playing it 20 times just on Friday. We're talking about a dramatic shift in supply and demand here. There may be close to 300 showings over the three-day weekend for Chicago moviegoers to choose from. The head scratcher is that there are no newspaper ads to support the expanded engagements, and I haven't seen any television ads either. Is Internet buzz going to fill theatres at 10:30 in the morning or 3:30 in the afternoon? Will a movie that was so cool and edgy with a full house at midnight have the same allure in the light of day where some people may be watching it in empty theatres? Is Paramount going to kill the golden goose by mishandling it? Are they testing whether just an Internet campaign can carry a film and old media isn't needed anymore? Are they arrogant, dumb or brilliant? Those are a lot of questions that will seemingly be answered on Monday morning when all the grosses are reported. A movie out of nowhere with the potential of "Paranormal Activity" comes around maybe once every five years. For the managers and marketers fortunate enough to be handling a film like this, every decision along the way becomes crucial to maximizing that potential and turning that movie into the biggest possible success it can be for both the distributor and the exhibitors. That is the art of distribution and when it's staged correctly, it's a beautiful thing to see. I have my doubts about what Paramount is doing or not doing this weekend, but stranger things have happened. We'll see what happens.

This Week at the Box Office: *Weekly Attendance: 19,963,599*

Universal may have finally caught a break and has the weekend to itself with the Vince Vaughn comedy "Couples Retreat" being the only national release set to open. Coupled with the fact that it's a three-day weekend for many people with the Columbus Day holiday on Monday, it's hard to believe that no other movie is opening against it, because "Couples Retreat" isn't exactly "Harry Potter." Paramount originally had "Shutter Island" on this date, which had caused a couple of the movies to move up to October 2nd. The studios are adept at taking advantage of all the three-day weekends, but there wasn't a counter move to get something else on this date after "Shutter Island" was moved to February. That could prove costly to some company. With only one new wide release, eyes will turn to those movies that opened last week to see how they hold up and whether or not they can show some "legs." The two movies I discussed last week, "Capitalism: A Love Story" and "Whip It," opened to lower grosses than expected and have a chance this weekend to show if they will have any staying power. If not, their fates will be sealed as disappointments.

Couples Retreat
Universal
Opening weekend: $22,100,820
Domestic gross: $112,735,375 63.5%
Foreign gross: $62,639,895 36.5%
Worldwide gross: $171,844,840
Widest release: 3,074

An Education
Sony Classics
Opening weekend: $159,017
Domestic gross: $12,574,914 48.2%
Foreign gross: $13,521,938 51.8%
Worldwide gross: $26,096,852
Widest release: 763 theatres

From Mexico with Love
Roadside
Opening weekend: $334,340
Domestic gross: $548,387 99.9%
Foreign gross: $708 0.1%
Worldwide gross: 279 theatres

The Damned United

Sony Classics

Opening weekend: $32,065

Domestic gross: $449,865 11.0%

Foreign gross: $3,641,513 89.0%

Worldwide gross: 45 theatres

Bronson

Magnolia

Opening weekend: $10,940

Domestic gross: $104,979 4.6%

Foreign gross: $2,155,733 95.4%

Worldwide gross: $2,260,712

Widest release: 8 theatres

Wedding Song

Strand

Opening weekend: $1,240

Domestic gross: $31,160

Foreign gross: N/A

Widest release: 4 theatres

Yes Men Fix the World

Shadow

Opening weekend: $10,940

Domestic gross: $104,979 4.6%

Foreign gross: $2,155,733 95.4%

Worldwide gross: $2,260,712

Widest release: 13 theatres

Visual Acoustics

Arthouse

Opening weekend: $3,517

Domestic gross: $102,463

Foreign gross: N/A

Widest release: 5 theatres

Adventures of Power

Variance

Opening weekend: $4,254

Domestic gross: $17,738

Foreign gross: N/A

Widest release: 3 theatres

Passport to Love

Variance

Opening weekend: $46,012

Domestic gross: $173,828

Foreign gross: N/A

Widest release: 9 theatres

Trucker

Monterrey

Opening weekend: $9,558

Domestic gross: $52,429

Foreign gross: N/A

Widest release: 13 theatres

Peter and Vandy

Strand

Opening weekend: $7,323

Domestic gross: $11,495

Foreign gross: N/A

Widest release: 3 theatres

2012 Update:
Universal Ends Deal with Hasbro

When Universal announced a deal with Hasbro to make a number of movies based on popular board games back in 2008, the announcement was met with a fair amount of derision in Hollywood. Had it come to this, "Candy Land: The Motion Picture"? Four years later, in January, 2012, the deal came to an end with only one movie made from the partnership, "Battleship," which crashed and sank at the box office in the summer of 2012 with a domestic gross of $64 million. As with many of the studios' big action blockbusters, the foreign grosses were much higher at $236 million, but with production and global marketing costs reported to be in excess of $300 million, the movie was considered an expensive misfire.

Week 41: Questions for Discussion

1. What does anti-trust law say about how distributors can sell their product in the marketplace?

2. What did Walmart do in reaction to lower consumer demand for DVDs in the fourth quarter of 2009? Was it good or bad news for distributors, and could they do anything about it?

PARANORMAL ACTIVITY: A NEW TWIST ON AN OLD RELEASE PATTERN

Week 42: October 16–22, 2009

The market demand will dictate to a distributor its course of action. The tricky part of it is not to get ahead of the marketplace or fall too far behind it.

Last weekend made me a believer of "Paranormal Activity." I admit I had my doubts on the way Paramount was handling the low budget sensation, expanding it into regular run theatres with up to 20 showtimes a day without any apparent traditional advertising to support the shift away from midnight shows. I posed the question, are they arrogant, dumb or brilliant? They sure aren't dumb, possibly arrogant, (distributors can get that way with theatre owners when they have a hot film on their hands), and I'd have to say they're pretty brilliant up to this point with their marketing and distribution strategies. I started working in the business in 1973, and I've seen everything that has happened in the modern era of the movie industry, and Paramount has accomplished something I've never seen done before, open a movie exclusively on midnight shows for two weeks, then shift into regular runs across the country with sold-out theatres everywhere. Let's recap the specific weekend numbers for the three weeks the movie has been in release:

September 25:
- 12 theatres (all midnight shows in college towns)
- 3 Day gross: $77,873 for a $6,489 per screen average
- 48th top ranking gross in country

October 2:
- 33 theatres (all midnight shows in larger cities)
- 3 day gross: $532,242 for a $16,129 per screen average
- 24th top ranking gross in country

October 9:
- 160 theatres (all regular show times throughout day)
- 3 day gross: $7,900,695 for a $49,379 per screen average
- 4th top ranking gross in country

October 16:
- Expansion to 800 theatres nationwide, opening in many new markets

To have a movie go from a $6,489 per screen average in its first week to a $49,379 average in its third week, while adding theatres, is an unprecedented occurrence, even if it did begin its life as midnight shows. It was easy to have doubts because there is really nothing to compare it to. A platform release is a staggered release where theatres are added slowly over weeks and at times even months with the idea of allowing word of mouth, critical acclaim and strong buzz to permeate into smaller markets before opening. In an era of wide releases and quick play off, the platform release remains an important strategy for distributors when handling smaller, harder to define films. So Paramount didn't invent a new release strategy, they just turned it on its head and gave it an innovative twist. The standard platform release has a handful of theatres open in New York and Los Angeles before expanding into markets like Chicago, Boston and San Francisco, then widening out in additional cities based on size and performance over a period of time. Instead of the weekend per screen average growing each successive week as the theatres increase, per screen averages fall as more theatres are added. A recent example is "A Serious Man," the latest Coen Brother's film, which opened October 2nd. The film opened very strong in six theatres in New York and Los Angeles averaging $41,890 a run. Focus Features expanded to 21 theatres last week, and the per screen average while still strong, fell off to $21,872. That's a typical type of performance and drop off.

Other films in the past have chosen to open away from the New York and Los Angeles markets, and other films have increased their per screen averages in later weeks, but they didn't open as midnight shows, and their box office increases were never as dramatic as what we're seeing with "Paranormal Activity." Paramount pulled off a gutsy, bold move because there was always the risk of marginalizing the movie as a cult item; that didn't happen because they moved swiftly and confidently into regular runs in a seamless fashion after creating an incredible Internet demand for the hard to find movie (more on this later). I recall the independent movie "Henry: Portrait of a Serial Killer" opening on midnight shows at the Music Box Theatre in Chicago for several weeks, and it was later picked up by a distributor for general release, but that's a different dynamic than "Paranormal Activity." More likely than not, the movies that have become successful at midnight were movies that failed in their original theatrical runs. By far the most successful midnight movie in history that followed that path is "The Rocky Horror Picture Show." In 1975, 20th Century Fox opened the movie in a traditional commercial way, and it immediately flopped at the box office. About six months later, a New York theatre owner started playing it on weekend midnight shows, and the rest is for the history books. "Rocky Horror" has been continuously playing somewhere in theatres at midnight for the last 34 years and has amassed over $150,000,000 from midnight shows, a feat so unthinkable and unreachable that it boggles the mind.

There have been plenty of past films that have had sensational platform releases. Ten years ago, Artisan opened "Blair Witch Project" in 50 theatres in the largest cities for two weeks, creating long lines and demand before blasting the movie out to 2,000 screens in the third week, eventually grossing $140 million. In 2002, "My Big Fat Greek Wedding" took a slower route to success. Distributor Bob Berney masterminded a release that had the film open on 108 screens in April of that year, and the movie never grossed over $2 million in a weekend until its 11th week when it was playing on 493 screens. The picture played in theatres for 10 months and grossed $241 million. For a distributor, managing a platform release is the most challenging and labor intensive release there is. When it's successful, there is no better satisfaction for a job well done. Last week "Paranormal Activity" set an all-time record for per screen average for that amount of theatres, breaking the record set by Orion's "Platoon" in 1987. Reports are that Paramount wants to be in 2,000 theatres next weekend. That's probably a smart move because you want to strike when the fire is hot and before the inevitable backlash of some negative word begins. There is already some muttering from people that the movie isn't that scary, but the same thing happened to "Blair Witch," and that didn't stop that movie from grossing $140 million. How fast or slow a movie expands is always dependent on prior box office performance. The market demand will dictate to a distributor its course of action. The tricky part of it is not to get ahead of the marketplace or fall too far behind it, and that's where the distribution pros make their living.

There are always a lot of casualties among platform releases, many of them good movies, when they just can't find enough critical and audience support to sustain an ongoing release. It has happened often in 2009. When a film falters, it's allowed to wither away for reasons tied to both distributors and exhibitors. For distributors, it's the thought of putting good money after bad, and they lose the motivation to continue spending money on additional prints and advertising and instead start preparing for the DVD release. On the exhibitor front, they lose the motivation to book an underperforming film at the expense of another; so both forces are in play, and the parties come to the same conclusion, let's move on to the next film. It always hurts, but it's the nature of the business.

Did Paramount set out to create this new type of platform release for "Paranormal Activity"? As more news about the release starts coming out, that doesn't seem to be the case. Paramount acquired the movie after DreamWorks bought the rights for $500,000, and the movie was left for them to distribute after the companies parted ways. If there was any movie to experiment with, this low-budget acquisition was the perfect one to do it with. Paramount's online marketing division was allowed to take a leading role in developing an Internet campaign built around social networking sites and a website which gave fans the opportunity to demand the movie play in their town. As far as anyone knows, this was the first time a major studio used a site like eventful.com to virally market one of their films. Marketing is going where the eyeballs are, and the findings of a recent survey show confirm the Internet is the place to be.

Where the Moviegoers Are:

▸ 94% are online.
▸ They spend more time online than watching television.
▸ 73% participate in online social networking.

Source: Stradella Road

The twelve original college towns chosen to play the film won the right to play it with fan voting, as did the 30 larger cities the following week. Strong college markets like Madison, Wis., Ann Arbor, Mich. and Durham, NC. were part of the original group that debuted the movie. All this was pretty ingenious. This was the rare case where the marketers drove the bus, and the distribution people were there responding to the demand and providing prints and cutting deals with theatre owners in those towns where fans were voting it to open. "Paranormal Activity" is destined to become a classic case study just as "Blair Witch Project" was. The difference is the full story remains to be written. Each week as "Paranormal" expands, it has to keep proving itself. We don't know yet where the story will end. When I questioned the lack of advertising last week, I wasn't aware of the television campaign that was being aired on MTV, Comedy Central and other cable stations. It makes sense that there was some strong traditional old media marketing reaching the core audience of 16 to 22 year olds to back up the Internet word of mouth. The Internet is powerful but not powerful enough to carry an entire national campaign. What still perplexes me is Paramount's continued refusal to have any newspaper ads, especially as it opens in 800 theatres. They have proven their point that newspaper ads weren't needed to open this movie, but with additional screens opening, what's the downside in announcing the movie's success and existence to a wider audience? The only newspaper ad I've seen was an excellent full page ad in last Sunday's *New York Times* with the topper 'Across the Country Audiences Have Demanded It! And Critics Agree ...' Newspapers may have fallen in readership and out of favor with studios as a primary way to reach audiences, but they should still be in the marketing mix when a picture like this is broadening out, especially when the movie is getting such surprisingly strong reviews. There is also a bit of hypocrisy here in regards to the major studios and their relationship with newspapers. The studios reap the benefits of both newspaper publicity articles and critics' reviews when it works to their interests but choose to run away from them when it comes to having a decent newspaper budget. Would the studios rather see newspapers disappear completely? There would be absolutely no advantage to anyone if that happens. Newspapers still serve a purpose and continue to have a loyal audience of seasoned moviegoers. It would make better sense for studios to remember that when putting marketing budgets together.

This Week at the Box Office: *Weekly Attendance: 23,167,669*

Where the Wild Things Are
Warner Brothers
Opening weekend: $32,695,407
Domestic gross: $77,333,467 77.2%
Foreign gross: $22,853,326 22.8%
Worldwide gross: $100,086,793
Widest release: 3,735 theatres

Law Abiding Citizen
Overture
Opening weekend: $21,039,502
Domestic gross: $73,357,727 57.9%
Foreign gross: $53,332,999 42.1%
Worldwide gross: $126,690,726
Widest release: 2,890 theatres

The Stepfather
Sony
Opening weekend: $11,581,586
Domestic gross: $29,062,561 93.2%
Foreign gross: $2,135,970 6.8%
Worldwide gross: $31,198,531
Widest release: 2,734 theatres

New York, I Love You

Vivendi
Opening weekend: $380,776
Domestic gross: $1,589,729 19.6%
Foreign gross: $6,507,581 80.4%
Worldwide gross: $8,095,596
Widest release: 118 theatres

The Maid

Elephant Eye
Opening weekend: $17,036
Domestic gross: $576,610 35.3%
Foreign gross: $1,056,397 64.7%
Worldwide gross: $1,633,005
Widest release: 19 theatres

The Little Traitor

Independent
Opening weekend: N/A
Domestic gross: $395,122
Foreign gross: N/A
Widest release: 6 theatres

Black Dynamite

Apparition
Opening weekend: $131,862
Domestic gross: $242,578 81.8%
Foreign gross: $53,979 18.2%
Worldwide gross: $296,557
Widest release: 70 theatres

Main Aur Mrs. Khauna

UTV
Opening weekend: $121,134
Domestic gross: $197,183 45.7%
Foreign gross: $234,447 54.3%
Worldwide gross: $431,630
Widest release: 59 theatres

Janky Promoters

Third Rail (Weinstein)
Opening weekend: $5,702
Domestic gross: $9,069
Foreign gross: N/A
Widest release: 22 theatres

OPA!

Cinedigm
Opening weekend: 52,453
Domestic gross: $52,453
Foreign gross: N/A
Widest release: 221 theatres

Food Beware

First Run
Opening weekend: $595
Domestic gross: $1,181
Foreign gross: N/A
Widest release: 1 theatre

The Ministers

Maya
Opening weekend: $2,844
Domestic gross: $4,447
Foreign gross: N/A
Widest release: 2 theatres

All the Best

Yasha Raj Films
Opening weekend: $96,054
Domestic gross: $120,713 80.6%
Foreign gross: $29,094 19.4%
Worldwide gross: $149,807
Widest release: 58 theatres

2012 Update:
The Legacy of "Paranormal Activity"

For what started out as a movie no one wanted and one that two different studios didn't really know what to do with once they had it, "Paranormal Activity" has since become one of those films from 2009 that has become more than its sturdy grosses. For such a small film, its impact has cast a large net, not only over Paramount but over the rest of the studios as well. First, let's look at the movies themselves. "Paranormal Activity" proved it was more than a one-hit wonder. It has become a very dependable new franchise for Paramount that has become an annual Halloween tradition, replacing the "Saw" movies after that franchise had run its course. The following are the domestic grosses for the first three films; they couldn't be steadier. The fourth one will be released in October 2012.

- ► Paranormal Activity (2009) - $107,918,810
- ► Paranormal Activity 2 (2010) - $84,752,907
- ► Paranormal Activity 3 (2011) - $107,028,807

If it was just the movies themselves and the arrival of a new franchise it would be impressive, but the movie's influence runs deeper because of events that occurred in the industry before the release and what has happened since. As 2009 began, Paramount had joined Warner Bros. in closing down their specialty art division, Paramount Vantage, and effectively getting out of that end of the business. It had simply gotten too risky for them as films like "There Will Be Blood" became too expensive and cost prohibitive at the same time the economy was in a freefall, leading to tighter credit and financing. Then along comes "Paranormal Activity." In a period of tighter money, high star salaries and industry cutbacks, Paramount releases a movie which they acquired for $500,000, and eight weeks later it passes $100 million and becomes one of the most profitable movies they've ever had. What's happening here? What happened is that soon after, Paramount decides to form another division just after they shut Paramount Vantage down, but instead of expensive, high-brow films made for upscale adults, this time it's all about going after teens and the young audience with micro-budgeted genre movies. They named their new experimental label Insurge, and the industry at large took notice. Over the last couple of years, Insurge has either developed or acquired several low-budget films that have done well, mostly in the horror and music concert categories, including one starring Justin Bieber. In January 2012, they released another horror film, "The Devil Inside," which the company acquired for $1 million and went on to gross $53 million. Other studios have since followed a similar business model of going after the teen audience on the Internet and through social networking sites. In February 2012, 20th Century Fox released their own low budget found footage feature, "Chronicle," which proceeded to gross $64 million. As the middle range adult $50 to $70 million dollar films continue to get squeezed out, the studios are finding a comfort level at both the very expensive end of the spectrum with their blockbuster movies and at the very low end with their teen genre movies marketed through Internet sites. Look for that trend to continue in the coming years.

Week 42: Questions for Discussion

1. Describe what a platform release is and how Paramount's "Paranormal Activity" turned this type of release on its head in a unique way?

2. How do distributors decide the amount of new theatres to open each week as a platform release evolves?

3. What would be two reasons a distributor would choose to go with a much wider release on a movie than originally planned?

THE BIGGEST OCTOBER WEEKEND IN HISTORY BRINGS LITTLE CHEER TO THE SPECIALTY BUSINESS

Week 43: October 23–29, 2009

---

*Only the strong survive, and out of the ashes comes a better
use of talent and resources in a different type of business.*

The fall season is referred to as the serious movie season where more quality films emerge, with the upscale audience coming out in force to support them. In a year when some type of industry record seems to be broken every month, including last weekend becoming the biggest October weekend in history, the independent, art, specialty, upscale, whatever you choose to call good, quality films for a discerning audience, haven't joined the party. Big commercial movies continue to drive the market, crowding out the smaller films in a month where they historically have had a better chance to succeed.

The thrill is gone. But why? Is this year's crop of specialty films having an off year? Is it because these films lack the "must see" aspect of past independent films? Is the core audience of baby boomers staying home more and going out to theatres less? What has been the impact of the studios losing interest in the specialty business and taking their marketing dollars with them? What part does Netflix and Video-on-Demand play in viewer habits? Have specialty films become more marketing driven than director driven? Have the remaining independent distributors become more complacent and even sloppy when distributing their films? Has the declining interest, readership, and loss of some top critics in newspapers had a major effect on box office? Are there younger audiences in line to replace the boomers in their support of independent films? Is the interest gone? Does anyone care?

Those are a lot of questions, and I'm not here to answer each and every one of them in this particular chapter, though I've touched on many of the issues throughout the various weeks. Even if I wanted to, I don't know all the answers. Before there can be answers, there have to be the right questions, and there's much to ponder and discuss about the plight of the independent film business, where it has been and where it's headed. There will always be quality films made outside the mainstream, but will there always be an entire industry infrastructure to support them as there has been for the last 30 years? That's the trickier question. In a competitive marketplace, there is an ebb and flow in each industry, where businesses form when there is consumer demand for a particular product or service. When that occurs, more companies and individuals appear and start chasing after profits, competition heats up, expenses can rise, profits may fall, and it's left to the marketplace to sort out the winners and losers based on risk/reward, success and failure. Only the strong survive, and out of the ashes comes a better use of talent and resources in a different type of business.

We are approaching the end of a cycle. Just as the years between 1930 and 1950 are considered the Golden Age of the Hollywood Studio System, 1980 – 2009 will be known as the Golden Age of the American Independent Film Industry. The golden years are over. What emerges will be something different than what we have now, a system that will depend less on theatrical and more on emerging distribution models. It is both an issue of demographics and economics. Let's begin with another question. Where have the adult moviegoers gone, the core audience that has supported the independent business for the last 30 years? As a card-carrying member of the baby boomer generation, I have to agree with a recent article stating that the baby boomers are finally starting to lose their influence and aren't the driving force of everything that's going on in the marketplace anymore. We're most important now as a generation that will be retiring in force in the next ten years and raising speculation over what that's going to do to the solvency of the Social Security

Program. We're getting older, slowing down a little, not willing to drive that extra mile to search out each and every art film, willing to wait for Netflix or pay for Video-on-Demand to watch it on our 50" widescreen, high-def televisions. Our generation helped build the independent industry, and our generation formed its core audience. We came out of the 1960s where we took dates to see the latest Fellini or Bergman film. We made "The Graduate" and "Easy Rider" into smash hits, and we rode high into the '70s as the first film generation and were rewarded with the films of Altman, Ashby, Coppola, Scorsese, Lucas, Allen, Mazursky and many other American auteurs. When the studios shifted gears in the late '70s to go after safer, commercial popcorn movies, we were there for John Sayles's "Return of the Secaucus Seven" in 1980, in my opinion the starting point for the entire independent film industry. The $60,000 film of a group of radical college friends getting together for a weekend as they were turning 30 years old spoke to us directly as we also were turning 30. That movie set the tone for years to come with many others to follow that were both important and relevant to our lives. Now we're turning 60. The problem is there doesn't seem to be another audience following us with the same size and passion to see independent films in theatres. The interest and buzz just isn't there. The younger audience's attention is elsewhere, either with the event movies or in new ways of watching movies away from the movie theatres.

Spending less is not the way to produce more hits and higher grosses.

It's an economic issue also. Three studios have already made the decision to pull out of the independent business because the dollars don't add up anymore. Costs are up, grosses are down, the audience base is dwindling, and the DVD market brings in less money than it used to, especially for the artier films. Some could say the studios used independent films, took over the business and abandoned it when the going got tough. That may be true, but they also have to be credited with helping to grow the business with their economy of size and the money they invested in filmmakers, films and marketing budgets. The point in time when independent films really took off was when Disney bought Miramax in 1993, and Harvey Weinstein used the studios' bankroll brilliantly in choosing the right projects, creating great marketing campaigns and then being able to buy larger newspaper ads and television spots to reach a wider audience than ever before. Other studios saw the results and jumped in to get a piece of the action. It's easy to rip the studios, but a lot of people made good money off them including filmmakers, sales agents, ad agencies, newspapers, publicists, film festivals and many others. The bottom line is that the studios grew the business. I've heard some people say the indie business can go back to where it was, but there is no going back; the genie has left the bottle. In the early to mid-'80s, while the business was still growing, little movies with minimal campaigns could get by. What I'm seeing today are smaller ads and marketing campaigns which is in response to lower expected revenues, but spending less is not the way to produce more hits and higher grosses in today's world. Sony Classics opened "An Education" today in Chicago with an 8-inch ad in the *Tribune* and a 4-inch ad in the *Sun-Times*. For such an accomplished film, that's a pitiful looking newspaper campaign. There's still close to a million people in Chicago reading the dailies, and that's how a potential Academy Award nominee is positioned? Film distributors are running scared, and it's not a pretty sight. No one likes to lose money, and they're watching every dollar.

2009 has been a record-breaking year for the studio movies, but the entire year has been lousy for specialty films. Dark clouds started forming when three Best Picture candidates, "Milk," "Frost/Nixon" and "The Reader" failed to get the expected bump at the box office after Oscar nominations were announced in February. It went from bad to worse from there, and even upscale adult dramas from the studios like "State of Play" and "Public Enemies" have fallen on hard times. September and October are months where solid independent films have opened and have played well into the Oscar season, movies like "Sideways," "Being John Malkovich," "Lost in Translation," and "The Queen," among many others. "The Queen" opened in October 2006, played five months and grossed $56,000,000. It was a huge success, but to keep the movie in the marketplace for five months cost Miramax (and Disney) $30 million in print and ad costs, which points to the expense involved in supporting a hit film regardless of whether it's a studio or independent film. Looking at what's playing in art theatres today, there are no films to compare to the above-mentioned titles. The buzz isn't there because the product isn't there. The films aren't as good or vital or as relevant as they have been in the past. It's an off year. Bob Berney, one of the best distributors in the business, has found that out after starting his latest company, Apparition. The company's first film, Jane Campion's "Bright Star," was a hot title from the Cannes and Toronto Film Festivals, opened in September with an aggressive marketing campaign and strong reviews, only to see the film stumble when widening out to additional theatres. The gross sits at about $3.5 million, and the film continues to lose theatres each week. It appears its theatrical run is sputtering out and has to be considered a big disappointment.

When famed art house directors like Spike Jonze and Wes Anderson turn to making family movies for studios, "Where the Wild Things Are" and "Fantastic Mr. Fox" respectfully, it has to be considered within the context of what's happening to the diminished fortunes of the independent film business and the credit crunch that's impacting the financing of more challenging subject matter. They can be making great films for wider audiences, but they're not specialty films, and that's a loss. Then when you see the one true breakout independent hit of the year, "Paranormal Activity," being distributed by a studio after being available at festivals for two years, that adds insult to injury. File the next item in the embarrassing category and how the mighty have fallen. Earlier in the chapter, I mentioned some sloppiness is creeping into the distribution business. When the Weinstein's ran Miramax, they ran it with an iron fist where no detail was too small to ignore. It may have been hell working for them as revealed by former employees through the years, but they kept their eye on the ball just about better than anyone else in the industry. Last weekend what happened in Chicago was not one of their proudest moments. Who knows; they may not even know about it yet. In the *Chicago Sun-Times*, two huge gaffes occurred. On the front page of the Friday movie section, Roger Ebert's review of Weinstein's "The Road" ran, but it doesn't open until later in the year. Perhaps it was the paper's fault, but it still looked very bad for the distributor and the movie itself. In the same paper, an ad ran for Weinstein's low brow "Janky Promoters," starring Ice Cube, which after checking all the theatre showtimes, also didn't appear to open this week. Situations like this should not happen. Having two mistakes from the same company on the same weekend is careless and inexcusable.

Two other independent films that have surprisingly underperformed this fall are "Capitalism: A Love Story" and "Whip It," both stuck at around $12,000,000. There was a great opportunity for both of them to gain some traction on their second weekends when only "Couples Retreat" opened, but they each landed up falling 40%, and their eventual fates were sealed. Michael Moore will have his worst gross of the decade, and the girl power of "Whip It" never materialized. When Fox Searchlight emphasized the mother/daughter relationship in its second week ad campaign, it just goes to show even the best of the distributors can stumble from time to time. That's been the story of 2009 for the independent film business, still breathing and hobbling along, pushing forward and wondering what changes are in store for them as a new decade looms ever closer.

This Week at the Box Office:

Weekly Attendance: 20,735,876

Saw VI

Lionsgate

Opening weekend: $14,118,444

Domestic gross: $27,693,292 40.6%

Foreign gross: $40,590,337 59.4%

Worldwide gross: $68,233,629

Widest release: 3,036 theatres

Astro Boy

Summit

Opening weekend: $6,702,923

Domestic gross; $19,551,067 49.0%

Foreign gross: $20,335,919 51.0%

Worldwide gross: $39,886,986

Widest release: 3,020 theatres

Amelia

Fox Searchlight

Opening weekend: $3,904,047

Domestic gross: $14,279,575 72.5%

Foreign gross: $5,396,598 27.5%

Worldwide gross: $19,642,013

Widest release: 1,070 theatres

Cirque Du Freak: Vampire's Asst.

Universal

Opening weekend: $6,293,205

Domestic gross: $13,869,515 35.4%

Foreign gross: $25,362,598 64.6%

Worldwide gross: $39,232,598

Widest release: 2,754 theatres

Antichrist

IFC

Opening weekend: $71,397

Domestic gross: $404,122 51%

Foreign gross: $387,745 49%

Worldwide gross: $791,867

Widest release: 19 theatres

Motherhood

Freestyle

Opening weekend: $50,081

Domestic gross: $93,388 12.9%

Foreign gross: $632,966 87.1%

Worldwide gross: $726,354

Widest release: 48 theatres

Ong Bak 2: The Beginning

Magnolia

Opening weekend: $25,195

Domestic gross: $101,215 1.1%

Foreign gross: $8,834,205 98.95

Worldwide gross: $8,936,663

Widest release: 12 theatres

(Untitled)

IDP/Samuel Goldwyn

Opening weekend: $18,002

Domestic gross: $230,600

Foreign gross: N/A

Widest release: 25 theatres

The Canyon

Trulie Indie

Opening weekend: $1,925

Domestic gross: $1,925

Foreign gross: N/A

Widest release: 1 theatre

Week 43: Questions for Discussion

1. Do you feel there are younger audiences in line to replace aging baby boomers in their support of theatrical independent films? Will you be one of them?

2. Filmmakers have to convince potential investors that there is an audience for their films and a chance that they can recoup their money. How is that done?

3. If specialty films become more marketing driven than director driven, is that a good or bad thing when it comes to searching for financing?

4. Look through the capsule history of the American independent film industry and write at least one paragraph on something that helped you to understand the indie business better.

HISTORY OF THE AMERICAN INDEPENDENT FILM BUSINESS

I've compiled facts and figures from a variety of sources through the years to come up with a capsule history of the American independent film business. I've worked and taught within the industry since the 1970s, so the later events listed are mostly through my own memory, notes and files. As you will notice, the industry didn't just spring up in 1980; it was taking shape and percolating for several decades before that. Before a fully independent business could be born, the infrastructure had to be established to support it, and when you look closely, you will be able to see all the elements slowly coming together, film festivals, distributors, art theatres, filmmakers, support organizations, magazines, media coverage, cable stations, producers reps, critics and financiers.

1896: First publicly screened motion picture in America

1903: Edison's "The Great Train Robbery" is first popular film

1908: The Motion Pictures Patent Corporation is formed to battle independents with patent suits

1915: D.W. Griffith's "Birth of a Nation" becomes America's first major independent feature film

1918: The Motion Pictures Patent Corporation is ruled an illegal restraint of trade by the federal government and is forced to close its doors

1919: Charlie Chaplin, Mary Pickford, Douglas Fairbanks Jr. and D.W. Griffith form United Artists Pictures

1921: More than 300 theatres in the country cater to 'race' films, black films made by black directors for black audiences. During this time, ethnic films, Yiddish films and Oriental films also being made outside the mainstream

1926: First art house theatres open in New York City and Washington D.C.

1927: Walt Disney starts out as a small independent film animator in Kansas City. For the next three decades his movies would be distributed through United Artists

1930: The Depression and expenses of sound technology hurt independent companies and ushers in the studio system

1930–50: During the golden age of the studio system, low budget B movies made by companies like Republic and Monogram constitute the bulk of the independent movies produced in the U.S.

1931: Venice International Film Festival opens

1932: Film Forum theatre in New York opens; New York Film Society is formed

1945: Only twelve art house theatres are operating in the United States

1947: The Cannes Film Festival is launched

1949: Studio system starts breaking down after Supreme Court's decision in the landmark Paramount Consent Decrees

1950: Berlin Film Festival begins; race picture industry fades away

1951: Lawyers Arthur Krim and Robert Benjamin take control of the faltering United Artists

1954:   American International Pictures (AIP) is formed and becomes a leader in the exploitation B movie arena for the next 25 years, starting the careers of Francis Coppola, Martin Scorsese, Joe Dante and Jonathan Demme and many other young filmmakers looking to break into the film business

Late '50s: U.S. art theatres play mostly foreign films led by those made by Fellini and Bergman

1957:   San Francisco International Film Festival becomes first major film festival in the United States

1960:   John Cassavetes's first film "Shadows" wins acclaim at the Cannes Film Festival; approximately 350 art houses in country

1962:   The New York Film Festival is born and opens with Louis Bunuel's "The Exterminating Angel."

1963:   Cinema 5 opens as an art film distributor in New York

1967:   No distributor would agree to distribute D.A. Pennebaker's Bob Dylan documentary "Don't Look Now," and he is forced to self-distribute it

1967:   "The Graduate," an independent film distributed by Embassy Pictures, becomes the biggest grossing movie of the year at $50 million. The American Film Institute is founded; New Line Pictures is formed

1968:   MPAA ratings system is instituted; Martin Scorsese's first film "Who's That Knocking at my Door" premieres at the Chicago Film Festival

1969:   "Easy Rider," shot in 16mm with independent financing, becomes the biggest non studio produced film since "Birth of a Nation" but is distributed by Columbia Pictures

1970:   John Cassavetes's "Faces" opens; Film Study programs accelerate in the United States

1971:   Melvin Van Peebles "Sweet Sweetbacks Badasses Song" grosses $15 million and ushers in the lucrative "Blaxploitation" wave of movies for the next five years, providing big city, downtown theatres a temporary lifeline

1974:   Cassavetes self-distributes his masterpiece "Woman Under the Influence" and has difficulty collecting his share of the box office from the theatres playing it.

1975:   Toronto and Seattle Film Festivals are founded

1977:   John Water's "Pink Flamingos" and David Lynch's "Eraserhead" open

1978:   A small film festival in Salt Lake City called the U.S. Film Festival is founded. John Carpenter's "Halloween" with a production cost of $320,000, grosses $40 million; Samuel Goldwyn Company is formed

1979:   Independent Film Project (IFP) and its Independent Film Market open for business; PBS starts funding films as part of its American Playhouse series

1980:   John Sayles's "Return of the Secaucus Seven," made for $60,000 and distributed by Cinecom, ushers in the modern era of the independent film movement

1981:   Robert Redford opens the Sundance Institute near Park City, Utah

1982:   Orion takes over Filmways/AIP

1984:   Jim Jarmusch's "Strangers in Paradise" starts a career, and John Cassavetes's "Love Streams" ends one. Redford takes control of the U.S. Festival and renames it the Sundance Film Festival and moves it to Park City, Utah

1985:   The Coen Brothers' first film "Blood Simple" is financed by Minneapolis dentists and debuts at Sundance

1986:   Spike Lee begins his career with "She's Gotta Have It;" Robert Townsend's "Hollywood Shuffle" is financed by credit cards, and the mainstream media gives the story tremendous coverage

1989:   Steven Soderbergh's "Sex, Lies, and Videotape" becomes the first major independent art film to emerge from the Sundance Film Festival as Miramax distributes it successfully to a $22 million box office; Strand Releasing formed; Michael Moore's "Roger and Me" is bought by Warner Bros. and grosses close to $7 million

1990:   Fine Line Features, a division of New Line, begins operations as an art film distributor

1991:   Filmmaker Magazine launches; John Singleton, ("Boyz 'N" The Hood") Richard Linklater ("Slacker") and Gus Van Sant ("My Private Idaho") debut their first films; Orion Pictures files for bankruptcy

1992:   Robert Rodriguez's "El Mariachi," with a reported $7,000 budget, creates a stir in the marketplace; Quentin Tarantino's first film "Reservoir Dogs" grosses $2 million in theatres but becomes a hit on video; Sony Pictures Classics is born

1993:   Miramax is bought by Walt Disney Studios

1994:   The Independent Film Channel is launched; Miramax's "Pulp Fiction" becomes fist independent film to gross $100 million; New Line Cinema is absorbed by Warner Bros.; Chicago based documentary "Hoop Dreams" wins Audience Award at Sundance and goes on to gross $7.8 million; Kevin Smith begins career with "Clerks."

1995:   Fox Searchlight is launched with Ed Burns's "Brothers McMullen" as its first film; Los Angeles Independent Film Festival is formed; Slamdance Film Festival begins; the Sundance Channel is created

1996:   The Internet reaches public mass; "Slingblade" costs $1.2 million and is sold to Miramax for $10 million, grosses $22 million

1997:   Lionsgate opens its own distribution company; October Films acquired by Universal

1998:   Artisan Entertainment and Paramount Classics founded; Darren Aronofsky's "Pi" launches career

1999:   "The Blair Witch Project," with a $40,000 budget, grosses $130 million to become the highest grossing independent film of all time while being recognized as the first Internet sensation for its viral marketing campaign

2000:   Filmmaking enters the digital age; 465 independent films are released as compared to 170 studio movies; 37,500 movie theatre screens in the U.S.

2002:   "My Big Fat Greek Wedding," made for $5 million and rejected by every distributor, grosses $222 million and overtakes "Blair Witch" as the largest grossing indie movie

2004:   "Fahrenheit 9/11" becomes the first documentary to gross over $100 million; "Passion of the Christ" becomes largest grossing independent film at $360 million; DVD sales and rentals generate $24 billion in revenue for all movies

2005: After leaving Miramax, Harvey and Bob Weinstein start Weinstein Films; the success of the Sundance Film Festival shows its dark side as national corporate sponsors and celebrity parties take over Park City and crowd out smaller films and their filmmakers

2006: Steven Soderbergh's "Bubble" becomes first film to debut simultaneously in the theatrical, DVD and pay cable markets. It grosses less than $200,000 at the box office with most mainstream theatres refusing to play the picture; "Crash" becomes the first film acquired at a film festival (Toronto) to win Best Picture of the Year.

2009: Paramount closes Paramount Vantage and joins Warner Brothers as studios without art divisions. The independent film business suffers through a terrible year at the box office; a number of small distributors close their doors; IFC Films announces that every acquisition will now go out on video-on-demand day and date with theatrical

2010: Disney leaves the specialty business and sells off Miramax to an investment firm for its library of films

2011: Total DVD sales and rentals fall to $18 billion; digital sales, including streaming movies, rises 50% from previous year to $3.4 billion, indicating a shift in distribution patterns and revenue streams while bringing new hope to the independent film industry.

2012: Lionsgate buys Summit Entertainment, putting the "Twilight" and "The Hunger Games" franchises under the same roof.

TICKETS AVAILABLE AT THEATRES EVERYWHERE

Week 44: October 30–November 5, 2009

Who would have thought that such cutting-edge marketing strategies
would be coming out of the studios on such a consistent basis?

"Tickets Available at Theatres Everywhere." With that simple copy line on top of all the advertising this week for Michael Jackson's "This Is It," Sony's Columbia Pictures changed their marketing campaign on a dime and proved once again that smart marketing is an essential element, if not the number one key, to achieving success in today's Hollywood. What? Aren't tickets always available everywhere when movies open in 3,500 theatres like "This Is It" is doing this weekend? Yes, they are, so why is it so special in this particular case? Well, after Sony created demand by positioning the movie more like a limited concert event than a regular film and pushed the fact that it would be playing in theatres for only two weeks, they started selling tickets a full month in advance, garnering huge amounts of publicity from every media outlet and Internet site imaginable. Mission accomplished. Fans came out in droves, camped out for days to buy tickets with the result being that more than 1,600 showings eventually sold out. When Sony's top brass started hearing rumbles from the marketplace that many people became certain that there were no tickets left, it was time for a simple, perhaps even subtle shift in their marketing strategy to remind people and to send them the message that the movie is available everywhere and that there is a seat for everyone to come out and see it. So simple, yet so brilliant. Often it's thinking of the small things that can make a big difference.

In this day and age of belt tightening by consumers, it's all about creating demand for your product. Instead of dropping prices like so many businesses and retail outlets have been forced to do to attract customers, movie studios are doing it the old fashioned way, creating ingenious distribution and marketing strategies that keep moviegoers coming out to their local movie houses. Just in the last month, Paramount and Sony created demand for their movies in totally different ways. With "Paranormal Activity," Paramount used a grass roots approach and the Internet to create interest and buzz by allowing college-age kids be a part of the campaign by allowing them to "demand" the movie come to their towns while adding more theatres each week in a slow rollout. Sony, on the other end of the spectrum, is betting big to win big and is staging a worldwide marketing blitz to create a global event. On the same night Los Angeles held the World Premiere of the movie this week, 15 cities around the world from Cairo to Moscow to Great Britain also hosted simultaneous world premiere events, highlighting the fact that it will be playing on 18,000 screens in 110 countries with the same marketing message we're seeing in the United States.

The size and scope of this venture is amazing, and considering the speed in which it was done and what Sony has accomplished in three months truly shows off the strength and power of a major studio with its economy of scale, deep pockets and all their multiple divisions at their disposal. It's easy to forget that this movie did not exist in anyone's mind until after Michael Jackson died suddenly in the summer. Most movies are on studios' release schedules for years before they are actually seen by the public, and the studios have months and months to plan their marketing campaigns. Plus, in an industry full of cookie cutter movies, "This Is It" does not have a precedent to draw from. It's not really a concert movie or a traditional documentary but sort of a combination of both. It's just a different animal pulled from over 100 hours of rehearsal footage and visual backdrops and turned into a movie in a very short period of time. Sony's deal to distribute the movie also came about quickly. The person who controlled the footage was the concert promoter for the 50 London shows Michael Jackson was rehearsing for. In mid-July, the promoter invited the heads of four major studios, Paramount, Sony, Universal and Fox, to watch 15 minutes of edited footage. Immediately following the screening a bidding war broke out, and Sony won the rights by offering $60 million for worldwide film rights, which includes DVD and television rights. Sony Music already was in control of most of Michael Jackson's music catalogue, so in that regard the purchase price makes sense. What may have seemed like a risky distribution decision isn't so risky anymore because of Sony's global approach and its ability to move so quickly and effectively in creating such a unique movie experience.

This follows Sony's masterful campaign for "District 9" in the summer where they turned an offbeat sci-fi movie shot in South Africa with no stars into a $100,000,000 hit. Who would have thought that such cutting-edge marketing strategies would be coming out of the studios on such a consistent basis, helping to fuel the record-breaking 2009 box office? In the past, independent distributors have been the ones who have been at the forefront of innovative release and marketing strategies from four-wall bookings to television saturations to Internet campaigns. The studios are often stuck in their old ways of doing business, producing more atrophy than innovation with their aversion to risk of going against established practices. Not this year. The studios are blowing away what the independents are doing. I posed the question in last week's chapter on whether or not independent films have to become or need to become more marketing driven than product driven. Without the right marketing, even the very best films don't have much of a chance these days. Simply put, independents will need to create better campaigns and be able to motivate their audience into believing their films need to be seen in theatres right here, right now. They only have to look at the studios for some inspiration on how it's being done.

This is the first year since 1998 that Halloween has fallen on a Saturday, and according to Box Office Guru, grosses over that weekend fell off 26% from the previous weekend. This is one holiday that presents problems for distributors when it falls on the biggest moviegoing night of the year. Too many costume parties, bar promotions, trick-or-treating, too many alternatives to moviegoing. Before Sony chose Halloween to open "This Is It," the only other movie scheduled for release was a minor film from Weinstein, which has now disappeared from the schedule. If there is a movie that can hold its own this weekend, it's one starring Michael Jackson. In a weird coincidence, Halloween was Jackson's favorite holiday, so it's perhaps fitting that his final swan song will be playing on the holiday, offering his fans an opportunity to dress up and have fun going to a movie theatre to watch his final performance.

"Saw" Wilts Under Pressure

As predicted, "Paranormal Activity" ended the five-year reign of "Saw" movies opening number one at the box office, but no one could have predicted it would do so poorly by grossing $14 million after debuting at $30 million or more for four straight years. Finally with some formidable competition to contend with, "Saw VI" wilted under pressure. The "Saw" franchise is the lone survivor for what was termed "torture porn," horror movies featuring gruesome, very explicit violent deaths and torture scenes, so it was good to see it brought to its knees by a horror movie which had more implied scares than explicit ones. It would be nice to report that we have seen the last of the franchise, but that's not the case because next Halloween audiences will be asked to endure "Saw in 3-D." Getting back to "Paranormal Activity" for a moment, becoming number one at the box office for the first time in its 5th week of release with a gross of $21 million is a rare feat to accomplish. I seemed to remember "My Big Fat Greek Wedding" achieving number one status in one of its later weeks, but in fact it's distinction is that it's the highest grossing movie ($241 million) in history to never have been at the top of the box office charts in any of its weeks. Another thing about "Paranormal" is that in its early weeks, a big chunk of its television campaign were spots on MTV, a sister company of Viacom's Paramount. A student asked me whether this would be considered self-dealing and if Paramount indeed paid the full amount to advertise on its station. These companies run separate businesses and do not cut any special deals with affiliated companies, so in this case it wouldn't be considered an example of self-dealing. Paramount most likely paid the going rate that any other company would pay, and they wouldn't have it any other way since all marketing expenditures are normal distribution expenses that are deductable right off the top of the distributor gross. That is, film rental collected from movie theatres. It goes back to the standard net profit deal in Hollywood between distributors and producers. By paying full freight, the money goes to MTV, which helps another

Viacom division, while Paramount has more legitimate charges to deduct before paying out any overages to the producers. But the way this movie is grossing, there should be more than enough dollars to carve up at the end of the day to keep all parties happy.

Living in the shadows of one of the all-time greats is a tough place to compete.

"Hoop Dreams" Anniversary

October marks the 15th anniversary of the release of "Hoop Dreams," a film whose legacy and singular achievement continue to grow in stature with each passing year. In 2007, the International Documentary Association (IDA) named "Hoop Dreams" the best documentary of all-time as selected by its 3,000 members from a list of some 700 films. (A list of the 25 best documentaries can be found at the end of this chapter.) I was thinking about "Hoop Dreams" as "More Than A Game," a documentary about LeBron James in his high school years, opened this month in select theatres. LeBron James is one of the NBA's biggest stars and gives the documentary some serious star power and an inside look at him growing into the player he would become as a professional. Distributed by Lionsgate, the most successful independent distributor, supported by strong critics' reviews and debuting in the same month "Hoop Dreams" did at the start of the NBA season, this was a documentary to keep an eye on to see if it could be a factor at the box office. After only a few weeks in limited release, the movie has failed to catch on and is showing no signs of any box office staying power. The movie will probably top out at around $1,000,000, far short of the $7,800,000 "Hoop Dreams" grossed in 1994's dollars. Putting it into a larger context, that's not too surprising because the sub genre of sports documentaries has been full of underachievers. In the last 35 years at least, "Hoop Dreams" is the top grossing sports documentary with "When We Were Kings" with Muhammad Ali, coming in second at $2,500,000. Another basketball documentary, "Year of the Yao" a few years ago, grossed only $35,000 before being taken out of release. You would think there would be more room for another basketball documentary to be successful, but that hasn't been the case. Even the biggest NBA stars can't draw audiences to their movies, and any documentary which tried following a team over the course of time, whether it was a women's team or Native American Indian basketball players, seemed to be crushed by being compared to "Hoop Dreams" or being relegated to copycat status or "been there, seen that." That's a shame because there have been some good basketball documentaries, but living in the shadows of one of the all-time greats is a tough place to compete.

This Week at the Box Office: *Weekly Attendance: 16,460,320*

There is no real precedent for "This Is It," so it's difficult to predict what the box office will be this weekend, but it should be somewhere around $30 million for five days. The bigger story is what it will do internationally where it is getting such a massive push from Sony. Most of the other movies in the marketplace will have to battle to overcome not only Halloween but also Saturday and Sunday night World Series games between two large Eastern market teams. This is the first year World Series games are being played this late in the year, and with Halloween falling on a weekend, it's not surprising that the other studios have decided to sit this weekend out. Other than "Paranormal Activity," look for "This Is It" to devour everything else in its path.

Michael Jackson's This Is It	*Boondock Saints II: All Saints Day*
Sony	Apparition
Opening weekend: $23,234,397	Opening weekend: $546,687
Domestic gross: $72,091,016 27.6%	Domestic gross: $10,273,187 96.6%
Foreign gross: $187,092,572 72.4%	Foreign gross: $356,133 3.4%

Worldwide gross: $261,183,588
Widest release: 3,481 theatres

London Dreams
Studio 18
Opening weekend: $207,969
Domestic gross: $300,293 51.8%
Foreign gross: $279,399 48.2%
Worldwide gross: $579,692
Widest release: 82 theatres

House of the Devil
Magnolia
Opening weekend: $25,195
Domestic gross: $101,215
Foreign gross: N/A
Widest release: 7 theatres

Storm
Film Movement
Opening weekend: $8,307
Domestic gross: $20,924
Foreign gross: N/A
Widest release: 3 theatres

Worldwide gross: $10,629,321
Widest release: 524 theatres

Gentlemen Broncos
Fox Searchlight
Opening weekend: $11,502
Domestic gross: $115,502 95.9%
Foreign gross: $4,810 4.1%
Worldwide gross: $118,492
Widest release: 18 theatres

Skin
Jour De Fete
Opening weekend: $24,134
Domestic gross: $203,305
Foreign gross: N/A
Widest release: 16 theatres

New Year's Parade
Independent
Opening weekend: $2,698
Domestic gross: $6,767
Foreign gross: N/A
Widest release: 1 theatre

25 BEST DOCUMENTARIES
AS VOTED BY THE INTERNATIONAL DOCUMENTARY ASSOCIATION

1. Hoop Dreams
2. The Thin Blue Line
3. Bowling for Columbine
4. Spellbound
5. Harlan County USA
6. An Inconvenient Truth
7. Crumb
8. Gimme Shelter
9. The Fog of War
10. Roger and Me
11. Super Size Me
12. Don't Look Back
13. Salesman
14. Koyaanisqatsi: Life Out of Balance
15. Sherman's March
16. Grey Gardens
17. Capturing the Friedmans
18. Born into Brothels
19. Titticut Follies
20. Buena Vista Social Club
21. Fahrenheit 9/11
22. Winged Migration
23. Grizzly Man
24. Night and Fog
25. Woodstock

Conversations with Industry Professionals

Jeff Blake – Vice Chairman of Sony Pictures, Los Angeles, CA

The following interview took place on March 30, 2011 in Las Vegas during the CinemaCon convention.

"Anyone who is going to have success in this business has to be enthusiastic for their movies. If you are going to make mistakes, it should be out of enthusiasm and pushing too hard, not too little."

Jeff Blake

Q: *Jeff, you have come a long way since you began your career in Chicago with Paramount in the 1970s. Can you talk about those days?*

JB: My first job was with Paramount in 1974 as a sales booker when three of the five best film nominees were "Godfather II," "Chinatown" and "The Conversation." My responsibility involved shipping film prints to theatres in Indiana and Wisconsin. I was so proud of that job because I was such a film buff growing up, and I was involved with the best movies from that time period. In 1978 I became the Chicago Branch Manager, and that same year I started going to DePaul Law School at night. I didn't tell anyone I was doing it, and it was hard, but it served me well, and that decision really helped me in the long run. I went to law school because there were some dark clouds on the horizon. I thought for the film business in general it became apparent to me that the branch system was going to really come down, offices were closing in Kansas City, Milwaukee, Des Moines. I did it to have a life preserver if things came crashing down and my film career ended with the closing of a branch. A lot of people's careers did eventually end, people who were highly thought of as good sales people, especially the branch managers. That whole localization process where managers knew their markets better than anyone else was really an attractive thing. We are so far removed from that now. When I start talking about this, young people don't want to hear about it. They don't know what the hell you are talking about.

Q: *Did you get your law degree from DePaul?*

JB: After two years at DePaul I did land up going to Los Angeles and took a job as Assistant General Sales Manager for Buena Vista in 1980, so I actually finished up law school in Los Angeles and got my degree there. Even though Paramount didn't close their Chicago office until the early '90s I tend to be a pessimist and felt I had to get to the West Coast. It's funny; now I think, "How do I get back to Chicago?" I kind of wish I was able to work in Chicago a little bit. I respect the fact that you were able to forge an entire film career in Chicago. It's a great city.

Q: *You have been at Sony for 20 years, and in addition to your role as Vice Chairman you are the head of global marketing and distribution for all of Sony's pictures. Can you talk to me about your responsibilities and how your career has evolved?*

JB: John Calley, the Chairman of Sony at the time, had the confidence in me to give me two things, one piece was the international piece and the other was marketing. International came in 1997, and that was a real blessing because it was far from my own experiences. I certainly had traveled to every city in the U.S., but international was a revelation to have the opportunity to get involved with international marketing and distribution. That was a huge learning curve with a lot of travel around the world; it just broadened my horizons tremendously when I visited the top 40 countries in the world. I get my top domestic people involved with international now. I want my top managers to discover this, to understand the international marketplace and think of themselves as part of the global film market. What I learned was that there is so much to learn. You can't just blow in to another country as an American and say this is how we do it in America. You learn so much more than you teach.

Q: *How many international sales offices does Sony have?*

JB: There are three different types of offices that we are connected with. Those that are owned and operated by Sony, about a dozen offices in larger territories like Japan, Germany, England. Then there are a lot of joint ventures with other studios, many of them with Disney, where you need a little more muscle. It's easier to justify overheads in places like Mexico, Brazil and Korea, and a combined release schedule gives you more strength with exhibitors. The last type is arrangements with local distributors who distribute for us. When you add them all up, it's more than 40 territories where we have something in place, and from those offices we cover the rest of the world, which totals over 100 territories.

Q: *What about the size of your domestic operation?*

JB: We have four sales offices, New York, Los Angeles, Toronto and Dallas. I think we are the only distributor still in Dallas. I never thought we would stay there, but every time we crunch the numbers it makes sense because it's efficient and cost effective for us. It would cost more if we moved people to Los Angeles because three of the biggest theatre chains are in Dallas, Knoxville and Denver, and a lot of their work would have them travelling back and forth.

Q: *Is the basic structure of the industry still in place, 30 branches, 4 divisions, that type of thing?*

JB: Yes, but in the last few years Sony and the other studios have really cut back staff, and we have people doubling and tripling their workload, with branch managers handling three to four branches instead of one. We still have four division managers overseeing different sections of the country. The one thing that has been lost is the local exhibitor relations department, and we do more in this area than other companies. Sony maintains a staff of more than a dozen people who are situated throughout the country, even in cities we no longer have a branch office like in Chicago, whose job it is to actually go to the theatres in the area to make sure the posters are up, the trailers are playing, to take the theatre manager to lunch to talk up the upcoming films, to make sure the standee has great placement and not stuck in some corner. It would seem that's a job we can cut, but it gives us a competitive advantage. Until I was on the marketing side I never realized how much money we spent making these materials, and to have their distribution so random and unreliable is something we consider in keeping our staff on the road. The creation and shipping of materials falls into the category of "basics" and often can total $8-10million. It's one of those hidden marketing costs that can really add up. And then we see our television advertising reach 90% of viewers who will never go to the theatre to see a particular movie, whether they are the youngest or oldest who make up the viewership or people who are time shifting through the commercials. It makes me really think back to my past and the importance of grass roots operations. Every exit poll we do when moviegoers are asked what made them see that movie, television spots always rank first, and trailers rank second. It's our best piece of advertising. Why wouldn't we throw money and overhead to make sure the trailer is playing with a picture with a full house rather than one down the hall with nobody in it?

Q: *The other studios pay outside checkers to do the same work, correct?*

JB: Most studios spend $3,000 a week to have their trailers checked. We [would] rather use our own people. We don't spend that much more than we would with a trailer checking company, which I always thought was a bit suspect.

These companies always gave us good news, and right away that makes me suspicious. You weren't fixing the problem, just doing the treatment.

Q: *Do you personally still push exhibitors hard on trailer placement?*

JB: Screaming at exhibitors about trailers every week used to be a ritual for me. Thanks to great people like Rory Bruer (pres w/w distribution) and Elizabeth Crotty (SVP exhibitor relations), I've now been able to retire from that.

Q: *Have you had any ideas that haven't worked?*

JB: I look back, and I'm surprised I'm still here because I've had some bad ideas. Probably the worst one was when I said we were going to charge 80% film rental on the first week of "Godzilla." There have been a few missteps along the way. Anyone who is going to have success in this business has to be enthusiastic for their movies. If you are going to make mistakes, it should be out of enthusiasm and pushing too hard, not too little.

Q: *Weren't you quoted once as saying, "If you don't ask, you don't get?"*

JB: Exactly.

Q: *How hard is it to open a movie successfully?*

JB: The thing about the movie business is that you are selling 20 different products a year, and you have to brand them from scratch. Whether you are in marketing or distribution you are selling to consumers, and I'm proud of the job we do at Sony; I feel we have a great, great team. The constant challenge is to motivate people to want to go to an opening movie on the first Friday, not next Friday. When you come down to it, the public has to show up opening weekend or the problems begin. To do that twenty times a year and to make that kind of investment without knowing the outcome, well, that's a pretty crazy business. Now I'm back to my pessimistic side when looking into the future, I wonder how we can continue to keep the current business model of spending a ton of money before we know or have any guaranteed type of returns whatsoever. With all the tracking, all the research, you still have to open the movie. I love the theatrical experience. I want it to live forever, and maybe it will, but certainly at times like these when the business is down you recognize this as a crazy model. When you hold back your content until we say you can see it, what other business does that? We say first you have to see it in theatres, then several months later you can buy the DVD, then you can see it on Pay Per View, then on cable, etc.

Q: *Haven't the exclusive windows worked pretty well over the last 30 years?*

JB: It has worked great, but you feel it every day, the ground moving from under you. You say to yourself this is a weird business. Who doesn't want things right away? How does our business model get away with saying you can't see something until we say you can? If I go into my optimistic mode, I think of all the content on the hundreds of cable channels that is so disposable, but what we put through theatres lives forever.

Q: *How do you stay current with today's marketplace?*

JB: I still call for grosses on Friday night. I have help, but I still make the calls every Friday even when Sony isn't opening a picture. I'll call executives, our talent, or leave emails and let them know what's happening in the theatres. The big joke is that I used to do a fax every weekend with my analysis, but I refuse to do that now. It's embarrassing because I can't even get my fax machine to work anymore. One of the true joys of the business for me is being able to put things in perspective. I used to spend every Friday night going to theatres when we opened a movie. If you weren't in Westwood on Friday night, you really didn't care that much. You saw how the trailers played, who showed up, the demographics, the size of the audience. The talent used to show up. We talked about the business. Showing up every Friday night in Westwood probably did more for my career than anything else, and it was doing what I would normally do anyway, which is going to the movies.

Q: *Did you ever have a more fun weekend than when "Spiderman" opened in 2002 and became the first movie in history to gross over $100 million dollars in its opening weekend?*

JB: No, that would be hard to top. I think we were the first to go out on the first Friday in May with a big important release, and we didn't have a goal of setting a new record, but the grosses from the opening shows just kept building through the weekend, and it was something special to experience. My faxes from that weekend were given to me as keepsake. The excitement kept building. To say there has never been a more enjoyable weekend would be true. The first Monday in May slot has now become one of the most important weekends of the year and the official start of the summer season. Our record of $116,000,000 has been beaten many times since. How high can the opening record go? $200 million? With higher ticket prices and 3D surcharges anything is possible.

Q: *Do you consider yourself an overall strategist for the company?*

JB: We have this fantastic electronic release schedule board in our conference room. We designed it like the Mirage in Las Vegas. It's spectacular. The old one used to be Velcro on a big board. The new one is very interactive. We can click on IMDB, read the synopsis of a competing film, click on trailers, move things around. If I make no other contribution, we live by the rhythm of the release schedule and never miss our target dates or our deadlines. We are staring at that damn board every meeting, and I think to myself, "What do we have to do for this particular movie to make it the biggest success it can be?"

Q: *Do you still have final say on the release dates?*

JB: I've kept two duties from the past, picking the release dates and reporting the grosses on Friday night. Those are mine.

Q: *Is choosing the right date still the most important distribution decision?*

JB: It is an important decision but in a way overrated as usually films do what they are meant to do one way or another. It's important because once you set the date it sets many things in motion. When you want your trailer up, what will be some good movies to put it with once you realize what you are up against, other factors like how do you get the female audience away from a competing movie and so on. A release date triggers a lot. It certainly is a big piece of setting the model of what you want your film to be.

Q: *In terms of a release schedule, is it harder to set movies at Christmas than in summer because the last couple of holiday seasons haven't been the greatest for Sony?*

JB: We joke about it. What can you do? You either laugh or cry. We have tremendous luck in February. In June we do great; other months are solid. For some reason Christmas has been tough. In 2010 with "How Do You Know," it was one of the most mystifying things where the movie died in a thousand little cuts. It was nothing like "Stealth" which was a tremendous loser. We missed on everything with that movie, bad marketing, the release date; it hit us between the eyes. "How Do You Know" was a quiet loser. The title wasn't really sticky, we avoided trying to come off as a typical romantic comedy, and we ended up with nothing. There were a lot of small mistakes that added up to a big failure. It won't go down in history as one of the big flops like "Ishtar;" it just quietly didn't make a dent. It was like a tree in a forest. We spent the normal big Christmas marketing money to open it, and nothing happened.

Q: *Is a final domestic gross of $100 million still as meaningful as it used to be?*

JB: Are you kidding me? "Green Hornet" and "Social Network" topped out at $97 million. I told my general sales manager if you don't get that last three million you better take a long trip. People like round numbers.

Q: *Let me ask you about 2009. What are some of your memories from that year?*

JB: We had a very well-rounded release schedule that year, all different kinds of genres, and pretty much we made most of them work. We started off the year with a picture no one saw coming, "Paul Blart." All the studios get three different tracking reports, all kinds of research; everyone is in the predicting business making pronouncements whether we meet expectations or not. These services and bloggers have taken some of the fun out of opening weekends. At times we put out a low number in what we think we will do; another studio might put out a high number out on us to make it seem we didn't meet expectations. It can get pretty cutthroat out there. But getting back to "Paul Blart," no one predicted that movie would open to over $30 million and land up grossing close to $150 million in domestic. It was a spectacular success and jump-started the year for us. That was a fun one.

Q: *Do you believe in momentum in the marketplace?*

JB: Yes. So much is about blocking and tackling. Do you have full houses seeing movies they like and trailers they like? It could be that simple. I think it's a great indicator when you get surprises when the theatres are full. The "Paul Blart" trailer played well; people thought it was funny. A lot of other movies were doing business in January of 2009, which got the ball rolling for the next few months. Kevin James became a star with that movie, and we'll be working with him again because we love to work with the same creative talent. Nora Ephron made "Sleepless in Seattle," and in 2009 she made "Julia and Julia." She made the perfect movie. There weren't any major hooks other than it was the perfect movie with the perfect star. That's it. We couldn't even cut a strong trailer for it. We had to just step back and acknowledge that Meryl Streep has a certain relationship with her audience, and she delivered again, one of the rare stars that seems to be getting more popular with age.

Q: *"District 9" was a pickup release for Sony that went on to gross over $100 million. What was the most important decision you made on that film?*

JB: We had a new head of marketing, a young guy named Mark Weinstock, and the best decision I made was to let him fly the plane on "District 9." He did things in viral marketing that everyone is now doing, but he invented them. He was smart enough to know you have to be patient with viral marketing. The movie didn't come out until August, but In March of that year at the ShoWest convention, all the elevators were covered with a marketing slogan with no title or release date, all the things that are usually important. Later with bus benches and other public places, he had slogans like, "When you see an alien, call this number," or, "This Bench is for Humans Only." I would ask him facetiously when is it going to open? Can you please put the release date on the marketing? Then the picture was featured at Comic-Con at the end of July. The fans were excited to see Peter Jackson. No one knew about the movie, then boom. He deserves the credit for an amazing campaign.

Q: *Peter Jackson was the executive producer, and the movie was independently made for $30 million. Is that about what the acquisition price was as well?*

JB: It was somewhere in that ballpark, and we couldn't have made it for that price. The movie was very profitable for us, and international was bigger than domestic. We are very proud of the movie; we received a Best Picture nomination for it.

Q: Let's turn to another Jackson, Michael Jackson's "This Is It." This movie came out of nowhere and wasn't on your 2009 release schedule. Were you in the room when the rights to the footage were auctioned off?

JB: I was there. You're right; it did come of nowhere. No one knew Michael Jackson was going to die in June 2009, and no one knew there was footage of his rehearsals. Out of the blue we get a call from AEG, the giant promoter of the London concerts, inviting us to see some assembled footage with several other studios to bid on. After we saw the twenty minutes, we knew we had to cut a deal. It was absolute dynamite.

Q: You sometimes plan up to three or four years in advance. This time you had three months. How did you do it?

JB: It was crazy, no doubt about it. We had to mobilize the whole world in a very short period of time. The first discussions were centered around a Thanksgiving release, but if we did we would be going up against "Twilight." We knew we had a powerful piece of entertainment, and there wasn't much to compare it to, but we had to apply it to the movie world and see what other movies would be playing against it. Sure, there's going to be tremendous interest in seeing Michael Jackson's final performance, but you don't have to open it against a proven blockbuster like "Twilight." We knew Jackson's favorite holiday was Halloween, and we decided on that date.

Q: Can you talk about the decision to sell the movie as if it was a concert, two weeks only with tickets sold in advance?

JB: The movie was like no other; it was a hybrid type of thing. I think most of our decisions were correct. Marketing it as two weeks only gave it an urgency. We had a lot of fun with that and created the demand. On the other hand, if I had to do it over again, I may not have done the advance tickets because I heard so many people say, "I heard it's all sold out." I was stopping people in the halls and screaming at them, "You are in the business. We are on 2,500 screens. Do you think they are really all sold out?" We did too good of a job convincing people it was a hot ticket. There were intelligent people walking around thinking it was sold out, and I said we have to push the other way. We were getting concert ideas from the concert promoters. I was throwing out some and keeping some. That's how I came up with the line "Tickets Available at Theatres Everywhere." We were able to regain ground and turn people's minds around.

Q: This was another one of your profitable 2009 releases?

JB: Very profitable. This one was very hard to predict, but look at the numbers. We grossed $72 million in North America and $187 million internationally. Almost three-quarters of our gross came from overseas, so everything we did on this picture was a global approach. Plus, it also bucked the DVD downspin, and it became our biggest DVD release of the year. We shipped almost 5 million units domestically. It was like the old days.

Q: How troubling has been the DVD decline?

JB: It's a big problem. To give you an example, on an action movie grossing $100 million we used to estimate 5 million units, now it's 4 million on its way to 3.5. When you do the math it starts adding up. No new technology has replaced those lost dollars. That's why everything is being tried, including Premium VOD, but one thing everyone knows is our product means more after it plays in theatres first, so that will always be a consideration.

Q: *What about the film deals with exhibitors?*

JB: Perhaps the best decision I ever made in distribution was when we went to firm terms. People outside the industry wouldn't believe we sold our movies one way, saw how it played, then changed the deal later, but that's how it was done for years. I don't know how we made money back then with theatre owners getting to keep more of the box office than distributors. Even with 90/10 deals, I remember sitting with Sumner Redstone and sometimes he wanted to pay only 25% film rental.

Q: *Can you share an important lesson you have learned through the years?*

JB: It's all about the movie. When distribution is handed a movie, it's a very collaborative process involving a lot of people doing their jobs. There are many little steps that have to be completed for success to happen. There are no short cuts. Once the release date is set, it becomes real, and the work begins in whatever arena we are playing in, whether it's going for the little chips or going after that big weekend. It's hard work, and it's amazing we can do it 20 times a year and create movies into events that serve each movie in its best way.

Q: *With all the traveling and responsibilities you have had to do over the years, was there a price to pay for your success with being away from home over long stretches?*

JB: Really good question. I actually think climbing up the ranks like I did allowed me in an odd way to be there for my family. When my kids were young, and I was the local distribution guy in Chicago and even in LA, I thought I was busy, but in reality the travel wasn't crazy, and showing up at theatres every Friday night was just what we all did together. By the time it got pretty hairy with lots of travel and stuff going on every night, they were older. I actually miss those Friday nights in Westwood where they'd see the movie, and I'd be in the lobby discussing its fate with the filmmakers; then we'd grab something to eat. Now I just check my handheld device from home and send an email.

Q: *What's most important in leading a global distribution operation?*

JB: To let everyone know what the goal is, to know what kind of movie we want it to be and who the audience is we want to reach. Everybody then has to do their part to make it happen. I have had a broad enough career to know the film business is a detail business. Making all the deadlines is crucial, like getting a trailer up in Germany you have to do it two weeks in advance because you have to dub the picture into German, and it's a big deal to do that. If someone misses the dubbing deadline or the subtitling deadline, and if nobody is doing the grassroots work to get it up on screen, it's not up. It comes down to attention to detail. I feel strongly that can make a difference between success and failure and helping a good picture become even bigger.

Q: *Is that ultimately how you are judged?*

JB: The easiest money in the world is making a big hit bigger; the hardest money is trying to find a way through the forest with a movie that is not working. So why wouldn't you take advantage of the best bets in the world like an Adam Sandler movie and work to make it bigger and not just making it bigger in the United States? What we are really proud of is that Adam Sandler has four $100 million hits in a row internationally. No other comedian has accomplished that. Maximizing what you have while paying attention to all the details, that's how I make a contribution.

Q: *Thank you for your time and insight. It was a pleasure seeing you again.*

Author's note: Jeff Blake's comment that a $200 million dollar weekend was a distinct possibility with higher ticket prices and 3D surcharges became reality when "The Avengers" grossed $207 million on the weekend of May 4, 2012, exactly ten years from the weekend when "Spiderman" broke through the $100 million dollar weekend barrier. In the ten years between 2002 and 2012, the following 22 movies opened to over $100 million on its first weekend with 11 of those opening in the month of May:

1. Marvel's The Avengers: $207,438,708 – May 4, 2012
2. Harry Potter and the Deathly Hallows: Part 2: $169,189,427 – July 15, 2011
3. The Dark Knight: $158,411,483 – July 18, 2008
4. The Hunger Games: $152,535,747 – March 23, 2012
5. Spider-Man 3: $151,116,516 – May 4, 2007
6. The Twilight Saga: New Moon: $142,839,137 – November 20, 2009
7. The Twilight Saga: Breaking Dawn, Part 1: $138,122,261 – November 18, 2011
8. Pirates of the Caribbean: Dead Man's Chest: $135,634,554 – July 7, 2006
9. Iron Man 2: $128,122,480 – November 19, 2010
10. Harry Potter and the Deathly Hallows: Part 1: $125,017,372 – November 19, 2010
11. Shrek the Third: $121,629,270 – May 18, 2007
12. Alice in Wonderland: $116,101,023 – March 5, 2010
13. Spider-Man: $114,844,116 – May 3, 2002
14. Pirates of the Caribbean: At World's End: $114,732,820 – May 25, 2007
15. Toy Story 3: $110,307,189 – June 18, 2010
16. Transformers: Revenge of the Fallen: $108,966,307 – June 26, 2009
17. Star Wars Episode III: Revenge of the Sith: $108,435,841 – May 20, 2005
18. Shrek 2: $108,037,878 – May 21, 2004
19. X-Men: The Last Stand: $102,750,665 – May 26, 2006
20. Harry Potter and the Goblet of Fire: $102,685,961 – November 18, 2005
21. Iron Man: $102,118,668 – May 2, 2008
22. Indiana Jones and the Kingdom of the Crystal Skull: $100,137,835 – May 22, 2008

Source: the-numbers.com as of June 20, 2012

Week 44: Questions for Discussion

1. What was the simple brilliance of Sony marketing "This Is It" as the movie was set to open, with the copy line "Tickets Available at Theatres Everywhere"? Before answering the question, consider the implications of this kind of decision, which has to be made from time to time by marketing executives.

2. Look at all the movies currently playing in your market, choose one movie and devise a five-word copy line not being used by the distributor to announce a simple, yet effective marketing message for that film.

3. Creating demand for your product is a crucial mantra for all marketers. Doing so without having to lower prices is even better. How are the studios being more effective than independents in this area? In 2009, why do you think the independents had fallen behind the studios in creating ingenious marketing campaigns for their films?

Do you think the situation has gotten any better for independents in today's market when it comes to cutting edge marketing campaigns?

4. Hollywood is known for copying success of other successful movies and genres, though no basketball documentary has been able to come close to duplicating the success of "Hoop Dreams," released in 1994. Why do you think that's the case? Shouldn't there be room for another similar type movie? Is it a marketing problem, the genre itself, the quality of films or a feeling of "been there, seen that"?

5. What does Jeff Blake mean when he says, "If you don't ask, you don't get," in relation to his work at Sony? What do you feel can be both a positive and a negative using that philosophy?

6. Choose any portion of the interview with Jeff Blake and discuss something that resonated with you, that you found to be valuable information or advice.

COMPETITION HEATS UP AT THE BOX OFFICE
FOR THE FINAL STRETCH RUN

Week 45: November 6–12, 2009

> *There are three stages of attracting audiences to a movie; creating*
> *awareness, creating want-to-see and motivating to go-to-see.*

All industries have their own particular annual business cycles, and the movie industry is no different. With Halloween in the rearview window and the pumpkins still out at the curb, the studios waste no time in turning their attention to the all-important final two months of the year. The month of November is the equivalent of May when the summer season opens and each of these months have evolved into prime playing time for some of the biggest, most anticipated movies the studios have to offer. It becomes a furious race to the end of the year, and the releases are broken into two parts, the November movies which peak over Thanksgiving weekend and the December movies which peak during the week between Christmas and New Year's Day. It took a number of years for distributors and exhibitors to work out a release arrangement that made sense for both parties. When movies used to open in mid-November, distributors expected theatre owners to hold those movies through the end of the year, but many of those movies faltered in the early parts of December, and it would become unrealistic for some theatres to keep them on the screen, leading to shouting matches, threats and a lot of chest pounding. The situation now is more rational and addresses the fact that movies have shorter theatrical runs. It becomes the law of the jungle. The strong movies will hold on and play as long as audiences are coming out to see them, and the movies that falter will fall on the wayside and be allowed to die in peace.

What a difference a week makes. Last week Sony's "This Is It" was the sole opener and did its thing to the tune of grossing $104 million worldwide, the only way to really approach the performance of this movie since the studio paid $60 million for world rights, and they blitzed over 100 countries day and date with North America. Sony didn't even wait until the weekend was over to announce the two-week limited engagement was being extended through Thanksgiving. That was a no-brainer. I don't remember a studio ever sticking to its announced theatrical limited time frame. You first create demand, then you extend the run. It works every time. The first weekend of November brings much more competition with four wide releases dueling for moviegoers, and looking at the titles, all the movies seem to share a strange connection to some form of paranormal activity, something that's pretty hot at the moment with the movie of the same name. Even though they are all different from each other, that's not necessarily good for business, but here is how the movies break down:

- ▶ Warner Bros. is opening "The Box," A Twilight Zone type thriller where a strange box is left at the doorstep of a character played by Cameron Diaz and her husband, where all they have to do is push a button to get a million dollars, but the catch is a stranger will die because of it.

- ▶ Universal has "The Fourth Kind," a sci-fi thriller about supposed true accounts of missing people who have been abducted by aliens.

- ▶ Overture is opening the weirdest sounding title of the year in "The Men Who Stare at Goats" with a good cast of George Clooney, Jeff Bridges and Kevin Spacey in a story about a U.S. military unit investigating telepathy and other phenomenon. The movie is being positioned to get laughs, but whether it's a farce, a satire or a dark comedy is hard to figure out, and its tagline "No Goats No Glory" doesn't help to decipher it. Even with that cast, if audiences don't know what it is, it's hard to be successful.

▶ Finally, Disney's big budget remake of "The Christmas Carol" kicks off the holiday season in the position to be this weekend's runaway box office champ, and even though it's a bit of a stretch, it also has the paranormal angle with the three ghosts visiting Scrooge. A romantic comedy would look pretty good about now. The key to big weekends with multiple releases is serving many niches, and this week will fall short in that category.

November is the best month to release a Christmas movie because of the lead time, and it's not unprecedented that one is opening on the first weekend of November ("Elf," Tim Allen's Santa Claus movies), but there is also an important consideration this year, maximization of all available 3D theatres in the country. Digital 3D has been a fantastic growth generator for studios and theatre owners, and there are only two 3D movies left to open in 2009, "A Christmas Carol" and the biggie, James Cameron's "Avatar" on December 18. Opening this weekend will give Disney six full weeks to control up to 2,000 locations, which is up from 900 theatres that had 3D capabilities at the beginning of 2009. That's impressive growth, over a 100% gain in 3D screens. With the potential of huge grosses for "Avatar," that number could reach 2,500 theatres by mid-December. Getting that extra $3.00 per admission is too good to pass up, but the question still remains what the long-term appeal for 3D will be. Is it here to stay, or will the public eventually tire of the process?

> *"The face of the industry is changing, and mass advertising isn't going to be enough anymore. It's getting harder to capture a broad audience because so many television stations and publications are niche-oriented today."*
>
> —*Robert Zemeckis*

I've always admired Robert Zemeckis and his movies from his early "Used Cars" to "Back to the Future" to "Who Framed Roger Rabbit?" to "Forrest Gump." Ever since he has gone to using capture motion technology, using real actors and then digitally animating them. I've cooled on him because of how the characters look in the process, somewhat creepy and unnatural looking. "A Christmas Carol" is his third movie in a row using this technology following "The Polar Express" and "Beowolf," both successful at the box office with grosses of $180 million and $82 million respectfully. Zemeckis has been a big commercial director in Hollywood for 25 years and has directed a lot of moneymakers for the studios and hopes to continue to deliver the hits, though I wouldn't mind it if he gave the capture motion process a rest. He also is a shrewd businessman and knows his marketing. His recent statement, "The face of the industry is changing, and mass advertising isn't going to be enough anymore. It's getting harder to capture a broad audience because so many television stations and publications are niche-oriented today," was in response to Disney's out-of-the-box marketing stunt of a six-month, whistle-stop tour promoting "A Christmas Carol." Following what other studios have been doing with movies like "District 9," Paranormal Activity" and "This Is It," the studios continue to impress, coming up with new creative ways to sell their movies. Disney just completed the train tour, which started in Los Angeles on Memorial Day weekend and ended last weekend at Grand Central Station in New York. It stopped in 40 cities, big and small, and stayed in each city for up to three days. The train was a six-car passenger train decorated on the outside with key art from the poster campaign and showcased different aspects of the production, a digital gallery, props from the movie, demonstrations of the technology used and interactive games for the entire family. It was free to the public. A train crisscrossing the country, town by town, city by city, harkens back to the earliest days of showmanship when the circus came to town and shows the studios are intent in pushing more non-traditional approaches to marketing to go along with their national T.V buys. When they are successful in creating awareness in other ways, that means they can cut back on their TV campaigns when they deem appropriate.

This Week the Box Office: *Weekly Attendance: 21,513,849*

November is also a month where some of the most prestigious, Oscar-worthy films of the year open in theatres. There is no movie arriving with more anticipation and festival acclaim than Lionsgate's "Precious," finally opening in theatres after conquering Sundance, Cannes and Toronto Film Festivals, the three most important and influential festivals on the circuit. "Precious" depicts the bleak story of an overweight black girl abused in every conceivable way by her parents and her subsequent struggle to rise above her situation with the help of a kind teacher. There is no other film out there that has the aura of social significance and importance that this film has. On the other hand, there is no other film with rougher subject matter, which would normally make it a very tough sell at the box office. This is the one to watch very closely, and I plan to see it this weekend with an audience in a big commercial theatre in the south suburbs of Chicago that caters to a sizable African American audience in addition to a somewhat smaller white audience. There is no better way to understand a film than going to a theatre on opening night to sit among the moviegoers and to be able to feel the vibe of the crowd. Several big questions will begin to be answered this weekend. How many people will show up in theatres to see it? What will be the makeup of the audience? Will Oprah Winfrey and Tyler Perry be successful in convincing the African American audience to pay to see what in its essence is a difficult black art film? Will the white upscale art audience be the primary audience, or will it be the rare film that is carried by both the art audience and the black audience? Will the very depressing subject matter, the relentless misery and ugliness the movie depicts, be too much for audiences who prefer their movies to be escapist entertainment? There are three stages of attracting audiences to a movie, creating awareness, creating want-to-see and motivating to-go-to-see. I think the first two stages are somewhat answered, but the final go-to stage is the one with the question mark. People can say they want to see something, but often they just don't quite get around to it and then figure they can catch it later on DVD or cable. I'm rooting for "Precious" to be successful because it's been a tough year for independents, and it would be great to see a big diverse audience come out to experience such a challenging film. Next week I'll be discussing "Precious" more in detail, my own experience in seeing it as well as its opening weekend theatrical performance.

Disney's A Christmas Carol

Disney
Opening weekend: $30,051,075
Domestic gross; $137,855,863 42.4%
Foreign gross: $187,430,783 57.6%
Worldwide gross: $325,286,6346
Widest release: 3,683 theatres

The Box

Warner Brothers
Opening weekend: $7,571,417
Domestic gross: $15,051,977 45.2%
Foreign gross: $18,281,554 54.8%
Worldwide gross; $33,333,531
Widest release: 2,635 theatres

The Fourth Kind

Universal
Opening weekend: $12,231,160
Domestic gross: $25,486,040 53.4%
Foreign gross: $22,223,153 46.6%
Worldwide gross: $47,709,193
Widest release: 2,530 theatres

Men Who Stare at Goats

Overture
Opening weekend: $12,706,654
Domestic gross: $32,425,665 47.0%
Foreign gross: $36,540,493 53.0%
Worldwide gross: $68,968,688
Widest release: 2,453 theatres

Precious

Lionsgate
Opening weekend: $1,872,458
Domestic gross: $47,566,524 74.7%
Foreign gross: $16,081,309 25.3%
Worldwide gross: $63,647,833
Widest release: 907 theatres

La Danse

Zipporah
Opening weekend: $14,000
Domestic gross: $567,493 51.2%
Foreign gross: $540,953 48.8%
Worldwide gross: $1,108,446
Widest release: 25 theatres

That Evening Sun

Freestyle
Opening weekend: $7,330
Domestic gross: $281,350

Collapse

Vitagraph
Opening weekend: $7,800
Domestic gross: $56,436

Lovely, Still

Monterey
Opening weekend: N/A
Domestic gross: $127,524 54.7%

Foreign gross: N/A

Widest release: 11 theatres

Foreign gross: N/A

Widest release: 6 theatres

Foreign gross: $105,519 45.3%

Worldwide gross: $233,083

Widest release: 17 theatres

The Bicycle Thief (60th Anniversary)

Independent

Opening weekend: $10,786

Domestic gross: $37,111

Foreign gross: N/A

Widest release: 1 theatre

Splinterheads

Paladin

Opening weekend: $10,515

Domestic gross: $16,392

Foreign gross: N/A

Widest release: 3 theatres

Endgame

Monterey

Opening weekend: $1,608

Domestic gross: $9,645

Foreign gross: N/A

Widest release: 14 theatres

Humble Pie

Monterey

Opening weekend: $1,083

Domestic gross: $3,389

Foreign gross: N/A

Widest release: 2 theatres

Week 45: Questions for Discussion

1. Are you ever influenced one way or another by a tagline for movie, whether it's on a poster, in a trailer, online, or in a newspaper or magazine? What is your opinion of the ad copy for "The Men Who Stare at Goats," *No Goats No Glory?*

2. What makes a movie poster memorable for you? Of all the movie posters currently in theatres and on the Internet, what has caught your attention that you think is good and makes you want to see the film? Do you think it's possible that a poster alone can create awareness, create want-to-see, and motivate someone to actually go to see a specific movie? Do you recall a poster that did that for you?

3. At the end of this chapter, you will find a number of taglines from 2009 movies that are listed in one column with all the movie titles listed in another column. Do your best to match up as many taglines to the movie titles themselves, utilizing each and every one of them. Then rank the taglines in order of what you feel are the ten best for their ability to help position the movie effectively in the minds of the moviegoer. Finally, choose one that you believe is the worst copy line of the year.

TAGLINES FOR 2009 MOVIES

Match the copy line with the appropriate movie on this page.

All She Ever Wanted Was a Little Credit...	The Hurt Locker
Everybody Pays	Adventureland
One Push Can Change Anything	Pink Panther
Inspect the Unexpected	Madea Goes to Jail
Death Saved the Best For 3-D	I Love You, Man
It Wants To Be Born... Now	Crank High Voltage
Life Tries to Break You. Love Holds You Together	Confessions of a Shopaholic
Don't Mess with His Mall	Sunshine Cleaning
The Story of the Man Behind the Legend	17 Again
She's an Executive on the Move. But Her Career Is Taking Her A Little Farther Than She Expected	Drag Me to Hell
The Race Is On	The International
Mother. Sister. Grandma. Gangster.	The Soloist
Life's a Messy Business	The Informers
If Bad People Hurt Someone You Love, How Far Would You Go to Hurt Them Back?	Obsessed
Are You Man Enough to Say It?	Push
New Model. Original Parts.	Management
She Has the Best of Both Worlds. Now She Has to Choose One.	Taking Woodstock
Long Hours. Low Pay. High Times.	Away We Go
One Woman Must Take a Stand	The Final Destination
He Was Dead...But He Got Better	The Proposal
No One Changes Anything by Playing It Safe	American Violet
Who Says You're Only Young Once?	Every Little Step
From the Author of American Psycho and Less Than Zero	The Unborn
All's Fair When Love Is War	The Hangover
A Touching Comedy	Not Easily Broken
Take the Trip This Summer	Year One
From Director Sam Mendes	Up in The Air
Some Guys Just Can't Handle Vegas	Paul Blart: Mall Cop
Right Place. Wrong Time.	The Morgans
The Journey of a Chorus Line	Notorrious
Christine Brown Has a Good Job, a Great Boyfriend, and a Bright Future. But in Three Days, She's Going to Hell	New in Town
Meet Your Ancestors	Race to Witch Mountain
Here Comes the Bribe	Hannah Montana The Movie
You Don't Have to Be a Hero to Do This Job. But It Helps.	Land of the Lost
This Is Not a Love Story. This is a Story about Love.	(500) Days of Summer
Based on Two True Stories	Julia & Julia
We're Not in Manhattan Anymore	Harry Potter and the Half-Blood Prince
His People Needed a Leader. He Gave Them a Champion	The Last House on the Left
The Story of A Man Ready to Make a Connection	Invictus
Dark Secrets Revealed	Fast & Furious

Match the copy line with the appropriate movie on this page.

Nothing Escapes Them	2012
There Are Two Sides to Every Family	Bruno
Frank Wanted the Holidays to Be Picture Perfect. What He Got Was Family.	Paranormal Activity
	The Cove
The Gift of Last Memories	A Christmas Carol
Sometimes When You Least Expect It	Couples Retreat
They Will Dream It. Earn It. Live It	Avatar
It's Not Rocket Science... Every Child Can Be Educated"	Precious
Fear What Happens Next	Inglourious Basterds
Nut Up Or Shut Up	The Stepfather
Be Your Own Hero	Everybody's Fine
The New Film by Joel and Ethan Coen	The Perfect Getaway
Daddy's Home	Crazy Heart
There's One in All of Us.	House of the Devil
The System Must Pay	Where the Wild Things Are
In a World Where Everyone Can Only Tell the Truth...This Guy Can Lie	The Box
A Comedy in Paradise They'll Never Forget	The Stepfather
He Helped Me.	The Providence Effect
Based on the Actual Case Studies	District 9
We Were Warned	Brothers
What Happens When You Sleep? Don't See It Alone	Zombieland
Based on the Extraordinary True Story	Whip It
Divorced...with Benefits.	Pirate Radio
Her Country. Her Heart. Her Majesty	Sherlock Holmes
The Harder the Life. the Sweeter the Song	Pandorum
From the Director of Terminator2 and Titanic	Gamer
Based on the Novel "Push" by Sapphire	The Invention of Lying
Inspired by True Events. Adored by Millions. Outlawed by the Government.	A Serious Man
See It in 3-D!	The Fourth Kind
You Are the Experiment	Funny People
You Are Not Welcome Here	Departures
A Basterd's Work Is Never Done	Saw VI
Who's Playing You?	It's Complicated
Shallow Water. Deep Secret.	The Blind Side
Let the Games Begin	Love Happens
The Third Film from the Director of the 40-Year-Old Virgin and Knocked Up	Fame
From the Man Who Brought You Borat	Law Abiding Citizen
Talk on the Phone. Finish Your Homework. Watch TV. Die	

A GRITTY URBAN DRAMA TURNS HEADS AND SETS RECORDS

Week 46: November 13–19, 2009

Behind every successful film are executives making astute decisions.

In the field of economics, the term "invisible hand" refers to the marketplace behaving as if some unseen force is guiding it, sorting out all the goods and services, winners and losers, in accordance to overall market demand. Perhaps it was time for the market to really embrace a serious independent film in 2009 after so many disappointments at the box office. If that was the case, the invisible hand didn't act alone last weekend; it received some big help from two outside forces. There were a lot of question marks surrounding the festival sensation "Precious" as it opened in 18 theatres in New York, Los Angeles, Atlanta and Chicago on November 6th. Many of them were answered with an exclamation point. When I drove to AMC's Country Club Hills Theatre in the south suburbs of Chicago on opening night for the 8:15 show, I didn't know what to expect. All I knew was something was doing business as I circled around a very crowded parking lot trying to find a place to park. When I finally walked into the theatre I had my answer. "Precious" opened to blockbuster business, selling out every show of the day and night, and I couldn't get in, so I left, deciding to come back Sunday morning to see it. Talking to the manager, he had already ordered two additional prints saying it projected out to be the biggest movie of the year for his theatre, and this is a theatre that plays every studio event movie released. The sellouts continued all weekend, and the theatre landed up grossing $150,000 over the weekend, one of four runs in the Chicago market, which totaled $443,000 between them. Nationally, the 18 theatres grossed an out-of-this-world $104,000 per theatre, an all-time industry record for any movie opening in more than five theatres.

The box office performance of "Precious" is a singular achievement never before seen in motion picture history. Whereas "Paranormal Activity" had recently set its own records, it had "Blair Witch Project" in a similar genre to compare it to. There is no such comparison to be made with "Precious." Grosses like this just don't happen with black art films, which in the past have made for a very small subcategory of films. "Precious" entered the Sundance Film Festival, like so many other independent films, looking for a distribution deal, and it snagged the richest deal, securing a $5.5 million deal with Lionsgate and emerging as the most heralded film of Sundance, winning two top awards. There have been countless other excellent films that have emerged from film festivals that couldn't catch a cold once they opened in commercial theatres. Just a year earlier at the 2008 Sundance Festival, "Ballast," another hard-edged drama with an African American cast, won two awards and had critics and audiences raving about it. The director decided to self-distribute his film after an earlier deal with a distributor broke down, and the movie went on to gross less than $100,000. Unfortunately, this is a typical performance for a gritty urban drama. It's tough to get audiences to come out to a movie theatre to see any independent film these days, much less one depicting a 16-year-old black girl experiencing every form of abuse you could imagine, much of it coming from her own mother and father. Four-star reviews and festival awards are not enough in most cases to insure success in the marketplace. Tough, depressing realism is a difficult sell however you slice it.

This is where the two outside forces I referred to earlier enter the picture. Oprah Winfrey and Tyler Perry, perhaps the two most influential African Americans in the entertainment industry, have been promoting "Precious" nonstop for the last eight months. Even though they weren't involved in making the film, their passionate praise and calls for support for the film helped create the intense demand seen in theatres last weekend. That kind of influence is real power marketing dollars can't buy. Their involvement didn't happened by chance. The producer's reps for the film, led by John Sloss, worked on getting a print to Tyler Perry to see in advance of Sundance, and after he saw it and was so moved by its subject matter and performances, he called Oprah and told her she had to see it at once. They were both emotionally moved enough to get involved to promote the film, and the strategy to get a print to Tyler Perry proved to be a masterful stroke that put the film in a much better position to succeed. Behind every successful film are executives making astute decisions. Winfrey's commitment to do multiple shows on the film and Perry's use of his 40,000 plus e-mail list provided the platform to get the word out that the vast majority of films could only dream of. Congratulations to director Lee Daniels and everyone involved in the making of this excellent, gut-wrenching and in the end, inspirational film. They won the lottery, and they earned it.

For agreeing to promote the film, Winfrey and Perry were given executive producer credits, generally reserved for those individuals or companies who actually finance movies, arrange for outside financing, or through their participation lead other investors to come on board. The actual investors of the film are a wealthy Denver couple, Gary Magness and Sarah Siegal-Magness, who invested $10 million to produce "Precious." In many ways they have been pushed aside by the high profile duo of Winfrey and Perry, but they also realize what their support has meant to the film and what it means for potential profits down the road. It looks like they're leaving their egos at the door, which is a good thing to see, and if the film somehow goes on to win Best Picture, the couple will share the stage to claim the prize. With a field of ten Best Picture nominees this year, "Precious" is a lock to be nominated. If it was still a field of five it would probably still be nominated; that's how good the entire package looks at this time. So attention turns to the distributor, Lionsgate, on how they're handling the distribution strategy. In the last couple of years, Lionsgate has moved away from smaller artier films and has concentrated on their bread and butter of mainstream action movies. It's interesting to note that the only film festival acquisition to ever go on to win Best Picture was "Crash," bought by Lionsgate at the 2003 Toronto Film Festival, but lately they haven't been active players in buying too many specialty films. That all changed for the company this year at Sundance after hearing Tyler Perry was on board to promote the film.

Being in the Tyler Perry business has been very good for Lionsgate, and they outbid Harvey Weinstein to make sure they acquired "Precious," knowing full well the potential of Perry's huge core audience of loyal fans. With Perry's base in Atlanta and Winfrey's base in Chicago, it made perfect sense to launch those markets along with the traditional New York and Los Angeles openings. I questioned the fact that none of the five theatres in the original Chicago run was a traditional art house with Landmark's two theatres in the market left out of the release. Lionsgate's most crucial decision, and the one which broadcast their belief in the film, was to choose the mainstream City North theatre in Chicago's important north side zone over one of the three main art theatres, Landmark's Century Centre, AMC's Pipers Alley or the independently operated Music Box. After the City North grossed $89,000 over the weekend, it would seem the distributor knew exactly what they were doing. They were putting their money more on the Tyler Perry audience than they were on the traditional art audience, and they were booking the theatres accordingly. The audience I saw the film with at the Country Club Hills theatre was made up of 95% African American women, the same audience for Tyler Perry's movies. That's good distribution. It was reported that the exit polls showed the overall weekend audience to be split 50/50 between black and white audiences, but I have my doubts about that, at least in Chicago. It appears that with the help of Winfrey and Perry, African American women were the primary target audience, while the white art audience was relegated to the secondary position. That's how I see it, and if that's the case, we're experiencing another first with an art film.

With the Oscars four months away, platform releases are very tricky affairs for films with Academy Award potential. Do you strike when the iron is hot and go wide, or do you stay small and gradually increase your runs, recognizing you are in it for the long haul? Lionsgate's decision is to be aggressive and push the envelope. For their second week, they are expanding from 18 to 174 theatres, opening up some additional large markets and adding a substantial number of theatres in the original four cities. In Chicago, it's going from 5 to 27 theatres, a strong push that will answer another important question, how deep will the suburban audience support be for this tough-minded film set in Harlem's ghetto? Since there is really no precedent to follow, Lionsgate is blazing its own path, forcing the issue and going after the larger audience that could make it into a true blockbuster. Will they be successful in capturing the mainstream audience? It's a week-to-week proposition, and you don't know unless you go for it. The film will be expanded to 900 runs across the country on November 20 in time for Thanksgiving. In a year of mostly disappointing news for independent films, "Precious" is the one film with heat and the one to keep an eye on.

Every weekend is pressure packed and a bit of a crapshoot.

This Week at the Box Office: *Weekly Attendance: 23,099,733*

The major studio release this weekend is Sony's disaster movie "2012," going out in over 3,400 domestic theatres and 13,000 theatres in 105 countries, the second time in three weeks following "This Is It" that Sony is blitzing the global marketplace looking for gold. This summer-like special effects blockbuster was actually originally slated to open in the summer on July 10 before Sony decided on switching it to November. They did it for two reasons; to stand out more as the only summer style movie of its kind at this time of the year and to take advantage of a month that has seen franchise films like Harry Potter and James Bond do blockbuster business. That looks good on paper, but it's impossible to know in advance if the results will match expectations. Big movies in November are asked to open to summer-like numbers, but that doesn't always happen, and instead of seven days of business in the summer, in November it comes down more to what happens over the three-day weekend with schools being in session. Every weekend is pressure packed and a bit of a crapshoot. Already November has started 14% behind 2008 because Disney's "A Christmas Carol" opened to less than half of "Madagascar: Escape 2 Arfica's" $63 million on the same weekend last year. New movies are released 51 out of the 52 weeks of the year, and they're compared to the previous year's output; sometimes the current ones just don't match up. With a $200 million production cost, there is a fair amount of pressure on "2012" to perform strong out of the gates, but even if it opens to $50-$60 million over the weekend, it still won't match last year's James Bond's "Quantum of Solace," which did $67 million. Whatever figure it opens to, the pressure is there in November more than it is in the summer to be more than a one-week wonder, so "2012" needs to show some staying power. Different times of the year, different set of dynamics. The huge thing it has going for it is that it's pure mindless entertainment, an over-sized grand spectacle where audiences can go to forget their problems for a couple of hours and watch the world end with a big box of popcorn in their hands. And for a lot of people, that's what movies are all about.

2012
Sony
Opening weekend: $65,237,614
Domestic gross: $166,112,167 21.6%
Foreign gross: $603,567,306 78.4%
Worldwide gross: $769,679,473
Widest release: 3,444 theatres

Pirate Radio
Focus
Opening weekend: $2,904,380
Domestic gross: $8,017,467 22.1%
Foreign gross: $28,330,867 77.9%
Worldwide gross: $36,348,784
Widest release: 882 theatres

Fantastic Mr. Fox
20th Century Fox
Opening weekend: $265,900
Domestic gross: $21,002,919 45.2%
Foreign gross: $25,468,104 54.8%
Worldwide gross: $46,471,023
Widest release: 2,034 theatres

The Messenger
Oscilloscope
Opening weekend: $44,523
Domestic gross: $1,109,660 72.9%
Foreign gross: $411,601 27.1%
Worldwide gross: $1,521,261
Widest release: 50 theatres

Four Seasons Lodge
First Run
Opening weekend: $11,667
Domestic gross: $58,334
Foreign gross: N/A
Widest release: 2 theatres

William Kunstler: Disturbing the Universe
Arthouse
Opening weekend: $10,332
Domestic gross: $57,569
Foreign gross: N/A
Widest release: 6 theatres

Uncertainty
IFC
Opening weekend: $13,075
Domestic gross: $36,689
Foreign gross: N/A
Widest release: 4 theatres

Dare
Image
Opening weekend: $13,200
Domestic gross: $18,087
Foreign gross: N/A
Widest release: 2 theatres

The End of Poverty?
Cinema Libre
Opening weekend: $12,593
Domestic gross: $57,324
Foreign gross: N/A
Widest release: 5 theatres

Oh My God
Mitropoulous
Opening weekend: $8,263
Domestic gross: $38,245
Foreign gross: N/A
Widest release: 7 theatres

Women in Trouble
Screen Media
Opening weekend: $12,784
Domestic gross: $18,251
Foreign gross: N/A
Widest release: 3 theatres

THE AMERICAN FILM MARKET

The American Film Market (AFM) in Santa Monica, California takes place every November and is one of the three major film markets in the world and the only one that stands alone without a major film festival attached to it. The other two are the markets that occur with the Cannes Film Festival in May and Berlin Festival in February. Despite 2009's downbeat economic climate and tighter money in the global marketplace, 8,000 industry professionals attended the market representing 70 countries. Even though there were a number of higher-profile films on display, the majority of the 4,000 movies in play each year at AFM are lower-budget movies looking for the same thing, either financing or distribution for their films. The global financial crisis posed the biggest problem because there were fewer institutions lending money. It was estimated that before the crisis there were 45 banks willing to lend money for film productions; at the time of AFM 2009 there were less than 12 banks left in that business. Hence, the 2009 AFM market was thought to be one of the quietest in history in terms of sales and completed deals. In addition, other reasons for the downturn in the independent film business have been documented and repeated throughout the book, the glut of films, television not buying films like they used to, international presales being extremely low, the increased importance and search for quality over quantity. As it had been for much of the industry, 2009 was a year in transition, and it certainly was that for the global independent film business looking for new avenues and revenue streams for their movies. The markets in 2010 and 2011 rebounded with more activity and deals, but the new revenue streams of VOD and streaming still haven't caught up with the decline in the theatrical, television and DVD revenues of the past.

Week 46: Questions for Discussion

1. Name the factors involved in the film "Precious" becoming a big box office success. How important was the release date and release pattern set by the distributor?

2. Discuss the various differences between "Precious" and "Paranormal Activity" in the marketplace from type of film, release strategy, distributor to target audience.

3. Analyze two current films in your market with platform releases, one that looks to be successful and the other having trouble drawing audiences. If you live in a city with no limited releases playing, discuss two titles from a national perspective.

WORLD SAVVY SUMMIT ENTERTAINMENT PROVES ITS METTLE IN HOLLYWOOD

Week 47: November 20–26, 2009

---

*The six major film studios control a lot, but they don't control everything, and
at times they make mistakes and allow projects to slip through their hands.*

The six major film studios control a lot, but they don't control everything, and at times they make mistakes and allow projects to slip through their hands. That has always been the beauty and challenge of the movie industry for independent film companies; opportunities are out there, and all they have to do is recognize what they are, what they can afford to do, and then make the correct decisions in figuring out how to capitalize on them. There are four commodities in Hollywood that matter most, power, money, talent and respect. For a distribution company, respect comes from having your own domestic organization and proving you can successfully distribute films in the United States over a solid period of time, still the crucial component that buyers everywhere look for in determining a film's value. Summit Entertainment had been a very successful foreign sales company since the early 1990s when they decided to start a U.S. distribution company in 2007. The key was to be able to strengthen their position by guaranteeing a U.S. release on all their movies they were selling internationally, something many other international sellers can't offer. A decision like this has buried companies in the past because marketing and distribution costs can make money disappear in a hurry, especially if box office success proves elusive. And the hits were elusive for Summit in their first year as a domestic distributor with flops like "Penelope," "Sex Drive" and "P2" opening and closing without a whimper.

Even as Summit's first wave of releases were tanking, they had an ace in the hole because the company had earlier bought the movie rights to the "Twilight Saga" books, taking advantage of Paramount choosing not to renew a $750,000 option they had on the property. At the time Summit picked up the option, the first book hadn't really taken off yet, so it was a speculative risk on their part. Being aggressive and jumping at the opportunity to purchase the rights to the four books proved to be a game changer for Summit. Exactly a year ago this weekend, "Twilight" opened to $69 million on its way to a domestic gross of $191,000,000, a tremendous success for a movie that cost $35 million with an unknown cast. The momentum just kept growing in 2009 when the "Twilight" DVD sold more than 8 million copies, more than any other movie of the year. The second installment, "New Moon," has a chance this weekend to surpass $100 million, which would really send Summit to the next level. Pre-sales for tickets have been through the roof, and "New Moon" has set the all-time record for pre-sold tickets on both Fandango and movietickets.com. There has been only one other movie in history to gross $100 million in its first three days in either November or December, and that was "Harry Potter: Goblet of Fire" in 2005 with $102 million. Look for that record to fall this weekend. It didn't take long, but after that very first weekend last year, "Twilight" became an instant franchise for Summit as they were sitting on three additional books to film. That's the holy grail for any distributor, finding new brands that have the potential to become franchises, and if that happens, maximize it to the fullest and try not to screw it up. So far they have been flawless in their execution, and they didn't waste any time getting more productions started, actually shooting the second and third films of the series back-to-back over the summer with the 3rd film, "Eclipse," scheduled to open June 30, 2010. All along they have been able to keep production costs down, $50 million for "New Moon" and $60 million for "Eclipse," and needless to say with their experience in international sales, Summit controls worldwide rights on all the properties and knows how to maximize those rights to the fullest. Worldwide revenues for "New Moon" should top a half billion dollars. Very impressive.

Without a doubt, Summit is building their company around this series of movies, and there is nothing wrong with that. Blockbusters of this kind can make up for a multitude of flops. But taking a closer look at the eight movies Summit

343

has released up to this point in 2009, without the "Twilight" series, they are a struggling independent with a 2.25% market share, with it they're a Hollywood player. The following are Summit's 2009 releases and their grosses:

- ► Push: $31 million
- ► Knowing: $79 million
- ► Next Day Air: $10 million
- ► The Brothers Bloom: $3 million
- ► The Hurt Locker: $13 million
- ► Bandslam: $5 million
- ► Sorority Row: $11 million
- ► Astro Boy: $17 million

It should take less than 10 days of release for "New Moon" to surpass the total grosses of all eight of the above movies. That's the power of the franchise movie, but it also points out the difficulty a distributor has in formulating a 12-month release schedule of diverse product that can deliver a profitable season. What they do from this point on will be interesting to follow. As the studios continue to withdraw from the specialty art business, there will be opportunities for other companies to pick up the slack on the upscale scripts and finished films that will be available to acquire. Summit has proven they can successfully handle a platform release when they nursed "The Hurt Locker" to a gross close to $13 million in the heat of the summer, not an easy task. There will be more money to mine with this film as it looks like a solid choice to be part of the Best Picture race. They also experienced how difficult it can be to make a star driven specialty title like "The Brothers Bloom" work in today's theatrical market, seeing it sputter out at the $3 million range despite giving it a strong marketing push. It would be good to see Summit as well as Overture Films ("Capitalism: A Love Story") become bigger players in festival type films because there will be plenty of quality films looking for distribution. Is the quality independent film just experiencing a temporary lull because the output of recent releases hasn't been as strong in past years? That's a question that will need to be answered by distributors like Summit and Overture as they map out their release schedules for the next couple of years. Summit at least will have a lot of those teen vampire dollars to spend as they look for which movies to back and take a gamble on. I'm hoping they choose more upscale films like "The Hurt Locker" rather than lowbrow fodder like "Sorority Row" and "Next Day Air."

From a pure distribution standpoint, when you have a sure thing like "New Moon," there is nothing quite like it in terms of the clout you gain in dealing with theatre owners. 4,000 theatres throughout the country are playing the movie, and they all wanted to play it; they all needed to play this movie. No convincing was necessary, no arm twisting was needed, and since every distributor has to sell their share of dogs, it's a sublime feeling when your movie is the one that is most in demand, and you have the power to demand a few things yourself. Especially when you are an independent like Summit. The following negotiation points are in play:

- ► The ability to set higher film rental terms to keep a larger piece of the box office pie. A distributor can literally say "take it or leave it" because no theatre can afford not to play it.

- ► Every theatre has their top auditoriums and various lesser ones. When you have the top film of the weekend, you play on all the best screens with the largest capacities.

- ► It becomes the movie that will wipe the books clean, that will get all the accounts receivables paid in full before the prints are shipped.

- ► It allows the distributor to quicken the payment of film rental to 14 days after each week of playtime for the duration of the engagement instead of the more normal 30 to 45 day payments.

I've handled my share of hot films, and it's an outstanding feeling knowing that you can call all the shots, get all your past bills paid off and demand and get quick payments on your new film. That's the way the game was played in the past, and that's the way the game is played now. When you have the upper hand in any negotiation, you have to be able to take advantage of it because you know the other side will when their opportunity comes up.

Summit Entertainment does a great job containing and cutting costs, and during the economic downturn, that that has been the mantra for businesses everywhere. The studios are no different in this area, and they have been addressing their costs in a couple of different ways. First, they're going after the big A-list actors offering them less money upfront. It's harder to get that $15 to $20 million dollar payday now, and even with backend participation for the creative talent, greater compensation is being awarded only after a movie breaks even and starts showing a profit. The studios want to see the stars earn their paychecks. Too many stars have failed to bring in audiences like they used to. Stars like Julia Roberts, Will Ferrel, Adam Sandler and Russell Crowe have had bad years, while at the same time movies like "Paranormal Activity," "The Hangover" and "District 9" have done huge business with no stars attached. Bad timing for the stars. The other thing the studios are doing is similar to what many other large companies have done, streamlining their organizational structures. Both Disney and Paramount have recently streamlined their marketing and distribution divisions, eliminating a number of separate divisions, now going to a single team to handle marketing movies every step of the way from theatres to DVD to pay television to digital downloads. What they are responding to are shorter windows and rapidly changing audience preferences. Formerly tall, deep organizations are becoming flatter, laying off mid-level managers and trying to be more efficient with fewer employees, jobs that will probably never return. This is good for the studios' bottom lines but bad news for employees and those who would like to find jobs with the studios someday. The Great Recession has sped up the dismantling of the American workforce, and it makes you wonder when the jobs will return and when companies will start hiring again. Film companies have always employed huge numbers of people. I remember back in the '80s when Orion Pictures had home offices in both New York and Los Angeles and employed 500 people, and Orion wasn't even a full-fledged studio. That's when there were still eight sales offices, but I still wondered what everyone did in the home offices. I guess it took the worst recession in 70 years for studios to wonder the same thing.

This Week at the Box Office: *Weekly Attendance: 50,700,751*

The week before Thanksgiving is one of the prime weekends of the year to release a major release, and that is why Summit claimed the date for "New Moon." It's a much better date than Thanksgiving week itself because the playing time is much stronger before the holiday than after the holiday. Most of the attention has centered on "New Moon" and rightfully so, but Warner Brothers is releasing an inspirational football drama called "The Blind Side" starring Sandra Bullock that has been gaining traction among exhibitors and audiences who have seen early previews. The weekend is big enough for two films to do well, and it will be fun to watch what happens.

The Twilight Saga: New Moon
Summit
Opening weekend: $142,839,137
Domestic gross: $296,623,614 41.8%
Foreign gross: $413,203,828 58.2%
Worldwide gross: $709,827,462
Widest release: 4,124 theatres

The Blind Side
Warner Brothers
Opening weekend: $34,119,372
Domestic gross: $255,959,475 82.8%
Foreign gross: $53,248,834 17.2%
Worldwide gross: $309,208,834
Widest release: 3,407 theatres

Planet 51
Sony
Opening weekend: $12,286,129
Domestic gross: $42,194,060 39.9%

Broken Embraces
Sony Classics
Opening weekend: $107,111
Domestic gross: $5,014,305 16.2%

Foreign gross: $63,453,042 60.1%

Worldwide gross: $105,647,102

Widest release: 3,035 theatres

Bad Lieutenant: Point of Call New Orleans

First Look

Opening weekend: $245,398

Domestic gross: $1,702,112 16.1%

Foreign gross: $8,886,990 83.9%

Worldwide gross: $10,589,102

Widest release: 96 theatres

Red Cliff

Magnolia

Opening weekend: $13,104

Domestic gross: $627,047 24.6%

Foreign gross: $1,918,865 75.4%

Worldwide gross: $2,548,912

Widest release: 42 theatres

The Missing Person

Strand

Opening weekend: $2,715

Domestic gross: $17,896

Foreign gross: N/A

Widest release: 3 theatres

Fix

Mangusta Prod.

Opening weekend: $5,951

Domestic gross: $9,890

Foreign gross: N/A

Widest release: 1 theatre

Foreign gross: $25,977,355 83.8%

Worldwide gross: $30,991,660

Widest release: 202 theatres

Kurbann

UTV

Opening weekend: $403,678

Domestic gross: $754,269 51.6%

Foreign gross: $707,343 48.4%

Worldwide gross: $1,461,611

Widest release: 83 theatres

The Sun

Lorber

Opening weekend: $11,588

Domestic gross: $77,303

Foreign gross: N/A

Widest release: 3 theatres

Defamation

First Run

Opening weekend: $4,725

Domestic gross: $12,038

Foreign gross: N/A

Widest release: 4 theatres

Mammoth

IFC

Opening weekend: $4,531

Domestic gross: $9,580

Foreign gross: N/A

Widest release: 1 theatre

2012 Update:
Lionsgate Buys Summit Entertainment

On January 13, 2012, Lionsgate announced it was purchasing Summit Entertainment for $412.5 million, combining the two largest independent production and distribution companies under the same roof. Summit will continue to run its own production label under the Lionsgate banner, but its distribution organization will no longer exist, as Lionsgate will be the sole distributor of a projected 10-14 films a year between the two production entities. The two leading executives of Summit, Patrick Wachsberg and Rob Friedman, were hired to stay on to run the entire domestic and foreign movie divisions at the newly merged Lionsgate. Something similar happened a few years ago when Paramount initially acquired DreamWorks, and many of the DreamWorks distribution executives replaced top Paramount management. It may sound unusual, but it happens. No one is safe when buyouts and mergers occur.

Summit may have gained respect when they opened their own domestic distribution company in 2007 and proved their mettle with the huge success of the "Twilight Saga," but perhaps gained even more respect for acknowledging the tough realities that they were going to be facing in the coming years. With the final "Twilight" movie set to open in November 2012, the reality of no longer having a big franchise movie anchoring their release schedules stared them directly in the eyes. Putting together a profitable 12-month release schedule for a privately owned company is a formidable task, and they surely thought back at the number of unsuccessful films they released before they hit the jackpot with "Twilight." They definitely knew when to hold them and when to fold them. Their five years as a domestic distributor will be remembered as an outstanding concentrated run. They avoided having a fall from grace, and in addition to the monumental success of the "Twilight" series, they even won a Best Picture Oscar for "The Hurt Locker," proving they could conquer both the commercial and art film markets.

Week 47: Questions for Discussion

1. What has been the road to success for Summit Entertainment? The path they took was unusual. Where did the company come from?

2. What is the best way a distributor earns respect in Hollywood, and if it arrives, what comes next?

3. What is the logic of continuing two production companies but not two distribution organizations after two companies merge? Couldn't they control more market share with two different distributors booking films into theatres?

A SEASON TO BE THANKFUL FOR

Week 48: November 27–December 3, 2009

Collecting $113 million on one film within 14 days is some very serious money. That is almost impossible for a distributor to duplicate anywhere else.

The weekend before Thanksgiving 2009 was one for the record books. The feeling going into it was that it was going to be big with the opening of "New Moon" and some tasty holdovers, but no one could have predicted that this particular weekend would become the second biggest box office weekend of all time, behind only the July 2008 frame when "The Dark Knight" debuted. Those weekends are usually found in the summer, not in a non-holiday November weekend. For that to happen a giant opening movie is a must, and this year the second installment of The Twilight Saga was the chosen one with numbers that were simply mind-boggling:

- ▸ Biggest midnight show debut: $26 million
- ▸ Biggest opening day: $72 million
- ▸ 3rd biggest weekend of all time: $142 million
- ▸ All-time biggest November/December opening ($38 million more than the 2005 Harry Potter)
- ▸ First week gross of $188 million, only $3 million short of the entire $191 million gross for "Twilight."

As the Thanksgiving weekend unfolds, there is a lot for the industry to be thankful for. When "New Moon" beat most estimates by $40 million, it was just the latest example of the various tracking services underestimating opening weekend numbers. It got me thinking about the overall marketplace in terms of the surprising movies we've seen just in the last five or six weeks, "Paranormal Activity," "Precious" and now "New Moon," and how they couldn't be more different from each other. A low-budget horror film, a gritty urban drama, a teen vampire love story, and it's interesting to note that none of these movies were in 3D getting higher admission prices to pad their grosses. Whereas the big numbers and new records are welcome news for the movie industry, I was wondering about the real meaning behind the eye-popping numbers. Was it mere coincidence that the three movies came out so close to each other in the October/November corridor and performed so well? Was it tied to superior marketing by the distributors? Was it because all three movies had large niche bases that they were able to reach? Certainly these were factors in the overwhelming success stories of the films, but I believe there's something else in play here. It's an affirmation of how healthy the theatrical business has been and how it continues to function at such a high level. As everyone worries about how to turn the Internet into a more profitable business model and wonders where other new technologies will fit in, movie theatres continue to generate huge returns for distributors. The approximately 40,000 movie screens are not going anywhere, and the Internet will not be bringing them down. As I've said before, the indisputable fact is that the movie theatre is an out-of-home experience, and the need for people to get out of the house will always be there. The Internet is mostly an in-home entertainment competing more against DVDs, television, cable and Video-on-Demand than it does with theatres.

The resiliency of the theatrical experience is impressive. It's not that everyone is a regular moviegoer or people enjoy every movie they go see. It's that the people who do go to the movies are loyal and go often. Every poll ever taken on moviegoing has shown that the frequent moviegoer (one who attends a movie at least once a month or more) makes up somewhere between 75%-80% of the total moviegoing population. That kind of support has been good enough to keep the theatre business humming along. When the market expands for specific movies and taps into the occasional moviegoer (one movie seen in theatres every 2-6 months) and the infrequent moviegoer (two to fewer movies seen every

12 months) that's when we see records fall and history being made. If the studios made better movies on a consistent basis, would more people become frequent moviegoers? Possibly, but patterns of behavior are pretty much established in people, so the percentage of frequent moviegoers might not change much with better quality movies. According to MPAA statistics, frequent moviegoing peaks between the ages of 18-24 with both the 12-17 and 25-39 age groups close behind. However, what can happen with those infrequent moviegoers when they find their way back to a theatre is that they can rediscover the joy of going to see a movie on the big screen. If they have an enjoyable experience, it makes it more likely they can return again sometime soon to see another film that's being promoted in the theatre. Good movies sometimes fail at the box office, and bad movies can find a big audience; that's the way it is. It's easy for critics and others to look down on audiences who support movies they feel are a waste of time, but it's tough for anyone to play God and question the personal preferences of others when it comes to their movie choices. They're paying customers, and it takes all kinds of audiences from highbrow to lowbrow to support the theatrical marketplace, and you have to admit they're doing a pretty good job of it in 2009.

As long as theatres keep pounding out the big grosses at the box office, theatre owners will continue to carry a lot of clout with the studios. A little simple math on the first week of "New Moon" shows why. The first week gross of $188 million will return to Summit Entertainment somewhere in the neighborhood of $113 million to be paid in full within 14 days of the completion of the first week. With the intense demand for the film, that assumed Summit was able to negotiate a minimum aggregate deal of 60% film rental for each week played on the picture, though it could even be a couple percentage points higher. Collecting $113 million on one film within 14 days is some very serious money that is almost impossible for a distributor to duplicate anywhere else. With a production cost of $50 million and a marketing cost in the $30 million range, profit was reached almost immediately with many weeks left to play, and that's not even figuring in international receipts and the DVD and television revenues to follow. Movie theatres are a cash business, and when something hits, cash flows back quickly to the distributors. There is no waiting around for quarterly financial statements to hit and payments to clear 60 days later. The speed at which revenue can be generated and money collected with no middlemen touching it first is a tantalizing business transaction. For that reason, the theatrical deal remains a solid one and is hard to beat.

This Week at the Box Office: *Weekly Attendance: 29,211,988*

The five-day Thanksgiving weekend is an important holiday for movies, but a pattern has been developing over the years where the studios don't wait until the day before Thanksgiving to open their strongest movies. They place their biggest November movies earlier in the month so they can play longer and build up steam leading up to the holiday weekend. The Friday after Thanksgiving is still one of the single biggest moviegoing days of the year, but the problem begins with the Monday after the holiday when business begins to fall off dramatically. It happens every year as the calendar shifts into December, and it takes a little time for movie theatre traffic to build up again. It's one of those seasonal cycles that is hard to buck. That's why the Wednesday before Thanksgiving never seems to be too exciting. Historically, comedies, animation and family movies have done the best on this date, but the only two true national releases this year are Disney's "Old Dogs," an older skewing comedy with Robin Williams and John Travolta, and Warner Brothers' "Ninja Assassin," an average looking action film. Neither will be setting any new records. The five-day window is just too short of time to risk a stronger commercial movie because early December can easily suck the momentum out of even the strongest movies. When fresh, stronger Christmas releases start getting rolled out in December, a late November film can become yesterday's news very quickly and fade from view. Disney is using the Thanksgiving weekend as a very limited launching pad for its animated "The Princess & the Frog," which will be playing in only two theatres as a high-ticket family experience which involves much more than the movie itself. The movie will be opening nationally December 10 at which time I'll be taking a closer look at the film.

Princess and the Frog

Disney
Opening weekend: $786,910
Domestic gross: $104,400,899 39.1%
Foreign gross: $162,644,866 60.9%
Worldwide gross: $267,045,765
Widest release: 3,475 theatres

The Road

Weinstein
Opening weekend: $1,502,231
Domestic gross: $8,114,270 29.4%
Foreign gross: $19,518,305 70.6%
Worldwide gross: $27,635,305
Widest release: 396 theatres

Private Lives of Pippa Lee

Screen Media
Opening weekend: $89,950
Domestic gross: $337,356 12.2%
Foreign gross: $2,433,585 87.8%
Worldwide gross: $2,770,941
Widest release: 26 theatres

Old Dogs

Disney
Opening weekend: $16,894,511
Domestic gross: $49,492,060 51.2%
Foreign gross: $47,261,636 48.8%
Worldwide gross: $96,753,696
Widest release: 3,425 theatres

Me and Orson Welles

Freestyle
Opening weekend: $63,638
Domestic gross: $1,190,003 50.9%
Foreign gross: $1,146,169 49.1%
Worldwide gross: $2,336,169
Widest release: 132 theatres

Small Change (reissue)

The Film Desk
Opening weekend: $4,624
Domestic gross: $34,578
Foreign gross: N/A
Widest release: 2 theatres

Ninja Assassin

Warner Brothers
Opening weekend: $13,316,158
Domestic gross: $38,122,883 61.9%
Foreign gross: $23,478,397 38.1%
Worldwide gross: $61,601,280
Widest release: 2,503 theatres

De Dan Dan

Eros
Opening weekend: $577,381
Domestic gross: $944,979 47.6
Foreign gross: $1,040,444 52.4%
Worldwide gross: $1,985,423
Widest release: 69 theatres

Home

Lorber
Opening weekend: $3,922
Domestic gross: $15,922
Foreign gross: N/A
Widest release: 2 theatres

TOP 10 NORTH AMERICAN MOVIE THEATRE CIRCUITS
(as of June 24, 2010)

Circuit	Headquarters	Screens	Sites
Regal Entertainment Group	Knoxville, TN	6,777	548
AMC Entertainment Inc.	Kansas City, MO	5,336	378
Cinemark USA, Inc.	Plano, TX	3,825	293
Carmike Cinemas, Inc.	Columbus, GA	2,268	242
Cineplex Entertainment LP	Toronto, ON	1,347	130
Rave Motion Pictures	Dallas, TX	936	62
Marcus Theatres Corp.	Milwaukee, WI	668	54
Hollywood Theatres	Portland, OR	546	49
National Amusements	Dedham, MA	450	34
Harkins Theatres	Phoenix, AZ	429	30

Source: National Association of Theatre Owners

Conversations with Industry Professionals

Doug Stone – President, Box Office Analyst for Movieline International, Kansas City

The following interview took place on March 29, 2011 in Las Vegas during the CinemaCon convention.

> *"The studios didn't mind if all their money was made in four weeks instead of twelve weeks because they got it faster. When it was stretched out over a longer time, distributors lost money on the interest that exhibitors were sitting on."*
>
> —*Doug Stone*

Q: Can you start off telling me how you became involved in the movie industry?

DS: My grandfather started a drive-in in Kansas City in 1948, and my first job was working concessions at the drive-in when I was 15 years old. I studied math in college and got my masters degree while still working at the drive-in booking second features. I taught high school for three years, then I went to work for the Mid-America circuit in Kansas City as the booker, and that lasted until 1989 when it was sold to AMC.

Q: What happened then?

DS: AMC offered me a job, and I moved back into my wheelhouse, which is analysis. I worked with the film department projecting numbers and built a new film system for the company. We would use it to analyze film rental terms, the best weeks of the runs, what a movie had to do to earn 90/10. I remember a letter my dad once wrote to a distributor asking why he should pay a certain amount, so I was always curious about how film rental was determined. The collapse of the exhibition industry in the late 1990s was a turning point. What distributors learned was that front-loading pictures gave them money a lot faster. Typically you settled a film, and it would be x number of weeks before you settled it. Going to 3,000 or 4,000 runs instead of 2,000 runs had distributors making more money and getting it faster. The studios didn't mind if all their money was made in four weeks instead of twelve weeks because they got it faster. When it was stretched over a longer time, distributors lost money on the interest that exhibitors were sitting on. This put pressure on the bottom line of exhibitors having to pay film rental at a quicker pace, and it also caused the retreat away from the 90/10 deal because the front-loaded deals were too damaging to theatres. What the studios are doing now is offering a choice between a couple different deals based on either an aggregate figure or a scale based on the final box office gross. I would analyze the two deals and make the choice on what I thought was the right deal for AMC to take.

Q: How often did you make the right choice?

DS: We were right a lot more times than when we wrong. When we see the movie in advance, you could see if it was good or bad and whether or not we thought it would have legs. The guys at AMC had seen a lot of movies over the years. We wouldn't make the deal until we saw the movie and generally didn't negotiate the final deal until the Monday for Friday of the opening week. One of the reasons we would wait was to see the results of the latest tracking reports. The deal could go down if the distributor saw less interest in the film tracking, which helps determine the price of a film.

Q: When did you join Movieline?

DS: In 2009 a new regime came into AMC, and I worked into the end of July. I wanted to continue as an analyst, and I contacted John Shaw who was running Movieline International, and I joined the company. We have about 200 clients, and the split is 70% exhibitors and 30% distributors who pay for information and analysis. We constantly put our butts on the line with long-term projections on future movies and our thoughts on where the industry is headed.

Q: In 2009 the industry had its first $10 billion dollar year at the domestic box office. What was the key to that year?

DS: I think the product came together real well. If you study statistical fluctuations, some years are going to turn out great, and other years it's not going to happen. There were a bunch of surprises that year. Who knew about "The Hangover," "The Proposal," "District 9" and "Paranormal Activity"? I think there was something with the recession that was going on. No one saw "Paul Blart" being a $160 million film. Audiences were craving for entertainment. I think I'm going to go back to see the Rotten Tomatoes scores of the 2009 movies and weigh them by gross. Even though critics and grosses don't always match, if I went back to 2009, I would bet most of those surprising films were getting pretty strong reviews. There were a bunch of good movies that year. One of the things 2009 had was an extraordinary fourth quarter; it ended with a bang in contrast to 2010 when a majority of the commercial movies underperformed.

Q: Do you believe in momentum in the marketplace?

DS: Definitely. Even when things are going bad, momentum can develop quickly. If there are a few pictures out there that a lot of people want to see, audiences start flocking to theatres, and momentum follows. They see a trailer they like, and they may be back the following week. It becomes contagious.

Q: How do you see movie attendance going forward?

DS: In 2002, the industry enjoyed a peak year of attendance. Why did this happen? The demographic age group between 10 and 20 years old correlated with very high attendance that year. That's the age group that goes to the movies the most, and the number of people in that age range has been slipping. The kids from 2002 are now 25 to 30 years old and starting to have kids and not going to movies as they once did; we lose them as active moviegoers. There are fewer ten to twenty year olds today, and they make up less of the total audience, so that's also affecting audience stagnation. Currently there is a big bump with baby boomers who are active moviegoers, but the next generation will be smaller as they age. What happens when people get older is that they become more selective, and the natural tendency is to see fewer movies. They have seen so many movies, every conceivable plot line. They are more discriminating with their choices. That's why studios make so few adult dramas, because older adults don't go out to see just anything. It has to be a good film, and it's execution dependent, which makes it more risky.

Q: So after saying that, do distributors and exhibitors have something else to worry about, future audience demographics and trends?

DS: I would say that if filmmakers and exhibitors are not sensitive to the changes in demographics, they risk losing their audience. On the theatre side, older audiences tend to be more discriminating and look for better venues that deliver good value. If you can't manage that in a theatre, an exhibitor will have something to worry about. On the film-making side, studios have to recognize while special effects and explosions can drive traffic and attract the youth market, the older audience (35 & over) is becoming a bigger, more important demographic. This age group will demand originality, cleverness, and themes that they can relate to, something that has been in short supply except for around the holiday and award seasons for the past decade.

Q: *What's your latest analysis on the state of digital 3D movies?*

DS: 3D is here to stay, and it will remain the standard for the majority of animated films. That being said, there have been some notable shifts. 3D was fresh in 2009 and 2010 with the top grossing film of all time driving the technology, but 2011 has seen a general decline in the domestic market in the percentage of gross on any given film that comes from 3D screens. As more and more inferior 3D movies came out, the love affair that audiences had with them declined. From my perspective, it's about quality, quantity and higher ticket prices. Distributors shot themselves in the foot by converting too many films to 3D after they were already shot, and the result was bad movies at higher ticket prices. 3D has declined on a per picture basis to about 40% of the total box office; in 2010 it was riding along at about 52%. This is definitely a result of more and more 3D films being released and poor quality 3D, or 3D that adds little to the film except for a higher ticket price. The international market is different. There seems to be a much greater acceptance of 3D overseas, and it hasn't fallen off nearly as much as it has here.

Q: *What are some of the fundamentals that haven't changed and lessons you have learned in your career?*

DS: One thing I go back to is the old adage you never go broke underestimating the intelligence of the American people. If you try to be too intellectual with your film, you will probably limit yourself. If you try to reach a broad audience, you have a better chance for success. If you make a quality film you improve your chances for success a thousand percent. If you throw something together just based on the concept without much of a story, the movie will have problems. The first "Iron Man" did great because the story was fundamentally solid. "Iron Man 2" did not meet expectations because the story wasn't there even though the production values were the same. It all comes down to the story.

Q: *What do you hear from your exhibitor clients? Are they optimistic about the future, or are they worried? Are their theatres on solid ground?*

DS: There is concern. This industry is not growing. Population rises, but attendance is flat, meaning people are going less and less to the theatres. The industry peaked in about 2002 in per capita visits. As I said before, part of this is due to demographic changes, but it can't all be explained away that simply. Competition from other entertainment options and cutting-edge technology is taking a toll. The digital conversion of theatres offers some promise if good alternative content can be piped in, but so far it's not adding much new meaningful revenue for theatre owners. Smaller exhibitors will be forced to make difficult decisions on the high cost of converting to digital as film prints start getting phased out in a couple of years.

Q: *What type of information and analysis is the most important for your exhibitor clients? What about for your distributor clients?*

DS: I'd have to say forecasting both long and short term in predicting future box office results. Our reports are a very concise and readable recap of a lot of information that my clients can understand; they are heavier in information than analytics. Where we make a difference is in our ability to help people plan their bookings and anticipate box office results.

Q: *Do you know if any of the exhibitors use your analysis in determining which choice to take on a film rental deal when presented a choice between an aggregate and a scale deal?*

DS: I expect that they would consider it as one factor in the decision-making process. I know that some do exactly that.

Q: What are the most important skills needed to become a good movie industry analyst? How do you think you separate yourself from other movie analysts?

DS: Experience in the industry and a talent for analytics. By luck of the draw I may be the only individual in the industry whose experience combines over 40 years in the film industry with a master's degree in mathematics. This combination gives me the fundamental knowledge of how the industry works on many levels with the ability to quantify, cut, slice, dice and analyze the data.

Q: Would you be able to put into proper perspective the 65 million weekly attendance of the last week of 2009. From the figures you had supplied to me, it looks like the average weekly attendance of 2009 was around 27 million. Would you be able to determine the last time the weekly attendance was that high? It just seems like an incredible figure since the same week in 2010 did 40 million, which is probably more the norm.

DS: The final week of 2009 was indeed spectacular and is perhaps an anomaly. A confluence of several things came together that year. One, the calendar was advantageous with Christmas Eve and New Year's Eve falling on a Thursday. Having Christmas Eve on Wednesday or Thursday is definitely the best, as it often results in an extended weekend for a large number of people. Add to that the openings of "Avatar" along with two other $200 million plus movies in "Sherlock Holmes" and "Alvin and the Chipmunks 2 [The Squeakquel]," and you had the stars aligned just right. I'm not sure I could actually pinpoint another time when it was that high. The closest I can find in recent years was Christmas 2003 when "Return of the King" was playing, and attendance was somewhere in the 50+ million range for the week.

Q: Thank you for your time and insight. I appreciate it.

DS: Thank you.

Week 48: Questions for Discussion

1. Would you consider yourself a frequent, occasional or infrequent moviegoer? How many movies do you see in theatres each year on the average? Is there anything that would motivate you to increase the amount of movies you attend?

2. What makes the Thanksgiving holiday a tricky date for distributors to maneuver around?

3. What does analyst Doug Stone say about future audience trends? Why does he state it's important for anyone involved in the movie business to be able to recognize these trends?

A TEN BILLION DOLLAR YEAR ALLOWS EXHIBITORS TO PLAY HARDBALL

Week 49: December 4–10, 2009

---

*A cold hard fact is that theatres will not be participating
in anything that could lead to their demise.*

You would think that after two record-breaking weekends at the box office and the holiday season upon us, peace and goodwill would be the order of the day with the studios and the exhibition community. But business is never as good as it seems or as bad as it seems. With distributors and exhibitors there is always a level of angst of what lies around the corner. For the studios, perhaps more than anything else, it's the dramatic fall off in DVD sales that has cast a dark shadow over profits. The studios have taken a big hit, and they realize some kind of change has to happen. For exhibitors, it's the growing experimentation by the studios that threatens to shorten the exclusive window theatres enjoy. The latest example is with Sony, the only major studio with a hardware component, which is making their animated hit, "Cloudy With a Chance of Meatballs" available through their own Internet enabled televisions, Bravia, free of charge a full month ahead of the DVD release. That's less than three months since its theatrical release, and that follows Paramount's DVD release of "G.I. Joe," which also had a similarly shortened time frame. Theatre owners monitor each DVD release closely and protest loudly when they see any departure from the slightly-over-four-month industry average currently in place. Exhibitors know full well that shorter windows can start affecting their business, especially since Premium Video-on-Demand will soon overtake earlier releases of DVDs as the number one threat to exhibition. With the domestic box office poised to pass $10 billion for the first time in history, theatre owners are adept at playing hardball with the studios. This is the nitty-gritty nature of the business, part of the inherent checks and balances, the tug of war where two large powerful forces are on different sides of the table but still depend on each other deeply.

It's timely that theatres are generating so much revenue this year; if that starts slipping, watch out, because that would give the studios reason to tweak things even more, similar to what we're seeing in the home market. When DVD sales were so strong for about a 10-year period between 1997 and 2007, studios would never have thought to upset Walmart, their most important customer, but now they are moving up Video-on-Demand dates and testing out other technology that directly impacts the big box retailers. Those retailers are losing some of their clout, not only because they're selling fewer DVDs, but also because of their decisions to decrease the aisle space afforded to DVDs. This has given the studios an opening to go ahead and make some changes that affect the exclusivity of the DVD window. When your customers start contracting, they have less reason to push back. The opposite is happening with movie theatres where the major circuits have spent hundreds of millions of dollars upgrading their theatres, continuing to add digital screens, 3D, ultra screens, restaurants and other upscale amenities that have played a huge part in keeping moviegoers in the habit of spending an evening outside the home watching movies in theatres. Those powerhouse grosses the studios are enjoying are happening for a reason. The studios have asked for improvements in theatres, and the theatres have delivered. Betraying that trust at this time would not be acceptable. Studios have always been respectful and protective of their relationship with theatres, sometimes even to their own detriment.

When I started in the business in the early 1970s, new patterns of distribution and exhibition were needed so movies could be delivered more quickly to audiences in a more convenient manner closer to where they lived in the suburbs. Big aging downtown theatres still existed, and they still needed product, and the circuits operating these theatres controlled many of the top grossing theatres in the country. They wielded enough power and clout to have a say where pictures opened, and the circuits had to protect their large investments in prime downtown real estate by insuring that enough of the top movies opened in them, including films like "The Godfather" and "Towering Inferno" which enjoyed exclusive engagements in major markets. Change was inevitable, and by the mid-'70s some of the downtown theatres started closing, never to be a force again. The point here is that exhibition has always had its needs, and distribution often has worked along with them to preserve important relationships forged over many decades of working together. Change eventually happened, but it took its own course.

But something different seems to be in the air now. The big, lumbering studios are moving more nimbly now, led by studio heads like Robert Iger of Disney, who would like to move into the digital age sooner than later and has shown a willingness to alter existing windows to accommodate a younger consumer audience who wants access to their entertainment in a more immediate fashion. Add to that this week's announcement of Comcast buying NBC/Universal and suddenly the movie business is looking at a potential new world order. A new set of dynamics enters the picture when the largest cable provider in the country buys one of the six major studios, an announcement no theatre owner was cheering. All of a sudden, the probability of a more aggressive Premium VOD policy takes on a whole new meaning and urgency. It's a certainty that Comcast will be squeezing the theatres with shorter exclusivity, and they have already indicated they would like to see a higher priced VOD tier in the neighborhood of $25.95 while movies are still playing in theatres. Anyone who thinks theatres would allow that to happen and be willing to play movies at the same time they're available inside the home is drinking some spiked Kool-Aid. That's not going to happen. It's weird sometimes that as more things change, the more they stay the same. There is a strange déjà vu quality to this. In 1983, Universal attempted a day and date release with "Pirates of Penzance" in theatres and on Pay-Per-View. That was very radical back then, and needless to say, all the major theatre circuits boycotted the movie and refused to play the picture, and it proceeded to disappear rather quickly. There wasn't much interest in the Pay-Per-View showing either. A strange movie to attempt a day and date release on well before it's time; I guess you can call it "The Bubble" of its day. One thing that hasn't changed 26 years later is the cold hard fact that theatres will not be participating in anything that could lead to their demise. Universal is only one of the major studios, so there will always be other movies to play.

Reports are that Comcast is ready to start calling the shots over at NBC/Universal even as the acquisition faces tough anti-trust scrutiny and has to be approved by federal regulators. That can take up to six months to a year. It has been that long since regulators have been looking over the merger of Live Nation and Ticketmaster, and there hasn't been a verdict on that one yet. The Obama administration came into office with a platform of being against big media mergers. I thought there was no way Live Nation and Ticketmaster would be allowed to merge because the elimination of competition could lead to some serious ticket price increases for consumers. I wonder what's taking so long to make a final decision. President Obama also was elected on an anti-war platform, and he's now sending 30,000 more troops into Afghanistan, so I guess anything is possible with the eventual decision on the Comcast deal.

Getting back to the current situation on the screens, the marketplace is ready for another of its breathers. There are points in the year when moviegoing levels drop off, and the first week of December is one of those weeks. Thirty to forty years ago some smaller theatres actually closed their doors in early December because there was nothing worth playing, and there was so little business. It was a dumping ground for orphan films and movies that were considered losers by their distributors that just had to get played off. When you think of it, it's a long three weeks until Christmas, and the whole idea of Christmas playtime is for a distributor to have its film in as strong a position as possible playing between Christmas Day and New Year's Day, the absolute best moviegoing week of the year. Why risk jeopardizing your December movie with an early knockout when you can place it on December 18th or 25th instead? The first film to buck this trend was when Paramount opened the first "Star Trek" on December 7, 1979 and grossed $17 million in its first three days, an incredibly strong gross at the time. Universal tried to duplicate the feat the following year on the same weekend with "Flash Gordon" and got burned. The movie was off the screens by Christmas. A hard lesson learned many times over the years. Even when a film shares the same genre and release date, there is absolutely no guarantee when it comes to box office performance and public acceptance.

A Small Town Wonder

I would be remiss if I didn't mention the incredible performance of Warner Brothers' "The Blind Side" after only two weekends in release. In a fourth quarter where there have already been several sleeper hits, this mainstream inspirational football film has accomplished some pretty impressive things of its own. With an 18% rise in ticket sales, it became the first wide release of the year that saw its gross grow in the second weekend. On the other hand, "New Moon" opened on the same weekend and saw its grosses fall by 70%. For grosses to rise in later weeks, superb word of mouth is needed, and exit polls proved that out. It was only the second film all year, along with "UP," which received an A+ grade from market research firm Cinema Score. Generally, big grosses are driven by big grossing theatres in the largest cities, but "The Blind Side" is performing just the opposite. The smaller the theatre, the bigger the gross. Theatres in Texas, Alabama, Tennessee and Indiana are leading the way and proving once again different movies perform in different ways as personified by "New Moon" and "The Blind Side" and that the theatrical marketplace continues to be full of surprises. Warner Brothers is enjoying the success of the film, but they would be enjoying it a lot more if they actually financed "The Blind Side." As the studios continue to lay off risk and allow independent production companies to totally finance some of their releases, studios are often content to take just their distribution fees. This is the case here when Acon Entertainment financed the movie at a cost of $35 million. Warner Brothers will still make a tidy profit on the film with all their distribution fees, but it's nothing compared to what they would have reaped if it was actually a Warner Brothers' in-house production.

This Week at the Box Office: *Weekly Attendance: 16,718,926*

The three national releases this week reflect the diminished expectations that early December offers. Miramax is opening "Everybody's Fine," a modest holiday offering starring Robert DeNiro as a father who decides to visit his four adult children scattered around the country after they couldn't find time to come see him. It has a chance to make it to Christmas if it's able to establish itself on the first weekend, but since Disney is downsizing Miramax, I wonder if there is going to be enough advertising support for it to make any kind of impact. Lionsgate's strategy to open "Brothers," their gritty wartime drama, wide on 2,000 screens is definitely risky and could be looked upon as an acknowledgement that the film will be a tough sell for audiences. They could have decided to use a platform release, but instead they are rolling the dice and taking the screens and seeing how far they can go. The difference between now and 30 years ago are the megaplexes with all their screens. That gives a film like "Brothers" a fighting chance to stay on some important screens during Christmas. The third movie is Sony's action movie "Armored" which might be considered the old dump and run and getting the picture played off before the big heavy hitters open later in the month. Look for business to start perking up again next week as we move closer to Christmas when I'll also take a look at the Oscar-caliber films opening in December. One of the top front runners for end-of-the-year awards is Paramount's "Up in the Air" which is opening on exclusive runs this weekend and will be playing wide around the country by Christmas Day. Much more next weekend on the challenges and strategies Paramount is facing with "Up in the Air" and how some of the other acclaimed films are being handled by their distributors during this final stretch of 2009.

Everybody's Fine	*Brothers*
Miramax	Lionsgate
Opening weekend: $3,852,068	Opening weekend: $9,527,848
Domestic gross: $9,208,876 56%	Domestic gross: $28,544,157 65.9%
Foreign gross: $7,234,733 44%	Foreign gross: $14,774,192 34.1%
Worldwide gross: $16,443,609	Worldwide gross: $43,318,349
Widest release: 2,141 theatres	Widest release: 2,088 theatres

Armored
Sony
Opening weekend: $6,511,128
Domestic gross: $15,988,876 69.7%
Foreign gross: $6,953,345 30.3%
Worldwide gross: $22,942,221
Widest release: 1,919 theatres

Paa
Big Pictures
Opening weekend: $199,228
Domestic gross: $199,228 86.5%
Foreign gross: $31,194 13.5%
Worldwide gross: $230,422
Widest release: 67 theatres

Until the Light Takes Us
Variance
Opening weekend: $7146
Domestic gross: $130,441
Foreign gross: N/A
Widest release: 3 theatres

One Peace at a Time
Monterey
Opening weekend: $4,138
Domestic gross: $11,698
Foreign gross: N/A
Widest release: 2 theatres

The Strip
Trulie Indie
Opening weekend: $5,107
Domestic gross: $5,107
Foreign gross: N/A

Up in the Air
Paramount
Opening weekend: $1,181,450
Domestic gross: $83,823,381 51.4%
Foreign gross: $79,403,690 48.6%
Worldwide gross: $163,227, 071
Widest release: 2,218 theatres

Serious Moonlight
Magnolia
Opening weekend: $11,636
Domestic gross: $25,339 7.5%
Foreign gross: $313,675 92.5%
Worldwide gross: $339,014
Widest release: 8 theatres

Transylmania
Full Circle
Opening weekend: $263,941
Domestic gross: $397,641
Foreign gross: N/A
Widest release: 1,005 theatres

Gigante
Film Movement
Opening weekend: $1,822
Domestic gross: $5,959
Foreign gross: N/A
Widest release: 1 theatre

2012 Update:

Throughout 2009, Miramax was being downsized by Disney and had very few releases. The handwriting was on the wall that the specialty division was no longer a priority for the studio and that Miramax did not fit into their future business model, especially with DreamWorks in the fold feeding them a variety of product including the occasional upscale adult film. It took a full year for Disney to unload the company when Disney completed a sale of Miramax to Colony Capital for $660 million in December 2010. Colony Capital purchased the company for its library of over 700 films with no plans to produce or distribute any new films. The sale ended Disney's 17-year ownership of Miramax, of which 13 of those years were led by Harvey and Bob Weinstein.

Looking Back on the "Bubble" Experiment

In January, 2006, Magnolia Pictures, owned by Mark Cuban and Todd Wagner, released Steven Soderbergh's $1.6 production "Bubble," becoming the first film to open in theatres, pay cable and DVD on the same day. All the major theatre chains refused to play the film, but since "Bubble" was a very small art house film with unknown actors, that was an easy call to make. Those theatres would not have played the film anyway. What made the experiment possible and low risk for Cuban and Wagner was that their company 2929 Productions enjoyed their own version of vertical integration in which they controlled all aspects of production and distribution. They financed the film; they played the film throughout their Landmark Theatres and the HDNet cable network, which they own, while also distributing the DVDS though their own company. On the surface, the release created a very small ripple in the marketplace despite getting tons of media coverage. "Bubble" only grossed $145,626 and didn't last long in theatres. The company reported DVD sales were good but didn't release any specific numbers in either the DVD or cable markets.

Despite the lackluster theatrical performance, it's conceivable the company recouped its costs and perhaps even made a profit on its simultaneous release, but as is often the case with privately owned companies, the real truth is hard to come by. One indisputable fact of the matter is that it wasn't much of a game changer. There were supposed to be a number of other low-budget films to follow the same type of release pattern but they never materialized. What it did ultimately lead to was day-and-date releases in the theatrical and VOD markets by not only Magnolia Pictures but IFC Films and other small distributors, with the DVD release being held back for a later date. These types of dual releases are here to stay for many smaller films and should only get more frequent in the coming years.

The Justice Department Approves Two Media Mergers

Despite the Obama administration's supposed opposition to big media mergers, the Justice Department ultimately approved the Ticketmaster/Live Nation merger in January 2010 and the Comcast/NBC Universal merger in January 2011. Exhibitors certainly didn't cheer the Comcast merger with a major movie studio and for good reason. In fall, 2011, the company announced a planned premium home Video-on-Demand experiment with Universal's action comedy, "Tower Heist," starring Ben Stiller and Eddie Murphy. How it was going to work was that Comcast digital subscribers in two markets, Portland and Atlanta, would have had the opportunity to rent "Tower Heist" in their homes just three weeks after its theatrical release on November 4, 2011 for $59.99. After a few national circuits threatened to not play the film in their theatres, Universal backed off and cancelled the VOD test. Exhibitors once again flexed their muscles and protected their turf, though Universal said they would continue to pursue premium VOD in the future.

Conversations with Industry Professionals

Tony Kerasotes – Chief Executive Officer of Kerasotes Showplace Theatres
Dean Kerasotes – Chief Operating Officer of Kerasotes Showplace Theatres
The following interview took place on June 24, 2011 in Chicago, IL.

> *"What I've learned in dealing with distribution is it's always been important not to take advantage of anybody because it always comes back to haunt you."*
> —*Tony Kerasotes*

> *"You can have the finest facility in the land, and if your staff is under par, you're not going to have a good theatre"*
> —*Dean Kerasotes*

Q: *What are the origins of Kerasotes Theatres?*

TK: People saw nickelodeons at the St. Louis World's Fair in 1908, and it spread from there. The family business was started in 1909 with a single storefront in downtown Springfield, IL, because all the nickelodeons were storefronts, and that particular storefront is still standing. The first movie theatres weren't special service buildings. Exhibitors used storefronts and put chairs in them. We're the third generation of family running the business.

Q: *When did each of you get started in the family business?*

TK: I worked in theatres in the summers during high school, doing clerical stuff, figuring out film rental, working on cut-off cards, a good way to learn the business. After I graduated from college I came back and started working as a booker, booking small towns outside the St. Louis region.

DK: I worked out of the office in the summer, too, on the operational side, and when I went to college in Champaign-Urbana I worked at our Co-Ed and Virginia theatres. I did everything from cashier to concessions. The management people showed me the ropes on managing a theatre. After college, I went on to manage one of our biggest multiplexes, which was three screens in 1972.

Q: *Tony, when did you take over as President of the company?*

TK: In 1985, after the split was completed with George Kerasotes, 26 years ago.

Q: *The announcement was made in January 2010 that the circuit was sold to AMC, so it was an exact 100 years for the circuit.*

TK: That's enough.

Q: *So the last full year was 2009, which was a record-breaking year at the box office. You sold while the business was at a high point.*

TK: That was an excellent year. In the spring we hired an investment banker to market the company. We finally reached a deal with AMC in the fall, and it wasn't announced until January when it became official.

DK: There was a period of time where we didn't think there was going to be any deal; we didn't know. But we finally did it. Even though 2009 was a very good year, it still wasn't the greatest time to sell. The prices were still down, and people were not paying that much for assets compared to what they had been paying. The multiple they paid on was less than it used to be.

Q: How difficult was it when you signed the deal?

TK: It wasn't that difficult. We had already decided to sell.

Q: How scary was it in the late1990s when 8 or 9 major circuits had to file for bankruptcy?

TK: Regal, UA, General Cinema, Edwards all went bankrupt, AMC was close, Cinemark was having difficulty, so it was a bad stretch for our industry. We weren't in bankruptcy, but the banks were so scared of the industry at that time we were having some difficulty in refinancing our debt obligations, we were tainted by all the problems going on in exhibition. It was the way banks regarded exhibition in general during that period.

Q: What was the name of the firm that bought into Kerasotes as an equity partner in the early 2000s?

TK: The private equity firm was Providence Equity Partners. They gave us a call, and we worked out a deal with them in 2003. They are in the business of buying and selling companies, so we knew that this day would eventually come.

Q: That outside equity money allowed you to really expand and upgrade the circuit, didn't it?

TK: Yes. We went from about 300 screens to close to 1,000 screens, and many of those theatres were small town twins or under five screens. We replaced most of those and built new theatres, the actual theatre count didn't change much; we had about 100 theatres before and had 100 theatres when we sold. All the original ones were replaced. The mix changed from three-screen theatres to an average of nine screens. We stayed in any market that was good for us and strengthened our presence with a more modern theatre and additional seating.

Q: Did you move your office to Chicago around this time?

DK: We moved our office from Springfield to Chicago in 1999. We were up here before we did the Providence deal.

Q: Can you talk about the economics of movie theatres?

TK: There is a lot more capital investment you have to make in order to be competitive. You remember all the old theatres people used to run and make a business out of. That was paid for a dozen times. Theatre owners used to cover up blemishes by installing new carpet or wall coverings or putting in some new seats. Now you have to build something good which is expensive. The risk is a lot higher than it used to be.

Q: What you don't hear about are theatres going out of business anymore.

TK: The product has been good; the over building has stopped. The companies left standing are mature companies with solid financials. Most of the good locations have already been taken. None of the circuits are in the predicament of the late 1990s or early 2000s when they had to replace older units with new stadium seating auditoriums. It was the perfect storm in the worst way. New builds were affecting older theatres, and there were a couple of bad years at the box office, boom, boom, boom. We were feeling the same crunch. We were replacing everything too.

Q: *Do you believe that every 20 years a new generation of theatres emerge?*

TK: Perhaps in the past that was the case, but looking ahead I don't see that. There has been an orderly progression from single screens to shopping twins, to eight plexes away from the malls to megaplexes, but I don't know how we can improve on what he have now. The final paradigm was stadium seating in the late 1990s. The most upscale theatres today with in-theatre dining and all digital screens will be tough to beat. I can't imagine what the next transformative change would be.

DK: There's nothing new. The Greeks invented stadium seating. Then it was done by the Romans. We had a theatre in Mount Vernon, IL called the Stadium that had stadium seating, and it was built in the 1940s. People elaborate and perfect older ideas, so they borrow from the past. A lot of things can change in 20 years, but I don't see any breakthrough in the design features and in the operation of movie theatres though filmmaking evolves and puts pressure on the technical aspects of exhibiting a movie.

Q: *Are concessions still the backbone of movie theatre profits?*

TK: I always disagreed with that line of thinking. I think it all works together. How much is your concession counter going to do if you don't have people in the theatre? In order to have people in the theatre, you have to have the right product; you have to run the movie; you have to staff it. When people say something like that, I think it's a warped view of accounting. You look at the margin of concessions, and you think that's where you are making all the money. I haven't seen somebody just open a concession stand and be successful. You need the whole capital investment, the overall structure of the theatre for the concession stand to work. I see it as one thing. Your gross margin is higher than anything else, but I think that's a false way at looking at the accounting.

Q: *Back in the day, studios like Paramount didn't like servicing bargain theatres because they felt the theatres were getting rich off their product by selling high priced concessions. People would spend $1.00 to get in and spend more than $4.00 or $5.00 at the concession stand.*

TK: The dollar theatres were something else. They were more dependent on concessions. Our experience was when we would convert our theatres to dollar theatres; overall we grossed more at the box office due to higher volume. We put a lot of people through the doors, and the distributors benefited from that business too.

Q: *How important is figuring out the proper pricing for each theatre? Did you play off what other theatres in the market were doing?*

TK: We would look at that, but sometimes we went our own way. I was always in the belief to encourage more volume we would perhaps be a little lower than our competitors and offer more discount programs than the other guy. We try to create a lot of value. Outside the ticket price we liked to offer free refills on all sizes of popcorn and soda, which creates value for the customer. It's important to keep an eye on maintaining and improving your volume. It's not like if we raise our price 50 cents we would make that much more money. The problem is you have a lot of corporate people making decisions on pricing where all they see is higher prices will equal higher revenue, and it doesn't always work that way.

There are two aspects of pricing, maintaining the value of your ticket and maintaining volume. Your primetime, adult admission fee is only part of the pricing structure. You have matinee, children and senior prices. You have to leave room for those who don't want to spend 10 or 11 bucks so they can still go see a movie. Movies are still a good value even though people always complain about what it costs.

Q: *A distribution executive told me he thought the art of film buying was gone. Can you comment on that?*

TK: The art of film buying has certainly taken a hit. We tend to play everything now except when distributors use platform releases and go out with fewer screens. Exhibitors still go to screenings to look at the movies; I don't know what for, you are going to play them anyway. I guess people go to kill time. There is still intelligence needed in how many prints or screens to use on certain movies and the number of 3D screens to commit to. Back in the days you mentioned, you had to have a strategy, you made choices on what to play and what not to play. You had to figure out how to transition from one film to another and block off certain number of weeks until the next booking. You had fewer screens and more choices; there was more of a strategy involved. With "Star Wars," I remember screening the movie, and I loved it. Fox was bidding at the time in competitive markets, and we bid and won the film in several of our markets. Other exhibitors weren't as high on the film and decided not to go after the film. I remember competitive bidding came back in the early '90s, but it got to be too cumbersome and didn't last too long. Distributors were closing regional sales offices during that period, and there was too much paperwork involved in the process.

Q: *Weren't those some pretty good years for exhibition in the late '70s/ early '80s with interest rates as high as 17%, many films with adjusted terms, some distributors being lax in collecting film rental? Exhibitors were known to hold onto their box office money as long as they could to earn that interest.*

TK: We didn't do that. We paid. We didn't sit on the distributors' money. General Cinema would sit on it, Redstone would sit on it. We didn't have the size of those circuits that we could do that.

Q: *Compare that to what is happening now with payments.*

TK: People pay like clockwork now.

Q: *Distributors finally have the upper hand now and are getting their biggest share of the pie after all these years.*

TK: The downside for the distributors with the 90/10 deal was the sliding scale aspect of the deals, which bottomed out at 35%, and it could stay there for weeks when theatres held on to the film. Now some companies give you the choice between a firm terms deal or an over/under deal based on the final domestic gross. We probably paid 53%, 54% aggregate when taking the full year into account from all our suppliers. It's higher than what we used to pay, but our mix of theatres changed with fewer small town situations.

Q: *Wouldn't you say it used to be a buyers' market, and now it's a sellers' market?*

TK: Yes, I think it is, but it's balanced by the three biggest circuits controlling so many screens that studios can't push them too far with the deals, but I do think some of the distributors take it out on the smaller guys.

Q: *You went from being the sixth-largest theatre circuit in the country to having three deluxe theatres in Chicago, Minneapolis and New Jersey. Do you see a difference now with your deals negotiating for only three theatres compared to 1,000 screens?*

TK: I haven't found our deals have changed much, probably due to our long-standing relationships that we have with distributors.

Q: *What's the average time frame for sending in your film rental payments to distributors?*

TK: Payments are due generally within 30 days, sometimes 45 days, and other times it's quicker for the bigger movies. We still have to process the payments, check them against our receipts, our bank statements and write the checks. We still write checks; we don't do direct deposit. I always resisted direct deposits, like it was putting money too quickly into the studios' pockets.

Q: Do you think there is one distinction over any other that makes for a successful theatre?

DK: It's the quality of your management and the people you have on the ground there. You can have the finest facility in the land, and if your staff is under par, you're not going to have a good theatre.

TK: You need a quality location, you need a good facility, but I agree with Dean; management makes the difference. Everybody can do stadium seating; there's not many secrets in building a theatre. Somebody can walk into a theatre, see the layout and go duplicate it somewhere.

Q: When you sold the circuit, what percentage of your theatres were successful in terms of being a profitable operation?

TK: Mostly all of them were profitable except for three or four theatres.

Q: Out of 100 theatres, that's a pretty good ratio.

Q: Your Icon theatres are all digital theatres. What's the upside for the industry moving away from 35mm projection to an all-digital future?

TK: Perhaps the biggest upside is that it gives you a better quality presentation for your customers. Handling a 35mm film in its pristine state was great, but it didn't stay pristine too long. The ease of moving prints around to other screens is a lot better. It gives a theatre more flexibility; you can program it on five screens, then go down to two in a hurry. Another upside is we can play alternative content, which can be fun. Some do well; other programming does terrible. I don't know if we make much money on alternative content, but servicing different audiences and getting them to sample the theatre is always a good thing.

Q: Any downside?

TK: The downside is cost, and since we are dealing with computers, when something doesn't work right it's trying to troubleshoot your computer system to see what's wrong with it. Problems can happen at different levels, and it takes time to figure out what happened and correct it. It can be a problem with the projector, the server or a specific screen rather than the entire auditorium.

Q: Are they theatres running without projectionists?

TK: It still doesn't run itself. When we downsized, we kept a technical person in each theatre. In the Chicago Icon Theatre one of my former technicians is one of the managers, and he works with the other managers on keeping everything running properly. We have to keep a close eye on it. The bigger circuits don't do that, and they have problems. Computers are not foolproof.

Q: What about digital 3D? It seems like it's in a slump. 85% of "Avatar's" gross came from 3D, but it's fallen under 50% for many movies now.

TK: It's a combination of product not really up to snuff, bad conversions, and cost to the public. A major recession is still going on, and for families, paying an extra $3 to $5 a person is too much. We charge $3.50, which is still under what some of the larger circuits get.

Q: Do you think 3D is here to stay?

TK: Of course, and I think filmmakers will get better using the 3D format, but the fact is 3D doesn't make a bad movie good.

Q: With your deluxe cinemas, you no longer have pre-show advertising. Talk to me about that end of the business. How profitable was it for you when you were running a circuit of 1,000 screens?

TK: It was more of a circuit wide deal tied to attendance, so it came down to bodies in the theatres watching those ads. We probably made $150,000 a year. When we promote a premium experience we get more on the admission price, not that much more, but why would we make someone watch a blue jean ad? Everyone started doing it, and we did it to remain competitive. If other theatres were making additional money on ads, it was difficult for us not to also partake in that extra revenue stream. I was never a big fan of theatre ads because I felt it denigrated the film experience.

Q: How about film piracy that originates in theatres?

TK: We have always been diligent in trying to stop any camcording. Prints are all watermarked so it can be tracked. Since we have been down to three theatres, I don't remember catching anybody. When we had more theatres, it certainly happened, and with the MPAA reward program, it gave extra incentive to the theatre staffs to be more diligent.

Q: Is Premium VOD something to be feared?

TK: What I can figure out, because distribution hasn't shared any information, is that the results of experiments they have done so far have been abysmal. I look at what the studios have done with Redbox and Netflix, making people wait a little longer and allow people to rent movies for a pittance. They have commoditized it, and there is no going back from that. When you wait 30 days or 60 days or 90 days following the theatre release, are people going to pay 30 bucks to see it. Studios are under a lot of pressure to replace the lost DVD revenue, and that revenue is irreplaceable. They have already given it away, so how can they reverse that and expect people to pay that kind of premium price. I'm not shedding too many tears for the DVD slide. The studios cry about it, but they don't talk about how their foreign revenues have skyrocketed. International revenue has gone berserk.

Q: So you don't fear it?

TK: I think it's a real stupid idea.

Q: What do you think of AMC and Regal forming their own distribution company?

TK: God bless them. The origins of distribution were in exhibition, so we have seen it all before. There's nothing new here.

Q: Let's talk about your beautiful Showplace Icon Theatre in Chicago. How long of a process was it from concept to opening? It seems like I first heard about Kerasotes planning a theatre in the south loop

years ago.

DK: The plans started in 2005, and we opened it in December 2009.

Q: *I always thought your choice of location on South Roosevelt Road was a bold move. Was that your first choice for a theatre in downtown Chicago?*

DK: There wasn't that much available. In a big city, there just aren't many spots available to build a large movie theatre complex. It took four years because it was a mixed-use development; it was a big development. It's typical in a big city like Chicago that a large development will take a long time. The developer had to present concept plans to the city; there were environmental issues; the wheels of city hall move slowly. We worked directly with the developer from the beginning. I started with the question how do we fit a large, modern, unusual shape theatre into this space. We were thinking 16 screens from the onset.

Q: *Did you plan on it being all digital?*

DK: No, we knew digital was coming, but we didn't know when. We kept changing the plans knowing we could go digital or film, so that's how we approached it. The biggest problem we were dealing with was how do we fit really good auditoriums into this space. We always knew it was a very good location. The biggest thing was working the business deal out with the developer. We knew we would have a free zone with only the River East and the 600 N. Michigan servicing the entire downtown area. It's a very unique theatre because there has never been a theatre serving the near south side up to Hyde Park along with the huge university community in the south loop and the near west side which has exploded in the last decade with condos and offices. There just wasn't anything there.

Q: *I hear you went on a road trip to look at deluxe theatres around the county?*

DK: Over the years, we took a look at most of the premium theatres in the country, the different concepts, and once again there wasn't much that was too new because people have done it in the past. You had Muvico with their VIP seating and restaurants, and you had the Archlight with their reserved seating, Alamo Drafthouses where you ate burgers and pizza and watched the movie and Gold Class theatres, with their small screens, high end food and very high ticket prices. So we saw what was working and made our decisions based on what we learned and what we wanted to do.

TK: We knew what we didn't want to do, and that was the small theatre sizes and very exclusive admission and food pricing. With the high labor costs, that would be a challenge, and I asked, "How do you make money if you sell mostly high priced food items and not regular concessions?" Also, with 40 to 60 seat auditoriums you become very limited in what the movies can gross. We have seen how much it costs to sell food and liquor.

Q: *Do you keep the dining dollars separate from the rest of the theatre's revenues?*

TK: Yes, they are separate, and we can analyze it separately. Per capita is based on total theatre admissions. We know what the average tab is, but that's not per capita. Our per capita is better at the Icon than we've ever experienced in our regular theatres because we get such a broad audience. They buy everything from yogurt to specialized coffee and teas to the usual popcorn, soda and candy.

Q: *What's a good range of per capita these days?*

TK: $3.50 to $4.00 per person.

Q: *What did the Icon cost to build?*

TK: About $35 million dollars.

Q: *I heard in the past the cost of a new giant, ultramodern theatre complex came out to about $1,000,000 per screen. Is that accurate?*

TK: I have heard that too, but I was never able to figure out if that was accurate. Each new build has its own characteristics.

Q: *So with the Icon, it was more like $2 million a screen.*

DK: Well, the physical plant was very expensive, plus it was a complicated construction project to boot. Construction costs in the middle of Chicago are very expensive.

Q: *Tony, you didn't blink when you said $35 million. You can buy a whole circuit for less, and I'm sure you have.*

TK: In 1988, we bought General Cinema units in Springfield, Terre Haute, Muncie and Michigan City in Illinois and Indiana, and all those theatres combined was $3 million bucks, and I think it was about 15 screens.

Q: *When you spend $35 million, how many years does it take to pay it down or show a profit? How do you look at that?*

TK: With this particular one, it was just fun to do; we didn't do any projections. There are different ways you can look at it. Do you think of it over a 10 or 20-year span, or return on investment or multiples of earnings?

Q: *You had said you wanted to do well the first year, better the second year and keep growing. How has that worked for you?*

TK: We are pretty much on track. I figure by the third year if we're getting a 15% cash return, that's as good as it will ever be. But we're still ramping up.

Q: *Did you figure on the money from the eventual sale of the circuit in your decision to proceed with such an expensive theatre?*

TK: We started the process years ago, so we weren't thinking about that.

Q: *It's the single most expensive thing you ever did?*

TK: Yes, and it will remain the single most expensive thing we ever do.

Q: *No more future $35 million Icons?*

TK: I don't think so.

Q: *Are you basically still product dependent? When you have a great theatre with so many amenities, do you still need strong product, or do the best theatres do business regardless?*

TK: You still need the product. If you have a better theatre, you do better regardless of what the level of product is.

Q: *In 2010, your first full year of operation, how did the theatre rank in gross in the Chicago area?*

TK: We were second behind AMC River East, which did in the $12 to $13 million dollar range, with the Icon a million less than that. In 2011, we are running number one and confident we will finish the number one grossing theatre in the Chicago area for the entire year.

Q: *When the general business was down in the first quarter of 2011, was the Icon down accordingly?*

TK: No, our business was up because the theatre was still growing and getting new audiences to the theatre. We have had some spectacular numbers this year. We just did $102,000 for the week on "The Green Lantern," which was 29th in the country. The River East had the next best gross at $69,000. "Hangover 2" did over $200,000 its first week, which ranked seventh in the U.S., so we're happy.

Q: *Those are impressive numbers. You are making the theatre indispensible for film companies.*

TK: There would be no reason for anyone to deny us. Distributors are in the business of collecting film rental.

Q: *And your dining portion has worked out?*

TK: The revenues have been terrific. We have made adjustments with our staff. When we opened the theatre, we had never done the dining thing before, so we wanted to make the experience the best possible for our patrons. We learned how to be more efficient with staffing by watching how the crowd flows when the movie begins. The dining area could be full one minute, and ten minutes later it could clear out.

Q: *When you opened the theatre, you offered free parking for a limited time in a large enclosed parking garage next to the theatre, and two years later it is still free. Free parking in downtown Chicago is unheard of. How important has this amenity been in growing your audience?*

TK: This came about because when the theatre opened, we were the only retailer open for business in the development, and that's still the case. It's been a slow process for the developer with the economy the way it's been, but the deal is when there are two restaurants open, that will be when we will begin to start charging for parking. There is no doubt free parking has been a big plus and a selling point in getting people to sample our theatre. Though it's been free to the public, it's costing us $20,000 a month in payment, and I would have to say it's been well worth it.

Q: *Do you think it will be shock to your patrons when they have to start paying for parking? Will you lose part of your audience?*

TK: I don't think so. It's always been advertised "for a limited time only," and people aren't stupid. The limited time has stretched for two years. When it changes, I'm told it will be a modest fee, perhaps $6.00 for three hours, which will still be a bargain. We are also near a lot of public transportation, so our patrons will have that option.

Q: *What's the makeup of your overall audience?*

TK: It's more of an adult audience, though we get our share of families too. We are much less a teen theatre than others because we have a restrictive policy that anyone under 17 years old has to be accompanied by a parent after 7:00 pm. Teens in the city are not a real important part of our potential audience, their strength is more suburban. In addition, the entire industry has been concerned about the falloff in teen attendance in general.

Q: *Speaking of that restrictive policy, I recall when you opened a new theatre at 22nd and Cicero some years ago, you not only had the same policy but instituted a policy that all teens 17 and under had to take Code of Conduct classes before they were able to attend the theatre. This garnered a fair share of negative publicity. Looking back, would you have done anything differently?*

TK: No. It was a very successful policy, and all that publicity helped make the theatre a family destination. We took some heat when we were called racist, but the area did have a gang problem. After things settled down, we were able to attract a good audience to the theatre made up of whites, blacks and Hispanics.

Q: *In closing, what's a lesson or basic truth about the industry you would like to share?*

TK: What I've learned in dealing with distribution is it's always been important not to take advantage of anybody because it always comes back and haunts you. Treat people as fairly as you can while still trying to do what's best for your own business. Don't mess with people just for fun, and we have all seen that happen. There's been some bad people in this business.

DK: It's really about taking care of your customer, working with our operations people, handling problems that people have, listening to them and trying to solve the problem quickly and fairly. You can't live and die with your policy all the time. I've learned you have to be flexible.

Q: *Thank you both for your time and insight.*

TK: Thank you.

Week 49: Questions for Discussion

1. What gives exhibitors the right to play tough with the studios, and what is the number one way they can wield their power?

2. In years past, why would some theatres actually close their doors during the first two weeks of December? Do you think this made sense at the time?

3. What was the overriding reason the Kerasotes theatre circuit was sold in 2009, and how does that point to a larger trend that has affected theatre circuits in the last two decades? How was the sale tied to the expansion of the circuit after 2003? Did that make the sale of the circuit inevitable?

4. What does Tony Kerasotes say about the art of modern day film buying? What are his views of paying film rental to distributors and his relationship with distributors over the years?

5. What makes the Showplace Icon in Chicago unique? From your moviegoing experiences, how does it compare and contrast to theatres in both cities and suburbs that you frequent? Name at least one detail of the theatre that surprised you and the reason it did.

AS CHRISTMAS DRAWS CLOSER, THE STAKES GET HIGHER

Week 50: December 11–17, 2009

There are strong egos to massage and relations to maintain.
Perception is everything in Hollywood.

With Christmas Day only two weeks away and as the temperature and snow fall through large parts of the country, both the Oscar race and the box office heat up as some of the most anticipated films of the year are set to open. There is always a debate about why the studios backload their best quality films in the last few weeks of the year, but when you look at the situation more closely, it comes down to rational decision making by distributors. It's just great positioning. The timing couldn't be more perfect with end-of-the-year critics awards, top ten lists and the Golden Globe nominations smothering these films with love and attention, which in turn creates extra awareness and want-to-see among moviegoers. Last year the five contenders for Best Picture all came out in the last seven weeks of the year with three of the five being December releases. It's too bad we have to wait until the absolute end of the year to see some of the best films, but it does make for excellent moviegoing during the holidays. The ante is raised this year with the Best Picture race being expanded from five to ten films, which gives more movies a chance at the top prize. To prove the point about December being crowded with potential award nominees, up to half of the Best Picture candidates could be opening within a three-week span in December. Take a look at the following films in the order they are being released this month:

- ▶ Up in the Air – Paramount
- ▶ Invictus – Warner Brothers
- ▶ The Lovely Bones – Paramount
- ▶ Nine – Weinstein
- ▶ Avatar – 20th Century Fox
- ▶ It's Complicated – Universal

These are some heavy hitters, and the competition is going to be fierce. I can't remember a December where so many Oscar candidates are coming from the studios rather than from independent distributors. At least two of the above films probably won't make the cut for Best Picture, but it still points to the fact the studios should be major players in this year's competition. A reduction in studio specialty divisions certainly plays a part in this dynamic. Not that independents won't be involved in the race. Earlier releases from independents such as "The Hurt Locker," "Precious" and "An Education" will no doubt be part of the mix also. An interesting movie that has an outside chance to work its way into the top ten is the Coen Brothers' "A Serious Man." If it accomplishes that, it will be due to Focus Feature's strategy of keeping the release very small and being able to retain its core art theatres, biding time until the field gets sorted out. There are two basic principles at play here. A distributor never wants to have one of their top candidates be considered a commercial failure. Recognizing soon after the film's limited debut that suburban runs would be a challenge, they made the smart decision not to push supply before demand to keep the perception that the movie was doing fine. In addition, it's much easier to book those good suburban theatres at a later date if they hadn't already played the film and failed with it. Focus has been engaging in the fine art of distribution.

One of the uncertainties in the Oscar race is whether or not one of the big commercial summer movies will be invited to the dance. The movie that is most mentioned as a possibility to be one of the ten nominations for Best Picture is "Star Trek," a very good and entertaining film. I wouldn't have a problem with that, but if there was one summer film to include, I would go with Michael Mann's "Public Enemies," one of my favorite movies of the year. The big mystery for me is how this film has never been part of the discussion and has been totally dismissed as having even a remote chance of getting nominated. The film received some excellent reviews including Manohla Dargis of the *New York Times* who called it "a grave and beautiful work of art," and it did fine commercially with just under $100 million in box office gross. I think it's a beautiful, stylish, hard-edged crime drama that delivers on a lot of levels and has a superb Johnny Depp performance at its center. The criticism I hear the most is that it lacks depth and character development, but I don't agree with that line of thinking. Universal must have read the tea leaves early on and has never attempted to position the movie as a Best Picture contender. Studios have to pick the movies they are going to push very carefully because it's both an economic and political decision. To support an Oscar campaign for several months is an expensive ordeal that can add millions of ad dollars to an already expensive campaign. This simply has to be done, especially with an earlier release because when a film is out of sight, it's also out of mind among Academy voters. A film company never wants to back the wrong horse. But that happens at times, and that's where it becomes political. Studios have close relationships with their creative partners, which includes producers, directors and stars, and those partners could get prickly when they perceive a studio is not supporting their baby the way they feel it should be supported. There are strong egos to massage and relationships to maintain. Perception is everything in Hollywood. "Public Enemies" is perceived to be a disappointment in Hollywood that didn't deliver on its full promise, and for that reason, above everything else, it will not be a factor in this year's race.

Just as the Oscar race is heating up, the box office is beginning to build up steam, even though mid-December is a time moviegoers are still busy with school, work, shopping and holiday activities. Two movies are opening wide this weekend, which matches the same output as last year when "The Day the Earth Stood Still" and "Nothing Like the Holidays" combined to gross $33 million between them. The weekend's two releases, Warner Brothers' "Invictus," and Disney's "Princess and the Frog," which is moving into national release, should beat that figure at somewhere over $40 million. These two movies couldn't be more different from each other, but they happen to be both dealing with the issue of race. Let's look at "Invictus" first. Clint Eastwood at the age of 80 continues to make important films, and his film on Nelson Mandela is almost certain to be in the running for Best Picture. Unlike last year when Warner Brothers opened "Gran Torino" on this very same week in only six theatres, "Invictus" is opening on over 2,000 screens. The difference in distribution strategy between the two films is striking. Warner Brothers' platform release of "Gran Torino" worked to perfection as they waited until early January to go wide, creating a huge demand and market for the film after they let the dust settle on the other big Christmas films. The curious thing is that "Gran Torino's" mass appeal blue-collar audience would seem to have been more conducive to a wide release, and "Invictus," with its subject matter and more upscale appeal, could have easily gone with a slower, more deliberate pattern. That could be true, but any second-guessing comes to a stop when a film achieves great success. "Gran Torino" became Eastwood's highest grossing movie at $148 million, a figure that "Invictus" has no real chance of approaching.

Each year's crop of films is different, and there are a number of considerations studios make in deciding how to release a film. Is Warner Bros. showing more confidence with "Invictus" by booking over 2,000 theatres from day one? That could be the case, or they may feel that their only shot of playing that many theatres is to book them all at once upfront. It may come down to having more marquee power with three major names, Eastwood, Morgan Freeman and Matt Damon to sell to the public rather than just Eastwood's name on "Gran Torino." Or Warner Bros. felt more comfortable in mid-December after sizing up the competition it will be facing in the next few weeks. With "Gran Torino" there was a bit of mystery of what the movie was actually about so a few extra weeks in limited release landed up helping to define the movie more and grow the buzz. Getting back to this weekend, "Invictus" is positioned nicely to capture the adult audience with the animated "Princess and the Frog" as its only new competition in the multiplexes. If the film can establish an audience base and open in the mid-teens with its gross, it could have many weeks to play because Eastwood's films generally have strong legs. However, a potential negative, which could derail the film's commerciality, is its title, which is not its strong suit and could prove to be a turnoff to mainstream audiences.

On the other end of the spectrum, Disney is positioned to pull in the family audience with their latest animated film. Two weeks ago "Princess and the Frog" opened one theatre in New York and one theatre in Los Angeles with a $25.00 ticket in exclusive engagements, which offered much more than just the movie. With interactive displays and Disney's stable of former movie princesses on hand, the movie has already amassed an unbelievable gross of $2.8 million, setting it up perfectly for its expansion. At this point, does it even matter that the movie stars Disney's first African American princess? If it delivers strong entertainment value for families, the color of the character's skin should not be a factor. What could be bigger issues to contend with is that the film is a return to 2D hand drawn animation, not the more popular computer animation which dominates today, and the princess storyline will not lend itself to the adult crossover that Pixar films enjoy. Disney has a lot riding on this movie and needs a big hit. Their ace in the hole is the fact that their princess merchandising line is a $4 billion annual business for the company, and so far the merchandising for "Princess and the Frog" has been jumping off the shelves. Who knows, it could be the right movie at the right time. These animated movies take years to make, so Disney had no idea who was going to be in the White House at the time of the release. Having the Obamas and their own princess daughters in Washington only adds to the sizzle.

It's the type of film we seldom see from a major studio anymore,
a story that actually deals with what's going on in today's world.
When a movie is bold and hits the zeitgeist it can go far.

Speaking of being timely, at this moment "Up in the Air" is the movie with the most Oscar heat and has to be considered a front-runner for Best Picture. That could change any time in the next couple of months, and it probably will since all the potential candidates haven't even opened yet. This may be a year when various films keep jockeying for position and trading off on the lead, and it stays a wide open race to the end. But in the space of a few days last week, everything came together for this George Clooney starrer about corporate downsizing. The day before "Up in the Air" opened in 15 exclusive theatres last weekend, the film was voted Best Film of the Year by the National Board of Review. It then proceeded to gross $79,000 a theatre with long lines and sellouts all weekend with critics and audiences praising its charms. Yes, people are still being laid off, it's still a tough economy, but a movie that's timely and rings true and is in the hands of an excellent director, in this case Jason Reitman, can become the movie of the moment. Audiences are connecting with it. It's the type of film we seldom see from a major studio anymore, a story that actually deals with what's going on in today's world. When a movie is bold and hits the zeitgeist it can go far. It reminds me of 30 years ago, Christmas 1979, when one of Columbia's holiday films was "Kramer vs. Kramer." Back then, the studios had two tracks at Christmas and labeled their releases "A" and "B" tracks based on box office potential with the "A" track films getting the better theatres. It was funny, but often the studios guessed wrong with their own movies, and the so-called "B" track movies became the more successful films. This is what happened with "Kramer vs. Kramer," a film that tapped into the era of working couples, a yuppie divorce and the eventual child custody fight. It didn't hurt to have Dustin Hoffman and Meryl Streep as its stars. Columbia didn't have much faith in the film and put it on their "B" track, and all it did was gross $109 million ($250 million in today's dollars) and win Best Picture of the Year. Will "Up in the Air" be this year's "Kramer vs. Kramer"? We'll see. By Christmas Day, the film will be playing everywhere in the country and the other films will also have had opened, so the Oscar picture may have another favorite by then. Then again, it may not.

This Week at the Box Office: *Weekly Attendance: $16,809,958*

Invictus

Warner Brothers
Opening weekend: $8,611,147
Domestic gross: $37,491,364 30.7%
Foreign gross: $84,742,607 69.3%
Worldwide gross: $122,233,971
Widest release: 2,170 theatres

A Single Man

Weinstein
Opening weekend: $217,332
Domestic gross: $9,172,425 36.8%
Foreign gross: $15,788,890 63.2%
Worldwide gross: $24,964,890
Widest release: 354 theatres

The Slammin Salmon

Anchor Bay
Opening weekend: $26,167
Domestic gross: $41,588
Foreign gross: N/A
Widest release: 11 theatres

The Lovely Bones

Paramount
Opening weekend: $116,610
Domestic gross: $37,491,364 47.1%
Foreign gross: $49,507,108 52.9%
Worldwide gross: $93,621,340
Widest release: 2,638 theatres

Town Called Panic

Zeitgiest
Opening weekend: $,2850
Domestic gross: $165,509 84.4%
Foreign gross: $30,667 15.6%
Worldwide gross: $196,176
Widest release: 10 theatres

Week 50: Questions for Discussion

1. How did Focus Features engage in the fine art of distribution with their handling of "A Serious Man"?

2. In what ways does perception matter in Hollywood? Do you believe in the saying, "Perception becomes reality"? Discuss.

3. What were the old "A" and "B" tracks that film distributors employed when there weren't as many strong theatre screens as there are now to book their films in. Was it an exact science? Discuss.

THE TIME IS NOW FOR "AVATAR"

Week 51: December 18–24, 2009

---

*If it seems like everything that has happened in 2009 has been
a prelude to this weekend, well, that's not too far from the truth.*

Finally. On the next to last weekend of the year, "Avatar" is set to open on about 20,000 screens around the world. In a year of big movies, this is the biggest, in scope, in budget and in expectations. If it seems like everything that has happened in 2009 has been a prelude to this weekend, well, that's not too far from the truth. If that's putting a lot of pressure on one movie, director James Cameron says "bring it on, I can handle it." That sounds like something a superstar athlete would say before a crucial game. The hype, of course, all begins with Cameron. It has been twelve years almost to the day that his last film "Titanic" opened, still the all-time box office champ at $1.8 billion worldwide and winner of 11 Oscars including Best Picture. We've been hearing about this film for years, and Cameron has been biding his time waiting for technology to catch up with his ideas, while also doing his part in developing and creating new camera systems and software to pull off his grand spectacle. The time is now. The question is, can he deliver again? When you think about it, the timing of "Avatar's" release couldn't arrive at a more crucial and opportune time for the industry, in the waning days of the first decade of the new millennium and as the cleanup hitter for the dozen 3D movies that have played in 2009. "Avatar" is being called the industry's first real 3D blockbuster, and everyone has been pointing to this movie all year saying it will validate the entire 3D business, for exhibitors to convert more of their screens to digital 3D and for audiences to prove that 3D is the real deal and the wave of the future. Since most of the prior 3D movies have been either animation or horror, the hope is that "Avatar" will hook more of the regular moviegoing audience and really bring it into the mainstream in a big way. In addition to being asked to be the exclamation point for the 3D movement, his movie is also being looked on to advance current film production with the technology that he helped to create. In essence, "Avatar" is being asked to carry the torch for the entire industry. That's a tall order for one movie to have on its shoulders.

I read one of the press interviews with Cameron where he referred to himself as being a modest man. I had to laugh at that one. The self-proclaimed "King of the World" is anything but, and that's what makes him who he is. He is bold, confident and knows he's good. He doesn't shy away from telling anyone who will listen that "Avatar" is groundbreaking and will change the way movies are made and how audiences will experience them. When someone in Hollywood achieves great success and openly brags about it, there are those who will openly root against a film or filmmaker to fail, the old build-him-up-tear-him-down syndrome. Throw in a dash of envy, jealousy and bitterness, and you have the recipe for Hollywood at its most spiteful. But that's not going on here with James Cameron and "Avatar." The man hasn't been around in twelve years. He made the most successful movie of all-time. Big movies help all companies; it brings people back to the theatres and eyeballs in front of trailers from competing distributors. He provided employment for 2,000 workers for three years – technicians, actors, camera operators, editors, caterers and special effects houses. Then there is the 3D factor. How can any distributor or producer not root for the movie that has a chance to be a game changer for the industry and solidify the process for years to come? 3D means higher revenues and hope for a stronger theatrical business for years to come. Thus Hollywood is coming together rooting for this movie to be as big as it can be, to propel the end of the year to record heights while pulling the rest of the films along with it. For once the industry is looking at the bigger picture, DVD sales are down, digital downloads aren't picking up the slack, the theatrical business, though attendance has been up throughout 2009, has been flat for a number of years. Specialty companies are being eliminated, studios are getting by with fewer workers. People are scared, worried about the future. Hollywood needs hits, the bigger the better. Hollywood needs visionary filmmakers, big ideas, giant productions that no other country can produce to fuel the global marketplace. Dream big, execute big and deliver big. They need James Cameron and "Avatar," right here, right now, to do killer business everywhere.

How much did "Avatar" cost to make, and how big of a risk is it for the studio? The guessing game of what the actual budget is for "Avatar" has gone to some ridiculous heights with a figure as high as $500 million being thrown around. This occurs in the press because studios seldom reveal their actual production budgets, and it's up to sources in the industry to conjecture about it. 20th Century Fox's co-chairman Jim Gianopulas is on record saying "Avatar" is the most expensive movie the studio has ever made and pegs the production at around $230 million, $30 million more than what "Titanic" cost. But no one believes that figure. The best estimate is that the movie cost somewhere between $250 and $300 million and that Fox is spending $150 million to market the movie around the world where it is opening in 106 territories. The $500 million figure comes from journalists who add production and marketing costs together, which is misleading. It's true that each of these costs is a recoupable distribution expense, but they are separate expenditures and are not the same line item. Nevertheless, Fox will have over $400 million riding on it that will need to be recouped. That's a tidy sum. It's even more of a gamble on paper because "Avatar" is not a pre-sold entertainment from best-selling books like "Lord of the Rings" or "Harry Potter," nor is it based on comic books like Batman or Spiderman. Rather it's an original story sprung from the mind of James Cameron. However, Fox is confident they will turn a profit and believe Cameron has delivered again. Does it have to do "Titanic" numbers for that to happen? No, I think Fox would take $300 million in North America and $600 to $700 million from foreign territories and they would be very happy with a global gross of a billion dollars with the real profits coming from ancillary markets like DVD and television. It has a long way to get there, and this weekend is just the start.

What does "Avatar" have to gross the opening weekend to put any worries at ease for 20th Century Fox? Well, it doesn't have to set any opening weekend records, and it probably won't. It is the week before Christmas, and people are still pretty busy getting ready for the holidays. Throw in a huge snowstorm scheduled to hit big Eastern cities over the weekend, and it becomes even harder to predict. Historically, this week is somewhat slow. It's interesting to remember that "Titanic" opened to only $28 million, but showed some of the best staying power in history by being number one for 14 weeks in a row on its way to a $600 million domestic gross. With 3,100 3D screens playing the picture with higher ticket prices and critics raving about it, "Avatar" will easily surpass the "Titanic" opening and should open to $70 million or more. It's not so much how it opens, it's how long it plays. Fox feels the key will be word of mouth and strong critics' reviews which is a whole lot different from most blockbusters which do it through pre-sold, massive marketing campaigns and merchandising tie-ins. Fox makes their tentpole sound more similar to the formula used by platform releases.

Be that as it may, Fox is not cutting corners on their marketing budget. Since it's an original story, the studio realizes it has to spend big money to make big money to establish the movie as a must-see with the public. In this era of global, high-priced blockbusters, spending too little on marketing is considered more risky than spending too much. In the U.S. alone, Fox is probably spending a minimum of $50 million on prints and advertising. The studio has been running longer length television commercials for a couple of months now, and it certainly looks like it's the most expensive media campaign of any 2009 movie. What has the marketing money bought them so far? Well, seemingly not the female audience. The appeal is predominantly male, and young men will initially drive the box office as it does for the majority of action-adventure blockbusters. This is what separates "Avatar" and "Titanic." The core audience for "Titanic" was women, and repeat business by younger women and teenage girls fueled the record gross.

"Avatar" will get its gross in a different way and hope that women will eventually come around as the result of good word of mouth and strong reviews. One of the problems Fox has had to deal with in their publicity campaign is the lack of a great single still image that makes the movie look interesting and compelling - one image, one scene from the movie that can capture its essence, become the face of the film and hook the audience at the same time. With "Titanic," the photo of Leonardo DiCaprio with his arms stretched out with Kate Winslet at his side on the front deck of the ship with a sunset in the background became the indelible image seen in publicity stories, on billboards, posters and newspaper ads. Romance, grand adventure, spectacle, freedom, the power of love, all of that captured in one photo. One of the challenges of movie campaigns is to find that one strong image that can sell the film. Sometimes it's just not there. The publicity power of the single image is missing in action with "Avatar." The main photo image that publications and the Internet has been running for months is a photo with the faces of a blue-skinned man and woman, which comes across as unreal and computer generated. I have heard women say they have no interest in seeing the film. As we have gotten closer to the film's opening, the face of the actor Sam Worthington has been used next to the female blue alien which is a bit more of a compelling image but still not very exciting. The problem with women being cold toward "Avatar" starts with that image. Is that a crippling blow for the film? Not at all because "Avatar" has so much else going for it, and the excitement level is so high for its debut. But I'm still surprised Cameron and 20th Century Fox couldn't come up with a more compelling single image to sell the movie's concept to the world.

With strong reviews and a Golden Globe nomination for Best Picture, "Avatar" seems destined to follow "Titanic" with an Oscar nomination for Best Picture. That would also be a boost for the movie industry and the Oscar broadcast since it would be the first blockbuster nominated for Best Picture since "The Lord of the Rings: Return of the King" swept the Oscars in 2003. It won't be the favorite, at least it isn't now, but it will be a player. Critics are calling "Avatar" tremendous and spectacular and also mention the strong story with its context of anti-war, pro-environment, anti-imperialism themes running through it. That's pretty heady stuff for a big, sci-fi film, and that's what separates it from the pack from all the other blockbusters that seem to always fall short in the Oscar race. The movie has some depth to go along with the spectacle, and that's what voters look for. When James Cameron accepted the Oscar for Best Picture for "Titanic," he screamed "I'm the King of the World." Maybe he'll prove he still is. And we'll see another return of the king.

This Week at the Box Office: *Weekly Attendance: 35,303,323*

The only studio that decided to go against "Avatar" with a national release was Sony with the comedy "Did You Hear About the Morgans?" starring Sarah Jessica Parker, which really isn't much competition at all. Three high profile independent films with Oscar aspirations will also be opening, "Crazy Heart," "Nine" and "The Young Victoria."

Avatar

20th Century Fox
Opening weekend: $77,025,481
Domestic gross: $760,507,625 27.3%
Foreign gross: $2,021,767,547 72.7%
Worldwide gross: $2,782,275,172
Widest release: 3,461 theatres

Did You Hear About the Morgans?

Sony/Columbia
Opening weekend: $6,616,571
Domestic gross: $29,062,561 34.7%
Foreign gross: $55,700,163 65.3%
Worldwide gross: $85,280,250
Widest release: 2,734 theatres

Nine

Weinstein
Opening weekend: $257,232
Domestic gross: $19,676,965 36.4%
Foreign gross: $34,321,841 63.6%
Worldwide gross: $53,998,806
Widest release: 1,412 theatres

The Young Victoria

Apparition
Opening weekend: $160,069
Domestic gross: $11,001,272 40.1%
Foreign gross: $16,408,617 59.9%
Worldwide gross: $27,409,889
Widest release: 476 theatres

Crazy Heart

Fox Searchlight

Opening weekend: $82,664

Domestic gross: $39,471,742 83.2%

Foreign gross: $7,941,260 16.8%

Worldwide gross: $47,405,566

Widest release: 1,361 theatres

Ricky

IFC

Opening weekend: $1,626

Domestic gross: $3,457 0.2%

Foreign gross: $2,268,418 99.8%

Worldwide gross: $2,271,875

Widest release: 1 theatre

The Lightkeepers

New Films

Opening weekend: N/A

Domestic gross: $18,463

Foreign gross: N/A

Widest release: 50 theatres

Week 51: Questions for Discussion

1. As "Avatar" was set to open, what was the main difference between the audience appeal of "Avatar" and "Titanic"? Do you think 20th Century Fox was worried about this? What marketing factors did Fox feel would occur that would be able to turn the thinking around?

2. The challenge for all marketing campaigns is to find that one strong image that can sell the film. After observing and researching the current movies by looking at posters in theatres, newspaper or magazine ads, bus shelters or billboards and Internet ads, choose one that you think is the best or most creative in capturing the essence, storyline and vibe of the film. Does that single image make you want to see the film?

2012 Update:
The Changing Face Of Product Delivery

The "Avatar" opening provides the perfect opportunity to get into a topic that is little known outside of the world of producers, filmmakers and distributors. The issue is Product Delivery, a complex process that involves a number of different materials that distributors need before they can actually distribute a film. When a studio produces and finances a movie as 20th Century Fox did with "Avatar," the studio is responsible for its own deliverables, which can often be a significant extra expense at the end of a long production process, which was certainly the case with "Avatar." With independent films that are either acquired by outside distributors or are released without a distributor in place, it is the producer's responsibility to produce, gather and pay for the materials that are necessary when someone wants to compete and release a film into the commercial marketplace. If a distributor purchases a film and offers an advance to a filmmaker, it is always predicated on the complete delivery of materials as listed in the distribution agreement. There have been a fair share of deals voided when certain items could not be delivered by the scheduled date. Delivery Schedules are divided into the following three sections:

- ▶ Technical materials
- ▶ Publicity/marketing materials
- ▶ Records and documentation

With the massive changes that have been occurring in the last several years from creating standard 35mm film release prints to today's digital prints and files, the area of technical materials has gone through the largest transformation, whereas for the most part, the other two sections of materials have basically remained the same. In the first part of this section, I'll focus on the highly complicated ordeal that James Cameron and Fox had to go through to produce the technical materials needed to service the global marketplace with "Avatar" prints. While in the second part, I'll detail what is changing and what has stayed the same for independent films, and what producers should know and concentrate on at all stages of a film's production, from pre-production to post-production to pre-release.

The trade publication Hollywood Reporter in March, 2010 wrote a very revealing piece on how "Avatar" was changing the rules of deliverables and proceeded to take the reader through the process of what James Cameron and Fox had to do in order to insure the highest quality presentation for each and every theatre playing the movie in whatever format it was. 2009 was a critical turning point for the industry in many ways, and that is the case here. The industry was stuck in the middle of an analog and digital marketplace with a large amount of theatre screens still projecting 35mm film prints, so there were many different kind of technical specifications needed to supply both 2D and 3D houses around the world. With the complicated technical nature of the film itself combined with James Cameron being a perfectionist and wanting to deliver the optimum theatre experience, the decision was made to complete the movie in three aspect ratios (2:39.1), flat (1:85.1) and Imax (1.43.1). Not too many directors go to this length in delivering their films.

According to the information the *Hollywood Reporter* gathered, "There were 18 different versions of "Avatar" created for the domestic market and an additional 92 for international markets, which were released in 47 languages. The international versions included more than 52 subtitled and 18 dubbed versions on film, 58 subtitled and 36 dubbed versions in digital 3D, nine subtitled and eight dubbed versions in digital 2D and 23 subtitled and 15 dubbed versions for IMAX. In the end, "Avatar" was finished in 10 parts, reel by reel, for more than 100 versions. Additionally, the IMAX film version was made up of 82 different reels.'

The breakdown of screens for "Avatar" was as follows:

- ▶ 17, 604 - 35mm screens
- ▶ 7,382 – digital 3D screens
- ▶ 553 – digital 2D screens
- ▶ 272 – Imax #D screens
- ▶ Total Worldwide Screens – 25, 811

    Source: *Hollywood Reporter*

This was an unprecedented ordeal and accomplishment, which will never be duplicated again as the movie industry moves closer and closer to an all-digital projection world. At the time of "Avatar's" release, what complicated matters was the fact that there were still more than 17,000 theatres around the world playing the film in 35mm along with the 8,000 or so theatres playing it digitally. The cost of producing this myriad of release prints was not revealed, but I wouldn't be surprised if it didn't amount to $30 million or more and that's not even figuring in the salaries of the large amounts of technicians working 24/7 for several months to complete the work. With a final worldwide gross of $2.7 billion, it would be an understatement to say that all the money and meticulous attention to detail paid to "Avatar" was money well spent.

On the other end of the spectrum are the countless independent features that are made each year. Whatever their cost, each film and its filmmakers have to confront the reality of supplying delivery materials for their films. Let's break it down into the three distinct areas of deliverables:

Technical Materials

As stated, the biggest change in deliverables has come in the area of technical materials. In the past, the vast majority of technical materials was tied to producing a 35mm print, regardless of what format it was filmed in, whether it was 16mm, super 16mm, 35mm or digital, because that was the industry standard for a hundred years. The materials consisted of an original picture negative, optical soundtrack negative, inter-positive, answer print, inter-negative, original mono magnetic soundtrack and music and effects (M&E) tracks. The entire process of blowing up a 16 or super 16mm print to 35mm was expensive, in the $35,000 to $50,000 range. With the announcement that Landmark Theatres, the largest theatre circuit for independent films, will have all their screens converted to digital by 2013, this will greatly ease the need of having to bother creating 35mm prints anymore. In addition, many smaller art house venues have cheaper digital capabilities, including Blu-ray projection, which works fine for smaller releases and is much cheaper to service. Even though there can be a significant savings in this area, it can still cost up to $10,000 or more to produce a professional high-def digital master. Evan as James Cameron had to deal with all the different technical specifications for various venues, the same problem to a lesser extent confronts independent filmmakers when they play their films on the Internet. A site like I-Tunes can have different specs and needs than Hulu or Netflix when working with aggregators to make video-on-demand and streaming deals. Producing acceptable prints for each site can amount to a few thousand dollars each so costs can add up.

Publicity/ Marketing Materials

This is a crucial area, which can be cost effective and controllable with a little hindsight and planning. The following elements help create a press kit for the film which becomes the centerpiece of the publicity campaign:

- ▶ Film Synopsis: A typewritten copy of the film's synopsis running at least 500 words.

- Cast and Crew List: A typewritten copy of a list of the cast and crew who worked on the film. It may sound like a simple task, but it's a task that should command attention to get it done right. On independent films, many people can work on a film for very little money, so getting all the names spelled correctly becomes very important, as that same list goes on the film prints.

- Press Kit Essentials: Typewritten copies of biographies of each member of the principal cast and production staff (director, producer, music supervisor, etc.) and copies of all available press clippings, production notes and anything else created which would help to sell the film.

- Photos: The most important deliverable in this section, bar none. Excellent professional photos can do more for a film than any other publicity item. They are used in a number of ways including in film festival catalogues, publicity stories, post cards, flyers, posters, Internet sites and DVD covers. Photos are the DNA of a marketing campaign, and much care and attention should be given to them. In the past, filmmakers had to generate both original black and white and color negatives and transparencies; now, high-def digital photos cover all needs.

Records and Documentation:
- Shooting script: One copy of the final shooting script.

- Final Titles: One typewritten copy of the final main and end titles of the film as they appear in the film.

- Music Cue Sheet: A copy of a music cue sheet includes the following:
  - The title of the musical compositions and sound recordings in the film
  - Names of composers and their performing rights society affiliation
  - Names of recording artists
  - Extent and exact timing of the uses of each piece of music in the film
- Music Licenses: Copies of all applicable sync, performance and master use licenses, and signed copies of all musicians' contracts agreeing to have their original music used in the film. This can become expensive, so contracting someone to write original music for the film at a reasonable price is an option that can save a lot of money and heartache, especially for anyone who uses music that's not properly cleared.

- Release Agreements: All licenses, agreements, contracts or written permissions from all the proper parties seen in the film, buildings identified and shown, artwork displayed and any other material such as products used in the production of the film.

- Paid Advertising Blocks: A producer's statement listing the names of all persons to whom the production is contractually obligated to accord credit on the screen or in any paid advertising or publicity of the film.

- Chain of Title: Chain of title documentation that shows any past owners of the script or property.

- Copyright Registration: One clear copy of the producer's registration of its claim to copyright the film in the Copyright Office of the Library of Congress.

- E&O Insurance: A certificate indicating coverage of the picture on a standard provider's errors and omissions liability insurance policy covering the picture. This is often overlooked in this era of self-distributed films, but before any cable station or Internet site plays your movie, they will request an E&O policy to protect themselves from any potential claim brought against the film. An all rights policy can cost in the area of $10,000.

▸ Certificate of Rating: A Certificate of Rating from the Motion Picture Association of America with a rating no more restrictive than "R" isn't absolutely necessary for a small theatrical release, but Cinemark, the third largest theatre chain, will not play a film without a proper rating. Where it becomes more necessary is in the DVD and television markets when a film is sold in those markets. The cost of procuring a rating is based on a movie's budget. For those movies under $500,000, the price of a Certificate of Rating is a reasonable $1,500. For the most expensive Hollywood movies, the cost for a rating is $15,000.

2012 Update: Questions for Discussion

3. Why does product delivery exist, and can a film be released without engaging in this process?

4. What was the most challenging deliverable that had to be created for "Avatar"? What made it so difficult of an ordeal?

5. For independent films, choose two deliverables that need to be completed, one that has gone through changes and one that has basically stayed the same. Discuss in your own words what they are, their importance, and what kind of approach should be taken to deliver quality items.

THE BEST IS SAVED FOR LAST: THE BOX
OFFICE RACES TO THE FINISH LINE

Week 52: December 25–31, 2009

---

*Out of this vast wasteland of empty parking lots and quiet solitude stand the
movie theatres, popping the popcorn and projecting the movies as usual, open
for business as they are for each of the 365 days of the year.*

Many things have changed in the Motion Picture Industry over the years, but one constant is the fact that the week between Christmas and New Year's remains the single best moviegoing week of the year. The best is saved for last with the quality and quantity of movies to see and the extra time people have on their hands after they get through with their holiday celebrations. The marketplace expands dramatically from Christmas evening to the end of New Year's weekend, a span of ten days, being able to absorb more movies to coincide with increased moviegoing availability. So on the 52nd week of the year, the movie business kicks into high gear, unlike so many other businesses, taking advantage of everyone else slowing down, schools being out, vacations being taken. Even with today's multitude of delivery platforms, one of the favorite traditions Americans enjoy during the holiday break is going out to their local movie theatre, relaxing, and watching movies. In addition, there is a lot more momentum going into Christmas this year. The week before Christmas in 2008 saw a Jim Carrey comedy, "Yes Man," as the top movie at $18 million. Last weekend "Avatar" opened to $77 million, despite the East Coast blizzard that kept attendance down in several major markets. With the box office already passing $10 billion for the first time earlier this week, distributors and exhibitors are in great position and looking forward to an explosive week at the ticket counters. This final stretch will determine how high the record will be; some are predicting as high as $10.5 billion.

When something unexpected like a blizzard hits big market cities during the opening weekend of a movie, that can spell doom for most movies and their distributors. The way the business is structured, new movies hit the marketplace each week, and the marketing campaigns are positioned to accomplish one objective, to deliver the biggest three-day gross possible before the next wave of releases open the following weekend. That's why we see a new number one movie almost every week. If a movie fails to maximize its opening gross for whatever reason, that lost business may never be recaptured, lost in the crunch of new competition. The adage goes, "A film has one chance to open, and you better get it right." Well, "Avatar" isn't most movies, and last weekend's blizzard is a mere hiccup that was easily shrugged off by its distributor 20th Century Fox. Fox knows they have the goods, and with that great holiday playtime looming ahead, every admission lost to the storm will find its way back to the theatres and then some in the next couple of weeks. "Avatar," which has been praised by Steven Spielberg as the best film he'd ever seen, is far from being a one-week wonder. After seeing it myself, this should be the dominant film well into next year, and where its eventual gross will land up is anybody's guess. If "Transformers" could gross $400 million, "Avatar" could surely match that and could even approach $500 million, especially with the higher 3D ticket prices. James Cameron dreamed big, and he hit it out of the park. It was an experience for me that was close to when I first saw "2001: A Space Odyssey" as an 18 year old. I saw some things on screen that I'd never seen before, and it blew me away. It looks like it could indeed be the game changer the industry was hoping for.

Just about every critic and moviegoer who has seen "Avatar" is raving about it, and repeat business is already being reported. The movie almost demands a second viewing because Cameron fills the screen with so many wonders you want to go back to see if you missed anything. The big question is how it will affect all the other movies, including the five films that will be going wide for the first time on Christmas Day. When a movie opens and grosses more than all the other movies combined, that's pretty formidable competition. Let's look at the five films opening across the country:

- ▶ "It's Complicated" – Universal
- ▶ "Sherlock Holmes" – Warner Brothers
- ▶ "Alvin and the Chipmunks: The Squeakuel" – 20th Century Fox
- ▶ "Up in the Air" – Paramount (national expansion)
- ▶ "Nine" – Weinstein (national expansion)

Each of these movies has their strengths or they wouldn't be opening or going wide on Christmas Day. Lionsgate found out the hard way last year when they chose to open the less than stellar "The Spirit" on Christmas and did very poorly, not able to compete with much higher-profile and star-driven films by the likes of Brad Pitt, Tom Cruise, Adam Sandler and Jennifer Anniston. This 2009 crop of movies should be able to hold their own, and the fact that many moviegoers plan to see several movies over the next ten days will turn many of the holiday movies into profitable successes for their studios and financial partners. Let's start with "It's Complicated." In a male dominated Hollywood, director Nancy Meyers is the industry's most successful woman director, and her latest has the look of a nice hit for Universal because its core audience of women 35 and over is the one demographic least interested in seeing "Avatar." Even though women make up half the population, Hollywood almost always seems surprised when women are able to carry a film by themselves. Last Sunday's *New York Times Magazine* cover story posed the question, "Can Anybody Make a Movie for Women?" The article was mostly a profile of Nancy Myers and pointed out she's one of only four or so women directors getting steady work in Hollywood. Myers knows her way around romantic comedies, and with a cast of Meryl Streep, Steve Martin and Alec Baldwin she can't lose on this one. The article also pointed out how difficult it is to make a winning romantic comedy. Sony's total misfire of "Did You Hear About the Morgans?" a week earlier with Sarah Jessica Parker and Hugh Grant confirms that as the movie received some of the worst reviews of the year and flopped with a $7 million gross. There always seems to be one studio every year that falls short at the end of the year, and this year it's Sony, whose only other December movie was the generic "Armored," which has come and gone after its December 4th launch.

Warner Brothers' "Sherlock Holmes" has matched the "Avatar" marketing campaign dollar for dollar, with each spending up to $50 million to open their films in North America. The strength of the studios remains their unmatched marketing and distribution organizations. They know how to get the job done on a massive scale. With their nonstop television commercials over the last two months, they've successfully repositioned the Sherlock Holmes brand as a witty, fast moving action franchise, which should pay off for today's audiences. Robert Downey Jr., between his two "Iron Man" stints, should help bring in both men and women. With all the adult films in the marketplace, Fox's "Alvin and the Chipmunks: The Squeakquel" may actually be in one of the better positions to compete against "Avatar" because there's little overlap with the two audiences. With Fox as the distributor of both films, no studio is in better shape to reap the rewards of the holiday season. Those who question the wisdom of another chipmunk movie only have to be reminded that the 2007 "Alvin and the Chipmunks" grossed over $200 million. The studio was chirping all the way to the bank with that one.

Of the two Golden Globe nominees going wide, "Up in the Air" and "Nine," the George Clooney starrer should be able to withstand the competition in the best fashion. For one thing, the reviews are much better for "Up in the Air" than they are for "Nine," and there's better momentum and want-to-see for the corporate comedy/drama than there is for the musical based on Fellini's "8 ½." They both add a touch of class to the marketplace, but both run the danger of running out of steam before the Oscar nominations are announced. Both movies are looking to establish a good base of support and word of mouth, which can carry them throughout January and into February. The competition across the board is fierce. In addition to "Avatar" and the other films opening this week, holdovers like "Invictus," "The Blind Side," "New Moon" and "Brothers" will continue to draw audiences. In the larger cities, another part of the mix are the upscale films opening in art houses with Oscar dreams themselves: Jeff Bridges in "Crazy Heart," Colin Firth in "A Single Man,"

Emily Blunt in "The Young Victoria" and Penelope Cruz in "Broken Embraces." This is the time of the year when movies for adults outnumber the ones for kids and teens. One of the laments heard often this time of year is why can't some of these films be spread out throughout the year. We'll be saying the same thing again next year, so all we can do now is enjoy what's out there right now.

Christmas Day is a day unlike any day of the year, regardless of a person's religious beliefs. There is an eerie silence when you venture out because the roads are fairly empty, and most everything is closed for the day. If a business is closed for one day of the year it's Christmas. People are home with their families. Out of this vast wasteland of empty parking lots and quiet solitude stand the movie theatres, popping the popcorn and projecting the movies as usual, open for business as they are for each of the 365 days of the year. Always open. Never closing. Dependable. Trustworthy. Often maligned, taken for granted, but there in a pinch when you need someplace to go to get out of the house, find some entertainment, mingle with people, to feel alive. Even as most studio heads and many executives from various production and distribution companies do slow down, take some much needed time off and go on vacation, there is no rest for the weary for those who work in movie theatres: theatre managers, operation execs, projectionists, ticket takers, ushers, concession workers, security personnel, the unsung heroes of the movie industry in which Christmas is not a day off but just another day on the job and a busy one at that. Some would call it the bottom of the food chain for those who toil in theatres, and perhaps it is, but it's a noble profession nevertheless and is essential work that has remained the primary and lead platform in the exhibition of movies for over 100 years. So when you go see some movies over the holidays, remember the workers who are there making it possible for you to enjoy yourself at a business that never closes. A thank you would be nice.

This is the world I began my film career in back in 1973 as one of the managers of the Woods Theatre in downtown Chicago. The last Christmas Day I worked was back in 1974 when Universal's "Willie Dynamite" played, and from what I recall, it was a full day of hard work and big crowds, which began at 9:00 in the morning and concluded around 6:00pm. By the time I reached my parent's house, Christmas was winding down and some relatives were already leaving. That's the life of the theatre manager, and every manager understands that's part of the deal when they take the job. In my case, my stint as a manager was only the start of a career that enabled me to do many things in the film business over the next 30 years. For that, I'm forever grateful. However, the business has changed much from the 1970s with consolidation of companies and technology, which has streamlined the work employees do, so the opportunities for theatre managers to advance in distribution and exhibition companies have been greatly reduced. Being a theatre manager now is more of an end job and a career rather than a steppingstone to something else in the industry. With over 5,600 theatres and close to 40,000 screens operating in a very stable industry in a still shaky economy, that's not something to scoff at. In the last of the interviews spread throughout the book, I talk to Kenny Bahr, a 28-year-old theatre manager in Yuma, Arizona who speaks passionately about being a theatre manager, what the job means to him and yes, what's it's like to work on Christmas Day.

In the 52-week cycle of the 2009 movie season, we end where we began with Christmas films playing, one year ending, another year about to begin. Looking back, distributors and exhibitors alike can take pride in the jobs they did and the parts they played in the record-breaking box office of the last twelve months. But when they get back to work after the first of the year, they have to do it all again and try to keep the good times rolling. That's the way it is.

This Week at the Box Office:

Sherlock Holmes
Warner Brothers
Opening weekend: $34,119,372
Domestic gross: $209,028,679 39.9%
Foreign gross: $315,000,000 60.1%
Worldwide gross: $524,028,679
Widest release: 3,626 theatres

Alvin and the Chipmunks: The Squeakquel
20th Century Fox
Opening weekend: $48,875,415
Domestic gross: $219,614,612 49.6%
Foreign gross: $233,525,393 50.4%
Worldwide gross: $443,140,005
Widest release: 3,447 theatres

It's Complicated
Universal
Opening weekend: $34,286,740
Domestic gross: $112,735,375 51.5%
Foreign gross: $106,368,280 48.5%
Worldwide gross: $219,103,655
Widest release: 2,955 theatres

The Imaginarium of Doctor Parnassus
Sony Classics
Opening weekend: $415,233
Domestic gross: $7,689,607 12.4%
Foreign gross: $54,119,168 87.6%
Worldwide gross: $61,808,775
Widest release: 607 theatres

3 Idiots
Reliance Big Ent.
Opening weekend: $1,645,622
Domestic gross: $6,533,849 60.8%
Foreign gross: $4,208,189 39.2%
Worldwide gross: $10,741,063
Widest release: 156 theatres

Police, Adjective
IFC
Opening weekend: $19,452
Domestic gross: $53,206 43.6%
Foreign gross: $68,771 56.7%
Worldwide gross: $121,977
Widest release: 8 theatres

Conversations with Industry Professionals

Kenny Bahr – Manager of Yuma Palms 14 Theatre, Yuma, Arizona

The following interview took place on July 7, 2011 and was updated in July, 2012.

> *"Every day is a new experience, there is never business as usual, and that's what makes the job what it is. And the days when everything is going as planned, that's when I'm on guard the most.*
>
> *Kenny Bahr*

Q: Tell me about yourself. How did you get started working in movie theatres?

KB: I'm 29 years old, and I started working in movie theatres when I was 18. I didn't know anything about the movie business when I began, but after a month on the job I was enjoying the fast-paced nature of the business. It was just a lot of fun. After about three years, I took a job with a larger theatre circuit, and my first job there was as a team leader, which is a first level supervisor. After about six months I was promoted to manager. I've spent a lot of time as a projectionist and became very good at working with 35mm projectors. At the same time, I was in charge of seat maintenance and repair and quickly grew to handling just about any maintenance or projection related problems. I would say that one of my strongest skills as a facilities manager is being able to walk into a rundown theatre with general wear and tear and bring it back to life. I've also done part-time work with an independent theater management company for my experience in many different areas, where I would go to different theatres for a short amount of time to either get a theatre open for business or to assist in training the employees.

Q: Are you still bouncing around various theatres?

KB: I manage one theatre now at the Yuma Palms 14, which has a 3,000+ seat capacity, and I'm in my seventh year at this theatre. I have regular manager duties along with the extra work I do keeping the projectors running properly. There are a total of 15 managers who work in this building, and many of them report to me depending on which department I'm in charge of on that shift, and I report to the general manager. On any given day I have anywhere between 15 and 60 employees reporting to me. It's a pretty big operation.

Q: How big of a market is Yuma, and what are your ticket prices?

KB: Yuma is a city with about 150,000 people with both an army base and a navy base located in town. There are also three or four surrounding small towns without a theatre, which we draw from as well as a large fluctuation of winter visitors. The admission prices are $8.50 for adults in the evening, $6.50 for matinees, $5.00 for children and seniors all day long, and when we play 3D, a $3.00 extra up-charge. There is a competing eight-screen theatre on Main Street, so there are 22 total screens in town. In the last few years both theatres have played together, so we play every film while becoming the dominant theatre due to our grossing potential and past performance.

Q: One of your specialties has been keeping 35mm projectors in good shape, but the entire industry is shifting to digital projection. What's your theatre mix between digital and 35mm?

KB: As of 2012, the entire complex has been converted to digital projection, and the conversion went smoother than I thought it was going to be. The new projectors still have some bugs to figure out, but overall it's a better presentation for our patrons. Three of our screens play digital 3D.

Q: How many hours a week do you work?

KB: I average about 50 hours a week, but it can be more during the summer and the week between Christmas and New Year's. There are no vacations or time off during the busy periods. I seem to be always working even when I'm not. I'll get a call in the morning and be asked to check a breaker valve or something because I'm the go-to guy for most everything. If I get a call, I'm there.

Q: Has working on Christmas Day been hard?

KB: It's been frustrating for my family. They want me to be home, but they have to understand this is my job, and theatres never close. I don't think I spent a Christmas at home in ten years. It's part of being a theatre manager, and it's a scheduling problem too because one week I may be opening the theatre, and then the next week I'll be closing the theatre, so it's hard to coordinate things with the family. Everyone who works in a movie theatre has to understand that. In our applications we state it very clearly that our industry does most of its business on weekends and holidays, and all employees are expected to work on those days. If they can't do that or don't want to, the job isn't for them, and we don't hire them.

Q: What do you recall about Christmas Day in 2009?

KB: In 2009 it was insane in our theatre. Our theatre ranked 332nd out of 4,000 theatres reporting box office grosses to Movieline International for Christmas week, so we were very, very busy. Our busiest day in history was Christmas Day 2009 where we put just under 8,000 people through the doors. For "Avatar" we had one 3D print and two 35mm prints and interlocked a third screen so we were playing it on four screens. I remember "Avatar's" first midnight show was nothing great with about 200 people, but word of mouth spread so quickly by the next day's matinees, we started selling out, and it was a picture that grew legs for the next three to four weeks. I worked that Christmas from 8:00am to 9:00pm, a thirteen-hour day, so there was no Christmas celebration for me that day. When my shift was over at 5:00pm, my boss asked me if I could stay over and help with crowd control because the lines were ridiculous, and I said sure, that's what I'm here for. I jumped into the middle of the fray managing the crowds, doing line control and dealing with the people looking for seats if they came five minutes before showtime. That's why I fell in love with the movie theatre, the action, the interaction of people, the excitement of a full house and long lines.

Q: In a way a theatre manager is on the front lines representing the entire industry. This is where the life of a movie begins, and you seem to get that and feed off it.

KB: Yes, I love that, it's a bit of magic with so many people showing up and wanting to enjoy the movie theatre experience with so many others. You live for movies like "Avatar" and being there to experience it because a lot of movies don't do so well and don't open with much excitement. Another way I look at it is that every person I know has a very fond memory of being in a movie theatre and seeing a movie they love. So in a way we are assisting them in creating a memory. I remind people who work with me if we do our jobs well, we are actually helping people to have great memories that could last for a lifetime.

Q: That's a very nice way of putting it.

KB: And that's just the audience. I haven't even talked about the bonding that goes on with fellow employees. I'm still friends today with the people I started with ten years ago. When you start in the trenches with somebody, you forge these lifetime bonds. To have things run as smoothly as possible, you have to rely on each other, if you don't, you can't be successful.

Q: *With so many people reporting to you, have you developed your own leadership style and philosophy of management?*

KB: I've developed my own style of leadership. I've watched how other managers have handled things over the years. There were always things that I didn't like about what my managers did and how they related to their employees, which I thought was counterproductive. When I promote someone, I say think about the things that managers did to you that you didn't like and try not to do the same thing. Don't become the person you didn't like. I had a particularly bad manager who was just plain mean and nasty when you came to her with a problem. I tell my employees who come to me with a problem that we'll find a way to fix this; let's work together to find a solution; don't freak out.

Q: *What's the best thing and worst thing about your job?*

KB: I think they are one and the same thing, the politics and relationships that go on between employees and guests. One manager may say something to another manager, and the employee does the complete opposite, which can put a big wrench in things. The one thing I love the best is taking young kids with their first jobs and putting them on the right path in the job market. Teaching them work integrity is one of the hardest things in my day but one of my most fulfilling parts of the job. These kids have no clue about a job, and then some turn into team leaders and even managers after starting out as a punk kid with little sense of responsibility. You can show them the right path, but if they don't see it, they won't take it. You have to explain to them why it's the correct way to do something, and then they understand. Once they understand, they become so enlightened its crazy to see how they turn around. The worst is difficult customers. Some people expect the world to be handed to them on a silver platter when they walk in the door. They demand people be removed from the seat they usually sit in, even if they just got there before the movie started and others waited an hour to get in. You learn about human nature. People in a group can be understanding to a certain extent, but once things start going wrong, it takes only one person to start a chain reaction. We have had to call in police to calm down an unruly crowd. There is an X factor in every crowd. I've learned if an emergency happens, get in there immediately and address the crowd, inform them what is happening, offer them passes to return, whatever it takes to diffuse the situation.

Q: *What's the one thing the public doesn't know about theatre managers?*

KB: The public doesn't realize a lot about what goes on inside a movie theatre. When there is a problem with a film, some people think you can just push the rewind button and press play. Audiences should give the theatre manager a break, especially when the power goes out or when the weather gets rough. It's not our fault when something like that happens; don't take it out on employees. People don't know what it takes to keep a theatre in operation. I love being the invisible man. You know you did a good job and it was a good night when there are no complaints and there isn't one call for anything, but then again I don't remember a day when everything went according to plan. Every day is a new experience. There is never business as usual, and that's what makes the job what it is. And the days when everything is going as planned, that's when I'm on guard the most.

Q: *Has audience behavior changed with Twitter and texting while a movie is playing?*

KB: We have a campaign going on right now with the code name NTDM, No Texting During Movies. Sometimes you look inside an auditorium and two-thirds of it is lit up with phones. We have 32 poster cases inside the theatre, and during the latest "Twilight" we took every poster down and put our no texting posters in them to drive the point home.

Q: *Is the campaign working?*

KB: It worked really well for "Twilight" with a lot less phone usage during the movie, but it takes constant diligence to keep it under control.

Q: *In your mind what makes for a successful movie theatre?*

KB: It starts with good management. I've been sent to problem theatres where managers didn't care, and it was bad. Things weren't fixed. The washrooms were a mess. Employees had no direction. I try to bring positive energy to work every day and hope it rubs off on people.

Q: *What's an important lesson you have learned?*

KB: I would say I've learned a few basic things on the job that I try to live by. It may sound boring, but number one is taking care of your feet. Wear insoles, arch support and properly fitted shoes. There is nothing worse than a busy Saturday night during primetime and having your feet ache when you're in the thick of it. The second thing is to stay calm. No matter how rough things are or are going to get, if you lose your cool or panic, it's just going to be that much harder to get through the day. Third, never assume or trust that a problem got resolved by someone else; always make sure for yourself. Finally, no matter how hard or long of a day you have ahead of you, eventually you will get to go home.

Q: *Working in Yuma, do you feel you are part of the overall Motion Picture Industry and what you do is important?*

KB: Yes, I feel I'm a small piece of the puzzle, and what we do is important because if it weren't for us, the distributors wouldn't be getting their product out like they want to and are used to. There are little things we do with placement of standees and posters for a movie we feel needs more awareness, and we put them in a primary spot to get noticed more, whereas a big pre-sold movie will do well regardless. If it weren't for us in the theatres promoting the movies and doing what we have to do, the industry wouldn't be what it is today.

Q: *Do you see being a theatre manager as a lifetime job, a career in itself?*

KB: This is something I'm good at, and I don't see myself leaving anytime soon, but I don't know if I would want to spend my whole career in this theatre. There are other jobs within an exhibition circuit that I may aspire to and go after down the road. I was fortunate once to be part of a survey crew accessing possible new locations, and my job was to go into a competing theatre and assess the operation of that theatre. I liked that very much. So as long as I continue to do my best in my current position, I feel there will be more opportunities for me in the future.

Q: *Do you think movie theatres will be around forever?*

KB: I hope so. I have a lot of years left in me.

Q: *I appreciate your time and insight. I hope you have a good, long career in the movie business.*

KB: Thank you.

Week 52: Questions for Discussion

1. How did Kenny Bahr make himself valuable to his employer in his role as a theatre manager?

2. In the interview, discuss something that impressed you with how Kenny Bahr approached his job.

3. With about 5,600 theatre locations in the country, the movie theatre industry is a steady employer of thousands of people. If you are interested in working in the motion picture marketplace, have you ever worked in a movie theatre or given any thought to working in this area of the film business? Discuss.

Closing Thoughts: A Look Ahead

As the 2009 movie season unfolded from week to week, the only certainty looming on the calendar was the huge anticipation for "Avatar" opening on December 18, the second to last week of the year. Other than that, I never really knew more than a couple of weeks in advance what I was going to be writing about. I followed where the marketplace took me, and I'm glad it ended where it did, inside a movie theatre on Christmas Day. In a way it came full circle for me, thinking back to that day in 1973 when I walked into the Woods Theatre to begin my own career. The final conversation in a series of interviews I conducted with industry professionals couldn't have been more timely and more deserved than the interview I did with Kenny Bahr, the 29-year-old theatre manager in Yuma, Arizona. I was blown away with the thoughtfulness of this young man and the way he articulated his excitement of being a theatre manager and how magical a place a movie theatre is. Kenny not only represents his theatre well with his enthusiasm, talent, and leadership skills, he represents what the future could be, should be, and hopefully will be for all those working in the theatrical marketplace. When I posed the question to him, "Do you think theatres will be around forever?" his reply "I hope so, I have a lot of years left in me," spoke to everyone who loves movies and the moviegoing experience.

After a very bumpy several years between exhibitors and distributors discussing the financial arrangements, necessity, and timetable of converting theatres to all-digital projection systems, issues have finally been resolved, and a new era is about to begin. In 2013, the majority of first run screens in the U.S. will be almost fully converted to digital with 35mm being phased out and becoming a relic of the past. This development, perhaps more than any other factor, should insure the continuance of theatres for many years to come. There has been so much time and money spent on the digital conversion by both distributors and exhibitors that neither side will allow theatres to fall by the wayside and become an afterthought. There's too much at stake and theatres are still too vital for that to happen. The fact that the digital picture looks and sounds fantastic and will be the same quality for someone who sees it in the fifth week as someone who sees the film on opening night is no small improvement for the theatrical experience. In time, after all the costs are paid for, the savings for the industry, especially for the studios that won't have to create and ship physical prints, will be tremendous. For theatre owners, digital projection adds great flexibility to add or subtract screen capacity on movies at the touch of a button as demand dictates. In addition, the hope is that the ancillary revenues that can be generated with digital alternative programming will become more meaningful and that their digital equipment won't have to be upgraded too often.

However, there is a downside to the digital era in exhibition. The high cost of digital conversion for a number of small town, independent and community theatres around the county is proving to be daunting, and there will certainly be a percentage of theatres that will be forced to close their doors once 35 mm prints are no longer made available. Even though the loss of revenue from these theatres may in fact prove to be negligible for the studios, their importance lies with the people they have served faithfully in their communities over the years. That special bond and connection that a movie theatre has with a community is turning impending gloom into happy endings for some of these theatres on the bubble. There have been reports that several theatres have decided to use crowdsourcing as a way to raise the $100,000 per screen needed to convert to digital projection. This method of financing involves asking donors for donations through one of the websites that facilitate these transactions, asking for a specific amount of money in a specific time frame that has to be raised in full for the financing to be successful. In August 2012, *The Daily Herald* in the northwest Chicago area reported on one such theatre, the 85-year-old Catlow Theatre in Barrington, IL. The owners requested $100,000 in contributions over a 60-day period through the website kickstarter.com and didn't know if that would be enough time to raise that kind of money. Well, it was. In seven days, 780 backers pledged a total of $100,294 to keep the theatre alive, which comes out to an average of $128 per donor. The power of the community spoke, and the Catlow Theatre will live on.

As much as the digital conversion has stabilized and improved movie theatre operations, that alone will not automatically guarantee the continued four-month, exclusive window theatres now enjoy with movies. The hot button issue of premium Video-on-Demand will continue to rage on. Studios will continue to push for more narrow windows and experiment with certain films as Universal attempted to do with "Tower Heist" in the fall of 2011, and exhibitors will continue to push back by threatening to pull all their theatres. So far that tactic has been effective in blocking any of these experiments from happening, but will that always be the case? There is a concern in this regard, and it stems from the fact that there is a slow changing of the guard happening within some distribution organizations, replacing retiring old school distribution executives with executives from either home entertainment or new media divisions taking on more prominent roles. These new executives don't have the same ties and relationships with theatrical exhibitors and may be more aggressive in implementing new premium viewing events with or without the consent of exhibitors. Would there be a film company willing to bite the bullet on losing a large number of screens to prove a point and set a precedent? No doubt there are many things on the table right now, but before a studio considers this route they would have to balance the risk and reward factor very carefully and remember one important fact – there are six major studios, and no one studio is indispensable.

It's a different set of dynamics for small, character-driven films and the art theatres that play them. One of the recurring themes from 2009 was the sad state of the independent business which basically hit rock bottom that year with tighter money for financing, fewer distributors left standing and question marks all over the place on the very future of the quality, specialized film in the theatrical marketplace. Things are still in the transitional phase for this segment, but there have been signs of improvement with new distributors emerging, a number of films breaking out and new revenue streams showing more promise. However, filmmakers of specialized films continue to find many hurdles in raising financing, maintaining creative control of their projects and finding good reliable distribution and success in the theatrical marketplace. For that reason, there is much more of a shift and acceptance of Video-on-Demand with independent films and the theatres that predominantly play them. There are a number of films that prove to be too small or obscure to be able to compete in the theatrical market, so going day and date with limited theatres or even offering Video-on-Demand before theatrical to create some buzz is becoming a new business model. The question becomes if a movie is too obscure to play in theatres, how many people will be able to find it in the cable universe and be willing to pay for it? Transparency remains an issue with new revenue streams, so it's difficult for filmmakers to know what potential money they could earn in this area because very few numbers are being reported. 2011's "Margin Call" was perhaps the highest profile film to go public when it was announced the VOD gross was $4 million to match its $4 million domestic gross. The question becomes how much did VOD limit its theatrical gross because with its star power and critical reviews, it looked like the film had the potential to play wider in the larger suburban theatres which have a policy against playing any films that are available inside the home. That question will continue to be debated. What have proven to be successful in the VOD market are low budget genre action or horror movies with titles like "Black Death" and "13 Assassins," which have little theatrical potential to begin with. Smaller films being able to have more options other than expensive theatrical releases is a positive development for filmmakers. It remains to be seen whether more reliable VOD figures will be released in the future as this market becomes more standardized.

Speaking of new distributors, Open Road Films was launched in March 2011 by the two largest U.S. theatre circuits, Regal Entertainment and AMC Entertainment. This isn't the first time that theatre circuits attempted to get into distribution; In the 1970s, General Cinema was one such circuit that became involved with a distribution venture. The reason for this was the same as it is now, having more movies available to play in their theatres. The studios have cut back their production output in the last several years, and there are a lot of 16-screen theatres that always need a fresh supply of product to play. They hired an experienced former distributor to head the company, and their business model is the mid-ranged commercial movie that can effectively play in suburban theatres. The film company's biggest success has been "The Grey" with a $77 million gross, a very solid performer. With AMC being acquired in 2012 for $2.6 billion by China's largest theatre circuit, time will tell if operating a distribution company will remain a part of the new owner's long-term business plan.

In 2009 there was a lot of discussion and hype surrounding digital 3D movies and whether or not they could become the game changer some people in the industry had predicted. Just as "Avatar" was the absolute peak of the 2009 season, it also looks like it was the absolute peak of 3D's popularity with moviegoers. Just about everyone had to see "Avatar" in 3D, and almost everyone did. An amazing 83% of its $760 million gross came from 3D tickets. Fast-forward to summer 2012. The *Hollywood Reporter* had a very interesting mid-year box office report which revisited the performance of 3D films. There has been a steady decline since "Avatar" in 3D's percentage of a film's gross. Six months after "Avatar," 56% of "Toy Story 3's" domestic gross came from 3D tickets; by the summer of 2012 the 3D percentage to gross had fallen to its lowest levels ever. Disney/Pixar's "Brave" set a record low of 32% and "Madagascar 3" wasn't much better at 38%. On paper, it would seem that the digital 3D movement may have been a passing fad, but that wouldn't tell the whole story. Families continue to be pinched in the pocketbook with the sluggish economy, and those three to four dollar extra surcharges per ticket are too much to stomach for many people, especially when the screen next to it is playing the same movie in regular 2D. What's the solution? Well, digital 3D movies aren't going away, though it's too early to say whether fewer of them will eventually be made. There will always be a 2D option in place because there are enough people who can't tolerate 3D for one reason or another, and distributors and exhibitors will never intentionally limit their audience. One solution may be to raise the regular ticket price slightly to include all films while eliminating the special 3D surcharges. If that happens there would surely be a reduction in the number of 3D movies being made. It begs another question. If you can't get extra for 3D, will it still be worth doing?

Plunging DVD revenues was also one of the crucial issues of 2009, and it remains one three years later, though home entertainment on the whole looks to be stabilizing. At its peak in 2004, home entertainment revenues stood at around $23 billion, most of that coming from DVD sales and rentals, with the remaining coming from the last remnants of the VHS video market. Beginning in 2005, DVDs started a slow decline which accelerated as the decade progressed until that $23 billion pie had fallen to under $19 billion by the end of 2009. That loss of over $4 billion in home entertainment revenue became a factor in fewer movies being produced and studios downsizing their work force because the profit margins were squeezed out with the loss of the once reliable DVD money. In 2010 and 2011, home entertainment revenue has somewhat stabilized in the $18.5 billion range, but now that figure includes DVD sales and rentals, Blu-ray sales and rentals and all Internet sales and rentals. In 2011, the Digital Entertainment Group revealed that the number of U.S. homes with Blu-ray players grew to 40 million, 38% higher in 2010, and sales of Blu-ray discs topped $2 billion for the first time. This is an important figure and if the growth continues the studios will be happy because Blu-ray's wholesale price of over $20 makes it the most profitable of the home entertainment options. Sales of movies on the Internet now are approaching $1 billion while Internet and cable Video-on-Demand surpass $2 billion. Spending on subscription streaming is also rapidly increasing largely due to Netflix shifting away from their DVD mail business. Added all together, the new revenue streams are building, and the trend is upwards. When a reliable cash cow business like DVDs starts freefalling as it did, it takes awhile for the sector to rebound with new forms of technology taking its place. Whether it can begin to approach where the DVD revenues once were is too early to say at this point.

In the second chapter, I made the argument that movie theatres, when it's all said and done, could be the most reliable and solid component of the entire movie revenue food chain. Even though 2010 and 2011 didn't match the $10.6 domestic gross of 2009, both years were still hovering over a steady $10 billion. More importantly, the international box office in 2011 topped $22 billion to make the theatrical business a $32 billion industry. International box office in U.S. dollars is up 35% over five years ago. Despite all the different ways people can view movies nowadays, movie theatres are here to stay. Movies and movie theatres may be the invention of the 20th century, but they have been recreated and reborn to endure in the 21st century. Will there continue to be debate on the long-term health and future of the theatrical business? Of course, but that's nothing new. History tells us that theatres have faced numerous threats since the advent of television in the late 1940s, pay television in the 1970s, video cassettes in the 1980s, DVDs and the rise of cable programming in the 1990s, wide screen HD televisions in the 2,000s and premium Video-on-Demand, Internet streaming and downloads of today. The pull of the theatrical marketplace remains strong and powerful. Even though filmmakers have a variety of alternative options outside theatrical, don't you think for an instant if you ask each and every one of those filmmakers if they had their choice of where they would prefer to have their movie play, they wouldn't all shout "on the big screen." The other key part of the equation are the moviegoers, all the people who will continue to love movies and the social experience of sitting in the dark with a theatre full of like-minded people allowing the super-sized images and sound to wash over them. As that wise theatre manager Kenny Bahr most eloquently put it, "creating happy memories that can last a lifetime."

Index of Industry Data

2009 ACADEMY AWARD WINNERS

Picture: "The Hurt Locker"

Actor: Jeff Bridges, "Crazy Heart"

Actress: Sandra Bullock, "The Blind Side"

Supporting actor: Christopher Waltz, "Inglourious Basterds"

Supporting actress: Mo'Nique, "Precious"

Director: Kathryn Bigelow, "The Hurt Locker"

Animated film: "Up"

Documentary: "The Cove"

Original script: "The Hurt Locker," Mark Boal

Adapted script: "Precious," Geoffrey Fletcher

Foreign film: "El Secreto de Sus Ojos" (Argentina)

Original song: "The Weary Kind" (from "Crazy Heart") by Ryan Bingham and T Bone Burnett

Original score: "Up," Michael Giacchino

Cinematography: Mauro Fiore, "Avatar"

Film editing: "The Hurt Locker"

Visual effects: "Avatar"

Art direction: "Avatar"

Costume design: "The Young Victoria"

Makeup: "Star Trek"

Sound mixing: "The Hurt Locker"

Sound editing: "The Hurt Locker"

Documentary short: "Music by Prudence"

Animated short: "Logorama"

Live action short: "The New Tenants"

2009 AVERAGE WEEKLY ATTENDANCE

A snapshot of the 2009 average weekly attendance is on the opposite page. Average weekly attendance remains a meaningful figure because unlike the box office, it can't increase merely due to higher ticket prices. It only measures the actual amount of fannies in the seats from year to year. 2009 turned into one of those special years when paid admissions rose 5.5% to 1.42 billion admissions, the first significant increase in attendance since 2002.

The Golden Age of Hollywood in the 1930s and 1940s was the height of moviegoing in the U.S. with an average between 75 million and 90 million people a week attending movies. To say that moviegoing was a weekly habit for Americans would not be an overstatement. With the U.S. population sitting at about 130 million during that period, over 60% of the population went to the movies weekly. The absolute peak of the curve came in the post World War II year of 1946, when the average weekly attendance was an astounding 90 million. Starting in the late 1940s, a steep decline in weekly movie attendance began as the first televisions entered U.S. homes and altered moviegoing habits forever. A new reality set in, and by 1960, weekly attendance had fallen to under 30 million and reached its lowest point in history in 1969 with weekly attendance falling under 18 million paid customers. By 1975, weekly attendance rebounded back to the 20 million range, and the 1980s and '90s averaged between 21 and 23 admissions a week, which worked out to about 1.1 billion tickets sold a year. In the late 1990s, massive changes occurred within the exhibition industry with a shift to the modern stadium seating megaplex replacing many older, smaller multiplexes. Though this transition was painful and expensive for many theatre circuits, it led to a jump in theatre screens (over 5,000 new screens in a five year period), a much better experience for moviegoers, and a dramatic increase in weekly admissions. Weekly attendance since 2000 has been averaging in the 27 million range. 2002 started a three-year period where weekly attendance averaged close to 30 million, but since 2005, attendance has fluctuated between 25 and 27 million weekly admissions.

According to the MPAA, over two-thirds of the population (67%) – or 217.1 million people went to the movies in 2009, accounting for the 1.42 billion in admissions (ticket sales). This averaged to 27.3 million tickets sold each week, but when you take a close look at the graph, there are very few weeks that hit that figure on the nose; the figures are generally either higher or lower, and that's the nature of the 52-week season. There are many peaks and valleys during the movie year due to seasonal viewing habits, holiday weekends and the vagaries of the movies themselves. The May-August summer season is consistently strong and represents 40% of the year's annual business, but then things really cool off quickly with September and October being the two weakest months for moviegoing. Even though a couple of weeks in the summer exceeded 40 million admissions, and the 18 weeks of summer playtime averaged 33 million weekly admissions, the two most attended weeks of the year were Thanksgiving week with 50 million and Christmas week with 65 million tickets sold. Led by "Avatar," "Sherlock Holmes," "Alvin and the Chipmunks: The Squeakuel," "It's Complicated" and other solid hits, the final week of 2009 was one for the ages. It's hard to pinpoint the last time that many tickets were sold in any one week, but available figures indicate it hadn't been done for many years. For that particular moment in time, those 65 million weekly admissions harkened back to Hollywood's Golden Age, when movie going was the center of the universe and when seemingly everyone went to the movies.

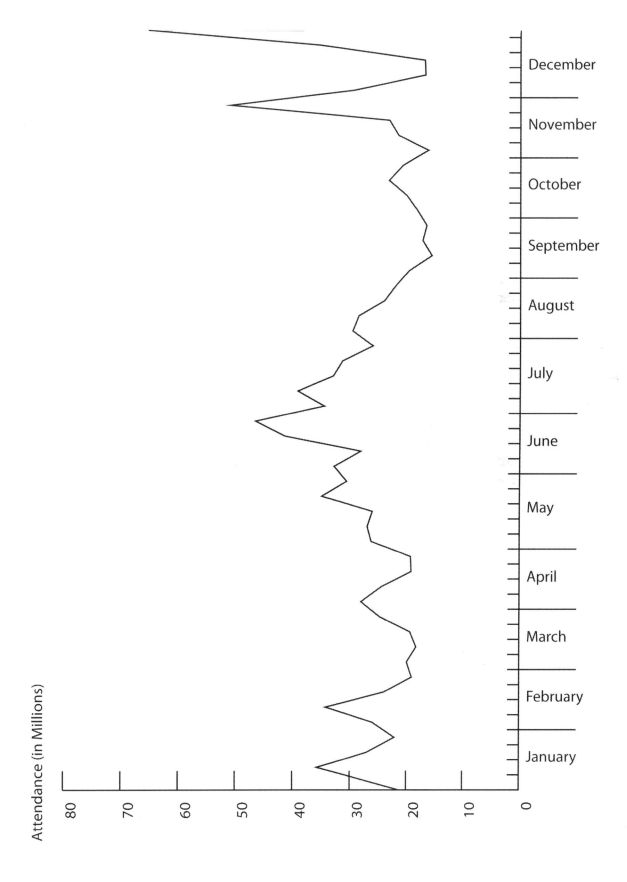